R. Gupta's®

POPULAR MASTER GUIDE

Guru Gobind Singh Indraprastha University (GGSIPU)

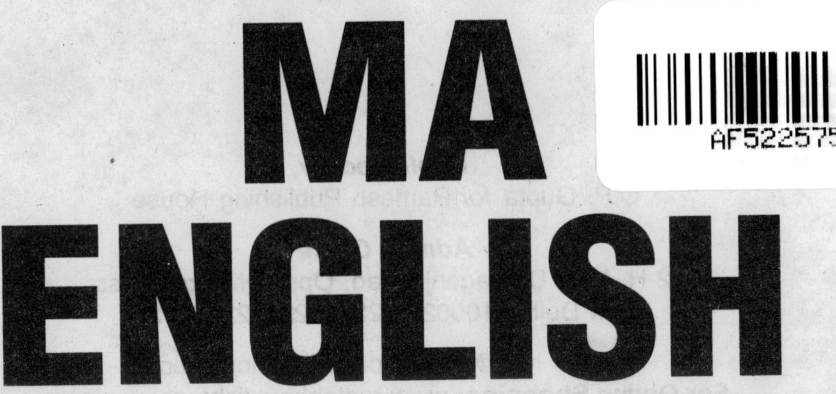

Common Entrance Test

by

RPH Editorial Board

RAMESH PUBLISHING HOUSE, NEW DELHI

Published by
O.P. Gupta *for* Ramesh Publishing House

Admin. Office
12-H, New Daryaganj Road, Opp. Officers' Mess,
New Delhi-110002 ✆ 23275224, 23245124

E-mail: info@rameshpublishinghouse.com
For Online Shopping: www.rameshpublishinghouse.com

Showroom
• Balaji Market, Nai Sarak, Delhi-6 ✆ 23253720, 23282525
• 4457, Nai Sarak, Delhi-6, ✆ 23918938

Book Code: R-1419

ISBN: 978-93-87604-92-6

Price: ₹ 340

Printed at: Deepak Offset, Delhi

Contents

SCHEME OF THE EXAMINATION

ELIGIBILITY:

Graduation in any discipline from a recognized University with aggregate of 50% marks.

SUBJECTS OF ENTRANCE TEST:

- **PART ONE (100 MCQ–400 MARKS)**

(*i*)	English Language & Comprehension	30%
(*ii*)	General Awareness and Culture	10%
(*iii*)	Literature	60%

- **PART TWO (ESSAY TYPE QUESTIONS–200 MARKS)**

Previous Paper (Solved)

Guru Gobind Singh Indraprastha University

GGSIPU – M.A. ENGLISH

Entrance Test 2019*

PART–A

OBJECTIVE TYPE QUESTIONS

1. Which one of the following statement is **not** true about Feminism?

(*a*) It is a complex, heterogeneous and a contradictory intellectual, ideological and activist baggage

(*b*) Its core is constituted by female-centered consciousness

(*c*) Mary Wollstonecraft, Dale Spender, Dorothy Richardson, Elaine Showalter, Julia Kristeva, Kate Millett, Luce Irigaray, Toril Moi are all feminists

(*d*) Most of the time feminists seem to speak from the vantage point of an already existing theoretical position

A. (*a*) & (*d*) B. (*c*) & (*d*)
C. All of these D. (*c*) only

2. Which one of the following is an **incorrect** statement?

(*a*) Theoretically, feminism emphasizes gender as a category of description

(*b*) Theoretically, feminism emphasizes gender as a tool of analysis

(*c*) Over time Feminism as a concept has been replaced by a more plural concept 'feminisms'

(*d*) At the level of praxis, feminism has evolved as a socio-cultural and political movement for ameliorating the condition of women

A. (*a*) only B. (*d*) only
C. (*c*) only D. none of these

3. As a theoretical category and concept 'gender' refers to:

(*a*) the trait that one's sex is determined by anatomy

(*b*) the traits that are largely, if not entirely, cultural constructs

(*c*) the practice that identifies woman as active, dominating, adventurous, rational, and creative

(*d*) a set of practices that brings reproductive distinctions between bodies into social processes

A. (*a*), (*b*), (*c*), (*d*) B. (*b*), (*c*), (*d*)
C. (*c*), (*d*), (*a*) D. (*d*) only

4. The three most influential ideas that govern 'gender difference' are:

(*a*) The idea of natural difference, which treats the body as a machine

(*b*) The idea of two separate realms of sex and gender

(*c*) The idea of gender as a discursive or symbolic system which treats body as a canvas on which society paints

(*d*) The idea is that gender is the only category through which one understands, describes and analyses woman's reality

A. (*a*), (*b*), (*d*) B. (*a*), (*b*), (*c*)
C. (*b*), (*c*), (*d*) D. (*c*), (*d*), (*a*)

*Exam held on 01-06-2019

5. It is said that various literary theories ask questions from the point of view of the writer, of the work/writing, and of the reader. Based on this assumption, match the following theories:

(*a*)	Writer	(*i*)	Romantic
(*b*)	Writing/Context	(*ii*)	Marxist
(*c*)	Reader	(*iii*)	Deconstructive
(*d*)	Work	(*iv*)	Formalistic

Codes:

	(*a*)	(*b*)	(*c*)	(*d*)
A.	(*i*)	(*ii*)	(*iii*)	(*iv*)
B.	(*ii*)	(*iii*)	(*i*)	(*iv*)
C.	(*iii*)	(*iv*)	(*i*)	(*ii*)
D.	(*iii*)	(*iv*)	(*ii*)	(*i*)

6. Find the correct match:

(*a*)	Franz Fanon	(*i*)	*The Myth of Sisyphus*
(*b*)	Ngugi wa Thiongo	(*ii*)	*Chronicle of a Death Foretold*
(*c*)	Albert Camus	(*iii*)	*Black Skin, White Masks*
(*d*)	Gabriel Garcia	(*iv*)	*Decolonising the Mind*

Codes:

	(*a*)	(*b*)	(*c*)	(*d*)
A.	(*i*)	(*ii*)	(*iii*)	(*iv*)
B.	(*ii*)	(*iii*)	(*i*)	(*iv*)
C.	(*iii*)	(*iv*)	(*i*)	(*ii*)
D.	(*iii*)	(*iv*)	(*ii*)	(*i*)

7. Which one of the following works is **not** authored by Elaine Showalter.

A. *A Literature of their Own: British Novelist from Bronte to Lessing*

B. *The Female Malady: Women, Madness, and English Culture*

C. *Hystories: Hysterical Epidemics and Modern Media*

D. *The Madwoman in the Attic: A Survey*

8. The term 'Androcentrism':

(*a*) Denotes a system of thought centred around male identity and values

(*b*) Denotes a system in which a female constitutes a deviation from the norm

(*c*) It also operates through language

(*d*) It is a defining feature of the patriarchal order.

A. (*a*), (*b*), (*c*) B. (*b*), (*c*), (*d*)

C. (*a*), (*b*), (*c*), (*d*) D. (*a*), (*c*), (*d*)

9. Which of the following statements is **not** correct about allegory?

(*a*) It is a narrative in prose, verse, or drama that self-consciously presents its meaning through concrete symbols

(*b*) The significance of a given symbol in allegory is determined by the conventions of the allegory as a whole

(*c*) A is a literary form with at least two levels of meaning: the literal level of the immediate narrative and the political, historical, philosophical or moral commentary the author intends to be recognized

(*d*) Thus allegories are generally non-didactic in focus

A. (*a*) only B. (*b*) only

C. (*c*) only D. (*d*) only

10. Which of the following statements does not capture the import of the term 'discourse' as it has been used by Foucault?

A. An authoritative way of describing, classifying and controlling desire and power

B. Discourses are propagated by specific institutions and dvide up the world in specific ways

C. In this way mastery is exerted over what appears to be the randomness of everyday reality

D. It is not possible to investigate these discourses that have been used to master reality and, in turn construct it, in the past

11. To what kind of reading practice do we associate the terms 'trace', paleonymy, aporia, and 'doubling commentary'?

A. Deconstructive Reading

B. Structuralist Reading

C. Formalistic Reading

D. Appropriatory Reading

12. Find the correct match:

(*a*) Kate Millet	(*i*) *Sexual/Textual Politics*
(*b*) Juliet Mitchel	(*ii*) *The Second Sex*
(*c*) Toril Moi	(*iii*) *Sexual Politics*
(*d*) Simone de Beauvior	(*iv*) *Psychoanalysis and Feminism*

Codes:

	(*a*)	(*b*)	(*c*)	(*d*)
A.	(*i*)	(*ii*)	(*iii*)	(*iv*)
B.	(*ii*)	(*iii*)	(*i*)	(*iv*)
C.	(*iii*)	(*iv*)	(*i*)	(*ii*)
D.	(*iii*)	(*iv*)	(*ii*)	(*i*)

13. Find the correct match:

(*a*) Liberal Feminism	(*i*) Examine the role that language plays in creating subjectivity and maintaining gender asymmetries
(*b*) Cultural Feminism	(*ii*) Attempts to reform or use existing political structures to advance women's interests along a civil rights model
(*c*) French Feminism	(*iii*) Attempts to recover lost of marginalized women's works and traditions and create an order that nurtures and supports women's experiences and values
(*d*) Material Feminism	(*iv*) Attempts to relate women's subordination to historical and class factors like the division of labour between men and women. Tends to focus on collaboration rather than identity politics

Codes:

	(*a*)	(*b*)	(*c*)	(*d*)
A.	(*i*)	(*ii*)	(*iii*)	(*iv*)
B.	(*ii*)	(*iii*)	(*i*)	(*iv*)
C.	(*iii*)	(*iv*)	(*i*)	(*ii*)
D.	(*iii*)	(*iv*)	(*ii*)	(*i*)

14. Find the correct match:

(*a*) Alexander Pope	(*i*) "The Function of Criticism"
(*b*) Mathew Arnold	(*ii*) "The Function of Criticism at the Present Time"
(*c*) T.S. Eliot	(*iii*) "Criticism as Speculation"
(*d*) J.C. Ransom	(*iv*) "An Essay on Criticism"

Codes:

	(*a*)	(*b*)	(*c*)	(*d*)
A.	(*i*)	(*ii*)	(*iii*)	(*iv*)
B.	(*iv*)	(*ii*)	(*i*)	(*iii*)
C.	(*ii*)	(*iii*)	(*i*)	(*iv*)
D.	(*iii*)	(*iv*)	(*i*)	(*ii*)

15. Who among the following was the theoretician of the drama of the absurd?

A. Samuel Beckett B. Martin Esslin
C. Harold Pinter D. Tom Stoppard

16. The line "she dwells with beauty–Beauty that must be" occurs in Keats":

A. "Odd to a Grecian Urn"
B. "Endymion"
C. "Ode on Melancholy"
D. "Ode to a Nightingale"

17. Negative Capability to Keats, means:

A. The ability to sympathize with others
B. Say bad thing, about others
C. To empathize
D. To be indifferent

18. Literature as "Art for Art's Sake" creed found its true adherent in:

A. William Wordsworth
B. Lord Byron
C. Robert Browning
D. Oscar Wilde

19. Which is the famous elegy written by Shelley?

A. In Memoriam B. Lycidas
C. Adonis D. Thyrsis

20. After who among the following is the Elizabethan Age named?

A. Elizabeth-I B. Elizabeth-II
C. Elizabeth-IV D. Elizabeth Browning

21. Which is the last of Shakespeare's great tragedies?

A. *Macbeth* B. *King Lear*
C. *Othello* D. *Hamlet*

22. Which among the following may be assumed as a date when Romanticism began?

A. Publication of "Intimations of Immortality"
B. The beginning of Queen Victoria's reign
C. The Reform Bill of 1832
D. Publication of "Lyrical Ballads" and its "Preface"

23. Which of the following would a Romantic poet be most likely to use?

A. A "feathered chorister"
B. A "bird"
C. A "tenant of the sky"
D. An "airy fairy"

24. Wordsworth's poetry invariably reflects a proclivity for:

A. The creation of abstract concepts
B. An endorsement of the scientific tradition
C. The creation of an original philosophy
D. An examination of extraneous matters

25. Choose the correct order of the following in a published book:

A. Index, Copyright Page, Bibliography, Footnotes
B. Copyright Page, Bibliography, Index, Footnotes
C. Copyright Page, Footnotes, Bibliography, Index
D. Bibliography, Copyright Page, Index, Footnotes

26. The following phrases from Shakespeare have become the titles of famous works by famous authors. Match them correctly:

(*a*) *Under the Greenwood Tree*	(*i*) Thomas Hardy
(*b*) *The Sound and the Fury*	(*ii*) Somerset Maugham
(*c*) *Rosencrantz and Guildenstern are Dead*	(*iii*) William Faulkner
(*d*) *Of Cakes and Ale*	(*iv*) Tom Stoppard

Codes:

	(*a*)	(*b*)	(*c*)	(*d*)
A.	(*i*)	(*iii*)	(*iv*)	(*ii*)
B.	(*iv*)	(*ii*)	(*i*)	(*iii*)
C.	(*ii*)	(*iii*)	(*i*)	(*iv*)
D.	(*iii*)	(*iv*)	(*i*)	(*ii*)

27. Identify the statement that is **not true** among the following that explain "stage directions" in drama:

A. Stage directions inform readers how to stage, perform or imagine the play.
B. The place, time of action, design of the set and at times characters' actions or tone of voice are indicated by stage directions.
C. Stage directions are often italicised in the text of a play in order to be spoken aloud
D. Stage directions may appear at the beginning of a play, before a scene or attached to a line of dialogue.

28. The emergence of the concept of "World literature" is associated with:

(*a*) Friedrich Schiller
(*b*) Johann Wolfgang von Goethe
(*c*) Johann Goltfried Herder
(*d*) Immanuel Kant

A. (*a*) & (*b*) B. (*c*) & (*d*)
C. (*b*) & (*c*) D. (*a*) & (*d*)

29. "The Waste Land" is:

A. An Allegory B. A Sonnet
C. Blank Verse D. None of these

30. Who considers Hamlet to be an Artistic failure?

A. Bradley B. Eliot
C. Kermode D. None of these

31. In Hardy's fiction Nature comes out as:

A. Friendly B. Indifferent
C. Vindictive D. None of these

32. Identify Browning's poem in which the line– 'Who knows but the world many end to-night'–occurs:

A. "The Last Ride Together"
B. "One Word More"
C. "The Last Duchess"
D. None of the above

33. "My soul had been a lawn besprinkled o'er with flowers, and Stirring Shades, and baffled dreams" is an example of:
A. Metaphor B. Simile
C. Personification D. Metonymy

34. "Iron, times of doubts, disputes, distraction and Fear" is an example of:
A. Oxymoron B. Conceit
C. Alliteration D. Metonymy

35. "Pleasant Pain" is an example of:
A. Metaphor B. Paradox
C. Oxymoron D. None of these

36. 'Proper study of Mankind is man'– who has said these words:
A. Pope B. Swift
C. Shelley D. Shakespeare

37. The word renaissance means:
A. Rebirth B. Revival
C. Renewal D. None of these

38. The essay, "Of Studies" is written by:
A. Francis Bacon B. Carlyle
C. Thomas Montaigne D. Samuel Johnson

39. Robert Frost is mainly known as:
A. a nature poet
B. Poet of country life
C. a poet of nature and country life
D. None of these

40. In *The Old Man and Sea,* Santiago is an illustration of:
A. Hemingway's respect for struggle
B. Hemingway's total view of life
C. Hemingway's philosophy of life
D. None of these

41. George Eliot's real name was:
A. George Evans B. Eliot Evans
C. Marian Evans D. Marian Eliot

42. The period of English literature from 1660 to the end of the century is called:
A. Renaissance B. Jacobean Period
C. Restoration Period D. Romantic Age

43. The phrase 'Stream of Consciousness' was first used by:
A. James Joyce B. William James
C. Virginia Woolf D. William Faulkner

44. Who is the author of the following works: *Ai ladki, Daar Se Bichhudi, Mitro Marjani*?
A. Amrita Pritam B. Krishna Sobti
C. Mridula Pandey D. None of these

45. Find the odd one out:
A. *Train to Pakistan* B. *Ashes and Petals*
C. *Azadi* D. *The Final Solution*

46. Identify the novel with the wrong subtitle listed below:
A. *Middle march, a Study of Provincial Life*
B. *Tess of the D'Urbervilles, A Pure Woman*
C. *The Mayor of Casterbridge, A Person of Character*
D. *Felix Holt, the Radical*

47. Identify the correctly matched pair:
A. Amitav Ghosh – *All About H. Halterr*
B. Anita Desai – *Inheritance of Loss*
C. Shashi Deshpande – *A Bend in the Ganges*
D. Salman Rushdie – *The Enchantress of Florence*

48. Find the correct match:

(*a*) Formalism	(*i*) John Crow Ransom
(*b*) New Critics	(*ii*) The Jugians
(*c*) Psychological Theory of the Value of Literature	(*iii*) Victory Shklovsky
(*d*) Literary Art as Archetypal Image	(*iv*) I.A. Richards

Codes:

	(*a*)	(*b*)	(*c*)	(*d*)
A.	(*i*)	(*ii*)	(*iii*)	(*iv*)
B.	(*ii*)	(*iii*)	(*i*)	(*iv*)
C.	(*iii*)	(*i*)	(*iv*)	(*ii*)
D.	(*iii*)	(*iv*)	(*ii*)	(*i*)

49. Modernism has been described as being concerned with "disenchantment of our culture with culture itself" Who is the critic?
A. Stephen Spender B. Malcolm Bradbury
C. Lionel Trilling D. Joseph Frank

50. Match the following names:
(*a*) William (*i*) Stern Eliot
(*b*) Robert (*ii*) Herbert Lawrence

(*c*) David (*iii*) Makepeace Thackeray
(*d*) Thomas (*iv*) Lousi Stevenson

Codes:

	(*a*)	(*b*)	(*c*)	(*d*)
A.	(*i*)	(*ii*)	(*iii*)	(*iv*)
B.	(*ii*)	(*iii*)	(*i*)	(*iv*)
C.	(*iii*)	(*i*)	(*iv*)	(*ii*)
D.	(*iii*)	(*iv*)	(*ii*)	(*i*)

51. Who is the author of the following lines?
"Where the mind is without fear and the head is held hight;
Where knowledge is free; ..."
A. Tennyson B. Shakespeare
C. Alfred Noyes D. Tagore

52. The quote "The child is father of the man" exemplifies the following figure of speech:
A. Metaphor B. Euphemism
C. Irony D. Epigram

53. The expression "uneasy lies the head that wears the crown is an example of:
A. Pun B. Euphemism
C. Synecdoche D. Epigram

54. Identify the rhetorical figure used in the following line by Tennyson: "Father unfaithful kept him falsely true":
A. Oxymoron B. Metaphor
C. Pun D. Synecdoche

55. Which of the following ideas cannot be associated with postmodernism?
A. Diversity B. Hierarchy
C. Surface D. Synchronicity

56. Arrange the following choice in an ascending/ chronological sequence:
(*a*) R.K. Narayan (*b*) Salman Rushdie
(*c*) Arvind Adiga (*d*) Arundhati Roy
A. *bcda* B. *abcd*
C. *abdc* D. *dcab*

57. Arrange the following choice in an ascending/ chronological sequence:
(*a*) Milton (*b*) Shakespeare
(*c*) Wordsworth (*d*) Alexander Pope
A. *bcda* B. *abcd*
C. *dcab* D. *abdc*

58. Arrange the following choices in an ascending/ chronological sequence:
(*a*) Pearl S. Buck (*b*) Leo Tolstoy
(*c*) R.K. Narayan (*d*) Alice Walker
A. *bacd* B. *abcd*
C. *abdc* D. *bcad*

59. Which one of the following figure of speech is based on sound in sense theory?
A. Hyperbole B. Pun
C. Onomatopoeia D. Simile

60. Who asserted: "Some books are to be tasted, others to be swallowed, and some few to be chewed and digested."
A. William Butler B. Francis Bacon
C. Russell D. Ben Jonson

61. Who wrote:
"But I have promises to keep
And miles to go before I sleep"
A. Robert Frost B. William Faulkner
C. Wallace Stevens D. Langston Hughes

62. How many Fundamental Rights are recognized by the Constitution?
A. Five B. Nine
C. Eight D. Seven

63. Choose the correct sequence in the process of film making:
A. shot, scene, sequence, film
B. scene, shot, sequence, film
C. sequence, shot, scene, film
D. scene, sequence, shot, film

64. Match the following:
(*a*) *Alam Ara* (*i*) Sohrab Modi
(*b*) *Raja Harishchandra* (*ii*) V. Shantaram
(*c*) *Jhansi Ki Rani* (*iii*) Ardeshir Irani
(*d*) *Jahanak Jhanak Payal Baje* (*iv*) Dadasaheb Phalke

Codes:

	(*a*)	(*b*)	(*c*)	(*d*)
A.	(*i*)	(*ii*)	(*iii*)	(*iv*)
B.	(*ii*)	(*iii*)	(*i*)	(*iv*)
C.	(*iii*)	(*i*)	(*iv*)	(*ii*)
D.	(*iii*)	(*iv*)	(*i*)	(*ii*)

65. Frankfurt school belongs to:
A. Marxist Scholars
B. Neo-Marxist Scholars

C. Structural Behaviourist Scholars
D. Post Modernist Scholars

66. Human Development Index was created by:
A. Mehboob-ul-Haq and Meghnad Desai
B. Mohammad Yunus and Amartya Sen
C. Amartya Sen and Mehboob-ul-Haq
D. Manmohan Singh and Kieth Griffin

67. Which is the first telefilm of India?
A. *Sadgati* B. *Pather Panchali*
C. *Pikoo* D. *Bala*

68. Name the 20th century Hindi poet whose poem was adapted into a song in 2015 Hindi film *Masaan*?
A. Jai Shankar Prasad
B. Sarveshwar Dayal Saxena
C. Dushyant Kumar
D. Mahadevi Verma

69. The film *Jungle Book* is based on the works of writer:
A. V.S. Naipaul B. E.M. Forster
C. Rudyard Kipling D. Jim Corbett

70. Which Indian author was also known as the 'Nightingale of India'?
A. Lata Mangeshkar
B. Mahadevi Verma
C. Subhadra Kumari Chauhan
D. Sarojini Naidu

71. Which of following is/are correct matched?
A. Vikram Samvat-began in 58 BC
B. Saka Samvat-began in 78 AD
C. Gupta era-began in 319 AD
D. All are correct

72. Identify the following sentence type:
"The father forgave the son his mistake."
A. It is a compound sentence
B. It is a complex sentence
C. It is a simple sentence
D. None of the above

73. Identify the following sentence type:
"He could not rise, for he never tried."
A. It is a compound sentence
B. It is a complex sentence
C. It is a simple sentence
D. None of the above

74. Identify the following sentence type:
She will come when you send her a message
A. It is a compound sentence
B. It is a complex sentence
C. It is a simple sentence
D. None of these

75. The passive form of the sentence "See to it." would be:
A. Let's see it B. Let it be seen to
C. See it D. All of the above

Directions (Qs. 76 to 80): *Read the following passage and answer the questions based on it:*

The last half of my life has been lived in one of those painful epochs of human history during which the world is getting worse, and past victories which had seemed to be definitive have turned out to be only temporary. When I was young, Victorian optimism was taken for granted. It was thought that freedom and prosperity would spread gradually throughout the world through an orderly process, and it was hoped that cruelty, tyranny, and injustice would continually diminish. Hardly anyone was haunted by the fear of great wars. Hardly anyone thought of the nineteenth century as a brief interlude between past and future barbarism.

76. The author feels sad about the latter part of his life because:
A. He was nostalgic about his childhood
B. The world had not become prosperous
C. The author had not won any further victories
D. The world was painfully disturbed during that period of time

77. The victories of the past:
A. Brought permanent peace and prosperity
B. Ended cruelty, tyranny and injustice
C. Proved to be temporary events
D. Filed men with a sense of pessimism

78. The word 'definitive' used in the passage means:
A. Defined B. Final
C. Temporary D. Incomplete

79. During the Victorian age people believed that:
A. Strife would increase

B. There would be unlimited freedom
C. Wars would be fought on a bigger scale
D. Peace would previal and happiness would engulf the whole world

80. 'A brief interlude between past and future barbarism' can be interpreted as:
A. A short period of time between past and future acts of savagery
B. A short space of time between two great events
C. An interval between cruel wars
D. A dramatic performance during wars

Directions (Qs. 81 to 84): *Supply the correct alternative (out of the four choices given) in the blank space to make a correct sentence.*

81. Study hard ____ you will fail the exam.
A. or B. if
C. unless D. lest

82. Bread and butter ____ a good breakfast.
A. makes B. make
C. are D. none of these

83. Mr. Bansal comes from Chandigarh, as ____ his supporters.
A. do B. are
C. come D. well

84. There are twenty candidates for ____.
A. lecturership
B. the post of lectureship
C. lectureship
D. the post of lecturership

85. A Parasol is:
A. Where birds are kept
B. Where grain is stored
C. An inscription on a tomb
D. A lady's umberalla

86. 'One who is indifferent to pains and pleasures of life' is:
A. Sadist B. Stoic
C. Cynic D. Pessimist

87. Find the odd one out:
A. Perception B. Pentration
C. Insinuation D. Discernment

88. Choose the one nearest in meaning of the word 'Muse'.
A. Ponder B. Infect
C. Appease D. Amuse

89. The opposite of 'elite' is:
A. Underprivileged B. Uncultured
C. Populace D. Rustics

90. Find the odd one out:
A. Night-Day B. Light-Dark
C. White-Black D. Sun-Moon

91. *Agoraphobia* is fear of:
A. Heights
B. Enclosed places
C. Open Spaces
D. Crowd

92. Choose an alternative that is opposite in meaning to the italicized word in the expression: 'I can hear this *discordant* note':
A. Pleasant B. Agreeable
C. Melodious D. Harmonious

93. Choose the odd one out:
A. lethargic B. torpid
C. sluggish D. turgid

94. 'One who is fond of fighting' is:
A. Bellicose B. Aggressive
C. Belligerent D. Militant

Directions (Qs. 95 to 98): *Identify the part of speech of the words in italics in the following sentence:*

95. 'He was *banking* on the help from the union'.
A. Adjective B. Verb
C. Noun D. Adverb

96. 'They have been walking *about* for too long'.
A. Noun B. Preposition
C. Adverb D. Conjunction

97. 'Can't you find a *leak* in the tank?'
A. Verb B. Adjective
C. Noun D. Adverb

98. 'Young people show the tendency to *flock* together at parties'.
A. Noun B. Adverb
C. Verb D. Adjective

Directions (Qs. 99 & 100): *In the following sentence which of the given alternatives would make a correct sentence, when supplied in the blank:*

99. *'He is stronger than ____ man'.*

A. any B. any other
C. all D. All of these

100. *'Many a man ____ drowned in the sea'.*

A. was B. were
C. have D. None of these

ANSWERS

1	2	3	4	5	6	7	8	9	10
C	D	A	B	A	C	D	C	D	D
11	**12**	**13**	**14**	**15**	**16**	**17**	**18**	**19**	**20**
A	C	D	D	B	C	C	D	C	A
21	**22**	**23**	**24**	**25**	**26**	**27**	**28**	**29**	**30**
A	D	D	C	C	A	*	C	C	B
31	**32**	**33**	**34**	**35**	**36**	**37**	**38**	**39**	**40**
B	A	A	C	C	A	A	A	C	A
41	**42**	**43**	**44**	**45**	**46**	**47**	**48**	**49**	**50**
C	C	B	B	D	C	D	C	C	D
51	**52**	**53**	**54**	**55**	**56**	**57**	**58**	**59**	**60**
D	D	C	A	B	C	C	A	C	B
61	**62**	**63**	**64**	**65**	**66**	**67**	**68**	**69**	**70**
A	*	A	D	B	A	A	C	C	D
71	**72**	**73**	**74**	**75**	**76**	**77**	**78**	**79**	**80**
D	C	A	B	B	D	C	B	D	A
81	**82**	**83**	**84**	**85**	**86**	**87**	**88**	**89**	**90**
A	A	A	C	D	B	B	A	A	D
91	**92**	**93**	**94**	**95**	**96**	**97**	**98**	**99**	**100**
C	D	D	A	B	B	C	C	B	A

PART–B

ESSAY TYPE QUESTIONS

1. Write a critical note on any one of the two poetic extracts/poems given below so as to showcase your skill in close textual reading (note more than 750 words):

Poets live to an old age
Thought they're always getting killed off
they are still around.
Making friends
with fools and lumpens in these selfish times
thrusting poetry books into their hands
poets laugh for days on end
they howl first and then turn silent
but the cursed poems never shut up

Poets find birds in children
and girls in birds
and flowers in girls

collect the seeds of all they've seen
and sow themselves together with the seeds
Pets hide like seeds
only to return in new forms

At least now their breed is in no danger of extinction.

OR

Lover and madmen have such seething brains,
Such shaping fantasies, that apprehend
More than cool reason ever comprehends.
The lunatic, the lover, and the poet
Are of imagination all compact:
One sees more devils than vast hell can hold,
That is the madman; the lover, all as frantic,
Sees Helen's beauty in a brow of Egypt:
The poet's eye, in a fine frenzy rolling,
Doth glance from heaven to earth, from to heaven;
And, as imagination bodies forth
The forms of things unknown, the poet's pen
Turns them to shapes, and gives to airy nothing
A local habitation and a name.
Such tricks hath strong imagination,
That, if it would but apprehend some joy,
It comprehends some bringer of that joy,
Or in the night, imagining some fear,
How easy is a bush supposed a bear!

2. Attempt a literary essay on any one of the following topics (not more than 750 words):
(*i*) Literary Culture
(*ii*) Story in the Digital Age
(*iii*) Poetry as Truth

ANSWERS

1. Lover and madmen have such seething brains, ...

Shakespeare probably wrote *A Midsummer Night's Dream* in 1595, a year in which he was likely excited by the reopening of the theaters (they had closed due to an outbreak of plague in 1593). At this time, Shakespeare was reaching his height as a writer of dramatic comedies and was writing his first major tragedy, *The Tragedy of Romeo and Juliet.* Many believe that *A Midsummer Night's Dream* is Shakespeare's finest comedy, revealing his fertile imagination at its best. Like most comedies of his day, the play centers around romantic relationships leading to marriage and derives much of its humour from the mishaps and misunderstandings the young couples experience before their romantic relationships are sorted out. The play draws its strength, however, not from the conventional story of young people hoping to find true love, but from the rich contrasts in the Athens of Shakespeare's imagination. There, Theseus, duke of Athens, rules and carries out the letter of the law in the city while mischievous fairies rule a kingdom of their own in the wild forest just outside the city. The story offers a wide array of characters: from the mischievous fairies to the witty noblemen and women, from unreasonable fathers to bumbling craftsmen. It is a place where identity itself is uncertain—in order to find their destiny the characters must essentially lose themselves for a time. It is a story of song, airy charm, and broad slapstick.

Many critics have speculated that *A Midsummer Night's Dream* was written and performed to celebrate an aristocratic wedding, and, indeed, there is much in the play to support such speculation. Its subject matter and themes would have been appropriate for a court wedding, and some have theorized that certain passages may have been intended as compliments to Queen Elizabeth. The play shares many elements with the court masque, a form of entertainment popular among the aristocracy of the period and characterized by music, song, dance, and fanciful characters. The play also contains an element of the masque made popular by Shakespeare's contemporary and rival dramatist Ben Jonson—the antimasque.

An antimasque, a burlesque comic sketch, took place before the masque itself, and the antimasque's grotesque elements were meant to contrast with the sophistication and elegance of the masque. With his customary ingenuity, however, Shakespeare places what can be considered his antimasque—the artisans' presentation of the Pyramus and This be story—at the end of *A Midsummer Night's Dream,* where it serves to comment on the action of the play as a whole.

Nevertheless, *A Midsummer Night's Dream* is much richer and broader in focus than any court masque. It raises questions about the difference between art and life, the theater and the everyday world, the dreaming and the waking world. Its characters are drawn not only from the nobility but from the common class, and while the "low" characters in the play—Bottom, Quince, Flute, and the other artisans—are burlesqued, their self-knowledge and kindliness often stands in contrast to the behaviour of the nobles. Also, Bottom, a mere commoner, is the only human character in the play allowed to glimpse and directly interact with the third group of characters in the play—the fairies. Thus, in *A Midsummer Night's Dream,* Shakespeare creates three separate but very interdependent worlds—the witty world of the aristocracy, the coarse humor of the well-meaning artisans, and the supernatural world of the fairies—for the audience to take delight in, compare and contrast, and view critically.

2. Poetry and Truth

Poetry and truth are related in this way. Poetry teaches us things we cannot learn from other sources. It speaks to us in a language that is different from the language of mathematics, logic and the natural sciences. And it puts us in touch with features of our life and environment – the inner and the outer world – to which we would have no access if it did not exist.

The language of poetry is the language of the imagination. It is a fact of human psychology that even the most abstract thoughts are accompanied by concrete images. By creating new images, poets enable us to think new thoughts, to reflect imaginatively on important aspects of our experience.

Not all poets succeed in doing this, but the best of them do. They convey important truths about life and death, joy and sorrow, childhood and old age, war and peace, love in all its forms, solitude, memory and the complexity of human emotions. And they convey these truths poetically, by using language in a special way, varying the patterns and rhythms of ordinary, everyday conversation, employing rhyme, assonance and alliteration, but, above all, by using simile and 'metaphor' to create striking and memorable images.

A simple example of the way thought and image are woven together in poetic texts is this Old Testament reflection from the Book of Job on the ephemeral character of man's life: "Man wastes away like rotten wood, like a garment eaten by moths. He rises like a flower, and withers away; he disappears like a shadow, never to be seen again."

There are four images in this short passage, where man's fragile existence is compared to rotten wood, a moth-eaten dress, a flower withering away, and a fleeting shadow. A few lines later the poet uses yet another image: "As water evaporates from a lake, and a river wastes away and dries up, so man goes to sleep and does not rise again."

It is by such accumulation of images that the poem succeeds in conveying its truth. Shorn of those images the central idea loses much of its force.

Poets were the first ecologists. All great poets, including the authors of the earliest sacred texts in both eastern and western cultural traditions, have found in the natural environment a constant source of inspiration.

Whether it was itself the subject of their poetic output, or whether it served as backdrop to it, nature always featured prominently in their works.

Before the great social upheavals brought about by urbanisation in the wake of the Industrial Revolution, people's ties to the natural environment were very strong – much stronger than they are today. But it would be wrong to think that such ties were severed for good, or that the poetic practice just referred to came to an abrupt end or was no longer possible.

Living in the middle of the urban jungle, contemporary writers can still borrow their imagery from nature and use it to good effect. In his famous two-line poem In a Station of the Metro, Ezra Pound compared the faces of people inside a subway station to petals on the branch of a tree. "The apparition of these faces in the crowd: petals on a wet, black bough."

As these lines show, poets do not limit themselves to describing Nature, they see psychological attitudes and states of mind reflected in it as they project their own moods and emotions onto it.

Iris Murdoch once wrote: "You may know a truth, but if it's at all complicated you have to be an artist not to utter it as a lie."

As is well known, Plato and Aristotle held contrasting views about poetry. While Plato insisted that poets were liars and wanted them banished from his Ideal State, Aristotle defended the claim of poetry to tell the truth.

There were other reasons for their disagreement. While Plato felt that the emotions belonged to the irrational soul and wanted them suppressed, Aristotle saw them as forming an integral part of the personality and considered an emotionless character as not really human at all. For him, poets in general, and dramatic poets in particular, played an important role in "directing the mind" to a better understanding of the emotions.

We can learn important truths about ourselves by watching Antigone or by reading Hamlet. In highlighting the role of action in the theatre we must not lose sight of the importance of the poetry; for unless we understand the words, the work loses much of its significance and will not produce its intended effect.

It is the poetry that conveys the rage of the disgraced protagonist in King Lear; and it is the quality of the language, the imagery and the rhythm of the verse that enable him to express his anger and grief at Cordelia's death with such poignancy and vigour. "Howl, howl, howl, howl! O! You are men of stones. Had I your tongue and eyes, I'd use them so/ That heaven's vaults should crack. She's gone for ever!"

The world is full of surprises, pleasant and unpleasant, and our emotions are extremely complex. That complexity, as Martha Nussbaum has emphasised, "cannot be fully and adequately stated in the language of conventional philosophical prose – a style remarkably flat and lacking in wonder – but only in a language and in forms themselves more complex, more allusive, more attentive to particulars" – precisely the language of the poet, the novelist, the artist.

In our search for the truth, in every attempt on our part to understand in some way the world's infinite variety and the complexity of the emotions, poetry plays a crucial role. Poets widen our perceptual field, they make us look at things in a new light, illuminating important aspects of reality and deepening our knowledge of the human condition. They evoke situations with which we can identify and provide us with images that stimulate fresh thoughts and from which we can learn. Contrary to what Plato claimed, poetry can be – and quite often is – a vehicle for truth.

English Language & Comprehension

Comprehension Passages

In the English language paper, questions on comprehension test are very important for the aspirants appearing in the competitive examinations. Therefore, you should try to learn how to solve these questions. Practice of solving these questions will greatly help you in the examination.

Comprehension means the act of comprehending or the capacity of the mind to understand. In the examination papers, questions on comprehension test are included to judge the ability of the aspirants to understand the given passage.

Directions: *In this chapter few passages for comprehension test are given. Read the passages carefully and answer the questions given after each passage. Each question is provided with four alternative answers and they are marked as 'A', 'B', 'C', and 'D'. Out of the four alternatives, choose the correct answer according to the context of the passage.*

PASSAGE-1

A need of tremendous significance, which has been discussed recurrently in educational literature, relates to the creation of a demand for education. Of course, the underlying assumption in this concern is that notwithstanding how poor people view education today, its widespread diffusion up to a minimal level is essential for national well-being. If this proposition is accepted, then it becomes, imperative that measures should be taken to create a feeling in the community that their future would be at stake if they do not look after the elementary education of their children. Because of the present apathy, there is total dependence on Government, and consequently, there is hardly any effort on the part of a village or the community leadership or at the level of block or district, to set up or even to help the proper running of schools. It is undeniable that, to a great extent, this is also because the school system is now a part of a gigantic bureaucratic set up which leaves no room for intervention at the local levels and is, in effect, equally frustrating to a teacher with some initiative. If the community is to be involved, local resources, knowledge and skills will have to help in setting up and managing the schools; school children of suitable age will have to participate in community work; and learning experience including skill development will have to be provided in other establishments where necessary, if the schools do not have the related facilities. The community will also have to assume responsibility for maintaining the school buildings and for arranging midday meals, uniforms (especially for girls) and books, etc., as these would greatly facilitate the retention of children in the schools. This would be facilitated if the community is also authorised to keep an eye on the performance of schools and specially of the teachers.

1. The community is not able to take active part in the running of schools largely because
   A. the community has no interest in the school system
   B. the present day school system does not allow any local intervention
   C. the teachers have no initiative for community work
   D. the community leaders depend on the government

2. Which of the following measures DOES NOT indicate community involvement in the school system?
   A. People in the community help in the setting up and management of schools
   B. Many learning experiences are provided to children in establishments outside school
   C. Schools become a part of the bureaucratic system
   D. People assume the responsibility of arranging midday meals, uniforms, etc.
3. "Its widespread diffusion up to minimal level is essential." Here DIFFUSION means
   A. dissemination B. proclamation
   C. publicity D. amplification
4. Today the most significant need in the area of education is that
   A. the schools should be run properly
   B. people should look after the education of their children
   C. education should be provided to all
   D. people should themselves demand education

PASSAGE-2

It is easy to accept Freud as an applied scientist, and indeed, he is widely regarded as the 20th century's master clinician. However, Marx is better understood for being an applied sociologist. Marx was no Faustian, concerned solely with understanding society, but a Promethean who sought to understand it well enough to influence and to change it. He was chiefly concerned with the social problems of a lay group, the proletariat, and there can be little doubt that this work is motivated by an effort to reduce their suffering, as he saw it. His diagnosis was that their increasing misery and alienation engendered endemic class struggle; his prognosis claimed that this would culminate in revolution. His therapeutic prescription was class consciousness and active struggle.

Here, as in assessing Durkheim or Freud, the issue is not whether this analysis is empirically correct or scientifically adequate. Furthermore, whether or not this formulation seems to eviscerate Marx's revolutionary core, as critics on the left may charge, or whether the formulation provides Marx with a new veneer of academic respectability, as critics on the right may allege, is entirely irrelevant from the present standpoint. In so far as Marx's or any other social scientist's work conforms to a generalised model of applied social science, and in so far as it is professionally oriented to the value and social problems of laymen in his society, he may be treated as an applied social scientist.

Despite Durkheim's intellectualistic proclivities and rationalistic pathos, he was too much the product of European turbulence to turn his back on the travail of his culture. "Why strive for knowledge of reality, if its knowledge cannot aid us in life," he asked. "Social science," he said, "can provide us with rules of action for the future." Durkheim, like Marx, conceived of science as an agency of social action, and was professionally oriented to the values and problems of laymen in his society. Unless one sees that Durkheim was in some part an applied social scientist, it is impossible to understand why he concludes his monumental study of *Suicide* with a chapter on "Practical Consequence," and why, in the Division of Labour, he proposes a specific remedy for anomie.

1. According to the author, which of the following did Marx and Durkheim have in common?
   A. Regard for practical application of science
   B. An interest in penology
   C. A belief in the importance of class struggle
   D. None of the above
2. What action did Marx prescribe for the proletariat?
   A. Alienation
   B. Passive resistance
   C. Class consciousness
   D. None of the above
3. Marx sought to
   A. Understand society
   B. Change the educational system
   C. Apply science to philosophy
   D. Both (A) and (B)

4. It may be inferred from the passage that the applied social scientist might be interested in all of the following except
A. the theory of mechanics
B. rehabilitation of delinquents
C. reduction of social tensions
D. industrial safety

PASSAGE-3

The social Darwinist conception of evolution is not that of the biologist but of the propagandist looking for justification for his political theories. The simplistic formulation of ferocious antisocial struggle finds no place in the theories of modern biologists. Even on the animal level the scientific picture is not that of "struggle" and ruthless elimination. If in the tropics a pigmented skin is an advantage, no one is swept to destruction in a fight for blackness. Modifications of that sort, which prove advantageous, gradually establish themselves without trouble. Even living on other animals for food does not imply savagery—fishermen are not unpleasant and aggressive persons; tribes living, as they once did, on shellfish are not haters of their kind; even pig breeders and chicken farmers can be kind to their neighbours and no worse than the rest of us. Lorenz, constantly quoted to defend innate aggression, points out that the predatory carnivores are not angry when bringing down an antelope. It is simply a matter of going to fetch the dinner. A lion can be angry, but not when going out to kill. One might go on and take the whole case to pieces bit by bit, but enough has been said to indicate that the picture of "nature red in tooth and claw" is the poet's view—the phrase was Tennyson's—not the scientist's: it is tendentious, controversial exaggeration, not objective science. Even the notion of the "survival of the fittest" begs the question. If we say that the fittest survive, we only mean that they do survive. It implies no other quality than survival ability. It holds just as well for the oyster or the flourishing flea as for the beautifully adapted camel or flying fox. It does not follow that the survivor is the fittest even in being the finest specimen of its kind, let alone of the kind that we would prefer to see flourish.

1. The instinct to kill in carnivores comes from their
A. need to survive
B. need to prove their might
C. inherently brutal nature
D. liking for flesh

2. The writer's attitude towards poets is that of
A. awe
B. scorn
C. anger
D. indifference

3. The term 'survival of the fittest' suggests the survival of the
A. mightiest
B. finest
C. best
D. prepared

4. By citing various examples the writer tries to establish the fact that savagery does not entail
A. killing of any kind
B. killing of lesser animals
C. killing dispassionately to serve an end
D. ruthless killing

5. The concept of ferocious antisocial struggle finds credence with
A. biologist
B. scientists
C. Lorenz
D. Darwin

PASSAGE-4

The difficulty in the education of young infants is largely the *delicate balance* required in the parents. Constant watchfulness and much labour are needed to avoid injury to health : these qualities will hardly exist in the necessary degree except where there is strong parental affection. But where this exists, it is very likely not to be wise. To the devoted parents, the child is immensely important. Unless care is taken, the child feels this and judges himself as important as his parents feel but later in life his social environment will not regard him so fondly and the habit of assuming that he is the centre of other people's universe will lead to disappointment. It is, therefore, necessary, not only in the first year, but afterwards also, that parents should be breezy, cheerful and rather matter-of-fact where the child's possible ailments are concerned. In old days, infants were too much patted, sung to, rocked and dandled. This was wrong since it turned them into helpless pampered parasities. The right rule is : encourage spontaneous activities but discourage demands on others. Do not let the child see how much you do for him or how much trouble you take. Let him, wherever possible, taste the joy of success, achieved by his own efforts, not extracted by tyrannising over the grown-ups.

1. 'Delicate balance' required in parents in sentence one refers to
   A. cautiousness B. possessiveness
   C. indifference D. matter-of-factness
2. In the past the excessively fondled children became
   A. troublesome B. mischievous
   C. parasites D. abnormal
3. For the possible ailments of the child, the writer advised the parents to be
   A. indifferent B. demanding
   C. unsympathetic D. matter-of-fact
4. The author wishes the parents to let the child
   A. manage his own things
   B. be absolutely free
   C. work under their guidance
   D. seek anybody's help if needed
5. A child pampered by his parents is likely to become
   A. disappointed B. demoralised
   C. dependent D. independent

PASSAGE-5

The world dismisses curiosity by calling it idle or mere idle curiosity—even though curious persons are seldom idle. Parents do their best to extinguish curiosity in their children because it makes life difficult to be faced everyday with a string of unanswerable questions about what makes fire hot or why grass grows. Children whose curiosity survives parental discipline are invited to join our university. With the university, they go on asking their questions and trying to find the answers. In the eyes of a scholar, that is what a university is for. Some of the questions which the scholars ask seem to the world to be scarcely worth asking, let alone answering. They asked questions too minute and specialised for you and me to understand without years of explanation. If the world inquires of one of them, why he wants to know the answer to a particular question, he may say, especially if he is a scientist, that the answer will in some obscure way make possible a new machine or weapon or gadget. He talks that way because he knows that the world understands and respects utility.

But to you who are now part of the university, he will say that he wants to know the answer simply because he does not know it, the way the mountain climber wants to climb a mountain, simply because it is there. Similarly, a historian asked by an outsider, why he studies history, may come out with the argument that he has learnt to repeat on such occasions, something about knowledge of the past making it possible to understand the present and mould the future. But if you really want to know why a historian studies the past, the answer is much simpler, something happened and he would like to know what. All this does not mean that the answers which scholars find to their questions have no consequences. They may have enormous consequences but these seldom form the reason for asking the question or pursuing the answers. It is true that scholars can be put to work answering questions for the sake of the consequences as thousands are working now, for example, in search of a cure for cancer. But this is not the primary function of the scholars. The consequences are usually subordinate to the satisfaction of curiosity.

1. The common people consider some of the questions that the scholars ask unimportant
   A. as they are too lazy and idle
   B. as they are too modest
   C. as it's beyond their comprehension
   D. as it is considered a waste of time
2. According to the passage, parents do their best to discourage curiosity in their children
   A. because they have no time
   B. because they have no patience to answer them
   C. because they feel that their children ask stupid questions continuously
   D. because they are unable to answer all their questions

3. According to the passage, the children make life difficult for their parents
   A. by their ceaseless curiosity
   B. by unceasing bombardment of questions
   C. by asking irrelevant questions
   D. by posing profound questions
4. Children whose curiosity survives parental discipline means
   A. children retaining their curiosity in spite of being discouraged by their parents
   B. children pursuing their mental curiosity
   C. children's curiosity subdued due to parents' intervention
   D. children being disciplined by their parents
5. A historian really studies the past
   A. to comprehend the present and to reconstruct the future
   B. to explain the present and plan the future
   C. to understand the present and make fortune
   D. to understand the present and mould the future

PASSAGE-6

I do not suggest that the cultural side of education should be ignored. On the contrary, I think, it is essential to the production of the sort of adult who best fits the modern world. But I think that what is important in cultural education should be conveyed, at any rate in the early stages, by methods far more attractive than those now usually practised. History and geography should be taught at first by means of the cinema. When taught this way, they will give pleasure; attention will be spontaneous and therefore the impression will be less temporary. In spite of reforming movements, there is still among educators a feeling that what is enjoyed without effort cannot have much educational value. I would have children made aware of the manners and customs of tribes and nations utterly remote from their own. Education conducted on these lines would do more than many books 'to cure provincialism in space and time' and to make children realize that actual human beings with actual feelings can be outwardly very different from the people among whom they live, but inwardly composed of the same human material. A Zulu would not appear strange, remote or savage but one like themselves.

1. The expression 'to cure provincialism in space and time' means to get rid of
   A. regional feelings B. obscure ideas
   C. narrow views D. selfish opinion
2. The writer thinks that the cultural side of education is needed to make man
   A. appreciate one's heritage
   B. appreciate other civilizations
   C. suitable for modern civilization
   D. admire his environment
3. The writer criticised traditional educators for not
   A. using cinema as a method of teaching
   B. making learning an enjoyable activity
   C. imparting information about remote tribes
   D. imparting information about various cultures
4. The response of the learners to teaching through cinema is
   A. absorbing B. long-lasting
   C. enthusiastic D. superficial
5. One of the goals of education should be to make children realise that
   A. human culture is diverse
   B. regional cultures should not be ignored
   C. they must respect values of alien culture
   D. there is a unified system of human values underneath cultural diversity

PASSAGE-7

Both plants and animals of many sorts show remarkable changes in form, structure, growth habits, and even mode of reproduction in becoming adapted to different climatic environment, types of food supply, or mode of living. This divergence in response to evolution is commonly expressed by altering the form and function of some part or parts of the organism, the original identity of which is clearly discernible. For example, the creeping foot of the snail is seen in related marine pteropods to be modified into a flapping organ useful for swimming, and is changed into prehensile arms that bear suctorial disks in the squids and other cephalopods. The limbs of various mammals are modified according to several different modes of life—for swift running (cursorial) as in the horse and antelope, for swinging in trees (arboreal) as in the monkeys, for digging (fossorial) as in the moles and gophers, for flying (volant) as in the bats, for swimming (aquatic) as in the seals, whales and dolphins, and for other adaptations. The structures or organs that show main change in connection with this adaptive divergence are commonly identified readily as *homologous* in spite of great alterations. Thus, the finger and wrist-bones of a bat and whale, for instance, have virtually nothing in common except that they are definitely equivalent elements of the mammalian limb.

1. The author provides information that would answer which of the following questions?

I. What factors cause change in organism?

II. What is the theory of evolution?

III. How are horses legs related to seals flipper?

A. I only B. II only

C. I and III only D. I, II and III

2. Which is the most appropriate title for the passage, based on its content?

A. Evolution

B. Our Changing Bodies

C. Adaptive Divergence

D. Changes in Organs

3. The author organises the passage by

A. comparison and contrast

B. general statements followed by examples

C. hypothesis and proof

D. definition of key terms

4. The author's style can best be described as

A. Objective B. Humorous

C. Esoteric D. Patronizing

5. Which of the following words, could best be substituted for 'homologous' (in bold type) without substantially changing the author's meaning?

A. Divergent B. Corresponding

C. Altered D. Tactile

PASSAGE-8

Shames and delusions are esteemed for soundest truths, while reality is *fabulous.* If men would steadily observe realities only, and not allow themselves to be deluded, life, to compare it with such things as we know, would be like a fairy tale and the Arabian Night's entertainments. If we respect only what is inevitable and has a right to be, music and poetry would resound along the streets. When we are unhurried and wise, we perceive that only great and worthy things have any permanent and absolute existence—that petty fears and petty pleasures are but the shadow of the reality. This is always exhilarating and sublime. By closing the eyes and slumbering and consenting to be deceived by shows, men establish and confirm their daily life of routine and habit everywhere, which still is built on purely illusory foundations. Children, who play life, discern its true law and relations more clearly than men, who fail to live it worthily, but who think that they are wiser by experience; that is by failure.

I have read in a Hindu book that there was a king's son who, being expelled in infancy from his native city, was brought up by a forester and growing up to maturity in that state, imagined himself to belong to the barbarous race with which he lived. One of his father's ministers, having discovered him, revealed to him what he was and the misconception of his character was removed and he knew himself to be a prince, "So soul," continues the Hindu philosopher, "from the circumstances in which it is placed, mistakes its own character, until the truth is revealed to it by some holy teacher and then it knows itself to be Brahma."

We think that is which appears to be. If a man should give us an account of the realities he beheld, we should not recognize the place in his description. Look at a meeting house, or a court house, or a jail, or a shop, or a dwelling house and say what that thing really is before a true gaze and they would all go to pieces in your account of them. Men esteem truth remote, in the outskirts of the system, being the farthest star, before Adam and after the last man. In entirety, there is indeed something true and sublime. But all these times and places and occasions are now and here. God himself culminates in the present moment and will never be more divine in the lapse of all ages. And we are enabled to apprehend at all what is sublime and noble only by the perpetual instilling and drenching of the reality that surrounds us. The universe constantly and obediently answers to our conceptions : whether we travel fast or slow; the track is laid for us. Let us spend our lives in conceiving, then. The poet or the artist never yet had so fair and noble a design but some of his posterity at least could accomplish it.

1. The author believes that children are often more acute than adults in their appreciation of life's relations because
A. children know more than adults
B. children can use their experience better
C. children's eyes are unclouded by failure
D. experience is the best teacher

2. The writer's attitude towards the arts is one of
A. indifference B. suspicion
C. admiration D. repulsion

3. The passage implies that human beings
A. cannot distinguish the true from the untrue
B. are immoral if they are lazy
C. should be bold and fearless
D. believe in fairytales

4. The author is primarily concerned with urging the reader to
A. mediate on the meaninglessness of the present
B. appraise the present for its true value
C. look to the future for enlightenment
D. spend more time in leisure activities

5. The word 'fabulous' in the passage means
A. wonderful B. delicious
C. birdlike D. illusion

PASSAGE-9

In this world of human affairs there is no worse nuisance than a boy at the age of fourteen. He is neither ornamental nor useful.

It is impossible to shower affection on him as on a little boy and he is always getting in the way. If he talks with childish lisp he is called a baby, and if he answers in a grown-up way he is called *impertinent.* In fact any talk at all from him is resented. Then he is at the unattractive, growing age. He grows out of his clothes with indecent haste, his voice grows hoarse and breaks, and quavers, his face grows suddenly angular and unsightly. It is easy to secure the shortcoming of early childhood, but it is hard to tolerate even unavoidable lapses in a boy of fourteen. The lad himself becomes painfully self-conscious. When he talks with elderly people he is either unduly forward, or else so unduly shy that he appears ashamed of his very existence.

Yet it is at this very age when in his heart of hearts a young lad most craves for recognition and love; and he becomes the devoted slave of any one who shows him consideration. But none dare openly love him, for that would be regarded as undue indulgence and therefore bad for the boy. So, what with scolding and chiding, he becomes very much like a stray dog that has lost his master.

For a boy of fourteen his own home is the only paradise. To live in a strange house with strange people is little short of torture, while the height of bliss is to receive the kind looks of women and never to be *slighted* by them.

1. How do grownups react to a boy of fourteen whenever he speaks?
A. They call him impertinent
B. They call him a baby
C. They resent it
D. They call him either a baby or an impertinent fellow and resent any talk at all from him

2. Point out the figure of speech in the first sentence
A. A metaphor
B. An alliterative sentence
C. Hyperbole
D. Exaggeration

3. Point out any two unavoidable lapses in a boy of fourteen
A. He grows painfully self-conscious and talk with a lisp

B. He craves for love and recognition and behave like a stray dog
C. His voice grows hoarse and breaks and quavers, his face grows suddenly angular and unsightly
D. He is neither antenatal nor useful

4. What does a boy of fourteen crave for?
A. Recognition
B. The height of bliss
C. Recognition and love
D. Love and indulgence

5. "He becomes the devoted slave of anyone who shows him consideration." Point out the figure of speech.
A. Simile B. Metaphor
C. Hyperbole D. Personification

6. "He becomes very much like a stray dog that has lost his master" is a:
A. metaphor B. good metaphor
C. bad simile D. good simile

7. "Impertinent" in the slang means:
A. happy-go-lucky B. care-a-hang
C. cheeky D. rowdy

8. "For a boy of fourteen his own home is the only paradise." Substitute another word for "Paradise".
A. Heaven B. Shelter
C. Haven D. Garden

9. "The height of bliss" indicates
A. excitement
B. the greatest joy and happiness
C. the greatest fear
D. the feeling of shyness

10. 'Slighted' is Synonymous with
A. insulted B. treated with love
C. beaten D. scolded

PASSAGE-10

Foot-racing is a popular activity in the United States. It is seen not only as a competitive sport but also as a way to exercise, to enjoy the *camaraderie* of like-minded people and to donate money for a good cause. Though serious runners may spend months training to compete, other runners and walkers might not train at all. Those not competing might run in an effort to beat their own time or simply to enjoy the fun and exercise. People of all ages, from those less than one year of age (who may be pushed in *strollers*) to those in their eighties, enter into this sport. The races are held in city streets, on college campuses, through parks and in suburban areas and they are commonly 5 to 10 kilometres in length.

The largest foot-race in the world is the 12 kilometre Bay to Breakers race that is held in San Francisco every spring. This race begins on the east side of the city near San Francisco Bay and ends on the west side at the Pacific Ocean. There may be 80,000 or more people running in this race through the streets and hills of San Francisco. In the front are the serious runners who compete to win and who might finish in as little as 34 minutes. Behind them are the thousands who take several hours to finish. In the back of the race are those who dress in costumes and come just for fun. One year, there was a group of men who dressed like Elvis Presley and another group consisted of fire-fighters who were tied together in a long line carrying a fire-hose. There was even a bridal party, in which the bride and the groom threw flowers to bystanders and they were actually married at some point along the route.

1. The word "camaraderie" could best be replaced by which of the following words?
A. Games B. Jokes
C. Companionship D. Views

2. The main purpose of the passage is
A. make fun of runners in costumes
B. give reasons for the popularity of foot-races
C. describe a popular activity
D. encourage people to exercise

3. As used in the passage the word "strollers" refers to:
A. carriages B. wheelchairs
C. wagons D. cribs

4. Which of the following is not the reason why people enter foot-races?
A. To exercise B. To enjoy
C. As a compulsion D. For charity

5. Which of the following is NOT implied by the author?
   A. Foot-races appeal to a variety of people
   B. Running is a good way to strengthen the heart
   C. Workers can compete for prizes
   D. Age and profession is no bar to enter footraces

PASSAGE-11

Culture is the cultivation of plant or garden, not the eradication of its roots. It is an understanding of the roots and seeds, their patient care and instructed nourishment. Culture is not knowledge, nor is it art; still less is it acquaintance with literature and art. By culture, I mean first of all what the anthropologists mean; the way of life of a particular people living together in one place. Culture is made visible in their arts, their social system, their habits, their customs and their religion. It is an aggregate of customs, institutions, manners, standards, tastes, morals and beliefs. Now these are transmitted rather by the family than by the school; hence when family life fails to play its part, we must expect our culture to deteriorate. It is a delusion to think that the maladies of the modern world can be put right by a system of instructions. On the contrary, universal education, by lowering standards, morals and tastes to a common denominator and by sharpening the wits rather than disciplining character, tends to breakdown existing checks and balances. Education should be the drawing forth of potential values; it should not be the destruction of the safeguards that tradition places around the young egos naturally inclined to willful and precarious flights.

1. According to this passage, education is
   A. the sharpening of wits
   B. tapping and encouraging the inherent values in man
   C. the substitution of old traditions with new ones
   D. the development of moral standards
2. The passage suggests that universal education
   A. is the solution to the problems in the modern world
   B. is, in fact, aggravating the existing problems of the modern world
   C. would help retain the cultural values
   D. would prevent us from transmitting culture to the future generations
3. The writer uses the term 'culture' to refer to
   A. one's acquaintance with literature and art
   B. the cultivation of a plant or garden by a community
   C. the way of life of a particular people living together in one place
   D. one's acquisition of knowledge
4. The culture of a community is said to deteriorate when
   A. there is a fall in its educational standards
   B. the family life fails to play its part
   C. there is universal education
   D. it adopts the modern system of instruction
5. The culture of a community is transmitted
   A. more by school than the family
   B. more by the family than school
   C. equally by both
   D. by the peer group

PASSAGE-12

Every survey ever held has shown that the image of an attractive woman is the most effective advertising gimmick. She may sit astride the mudguard of a new car, or step into it ablaze with jewels, she may lie at the man's feet stroking his new socks, she may hold the petrol pump in a challenging pass, or dance through woodland glades in slow motion in all the glory of a new shampoo. Whatever she does, her image sells. The *gynolatry* of our civilization is written large upon its face, upon hoardings, cinema screens, television, newspapers, magazines, tins, packets, cartons, bottles, all consecrated to the reigning deity, the female fetish. Her dominion must not be thought to entail the rule of women, for she is not a woman. Her glossy lips and matt complexion, her unfocused eyes and flawless fingers, her extraordinary hair all floating and shining, curling and gleaming, reveal the inhuman triumph of cosmetics, lighting, focussing and printing. She sleeps unruffled, her lips red and juicy and closed, her eyes as crisp and black as if newly painted and her false lashes immaculately curled. Even when she washes her face with a new and creamier toilet soap her expression is as tranquil and vacant, and the paint as flawless as ever. If ever she should appear tousled and troubled, her features are miraculously smoothed to their proper veneer by a new washing powder on a bouillon cube. For, she is a doll : weeping, pouting or sinking, running or reclaiming, she is a doll.

1. The author's primary purpose in this passage is
A. to ridicuie women
B. to show the dominance of women in advertising
C. to portray the obsession of women with trivial thing
D. to depict the emancipation of women

2. What point is the writer trying to make when he says "she may lie at a man's feet stroking his new socks"?
A. Women like being subservient
B. Women are observed with clothes
C. This is a typical posture of women in advertising
D. Women enjoy this kind of intimacy

3. The 'gynolatry' of one civilization would suggest all the following except that
A. women enjoy immense power in modern society
B. the image of women boost sales as few other things can
C. women worship is all pervasive in advertising
D. glamorous and attractive women are the forte of modern advertising

4. By saying that women depicted in an advertisement is 'not a woman' the author implies that
A. in real life women are less attractive
B. the depiction of women in advertisement is grossly artificial and unreal
C. in real life women are more dominant
D. in advertisement, a woman is a mere commercial symbol

5. In the last sentence of the paragraph, the word 'doll' is meant to express
A. tenderness
B. delicacy
C. contempt
D. beauty

PASSAGE-13

Today, every major *anthology* of ninenteenth century poetry includes examples of the work which Christina Rossetti produced during her long literary *career.* Born in 1830, she began composing verse at the age of eleven and continued to write for the remaining fifty three years of her life. Her brother Dante Gabriel Rossetti, himself a poet and painter, soon recognised her genius and urged her to publish her poems. By the time of her death in 1894, Christina had written more than eleven hundred poems and had published over nine hundred of them. Although her work has earned her recognition as the greatest woman poet of the Victorian Age, there is still no authoritative edition of her poetry.

1. Christina Rossetti began writing poetry
A. only after her brother urged her to do so
B. when she was fifty-three years old
C. when she was very young
D. when her genius was recognised

2. Christina's brother was probably a good judge of her work because
A. he loved his sister very much
B. he himself published poems
C. he was a poet
D. he was a famous painter

3. At the time this passage was written, Christina Rossetti's poetry
A. was almost unknown
B. was rarely published
C. had made her known as the greatest woman poet of the eighteenth century
D. had not been collected in an authoritative edition

4. By 1894, Christina had
A. published only a few of the many poems she had written
B. published all the poems she had written
C. published more than eleven hundred poems
D. published over nine hundred poems

5. The word "anthology" probably means
   A. writer   B. collection
   C. poem   D. poet

PASSAGE-14

Several years ago my parents, my wife, my son and I ate at a restaurant. After a wonderful dinner, the waiter set the bill in the middle of the table. That's what it happened, my father did not reach for the bill.

Conversation continued. Finally, it dawned on me. I was supposed to pay the bill. After hundreds of restaurant meals with my parents after a lifetime of thinking of my father as the one with the money, it had all changed. I reached for the bill and my view of myself suddenly altered; I was an adult.

Some people mark off their lives in years, I measure mine in small events—in rites of passage. I did not become a young man at a particular age, like 13, but rather when a boy strolled into the shop where I worked and called me "mister". The realization hit me like a punch; I was suddenly a mister.

I never thought that I would fall asleep in front of the television set as my father did. Now it's what I do best. I never thought I would prefer to stay at home, but now I find myself foregoing parties. I used to think that people who watched birds were weird, but this summer I found myself watching them, and may be I'll get a book on the subject. I yearn for a religious conviction that I never thought I'd want to feel close to my ancestors long gone, and echo my father in arguments with my son; I still lose.

One day I became a father, and not too long after that I picked up the bill for my own father. I thought then it was a rite of passage for me. But one day, when I was little older, I realized it was one for him too.

1. Which of the following does the author consider a rite of passage for him?
   A. Becoming thirteen years old
   B. Going to a restaurant with his parents, wife and son
   C. Being called 'mister' by the boy in the shop
   D. Working in a shop as a young boy

2. The author's father expected his son to pay the restaurant bill because
   A. he did not have enough money
   B. he acknowledged that his son was now an adult
   C. it was the first time the family was eating out together
   D. the waiter had set the bill in the middle of the table

3. "Rites of passage" for the author generally refers to
   A. events that mark the passage of time
   B. imitating his father as he grows older
   C. slowing down in his pace of living
   D. the act of growing old with time

4. In the fourth paragraph, the author makes the point that as people grow older they
   A. become lazier and less adventurous in their behaviour
   B. have to take on many more financial responsibilities
   C. turn to their children more for help and advice
   D. behave in the same way as their elders even if they never thought they would

5. In the fourth paragraph, 'foregoing parties' means
   A. going early to parties
   B. hosting many parties
   C. giving up parties
   D. going to many parties

PASSAGE-15

Language, they say, is the lens through which human beings perceive the world. If so, English is perhaps the most distorting lens through which to see animals. It has perpetuated a cross-eyed view of birds, beasts, fish and fowl. The very word 'animal' connotes the brutish and the sensual. Animal instinct implies baseness and vulgarity. The language transfers negative human traits to animals, making the former appear as characteristics of the latter. Thus, the chicken is cowardly, frightened, faint-hearted; the goat lustful and foolish; the bear rough and ill-bred. Butterflies are flighty, seals slippery and foxes notorious for craftiness and cunning. Much the worst are the reptiles particularly the snake, creeping, base, malignant, abject, ungrateful and treacherous. Always the snake in the grass.

Each species carries its denigration forever embedded in its English name giving the language as many unpleasant adjectives as it could possibly want. To be bull-headed is to be impetuous and obstinate; the cattish woman is spiteful and backbiting. An elephant's walk is ungainly, bird-brains are to be ridiculed and the herd mentality draws only contempt. You can be as blind as a bat, and batty if you are crazy as well.

1. According to the passage, the chicken is
A. cowardly, the goat cunning and the bear ill-bred
B. simple, the goat foolish and the bear rough
C. cowardly, the goat lustful and foolish and the bear rough and ill-bred
D. faint-hearted, the goat lustful and ill-bred and the bear crafty

2. According to the passage, English language is the lens
A. through which people see a correct picture of the world
B. that does not permit one to see a correct picture of the world
C. through which people see a distorted animal world
D. through which people see the beautiful animal world

3. In the English language, the animals are
A. used for uninteresting comparisons
B. used for unpleasant comparisons
C. used for pleasant comparisons
D. not used for any comparisons

4. The phrase, "Always the snake in the grass" implies
A. the snake hiding in the grass for its victims
B. a dangerous person
C. a person secretly working against you
D. a harmless person

5. According to this passage, elephant walk is
A. ungainly, bird brains ridiculous and herd mentality contemptible
B. beautiful, bird brains ridiculous and herd mentality contemptible
C. ugly, bird brains beautiful and herd mentality good
D. ugly, bird brains ridiculous and herd mentality good

PASSAGE-16

Among the natural resources which can be called upon in national plans for development, possibly the most important is human labour. Since the English language suffers from a certain weakness in its ability to describe groups composed of both male and female members, this is usually described as 'manpower'.

Without a productive labour force, including effective leadership and intelligent middle management, no amount of foreign assistance or of natural wealth can ensure successful development and modernisation.

The manpower for development during the next quarter-century will come from the world's present population of infants, children and adolescents. But we have no assurance that they will be equal to the task. Will they have the health, the education, the skills, the socio-cultural attitudes essential for the responsibilities of development?

For far too many of them the answer is no. The reason is basic. A child's most critical years, with regard to physical, intellectual, social and emotional development, are those before he reaches five years of age. During those critical formative years he is cared for almost exclusively by his mother and in many parts of the world the mother may not have the capacity to raise a superior child. She is incapable of doing so by reason of her own poor health, her ignorance and her lack of status and recognition, of social and legal rights, of economic parity, of independence.

One essential factor has been overlooked or ignored. The forgotten factor is the role of women. Development will be handicapped as long as women remain second-class citizens, uneducated, without any voice in family or community decisions, without legal or economic status, married when they are still practically children, and henceforth producing one baby after another, often only to see half of them die before they are school-age.

We can enhance development by improving "womanpower," by giving women the opportunity to develop themselves. Statistics show that the average family size increase in inverse ratio to the mother's years of education—is lowest among college graduates, highest among those with only primary school training or no education. Malnutrition is most frequent in large families, and increases in frequency with each additional sibling.

The principle seems established that an educated mother has healthier and more intelligent children and that this is related to the fact that she has fewer children. The tendency of educated, upperclass mothers to have fewer children operates even without access to contraceptive service.

The educational level of women is significant also because it has a direct influence upon their chances of employment; and the number of employed women in a country's total labour force has a direct bearing on both the Gross National Product and the disposable income of the individual family. Disposable income, especially in the hands of women, influences food purchasing and therefore the nutritional status of the family. The fact that this additional income derived from the paid employment of women provides a logical incentive to restrict the size of the family.

1. The writer made only one of the following statements; indicate which one?
   A. The world's present population of infants, children and adolescents is very healthy
   B. The world's present population of infants, children and adolescents is very sickly
   C. The world's present population of infants, children and adolescents may not be equal to its task
   D. The world's present population of infants, children and adolescents is likely to go morally bankrupt

2. Among the natural resources which can be called upon in national plans for development?
   A. The most important is certainly human labour
   B. The most important is possibly human labour
   C. The least developed is certainly human labour
   D. The least developed is undoubtedly human labour

3. Without a productive labour force, including effective leadership and intelligent middle management
   A. No productive work is possible
   B. Entrepreneurs will incur heavy losses
   C. Economic development will not keep pace with nationalist movements
   D. No amount of foreign assistance or of natural wealth can ensure successful development and modernization

4. According to the writer, we can enhance development by
   A. giving women the opportunity to develop themselves
   B. making greater capital investments in agriculture and industry
   C. establishing Ministry of Economic Planning and Development
   D. increasing wages and improving general condition of service for all workers

5. The manpower development during the next quarter-century
   A. will be adversely affected by the threat of war
   B. will come from the world's present population of infants, children and adolescents
   C. Will be well taken care of by the current emphasis on free education for women
   D. Will be adversely affected by the country's economic losses and political instability

ANSWERS

PASSAGE-1

1	2	3	4
B	C	A	B

PASSAGE-2

1	2	3	4
A	C	D	A

PASSAGE-3

1	2	3	4	5
A	D	A	C	D

PASSAGE-4

1	2	3	4	5
A	C	D	A	C

PASSAGE-5

1	2	3	4	5
C	D	A	A	D

PASSAGE-6

1	2	3	4	5
C	C	B	C	D

PASSAGE-7

1	2	3	4	5
C	C	B	A	B

PASSAGE-8

1	2	3	4	5
C	C	B	B	D

PASSAGE-9

1	2	3	4	5
A	B	C	C	B
6	**7**	**8**	**9**	**10**
B	C	B	B	A

PASSAGE-10

1	2	3	4	5
C	C	B	C	C

PASSAGE-11

1	2	3	4	5
B	B	C	B	B

PASSAGE-12

1	2	3	4	5
B	C	B	B	D

PASSAGE-13

1	2	3	4	5
C	C	D	D	B

PASSAGE-14

1	2	3	4	5
C	A	A	D	C

PASSAGE-15

1	2	3	4	5
C	C	B	C	A

PASSAGE-16

1	2	3	4	5
C	B	D	A	B

●●●

2 Spot the Error

The most common errors in English are of spellings, grammar and usage of words. By regular practice, the errors can be easily spotted and minimised.

COMMON ERRORS WITH NOUNS AND NOUN-PHRASES

	Incorrect	Correct
1.	I have bought new *furnitures.*	I have bought new *furniture.*
2.	The wages of sin *are* death.	The wages of sin *is* death.
3.	She told these *news* to her mother.	She told her mother this *news.*
4.	He took *troubles* to do his work.	He took *trouble* (or pains) over his work.
5.	The *cattles* were grazing.	The *cattle* were grazing.
6.	He showered *many abuses* on me.	He showered *much abuse* on me.
7.	I spent the holidays with my *family members.*	I spent the holidays with my *family.*
8.	There is no *place* in this compartment.	There is no *room* in this compartment.
9.	Write this new *poetry* in your *copy.*	Write this new *poem* in your *note-book.*
10.	He took *insult* at this.	He took *offence* at this.
11.	Put your *sign* here.	Put your *signatures* here.
12.	She is my *cousin sister.*	She is my *cousin.*
13.	*Sunil's* my *neighbour's* house was burgled.	*Sunil* my *neighbour's* house was burgled.
14.	I lost a *ten-rupees* note.	I lost *a ten-rupee* note.
15.	Road closed for *repair.*	Road closed for *repairs.*
16.	His house is out of *repairs.*	His house is out of *repair.*
17.	What is the *reason* of an earthquake?	What is the *cause* of an earthquake?
18.	This building is made of *stones.*	This building is made of *stone.*
19.	I disapprove of *these kinds* of games.	I disapprove of *this kind* of games.
20.	Veena's and Sheela's father is ill.	Veena and Sheela's father is ill.
21.	His *son-in-laws* are doctors.	His *sons-in-law* are doctors.
22.	*Alms* is given to the *poor.*	*Alms* are given to the poor.

	Incorrect	Correct
23.	He always keeps his words.	He always keeps his *word.*
24.	I carried the *luggages.*	I carried the *luggage.*
25.	*Two-third* of the work is left.	*Two-thirds* of the work is left.

COMMON ERRORS WITH PRONOUNS

	Incorrect	Correct
1.	Both did not go.	Neither went.
2.	We all did not go.	None of us went.
3.	Each of these boys play.	Each of these boys plays.
4.	Whoever does best he will get a prize.	Whoever does best will get a prize.
5.	One should not waste his time.	A man should not waste his time.
6.	I and she are sisters.	She and I are sisters.
7.	He is wiser than me.	He is wiser than I.
8.	Between you and I, Anil is not to be trusted.	Between you and me, Anil is not to be trusted.
9.	Nobody was there but I.	Nobody was there but me.
10.	Who is there ? It is me.	Who is there ? It is I.
11.	Only he and me can use this card.	Only he and I can use this card.
12.	Let you and I go now.	Let you and me go now.
13.	Everyone got one's pay.	Everyone got his pay.
14.	Everyone is frightened when they see a tiger.	Everyone is frightened when he sees a tiger.
15.	These two friends are fond of one another.	These two friends are fond of each other.
16.	I did not like him coming at that hour.	I did not like his coming at that hour.
17.	Who do you think I met?	Whom do you think I met?
18.	You should avail this opportunity.	You should avail yourself this opportunity.
19.	When you have read these books, please return the same to me.	When you have read the books, please return them to me.
20.	They that are humble need fear no fall.	Those that are humble need fear no fall.

COMMON ERRORS WITH ADJECTIVES

	Incorrect	Correct
1.	These all oranges are good.	All these oranges are good.
2.	He held the book in the both hands.	He held the book in both hands.
3.	Both men have not come.	Neither man has come.
4.	That man should do some or other work.	That man should do some work or other.

	Incorrect	Correct
5.	He is elder than I.	He is older than I.
6.	Shakespeare is greater than any other poets.	Shakespeare is greater than any other poet.
7.	He is a coward man.	He is a cowardly man.
8.	Many villagers cannot write his own name.	Many villagers cannot write their own name.
9.	Each of us loves our home.	Each of us loves his home.
10.	Much efforts bring their reward.	Much effort brings its reward.
11.	He found hundred rupees.	He found a hundred rupees.
12.	He had leave of four days.	He had four days leave.
13.	This is a worth seeing sight.	This is a sight worth seeing.
14.	He will spend his future life here.	He will spend the rest of his life here.
15.	There is a best teacher in that class.	There is a very good teacher in that class.
16.	Of the two plans this is the best.	Of the two plans this is the better.
17.	He is becoming strong every day.	He is becoming stronger every day.
18.	He is worst than I.	He is worse than I.
19.	Jaipur is hot than Delhi.	Jaipur is hotter than Delhi.
20.	In our library the number of books is less.	In our library the number of books is small.
21.	From the three he is more clever.	He is the cleverest of the three.
22.	India is the first peace-loving country in the world.	India is the foremost peace-loving country in the world.
23.	Verbal instruction will not do.	Oral instruction will not do.
24.	Her command over French is most excellent.	Her command over French is excellent.
25.	He has not some money with him.	He has not any money with him.
26.	I have visited Bombay many a times.	I have visited Bombay many a time.
27.	Death is more preferable to dishonour.	Death is preferable to dishonour.
28.	I gave him a few books I had.	I gave him the few books I had.
29.	If he wants farther help send him to me.	If he wants further help, send him to me.
30.	She is so cunning as a fox.	She is as cunning as a fox.

COMMON ERRORS WITH VERBS

	Incorrect	Correct
1.	He asked had we taken our luggage.	He asked if we had taken our luggage.
2.	She asked what are you doing.	She asked what we were doing.
3.	Rama asked to Anil why he is angry.	Rama asked Anil why he was angry.
4.	He does not care for his money.	He does not take care of his money.
5.	He does not care for his work.	He takes no care over his work.
6.	No one cared for him after his mother died.	No one took care of him after his mother died.
7.	He got angry before I said a word.	He got angry before I had said a word.

	Incorrect	Correct
8.	I met a man who was my tutor 20 years ago.	I met a man who had been my tutor twenty years ago.
9.	I had been for walking yesterday.	I went for a walk yesterday.
10.	If I shall do this I shall be wrong.	If I do this I shall be wrong.
11.	I have left trekking.	I have given up trekking.
12.	I came to know as to how he did this.	I learnt how he did this.
13.	I came to know why he was sad.	I found out why he was sad.
14.	He knows to swim.	He knows how to swim.
15.	The criminal's head was cut.	The criminal's head was cut off.
16.	I said to him to go.	I told him to go.
17.	I told the teacher to excuse me.	I asked the teacher to excuse me.
18.	He is troubling me.	He is giving me trouble.
19.	I have got a hurt on my leg.	I have hurt my leg.
20.	She gave a speech.	She made a speech.
21.	He has given his examination.	He has sat for his examination.
22.	He took out his shoes.	He took off his shoes.
23.	I have ordered for a new car.	I have ordered a new car.
24.	He would not hear me.	He would not listen to me.
25.	I struck a blow on his face.	I struck him in the face.
26.	He denied to come.	He refused to come.
27.	He lived there for a day.	He stayed there for a day.
28.	The book is not found.	The book is lost.
29.	Shut the light.	Turn off the light.
30.	I must revenge my brother.	I must avenge my brother.

COMMON ERRORS IN SUBJECT-VERB AGREEMENT

	Incorrect	Correct
1.	The owners of this factory *is* very rich.	The owners of this factory *are* very rich.
2.	The pleasures of nature that one can experience at Shimla *is* beyond description.	The pleasures of nature that one can experience at Shimla *are* beyond description.
3.	There *is* no street lights in our colony.	There *are* no street lights in our colony.
4.	He and I *am* entrusted with the job.	He and I *are* entrusted with the job.
5.	Rice and curry *are* his favourite dish.	Rice and curry *is* his favourite dish.
6.	The honour and glory of our country *are* at stake.	The honour and glory of our country *is* at stake.
7.	Time and tide *waits* for none.	Time and tide *wait* for none.
8.	All the passengers with the driver *was* killed.	All the passengers, with the driver, *were* killed.

	Incorrect	Correct
9.	The teacher, with her students, *were* going out.	The teacher, with her students, *was* going out.
10.	I as well as they *am* tired.	I as well as they *are* tired.
11.	Not only the soldiers but their captain also *were* captured.	Not only the soldiers but their captain also *was* captured.
12.	Neither you nor I *were* selected.	Neither you nor I *was* selected.
13.	Either of these two applicants *are* fit for the job but neither want to accept it.	Either of these two applicants *is* fit for the job but neither wants to accept it.
14.	One of these students are sure to stand first.	One of these students *is* sure to stand first.
15.	Everyone of these workers want a raise.	Everyone of these workers wants a raise.
16.	None of these letters has been answered so far.	None of these letters *have* been answered so far.
17.	None of the girls were present at the party.	None of the girls *was* present at the party.
18.	Many a battle were fought on Indian soil.	Many a battle *was* fought on Indian soil.
19.	A lot of work remain to be done.	A lot of work *remains* to be done.
20.	The majority of these girls likes music.	The majority of these girls *like* music.
21.	The number of admissions are encouraging.	The number of admissions *is* encouraging.
22.	A large number of boys was present.	A large number of boys *were* present.
23.	A variety of books was on display.	A variety of books *were* on display.
24.	Variety are the spice of life.	Variety *is* the spice of life.
25.	If my estimates are correct. I will need another hundred rupees.	If my estimate is correct, I will need another hundred rupees.
26.	Mathematics *are* my favourite subject.	Mathematics *is* my favourite subject.
27.	'Gulliver's Travels' *are* written by Swift.	'Gulliver's Travels' *is* written by Swift.
28.	Ten miles *are* a long distance to cover on foot.	Ten miles *is* a long distance to cover on foot.
29.	A new pair of shoes *are* to be purchased.	A new pair of shoes *is* to be purchased.
30.	The Committee *have* issued its report.	The Committee *has* issued its report.
31.	I, who am your friend, *has* always been on your side.	I, who am your friend, *have* always been on your side.
32.	I am the person who *have* always stood by you.	I am the person who *has* always stood by you.
33.	This is one of the best novels that *has* been published this year.	This is one of the best novels that *have* been published this year.
34.	Less than half the amount *have* been wasted.	Less than half the amount *has* been wasted.
35.	A lot of people *has* turned up for the show.	A lot of people *have* turned up for the show.
36.	Much of their honour *are* un-deserved.	Much of their honour *is* un-deserved.
37.	More than a decade *have* passed since this house was built.	More than a decade *has* passed since this house was built.
38.	Either she or he *are* mistaken.	Either she or he *is* mistaken.
39.	Plenty of information *are* available on the subject.	Plenty of information *is* available on the subject.
40.	Plenty of pamphlets *is* available on the subject.	Plenty of pamphlets *are* available on the subject.

COMMON ERRORS IN USE OF WILL, SHALL, WOULD, SHOULD, MAY, MIGHT, MUST

	Incorrect	Correct
1.	When I shall see him I shall tell him this.	When I *see* him, I shall tell him this.
2.	If I should do wrong, he would punish me.	If I *did* wrong, he would punish me.
3.	Until he will have confessed his fault, he will be kept in prison.	Until he *has* confessed his fault, he will be kept in prison.
4.	She will obey me.	She *shall* obey me.
5.	You would work hard.	You *should* work hard.
6.	You shall find him in the garden.	You *will* find him in the garden.
7.	He must have died of exposure, but we cannot be certain.	He *might* have died of exposure, but we cannot be certain.
8.	You might not show disrespect to your elders.	You *must* not show disrespect to your elders.
9.	You may take exercise in order to maintain good health.	You *must* take exercise in order to maintain good health.
10.	He must be a crook for all we know.	He *may* be a crook for all we know.

COMMON ERRORS IN THE USE OF ADVERBS

(Very, Much, Too, Enough, Quite, Hardly, Scarcely, Before, Ago, Since, Yet, Still, etc.)

	Incorrect	Correct
1.	He is very much angry.	He is *very* angry.
2.	She was very good enough to help me.	She was *good enough* to help me.
3.	She runs much fast.	She runs *very* fast.
4.	She runs very faster than Seema.	She runs *much* faster than Seema.
5.	It is bitter cold today.	It is *bitterly* cold today.
6.	He is a much learned man.	He is a very learned man.
7.	She is thinking very hardly.	She is thinking very hard.
8.	To tell in brief the film was boring.	*In short* the film was boring.
9.	He told the story in details.	He told the story *in detail.*
10.	I did it anyhow.	I *managed to do* it somehow.
11.	Aeroplanes reach Europe soon.	Aeroplanes reach Europe quickly.
12.	Before long there were dinosaurs on the earth.	*Long ago,* there were dinosaurs on the earth.
13.	This book is too interesting.	This book is *very* interesting.
14.	He lives miserly.	He lives in *a miserly* way.
15.	Just I had gone when she came.	I had just gone when she came.
16.	He sings good.	He sings *well.*
17.	He sings good than I.	He sings *better* than I.

	Incorrect	Correct
18.	Really speaking it is cold.	*As a matter of fact* it is cold.
19.	He is enough tall to reach the ceiling.	He is *tall enough* to reach the ceiling.
20.	He went directly to his college.	He went *direct* to his college.
21.	He is presently at Delhi	He is at Delhi *at present.*
22.	Last night she returned lately.	Last night she *returned late.*
23.	He was even blamed by his friends.	He was *blamed even* by his friends.
24.	I only employed him for a week.	I employed him for a week only.
25.	I met him four months before.	I met him four *months ago.*
26.	Anil seldom ever goes to school.	Anil *seldom goes* to school.
27.	I will wait here until you do not go.	I will wait here until *you go.*
28.	I never remember having met her before.	I *do not remember* having met her before.
29.	She has not been here too long to have many friends.	She has not *been here long* enough to have many friends.
30.	Hardly I have had any rest since one week.	Hardly have *I had* any rest for a week.
31.	Scarcely the water crossed the danger level, the warning signals were sounded.	Scarcely *had the* water *crossed the* danger level, when the warning signals were sounded.
32.	She is neat but fairly slow.	She is *neat* but rather slow.
33.	It is a rather good film.	It is a *fairly good* film.
34.	We yet have time to catch the bus.	We *still have* time to catch the bus.
35.	She has not still spent all her money.	She has *not yet* spent all her money.

COMMON ERRORS IN THE USE OF CONJUNCTIONS

	Incorrect	Correct
1.	As he is fat so he runs slowly.	As he is fat *he* runs slowly.
2.	If he is fat then he will run slowly.	If he is fat, he will run slowly.
3.	Though he is fat still he runs fast.	Though he is fat, *he runs* fast.
4.	*As* I pulled the trigger at the sametime he shook my arm.	As I pulled the trigger, he shook my arm.
5.	No sooner I had spoken than he left.	No sooner *had* I spoken than he left.
6.	Not only he will go, but also he will stay there.	Not only *will he* go, but he *will also* stay there.
7.	Neither he comes nor he writes.	Neither *does he* come nor *does he* write.
8.	Scarcely he entered the room than the telephone rang.	Scarcely *had* he entered the room *when the* telephone rang.
9.	Hardly she had left the house than it began to rain.	Hardly *had she* left the house *when* it began to rain.
10.	He is the fastest runner and he comes last.	He is the fastest runner *but* he comes last.
11.	She is as innocent as if she looks.	She is as innocent as she looks.

	Incorrect	Correct
12.	Until he does not try he must be punished.	He must be punished unless he tries.
13.	I want to know as to why you are late.	I want to know why you are late.
14.	I am fond of Chinese food as for example sweet and sour prawns.	I am fond of Chinese food, for example, sweet and sour prawns.
15.	He was angry therefore I ran away.	He was angry so I ran away.
16.	I was trying to work, at that time he was disturbing me.	While I was trying to work, he was disturbing me.
17.	Supposing if he is late, what will happen?	Supposing he is late (or if he is late) what will happen?
18.	He asked me that why I was late.	He asked me why I was late.
19.	Let us catch a taxi lest we should not get late.	Let us catch a taxi lest we should get late.
20.	She dresses herself like the teacher does.	She dresses herself as the teacher does.
21.	Wait while I come.	Wait *until* (or *till*) I come.
22.	Until, there is corruption in India, there can be little progress.	*As long* as there is corruption in India there can be little progress.
23.	I have never told a lie nor cheated anybody.	I have never told a lie *nor have I* cheated anybody.
24.	Both Mohan as well as Arun are responsible for this action.	Both Mohan *and* Arun are responsible for this action.
25.	Hindus and Muslims both are to blame for the riots.	*Both Hindus* and Muslims are to blame for the riots.
26.	I have bought paintings, books, records, and etc.	I have bought paintings, books *and records etc.*
27.	He as well as you is a fool.	He as well as you *are* a fool.
28.	He is so poor and he cannot save anything.	He is so *poor that* he cannot save anything.
29.	Such a book that you want is not available.	Such a book *as* you want is not available.
30.	Such was her condition as everyone was moved to pity.	Such was her condition that everyone was moved to pity.

COMMON ERRORS IN THE USE OF PREPOSITIONS

	Incorrect	Correct
1.	I will not listen him.	I will not listen *to* him.
2.	Copy this word by word.	Copy this word *for* word.
3.	He enquired from her where she lived.	He enquired *of* her where she lived.
4.	Sign here with ink.	Sign here *in* ink.
5.	Has she come in train or by foot?	Has she come *by* train or *on* foot?
6.	She said this at his face.	She said this *to* his face.
7.	Open the book on page one.	Open the book *at* page one.

	Incorrect	Correct
8.	I was invited for lunch.	I was *invited to* lunch.
9.	I am ill since three months.	I have been *ill for* three months.
10.	This paper is inferior than that.	This paper is inferior *to* that.
11.	This resembles to that.	This *resembles* that.
12.	My brother is superior than you in strength.	My brother is superior *to* you in strength.
13.	He wrote me.	He wrote *to* me.
14.	I shall explain them this.	I shall explain this *to* them.
15.	Send this letter on my address.	Send this letter *to* my address.
16.	He suggested me this.	He suggested this *to* me.
17.	He goes *on his* work.	He goes *to his* work.
18.	He *reached to* Nagpur.	He *reached* Nagpur.
19.	He told *to me* to go.	He told *me* to go.
20.	The term begins *from* July 1st.	The term begins *on* July 1st.
21.	There are many advantages *from* this.	The advantages *of* this are many.
22.	We waste much time *in* trifles.	We waste much time *on* (or *over*) trifles.
23.	He sat *on* a tree.	He sat *in* a tree.
24.	This is a comfortable house to *live*.	This is a comfortable house to *live in*.
25.	This is the road to *go*.	This is the road to *go by*.
26.	He married *with* an Indian lady.	He *married an Indian* lady.
27.	He accompanied *with* his friend.	He *accompanied his* friend.
28.	He went *for doing some* business.	He went away *on* business.
29.	He went for *riding*.	He went *for a ride*.
30.	I *pitied on* him.	I *pitied* him.
31.	When this was searched it was found.	When this was searched *for* it was found.
32.	I shall inform them *this*.	I shall inform them *of* this.
33.	*Due to illness* I cannot go to school.	*Owing* to illness I cannot go to school.
34.	He went *to the back side* of the house.	He went *behind* (or to the back of) the house.
35.	I must go; there is no *help*.	I must go; there is no help *for it*.
36.	I *met with your* friend there.	I *met your* friend there.
37.	The First World War was fought *during* 1914-1918.	The First World War was fought *between* 1914-1918.
38.	England grew prosperous *between* Queen Victoria's reign.	England grew prosperous *during* Queen Victoria's reign.
39.	He asked a holiday.	He asked *for* a holiday.
40.	I am obliged of you for this good turn.	I am obliged *to* you for this good turn.
41.	There is no harm to try.	There is no harm *in trying*.

MISCELLANEOUS ERRORS

(Including Ambiguities and Indianisms)

	Incorrect	Correct
1.	Many *homes* are lying vacant.	Many *houses* are lying vacant.
2.	It is cool in the *shadow* of the tree.	It is cool in the *shade* of the tree.
3.	She *keeps* good health.	She *enjoys* good health.
4.	My leg is *paining*.	*I am feeling pain* in my leg.
5.	*See* this word in the dictionary.	*Look up* this word in the dictionary.
6.	The train will arrive *just now*.	The train will arrive *shortly*.
7.	They are *pulling* on well.	They are *getting* on well.
8.	The river has *over flown* its bank.	The river has *over flown* its banks.
9.	He was appointed *on* the post.	He was appointed *to* the post.
10.	Last but not *the least,* we have to discuss the problem of over population.	Last but not *least,* we have to discuss the problem of over population.
11.	*Cities* after *cities* fell.	*City* after *city* fell.
12.	What is the use Munir going there?	What is the use of Munir going there?
13.	He *did many mischief.*	He *made much mischief.*
14.	It is exact five *in* my watch.	It is exact five *by* my watch.
15.	I will dine with them on *next Sunday.*	I will dine with them *Sunday next.*
16.	Misfortunes when faced bravely and *manly* become less troublesome.	Misfortunes when faced bravely and *manfully* become less troublesome.
17.	I am *laid down* with fever.	I am *laid up* with fever.
18.	He is habituated to smoking.	He is *addicted* to smoking.
19.	*According to my opinion* he is right.	*In my opinion* (or according *to me)* he is right.
20.	Could you please *open* this knot?	Could you please *untie* this knot?

MULTIPLE CHOICE QUESTIONS

Directions: *In this section, each sentence has three parts, indicated by (A), (B) and (C). Read each sentence to find out whether there is an error. If you find an error in any one of the parts (A, B, C), indicate your response by marking the letter related to that part. If a sentence has no error, indicate this by marking '(D)' which stands for "No error". Errors may belong to grammar, usage or idiom. Ignore errors of punctuation, if any.*

1. (A) We are meeting today afternoon/(B) to discuss the matter/(C) and reach a compromise./ (D) No error.

2. (A) Either Ram or/(B) you is responsible/(C) for this action./(D) No error.

3. (A) The student flatly denied/(B) that he had copied/(C) in the examination hall./(D) No error.

4. (A) By the time you arrive tomorrow/(B) I have finished/(C) my work./(D) No error.

5. (A) The speaker stressed repeatedly on/(B) the importance of improving/(C) the condition of the slums./(D) No error.

6. (A) The captain with the members of his team/(B) are returning/(C) after a fortnight./(D) No error.

7. (A) After returning from/(B) an all-India tour/(C) I had to describe about it/(D) No error.

8. (A) The teacher asked his students/(B) if they had gone through/(C) either of the three chapters included in the prescribed text./(D) No error.

9. (A) Although they are living in the country/(B) since they were married/(C) they are now moving to the town./(D) No error.

10. (A) Do you know/(B) how old were you/(C) when you came here?/(D) No error.

11. (A) Beware of/(B) a fair-weather friend/(C) who is neither a friend in need nor a friend indeed/(D) No error.

12. (A) Copernicus proved/(B) that Earth/(C) moves round the Sun./(D) No error.

13. (A) Seldom we have been treated/(B) in such a rude manner/(C) by the police personnel./(D) No error.

14. (A) Some men are born great,/(B) some achieve greatness/(C) and some had greatness thrust on them./(D) No error.

15. (A) The property/(B) was divided/(C) among the two brothers./(D) No error.

16. (A) I am quite certain/(B) that the lady is not only greedy/(C) but miserly./(D) No error.

17. (A) The aircraft overloaded/(B) there was something wrong of the battery/(C) and the engine was making a queer noise/(D) No error.

18. (A) A thorough inquiry of the misappropriation of funds/(B) is now imperative/(C) to bring the guilty to book/(D) No error.

19. (A) The brilliant success in the examination/(B) as well as his record in sports/(C) deserves high praise/(D) No error.

20. (A) While travelling by a train/(B) on a cold winter night/(C) an argument rose between two passengers in our compartment/(D) No error.

21. (A) I cannot find/(B) where has he gone/(C) though I have tried may best/(D) No error.

22. (A) If I was/(B) the Prime Minister of India/(C) I would work wonders/(D) No error.

23. (A) Amit's severe bout of flu/(B) debilitated him so much/(C) that he was too tired to do for work for a week./(D) No error.

24. (A) This is the crux of the entire problem;/(B) everything centres on/(C) it being resolved./(D) No error.

25. (A) One of the major aims of the Air Force/(B) was the complete demolition of all means of transportation/(C) by the bombing of rail lines and terminals./(D) No error.

26. (A) His strong voice cut over/(B) the hum of conversation/(C) like a knife through butter./(D) No error.

27. (A) Even though they weren't expecting us/(B) they managed to knock up/(C) a marvellous meal./(D) No error.

28. (A) The celebrated singer was/(B) surrounded by the usual crowd/(C) of lackeys and hanger-ons./(D) No error.

29. (A) If it weren't/(B) for you,/(C) I wouldn't be alive today./(D) No error.

30. (A) He looked like a lion/(B) baulked from/(C) its prey./(D) No error.

31. (A) Widespread flooding/(B) is effecting/(C) large areas of the villages./(D) No error.

32. (A) She regards/(B) negotiating prices with customers/(C) as her special preserve./(D) No error.

33. (A) Often in political campaigns, a point is reached at which/(B) the candidates take out their gloves./(C) and start slugging with bare fists./(D) No error.

34. (A) If we really set to/(B) we can get the whole house/(C) cleaned in an afternoon./(D) No error.

35. (A) Pieces of rock plummeted/(B) down the mountainside/(C) in the ground below./(D) No error.

36. (A) Since the two parties each won/(B) the same number of seats,/(C) the minority party holds the balance of power./(D) No error.

37. (A) It's arrogant for you/(B) to assume you'll/(C)win every time./(D) No error.

38. (A) We've paid for our travel and accommodation,/(B) so we need only to take/(C) some pocket-money with us./(D) No error.

39. (A) There's no evidence to show/(B) that information technology secrets are more/(C) vulnerable in India than Britain or the US./(D) No error.

40. (A) It is shameful that hunting/(B) is still considered sport/(C) by some unscrupulous people in the civilized world./(D) No error.

41. (A) The Prime Minister's good looks won him/(B)the election but he has still to prove/(C) that he's not a just pretty face./(D) No error.

42. (A) The two books are the same/(B) except for the fact that this/(C) has an answer in the back./(D) No error.

43. (A) He estimated his income tax bill/(B) by extrapolation over figures/(C) submitted in previous years./(D) No error.

44. (A) The modern office block/(B) sticks out like a sore thumb/(C) among the old buildings in the area./(D) No error.

45. (A) I will try to put over/(B) some feelers to gauge/(C) people's reactions to our proposal./(D) No error.

46. (A) A major contribution of Mathura sculptors/(B)of that period were the creation and popularization/(C) of the Buddha's image in human form./(D) No error.

47. (A) Amit has been deceiving Mona/(B) for many years but she/(C) has not still tumbled to it. (D)/No error.

48. (A) Mahavira was an advocate of nonviolence and vegetarianism,/(B) who revived and reorganized the Jain doctrine/(C) and established rules for their monastic order. (D) No error.

49. (A) Microwaves are the principle carriers/(B) of television, telephone and data transmissions/(C)between stations on earth and between the earth and satellites./(D) No error.

50. (A) An unit is an abstract idea,/(B) defined either by reference to/(C) a randomly chosen material standard or to a natural phenomenon./(D) No error.

51. (A) With the crisis deepening,/(B) the critics sense an opportunity/(C) about putting in place a more radical strategy./(D) No error.

52. (A) The salesman gave us/(B) a big spiel about why/(C) we should buy his product./(D) No error.

53. (A) I will need several weeks/(B) to invent the lie of the land before/(C) I can make any decision about the future of the business./(D) No error.

54. (A) You should be cautious/(B) and make a few discrete enquiries about/(C) the firm before you sign anything./(D) No error.

55. (A) Your husband doesn't/(B) believe that you are older/(C) than I./(D) No error.

56. (A) There is a beautiful moon out tonight/(B) and Neeta and I are going for a stroll/(C) — would you like to come along with she and I?/(D) No error.

57. (A) The data on/(B) the divorce case is/(C) on the judge's desk./(D) No error.

58. (A) The stood off/(B) from the crowd/(C) because of her height and flaming red hair./(D) No error.

59. (A) It's stupid to go/(B) to the expense of taking/(C) music lessons if you never practise/(D) No error.

60. (A) You will find it difficult/(B) to explain of your use/(C) of such offensive language/(D) No error.

61. (A) Because of the/(B) extenuating circumstances/(C) the court acquitted him out of the crime/(D) No error.

62. (A) The carpet was badly stained/(B) to such an extent that/(C) you couldn't tell its original colour/(D) No error.

63. (A) It is greatly to Amit's credit/(B) that he gave back the money he found/(C) his honesty does for him credit/(D) No error.

64. (A) A terrific hue and cry/(B) was raised/(C) at the new tax proposals/(D) No error.

65. (A) The former General was/(B) exiled of his country because of/(C) his part in the plot against the government/(D) No error.

66. (A) The company has/(B) set off itself some stiff production/(C) goals for this year/(D) No error.

67. (A) The music was so loud/(B) that we had to bellow over each/(C) other to be heard./(D) No error.

68. (A) When this beautiful girl arrived/(B) all the men in the room/(C) gravitated over her./(D) No error.

69. (A) The children are/(B) really in their element/(C) playing on the beach./(D) No error.

70. (A) The refugees are/(B) badly off for blankets,/(C) and even worse for food./(D) No error.

71. (A) From their vintage-point on the cliff,/(B) the children could watch/(C) the ships coming and going./(D) No error.

72. (A) A cogent remark/(B) compels acceptance because/(C) of their sense and logic./(D) No error.

73. (A) Credit cards have/(B) brought about a revolution/(C) in people's spending habits./(D) No error.

74. (A) In financial matters/(B) it is important to/(C) get disinterested advice./(D) No error.

75. (A) Some women admit that/(B) their principle goal in life/(C) is to marry a wealthy man./(D) No error.

76. (A) Take two spoonsful/(B) of this medicine/(C) every three hours./(D) No error.

77. (A) The film was so disjointed/(B) that I could not tell you/(C) what the story was about./(D) No error.

78. (A) He had been/(B) saved of death as if/(C) by divine intervention./(D) No error.

79. (A) I informed the principal/(B) that I was running temperature/(C) and, therefore, could not attend the meeting./(D) No error.

80. (A) The lady was broken with grief/(B) when she heard the sad news of the train disaster/(C) in which her brother was killed./(D) No error.

81. (A) The farmer is irrigating/(B) his fields/(C) since morning./(D) No error.

82. (A) I could not/(B) answer to/(C) the question./(D) No error.

83. (A) Two years passed/(B) since/(C) my cousin died./(D) No error.

84. (A) He hesitated to accept the post/(B) as he did not think/(C) that the salary would be enough for a man with a family of three (D)/ No error.

85. (A) Have you gone through/(B) either of these three chapters/(C) that have been included in this volume?/(D) No error.

86. (A) I am learning English/(B) for ten years/(C) without much effect/(D) No error.

87. (A) Ramesh has agreed/(B) to marry with the girl/(C) of his parent's choice (D) No error.

88. (A) The pity is that/(B) no sooner he had left the place/(C) than the fire broke out/(D) No error.

89. (A) When he was arriving/(B) the party was/(C) in full swing/(D) No error.

90. (A) The Dean wrote he constituted a committee of experts/(B) comprising of five members/(C) before the next meeting took place/(D) No error.

91. (A) Inflation and shortages/(B) have made it very difficult for him/(C) to make his both ends meet./(D) No error.

92. (A) The most studious boy/(B) in the class/(C) was made as the captain./(D) No error.

93. (A) I am participating/(B) in the two-miles race/(C) tomorrow morning./(D) No error.

94. (A) The sum and substance/(B) of his speech/ (C) were essentially anti-establishment./(D) No error.

95. (A) It has been such a wonderful evening/(B) I look forward to meet you again/(C) after the vacations./(D) No error.

96. (A) When the boy committed a mistake/(B) the teacher made him to do/(C) the sum again./ (D) No error.

97. (A) Unless the government does not revise its policy of liberalization/(B) the growth of the indigenous technology/(C) will be adversely affected./(D) No error.

98. (A) Supposing if you get/(B) a seat in the plane/ (C) you will not take more than two hours to reach Mumbai./(D) No error.

99. (A) Whenever a person lost anything/(B) the poor folk around/(C) are suspected./(D) No error.

100. (A) Still impressive is that/(B) we achieve this selective attention/(C) through our latent ability to lip-read./(D) No error.

101. (A) The brakes and steering failed/(B) and the bus ran down the hill/(C) without anyone being able to control it./(D) No error.

102. (A) The polling was marred/(B) at many a place/(C) by attempts at rigging./(D) No error.

103. (A) He wanted to work all right/(B) but we saw that he was completely worn/(C) and so we persuaded him to stop./(D) No error.

104. (A) When a whale is washed ashore by the tide,/(B) the people flock together to see it./ (C) wondering how so huge an animal can swim about in the water./(D) No error.

105. (A) Few scientists changed/(B) people's ideas as much as/(C) Darwin with his Theory of Evolution./(D) No error.

106. (A) Were he/(B) to see you,/(C) he would have been surprised./(D) No error.

107. (A) The number of marks carried by each question/(B) are indicated/(C) at the end of the question./(D) No error.

108. (A) An animal/(B) can be just as unhappy in a vast area/(C) or in a small one/(D) No error.

109. (A) It is time/(B) we did something/(C) to stop road accidents./(D) No error.

110. (A) A free press is not a privilege/(B) but the organic necessity/(C) in a free society./(D) No error.

111. (A) The Indian radio./(B) which was previously controlled by the British rulers./(C) is free now from the narrow vested interests./(D) No error.

112. (A) Because of the emergency help/(B) that the patient received./(C) he would have died/ (D) No error.

113. (A) At present juncture,/(B) however, the super-computer/(C) would be a costly toy./(D) No error.

114. (A) Students should not take part/(B) in party politics and political demonstrations/(C) as they interfere in serious study./(D) No error.

115. (A) Wherever they go/(B) Indians easily adapt to/(C) local circumstances./(D) No error.

116. (A) According to the Bible/(B) it is meek and humble/(C) who shall inherit the earth./(D) No error.

117. (A) I was there/(B) many a time/(C) in the past./(D) No error.

118. (A) As much as I admire him for his sterling qualities./(B) I cannot excuse him for/(C) being unfair to his friends./(D) No error.

119. (A) Were you/(B) given a choice/(C) or you had to do it?/(D) No error.

120. (A) When he was asked what is wrong with him,/(B) he said that he was not well,/(C) and asked for leave of absence for one day./(D) No error.

121. (A) At the end of the year/(B) every student who had done adequate work/(C) was automatically promoted./(D) No error.

122. (A) Many times the news has been published/ (B) in the papers that the end of the world will be certain/(C) if a nuclear war breaks out./(D) No error.

123. (A) Happily, zoos were/(B) unwilling to cooperate/(C) in a scheme that was potentially harmful to animal welfare./(D) No error.

124. (A) We discussed about the problem so thoroughly/(B) on the eve of the examination/ (C) that I found it very easy to work it out./(D) No error.

125. (A) She reluctantly said that/(B) if nobody else was doing it/(C) she will do it./(D) No error.

126. (A) He will end up his work/(B) in the city/(C) by the end of the year./(D) No error.

127. (A) Though child marriage/(B) has been banned,/(C) the custom still prevailed among some groups in India./(D) No error.

128. (A) Supposing if/(B) there is no bus,/(C) how will you get there?(D) No error.

129. (A) At the moment the house/(B) was burgled the family/(C) attended a night party in the neighbourhood./(D) No error.

130. (A) On a holiday/(B) Sudha prefers reading/ (C) than going out visiting friends/(D) No error.

131. (A) Neither he/(B) nor his father is interested/ (C) in joining the party./(D) No error.

132. (A) A group of friends/(B) want to visit/(C) the new plant as early as possible./(D) No error.

133. (A) May I/(B) know who you want/(C) to see please/(D) No error.

134. (A) Myself and Gopal/(B) will take care of/(C) the function on Sunday./(D) No error.

135. (A) I could not put up in a hotel/(B) because the boarding and lodging charges/(C) were exorbitant./(D) No error.

136. (A) He is not coming tomorrow/(B) as he is having a pain in the chest/(C) and has to see a doctor./(D) No error.

137. (A) They have been/(B) very close friends/(C) until they quarrelled./(D) No error.

138. (A) Since India has gained Independence/(B) 49 years ago,/(C) much progress has been made in almost every field./(D) No error.

139. (A) The party chief made it a point to state that/(B) the Prime Minister and the Union Home Minister should also come/(C) and they see what his party men had seen./(D) No error.

140. (A) Due to me being a newcomer/(B) I was unable to get a house/(C) suitable for my wife and me./(D) No error.

141. (A) The reason why/(B) he was rejected/(C) was because he was too young./(D) No error.

142. (A) The scientist must follow/(B) his hunches and his data/(C) wherever it may lead./(D) No error.

143. (A) Firstly you should/(B) think over the meaning of the words/(C) and then use them./ (D) No error.

144. (A) Scarcely had/(B) I arrived than/(C) the train left./(D) No error.

145. (A) Unless you stop to make noise at once/(B) I will have no option but to/(C) bring the matter to the attention of the police./(D) No error.

146. (A) He couldn't but help/(B) shedding tears at the plight of the villagers/(C) rendered homeless by a devastating cyclone./(D) No error.

147. (A) Since it was his first election campaign, the candidate was confused;/(B) none could clearly understand/(C) either the principles he stood for or the benefits he promised./(D) No error.

148. (A) It is an established fact that the transcendental American poets and philosophers,/(B) who lived in the latter half of the nineteenth century,/(C) were more influenced by Indian philosophy, in particular by Upanishadic Philosophy./(D) No error.

149. (A) The crew were on board/(B) and they soon busied themselves/(C) in preparing to meet the storm./(D) No error.

150. (A) One of the members/(B) expressed doubt if/ (C) the Minister was an athiest./(D) No error.

151. (A) A body of volunteers/(B) have been organised/(C) to spread the message of the saint./(D) No error.

152. (A) If I will have the time/(B) I shall try and make it/(C) to the zoo this afternoon./(D) No error.

153. (A) To facilitate exports and improve sales in the domestic market/(B) some of the improvised fabrics and garments fabricated out from them/(C) are displayed in the main pavilion./(D) No error.

154. (A) He gave them no money/(B) nor did help them/(C) in any way./(D) No error.

155. (A) Azharuddin is one of the finest batsmen/ (B) that India have produced/(C) over the decades./(D) No error.

156. (A) An Indian ship/(B) laden with merchandise/ (C) got drowned in the Pacific./(D) No error.

157. (A) Though senior in age,/(B) his father is junior than/(C) my father in service./(D) No error.

158. (A) If I am you/(B) I would have seen to it/(C) that I won the prize./(D) No error.

159. (A) His father died of cholera/(B) but his mother also,/(C) though very weak, is out of danger./(D) No error.

160. (A) He asked me/(B) why did I call/(C) him a rogue./(D) No error.

161. (A) I have got/(B) my M.Sc. degree/(C) in 1988./(D) No error.

162. (A) They/(B) enjoyed thoroughly/(C) at the party./(D) No error.

163. (A) After the humiliating exposure/(B) he hanged his head/(C) in shame./(D) No error.

164. (A) Kamala's fountain-pen/(B) is as expensive/(C) as Shyama./(D) No error.

165. (A) I shall certainly/(B) write you/(C) when I shall reach New Delhi./(D) No error.

166. (A) The criminal was/(B) caught, convicted the hung/(C) in a short period of time./(D) No error.

167. (A) You will get/(B) all the information/(C) if you read this booklet carefully./(D) No error.

168. (A) She sang/(B) very well/(C) isn't it?/(D) No error.

169. (A) He is working in/(B) a bank is New Delhi/ (C) for the past several months./(D) No error.

170. (A) There is no question/(B) of my failing/(C) in the examination./(D) No error.

171. (A) He managed to make sense of the book/ (B) even though it was the first time/(C) he read anything on the subject./(D) No error.

172. (A) A large scale exchange of nuclear weapons/(B) will produce unprecedented amounts of radiation/(C) that can penetrate into the biological tissue./(D) No error.

173. (A) No sooner did I open the door/(B) when the rain, heavy and stormy, rushed in/(C) making us shiver from head to foot./(D) No error.

174. (A) After opening the door/(B) we entered into the room/(C) next to the kitchen/(D) No error.

175. (A) Locke's treatises on government toleration and education/(B) show a mind fully awake in /(C) the possibilities of social reconstruction./ (D) No error.

176. (A) There was very heavy rain last night,/(B) and the rivers have overflown their banks/(C) causing severe hardship to the people living by them./(D) No error.

177. (A) A leading textile manufacturer, one of the fastest growing in the industry,/(B) is looking for a marketing manager/(C) to look up the marketing network of the company./(D) No error.

178. (A) Last month we celebrated/(B) the wedding of our sister for whom/(C) we have been looking for a suitable alliance for three years./ (D) No error.

179. (A) The method suggested in the lecture/(B) enables a student to learn more quickly/(C) and to have remembered for a longer period of time./(D) No error.

180. (A) She is/(B) no longer popular as she has/ (C) a friends./(D) No error.

ANSWERS

1	2	3	4	5	6	7	8	9	10
A	B	D	B	A	B	C	C	B	D
11	**12**	**13**	**14**	**15**	**16**	**17**	**18**	**19**	**20**
D	B	A	C	C	C	B	A	D	C
21	**22**	**23**	**24**	**25**	**26**	**27**	**28**	**29**	**30**
B	A	C	C	B	A	A	C	C	C
31	**32**	**33**	**34**	**35**	**36**	**37**	**38**	**39**	**40**
C	A	A	A	C	A	A	B	D	B
41	**42**	**43**	**44**	**45**	**46**	**47**	**48**	**49**	**50**
C	C	C	D	A	B	C	C	A	A
51	**52**	**53**	**54**	**55**	**56**	**57**	**58**	**59**	**60**
C	D	D	D	C	C	D	A	B	B
61	**62**	**63**	**64**	**65**	**66**	**67**	**68**	**69**	**70**
C	A	C	A	B	B	B	C	B	D
71	**72**	**73**	**74**	**75**	**76**	**77**	**78**	**79**	**80**
A	C	D	D	D	A	B	B	B	A
81	**82**	**83**	**84**	**85**	**86**	**87**	**88**	**89**	**90**
A	B	A	D	B	A	B	B	A	B
91	**92**	**93**	**94**	**95**	**96**	**97**	**98**	**99**	**100**
C	C	B	C	B	B	A	A	A	C
101	**102**	**103**	**104**	**105**	**106**	**107**	**108**	**109**	**110**
C	D	B	D	A	A	B	C	D	B
111	**112**	**113**	**114**	**115**	**116**	**117**	**118**	**119**	**120**
C	A	A	C	B	B	A	A	A	A
121	**122**	**123**	**124**	**125**	**126**	**127**	**128**	**129**	**130**
D	D	C	A	C	A	C	A	A	C
131	**132**	**133**	**134**	**135**	**136**	**137**	**138**	**139**	**140**
D	B	B	A	A	C	A	A	C	A
141	**142**	**143**	**144**	**145**	**146**	**147**	**148**	**149**	**150**
C	C	A	B	A	A	D	C	C	B
151	**152**	**153**	**154**	**155**	**156**	**157**	**158**	**159**	**160**
B	A	B	B	B	C	B	A	B	B
161	**162**	**163**	**164**	**165**	**166**	**167**	**168**	**169**	**170**
A	B	B	C	C	C	A	C	A	B
171	**172**	**173**	**174**	**175**	**176**	**177**	**178**	**179**	**180**
C	C	B	B	B	B	C	C	C	C

●●●

3 Correct Sentence Selection

One may use the same words in many ways but the best way is only one that makes the perfect usage of the words and conveys the proper meaning of the expression. Try it yourself in this exercise.

MULTIPLE CHOICE QUESTIONS

Directions: *There are four sentences in each of the following questions. One of the sentences is correct, and the rest are incorrect. You have to select the correct sentence in each question.*

1. A. She is either right nor wrong.
B. She is nor right or wrong.
C. She is neither right or wrong.
D. She is neither right nor wrong.

2. A. He went to Nepal five years ago.
B. He went to Nepal five years back.
C. He went to Nepal five years before.
D. He went to Nepal five years past.

3. A. Before leaving home, it began to rain.
B. As since I was leaving home, it began to rain.
C. As I was leaving home, it began to rain.
D. When leaving home, it began to rain.

4. A. I have given up alcoholic drinks two years before.
B. I have given up alcoholic drinks two years since.
C. I have given up alcoholic drinks two years ago.
D. I had given up alcoholic drinks two years ago.

5. A. I told to her to give me that book.
B. I said her to give me this book.
C. I said to her that to give me that book.
D. I asked her to give me that book.

6. A. My maternal grandmother said to me not go without having a cup of tea.
B. My material grandmother asked me not go without having a cup of tea.
C. My material grandmother asked me to go not without having a cup of tea.
D. My material grandmother asked me not to go without having a cup of tea.

7. A. His sister told me that he likes my new car.
B. His sister said me that she likes my new car.
C. His sister told me I like your new car.
D. His sister told me that she liked my new car.

8. A. The teacher asked me where was I going?
B. The teacher asked me where I am going.
C. The teacher asked me where I go.
D. The teacher asked me where I was going.

9. A. Your conduct admits no excuses.
B. Your conduct admit no excuse.
C. Your conduct is inexcusable.
D. Your conduct admit of no excuses.

10. A. The young woman tried on two coats and finally decided to buy the most expensive one.
B. The young woman tried on two coats and finally decided to buy the more expensive one.
C. The young woman tried on two coats and finally decided to buy the expensive one.
D. The young woman tried on coats two and finally decided to buy the very expensive one.

11. A. She is anxious about my health.
B. She is anxious of my health.
C. She is anxious for my health.
D. She is anxious with my health.

12. A. My youngest son had no difficulty with solving the problem.
B. My youngest son had no difficulty to solve the problem.
C. My youngest son had no difficulty in solving the problem.
D. My youngest son had no difficulty for solving the problem.

13. A. The plane had left before I reached the airport.
B. The plane left before I reached the airport.
C. The plane was leaving before I reached the airport.
D. The plane will leave before I reached the airport.

14. A. The four dacoits distributed the loot with themselves.
B. The four dacoits distributed the loot between themselves.
C. The four dacoits distributed the loot among themselves.
D. The four dacoits distributed the loot upon themselves.

15. A. What out country needs today is a number of selfless and competent leaders.
B. What our country need today is a number of unscrupulous leaders.
C. What our country needs today are a number of selfish leaders.
D. What our country needs today is a number of motivated leaders.

16. A. I am very sorry to learn that you lose the match yesterday.
B. I am very sorry to learn that you loosed the match yesterday.
C. I am very sorry to learn that you lost the match yesterday
D. I am very sorry to learn that you have lost the match yesterday.

17. A. It is our bounden duty to instil a sense of responsibility into people of the country.
B. It is our bounden duty to instigate a sense of responsibility into the people of the country.
C. It is our bounden duty to excite a sense of responsibility into the people of the country.
D. It is our bounden duty to incite a sense of responsibility into the people of the country.

18. A. He is over seventy years of age and are still alert and strong.
B. He is over seventy years of age but who is still alert and strong.
C. He is a man over seventy years of age but who is still alert and strong.
D. He is over seventy years of age, but is still alert and strong.

19. A. She told me that it is better to fail than pass by unfair means.
B. She told me it was better to fail than passing by unfair means.
C. She told whether it was better to fail than pass by unfair means.
D. She told me that it was better to fail than to pass by unfair means.

20. A. She asked me to name the capital of Nepal.
B. She asked me which is the capital of Nepal.
C. She asked me what is the capital of Nepal.
D. She told me in the capital of Nepal.

21. A. She heartily congratulated me about my splendid success in the examination.
B. She heartily congratulated me on my splendid success in the examination.

C. She heartily congratulated me for my splendid success in the examination.
D. She heartily congratulated me at my splendid success in the examination.

22. A. He replied that he will call on me tomorrow.
B. He replied that he would call on me tomorrow.
C. He had replied that he would have called on me tomorrow.
D. He replied that he will have called on me tomorrow.

23. A. I am sorry to say that she made me do the dirty job.
B. I am sorry to say that she made me to do the dirty job.
C. I am sorry to say that she would make me to do the dirty job.
D. I am sorry to say that she did me to do the dirty job.

24. A. Will you please excuse my dropping in at this untimely hour?
B. Will you please excuse me dropping at this untimely hour?
C. Will you please excuse my dropping at this untimely hour?
D. Will you please excuse my dropping by this untimely hour?

25. A. Now I must beg of your leave.
B. Now I must beg off your leave.
C. Now I must beg your leave.
D. Now I must beg leave of you.

26. A. When narrating the road accident, she was in tears.
B. As narrating the road accident, she was in tears.
C. In narrating the road accident, she was in tears.
D. When she was narrating the road accident, she was in tears.

27. A. A long period of ten years have passed since he has passed away.
B. A long period of ten years has passed since he passed away.
C. A long period of ten years passed since he has passed away.
D. A long period of ten years have passed since he had passed away.

28. A. Can you do it more quick than I?
B. Can you do it more quicker than I?
C. Can you do it more quickly than I?
D. Can you do it more quick than I can?

29. A. This coat is too small for her.
B. This coat is to small for her.
C. This coat is too much small for her.
D. This coat is much too small for her.

30. A. My boss was kind enough to grant me leave of absence for ten days.
B. My boss was enough kind to grant me leave of absence for ten days.
C. My boss was kindly enough to grant me leave of absence for ten days.
D. My boss was enough kind for granting me leave of absence for ten days.

31. A. You should work had lest you may fail in the examination.
B. You should work hard lest you should fail in the examination.
C. You should work hard lest you might fail in the examination.
D. You should work had lest you fail in the examination.

32. A. When entering the class-room, each of the boys kept quiet.
B. Entering the class-room, each of the boys kept quiet.
C. On entering the class-room, each of the boys kept quiet.
D. Since entering the class-room, each of the boys kept quiet.

33. A. She asked that why her son shall be punished.
B. She asked that why her son should be punished.
C. She asked why her son should be punished.
D. She asked on why her son shall be punished.

34. A. She gives me such troubles which I cannot endure them.
B. She gives me such troubles as I cannot endure them.
C. She gives on me such troubles that I cannot endure them.
D. She gives at me such troubles which I cannot endure.

35. A. I have not seen her long since.
B. I have not seen her since long.
C. I have not seen her since a long.
D. I have not seen her from a long time.

36. A. This is the same book which I lost a few weeks ago.
B. This is the same book that I lost a few weeks ago.
C. This is the same books that I lost a few weeks before.
D. This is the same book which I lost a few weeks past.

37. A. This cloth is more preferable than that.
B. This cloth is more preferable than that.
C. This cloth is more preferable to that.
D. This cloth is preferable to that.

38. A. I seldom or ever make a mistake.
B. I seldom and never make a mistake.
C. I seldom or never make a mistake.
D. I seldom that never make a mistake.

39. A. His command in the English language is very unique.
B. His command of the English language is unique.
C. His command of the English language is perfectly unique.
D. His command of the English language is totally unique.

40. A. Her speech was so halting that the stopped between each word.
B. Her speech was so halting that she stopped after each word.
C. Her speech was so halting that she has stopped each word.
D. Her speech was so halting that she was stopping between each word.

41. A. I do not know who you consider the best man of the two.
B. I do not know whom you consider to be the man of the two.
C. I do not know whom you consider better of the two.
D. I do not know who you consider as the best of the two.

42. A. Do you bathe yourself daily?
B. Do you bathe daily?
C. Do you bathe daily?
D. Do you daily bath?

43. A. Being a cold day, I did not go out to the house.
B. It being a cold day, I did not go out of the house.
C. Being a cold day, I have not gone out of the house.
D. It being a cold day, I had not gone out of the house.

44. A. One should do his duty honestly and efficiently.
B. One should do one's duty honestly and efficiently.
C. One should do his responsibility honestly and efficiently.
D. One should act his responsibility honestly and efficiently.

45. A. She is one of those girls who cannot control her anger.
B. She is one of those girls which cannot control her anger.
C. She is one of those girls that cannot control her anger.
D. She is one of those girls who cannot control their anger.

46. A. You should attentively listen what he says.
B. You should attentively listen to what he says.
C. You should attentively listen to what he say.
D. You should attentively listen to what he says.

47. A. If she will come, I shall certainly give her five hundred rupees.
B. If she will come, I shall certainly give with her five hundred rupees.
C. If she comes, I shall certainly give five hundred rupees upon her.
D. If she comes, I shall certainly give her five hundred rupees.

48. A. She asked me if I broke the mirror.
B. She asked me if I have broken the mirror.
C. She asked of me if I have broken the mirror.
D. She asked if I had broken the mirror.

49. A. Workers are prohibited to bring their cycles inside the factory premises.
B. Workers are prohibited from bringing their cycles inside the factory premises.
C. Workers are prohibited to bringing their cycles inside the factory premises.
D. Workers are prohibited from to bring their cycles inside the factory premises.

50. A. Do you remember the date of him leaving India for Japan?
B. Do you remember the date of his leaving India for Japan?
C. Do you remember the date from his leaving India for Japan?
D. Do you remember the date by his leaving India for Japan?

51. A. She expected to have passed in the examination.
B. She expected to have pass in the examination.
C. She expected in passing the examination.
D. She expected to pass the examination.

52. A. I have visited him four hours ago.
B. I have visited him four hours before.
C. I have visited him four hours since.
D. I visited him four hours ago.

53. A. I did not go out of the house after I wrote the letter.
B. I did not go out of the house since I wrote the letter.
C. I did not go out of the house after I had written the letter.
D. I did not go out of the house after I have written the letter.

54. A. The murderer was tried, convicted and hung.
B. The murderer was tried, convicted and was hung.
C. The murderer was tried, convicted and hunged.
D. The murderer was tried, convicted and hanged.

55. A. The sceneries of Kashmir are very beautiful.
B. The sceneries of Kashmir is very beautiful.
C. The scenery of Kashmir is very beautiful.
D. The scenery of Kashmir are very beautiful.

56. A. Unless you do not work hard, you will not achieve success in life.
B. Unless you work hard, you will not achieve success in life.
C. Unless you do not work hard, you will achieve success in life.
D. Unless you work hardly, you will not achieve success in life.

57. A. Every one of my children are intelligent and healthy.
B. Every one of my children is intelligent and healthy.
C. Every one of my childs are intelligent and healthy.
D. Every one of my childs is intelligent and healthy.

58. A. Neither of the two candidates are suitable for the job.
B. Neither of the two candidate is suitable for the job.
C. Neither of the two candidates is suitable for the job.
D. Neither of the two candidates is suit for the job.

59. A. As I am ill, so I shall not be able to attend the meeting.
B. As I am ill, so I shall not to be able to attend the meeting.
C. As I am ill, so I shall not be able for attending the meeting.
D. As I am ill, I shall not be able to attend the meeting.

60. A. She never has and never will disobey me.
B. She never have and never will disobey me.
C. She never has disobeyed, and never will disobey me.
D. She never have disobeyed and never will disobey me.

61. A. This is the third time he broke a cup.
B. This is the third time when he broke a cup.
C. This is the third time he had broken a cup.
D. This is the third time he has broken a cup.

62. A. Let you and I be friends again.
B. Let you and myself be friend again.
C. Let you and I become friends again.
D. Let you and me be friends again.

63. A. I have come for seeing you.
B. I have come on seeing you.
C. I have came to seeing you.
D. I have come to see you

64. A. I am true to my words.
B. I am true with my words.
C. I am true at my words.
D. I am true to my word.

65. A. She is very anxious with my health.
B. She is very anxious at my health.
C. She is very anxious about my health.
D. She is very anxious after my health.

66. A. This is one of the best books that has been published so far.
B. This is one of the best books which has been published so far.
C. This is one of the best books that have been published so far.
D. This is one of the best books which had been published so far.

67. A. She is taller than all the girls in the college.
B. She is taller then all the girls in the college.
C. She is taller than other girls in the college.
D. She is taller than all other girls in the college.

68. A. As far I am concerned, you are free to go anywhere you like.
B. As far I am concerned, you are to free go anywhere you like.
C. As far as I am concerned, you are free to go anywhere you like.
D. As far as I concerned, you are free to going anywhere you like.

69. A. He is confined to bed for about a week.
B. He was confined to bed for about a week.
C. He has been confine to bed for about a weak.
D. He has been confined to bed for about a week.

70. A. Subhash Bose was one of the greatest patriot of India.
B. Subhash Bose has been one of the greatest patriot of India.
C. Subhash Bose has been one of the greatest patriot of India.
D. Subhash Bose was one of the greatest patriots of India.

71. A. She is as good and even better than you.
B. She is as good as, or even better than, you.
C. She is as good as or even batter than you.
D. She is as good as and better than you

72. A. They said to me that the General English paper is difficult.
B. They said me that the General English paper is difficult.
C. They said to me that the General English paper was difficult.
D. They said to me that the General English paper has been difficult.

73. A. May I have some words with you?
B. May I have a few words with you?
C. Can I have words with you?
D. May I have a word with you?

74. A. Our General Manager asked me as to why I am late.
B. Our General Manager asked me as to why am I late.
C. Our General Manager asked me why I am late.
D. Our General Manager asked me why I was late.

75. A. The story should not exceed more than five hundred words.
B. The story should not exceed than five hundred words.
C. The story should not exceed five hundred words.
D. The story should not accede five hundred words.

76. A. What is the good of him trying to do that work?
B. What is the good of his trying to do that work?
C. What the good is of him trying to do that work?
D. What is the good at his trying to do that work?

77. A. He does his best to find faults with my work.
B. He does his best in finding faults with my work.
C. He does his best to find fault with my work.
D. He does his best to find faults of my work.

78. A. This is a most unique opportunity for you to go abroad.
B. This is the most unique opportunity for you to go abroad.
C. This is a unique opportunity for you to go abroad.
D. This is a unique opportunity with you to go abroad.

79. A. Will you please say my compliments to your father?
B. Will you please say my complements to your father?
C. Will you please tell my compliments to your father?
D. Will you please pay my compliments to your father?

80. A. I always have and shall be your fast friend.
B. I always have been and shall be your fast friend.
C. I always was and shall be your fast friend.
D. I always had been and shall be your fast friend.

81. A. Tell me whether she loves you or not.
B. Tell me whether she loves you or knot.
C. Tell me whether or not she loves you.
D. Tell me whether she love you or not.

82. A. Tagore was greater than any poet.
B. Tagore was great than any poet.
C. Tagore was greater then any poet.
D. Tagore was greater than any other poet.

83. A. Going up the hill, an old temple was seen.
B. Going up to the hill, an old temple was seen.
C. On our going up the hill, an old temple was seen.
D. By going up to the hill, an old temple was seen.

84. A. The reason of her failure last time was due to her negligence.
B. The reason of her failure last time is due to her negligence.
C. Her failure last time was due to her negligence.
D. Her failure last time is on account of her negligence.

85. A. Nothing is more deplorable as dishonesty of this kind.
B. Nothing is so deplorable as dishonesty of this kind.
C. Nothing is such deplorable like dishonesty of this kind.
D. Nothing is more deplorable than dishonesty of this kind.

86. A. My cousin asked me that why did I not write to him?
B. My cousin asked me why did I not write to him?
C. My cousin asked me as to why did I not write to him?
D. My cousin asked me why I did not write to him.

87. A. She has no other ambition but only to pass the examination.
B. She has no ambition but only to pass the examination.

C. She has no ambition other than to pass the examination.
D. She has no other ambition other then to pass the examination.

88. A. If I could have worked hard, I would have passed the examination.
B. If I could work hard, I would have passed the examination.
C. If I might have worked hard, I would have passed the examination.
D. If I had worked hard, I would have passed the examination.

89. A. Four men were suspected of the crime but none of them confessed their guilt.
B. Four men were suspected of the crime but none of them accepted their guilt.
C. Four men were suspected of the crime but none of them admitted their guilt.
D. Four men were suspected of the crime, but none of them confessed his guilt.

90. A. Sita is younger to Rita but senior than her (Rita) in service.
B. Sita is younger to Rita but more senior to her (Rita) in service.
C. Sita is younger than Rita, but senior to her (Rita) in service.
D. Sita is more younger than Rita but senior to her (Rita) in service.

91. A. Tell me how are you?
B. Say me how are you?
C. Tell to me how are you?
D. Tell me how you are?

92. A. He denied that he was not a dacoit.
B. He denied that he not was a dacoit.
C. He denied he was not a dacoit.
D. He denied that he was a dacoit.

93. A. She insisted to go to Kuala Lumpur.
B. She insisted for going to Kuala Lumpur.
C. She insisted on going to Kuala Lumpur.
D. She insisted at going to Kuala Lumpur.

94. A. She gave me a chair to sit.
B. She gave me a chair for sitting.
C. She gave me a chair to be seated.
D. She gave me a chair to sit on.

95. A. He is one of the wisest persons who has ever lived.
B. He is one of the wisest persons who have ever lived.
C. He is one of the wisest persons which has ever lived.
D. He is one of the wisest persons which have ever lived.

96. A. Nobody in their senses could do such a nasty work.
B. Nobody in their senses could do such a good work.
C. Nobody in his senses could do such a nasty work.
D. Nobody in their senses could do such a nasty work.

97. A. Please tell me where is the Birla Temple?
B. Please say me where is the Birla Temple?
C. Please tell to me where is the Birla Temple?
D. Please tell me where the Birla Temple is?

98. A. They have and are still doing excellent work.
B. They have and have still doing excellent work.
C. They have and have still been doing excellent work.
D. They have done and are still doing excellent work.

99. A. All our family member have gone to Calcutta.
B. All our family member has gone to Calcutta.
C. All our family member have gone to Calcutta.
D. All the members of our family have gone to Calcutta.

100. A. Although we are living in Delhi for fifty years, we have not seen the Red Fort.
B. Although we are living in Delhi for fifty years, we had not seen the Red Fort.
C. Although we have been living in Delhi for fifty years, we have not seen the Red Fort.
D. Although we live in Delhi for fifty years, we had not seen the Red Fort.

ANSWERS

1	2	3	4	5	6	7	8	9	10
D	A	C	D	D	D	D	D	C	B
11	**12**	**13**	**14**	**15**	**16**	**17**	**18**	**19**	**20**
A	C	A	C	A	C	A	D	D	A
21	**22**	**23**	**24**	**25**	**26**	**27**	**28**	**29**	**30**
B	B	A	A	D	D	B	C	D	A
31	**32**	**33**	**34**	**35**	**36**	**37**	**38**	**39**	**40**
B	C	C	B	B	B	D	C	B	B
41	**42**	**43**	**44**	**45**	**46**	**47**	**48**	**49**	**50**
C	C	B	B	D	D	D	D	B	B
51	**52**	**53**	**54**	**55**	**56**	**57**	**58**	**59**	**60**
D	D	C	D	C	B	B	C	D	C
61	**62**	**63**	**64**	**65**	**66**	**67**	**68**	**69**	**70**
D	D	D	D	C	C	D	C	D	D
71	**72**	**73**	**74**	**75**	**76**	**77**	**78**	**79**	**80**
B	C	D	D	C	B	D	C	D	B
81	**82**	**83**	**84**	**85**	**86**	**87**	**88**	**89**	**90**
C	D	C	C	D	D	C	D	D	C
91	**92**	**93**	**94**	**95**	**96**	**97**	**98**	**99**	**100**
D	D	C	D	B	C	D	D	D	C

4 Synonyms and Antonyms

English is the most popular language of the world. It comprises thousands of words. No one can remember all the words and their meanings but everyone must try to read and learn the maximum number of words and their meanings. Readers must keep and use a dictionary religiously. Several important words are listed below with their synonyms and antonyms. Learn as many as you can.

ABANDON
Syn.: discard, desert, discontinue, renounce, relinquish, abnegate, forsake, surrender, give up, quit.
Ant.: retain, maintain, uphold, stay, remain.

ABATE
Syn.: lessen, decrease, diminish, subside, slacken, subside, allay, reduce, curtail.
Ant.: increase, enlarge, heighten, intensify, raise.

ABBREVIATE
Syn.: shorten, abridge, compress, curtain, condense, contract, prune, truncate, reduce.
Ant.: enlarge, expand, lengthen, extend, elongate, prolong, protract.

ABILITY
Syn.: competence, aptitude, capability, talent, intelligence, cleverness, capacity.
Ant.: inability, incompetence, incapacity, incapability, inaptitude.

ABLE
Syn.: capable, competent, intelligent, talented, efficient, skilful.
Ant.: unable, incapable, inefficient, incompetent.

ABRUPT
Syn.: sudden, curt, steep, hasty, unexpected, disconnected, disjointed, brusque, rough.
Ant.: expected, anticipated, gradual, courteous, smooth.

ABSURD
Syn.: illogical, irrational, inconsistent, silly, inane, unreasonable, funny, ridiculous, laughable, ludicrous, nonsensical, fatuous.
Ant.: logical, reasonable, rational, consistent, sensible, sound, proper, sane.

ACCURATE
Syn.: exact, precise, correct, actual, just, right, correct.
Ant.: incorrect, inexact, improper, fallacious, inaccurate, misleading, erroneous.

ADEQUATE
Syn.: ample, abundant, enough, sufficient, plentiful, copious.
Ant.: inadequate, insufficient, meagre, scant, scantly, skimpy.

AFFABLE
Syn.: urbane, polite, friendly, courteous, amiable, suave, good-tempered.
Ant.: impolite, unfriendly, discourteous, haughty.

AKIN
Syn.: kindred, similar, allied, cognate, alike, related, analogous.
Ant.: dissimilar, unrelated, unallied, unconnected, different, unlike, separate.

ALERT
Syn.: wary, vigilant, watchful, attentive, heedful, cautious, lively, fully awake.
Ant.: unwatchful, sluggish, relaxed, quiet, restful.

ABNORMAL

Syn.: unusual, irregular, anomalous, unnatural, odd, strange, erratic.

Ant.: usual, regular, natural, normal, customary.

ACTIVE

Syn.: brisk, energetic, lively, nimble, agile.

Ant.: inactive, indolent, sluggish, lazy, passive, torpid.

ACTUAL

Syn.: real, genuine, authentic, true, concrete, factual, existing.

Ant.: unreal, implied, assumed, false, imaginary, fictitious.

AMBIGUOUS

Syn.: vague, uncertain, undecided, undefined, obscure, doubtful, indistinct, dubious, perplexing.

Ant.: lucid, plain, clear, obvious, unambiguous, unmistakable, indisputable.

APT

Syn.: appropriate, apposite, suitable, fitting, pertinent, germane, relevant, congruent, harmonious, congruous.

Ant.: inapt, inappropriate, incongruous, improper, unsuitable, inapposite, irrelevant.

ARDENT

Syn.: fervid, fervent, warm, impassioned, plowing, intense, eager, earnest, passionate, hearty, cordial, enthusiastic.

Ant.: cool, indifferent, apathetic, nonchalant, unimpassioned.

ATROCIOUS

Syn.: nefarious, heinous, cruel, outrageous, beastly, horrible, horrendous.

Ant.: noble, humane, honourable, laudable, admirable, moral.

AUDACIOUS

Syn.: bold, daring, fearless, impudent, brash, rash, reckless, impertinent, madcap, insolent, brave, disrespectful, intrepid.

Ant.: cowardly, timid, fearful, meek, humble, afraid, frightened, scared, different, panicky, apprehensive, shy, mousy, timorous, fidgety.

AUTHENTIC

Syn.: genuine, real, trustworthy, true, reliable, accurate, authoritative, sound, tangible, definite, actual, precise, exact, correct, factual, veritable, sterling.

Ant.: apocryphal, unreliable, spurious, false, fictitious, fake, sham, imaginary, counterfeit, baseless, untrue.

BEAUTIFUL

Syn.: catching, prepossessing, fetching, cute, enticing, engaging, attractive, charming, fascinating, captivating, alluring, tempting, lovely, bewitching, reductive, pretty, enchanting, winning, comely.

Ant.: ugly, unattractive, unprepossessing, repulsive, gaunt, haggard, unpleasing, revolting, hideous.

BITTER

Syn.: tart, harsh, pungent, unpalatable, acrid, spiteful, cutting, stinging, sour, unpleasant, sarcastic, resentful, biting, sardonic, caustic, severe, acrimonious, poignant, distasteful.

Ant.: tasty, toothsome, tasteful, palatable, pleasant, delicious, warm.

BRIGHT

Syn.: brilliant, shining, luminous, lustrous, radiant, sparkling, quick-witted, cheerful, clever, resplendent, flashing, lucid, limpid, sagacious, keen, astute, shrewd, brainy, intelligent.

Ant.: dull, ignorant, cheerless, imbecile, murky, dark, gloomy, sullen.

BRIEF

Syn.: compendious, concise, short, terse, laconic, curt, succinct, condensed, compact, pithy.

Ant.: long, lengthy, prolonged, protracted, elongated, lengthened, extended, detailed, prolix, verbose, wordy.

BRUTAL

Syn.: atrocious, savage, beastly, brutish, fiendish, devilish, barbarous, cruel, ruthless, merciless, crude, ferocious, bestial, heinous.

Ant.: humane, gentle, civilised, merciful, polished, sympathetic, tender, liberal, considerate, good-natured.

CANDID

Syn.: frank, outspoken, sincere, impartial, honest, artless, ingenuous, straightforward.

Ant.: sly, wily, insincere, reserved, unfair, evasive.

CAPRICIOUS

Syn.: unpredictable, impulsive, fickle, changeable, inconstant, whimsical.

Ant.: constant, firm, steadfast, unswerving.

CARELESS

Syn.: heedless, inattentive, indifferent, negligent, remiss, lax, unmindful.

Ant.: cautious, vigilant, careful, mindful, attentive.

CERTAIN
Syn.: indisputable, reliable, sure, definite, undisputed, unmistakable, positive, absolute.
Ant.: uncertain, disputable, doubtful, indefinite, ambiguous, dubious, questionable.

CHEEK
Syn.: impudence, impertinence, effrontery, gall, temerity, audacity, insolence, sauce, sass.
Ant.: politeness, courtesy, humility, gentleness, respect.

☛ *Cheek* also means either side of the face below the eye.

Examples: She has healthy rosy *cheeks*.
They are dancing *cheek* to *cheek*.

CHEERFUL
Syn.: genial, happy, jolly, merry, jovial, pleasant, lively, cheery, sunny, jocund, gay.
Ant.: cheerless, joyless, dejected, unhappy, doleful, sorrowful, mournful, glum, dreary, dismal.

CHARM (Verb)
Syn.: fascinate, attract, please, delight, influence, entice, enchant, entrance, enrapture, allure, captivate, bewitch, ravish, tempt, lure, seduce, beguile, enthral, thrill.
Ant.: repel, repulse, rebuff, snub, disgust, deter, disturb, irritate, annoy, alarm, frighten, terrify.

COMFORTABLE
Syn.: cosy, snug, pleasant, pleasing, pleasurable, satisfied.
Ant.: uncomfortable, disagreeable, dissatisfied, disturbed, displeasing, irritating, miserable, wretched, troubled, cheerless.

COMPLETE (Adj)
Syn.: whole, thorough, total, entire, full, perfect, exhausive, consummate.
Ant.: incomplete, imperfect, partial, unfinished, uncompleted, unaccomplished, deficient, skimpy, sketchy.

CORDIAL
Syn.: sincere, friendly, earnest, warm, hearty, ardent, heartfelt, amiable, affable.
Ant.: unfriendly, insincere, cold, distant, formal, reserved.

COURAGE
Syn.: bravery, boldness, valour, heroism, fearlessness, intrepidity, nerve, gallantry, pluck, fortitude, daring.
Ant.: cowardice, timidity, pusillanimity, fear, funk.

CURIOUS
Syn.: inquisitive, inquiring, prying, strange, unusual, nosey, meddlesome.
Ant.: incurious, uninquiring, uninquisitive, uninterested, unconcerned, indifferent, common, usual.

CORRECT (Adj)
Syn.: accurate, proper, exact, precise, right, true, regular, perfect.
Ant.: incorrect, improper, inexact, wrong, untrue, irregular, imperfect.

DAFT
Syn.: silly, crazy, irrational, foolish, unreasonable, reckless, insane, imbecile, lumpish.
Ant.: sane, sound, sensible, deft, rational, reasonable.

DAINTY
Syn.: pretty, neat, delicate, refined, tasty, delicious, fastidious, elegant, toothsome, exquisite, cute, tasteful, palatable.
Ant.: inelegant, coarse, vulgar, rough, crude, rude, nasty, dirty.

DEEP
Syn.: abstruse, profound, intense, learned, sagacious, extreme, devious, vivid, submerged, bottomless, unfathomable, abysmal, mysterious, knotty, astute, recondite, intricate.
Ant.: shallow, apparent, familiar, artless, commonplace, ordinary, trite, naive, superficial, cursory, simple, banal.

DELIGHT
Syn.: joy, pleasure, rapture, ecstasy, enjoyment, bliss, gratification, gusto, comfort.
Ant.: displeasure, discomfort, sorrow, distress, misery, anguish, suffering, agony, woe, despair, depression.

DETRIMENTAL
Syn.: harmful, injurious, hurtful, pernicious, damaging, noxious.
Ant.: good, beneficial, valuable, useful, profitable, harmless, inoffensive, unobnoxious.

DIFFICULT

Syn.: hard, troublesome, perplexing, tough, laborious, irksome, toilsome, arduous, knotty, burdensome, uphill, herculean, enigmatic.

Ant.: easy, uncomplicated, intelligible, lucid, plain, simple, facile, manageable, tractable, elementary, rudimentary.

DILIGENT

Syn.: industrious, laborious, hard-working, attentive, assiduous, observant, mindful, vigilant, watchful, wakeful, careful.

Ant.: careless, heedless, inattentive, indifferent, unobservant, unmindful.

DISHONEST

Syn.: untrustworthy, false, fraudulent, deceitful, crooked, tricky, deceptive, treacherous, unjust, unfair, unreliable.

Ant.: trustworthy, reliable, fair, just, candid, frank, sincere, upright, truthful, veracious, honest.

DOCILE

Syn.: pliant, tractable, amenable, teachable, yielding, compliant, tame, submissive, gentle, unresisting, dutiful, passive, acquiescent, unassertive, manageable, governable, obsequious.

Ant.: obstinate, stubborn, intractable, self-willed, dogged, defiant, insolent, resistant, resisting, obdurate, disobedient, wilful, uncompromising, unyielding, refractory, recalcitrant.

DOUBTFUL

Syn.: questionable, uncertain, unsure, unlikely, improbable, disputable, debatable, dubious, controversial, fishy, moot, ambiguous.

Ant.: certain, sure, probable, indisputable, unquestionable, positive, absolute, definite, clear, unmistakable, reliable, trustworthy, undoubted, undeniable, indubitable.

DROLL

Syn.: amusing, laughable, funny, comic, sarcastic, whimsical, comical, odd, queer, farcical, ludicrous, ridiculous, absurd, diverting, rompish.

Ant.: sad, lamentable, lugubrious, tragic, painful, dolorous, hurtful, distressing, grievous, woeful, rueful, mournful, deplorable, touching.

DULL

Syn.: stupid, boring, monotonous, foolish, unintelligent, cheerless, gloomy, uninteresting, spiritless, blunt, doltish, sad, stolid, dismal, dowdy, drab, unfashionable, insensible.

Ant.: sensible, cheerful, bright, intelligent, clever, lively, animated, brilliant, sharp, talented, jolly, merry, joyful, gay, jocund, energetic, keen, active, intense, brisk, lively, trenchant, rousing.

EAGER

Syn.: ardent, earnest, zealous, keen, fervent, fervid, vehement, intent, agog, avid, excited, impatient, curious, anxious, enthusiastic, wistful, hearty, cordial, desirous.

Ant.: indifferent, disinterested, cool, loath, unconcerned, apathetic, reluctant, unwilling, disinclined.

EFFICIENT

Syn.: capable, able, competent, gifted, effective, effectual, efficacious, skilful, proficient, talented, intelligent, adept.

Ant.: inefficient, incompetent, ineffectual, unskilled, inexpert.

ELIGIBLE

Syn.: fit, suitable, desirable, worthy, qualified, acceptable, right.

Ant.: unfit, unsuitable, unworthy, unacceptable, undesirable, unqualified.

EMPHEMERAL

Syn.: short-lived, transitory, transient, fleeting, momentary, fugitive, evanescent, fugacious, temporary.

Ant.: eternal, perpetual, perennial, permanent, intransient, lifelong, everlasting, long-lived, prolonged, protracted.

ENORMOUS

Syn.: immense, gigantic, colossal, huge, vast, gargantuan, monstrous, prodigious, stupendous, plentiful, plenteous, copious.

Ant.: trivial, insignificant, ordinary, average, small, little, tiny, diminutive.

ENOUGH

Syn.: plenty, ample, sufficient, abundant, adequate.

Ant.: insufficient, inadequate, meagre, scanty, deficient, scant, jejune, skimpy.

ENTHUSIASM

Syn.: verve, ardour, zeal, fervour, fanaticism.

Ant.: apathy, indifference, detachment, ennui, unconcern, lethargy, weariness, exhaustion, lassitude, languor.

EXPERT (Adj)

Syn.: adept, skilled, adroit, proficient, skilful, deft, dexterous, versed, accomplished.

Ant.: inexpert, unskilful, unskilled, maladroit, clumsy, lungling, unqualified, raw, inexperienced, green, incompetent.

FACE (V)

Syn.: confront, oppose, defy, meet, encounter, resist.

Ant.: avoid, shun, elude, avert, eschew.

FAITHFUL

Syn.: loyal, trustworthy, conscientious, true, accurate, devoted, exact, reliable, staunch, steadfast, constant, dependable, compliant.

Ant.: disloyal, untrustworthy, inaccurate, inexact, unreliable, unfaithful, treacherous, undependable, untrue, fickle.

FICKLE

Syn.: inconstant, disloyal, unfaithful, capricious, impulsive, unpredictable, changeable, unstable, variable, vacillating, wavering, fanciful, whimsical, mutable, irresolute, erratic, unreliable, fitful.

Ant.: steady, steadfast, unchangeable, unwavering, constant, loyal, faithful, reliable, dependable, stable, immutable, invariable.

FIT (Adj)

Ant.: suitable, appropriate, proper, advantageous, sound, well, meet, becoming, fitting, qualified, apt, apposite, decent, decorous, congruent, congruous, concordant, harmonious, eligible.

Ant.: unfit, unsuitable, unbecoming, disadvantageous, unwell, indecent, indecorous, improper, inappropriate, inapt, incongruent, ineligible.

FOOLISH

Syn.: silly, stupid, unwise, ridiculous, absurd, asinine, imbecile, indiscreet, irrational, idiotic, brainless, senseless, nonsensical, witless, preposterous, inane, fatuous, imprudent, inconsistent, illogical, laughable, paradoxical, dotty.

Ant.: wise, sane, prudent, discreet, sound, sensible, rational, sagacious, judicious, sage.

FRIENDLY

Syn.: kindly, pleasantly, amicable, cordial, hearty, warm-hearted, affable, genial, well-inclined, good-tempered, amiable, favourable, pleasing, sociable, companionable, nice, neighbourly, benevolent, well-disposed.

Ant.: hostile, unsociable, unfavourable, unfriendly, adverse, inimical, antagonistic, distant, reserved, cool, ill-inclined, ill-disposed, resistant, opposed.

FUNDAMENTAL

Syn.: basic, primary, essential, cardinal, indispensable, original, rudimentary, elementary, radical, most important, prime, chief.

Ant.: secondary, subordinate, minor, inferior, resultant, second-rate, subsidiary.

FUNNY

Syn.: amusing, jocular, jocose, laughable, eccentric, absurd, droll, comical, comic, playful, ludicrous, farcical, humorous, ridiculous, odd, queer, diverting, strange.

Ant.: sad, serious, solemn, sober, sedate, staid, grave, sorrowful, mournful.

GARRULOUS

Syn.: talkative, chatty, verbose, loquacious, communicative, glib, voluble, prolix, wordy, long-winded, diffuse, profuse, discussive, rambling, circumlocutory, maundering, periphrastic.

Ant.: laconic, reticent, silent, taciturn, uncommunicative, terse, reserved, short-spoken.

GENUINE

Syn.: authentic, sound, true, real, pure, veritable, unadulterated, unalloyed, unaffected, natural, factual, actual, legitimate, undistorted, tangible, valid, sterling.

Ant.: sham, spurious, fictitious, artificial, adulterated, alloyed, impure, apocryphal, untrue, fallacious, unsound, invalid.

GIFTED

Syn.: talented, intelligent, sagacious, competent, wise, able, proficient, efficient, capable, shrewd, inventive, skilful, ingenious, experienced.

Ant.: foolish, doltish, silly, stupid, idiotic.

GLORIOUS

Syn.: famous, beautiful, splendid, magnificent, enjoyable, pleasant, grand, exalted, lofty, majestic, sublime, noble, bright, radiant, renowned.

Ant.: base, ignoble, low, ordinary, ridiculous.

GOOD (N)

Syn.: benefit, profit, advantage, virtue, boon, weal, prosperity, blessing, gain, welfare, righteousness, merit.

Ant.: harm, injury, corruption, wickedness, depravity, detriment, disadvantage, ill, calamity, loss, evil, curse.

GRACEFUL

Syn.: elegant, pleasing in style and attitude, polite, considerate, comely, beautiful, attractive, lithe, lissom, svelte, sylphlike, willowy.

Ant.: ungainly, awkward, lumbering, uncouth, ill mannered, not refined.

GRAND

Syn.: august, exalted, stately, splendid, majestic, lofty, superb, imposing, dignified, noble, princely, magnificent, big, pompous, gorgeous, sublime, impressive.

Ant.: mean, common, insignificant, secondary, inferior, unimportant, little, undignified, unimposing, petty, paltry, beggarly, lowly.

GRIM

Syn.: fearful, stern, fierce, ruthless, horrible, determined, strong-willed, horrid, repellent, frightful, ghastly, gristly, gloomy, severe, unrelenting, unpleasant, depressing, determined, repulsive, dingy, drab, savage, appalling, ferocious, ugly, sullen, hideous.

Ant.: handsome, pretty, graceful, elegant, gentle, gracious, friendly, humane, benign, mild, docile, attractive.

GRUFF

Syn.: rough, surly, blunt, harsh, rude.

Ant.: affable, courteous, mild, smooth.

HARMFUL

Syn.: detrimental, pernicious, prejudicial, deleterious, injurious, noxious, hurtful, mischievous, obnoxious, inauspicious, oppressive, baneful, baleful, menacing, malignant, unhealthful, vitiated, damaging.

Ant.: helpful, profitable, beneficial, advantageous, harmless, useful, favourable, good, salutary, healthful, inoffensive, unobnoxious.

HARMONIOUS

Syn.: congruous, concordant, uniform, proportioned, consistent, tuneful, melodious, sweet-sounding, agreeable, friendly, amicable, cordial.

Ant.: unfriendly, hostile, unfavourable, adverse, opposing, opposed, antagonistic, contrary, discordant, conflicting, inconsistent.

HARSH

Syn.: rough, stern, cruel, severe, blunt, coarse, gruff, discordant, raucous, hoarse, rugged, severe, shrill, strident, austere, acrimonious, ungenial, sharp, sour, ungracious, brutal, heartless.

Ant.: gentle, mild, smooth, soft, melodious.

HEALTHY

Syn.: robust, strong, vigorous, lusty, hearty, sound, well, hygienic, salubrious, wholesome, salutary, bracing, invigorating, harmless, healthful, hale and hearty, inoffensive, laudable, moral.

Ant.: diseased, delicate, infirm, injurious, frail, noxious, sick, ailing, ill, sick.

HEARTY

Syn.: warm, earnest, sincere, heartfelt, cordial, sound, ardent, friendly, enthusiastic, cheerful, healthy, fervent, fervid.

Ant.: cool, reserved, taciturn, insincere.

HONEST

Syn.: frank, sincere, direct, fairly earned, truthful, upright, virtuous, right, sincere, genuine, trustworthy.

Ant.: dishonest, untrustworthy, tricky, deceitful, fraudulent, insincere.

HONOUR (N)

Syn.: privilege, probity, integrity, glory, distinction, great respect, glory, dignity, reverence, grandeur, high-mindedness, eminence, renown, fame.

Ant.: dishonour, disrespect, contempt, irreverence, disgrace, degradation, slight, infamy, perfidy, treachery, improbity, scorn, disdain.

HUMOROUS

Syn.: droll, amusing, ludicrous, funny, jocular, merry, comic, jocose, waggish, farcical.

Ant.: solemn, serious, sober, grave, composed, sedate, dignified.

IDLE

Syn.: indolent, lazy, inactive, unemployed, useless, unoccupied, slothful, futile.

Ant.: active, busy, occupied, working, industrious, employed.

INDUSTRIOUS

Syn.: diligent, hard-working, laborious, assiduous, sedulous.

Ant.: lethargic, inactive, apathetic, lazy, idle, indolent, slothful, torpid, sluggish, shiftless, slack, lax, supine.

IMPORTANT

Syn.: significant, valuable, weighty, influential, momentous, prominent, material, essential, remarkable, eventful.

Ant.: insignificant, unimportant, petty, trivial, mean, secondary, minor, uninfluential, worthless, valueless, immaterial, inferior.

INGENIOUS

Syn.: adroit, clever, dexterous, quick-witted, skilful, talented, smart, bright, sharp, adept, original, inventive, expert, intelligent.

Ant.: unskilled, dull, foolish, clumsy, awkward, stupid, unskilful, inexpert, maladroit, incompetent, inexperienced, unconversant, ungainly.

INGENUOUS

Syn.: innocent, open, candid, frank, sincere, straightforward, truthful, artless, honest, naive, simple, trusting, unaffected, outspoken.

Ant.: insincere, reserved, sly, wily, contrived, disingenuous, mean, pretentious, sham, affected, priggish.

INFINITE

Syn.: boundless, endless, unlimited, unbounded, limitless, immeasurable, interminable, stupendous, eternal, immense, vast, incalculable, numberless, countless, bottomless, unfathomable, inexhaustible, indefinite, perpetual.

Ant.: finite, limited, restricted, bounded, conditioned, confined, definite, determinate, circumscribed.

INTELLIGENT

Syn.: brainy, clever, bright, brilliant, keen, sagacious, quick-witted, discerning, sharp, shrewd, astute, canny, perspicacious, perceptive, nimble, well-informed, enlightened.

Ant.: foolish, doltish, dull, stupid, unintelligent, stolid, obtuse, silly, inane.

INTEGRITY

Syn.: honesty, probity, uprightness, rectitude, truthfulness, sincerity, trustworthiness, fairness, wholeness, completeness, oneness, totality, entirety, indivisibility.

Ant.: dishonesty, duplicity, unfairness, deceit, fraud, improbity.

IRRITABLE

Syn.: peevish, touchy, irascible, testy, short-tempered, fretful, splenetic, petulant, grumpy, pettish, snappish, choleric, peppery, churlish, cantankerous, fractious, crabbed.

Ant.: calm, composed, agreeable, gracious, cheerful, genial, good-natured, blithe, jaunty, buoyant, lively, animated.

JEALOUS

Syn.: envious, invidious, suspicious, resentful, covetous, jaundiced, distrustful, apprehensive, intolerant.

Ant.: unenvious, unjealous, tolerant, liberal, genial, indifferent, unsuspecting.

JOLLY

Syn.: genial, jovial, jubilant, lively, gay, joyful, merry, mirthful, cheerful, light-hearted, jocular, jocund, blithe.

Ant.: cheerless, joyless, sad, mournful, gloomy, morose, sullen, lugubrious, sorrowful, melancholy, dismal, unhappy.

JUST

Syn.: fair, honest, proper, right, reasonable, well-founded, deserved, impartial, true, upright, exact, precise, proportioned, normal.

Ant.: unfair, unjust, improper, unreasonable, partial, untrue, inexact, abnormal, ill-proportioned, prejudiced, biased.

KEEN

Syn.: acute, sharp, penetrating, astute, clever, cunning, quick, shrewd, wily, eager, enthusiastic, intense, deep, strong, cutting, ardent, nippy, avid, fervent.

Ant.: indifferent, blunt, dull, languid, indifferent, cool, careless, half-hearted, unconcerned, lukewarm, impervious, insouciant.

KIND (Adj)

Syn.: friendly, gentle, mild, obliging, benign, lenient, helpful, sympathetic, favourable, benevolent, amiable, good-natured, cordial, courteous, gracious, warm-hearted, humane, compassionate, generous, philanthropic.

Ant.: unfriendly, unfavourable, discourteous, unkind, harsh, severe, hard, callous, cruel, inhumane.

KNOWLEDGE

Syn.: understanding, learning, information, instruction, acquaintance, cognition, cognizance, awareness, comprehension, apprehension, consciousness, familiarity, ken, enlightenment, experience, attainments, scholarship, education.

Ant.: ignorance, nescience, illiteracy, incomprehension, inexperience, unawareness.

LABORIOUS

Syn.: diligent, hard-working, industrious, toilsome, tedious, tiresome, irksome, arduous, assiduous, wearisome, strenuous, painstaking, uphill.

Ant.: easy, light, feasible, indiligent, lazy, indolent, simple, idle.

LACONIC

Syn.: curt, terse, concise, pithy, short, brief, succinct, crisp, compendious, compact.

Ant.: lengthy, prolix, wordy, circumlocutory, verbose, discursive, long-winded, rambling, roundabout, copious, diffuse.

LAX

Syn.: negligent, careless, remiss, sluggish, inattentive, neglectful, heedless, vague, desultory, unmethodical, loose, slack, relaxed.

Ant.: careful, meticulous, attentive, methodical, severe, strict, heedful, regardful, cautious, prudent, discreet.

LESSEN

Syn.: shorten, abate, curtail, decrease, reduce, diminish, abridge, mitigate, contract, deduct, subtract, shrink, allenuate.

Ant.: increase, enlarge, augment, extend, expand, grow, amplify, enhance, magnify.

LIVELY

Syn.: high-spirited, vigorous, energetic, active, animated, brisk, bright, blithe, frolicsome, merry, playful, spirited, forceful, sprightly, vivacious, joyous, joyful, gay.

Ant.: dull, listless, insipid, vapid, inactive, uninteresting, depressed, languid, torpid, apathetic, indifferent, sluggish, dejected, joyless, cheerless, unlively, spiritless.

LOGICAL

Syn.: cogent, convincing, sound, valid, effective, reasonable, natural, rational, sane, relevant.

Ant.: illogical, invalid, ineffective, unreasonable, unnatural, irrational, insane, irrelevant, fallacious.

MADDEN

Syn.: infuriate, enrage, incense, derange, craze, anger, offend, displease, embitter, exasperate, rankle, affront, irritate, provoke, nettle, inflame, annoy.

Ant.: placate, pacify, soothe, calm, assuage, appease, mollify.

MALICIOUS

Syn.: spiteful, malignant, malevolent, evil-minded, hostile, rancorous, virulent, wicked, malign, pernicious, vicious, harmful, maleficent, ill-disposed, ill-intentioned.

Ant.: benign, kind, good-natured, benevolent, cordial, unselfish, sympathetic, gracious, well-intentioned, humane, warm-hearted, affectionate.

MASTERLY

Syn.: skilful, adept, deft, dexterous, expert, skilled, consummate, perfect, masterful, dominating.

Ant.: unskilled, maladroit, clumsy, inexpert.

METHODICAL

Syn.: orderly, logical, systematic, regular, procedural, planned, arranged, tidy.

Ant.: disorderly, illogical, irregular, unsystematic, unmethodical, untidy, desultory, unarranged, disarranged, sloppy, chaotic, anarchical.

MODEST

Syn.: moderate, inexpensive, not showy or splendid in appearance, not vain or boastful, shy, bashful, humble, meek, reserved, unassuming, unpretentious, diffident, unobtrusive, coy.

Ant.: immodest, showy or splendid in appearance, vain, boastful, ostentatious, pretentious, proud, arrogant, bold, conceited, haughty, disdainful, pert, imperious, domineering, priggish, smug, self-satisfied, egotistic, self-important.

MOMENTOUS

Syn.: important, prominent, significant, weighty, material, pressing, influential, grave, consequential, serious, notable, solemn, memorable, remarkable.

Ant.: unimportant, immaterial, inconsequential, insignificant, mean, petty, trivial, slight, niggling, trifling.

NATURAL

Syn.: innate, inherent, original, normal, spontaneous, unaffected, characteristic, typical, native, unstudied, inborn, naive, ingenuous, inbred, ingrained, usual, intrinsic.

Ant.: unnatural, abnormal, artificial, affected, forced, irregular, unusual, inconsistent, fictitious.

NECESSARY

Syn.: requisite, needful, essential, inevitable, unavoidable, indispensable.

Ant.: unnecessary, optional, unessential, dispensable, voluntary, discretional, casual.

NICE

Syn.: pleasant, agreeable, friendly, kind, fine, subtle, respectable, scrupulous, dainty, attractive, fastidious, tasteful, delicate, choosy, refined, palatable, delectable, pleasing, pleasurable.

Ant.: disagreeable, coarse, unscrupulous, rough, nasty, rueful, mournful, woeful, deplorable, distressing.

NIMBLE

Syn.: agile, sharp, active, brisk, lively, spry, quick.

Ant.: slow, sluggish, clumsy, inert, lazy, indolent, awkward, slothful.

NOVICE

Syn.: beginner, tyro, neophyte, apprentice, greenhorn, learner, acolyte, rookie.

Ant.: expert, adept, master, teacher, trainer, instructor.

OBEDIENT

Syn.: observant, dutiful, complying, compliant, loyal, faithful, devoted, fractable, docile, submissive, pliable, pliant, yielding.

Ant.: disloyal, unfaithful, intractable, uncomplying, uncompliant, unruly, unsubmissive, refractory, resisting, contumacious, recalcitrant.

OBSTINATE

Syn.: stubborn, obdurate, dogged, tenacious, persistent, insistent, headstrong, pertinacious, unyielding, determined, self-willed, wilful, resolute.

Ant.: irresolute, subservient, yielding, submissive, amenable, wavering.

OFFENSIVE (Adj)

Syn.: insulting, annoying, disgusting, repulsive, aggressive, distasteful, foul, aggressive, obnoxious, nasty.

Ant.: pleasant, defensive, inoffensive, harmless, blameless, unaggressive, innocuous.

OWN (V)

Syn.: possess, confess, admit, avow, acknowledge, have, hold, concede.

Ant.: deny, disclaim, disavow, renounce, disown, abjure, abandon.

PEEVISH

Syn.: irritable, touchy, testy, tetchy, irascible, fretful, bad-tempered, crabbed, pettish, petulant, snappish, waspish, fractious, hot-headed, crabby, churlish.

Ant.: affable, genial, good-natured, good-tempered, pleasant, cordial, hearty, jolly, soft-spoken, polite, urbane.

PERFECT (Adj)

Syn.: complete, excellent, ideal, exact, precise, total, absolute, thorough, faultless, indefective, indeficient, immaculate, impeccable, sound, spotless, entire, utter, consummate.

Ant.: imperfect, incomplete, inexact, deficient, faulty, unsound, deformed, impaired, blemished, crude.

PLEASANT

Syn.: enjoyable, polite and friendly, pleasurable, agreeable, pleasing, delectable, palatable, delightful, cheerful, delicious, jocular, merry.

Ant.: unpleasant, disagreeable, unlively, lugubrious, dismal, sad, mournful, offensive, unpleasing, disgusting, obnoxious, nasty.

PLENTIFUL

Syn.: ample, abundant, copious, profuse, plenteous, prolific, bounteous, bountiful, lavish.

Ant.: scanty, meagre, limited, skimpy, insufficient, sparing, scarce, deficient, rare.

POMPOUS

Syn.: self-important, ostentatious, high-flown, bombastic, grandiose, arrogant, haughty, grand, imposing, lofty, magnificent, majestic, stately, sublime, dignified, showy, pretentious, assuming, turgid, magniloquent.

Ant.: unassuming, plain-mannered, unpretending, modest, unobtrusive, humble-minded, unpreten-tious, bashful, coy.

PRECISE

Syn.: exact, accurate, definite, correct, punctilious, fastidious, particular, proper.

Ant.: inexact, inaccurate, indefinite, incorrect, improper, vague, ambiguous, rough, circumlocutory.

PREPOSSESSING

Syn.: attractive, charming, taking, alluring, engaging, winning, appealing, winsome.

Ant.: unattractive, repulsive, ugly, unprepossessing, ill-looking.

PREPOSTEROUS

Syn.: outrageous, absurd, unreasonable, ridiculous, foolish, silly, stupid, inconsistent, irrational, nonsensical, laughable, idiotic, illogical, ludicrous.

Ant.: consistent, reasonable, rational, logical, sensible, sound, just, fair, right, moderate.

PRINCIPAL (Adj)

Syn.: chief, main, foremost, prime, leading, most important, pre-eminent, outstanding, excellent, conspicuous, highest, first-rate, cardinal, fundamental, primary, paramount, supreme, predominant.

Ant.: minor, inferior, subordinate, secondary, auxiliary, subsidiary.

PUSHY

Syn.: aggressive, offensive, forceful, belligerent, bold, impudent, rude, disrespectful, insolent, self-assertive.

Ant.: cowardly, timid, defensive.

QUESTIONABLE

Syn.: doubtful, uncertain, suspicious, dubious, disputable, debatable, arguable, fishy, controversial.

Ant.: certain, indisputable, obvious, evident, unquestionable, sure.

QUICKEN

Syn.: hasten, hurry, speed, accelerate, refresh, animate, rush, expedite.

Ant.: retard, slacken, moderate, curb, shorten, slow, relax, delay, impede, hinder, obstruct.

QUIET (Adj)

Syn.: calm, peaceful, serene, hushed, silent, modest, restrained, subdued, gentle, unostentatious, restful, relaxed, leisurely, unhurried, reposeful, tranquil, quiescent, unobtrusive, passive, undisturbed, motionless, still, mild, modest.

Ant.: loud, agitated, disturbed, perturbed, noisy.

QUIET (N)

Syn.: calm, calmness, hush, peace, repose, rest, silence, stillness, tranquility, serenity, quiescence, quietude.

Ant.: agitation, disturbance, uproar, noise, din, noisiness, loudness, tumult, excitement, turmoil, commotion, unrest.

RAPID

Syn.: speedy, quick, swift, fast, prompt, expeditious, hasty, hurried.

Ant.: slow, sluggish, slack, tardy, leisurely, gradual, languid.

REASONABLE

Syn.: sensible, logical, moderate, tolerable, acceptable, average, sound, fair, rational, inexpensive, sober, temperate.

Ant.: unreasonable, absurd, unfair, illogical, irrational, intolerable, immoderate, expensive, senseless, preposterous, ridiculous, silly, excessive, obstinate.

REGULAR

Syn.: proper, systematic, symmetrical, normal, usual, habitual, constant, orderly, steady, methodical, consistent.

Ant.: irregular, improper, abnormal, unusual, disorderly, inconstant, desultory, unmethodical, changeable, erratic, sporadic.

REMARKABLE

Syn.: unusual, exceptional, august, impressive, extra-ordinary, uncommon, splendid, singular, notable, noteworthy, striking, distinguished, wonderful, famous, prominent, conspicuous, imposing.

Ant.: ordinary, average, inconspicuous, normal, usual, common, customary, undistinguished.

RESPONSIBLE
Syn.: answerable, trustworthy, dependable, accountable, liable, chargeable, reliable.
Ant.: irresponsible, untrustworthy, undependable, unreliable, unaccountable, unanswerable.

RICH
Syn.: wealthy, affluent, prosperous, opulent, nourishing, abundant, ample, fruitful, fertile, luxuriant, vivid, bountiful, sumptuous, gorgeous, sonorous, well-to-do, plentiful, fecund, well-heeled, productive, wholesome, nutritious.
Ant.: poor, needy, penniless, beggarly, indigent, destitute, barren, sterile, unfruitful, unproductive, impecunious, hard up, necessitous.

SCHOOL (V)
Syn.: train, teach, direct, lead, guide, educate, instruct, control, discipline, inform, enlighten, tutor.
Ant.: misdirect, mislead, misguide, deceive, delude.

SCRUPULOUS
Syn.: absolutely honest, extremely careful and thorough, paying great attention to details, exact, meticulous, punctilious, upright, moral, conscientious, veracious, truthful, right-minded, high-principled.
Ant.: dishonest, deceitful, tricky, fraudulent, unscrupulous, careless, unprincipled, conscienceless, knavish.

SILLY
Syn.: foolish, doltish, indiscreet, stupid, unwise, childish, inane, fatuous, senseless, absurd, ridiculous, idiotic, nonsensical, irrational, preposterous, outrageous, imprudent.
Ant.: wise, prudent, rational, sane, discreet, sound, intelligent, sensible, sapient, sagacious, discerning, perspicacious, brainy, brilliant, well-advised, judicious, astute, shrewd.

SLY
Syn.: foxy, wily, crafty, cunning, deceitful, secretive, furtive, roguish, mischievous, stealthy, underhand, surreptitious.
Ant.: open, frank, candid, ingenuous, sincere, artless.

SOFTEN
Syn.: mollify, soothe, ease, calm, comfort, quiet, temper, moderate, mitigate, abate, allay, alleviate, assuage, diminish, lessen, extenuate, relieve.
Ant.: harden, stiffen, augment, irritate, increase, aggravate, worsen, enhance, heighten, intensify, infuriate, indurate.

SUITABLE
Syn.: appropriate, proper, fitting, right, becoming, apposite, eligible, seemly, apt, meet, decorous, seasonable.
Ant.: unsuitable, improper, unbecoming, inapt, indecorous, unseemly, ineligible, inappropriate, inapposite.

TEDIOUS
Syn.: boring, tiresome, wearisome, irksome, monotonous, dreary, uninteresting, dull, humdrum, drab.
Ant.: interesting, amusing, entertaining, exciting, delightful, brisk.

TERRIBLE
Syn.: horrible, alarming, fearful, shocking, frightful, awesome, appalling, dreadful, terrifying, frightening, formidable, terrific, horrid, terrible, fearsome.
Ant.: pleasing, encouraging, safe, secure, joyous, informidable, unastounding.

TOLERABLE
Syn.: endurable, bearable, passable, sufferable, acceptable.
Ant.: intolerable, unbearable, unacceptable, unendurable.

TOTALLY
Syn.: fully, wholly, completely, entirely, absolutely, thoroughly, perfectly, utterly.
Ant.: partially, partly, incompletely, somewhat.

TRUE
Syn.: accurate, actual, unerring, correct, authentic, exact, real, veracious, constant, faithful, loyal, genuine, precise, veritable, reliable, rightful, sincere, factual, legitimate.
Ant.: untrue, inaccurate, incorrect, inexact, unreal, unfaithful, disloyal, unreliable, insincere, false, spurious, fictitious, erroneous, inconstant, fickle, fallacious, apocryphal.

UNASSUMING
Syn.: modest, reserved, retiring, humble, diffident, bashful, shy, coy, unpretentious, unostentatious.
Ant.: arrogant, boastful, haughty, proud, vain,

immodest, pretentious, ostentatious, pert, vainglorious, imperious, smug, priggish, domineering.

URBANE

Syn.: suave, affable, polite, civil, courteous, refined, well-bred, well-mannered, accomplished, sophisticated, courtly, amiable.

Ant.: uncivil, uncouth, rude, ill-mannered, discourteous, impolite, boorish, impertinent.

UTTER (Adj)

Syn.: complete, entire, thorough, full, whole, perfect, absolute, sheer, total, downwright, consummate, arrant.

Ant.: incomplete, imperfect, partial, meagre, lacking, wanting, deficient, sketchy, skimpy.

VALID

Syn.: binding, sound, legal, logical, effective, cogent, operative, weighty, well-grounded, just.

Ant.: invalid, illegal, illogical, unjust, unsound, ineffective, null and void, inoperative.

VANITY

Syn.: pride, egotism, arrogance, conceit, immodesty, self-esteem, smugness, priggishness, vainglory, boasting, boast, bombast, bluster, brag, rodomontade.

Ant.: modesty, humility, meekness, simplicity, unostentatiousness.

VIGOROUS

Syn.: energetic, active, strong, potent, powerful, mighty, forceful, animated, lively, spirited, sprightly, brisk, vivacious, intense.

Ant.: powerless, ineffective, ineffectual, dull, feeble, unsound, impotent, flabby.

VITAL

Syn.: essential, indispensable, necessary, basic, cardinal, paramount, energetic, lively, dynamic.

Ant.: unessential, unimportant, dispensable, immaterial, insignificant.

WELCOME (Adj)

Syn.: pleasing, agreeable, acceptable, gratifying, pleasant, pleasurable.

Ant.: unwelcome, unacceptable, disagreeable, distasteful, unpleasant, offensive, repugnant, repulsive, unpalatable.

WISE

Syn.: prudent, sagacious, sage, learned, profound, well-advised, judicious, scholarly, well-informed, well-read, shrewd.

Ant.: unwise, foolish, shallow, silly, stupid, inane, fatuous, injudicious, imprudent, ill-advised, doltish, uneducated, unschooled.

WRONG (Adj)

Syn.: erroneous, incorrect, unjust, inaccurate, mistaken, faulty, untrue, unprecise, improper, bad, amiss, inappropriate, unsuitable, false, unfair, unfit.

Ant.: right, correct, true, proper, suitable, exact, just, precise, fair, accurate.

YEARLING

Syn.: youngling, colt, filly, cub, whelp, puppy.

Ant.: elder, doyen, old-timer, veteran.

YEARN

Syn.: desire, strongly, pine, long, hanker, grieve, mourn.

Ant.: hate, detest, despise, loathe, dislike, abominate.

YIELDING

Syn.: pliant, tractable, docile, submissive, compliant, flexible, soft, manageable.

Ant.: intractable, unmanageable, awkward, stubborn, obstinate, obdurate, unyielding, inflexible, hard, unruly, recalcitrant.

YOUNG

Syn.: youthful, new, fresh, inexperienced, immature, youngish, teen-age, juvenile, adolescent, green, puerile.

Ant.: old, elderly, experienced, aged, senior, mature, full-grown.

ZANY (Adj)

Syn.: ridiculous, eccentric, amusing, ludicrous, foolish, doltish, silly, inane, fatuous, stupid, droll, funny, whimsical, dull, drab.

Ant.: wise, intelligent, accomplished, well-informed, shrewd, brisk, active.

ZANY (N)

Syn.: merry-andrew, buffoon, clown, madcap, fool, comedian, jester, nitwit, dunce, dolt, nincompoop, ninny, simpleton, numbskull, oaf, loon, dullard, dunderhead, blockhead, goof, idiot, booby, bonehead, dunce, imbecile.

Ant.: sage, scholar, genius, wise person, intelligent person.

ZEAL

Syn.: enthusiasm, energy, verve, keenness, vim, vigour, heartiness, earnestness, spirit, eagerness, warmth, ardour, fervour, devotion, dash, briskness, alacrity, intensity, vehemence.

Ant.: apathy, indifference, unconcern, ennui, detachment, coldness, torpor, torpidity.

ZEALOUS

Syn.: eager, keen, enthusiastic, deep, strong, intense, earnest, passionate, spirited, ardent, warm, energetic, fervent, fervid, impassioned, vehement.

Ant.: cold, apathetic, indifferent, nonchalant, calm and casual, cool.

ZENITH

Syn.: acme, top, summit, apex, climax, vertex, culmination, peak, prime, highest point.

Ant.: nadir, lowest point or part, base, bottom, foot.

ZEST

Syn.: gusto, relish, enthusiasm, exhilaration, thrill, great enjoyment or excitement.

Ant.: distaste, disrelish, dislike, insipidity.

MULTIPLE CHOICE QUESTIONS

Directions (Qs.1 to 50): *Choose the words which are most nearly the SAME in meaning to the words given in capital letters.*

1. CARP
   A. to find fault unreasonably
   B. to hone
   C. to twist a meaning unfairly
   D. to jump to a conclusion

2. GIBE
   A. sneering remark B. praise
   C. expose D. measure

3. IMPALPABLE
   A. bad taste B. bad odour
   C. cannot be felt D. wholly false

4. DISQUISITION
   A. uncomfortable B. formal discourse
   C. deprived D. cross-examination

5. PROSCRIBE
   A. to order B. to declare
   C. to protect D. to prohibit

6. OSTRACIZE
   A. to expand B. to describe
   C. to exclude D. to curtail

7. INVEIGH
   A. to encroach B. to murder
   C. to hurt D. to rail

8. CONCOCT
   A. to blame
   B. to falsify
   C. to prepare or make up
   D. to make fool

9. BURGEON
   A. to sprout B. to begin
   C. to diminish D. to intrude

10. CAJOLE
    A. to scold B. to ridicule
    C. to wheedle D. to scorn

11. ARCHAIC
    A. damaged
    B. belonging to an earlier period
    C. neophyte
    D. lame

12. ATTENUATE
    A. to support B. to pay attention
    C. to brood D. to weaken

13. PERFUNCTORY
    A. half-hearted B. orator
    C. performer D. stern

14. INTERNECINE
    A. insincere B. peaceful
    C. deadly D. unreliable

15. PROLETARIAT
    A. wealthy class B. trade agreement
    C. intellectual class D. working class

16. PALLIDNESS
    A. wanness B. obsess
    C. egress D. transgress

17. IMPECUNIOUSNESS
A. habitual poverty B. aloofness
C. impulsiveness D. peerless

18. REPARTEE
A. irrelevant B. sarcasm
C. witty retort D. introvert

19. TENOR
A. timid B. topical
C. support D. purport

20. TERMAGANT
A. selfish B. shrewish woman
C. self-dependent D. brave

21. RELEGATE
A. retaliation B. banish
C. repeat D. bold

22. UBIQUITOUS
A. universal B. frenzied
C. omnipresent D. absent

23. UNTRAMMELLED
A. unfettered B. unwearied
C. indubitable D. unbroken

24. CHURLISH
A. sophisticated B. childish
C. rude D. polite

25. GUMPTION
A. common sense B. guilt
C. insidious D. idealistic

26. QUISLING
A. cheat B. partriot
C. traitor D. loyal

27. ARDUOUS
A. strange B. difficult
C. unique D. antique

28. DOUGHTY
A. coarse B. stupid
C. impudent D. strong and able

29. COGNIZANT
A. suitable B. aware
C. ignorant D. substitute

30. OVERTURE
A. tentative proposal B. declaration
C. exaggeration D. treaty

31. ABASH
A. lowered B. humiliate
C. embarass D. appreciate

32. ABSOLVE
A. solution B. resolve
C. confusion D. pardon

33. ACCOLADE
A. accomodation B. allotment
C. award of merit D. punishment

34. IMPUTATION
A. impending B. attribution
C. impression D. insistent

35. IMBUE
A. to force B. to attack
C. to charge D. to saturate

36. IMBROGLIO
A. complicated situation
B. climax
C. beginning
D. conclusion

37. OBFUSCATE
A. to surrender B. to confuse
C. to argue D. to punish

38. ENTHRALL
A. to exclude B. to idealize
C. to captivate D. to point out

39. EXCULPATE
A. murder
B. to sentence to death
C. to involve in crime
D. to free from blame

40. RIPOSTE
A. resignation B. re-appointment
C. commitment D. clever retort

41. RETRENCHMENT
A. forced withdrawal
B. encroachment
C. official order
D. reduction of expenses

42. SUPERCILIOUS
A. arrogant B. misbehaved
C. urbane D. sophisticated

43. MENDACITY
A. sincerity B. falsehood
C. gaiety D. consciousness

44. RETICENCE
A. cruelty B. simplicity
C. secretiveness D. honesty

45. RENDITION
A. artistic interpretation
B. summarize
C. illustration
D. elucidation

46. FEUD
A. conference B. debate
C. dual D. bitter quarrel

47. TRITE
A. unusual B. commonplace
C. widespread D. unique

48. SUPPLICATE
A. to entreat B. to provide
C. to intimate D. to affiliate

49. HIRSUTE
A. horrible B. hostile
C. humorous D. hairy

50. VICISSITUDE
A. unfortunate B. misfortune
C. change of fortune D. change of mind

Directions (Qs. 51 to 100): *Choose the words which are most nearly the OPPOSITE in meaning to the words given in capital letters.*

51. ODIUM
A. affection B. hatred
C. fulfilment D. scarcity

52. COMPOSURE
A. wordiness B. tranquility
C. noisiness D. perspicuity

53. INEQUITY
A. balance B. justice
C. justified D. unequal

54. PERVERSE
A. appropriate B. exact
C. similar D. reasonable

55. EXTRINSIC
A. inherent B. extraordinary
C. god-gifted D. appreciating

56. ASSENT
A. indifferent B. descent
C. disagreement D. consent

57. FICTITIOUS
A. artificial B. illusive
C. deceiving D. real

58. DISINGENUOUS
A. sincere B. genius
C. practical D. sensible

59. ABBREVIATE
A. epitomize B. abdicate
C. amplify D. abate

60. ABHORRENCE
A. detest B. abduct
C. respect D. sympathy

61. CALUMNY
A. vituperation B. eulogy
C. obloquy D. disturbed

62. CALEFACTION
A. separation B. calid
C. cooling D. warmth

63. CARIOUS
A. careful B. putrid
C. anxious D. fresh

64. DISENCUMBER
A. burden B. free
C. discharge D. able

65. HORTATIVE
A. disappointing B. hostile
C. pleasant D. deterring

66. OBLITERATE
A. restore B. refractory
C. highly qualified D. rural

67. RETICENT
A. resonant B. relinquish
C. taciturn D. garrulous

68. VENGEANCE
A. subdued B. submissive
C. forgiveness D. forgetfulness

69. FLAUNT
A. covered B. hide
C. curtailed D. apparent

70. EXPURGATE
A. insert B. stain
C. scrutinize D. exterminate

71. DAWDLE
A. fiddle B. dally
C. hurry D. dauby

72. DISCOUNTENANCE
A. credit B. encourage
C. appreciate D. entertain

73. INSURRECTION
A. exhume B. sedition
C. surrender D. subjection

74. PERMUTATION
A. refusal B. rejection
C. transference D. sequence

75. SAUNTER
A. shelter B. linger
C. wander D. hasten

76. MOURNFUL
A. cheerful B. humorous
C. jolly D. joyous

77. DESSICATE
A. exonerate B. concenterate
C. saturate D. propagate

78. SPUNK
A. strong B. timidity
C. bold D. miser

79. PREVARICATE
A. exaggerate B. state truthfully
C. irrelevant D. illustrate

80. FLEDGLING
A. childish B. energetic
C. old man D. experienced person

81. BILK
A. small in size B. balance to pay
C. pay in full D. credit

82. CHARY
A. brash B. slow
C. lethargic D. exhausted

83. CRASS
A. refined B. garrulous
C. boastful D. introvert

84. SPLENETIC
A. distant B. cordial
C. strange D. unfamiliar

85. ADHERENT
A. oppose B. revengeful
C. rival D. opponent

86. UNASSUAGED
A. harmful B. satisfied
C. soothed D. kind

87. PULCHRITUDE
A. tranquility B. unknown
C. unsightliness D. pleasant

88. VOUCHSAFE
A. scholarship B. admit
C. permit D. prohibit

89. TESTY
A. even-tempered B. difficult
C. puzzled D. cheerful

90. JETTISON
A. burden B. overloaded
C. submerge D. salvage

91. GADFLY
A. joyous B. thoughtful
C. nuisance D. tranquility

92. FURORE
A. sensitive B. discomposure
C. calmness D. excitement

93. FRUGALITY
A. economy B. extravagance
C. futility D. furitive

94. GERMANE
A. apposite B. pertinent
C. irrelevant D. ovum

95. GRANDILOQUENT
A. simplicity B. turgidity
C. bombastic D. dumbness

96. GULLIBLE
A. incredulous B. shrewdness
C. circumvent D. beguile

97. HALCYON
A. serene B. stormy
C. robust D. delusion

98. HARANGUE
A. annoy B. oration
C. mumble D. blissful

99. INCONGRUITY
A. constant B. convenient
C. consequent D. consistent

100. PIQUANT
A. irritating B. sarcastic
C. soothing D. enviable

ANSWERS

1	2	3	4	5	6	7	8	9	10
A	A	C	B	D	C	D	C	A	C
11	**12**	**13**	**14**	**15**	**16**	**17**	**18**	**19**	**20**
B	D	A	C	D	A	A	C	D	B
21	**22**	**23**	**24**	**25**	**26**	**27**	**28**	**29**	**30**
B	C	A	C	A	C	B	D	B	A
31	**32**	**33**	**34**	**35**	**36**	**37**	**38**	**39**	**40**
C	D	C	B	D	A	B	C	D	D
41	**42**	**43**	**44**	**45**	**46**	**47**	**48**	**49**	**50**
D	A	B	C	A	D	B	A	D	C
51	**52**	**53**	**54**	**55**	**56**	**57**	**58**	**59**	**60**
A	C	B	D	D	C	D	A	C	D
61	**62**	**63**	**64**	**65**	**66**	**67**	**68**	**69**	**70**
B	C	D	A	D	A	D	C	B	B
71	**72**	**73**	**74**	**75**	**76**	**77**	**78**	**79**	**80**
C	B	A	D	A	D	C	B	B	D
81	**82**	**83**	**84**	**85**	**86**	**87**	**88**	**89**	**90**
C	A	A	B	D	C	C	D	A	D
91	**92**	**93**	**94**	**95**	**96**	**97**	**98**	**99**	**100**
D	C	B	C	A	A	B	C	D	C

●●●

5 One Word Substitution

There are many words in English language which can be perfectly used for a number of words. These words help in expressing ideas in a short and correct manner for the right occasion. Such words not only enhance the vocabulary but also enable you to economise in the use of words to a great extent. Here is a categorywise list of many such words.

Pertaining to Government

To give up a throne or other office of dignity	*abdicate*
Absence of government	*anarchy*
Government by Sovereign of uncontrolled authority	*autocracy, despotism*
Government by departments of states	*bureaucracy*
Government of the people, for the people and by the people	*democracy*
Government by the nobility	*aristocracy*
The right of self-government	*autonomy*
Government by a few	*oligarchy*
Government by the wealthy	*plutocracy*
Government by divine guidance	*theocracy*
To decide a political question by the direct vote of the whole electorate	*referendum*
Sweeping governmental change	*revolution*
The science of government	*politics*

Pertaining to Religion

One who believes that man can have no knowledge of God but only of natural phenomena	*agnostic*
One who renounces his religious vows or forsakes his religious principles	*apostate*
One who does not believe in existence of God	*atheist*
One intolerantly devoted to a particular creed	*bigot*
To utter profane language against God or anything holy	*blaspheme*
A breaker of church images	*iconoclast*
Worship of images or idols	*idiolatory*
One who believes in one God	*monotheist*
One who believes in many Gods	*polytheist*

Pertaining to Marriage and Children

One who marries a second wife or husband while the legal spouse is alive	*bigamist*
One vowed to a single or unmarried life	*celibate*
One engaged to be married	*fiancé, fiancee*
A child whose parents are dead	*orphan*
A hater of marriage	*misogamist*
One who has more than two wives at a time	*polygamist*

Pertaining to Death

Dead and decaying flesh (esp. of animals)	*carrion*
A monument set up for persons who are buried elsewhere	*cenotaph*
To preserve a dead body from putrefaction	*embalm*
Words inscribed on a tomb	*epitaph*
An examination of dead body	*postmortem, autopsy*
An account in the newspaper of the funeral of one deceased	*obituary*
The property left to someone by a will	*legacy*
Occurring after death	*posthumous*
The act of killing a human being	*homicide*
Murder of a new born child	*infanticide*
Murder of a brother	*fratricide*
Murder of a sister	*sororicide*
Murder of a mother	*matricide*
Murder of a father	*patricide*
Murder of a parent	*parricide*
Murder of a king	*regicide*

Pertaining to the Literary Sphere

A work whose writer is unknown	*anonymous*
A record of one's life written by oneself	*autobiography*
The history of the life of a person	*biography*
The heading or short description of a newspaper article, chapter of a book etc.	*caption*
A humorous play, having a happy ending	*comedy*
A list of books in a library	*catalogue, bibliography*
A book in which the events of each day are recorded	*diary*
A books containing the words of a language with their definitions, in alphabetical order	*dictionary*
A book of names and addresses	*directory*
A short speech by a player at the end of a play	*epilogue*
A brief summary of a book	*epitome*

A book containing information on all branches of knowledge	*encyclopaedia*
To remove the offensive portions of a book	*expurgate*
A speech delivered without earlier preparation	*extempore*
A noisy or vehement speech intended to excite passions	*harangue*
A written account, usually in book form of the interesting and memorable experiences of one's life	*memoirs*
A note to help the memory	*memorandum*
A declaration of plans and promises put forward by a candidate for election, political party or a sovereign	*manifesto*
A short speech by a player at the beginning of a play	*prologue*
Literary theft, or passing off an author's original work as one's own	*plagiarism*
Speaking aloud to oneself	*soliloquy*
A play with a sad or tragic end	*tragedy*

Pertaining to Sciences and Arts

The study of all heavenly bodies and the earth in relation to them	*astronomy*
The science of land management	*agronomics*
The study of mankind	*anthropology*
The study of physical life or living matter	*biology*
The study of plants	*botany*
The art of beautiful hand-writing	*calligraphy*
The science which deals with the varieties of human race	*ethnology*
The study of the origin and history of words	*etymology*
The study of coins	*numismatics*
The study of human face	*physiognomy*
The art of making fireworks	*pyrotechnics*
The study of birds	*ornithology*
The study of languages	*philology*
At home equally on land or in water	*amphibious*
The inside of a nut	*kernel*
The central or innermost part of fruit	*core*
The animals of a certain region	*fauna*
The plants and vegetation of a certain region	*flora*
Absence of rain for a long time	*drought*
To supply land with water by artificial means	*irrigate*
One who studies plant and animal life	*naturalist*
A cud-chewing animal, *e.g.* the cow	*ruminant*
A gnawing animal, *e.g.* the rat	*rodent*
A four-footed animal	*quadruped*
Animals which carry their young in a pouch, *e.g.* kangaroo	*marsupials*

Soil composed largely of decayed vegetable matter	*humus*
A preparation for killing insects	*insecticide*
A plant or animal growing on another	*parasite*
Living for many years	*perennial*

Pertaining to Medicine

A substance which destroys or weakens germs	*antiseptic*
Any medicine which produces insensibility	*anaesthetic*
A medicine to counteract poison	*antidote*
Want or poorness of blood	*anaemia*
A medicine which alleviates pain	*anodyne*
To cut off a person's body a part which is infected	*amputate*
One who is recovering from illness	*convalescent*
To be able to tell the nature of disease by its symptoms	*diagnose*
A disease affecting many persons at the same place and time	*epidemic*
A disease confined to a particular district or place	*endemic*
To disinfect by smoke	*fumigate*
Free or exempt from infection	*immune*
A person who is sick	*invalid*
A cure for all diseases	*panacea*
A disease widely epidemic	*pandemic*
Confinement to one place to avoid spread of infection	*quarantine*

Pertaining to War

An unprovoked attack by an enemy	*aggression*
Shells, bombs, military stores	*ammunition*
A place where naval or military weapons are made or stored	*ordnance*
An agreement between belligerents to stop fighting	*armistice*
A general pardon of offenders	*amnesty*
To reduce to nothing	*annihilate*
Nations carrying on warfare	*belligerents*
To surround a place with the intention of capturing	*besiege*
To camp in the open air without tents or covering	*bivouac*
To seize for military use	*commandeer*
A person who is forced by law to become a soldier	*conscript*
An order prohibiting ships to leave the ports	*embargo*
A number of firearms being discharged continuously	*fusillade*
To make an examination or preliminary survey of enemy territory or military objectives	*reconnoitre*

Pertaining to Professions

One who attends to the diseases of the eye	*oculist*
One who tests eyesight and sells spectacles	*optician*
One who attends to the teeth	*dentist*
One skilled in the care of hands and feet	*chiropodist*
A physician who assists women at child-birth	*obstetrician*
One who drives a motor-car	*chauffeur*
One who makes or sells candles	*chandler*
One who preserves the skins of animals and mounts them so as to resemble the living animals	*taxidermist*
One who compiles a dictionary	*lexicographer*
One who writes books	*author*
One skilled in the treatment of diseases of animals	*veterinarian*
A tradesman who manages funerals	*undertaker*
One who draws up contracts and lends money on interest	*scrivener*
One who lends money and keeps goods as security	*pawnbroker*
A teacher who travels from place to place to give instruction	*peripatetic*
One who travels from place to place selling miscellaneous articles	*hawker, pedlar*
One who collects postage stamps	*philatelist*
One who lends money at exorbitant interest	*usurer*
One who takes care of a building	*janitor*
One who sells sweets and pastries	*confectioner*
One who works in a coal-mine	*collier*
One who flies an aeroplane	*pilot, aviator*
One who studies rocks and soils	*geologist*
One who shoes horses	*farrier*
A professional rider in horses races	*jockey*
One who deals in silks, cotton, woollen, and linen goods	*mercer*
One who deals in wines	*vintner*
One who deals in fish	*fishmonger*
One who deals in iron and hardware	*ironmonger*
One who sells fruits, vegetables, etc. from a barrow	*costermonger*
One who sets type (in a printing office)	*compositor*

Pertaining to Characteristics and Actions

One who devotes his life to the welfare and interests of other people	*altruist*
One who can use both hands with equal case	*ambidexterous*
One who fishes with a rod	*angler*

One who kills secretly or by surprise	*assassin*
A person who collects things belonging to ancient times	*antiquary*
One who is always finding faults	*censorious*
One living at the same time as another	*contemporary*
One who sneers at the aims and beliefs of his fellowmen	*cynic*
One who delights in speaking about oneself	*egotist*
One who exalts his own opinion	*egoist*
One who dies for a noble cause	*martyr*
One who retires from society to live a solitary life	*recluse, hermit*
One who maliciously sets fire to buildings	*incendiary*
One who is banished from his home or his country	*exile*
One who takes refuge in a foreign country	*refugee, alien*
One who runs away from justice or the law	*fugitive*
One who walks in his sleep	*somnambulist*
One who looks on the bright side of things	*optimist*
One who looks on the dark side of things	*pessimist*
A hater of mankind	*misanthropist*
One who knows everything	*omniscient*
One who is all powerful	*omnipotent*
One who is present everywhere	*omnipresent*
One who devotes his service or wealth for the love of mankind	*philanthropist*
One new to anything	*novice, tyro, neophyte*
One who engages in any pursuit for the love of it, and not for gain	*amateur*
One who journeys to a holy place	*pilgrim*
A leader of the people who can sway his followers by his oratory	*demagogue*
One who has special skill in judging art, music, tastes, etc.	*connoisseur*
One whose reasoning is clever yet false	*sophist*
One who makes a display of his learning	*pedant*
One who is indifferent to pain or pleasure	*stoic*
One who loves his country and serves it devotedly	*patriot*
One devoted to the pleasures of eating and drinking	*epicure*
One who poses to be what he is not	*hypocrite, impostor*
One who foretells events	*prophet*
One who pretends to know a great deal about everything	*mountebank, charlatan, quack*
One versed in many languages	*linguist*
One who cannot pay one's debts	*insolvent*
One who takes over after another in office or employment	*successor*
One who has been before another in office or employment	*predecessor*

One who is opposed to intellectual progress	*obscurant*
One who abstains from alcoholic drinks	*teetotaller*
One who hides away on a ship to obtain a free passage	*stowaway*
One who spends very little	*miser*
One who spends too much	*spendthrift*

Denoting Numbers

A collection of poems	*anthology*
A number of merchant ships protected by warships (in war-time)	*convoy*
A number of stars grouped together	*constellation*
A number of hired applauders, *i.e.* persons paid to clap	*claque*
A number of people at church	*congregation*
A number of people gathered together for some common purpose	*gathering, assembly, society*
A group of people who get together to work for some cause of common interest	*coterie*
A number of workmen, prisoners, thieves	*gang*
A number of sheep	*flock*
A number of geese	*gaggle*
A number of leopards	*leap*
A number of lions, monkeys	*pride, troop*
A number of herrings, mackerel	*shoal*
A number of fish taken in a net	*catch, haul*
A number of whales, porpoises	*school, gam*
A number of oxen or horses (two or more) harnessed together	*team*
A number of ships	*fleet*

Denoting Places

A place where bees are kept	*apiary*
A place where birds are kept	*aviary*
A place where fishes are kept	*aquarium*
A dwelling-place of an animal underground	*burrow*
A squirrel's home	*drey*
A nest of a bird of prey	*eyrie, aerie*
A place where spirituous liquors are produced	*distillery*
A place where clothes are washed and ironed	*laundry*
A place where Government records are kept	*archives*
A place where treasures of art, curiosities, etc. are preserved or exhibited	*museum*
A place where fruit trees are grown	*orchard*

Miscellaneous

Loud enough to be heard	*audible*
Not distinct enough to be heard	*inaudible*
Fit for food	*edible*
Unfit for human consumption	*inedible*
Fit to be chosen or selected	*eligible*
Not having the qualities for being chosen	*ineligible*
(Writing) that is easy to read	*legible*
Writing that is difficult to decipher	*illegible*
Able to read	*literate*
Unable to read	*illiterate*
Born of married parents	*legitimate*
Born of unmarried parents	*illegitimate*
To send back a person to his own country	*repatriate*
To banish from one's country	*expatriate*
To move from one country to another	*migrate*
One who leaves his country to settle in another	*emigrant*
One who comes into a foreign country to settle there	*immigrant*
Incapable of being redeemed from evil, *i.e.* beyond correction	*incorrigible*
That which cannot be rubbed out or blotted out	*ineffaceable, indelible*
That which cannot be conquered	*invincible*
Incapable of making errors	*infallible*
That which cannot be avoided or prevented	*inevitable*
Incapable of being burnt	*incombustible*
That which easily catches fire	*inflammable, flammable*
That which cannot be seen	*invisible*
Living for ever	*immortal*
Increase the gravity of an offence	*aggravate*
Ordinary or commonplace remark	*platitude*
That which cannot be satisfied	*insatiable*
That which cannot be repaired	*irreparable*
That which cannot be imitated	*inimitable*
Persons (or efforts) that cannot be wearied	*indefatigable*
One who eats too much	*glutton*
To destroy completely	*annihilate*
A statement open to more than one interpretation	*ambiguous*
A round about way of speaking	*circumlocution*
Cautious observation of events, etc.	*circumspection*
That which cannot be hurt	*invulnerable*

MULTIPLE CHOICE QUESTIONS

Directions: *Below are given some statements each of which is capable of being expressed by one word only. Each statement is followed by four such words of which only one is correct. Out of the given alternatives A, B, C and D choose the correct word which very closely fits each definition.*

1. One who does not believe in the existence of God:
   A. atheist B. altruist
   C. agnostic D. flippant
2. The large money paid for an early retirement:
   A. gold mine
   B. golden handshake
   C. gratuity
   D. lion's share
3. A hater of learning and knowledge:
   A. misologist B. misogynist
   C. philologist D. philanthropist
4. One who lives and acts for the welfare of others:
   A. misanthrope B. credulous
   C. altruist D. gregarious
5. Mental weariness for want of occupation:
   A. desperate B. depression
   C. fatigue D. ennui
6. That which makes it difficult to recognise the presence of real of somebody or something:
   A. cover B. mask
   C. make-up D. camouflage
7. To *bear a hand* in one's new business.
   A. partnership B. interfere
   C. assist D. join
8. One who renounces the world and practices self- discipline in order to attain salvation:
   A. devotee B. ascetic
   C. theist D. parsimonious
9. A place where gambling is practiced:
   A. hotel B. motel
   C. casino D. stadium
10. A sad song is a:
    A. dirge B. elegy
    C. ditty D. knell
11. A set of papers giving information about a person or event:
    A. editorial B. agenda
    C. dossier D. clippings
12. List and explanations of technical, difficult, etc. terms:
    A. preface B. glossary
    C. bibliography D. appendix
13. One who pays too much care to his clothes and personal appearance:
    A. conscious B. dandy
    C. cynosure D. leer
14. A child born after death of father:
    A. effeminate B. immature
    C. fatherless D. posthumous
15. A person who is hard to please:
    A. insensible B. hypocrite
    C. egoist D. fastidious
16. Complete failure in something attempted:
    A. fiasco B. vain
    C. falsies D. flop
17. A word which can be interpreted in any way:
    A. confusing B. misnomer
    C. ambiguous D. precise
18. A group of persons united by common interests:
    A. society B. class
    C. clique D. coterie
19. A person who is inexperienced and easily deceived:
    A. fool B. immature
    C. blackhorn D. greenhorn
20. Instruction by question and answer:
    A. interrogatory B. catechism
    C. bulletin D. alibi
21. Record of events by someone with first hand knowledge:
    A. novice B. report
    C. memoir D. itinerary
22. A mode of talk familiar to a particular group or profession:
    A. jargon B. colloquial
    C. slang D. abuses

23. Person who is crazy:
A. lackadaisical B. tarter
C. scrupulous D. loony

24. A person who readily believes others:
A. hasty B. immature
C. credulous D. credible

25. One who eats human flesh:
A. beast B. cannibal
C. maneater D. carnivorous

26. Intentional destruction of racial groups:
A. genocide B. homicide
C. fratricide D. communal riot

27. One with weakness of mind caused by old age:
A. dastard B. dotard
C. fop D. philanderer

28. Study of insects:
A. zoology B. philology
C. entomology D. etymology

29. A critical judge of any art particularly fine arts:
A. connoisseur B. veteran
C. philistine D. dilettante

30. One who introduces items of an entertainment:
A. consort B. compere
C. director D. introducer

31. A combination of business firms:
A. enterprise B. franchise
C. cartel D. autonomous

32. Freeing of suppressed emotions:
A. catastrophe B. catharsis
C. epilogue D. chagrin

33. One who believes in the power of fate:
A. optimist B. pessimist
C. fearful D. fatalist

34. The murder of brother:
A. genocide B. homicide
C. salvage D. fratricide

35. Additional to proper payment:
A. premium B. overtime
C. ex-gratia D. fringe

36. A person or thing used to tempt somebody into a position of danger:
A. decoy B. provocateur
C. jinx D. scapegoat

37. Custom of having more than one husband at the same time:
A. polygamy B. polyandry
C. bigamy D. sexagenary

38. A person of refined taste in food and drink:
A. emeritus B. epicure
C. glutton D. gourmand

39. A tombstone inscription:
A. epithet B. encomium
C. epistle D. epitaph

40. An office which has no work but high salary:
A. fortuitous B. gratuitous
C. sinecure D. ceremonial

41. One who is indifferent to pains and pleasure of life:
A. stoic B. metaphysical
C. pessimist D. sceptic

42. List of names of persons showing duties to be performed by each in turn:
A. notice B. bulletin
C. roster D. agenda

43. Long angry speech of criticism or accusation:
A. track record B. tirade
C. taut D. outburst

44. One who is in favour of never drinking alcoholic drinks:
A. idealist B. uxorious
C. teetotaller D. unalcoholic

45. Trying to win favour by flattery and charm:
A. smarmy B. shrewish
C. toady D. loquacious

46. A decision on which one cannot go back:
A. incorrigible B. irrevocable
C. rigid D. invulnerable

47. The science that studies the varieties of human race:
A. phrenology B. physiology
C. sociology D. ethnology

48. A person who hates women:
A. philogynist B. philatelist
C. misogamist D. misogynist

49. A group of people in a particular grade in an organisation:
A. colleague B. staff
C. echelon D. commission

50. Honourably discharged from service:
A. emeritus B. latitudinarian
C. infallible D. meritorious

51. Incapable of being wounded:
A. inevitable B. invulnerable
C. indomitable D. indefatigable

52. A short description of a picturesque scene or event of rural life:
A. narration B. panorama
C. idyll D. passage

53. The act of violating the sanctity of church:
A. sacrilege B. dissenter
C. immorality D. desecration

54. A dishonest dealing:
A. hanky-panky B. hocus-pocus
C. hoity-toity D. hilly-billy

55. A short and stout person:
A. lilliput B. hussy
C. humpty-dumpty D. paragon

56. Word that reads the same backwards as forwards (like did, dad, noon):
A. paradox B. palindrome
C. kowtow D. ragtag

57. Walking in sleep:
A. delusion B. somniloquism
C. somnabulism D. lethargic

58. Glamour and excitement:
A. razzle-dazzle B. razzmatazz
C. kudos D. winsome

59. Violent and bad tempered woman:
A. virago B. moll
C. concubine D. profane

60. One who pays excessive attention to preserving his health:
A. pagan B. bellicose
C. sycophant D. fop

61. Talking to one's own self:
A. pessimism B. introvert
C. soliloquy D. brooding

62. One who pretends to have more knowledge than he really has:
A. hypocrite B. charlaton
C. paragon D. lackadaisical

63. Brief biography of a person:
A. profile B. bibliography
C. synopsis D. resume

64. Very small allowance or wage:
A. lumpsum B. consolidated
C. pittance D. paltry

65. Purely spiritual love:
A. devotion B. platonic
C. passionate D. divine

66. Place where people often meet:
A. common room B. discotheque
C. roster D. rendezvous

67. A completely perfect person:
A. upright B. straightforward
C. paragon D. intellectual

68. Commencement of words with the same alphabet:
A. symmetry B. pun
C. phonetic D. alliteration

69. A person who loves everybody:
A. ascetic B. philander
C. philistine D. cosmopolitan

70. A government where the powers are concentrated in the hands of one person:
A. dictatorship B. autocracy
C. plutocracy D. anarchy

71. That which is outdated or out of use or fashion:
A. discarded B. obsolete
C. classic D. antic

72. Calendar giving information about sun, moon, stars and sometimes also the future:
A. almanac B. appendix
C. horoscope D. chronology

73. Collection in one volume of works by various authors:
A. panorama B. anthology
C. autobiography D. bibliography

74. One who takes part in a study, game, etc. for the love of it and not for professional gain:
A. apologist
B. august
C. amateur
D. avant-garde

75. A thing that causes annoyance:
A. bugbear B. arduous
C. anathema D. shrill

76. An allowance for support made to a wife by her husband after their legal separation:
A. alimony B. compensation
C. settlement D. ex-gratia

77. Place for hiding treasure, food, weapons, etc.:
A. store B. cache
C. stock D. armoury

78. A person who is stubborn in resisting change:
A. irresistible B. die-hard
C. dead beat D. terse

79. Able to use the left hand or the right hand equally well:
A. ambidextrous B. epicurean
C. apostle D. arbiter

80. A man who rarely speaks the truth:
A. liar B. unreliable
C. hypocrite D. bellicose

81. Partial or total loss of memory:
A. alexia B. anorexia
C. anexia D. amnesia

82. A word made by rearranging the letters of another word like eat–tea:
A. acronym B. anagram
C. byword D. dossier

83. A mass of snow and ice sliding down from a mountain:
A. avalanche B. glacier
C. icebery D. azure

84. To speak irreverently of God:
A. impious B. irreligious
C. immoral D. blasphemy

85. Sudden increase in business:
A. bonanza B. boom
C. bounce D. booze

86. Object of laughter or ridicule:
A. butt B. but
C. divert D. hurtle

87. A pioneer of a reform movement:
A. sinecure B. sycophant
C. gallant D. apostle

88. Art of handwriting:
A. cartography B. choreography
C. calligraphy D. graph

89. One who takes a low view of human nature:
A. coquette B. cynic
C. crony D. coy

90. Document that is handwritten by the author:
A. autograph B. holograph
C. editorial D. preface

91. A person who forsakes religion:
A. irreligious B. non-religious
C. fatalist D. apostle

92. Speaker or agitator who can stir the emotions of the masses:
A. demagogue B. dexterous
C. diligent D. reformist

93. Uncontrollable craving for alcohol:
A. dyspepsia B. delirium
C. edict D. dipsomania

94. A lady who remains unmarried:
A. concubine B. alien
C. spinster D. damsel

95. State payment to an unemployed person:
A. pension B. dole
C. increment D. grant in aid

96. Person slow at learning:
A. adroit B. dubious
C. dunce D. agile

97. One who has a good taste for food and enjoys it:
A. gourmet B. sensitive
C. deleterious D. debonair

98. One who is fond of gossip:
A. flippant B. flibbertigibbet
C. fuddy-duddy D. gregarious

99. A long, loud and angry speech:
A. incongruous B. hyperbole
C. hullabaloo D. harangue

100. A person chosen by the opposing parties to settle their differences:
A. mediator B. prude
C. paramour D. arbitrator

ANSWERS

1	2	3	4	5	6	7	8	9	10
A	B	A	C	D	D	C	B	C	A
11	12	13	14	15	16	17	18	19	20
C	B	B	D	D	A	C	C	D	B
21	22	23	24	25	26	27	28	29	30
C	A	D	C	B	A	B	C	A	B
31	32	33	34	35	36	37	38	39	40
C	B	D	D	D	A	B	B	D	C
41	42	43	44	45	46	47	48	49	50
A	C	B	C	A	B	D	D	C	A
51	52	53	54	55	56	57	58	59	60
B	C	D	A	C	B	C	B	A	A
61	62	63	64	65	66	67	68	69	70
C	B	A	C	B	D	C	D	D	B
71	72	73	74	75	76	77	78	79	80
B	A	B	C	A	A	B	B	A	C
81	82	83	84	85	86	87	88	89	90
D	B	A	D	B	A	D	C	B	B
91	92	93	94	95	96	97	98	99	100
D	A	D	C	B	C	A	B	D	D

●●●

6 Idioms & Phrases

An idiom is a group of words established by usage as having a meaning different from the individual words.
A phrase is a small group of words standing together as an idiomatic expression.
The use of idioms and phrases makes your expression more effective and powerful.
Learn and practise as many as you can.

An angel: A person who is gentle and kind to others

A devil: A particularly wicked or mischievous person

A giant: A person who is very large

A wizard: A clever and skillful person

An Adonis: A very handsome man

An Apollo: A man with a perfect physique or body shape

A Hercules: A very strong man

A Goliath: An extremely large man

A Judas: A mean traitor

A Samson: A very strong man

A Solomon: A very wise man

A dog: A worthless person; someone who is despised

A cat: A malicious, person. usually referring to females

A bear: A clumsy, rough person

A fox: A crafty, cunning person

A goose: A silly person

A lamb: An innocent harmless person

A monkey: A child who is lively and full of mischievous tricks

A mule: A very stubborn person

A wolf: A greedy and cunning person

A snake/serpent: A treacherous, dangerous person

A parrot: A person who learns things off by heart without understanding the real meaning

A pest: A troublesome person; one who annoys and pesters others

A pig: A greedy and dirty person

A shark: A greedy and cunning person; one who swindles others

A parasite: A person who lives off others and gives nothing in return

An ape: A person who foolishly imitates others

An ass/donkey: A stupid person

An elephant: A huge, clumsy, ungainly person

A wet blanket: A person who discourages others or prevents them from enjoying what they are doing

A stag party: A party where only men are allowed to be present

A hen party: A party where only women are allowed to be present

A working lunch/dinner: A meal at which the people who attend, discuss business

A working knowledge: Enough practical knowledge to do something

A willing horse: A helpful person who often gets all the work to do

A wild goose chase: A search for something which has no chance of being successful

A trend-setter: A person who starts a new fashion which becomes popular

A thick-skinned person: A person who is not easily offended

Teething troubles: Troubles and difficulties which occur during the early stages of an activity or enterprise, but which will lessen with time

A sweeping statement: A statement which is not careful or correct in its details; a generalisation

A spending spree: An outing during which one spends a lot of money

A tall order: A request which is unreasonably difficult to grant or carry out

A soft spot: A feeling of special fondness for something or someone

A sore point: A matter which irritates or hurts when it is mentioned

The small hours: The early morning hours just after midnight

A sleeping partner: A business partner who provides a share of the capital for a venture but does not take an active part in its operation

Small talk: Trivial, light conversation on unimportant topics

Second nature: Some acquired habit or skill which seems perfectly natural to someone; a very firmly fixed habit

A shady character: A person of very doubtful honesty or character

Second thoughts: A change of mind, attitude or decision after thinking about the matter

A security risk: A person who is a risk to a country's security because of his political activities; one whose loyalty is doubted

A jail bird: A man who has spent a lot of time in prison

A ladies' man: A man who likes to be with women or who likes to please them

A last fling: The last opportunity for pleasure or amusement before having to stop

An inside job: A theft committed by someone inside a building, i.e., by an employee, not a stranger

A knowing look: A look which suggests that, the person is well-informed of a matter

A hushed-up affair: An affair or matter that is kept secret by forcing silence about it

Hush money: A bribe paid to keep a matter secret from the public

A hot line: A direct telephone line between heads of governments, to be used at times of great difficulty

Hot news: Very recent, important or sensational news

High time: At the most important point of time

Fast living: A person who spends too much money in enjoying life

A fishy story: An untrue tale; an unlikely story

Half-hearted: Having no enthusiasm for a particular task

An iron will: A very strong will

Hot water: Trouble

A laughing stock: A person who is unkindly laughed at by everyone

A light-fingered person: A person who is in the habit of stealing small things

Pin money: A wife's allowance for her personal needs

Plain sailing: A plan or action that is simple and free from trouble

A pep talk: A friendly talk to give encouragement to win a game, etc. or to complete something well

A package tour: A completely planned holiday at a fixed price arranged by a company

A passing fancy: A temporary liking for something or someone

An open secret: Something supposed to be a secret but which in fact is known to everyone

A package deal: An offer or agreement which includes a number of things all of which must be taken

Plain dealing: Truthfulness and honesty, especially in business

A pet aversion: Something or someone much disliked

A sideline: Work one does apart from one's regular job

Second sight: An ability to foresee future events

A rolling stone: Person who travels around a lot without staying in any one place or job for long

A raw deal: An unjust or cruel treatment

In a rash moment: Doing something hastily without thinking of the results

A practical joke: A trick played on a person to make him look silly and to give amusement to others

A sugar daddy: An older man who has a relationship, especially sexual, with a younger woman, providing her with money and presents

Take-home pay/wages: The amount a person receives after taxes have been deducted

backstairs influence: Secret and usually unfair influence

Bad blood: Bad feelings or unfriendliness between two persons

A bad egg/a bad penny: A bad character

A false alarm: A warning of something bad, which does not happen

Elbow room: Space, in which to move and act freely

A double agent: A person who works secretly for two opposing sides without either of the sides knowing

A dead-end job: A job without prospects; a job that leads to nothing further

A dark horse: A person who competes successfully against another although little is known about him

A confirmed bachelor: A man who has no desire to marry

A burning question: A matter having to be dealt with at once; an urgent important matter

A big shot: An important person, usually someone who is wealthy and influential

A blind date: A social meeting of two persons, usually a boy and a girl who have not met before

Broken English: Imperfect, ungrammatical English

A chicken-hearted person: A timid, cowardly person

A close-fisted person : Someone who is stingy; a miser

A country cousin: A person who is simple and inexperienced and not used to city life

A close shave: A narrow escape from danger, an accident, etc.

A light sleeper: A person who is easily awakened from sleep

A cock-and-bull story: An invented story

A cold war: A serious political struggle between countries which does not actually result in fighting

A dog-eared book: A book where the corners of the pages have been turned down with use

An easy victim/mark: Somebody who can easily be cheated or treated badly

A bosom friend: A very close, trusted friend

Crocodile tears: Pretended sorrow; insincere tears

A fast colour: A colour which does not run out of the material when washed or dried

A fair copy: A neat, legible copy

An armchair critic: A person who critically judges others' work and gives advice, but who has not himself experienced doing the work

Apple-pie order: In perfect order

An absent-minded person: A forgetful, inattentive person

A flying visit: A very short visit

Forty winks: A short nap or sleep

Hard labour: Hard, manual work usually done as a punishment

Hard cash: Actual money, not a cheque, etc.

A hard drinker: A person who drinks large quantities of alcohol

A golden opportunity: A very good opportunity

A going concern: A successful, thriving business

A foregone conclusion: A result that is certain, sure

The naked eye: The eye unaided by any instrument

An odd-job man: A man who does various types of work, usually manual, for pay

Old hat: No longer fashionable

A grass widow: A wife who is alone because her husband is away temporarily

A good samaritan: A person who helps a stranger in difficulties

French leave: Absence from work that is taken without permission

The generation gap: The difficulties arising when younger and elder people do not understand each other's way of life

The happy medium: The middle course of doing something when opposite ways are suggested

A henpecked husband: A husband who is dominated and nagged by his wife

A hard and fast rule: A rule that cannot be changed; fixed, unchangeable rule

One-track mind: A person's mind that is limited and thinks of only one thing at a time

A short cut: An easier method of doing something or getting somewhere; a quicker, more direct way

A small-time business: A business limited in activity and profits

A splitting headache: A very severe and painful headache

A square deal: A fair bargain or fair treatment

A square meal: A meal with adequate good; a satisfying meal

Strong language: Angry language consisting of many swear words

Tall talk: Boastful talk

A tight spot/corner: A difficult situation

Tough luck: Bad luck; hard luck

Ready money: Money which is immediately available in coins or notes

Second best: Next to the best; second in value or importance

The writing on the wall: An indication that something bad or difficult is about to happen

A storm in a teacup: A big fuss made over a small, trivial event

The talk of the town: A person or event that is causing great excitement and is the subject of much discussion

A snake in the grass: A cunning, harmful person who pretends to be a friend; a false friend

A shot in the dark: A guess which is not supported by arguments; a wild guess

The tricks of the trade: The best and most successful ways of doing good business

The bottom of the ladder: In the least important position

A shot in the arm: Something which acts to bring back a happy state or condition

The man in the street: The ordinary, average man

The gift of the gab: A person fluent in speech; a persuasive speaker

A man about town: A man who is used to living in the city and associating with well-known fashionable people

The life and soul: The person who is the centre of attaction because he is amusing and lively

The lion's share: The greater part; an unfairly large share

The long arm of the law: The police

A bear hug: A rough, tight hug

A brain wave: A clever idea; sudden inspiration

A bone of contention: Something that causes argument

Birds of a feather: People of the same kind (often bad) who like each other's company

A feather in one's cap: A deserved honour that one is proud of

Castles in the air: Plans which cannot be carried out or which will probably not succeed

A fish out of water: A person who feels uncomfortable because he is in a strange place, or among people who are very different from himself

The ups and downs: The good and bad times, the happy and sad times

A stone's thorw: A short distance

A slip of the tongue: Something said unintentionally

A slap in the face: A rebuff

The rank and file: Ordinary people without special positions; the masses

A man of means: A rich man

A man of iron: A cruel, hard person

A jack of all trades: A person who can do many different kinds of work but who may not be good at any of them

By hook or by crook: By any means possible

By fits and starts: At irregular intervals

A pack of lies: A whole lot of untruths

A clean bill of health: A certificate or announcement that someone is healthy

A happy-go-lucky person: Someone who does not think or plan carefully

A stay-at-home person: A person who is in the habit of staying at home, and not liking to travel

A smash-and-grab robbery: A robbery done quickly, usually by breaking windows or showcases taking away valuables, and running away

A hit-and-run driver: A driver who drives away after an accident without stopping to find out about damage or injuries

A run-of-the-mill job: An ordinary unexciting job

A round the-clock service: A twenty-four hour service

An out-of the way place: A place that is distant and far away from people and places

A much-talked-of affair: Something which is the subject of much discussion

A nine to six job: A job in which the working hours are from nine in the morning to six in evening

An open and shut case: A case which is easy to settle or solve

Bumper-to-bumper traffic: Cars that are very close together one after another

A hand-me-down dress: A dress used by someone after belonging to another

A well-to-do man/woman: A rich person

Again and again: Repeatedly; continually; very often

Back and forth/backward: Moving first in one direction and then in the opposite direction and forwards

By and by: Soon; before long

By and large: On the whole; in general; all things considered

Far and away: Very much

Far and near/far and wide: Everywhere

First and foremost: In the first place; firstly

Here and there: In various places; firstly

Here, there and everywhere: In all possible places; everywhere

In and out: Sometimes inside and sometimes outside

Up and about: On one's feet; up again after an illness

To-and fro: Backwards and forwards; from side to side

Through and through: Completely; entirely; in every way

Out and out: Complete, thorough; total

Out and away: By far

Over and over again: Again and again; repeatedly

Round and round: Repeatedly moving round

Once and for all: Finally; for the last time

On and on: Without stopping

Off and on: From time to time; occasionally

Every now and then/again: From time to time; at times

Now and again: Sometimes; occasionally; not very often

Nowadays: In these times

To backbite a person: To speak ill of someone

To back chat: To be cheeky; to talk back to someone

To be a bag of bones: To be extremely thin

To be a blockhead: To be an idiot

To be a great hand at: To be an expert

To be a sight for sore eyes: Something or someone who appears before another and is very welcome

To be all ears: To be eager to listen

To be armed to the teeth: Fully armed or protected

To be at one's wits' end: Completely puzzled

To be close-fisted: To be mean; miserly

To be double-faced: Insincere

To be down in the mouth: To feel depressed and unhappy

To be head and shoulders above someone else: To be very much better or superior

To be out of one's mind: To be mad; crazy

To be someone's blue-eyed boy: To be someone's favourite

To be the apple of someone's eye: To be someone's favourite

To bite someone's head off: To speak abruptly or sharply to another

To burn one's fingers: To get into trouble

To catch someone's eye: To suddenly exchange glances with another

To change hands: To pass from one owner to another

To dig someone in the ribs: To make unkind remarks or insinuations about another

To eat one's heart out for another: To long for someone who is unattentive

To foot the bill: To pay the bill, especially for some social outing

To get on someone's nerves: To irritate someone very greatly

To get something off one's chest: To confess to something

To get the upper hand: To gain mastery over an opponent

To give someone the cold shoulder: To ignore someone; to slight another

To give someone the sharp: To thoroughly scold another person edge of one's tongue

To go on all hands: To crawl on hands and knees

To have a chip on one's shoulder: To bear a grudge against the world/society

To have a finger in every pie: To have many business interests

To have a head like a sieve: To have a very poor memory

To have a skeleton in the cupboard: To have a guilty secret, especially a family scandal

To have at one's fingertips: To know thoroughly

To have cold feet: To be afraid

To have no backbone: To be a weak, spineless person

To have one's head screwed on: To be very sensible

To have someone under one's thumb: To dominate another

To have the upper hand: To be in command/charge; to be someone in power

To have two left hands: Someone who is clumsy

To hold one's tongue: To keep silent even though there is an urge to talk

To hold up one's head: To be able to look people in the face

To jump out of one's skin: To get a sudden fright

To keep a cool head: To keep calm, especially in an emergency

To keep a stiff upper lip: To remain calm and courageous

To keep one's fingers crossed: To hope for luck

To keep one's hair on: To keep cool and patient

To keep one's head above water: To avoid getting into debt or trouble

To keep someone at arm's length: Not too friendly with another

To knock something on the head: To suddenly stop an idea/project

To know something by heart: To be able to say something from memory

To lay hands on someone: To handle someone roughly

To lend a hand: To help

To let the grass grow under one's feet: To be inactive and uninvolved

To live from hand to mouth: To live in hardship with the barest essentials

To lose face: To lose one's reputation/honour

To lose heart: To be discouraged

To lose one's head: To be very angry; to lose control of oneself

To make a clean breast of something: To confess to something; to reveal all

To make neither head nor tail of something: To understand nothing of a particular issue

To pat someone on the back: To give praise and encouragement to another

To pay through the nose for something: To pay an excessively high price for something

To poison someone's mind: To turn someone against another person

To pull one's weight: To do one's share of work

To pull someone's leg: To play a joke on someone

To pull the wool over someone's eyes: To deceive another

To put one's back into it: To work hard

To put one's foot down: To be firm about an issue

To put one's shoulder to the wheel: To work hard and earnestly

To put someone's nose out of joint: To make someone jealous by taking his place as the centre of attraction

To rack one's brains: To try to recall or remember something

To receive with open arms: To welcome warmly

To save face: To save one's honour/reputation/name

To show a clean pair of heels: To escape by running

To snap someone's head off: To speak abruptly

To stand on one's own feet: To do things without help; to be independent

To sweep someone off his/her feet: To flatter and woo someone, usually a girl

To take matters into one's own hands: To do something independently without help

To take something to heart: To take something seriously

To take to one's heels: To run away

To throw dust in someone's eyes: To try to deceive someone

To tread in someone's foot steps: To follow the example of another, usually of talent/occupation

To tread on someone's toes: To offend another person

To try one's hand at: To try doing something for the first time

To turn a blind eye: To refuse to see

To turn a deaf ear: To refuse to hear

To turn up one's nose at something: To treat with contempt

To twist someone's arm: To force someone into doing something for you

To wash one's hands of something: To have nothing to do with a particular matter

The green-eyed monster: Jealousy

To scream blue murder: To complain loudly

Out of the blue: Suddenly; without warning

Once in a blue moon: Very rarely

To feel blue/have the blues: To be sad or depressed

A bolt from the blue: A complete surprise

Blue blood: Royal or noble blood

To blackmail someone: To threaten to reveal someone's misdeeds unless he pays money

In someone's black books: Out of favour with someone

A black sheep: A bad character who disgraces his family

A blacklist: A list of people groups, etc. who have done something wrong

Black and blue: Badly bruised after a beating/a fall

In black and white: In writing or print

A greengrocer: A person who sells fruit and vegetables

A greenhorn: An inexperienced person

The green light: The signal to proceed

Green with envy: Tilled with jealousy

Grey matter: Common sense; brains

In the pink of health: In excellent health

Purple with rage: So angry that the face becomes purple

To be caught red-handed: To be caught in the act of committing a crime

A red carpet welcome: A special ceremonial welcome to guest

The red flag: A flag used as a danger signal

A red-letter day: A notable, fortunate day that will be remembered

The red light: A signal to stop; a danger signal

Red tape: Official rules which cause delay in settling one's problems

To jump out of the frying-pan into the fire: To get out of one bad situation and fall into another worse situation

To see red: To lose control of oneself in anger

A white-collar job: An office job

A white elephant: A worthless possession which the owner wants to get rid of

The white flag: A sign that one accepts defeat or surrenders

To show the white feather: To show signs of cowardice

Yellow at heart: Cowardly

To be/feel off colour: To be unwell or rather ill

To come off with flying colours: To achieve great success

To have a high colour: To appear very red in the face

To show one's true colours: To show what one is really like; to show one's true character

A blue-collar job: A factory job

To act the goat: To behave foolishly

To air one's opinion: To express one's feelings in public

To be a chip off the old block: A son who is very much like his father in appearance, character, habits, etc

To be as fit as a fiddle: To be in excellent health

To be at a loose end: To have nothing to do

To be at a loss for words: Not knowing what to say; to be speechless

To be at death's door: To be so ill as to be near death

To be at sixes and sevens: To be in confusion and discord

To be at the end of one's teeter: To be at a loss as to what to do

To be born under a lucky star: To have considerable luck in whatever one does

To be born with a silver spoon in one's mouth: To be born into a rich family

To be dead beat: To be worn out by fatigue

To be in hot water: To be in serious trouble

To be in someone's bad/good books: To be out of/in favour with someone

To be in the doldrums: To be in low spirits

To be in the same boat: To have the same troubles/ circumstances

To be mad about someone: To like someone very much

To be made of money: To have plenty of money; to be well-off

To be on tenterhooks: To be in a state of suspense and anxiety

To be on the ball: To be alert, up-to-date, prepared

To be on the horns of a dilemma: Not knowing what to do from several courses of action

To be on the rocks: To be in danger of failing, collapse, especially a business, a marriage, etc

To be on top of the world: To be very happy; to be in high spirits

To be out of the woods: To be out of danger, especially a serious illness

To be quick on the uptake: To be alert and quick to do or say something

To be rolling in money: To be rich; to have plenty of money

To be scared to death: To be extremely frightened of something

To be slow on the uptake: Slow to do or say something

To be too big for one's boots: To think very highly of oneself

To bear the brunt of: To bear the main force or strain of some action

To beat about the bush: To be indecisive; not coming to the point

To blow hot and cold: To do one thing at one time and the opposite soon after

To blow one's own trumpet: To boast about one's abilities, achievements etc.

To break the ice: To take the first step; to be the first to begin, especially a conversation

To bring down the house: To cause loud and long applause through one's skill

To bring to light: To disclose, reveal

To build castles in the air: To think of things impossible to realize

To burn the candle at both ends: To use one's energy in two directions at the same time

To burn the midnight oil: To work till late at night

To call a spade a spade: To speak out bluntly and frankly

To clip one's wings: To deprive one of power and/ or freedom

To cook an account: To tamper with/falsify an account

To come down on someone like a: To harshly criticise another ton of bricks

To come of age: To reach adulthood

To come to grief: To meet with danger

To come to light: To become known

To count-sheep: To try various methods to get to sleep

To cry over spilt milk: To be unhappy about something that can no longer be remedied

To curry favour: To seek/win favour by flattery or gifts

To cut off in its prime: To destroy something when it is at its best

To cut one's coat according to: To live within one's income one's cloth

To cut someone down to size: To put someone in his place especially a person who thinks too highly of himself

To do a city/the sights: To visit a city and see its well-known places

To do a thing by fits and starts: To work intermittently on something

To do a thing by hook or by crook: To do something by any means, fair or foul, direct or indirect

To do something on the spur of the moment: To suddenly decide to do something

To drop a brick: To say or do something very tactless and unexpected

To drop a hint: To make veiled and subtle suggestions

To eat like a horse: To eat a lot

To eat one's words: To take back what one has said; to apologise

To egg on: To spur on to further action

To face the music: To meet the worst; to face punishment for doing something wrong

To fall out with someone: To quarrel with someone

To fall through: To fail, especially a plan, project, etc.

To fancy someone/something: To take a great liking to someone/something

To fight shy of: To avoid

To fire someone: To dismiss someone from employment

To flog a dead horse: To try fruitlessly to revive interest in something

To follow the crowd: To follow unthinkingly; to believe or act as most people do

To follow suit : To do the same thing as another person

To gain ground: To make progress in an undertaking

To get away with something: To escape detection despite doing something wrong

To get blood out of stone: To get more than is fair out of someone

To get down to work: To start on the task in hand

To get even with someone: To take revenge of someone

To get hitched: To get married

To get into a flap: To get worried and nervous

To get into hot water: To be in/to get into trouble

To get off scot-free: To escape punishment; to be let off payment

To get out of bed on the wrong side: To start the day in a bad temper

To get the sack: To be dismissed from employment

To get wind of: To hear a rumour of

To get the wind up: To get worried and nervous; to get a fright

To give someone a telling-off: To scold someone

To give someone the slip: To manage to avoid someone who is looking for you

To give the game away: To let out a secret

To give up the ghost: To die; to cease trying

To go a long way: To excel; to go far, especially in a career

To go off at a tangent: To change suddenly to a different course of thought or action

To go like a bomb: To go fast; to function well, especially a vehicle

To go to rack and ruin: To fall into a ruined or disorganised state

To grin and bear it: To make the best of a bad job; to put up with something

To haul someone over the coals: To reprimand someone

To have a bee in one's bonnet: To be strong-minded over certain issues

To have a soft spot for: To be very fond of someone or something

To have an axe to grind: To have a selflsh motive for doing something

To have one's knife in someone: To be always finding fault with another person

To hit below the belt: To attack an opponent unfairly

To hit the nail on the head: To do or say exactly the right thing

To jog someone's memory: To remind someone of something

To keep a person in the dark: To keep something hidden from someone

To keep open house: To encourage visitors to come at any time

To keep one's pecker up: To keep one's courage up

To keep one's shirt on: To keep cool and calm in a dispute

To keep the ball rolling: To keep a conversation going

To keep up appearances: To pretend to be well-off and to live in a certain style

To kick the bucket: To die

To kid someone: To tease

To kill two birds with one stone: To accomplish two things with one action

To knock off work: To stop working

To know the ropes: To be thoroughly familiar with a particular situation

To knock someone down with a feather: To surprise someone very much

To kowtow to someone: To act in a very servile manner hoping for favour

To lay down the law: To speak in an authoritative way

To lead someone up the garden path: To deceive someone by hiding the real intention

To leave someone in the lurch: To desert someone in time of difficulties

To let bygones be bygones: To let things that are past and gone remain untouched and forgotten

To let the cat out of the bag: To reveal a secret; to expose a trick

To look like a wet week: To look miserable and depressed

To make a go of something: To try one's best to succeed in something

To make a hash/a mess of something: To fail at a task

To make believe: To pretend

To make both ends meet: To be able to manage on one's income

To make hay while sun shines: To take advantage of an opportunity

To make much ado about nothing: To make a great fuss about something unimportant

To make oneself scarce: To disappear

To nip something in the bud: To stop something before it can develop into something serious

To pass the buck: To pass on the responsibility

To pick holes in something: To find fault with

To pick to pieces: To analyse critically

To pick and choose: To make a careful selection

To play a double game: To do one thing openly and a different thing in secret

To play fast and loose: To disregard one's promises

To play second fiddle: To take a subordinate position

To pooh-pooh an idea: To express contempt for an idea

To pull strings: To use friends in influential positions, or to use one's own influence, to secure favours

To put the cart before the horse: To do the wrong thing first

To put two and two together: To arrive at a conclusion

To put a spoke in one's wheel: To hinder; to obstruct progress

To rain cats and dogs: To rain very heavily

To read between the lines: To detect the hidden meaning

To rule the roost: To domineer over others

To run in the blood: Inherited qualities

To see something through coloured spectacles: To see only the best points about a thing

To see the light: To begin to understand

To sit on the fence: To take neither side in a dispute; to remain neutral

To smell a rat: To become suspicious about something

To steer clear of: To avoid

To take French leave: To be absent from work without permission

To take someone for a ride: To deceive someone

To take the bull by the horns: To meet a difficulty with courage

To take the law into one's own hands: To punish a person, usually by force, witnout his being tried in a law court

To take with a pinch of salt: To accept what someone has said with doubt and misgiving

To talk nineteen to the dozen: To speak a lot

To talk the hind legs of a donkey: To talk a great deal at great length

To tear a strip off someone: To scold harshly

To throw cold water upon: To discourage effort

To turn over a new leaf: To give up one's bad ways, and lead a better life

To turn the tables on someone: To defeat someone who has previously defeated you

To upset the apple cart: To disturb the routine of something

MULTIPLE CHOICE QUESTIONS

Directions: *Select the options which express the correct meaning of the given Idioms/Phrases.*

1. Cats' paw
A. a person who is used as a tool by another person
B. very slowly and quietly
C. very cleverly
D. to share a responsibility

2. To catch a tartar
A. to overcome a serious problem
B. to attack one who turns out to be stronger than is expected
C. to achieve the goal
D. to struggle hard

3. Cheek of jowl
A. very soft
B. close together
C. intimate relationship
D. low in status

4. A chip of the old block
A. a symptom of a serious disease
B. a child of a parent
C. a part of a whole
D. offsprings who display characteristics of their parents

5. To cool one's heels
A. to be kept waiting
B. to give a cold response to somebody
C. to follow somebody
D. to answer all the queries of somebody

6. To cleanse the Augean stables
A. to clean something which has not been cleaned for a long time
B. to wind up a joint business
C. to remove the stains of blood
D. to remove the traces of murder

7. A cry in wilderness
A. The cry of the poors
B. a warning that goes unheeded
C. A speech made by a less important leader
D. A cry out of deep sorrow

8. To cut one's coat according to one's cloth
A. to work according to one's capacity
B. to allot portfolio according to one's capability
C. to live within one's means
D. to live as one desires

9. Chicken hearted
A. coward
B. brave
C. kind
D. mortal

10. To clip one's wings
A. to lessen one's power
B. to defame
C. to dismiss
D. to punish

11. To come round
A. to agree with another's point of view
B. to come back to the point of origin
C. a circular movement
D. to wander

12. To call to order
A. a command
B. to rebuke for improper or incorrect behaviour
C. to obey an order
D. to show superiority

13. To cover one's tracks
A. to maintain the secrecy
B. to hide one's weaknesses
C. to carefully hide all traces of one's actions
D. to conceal the falsity

14. To throw up one's cards
A. To make a last effort
B. to cease to struggle
C. to end up the game
D. to come out victorious

15. To let the cat out of the bag
A. to disclose a secret
B. to set free
C. a person without a shelter
D. to permit the thief to run away

16. To cave in
A. to interfere B. to prohibit
C. to find a way D. to give way

17. To chuck up
A. to abandon
B. to decorate
C. to summarize
D. to cut into pieces

18. A dead letter
A. a delayed report
B. a false report
C. something exaggerated
D. something which is null and void

19. To die in harness
A. to die in office
B. to die with great pain
C. a premature death
D. a cruel murder

20. At the drop of a hat
A. without fail
B. without delay
C. against the self-respect
D. against the will

21. Day in and day out
A. always
B. forever
C. to break a promise done earlier
D. to remain busy always

22. Champ at
A. to pounce at
B. be impassioned
C. be composed
D. be eager or impatient

23. Burn one's fingers
A. to get oneself into trouble
B. to commit a blunder
C. a heavy monetory loss
D. to be in great rage

24. Down in the dumps
A. in a solitary mood
B. in a bad mood
C. to be in an unfavourable situation
D. to decline

25. To beg the question
A. to beg the pardon
B. to request for some extra-time to finish the work
C. unanswerable
D. to assume in the premises somethign which is to be proved

26. To carry the day
A. to be victorious
B. an on-going discussion
C. a memorable day
D. a miserable phase of life

27. At death's door
A. on the point of expiring
B. on the point of gun
C. to show bravery
D. a gradual deterior

28. To pay the debt of nature
A. to die
B. to give birth
C. to safeguard the natural things
D. to avoid environmental pollution

29. To do up
A. to finish off B. to mend
C. to improve D. to make tidy

30. To do away with
A. to break B. to destroy
C. to get rid of D. to forget

31. To have to do with
A. to be interested in
B. to do something under compulsion
C. work done unenthusiastically
D. to complete

32. To egg on
A. just a beginning
B. to urge on
C. to develop something
D. an initial stage

33. To face the music
A. to face the consequences
B. to get filled with ecstasy
C. to be lucky
D. to lead a happy life

34. To end in smoke
A. all efforts in vain
B. the end of life
C. to come to nothing
D. to end the enmity

35. Eye to eye with
A. agree completely
B. a confrontation
C. full of anger
D. a quarrel between the two persons

36. To eat humble pie
A. to harass a humble person
B. a celebration or a treat without any cause
C. to confess that one is in the wrong
D. food provided to the needy or poor

37. Easy come easy go
A. what is gained without difficulty is spent without much thought
B. anything which is surplus
C. without any difficulty
D. to achieve something without any struggle

38. To eat out one's heart
A. to break one's heart
B. to deceive someone
C. to get deceived
D. to suffer intensely

39. To see with half an eye
A. to see with great ease
B. to dislike
C. to see stealthily
D. to feel jealous

40. A fair-weathered friend
A. A friend always eager to help
B. A friend who deserts one in times of adversity
C. a selfish friend
D. a true friend

41. A far cry
A. an unfulfilled desire
B. a very low voice
C. remote from
D. a distant place

42. To feather one's nest
A. to provide for one's own comfort
B. to be proud
C. to succeed again
D. to decorate one's house

43. To fish in troubled waters
A. to be in trouble
B. to make capital out of other's troubles
C. to be in trouble because of other's fault
D. to laugh at other's trouble

44. To follow suit
A. to follow the command
B. to obey the rules
C. to work in accordance with
D. to behave in the same manner

45. To get the hang of a thing
A. to understand the implications of something
B. to get a trace of theft
C. to find a new resource
D. to have some indications

46. To get wind of
A. to get news about something much before the event actually takes place
B. to forget the event that had taken place
C. to spread a rumour
D. to have some idea of a conspiration

47. French leave
A. a long leave
B. a small leave
C. absence from one's place of work without prior information
D. to leave the place forever

48. To steal a march upon
A. to outshine somebody
B. to rob
C. to move forward
D. to crush the enemy

49. A long face
A. a sad or mournful countenance
B. a very shameful defeat
C. a shameful act
D. an ugly face

50. To set one's face against
A. to criticise openly
B. to oppose with determination
C. a biased disapproval
D. to show disappointment

51. To fall away from
A. to decline
B. to desert
C. to avoid
D. to leave

52. To fall flat
A. to cause no amusement or interest
B. to lie down
C. to defeat the opponent
D. to plead

53. To have a finger in the pie
A. to be mixed up in any affair
B. to interfere in other's work
C. to have a share in the profit
D. to be a member of an organisation

54. In full cry
A. in full volume
B. in hot pursuit
C. a verbosity
D. manifestation of grief

55. To give a piece of one's mind
A. to rebuke
B. to give an idea
C. to present one's view
D. to judge one's intelligence on the basis of his work or contributions

56. Gift of the gab
A. the ability of verbosity
B. the ability of writing creatively
C. the ability to speak in an impressive manner
D. a man of versatile genius

57. To give the cold shoulder
A. to give support
B. to be indifferent
C. to express anger silently
D. to behave in a cold manner with someone

58. To give devil his due
A. to give an evil person credit for whatever good he has done
B. to punish one who has committed sin
C. an evil person meeting a tragic end
D. to give devil his share

59. To give up the ghost
A. to die
B. to sacrifice
C. to murder
D. to convert from vicious to virtuous

60. To give wide berth to
A. to give more space
B. to keep far away from
C. to appreciate more than what one deserves
D. to maintain a distance

61. To go to pieces
A. to tear
B. to feel disheartened
C. to be wrecked completely
D. to dismantle

62. To have too many irons in the fire
A. to be engaged in too many things
B. to handle more than one work at the same time
C. to have lot of energy
D. to have various plans in the mind

63. To put a spoke in one's wheel
A. to obstruct one in his work
B. to assist one in his work
C. to interfere one in his work
D. to increase the strength of a team

64. On the rack
A. in a dilemma
B. tortured by anxiety
C. highly curious
D. to be in a disadvantageous position

65. To get into hot water
A. an acute pain
B. to be in trouble
C. to face a short-tempered person
D. to be in hypertension

66. Fish and blood
A. by extreme means
B. by unlawful ways
C. human nature
D. life-like

67. From hand to mouth
A. to harm and humiliate
B. to be a bankrupt
C. to spend all that is earned
D. to feed someone

68. Hit the nail on the head
A. to take revenge openly
B. to insult on the face
C. to do a wrong thing
D. to do exactly the right thing

69. Put the cart before the horse
A. to reverse the natural order
B. to put obstruction
C. to cause problem for others
D. to stop one's advancement

70. Pay back in one's own coin
A. to save money
B. to treat in the same way as one has been treated
C. to get the return of the investment
D. to give a befitting reply

ANSWERS

1	2	3	4	5	6	7	8	9	10
A	B	B	D	A	A	B	C	A	A
11	**12**	**13**	**14**	**15**	**16**	**17**	**18**	**19**	**20**
A	B	C	B	A	D	A	D	A	B
21	**22**	**23**	**24**	**25**	**26**	**27**	**28**	**29**	**30**
A	D	A	B	D	A	A	A	D	C
31	**32**	**33**	**34**	**35**	**36**	**37**	**38**	**39**	**40**
A	B	A	C	A	C	A	D	A	B
41	**42**	**43**	**44**	**45**	**46**	**47**	**48**	**49**	**50**
C	A	B	D	A	A	C	A	A	B
51	**52**	**53**	**54**	**55**	**56**	**57**	**58**	**59**	**60**
B	A	A	B	A	C	D	A	A	B
61	**62**	**63**	**64**	**65**	**66**	**67**	**68**	**69**	**70**
C	A	A	B	B	C	C	D	A	B

●●●

7 Figures of Speech

It is a common saying that a picture is worth a thousand words. Same goes with the figures of speech as they elaborate the meaning of words.

FIGURATIVE LANGUAGE

One meaning of "figure" is "drawing" or "image" or "picture". Figurative language creates figures (pictures) in the mind of the reader or listener. These pictures help convey the meaning faster and more vividly than words alone.

We use figures of speech in "figurative language" to add colour and interest, and to awaken the imagination. Figurative language is everywhere, from classical works like Shakespeare or the Bible, to every day speech, pop music and television commercials. It makes the reader or listener use their imagination and understand much more than the plain words.

Figurative language is the opposite of literal language. Literal language means exactly what it says. Figurative language means something different to (and usually more than) what it says on the surface. *e.g.,*

- He ran fast. (literal)
- He ran like the wind. (figurative)

In the above example "like the wind" is a figure of speech (in this case, simile). It is important to recognize the difference between literal and figurative language.

There are many figures of speech that are commonly used and which you can learn by heart. At other times, writers and speakers may invent their own figures of speech. If you do not recognize them as figures of speech and think that they are literal, you will find it difficult to understand the language.

In this chapter we will discuss four common types of figures of speech :

- Simile
- Metaphor
- Hyperbole
- Oxymoron

Simile

A simile is a figure of speech that says that one thing is like another different thing. We can use similes to make descriptions more emphatic or vivid.

We often use the words *as....as* and like with similes.

Common patterns for similes, with example sentences, are :

- Something AS *adjective* AS *something*
  His skin was as cold as ice.
  It felt as hard as rock.
  She looked as gentle as a lamb.
- Something LIKE something
  My love is like a red, red rose.
  These cookies taste like garbage.
  He had a temper (that was) like a volcano.

- Something LIKE something
  He eats like a pig.
  He smokes like a chimney.
  They fought like cats and dogs.

Here are some more examples of well known similes :

AS *adjective* **AS** *something*	**Meaning**
as blind as a bat	completely blind
as cold as ice	very cold
as flat as a pancake	completely flat
as gentle as a lamb	very gentle
as light as a feather	very light
as old as the hills	very old
as sharp as a knife	very sharp
as strong as a bull	very strong
as white as snow	pure white
as wise as an owl	very wise

LIKE *something*	**Possible meaning (depending on context)**
like a rose	beautiful
like a volcano	explosive
like garbage	disgusting
like an animal	inhuman
like spaghetti	entangled
like dewdrops	sweet and pure
like golddust	precious
like a tip	very untidy (tip = garbage dump)
like a dream	wonderful, incredible
like stars	bright and beautiful

LIKE something	**Meaning**
to drink like a fish	to drink a lot
to eat like a bird	to eat very little
to eat like a horse	to eat a lot
to eat like a pig	to eat impolitely
to fight like cats and dogs	to fight fiercely
to sing like an angel	to sing beautifully
to sleep like a log	to sleep well and soundly
to smoke like a chimney	to smoke heavily, all the time
to soar like an eagle	to fly high and free
to work like a dog	to work very hard

Note that with the AS...AS pattern, the first AS is sometimes suppressed, for example :

His skin was cold as ice.

The above patterns of simile are the most common, but there are others made with adverbs or words such as than and as if, for example :

- He ran as fast as the wind.
- He is larger than life.
- They ran as if for their lives.

Similes can include other figures of speech. For example. "He ran like greased lightning" is a simile that includes hyperbole (greased lightning).

Similes often make use of irony or sarcasm. In such cases they may even mean the opposite of the adjective used.

Look at these examples :

- His explanation was as clear as mud. (not clear at all since mud is opaque)
- The film was about as interesting watching a copy of Windows download. (long and boring)
- Watching the show was like watching paint dry. (very boring)

Similes are often found (and they sometimes originate) in poetry and other literature. Here are a few examples :

- A woman without a man is like a fish without a bicycle—Irina Dunn
- Dawn breaks open like a wound that bleeds afresh—Wilfred Owen
- Death has many times invited me : it was like the salt invisible in the waves—Pablo Neruda

- Guiltless forever, like a tree
—Robert Browning
- Happy as pigs in mud—David Eddings
- How like the winter hath my absence been—William Shakespeare
- As idle as a painted ship upon a painted ocean—Samuel Taylor Coleridge
- Jubilant as a flag unfurled—Dorothy Parker
- So are you to my thoughts as food to life—William Shakespeare
- Yellow butterflies flickered along the shade like flecks of sun—William Faulkner

Metaphor

A metaphor is a figure of speech that says that one thing is another different thing. This allows us to use fewer words and forces the reader or listener to find the similarities.

The word metaphor comes from the Greek word *metapherin* (meaning "transfer").

The simplest form of metaphor is : "The [first thing] is a [second thing]."

Look at this example :

Her home was a prison.

In the above sentence, we understand immediately that her home had some of the characteristics of a prison. Mainly, we imagine, she could not leave her home. She was trapped inside. Why it was a prison we do not know, but that would be clear from the context—perhaps her husband forced her to stay at home, perhaps she was afraid of the outside. We don't know, but the rest of the story would tell us. What is important here is that in five simple words we understand a lot about her environment, how she felt and how she behaved. In this sentence, "prison" is a metaphor.

Look at another example :

George is a sheep.

What is one characteristic of sheep? They follow each other. So we can imagine that George is a follower, not a leader. In this sentence "sheep" is a metaphor.

Metaphors are very common in everyday language. But poets also like to use metaphors.

Look at these examples of metaphors with sample sentences and meanings :

Metaphor example	Metaphorical sense	Original sense
I'm not an angel, but I wouldn't behave like that.	exemplary person	a spiritual being believed to be a messenger of God
America is a melting pot.	place where different peoples, styles and cultures are mixed together	a container in which metals or other materials are melted and mixed
John is a real pig when he eats.	greedy person	a four-legged animal kept for meat (pork)
My father is a rock.	very strong or reliable person	a hard, mineral material made of stone
How could she marry a snake like that!	traitor	a long, limbless reptile (e.g., cobra, python, viper)
The policeman let him off with a yellow card.	warning	(in soccer) a yellow card that the referee shows to players when cautioning them

All the above metaphors (the simplest form) are nouns. But there are other ways of making metaphors, for example with verbs or adjectives. Here are some examples :

Metaphor example	Original sense of the word (example)
The committee **shot** ideas **down** one by one.	Anti-aircraft guns that shoot down planes.
The private detective **dug** up enough evidence to convince the police to act.	Dugs like to bury bones and dig them up later.
He **broke into** her conversation	Burglars break into buildings.
The new movie was very popular. People **flocked** to see it.	Birds flock together before they migrate.
His head was **spinning** with ideas.	Some computer hard drives spin at over 10,000 revolutions per minute.
Reading that book **kindled** my interest in branches when you kindle a camp fire.	You need to start with twigs and small politics.
Tim lost his job after a **heated** argument with his boss.	We have a heated swimming pool.
The new car's **sexy** design increased sales for the company.	Some women think that lipstick makes them look sexy.
He was dressed rather vulgarly in a **loud** checked suit.	I can't hear you because the radio is too loud.
It wasn't long before their relationship turned **sour**.	Sour food has an acid taste like lemon or vinegar.

Difference Between Metaphor and Simile

Both similes and metaphors link one thing to another. A simile usually uses "as" or "like". A metaphor is a condensed simile, a shortcut to meaning, which omits "as" or "like". A metaphor creates a relationship directly and leaves more to the imagination. With simile, A is like B. With metaphor, *A* is *B*.

Simile	Metaphor
Your eyes are like sun.	You are my the sun-shine.
He eats like a pig.	He is a pig.
He lives like a pig.	He is a pig.

Dead Metaphors

In the phrase "to grasp the concept" the physical action "to grasp" is used as a metaphor for "to understand" (which is non-physical). But this phrase has been used so often that most English speakers do not have an image of the physical action in their mind. This metaphor is a "dead metaphor".

Mixed Metaphors

The awkward use of two or more different metaphors at the same time is normally best avoided. It creates conflicting images in the reader or listener's mind, reduces each metaphor's impact, and generally causes confusion.

Look at this example :

America is a **melting pot** where new ideas are **kindled**.

Hyperbole

Hyperbole is a figure of speech that uses an exaggerated or extravagant to create a strong emotional response. As a figure of speech it is not intended to be taken literally. Hyperbole is frequently used for humour.

Examples of hyperbole are :

- They ran like greased lightning.
- He's got tons of money.
- Her brain is the size of a pea.
- He is older than the hills.
- I will die if she asks me to dance.
- She is as big as an elephant!
- I'm so hungry I could eat a horse.
- I have told you a million times not to lie!

The media and the advertising industry often use hyperbole (which may then be described as hyper or media hype).

Oxymoron

An oxymoron is a figure of speech that deliberately uses two contradictory ideas. This contradiction creates a paradoxical image in the reader or listener's mind that generates a new concept or meaning for the whole. Some typical oxymorons are :

- a living death
- sometimes you have to be cruel to be kind
- a deafening silence
- bitter-sweet
- The Sounds of Silence (song title)
- make haste slowly
- he was conspicuous by his absence

Pseudo Oxymorons

In the standard meaning of oxymoron the contradiction is deliberate. However, in popular usage oxymoron is sometimes used to mean "contradiction in terms", where the contradiction is unintentional. Such expressions, unlike real oxymorons, are commonly used without any sense of paradox in everyday language, for example :

- anecdotal evidence
- friendly fire
- pretty ugly

A common attempt at humour is to describe a certain phrase as an oxymoron, implying that the two parts of the phrase are mutually exclusive and that consequently the phrase as a whole must be nonsensical :

- airline food
- American culture
- eco-tourism
- Microsoft security
- military intelligence

The following are the other major Figures of Speech :

1. **Personification**—In Personification inanimate objects and abstract notions are spoken of as having life or intelligence.
2. **Onomatopoeia**—Onomatopoeia is that artifice of language by which the sound of words is made to suggest or echo the sense.
3. **Apostrophe**—An Apostrophe is a direct address to the dead, to the absent, or to a personified object or idea.
4. **Alliteration**—Alliteration consists in the repetition of the same sound or syllable at the beginning of two or more words.
5. **Irony**—Irony is a mode of speech in which the real meaning is exactly the opposite of that which is literally conveyed.
6. **Pun**—This consists in a play on the various meanings of a word, and is seldom used except as a joke.
7. **Metonymy**—In Metonymy an object is designated by the name of something which is generally associated with it.
8. **Synecdoche**—In Synecdoche a part is used to designate the whole, or the whole to designate a part.
9. **Antithesis**—In Antithesis a striking opposition or contrast of words or sentiments is made in the same sentence. It is employed to secure emphasis.
10. **Transferred Epithet**—In this figure an epithet is tranferred from its proper word to another that is closely associated with it in the sentence.

MULTIPLE CHOICE QUESTIONS

Directions (Qs. 1 to 20) : *Select the correct option for each of the following questions.*

1. Recognize the figure of speech in the following statement.
   He is the Newton of our class.
   A. Simile B. Hyperbole
   C. Metaphor D. Climax
2. Which of the following statements shows oxymoron:
   A. He is leading a busy life.
   B. He is leading a highly busy-idle life.
   C. He is leading an idle life.
   D. How happy I am!
3. Recognize the figure of speech in the following:
   The Child is father of the Man.
   A. alliteration B. hyperbole
   C. paradox D. metaphor
4. Which of the following shows Metonymy:
   A. Have you read the whole of George Eliot?
   B. Which building in Delhi do you like most?
   C. Whose acting do you like most among the Bollywood actors?
   D. Why are day and night equal on 21 March?
5. Recognize the figure of speech in the following statement.
   I wandered lonely as a cloud.
   A. Simile B. Metaphor
   C. Alliteration D. Hyperbole
6. Which of the following phrases shows onomatopoeia:
   A. living like a king.
   B. looking beyond the horizon.
   C. burning the candle at both ends.
   D. murmuring of innumerable bees.
7. Recognize the figure of speech in the following:
   Five miles meandering in mazy motion.
   A. oxymoron B. climax
   C. anticlimax D. alliteration
8. Which of the following shows 'climax':
   A. I walk, I jump, I dance.
   B. I run, I walk, I sit.
   C. He lies, runs and sits.
   D. She thinks, writes and observes.
9. Recognize the figure of speech in the following:
   Lightly, O lightly, they bear her along.
   A. Hyperbole B. Onomatopoeia
   C. Climax D. Repetition
10. Which of the following shows 'Hyperbole':
    A. You will have to speak for a hundred thousand years to describe her beauty.
    B. Love begets love.
    C. Better alone than in bad company.
    D. Nothing can be decided by war.
11. What Figure of Speech is used when a statement is made emphatic by over statement?
    A. Apostrophe B. Hyperbole
    C. Personification D. Antithesis
12. What Figure of Speech is used when two contradictory qualities are predicted at once of the same thing?
    A. Antithesis B. Onomatopoeia
    C. Oxymoron D. Hyperbole
13. In which Figure of Speech the sense is conveyed by the sound of words?
    A. Metonymy B. Synecdoche
    C. Alliteration D. Onomatopoeia
14. In which Figure of Speech is there a play on the various meanings of a word?
    A. Pun B. Metaphor
    C. Transferred EpithetD. Irony
15. Which Figure of Speech is produced when the same sound is repeated more than twice at the beginning of a word?
    A. Onomatopoeia B. Alliteration
    C. Metonymy D. Synecdoche
16. Which of the following is an example of Onomatopoeia?
    A. Sweet-bitter tears flowed from her eyes
    B. The beetle wheels his droning flight
    C. A load of learning lumbering in his head
    D. Fair is that fair does

17. Which of the following is an example of Oxymoron?
A. There is kind cruelty in the surgeon's knife
B. Ruin seize thee, ruthless king!
C. And Brutus is an honourable man!
D. Kalidas is the Shakespeare of India

18. Which of the following is an example of Antithesis?
A. Who is to blame but you!
B. Fair is foul, and foul is fair!
C. As you sow, so will you reap
D. Forget me not!

19. Which of the following is an example of Apostrophe?
A. Barking dogs seldom bite
B. My misfortune is your fortune
C. O Solitude! Where are thy charms?
D. I am the monarch of all I survey

20. Which of the following is an example of Alliteration?
A. Sweet are the uses of adversity!
B. Thus idly busy rolls their world away
C. He is the heir apparent
D. With beaded bubbles winking at the brim

Directions (Qs. 21 to 50) : *In each of the following sentences or verses a Figure of Speech has been used. You have to choose the correct Figure of Speech out of the four choices given under each :*

21. Rivers of blood flowed on the battlefield :
A. Simile B. Metaphor
C. Hyperbole D. Alliteration

22. Camel is the ship of the desert :
A. Metaphor B. Simile
C. Pun D. Personification

23. 'O my love's like a red, red rose, that's newly sprung in June':
A. Alliteration B. Metaphor
C. Simile D. Hyperbole

24. "Opportunity knocks at the door but once."
A. Hyperbole B. Metaphor
C. Antithesis D. Personification

25. "Death lays his icy hand on Kings" :
A. Personification B. Antithesis
C. Metaphor D. Oxymoron

26. "The murmurous haunt of flies on summer eves."
A. Hyperbole B. Alliteration
C. Onomatopoeia D. Personification

27. "Milton! thou should'st be living at this hour."
A. Personification B. Apostrophe
C. Alliteration D. Irony

28. How high his honour holds his haughty head!
A. Oxymoron B. Personification
C. Alliteration D. Irony

29. "Yet Brutus says he was ambitious. And Brutus is an honourable man."
A. Irony B. Oxymoron
C. Apostrophe D. Pun

30. Is life worth living? That depends upon the liver.
A. Pun B. Alliteration
C. Irony D. Metaphor

31. The pen is mightier than the sword.
A. Simile B. Metaphor
C. Metonymy D. Irony

32. A reeling road, a rolling road, that rambles round the shire.
A. Alliteration B. Metonymy
C. Personification D. Apostrophe

33. "The ploughman homeward plods his weary way."
A. Oxymoron
B. Synecdoche
C. Transferred Epithet
D. Pun

34. To err is human, to forgive divine :
A. Oxymoron
B. Antithesis
C. Transferred Epithet
D. Pun

35. He passed a sleepless night :
A. Transferred Epithet
B. Antithesis
C. Synecdoche
D. Oxymoron

36. The best brains assembled there :
A. Oxymoron B. Synecdoche
C. Irony D. Pun

37. I have many mouths to feed :
A. Synecdoche B. Irony
C. Pun D. Oxymoron

38. Man proposes, God disposes :
A. Synecdoche B. Antithesis
C. Pun D. Irony

39. O Death! Where is thy sting?
A. Metaphor B. Oxymoron
C. Personification D. Apostrophe

40. "Life is a tale told by an idiot,
Full of sound and fury ...."
A. Simile B. Personification
C. Metaphor D. Apostrophe

41. "Thy soul was like a star, and dwelt apart."
A. Metaphor B. Personification
C. Simile D. Onomatopoeia

42. He can devour mountains of food, and drink rivers of whisky.
A. Onomatopoeia B. Hyperbole
C. Metaphor D. Personification

43. "There Honour comes a pilgrim grey" :
A. Metaphor
B. Apostrophe
C. Personification
D. Onomatopoeia

44. An ambassador is a man who lies abroad for the good of his country :
A. Metonymy B. Personification
C. Pun D. Irony

45. "Husbands had she five on the holy altar" :
A. Hyperbole B. Metaphor
C. Irony D. Pun

46. His honour rooted in dishonour stood :
A. Antithesis B. Oxymoron
C. Irony D. Personification

47. "Sceptre and crown must tumble down."
A. Metonymy B. Antithesis
C. Irony D. Oxymoron

48. A lie has no legs :
A. Apostrophe B. Pun
C. Personification D. Irony

49. Youth is full of pleasure; Age is full of care :
A. Antithesis B. Pun
C. Metaphor D. Personification

50. The righteous shall flourish as the palm trees :
A. Simile
B. Transferred Epithet
C. Antithesis
D. Synecdoche

ANSWERS

1	2	3	4	5	6	7	8	9	10
C	B	C	A	A	D	D	A	D	A
11	12	13	14	15	16	17	18	19	20
B	C	D	A	B	B	A	B	C	D
21	22	23	24	25	26	27	28	29	30
C	A	C	D	A	C	B	C	A	A
31	32	33	34	35	36	37	38	39	40
C	A	C	B	A	B	A	B	D	C
41	42	43	44	45	46	47	48	49	50
C	B	C	C	C	B	A	C	A	A

●●●

ENGLISH LITERATURE

1 English Literature : At A Glance

THE OLD ENGLISH PERIOD

ANGLO-SAXON PERIOD (450-1050)

Beowulf is probably the oldest epic of the Teutonic world. It is believed to be belonging to the first half of the sixth century.

Some important works of the Anglo-Saxon period (Pre-Christian Era).

Some important works of the Anglo-Saxon period are: *The Ruined Burg, The Lover's Message. The Maiden's Complaint, The Wanderer* and *the Seafarer.*

'The Wanderer is also known as *'Widsith'*. The work is based on the wandering life of the gleeman.

Belonging to this period, we also have *"Deor's Lament"*, which, according to Long is, "much more poetic than *'Widsith,'* and is the one perfect lyric of the Anglo-Saxon period."

In the *Seafarer*, we have glimpses of hard sea life along with the call of the sea, which we, in our times, find more pronouncedly, but perhaps less picturesquely, in Masefield's *"Sea-Fever"*.

Some Christian writers of the Anglo-Saxon period.

Whereas the pagan literature of the Anglo-Saxon period was chiefly in the form of oral legends which they had brought with them from the foreign lands which they previously inhabited, the Christian writing mainly came into existence as a result of the teachings of the monks who had come under the influence of two schools—the Augustinian School (from Rome) and Northumbrian School (from Ireland).

While the former, did not produce much lasting works, the latter produced a number of good and great writers, *e.g.,* **The Venerable Bede (673-735), Caedmon (seventh century)** and **Cynewulf (eighth century)**.

Besides the poets mentioned above, we have **Alfred (848-90)** who is chiefly known as a translator.

ANGLO-NORMAN PERIOD (1066-1350)

Some important works of the Anglo-Norman period.

One important work of this period is *Geoffrey's "Historic Regum Britanniae"* (1137) commonly known as *"History"*. Geoffrey is believed to have died in 1154.

Geoffrey's work which became immensely popular in his own life, is a mixture of pagan and Christian legends and is based more on lies than on real historical events.

However, the said work has its literary value for its poetry and romance pertaining to king Arthur and his Knights, and hence, it became a source of inspiration and scintillating subject matter for such illustrious authors as Malory, Shakespeare and Tennyson.

Geoffrey's work was in Latin verse. Thereafter appeared *"Layman's Brut"* (c. 1200) which has its main interest in giving Arthur's legends in (Anglo-Saxon) English itself.

Then there appeared what are known as *"Metrical Romances"* which were based on the "matter" of France, Rome and Britain.

While in the *Matter of France,* **Charlemagne's** exploits dominated and in the *Matter of Rome* Alexander's adventures and the war of Troy were the main subjects, in the *Matter of Britain*, exploits of Arthur and his knights of the Round Table were chief subject matter. There were a number of cycles pertaining to the knights of Arthur, among them being **Sir Gawain (1350)** *Quest of the Holy Grail, Death of Arthur, Merlin, etc.*

Besides the above, other works of the period included ballads, lyrics and such poems as the *Owl and the Nightingale, Ormulum, Cursor Mundi* (*1320*), *The Pearl, Patience, Cleanness, etc.* Also **Roger Bacon's** *"Opus Majus"* appeared in 1267.

THE AGE OF CHAUCER (1340-1400)

The Hundred years war between England and France had already started in 1338 when **Chaucer** was born in **1340**.

In the earlier years of the war, England was all-powerful and under Edward III it won victories over France at Sluys in 1340 and Crecy in 1346, culminating in the capture of Calais in 1347.

Another thumping victory was won by the Black Prince, Edward III's son in 1356 by defeating the French at Poitiers.

As a result of the English victories, the English foreign trade began to flourish, particularly in the export of wool to Flanders, which filled the coffers of the English king and the people also became richer, as we notice conspicuously in **Chaucer's** *Canterbury Tales* when we consider the lot of so many acters, particularly those belonging to landed aristocracy.

This picture is also graphically depicted in **Trevelyan's** *British History of Six Centuries.*

It was unfortunate for England that in the moment of its glory it was overtaken by plague, the Black Death which took a heavy toll of life all over Europe in 1348-49.

As a result of the Black Death, most of the labourers who escaped death, left the country, and this caused an intense scarcity of the availability of essential commodities at cheap rates. To meet this menace, the Parliament tried to force the labourers to accept the same wages as they were getting before the Black Death, and it all finally precipitated into the well-known Peasants' Revolt during the reign of Richard II.

In spite of the passage of certain statutes purported to safeguard the English clergy against the undue domination of the Pope, the low simmering of wrath among the clergymen for several reasons, there emerged in the "Lollards Movement" under the leadership of the redoubtable Wyclif.

Another prominent feature, this one in the literary world, was the slow advent of the spirit of New Learning from Italy and drastic changes in the structure of the English language which had already been continuing as the inevitable outcome of the Norman conquest at Hastings in 1066.

These were the general conditions in which the most significant writers of the age—**Chaucer, Langland, Dunbar,** etc. lived and flourished, thus heralding a new age slowly, but boldly and surely.

MAJOR AUTHORS AND THEIR WORKS OF CHAUCER'S AGE

Sir Thomas More (1478-1535)

Utopia (*English Version*)

William Tyndale (1485-1536)

New Testament

Geoffrey Chaucer (1340-1400)

The Boke of the Duchesse

The Romaunt of the Rose

The House of Fame

Troylus Cryseyde

The Canterbury Tales
Legends of Good Women
The Parliament of Fouls
Wyclif (1320-1384)
The Bible

John Heywood (1564-1627)
Four P's
Thomas Sackville and Thomas Norton : (1536-1608) (1532-1584)
Gorboduc

THE SEVENTEENTH CENTURY

THE RENAISSANCE (1578-1625)

The Renaissance of English Literature coincides with the Age of Queen Elizabeth I. Hence, in the history of English literature, this period is also called as the *Elizabethan Age*. The inspiration for the great works of this period came from the prolific translations into English of works of ancient Rome and Greece. Thus, **Plutarch's** *Lives* was translated by **Sir Thomas North (1579)** from the French version. Montaigne's Essays was translated by **John Florio (1603)**. In verse, **Ovid's** *Metamorphoses* was translated by **Arthur Golding (1565, 1567)**. Among other works of foreign origin translated into English were Ariosto's *Orlando Furioso* by **Harrington (1591)**, and Homer's *Iliad* by **George Chapman (1598)**.

The rising English stage and the English novel borrowed from Boccaccio, Cinthio, Bandello and Straparola — the Italians. Attracted though England was to Italian art, it resisted the evil influences of debauchery, crime and passions that the Italian spirit represented. Yet, the time was ripe in England for the full development of every art and literary form. Renaissance means *a flowering again of art and culture*. It inculcated a sense of wonder in things. England also wanted to rival Spain, France and Portugal in her navigational triumphs. Thus in 1578, Sir Francis Drake circumnavigated the world, and in 1588, the English navy destroyed the Armada. The same spirit of adventure moved literature. In *Apologie for Poetrie*, Sidney described the poet — of all sciences 'the monarch'. Poets were encouraged to innovate new styles and rhythms.

Poetry

Three great men of letters led the Renaissance in England — Spenser, Sidney and Lyly.

Edmund Spenser (1552-1599) wrote the *Shepheardes Calendar* (1579)—an allegory. The union of line and metre is varied and rich. In *Hymnes In honour of Love and Beautie*, he sets forth his philosophy, the conflict in his mind between paganism and Christianity. He also wrote a satire named, *Mother Hubberd's Tale* to denounce the neglect of arts and letters. His pastoral, *Colin Clout's Come Home Again* describes his stay in London in 1589. His *Amoretti* (1595) are sonnets on love and his *Epithalamion* is an ode, but his masterpiece is the *Faerie Queene* (1589, 1595), an allegory in which characters represent virtues and vices. In it his lyrical quality and colour-effects are at their best. The *Faerie Queene* is Queen Elizabeth. The nine-line stanza he used is now called the *Spenserian stanza*.

Sir Philip Sidney (1554-1586) was a scholar, knight and courtier. In 1580 he wrote *Arcadia* which has a blend of pastoral and heroic elements. It is a romance of chivalry and love. The language is characterized by *pathetic fallacy* — endowing inanimate objects with feelings and sensations. William Shakespeare borrowed from this style. His other poem, *Astrophel and Stella* (1591) describes his lost love for the daughter of an Earl. His *Apologie for Poetrie* (1595) written in an unaffected prose, is a plea for poetry.

John Lyly (1554-1606) invented an artistic, flowery style called *euphuism* through his famous romance, *Euphues, the Anatomy of Wit* (1579). This style was adopted by the refined people of the Court. The style is characterized by the use of alliteration and antithesis, fantastic metaphors and similes based on mythology, and natural history of flora and fauna.

The works of these three trail-blazed many poets and sonneteers like Samuel Daniel, Michael Drayton, Thomas Watson, Henry Constable and Thomas Lodge. Notable works from 1590 to 1603 were **Samuel Daniel's (1562-1619)** *The Civil Wars* (1595) describing the *War of the Roses*, **Michael Drayton's (1563-1631)** *Idea, the Shepherd's Garland, The Baron's Wars, England's Heroicall Epistles* (1603) and *Poly-Olbion*, a long description of England in 15,000 alexandrines or lines of twelve syllables. England came to be known as *"a nest of singing birds"* because of the great number of lyrics and poems written in this period. **Thomas Campion (1567-1620)** published an anthology called *Two Books of Ayres* (1612). Many of the best poems are found in plays by Ben Jonson, Thomas Dekker, Beaumont and Fletcher, and Webster. But those of William Shakespeare are probably the most beautiful. In his *Sonnets*, he describes his love for a married woman who betrays him. Other poems of this period are Marlowe's Hero and Leander (1598), Shakespeare's *Venus and Adonis* (1593) and *The Rape of Lucrece* (1594).

After Elizabeth's reign, in James I rule, poetry became religious and didactic. The Protestant spirit dominated the literary works. The poems of George Wither, William Browne, the Fletcher brothers and William Drummond show the influence of Spenser still.

Ben Jonson (1573-1637) was the greatest humanist of the time. He was mainly a playwright but wrote poems also. His poetry is found in collections like *Epigrams* and *The Forest* (1616) and *The Underwoods* (1640). He was a satirist and neo-classicist being influenced by the Latin classics.

John Donne's (1573-1631) poetry is revolutionary. He disobeys the laws of rhythm and uses a device called the metaphysical conceit in which strangely opposite ideas are juxtaposed.

Prose

Much of the prose of the period is poetical, influenced by euphuism. Robert Greene, Thomas Lodge, Thomas Nashe, Thomas Deloney, and Thomas Dekker are the major writers. **Robert Greene's (1558-1592)** works include *Mamilia* and *Menaphon* and **Thomas Lodge's (1558-1625)** include *Rosalynde: Euphues Golden Legacie* (1590). **Thomas Nashe (1567-1601)** wrote pamphlets like The *Anatomie of Absurdities* and *The Terrors of the Night*. **Thomas Dekker's (1572-1632)** *The Gils Horne booke* is famous for its picturesque prose. Most of the poets and prose writers of this period were also dramatists. Shakespeare used prose for homely and humorous scenes and verse for tragic ones.

Many writers of the English Renaissance were inspired by the literary criticism of the Continent to write some themselves. Stephen Gosson's *The Schoole of Abuse* (1579) and *Sidney's Apologie for Poetrie* are good examples. Sidney eulogizes the poet as a law-giver. The period also saw works of religious prose. **Richard Hooker's (1554-1600)** pamphlet on the Marlin Marprelate controversy is a famous one. Hooker's *Of the Laws of Ecclesiastical Polity* (1594) is a masterpiece of English prose. The most seminal work of the period is the authorized version of the Bible published in 1611. The work was commissioned by James I. A beautiful prose minus archaism is used by the revisers. The diction was to influence the English language very deeply. It is the language of daily speech, yet fresh and lofty.

Side by side with religious literature, secular and philosophical literature, mostly written by **Francis Bacon (1561-1626)**, came out. He had taken all knowledge as his province and elaborated his doctrines in his *Novum Organum* (1620). His ideas influenced the formation of *The Royal Society for Improving Natural Knowledge* in 1645. His most popular work is his *Essays* written on diverse topics in a terse, epigrammatic style. The English writers quote copiously from Bacon today. His sentences are household terms. Take for example, "*He that hath wife and children hath given hostages* *to fortune*". "*Some books are to be tasted, others to be swallowed and some few to be chewed and digested*".

Another great prose-writer of the period was **Robert Burton (1577-1640)** whose *The Anatomy of Melancholy* (1621) is full of pedantry. He borrowed from numerous sources and is full of melancholy and jests; his style abounds in synonyms and epithets.

Drama

Drama thrived in the Renaissance. Foreign influence, especially of Italy, predominated. Plays were written so that the public would enjoy them and applaud the stage. There was a great variety of plays written — pure tragedy, tragi-comedy, historical drama, romantic comedy, comedy of errors, farce, pastoral, etc. The stage was a simple structure, circular in form with a courtyard open to the sky. A platform projected into the courtyard. Boys played the female roles. The public consisted of groundlings and courtiers on galleries. The unities of time, place and action were disregarded. Farce and tragedy were found in succession.

Several mythological allegories were acted before the court. **John Lyly's** euphuistic romances like *Campaspe* (1584), *Sapho and Phao, Endymion* (1592), *Midas* were praises of the queen. **George Peele (1558-1598)** wrote *The Araygnement of Paris* (1584) and *The Old Wives' Tale*. There were violent plays like **Thomas Kyd's (1558-1594)** The *Spanish Tragedie* (1585) and **Christopher Marlowe's (1564-1593)** *Tamburlaine, the Great* (1587) and *Doctor Faustus* (1592). *Doctor Faustus* is an allegory on the Renaissance love of power. It shows how Doctor Faustus, the scientist, sells his soul to the devil for twenty-four years of full power to satisfy every desire. In the end his agony increases as the devil approaches to claim his soul. Marlowe also wrote *The Jew of Malta*, which shows the unbridled love for wealth, and the historical play Edward II. Marlowe crafted the blank verse (mighty line as Shakespeare called it and used). This was suited to the fiery speeches of his characters.

The towering genius of the age was certainly **William Shakespeare (1564-1616)**. He was versatile and wrote about 36 plays and 144 sonnets. "Shakespeare was not of an age but for all times" and "Poets are born not made", wrote Ben Jonson about him. He created a gallery of nearly 800 characters who typify personalities found through human history. Julius Caesar's pride and ambition, Macbeth's unbridled ambition, King Lear's dotedness, and Othello's susceptibility to suspicion against his wife — are tragic flaws that govern men even today.

Shakespeare was not educated except for a few years at a grammar school. He had 'little Latin and less Greek' and read books in translation from Latin and Greek. He adapted the stories into a World entirely his own, instinct with life and vibrancy. Shakespeare began his career by acting for the stage. Then he wrote plays and staged them, mainly to seek court patronage. His great success made him the envy of his contemporaries like Robert Greene. In his tragedies he depicts the fall of great men owing to a tragic flaw in their character. Although they had the will to change their destiny, a fate controlled them. He used the beliefs of his time like the supernatural powers and phenomena to capture the interest of his audience. Some of his historical plays are *Richard II* (1596) and *King John* (1595). Among the romantic comedies *As You Like It* (1600), *The Merchant of Venice* (1596) and *Twelfth Night* (1601) are popular. *A Midsummer Night's Dream* (1595) is a fairy play. *Romeo and Juliet* (1594) is a tragicomedy. He used prose and blank verse.

His *Henry IV* (I & 2) (1597, 1598) contain much more blank verse than his other plays. In depth of psychological insight, and power of style *Hamlet* (1601), one of Shakespeare's great tragedies, stands supreme. *The Tempest* (161I) is one of his last plays which shows the dramatist's mellowed maturity.

Even after 400 years, Shakespeare's plays are very popular, being translated into almost every important language. "*Age cannot wither her nor custom stale her infinite variety*"; Shakespeare described Cleopatra in these words. The same may be said about his plays also.

Ben Jonson was Shakespeare's antithesis. He borrowed the style of the classics and was very erudite. He carefully studied society and wrote about it. He took the different 'humours' or dominating characteristics of men and satirized them in *Every Man in his Humour* (1598) and *Every Man out of his Humour* (1599), *Volpone, or the Fox* (1605) and *The Alchemist* (1605). He also wrote the historical tragedies, *Sejanus His Fall* (1603) and *Catiline His Conspiracy* (1611). The plays are very true to history. John Marston, Thomas Dekker, Thomas Heywood and Middleton were other playwrights of the age. John Webster (1580-1625) is famous for horror plays like *The White Devil* (1609-1612) and *The Duchess of Malfi* (1613-1614).

MAJOR AUTHORS AND THEIR WORKS

Edmund Spenser (1552-1599)

The Faerie Queene
The Shepheardes Calendar
Amoretti
Epithalamion
Prothalamion
Mother Hubberd's Tale
The Ruins of Time
The Tears of the Muses
Astrophel

Phillip Sidney (1554-1586)

Arcadia
Astrophel and Stella
An Apologie for Poetrie

Ben Jonson (1573-1637)

Every Man in His Humour
Every Man Out of His Humour
Volpone Or the Fox
Cynthia's Revels
The Alchemist
Bartholomew Fayre
Epicaene or the Silent Women
Sejanus His Fall
Catline His Conspiracy
The Poetaster
The Devil as an Ass
The Masque of Beauty

Samuel Daniel (1562-1619)

Delia
Civil Wars between the Two Houses of Lancaster and York

Michael Drayton (1563-1631)

The Battle of Agincourt
England's heroic Epistles
The Barons' Wars
Polyolbion

William Shakespeare (1564-1616)

The Two Gentlement of Verona
The Merry Wives of Windsor
Measure for Measure
The Comedy of Errors
Love's Labour's Lost
The Taming of the Shrew
All's Well that Ends Well
A Midsummer Night's Dream
The Merchant of Venice
Much Ado About Nothing
As You Like it
Twelfth Night
Romeo and Juliet
Macbeth
Hamlet
King Lear
Othello
Antony and Cleopatra
Julius Caesar
Timon of Athens
Coriolanus
Titus Andronicus
Troilus and Cressida
King John
King Richard the Second
King Henry the Fourth-Part First
King Henry the Fourth-Second Part
King Henry the Fifth
King Henry the Sixth-First Part
King Henry the Sixth-Second Part
King Henry the Sixth-Third Part

King Richard the Third
King Henry the Eighth
Cymbeline
Pericles
The Winter's Tale
The Tempest
Venus and Adonis and Rape of Lucrece (Narrative Poems)
Sonnets (154 in number).

Christopher Marlowe (1564-1593)
Tamburlaine the Great
Edward II
Doctor Faustus
The Jew of Malta
The Tragedy of Dido, Queen of Carthage.

George Peele (1558-1597)
The Araygnement of Paris
The Famous Chronicle of King Edward I

Robert Greene (1560-1592)
Frier Bacon and Frier Bungey
Orlando Furioso
Pandosto

Thomas Nashe (1567-1601)
The Unfortunate Traveller Or The Life of Jack Wilton

Thomas Lodge (1558-1625)
The Wounds of Civil War
Rosalynde

Thomas Kyd (1557-1595)
The Spanish Tragedy

John Lyly (1554-1606)
Euphues, The Anatomy of Wit
Euphues and His England
Endymion

Francis Bacon (1561-1626)
Essays
The Advancement of Learning
The New Atlantis
Novum Organum

John Webster (1580-1625)
The White Devil
The Duchess of Malfi
The Devil's Law Case.

Thomas Heywood (1575-1650)
A Woman Killed with Kindness
The English Traveller
The Captives

Robert Burton (1577-1640)
The Anatomy of Melancholy

Sir Thomas Browne (1605-1682)
Religio Medici
Vulgar Errors
Hydrotaphia or Urne Burriale
Christian Morals

Thomas Hobbes (1588-1679)
Leviathan

Jeremy Taylor (1613-1667)
The Liberty of Prophesying
Holy Living
Holy Dying

END OF THE RENAISSANCE (1625-1660)

Prose

Puritanism set the trend for the literature during the reign of Charles I. The Bible was the guiding spirit which may be best seen in Milton's works. The zealous Calvinists enforced Presbyterianism. The passionate curiosity for life which characterized the Renaissance gave place to a search for salvation. **Sir Thomas Browne (1605-1682)** was a scientist, but in his *Pseudodoxia Epidemica or Vulgar Errors* (1646), we see his belief in miracles. His *Religio Medici* (1642) speaks of the vanity of earthly life. **George Herbert's (1596-1633)** *The Country Parson* and **Jeremy Taylor's (1613-1667)** *Holy Living* (1650) and *Holy Dying* (1651) are sermons championing religious freedom. **John Milton (1608-1674)**, who is famous as a poet, wrote numerous pamphlets in favour of divorce which are models of beautiful prose. His *Areopagitica* (1644) is a speech for the liberty of unlicensed writing.

Another great prose-writer was **Thomas Hobbes (1588-1679)** whose *Leviathan* (1651) is a famous work. He was an empiricist and realist and believed that sensations and ideas are caused by physical reasons. Numerous works of ethics, sociology and history were written. *The History of the Rebellion and Civil Wars in England* was written by **Edward Hyde (1609-1674). Izaac Walton (1593-1683)** wrote the biographies of John Donne and George Herbert. *The Compleat Angler* (1653) is his famous work on the post-Civil War scene and contains descriptions of the English countryside.

Poetry

Two types of poets existed then — the Cavaliers, who were the Royalists, and the religious or Metaphysical poets. Thomas Carew, Sir John Suckling, John Cleveland, Robert Herrick were Cavalier poets who displayed epicurean tastes. Imagination and sensuous imagery predominate their poems. Among the religious poets, Herbert, Crashaw, Vaughan and Marvell stand out. They were mystics. **George Herbert's (1593-1633)** style is simple and expresses Christian piety in his anthology The Temple (1633). His poems *The Pulley and Love* are very popular. **Richard Crashaw (1613-1649)** used fantastic conceits; e.g. he describes the maudlin St Mary Magdalene's eyes as "walking baths, compedious oceans", **Henry Vaughan (1622-1695)** was a mystic and his poem The Retreat is a nostalgic longing for the blissful heavenly state of childhood.

John Milton's greatest achievement was his *Paradise Lost* (1667). In theme it deals with the fall of man. In form, it follows the strict unity of the classical epic. His other poems are *L'Allegro* (1632), *Il Penseroso* (1632), *Comus* (1634), *Lycidas* (1637), *Samson Agonistes* (1671), etc.

RESTORATION LITERATURE (1620-1734)

Prose

In 1660, Charles II returned to the throne and the Puritan republic ended. The year is also marked as the beginning of the modern literature. **John Bunyan's (1628-1688)** works, *Grace Abounding* (1666) and *The Pilgrim's Progress* (1678) are the last surviving works of Puritan faith. The Pilgrim's Progress is an allegory describing the trials and tribulations on the way to salvation as faced by a Christian. Bunyan's prose is a blend of common speech and the grandeur of the revised Bible.

The scientific spirit took over the reign. The Royal Society of London for the Improvement of Natural Knowledge, to which Bacon and William Harvey (who discovered the circulation of blood) had contributed, now had many learned men. **Sir Isaac Newton** published Principia in 1687. He discovered the laws of gravity, of the diffraction of white light and the theory of fluxions.

John Locke (1632-1704) propounded a new philosophy of commonsense and intelligent reasoning in his *An Essay Concerning Human Understanding* (1690). It lays stress on development of character. It was to influence the English thought. Voltaire was one of his French disciples.

Poetry

Restoration literature was derived from pre-Commonwealth national literature and was a reaction against Puritan oppression. It rejected severe moral codes of conduct and was chiefly satiric in nature. **Samuel Butler's (1612-1680)** poem, *Hudibras* published in three parts (1663, 1664 & 1678), is a typical work of this period. It is inspired by *Don Quixote*. He satirizes Sir Hudibras as a grotesque Presbyterian with a squire called Ralpho. It lays bare all the human follies in octosyllabic couplets. Many court poets like **Andrew Marvell (1621-1678)** and **John Oldham (1653-1683)** were veterans of the Republican era and satirize the follies of the new age.

The great poet of the period was **John Dryden (1631-1700)**. He excelled in almost every kind of composition. He wrote a series of heroic stanzas in honour of Cromwell on his death. He was a disciple of the metaphysical poets displaying their far-fetched images and conceits. In *Astraea Redux* (1660), he celebrated the return of Charles II and in *Annus Mirabilis* (1667) he commemorated the Great Fire of London and the war with Holland. He was a staunch Tory and his famous satires are *Absalom and Achitophel* (1681), *The Medal and Mac-Flecknoe*. In this last work he satirizes Shadwell, the Whig poet. *The Hind and the Panther* (1687) is an allegory on Catholicism and Anglicanism. Dryden also translated the classics, chiefly Persuis and Juvenal. He turned Virgil's *Aeneid* into brilliant couplets. His *Alexander's Feast* is an ode in honour of St. Cecilia.

Drama

The dramatic works of the Restoration were licentious and full of cynicism. They regarded the moral code of the Puritans as a matter of ridicule. Scenery now played an important part on the stage and actresses, not boys, played the female roles. The theatre was regarded as a place of vice and evil. Shakespeare's plays were rewritten and his tragedies like *Romeo and Juliet* given happy endings. French influence dominated and extraordinary superhuman feats were described. Heroes were presented as ideals and were made to give pompous speeches.

Dryden wrote many plays like *Aureng-zebe* or *The Great Mogul* (1675) and The Conquest of Granada (1669, 1670) which abound in rhetoric.

The tragedians were **Thomas Otway (1651-1685)**, Nathaniel Lee (1653-1692) and **Nicholas Rowe (1674-1718)**. The comedy of this period reflects the gay intrigues of the society. Caricature and farce were used and obscenity also touched it. The main aim was to amuse. **Sir George Etheredge (1635-1691)** was an innovator and **William Wycherley (1640-1715)** was a moralist playwright. **William Congreve (1670-1729)** wrote a series of masterpieces including *The Way of the World* (1700). **John Vanbrugh** (1664-1726) and **George Farquhar (1678-1707)** were other comedy writers of the period.

Criticism

Dryden was the first English critic. *The Essay of Dramatick Poesie* (1668) is his longest single prose work and a major piece of English literary criticism. It is in the form of a discussion between four characters, one of whom is Dryden himself. It deals with topics related to theatre and evaluates the works of the Elizabethan dramatists, especially of Shakespeare.

The Diarists of the Restoration Period

One of the sources of information and genres of prose writing during the Restoration were diaries. The important names are those of John Evelyn, Samuel Pepys and Roger North. **John Evelyn (1620-1706)** was a rich man who had cultured tastes. He was a member of the Royal Society and had wide interests in diverse fields like gardening, forestry, navigation and architecture. His *Diary* which was written almost throughout his lifetime throws a floodlight on the major social and national events of the time like the Galley Slaves and the Great Fire. It is written in a plain, graphic style. **Samuel Pepys (1633-1703)** had a chequered career. Coming from the middle classes, he joined the civil services and rose to be the secretary of the Admiralty. He also became the President of the Royal Society and a member of Parliament. His famous *Diary*, covering a period of ten years, is in the form of confessions. It was written in laconic sentences like the messages of a telegram and was in a sort of code which was deciphered only in 1825. The diary shows him to be a man of versatile interests like music, science and literature. But the most controversial aspect is the detailed confessions of his life. Nobody seemed to guess he was a libertine, a morally debauched character who could stoop to low means. When we read the diary, it seems he is writing of another person. **Roger North** belonged to an elite family. He was a Tory gentleman and was engaged in the politics of the times. His famous work is *North's Lives of the Norths* containing biographies of three relatives and an autobiography. His pen pictures and anecdotes are in colloquial style.

MAJOR AUTHORS AND THEIR WORKS

Robert Herrick (1591-1574)

Noble Numbers

Hesperides

Thomas Carew (1598-1639)
Poems
'He that loves a rosy cheek'

Sir John Suckling (1660-1642)
'Ballad upon a Wedding'
'Why so pale and wan, Fond Lover'?

Andrew Marvell (1621-1678)
'To His Coy Mistress'
'The Rehearsal Transprosed'
'Ode upon Cromwell's Return from Ireland'
New Letters (*a Prose Work*)

George Herbert (1593-1633)
The Temple
Affliction
Easter Wings
The Collar
Man

Richard Crashaw (1613-1649)
Carmen Deo Nostro
The Infant Morturs
Steps to the Temple

John Milton (1608-1674)
Paradise Lost (*in twelve Books*)
Paradise Regained
Comus
Lycidas
Samson Agonistes
L'Allegro
Ill Penseroso
Areopagitica (*Prose Work*)
Ode on the Morning of Christ's Nativity
Sonnets (*including*) :
'On His Blindness'
'On the Late Massacre in Piedmont'
'When the Assault was Intended to the City'
'On His Having Arrived at the Age of Twenty-three'
A large number of Tracts and Pamphlets in support of the Parliament

John Donne (1573-1631)
Songs and Sonnets
Aires and Angels
A Nocturnall upon Lucies Day
A Valediction : Forbidding Mourning
The Extasie
Devotions (*Sermon in Prose*)
Ignatius His Enclave (*a Prose Work*)
Of the Progress of the Soul
Death's Duell

Abraham Cowley (1618-1667)
Pyramus and Thisbe
The Mistress
The Davideis
Pindarique Odes
Constantia and Philetus
Discourse by Way of Vision
Concerning the Government of Cromwell (a Prose Work)

Henry Vaughan (1622-1695)
Poems
Regeneration
The Retreat
Olor Iscanus
Thalia Redivia
Silex Scintillans

John Dryden (1631-1700)
(*i*) *Heroic Stanzas on the Death of Oliver Cromwell*
Astraea Redux (on the Restoration of Charles II)
Absalom and Achitophel
Religio Laici
The Hind and the Panther
The Fables
Annus Mirabilis
The Medal
Mac Flecknoe
Alexander's Feast
Prefaces to His Plays (in Prose)
An Essay of Dramatic Poesy
(*ii*) *Dryden's Plays*
Tyrannic Love
Conquest of Granada

All for love
The Rival Ladies
The Indian Emperor
Aureng-Zeb
Don Sebastian
Cleomenes
Love Triumphant

John Vanbrugh (1664-1726)
The Relapse
The Provoked Wife
The Confederacy

George Farquhar (1678-1707)
The Recruiting Officer
The Beaux Stratagem

Thomas Otway (1652-1685)
Orphan
Venice Preserved
Don Carlos
Alcibiades

Nathaniel Lee (1653-1692)
Nero
The Rival Queens
Sophonisba

John Bunyan (1628-1688)
The Pilgrim's Progress
Grace Abounding
The Life and Death of Mr. Badman
The Holy War

John Locke (1632-1704)
Essay on the Human Understanding
Treatise on Government
Thoughts on Education

John Evelyn (1620-1706)
Diary

Samuel Pepys (1633-1703)
Diary

MULTIPLE CHOICE QUESTIONS

1. Who wrote the *Faerie Queene?*
A. John Lyly
B. Edmund Spenser
C. Ben Jonson
D. Shakespeare

2. What is the nine-line stanza used in the *Faerie Queene* called?
A. Alexandrine B. Shakespearean
C. Spenserian D. Petrarchan

3. *The Anatomy of Melancholy* is written by:
A. Robert Burton B. John Dryden
C. Thomas Dekker D. Milton

4. *Doctor Faustus* is a story of:
A. a scientist
B. revenge
C. the Renaissance love of power
D. a greedy Jew

5. Marlowe invented:
A. sprung rhythm B. sonnet
C. allegory D. blank verse

6. *Romeo and Juliet* is a:
A. tragedy B. comedy
C. tragi-comedy D. history

7. *Every Man in His Humour* is written by:
A. Ben Jonson B. Dryden
C. John Donne D. Marston

8. Dryden wrote:
A. *Sejanus*
B. *The Compleat Angler*
C. *Aureng-zebe*
D. *Principia*

9. The song *Drink to me only with thine eyes* is written by:
A. Lyly
B. Ben Jonson
C. Shakespeare
D. Spenser

10. The Puritan Parliament closed the theatres in:
A. 1638 B. 1632
B. 1606 D. 1642

11. *The Shoemaker's Holiday* is a play written by:
A. Shakespeare
B. Marlowe
C. Thomas Dekker
D. Marston

12. Ben Jonson's *The Poetaster* is a satire on:
A. Marston and Dekker
B. Marlowe
C. Kyd
D. Greene

13. The main theme of Webster's plays is his:
A. humour
B. satire
C. preoccupation with death
D. social life

14. Marlowe, Kyd, Lyly and Greene were known as:
A. Humorists
B. University Wits
C. The Rivals of Shakespeare
D. The Decadents

15. The person who collaborated with Beaumont for many plays was:
A. Fletcher
B. Shakespeare
C. Marston
D. Greene

16. Herrick, Carew, Suckling and Lovelace were collectively called:
A. Metaphysical Poets
B. Religious Poets
C. Puritans
D. Cavalier Poets

17. The *Horatian Ode* by Andrew Marvel is addressed to:
A. Cromwell B. Charles II
C. Queen Elizabeth D. Shakespeare

18. *Comus* by Milton is a/an:
A. masque B. ode
C. epic D. lyric

19. *Lycidas* is an elegy by Milton on:
A. Arthur Hallam B. Edward King
C. Cromwell D. Ben Jonson

20. *The Compleat Angler* is written by:
A. Milton B. Robert Burton
C. Izaak Walton D. Thomas Fuller

21. *Leviathan* is written by:
A. Milton B. Marvel
C. Thomas Hobbes D. Farquhar

22. *The Pilgrim's Progress* by John Bunyan is a/an:
A. book of philosophy
B. treatise on education
C. masque
D. allegory

23. Samuel Butler's satire on Puritanism is:
A. *Hudibras* B. *Way of the World*
C. *Utopia* D. *Paradise Lost*

24. John Evelyn's *Diary* is famous for:
A. describing major social events of his times
B. describing personal experiences
C. scholarly research
D. noting facts and figures

25. Samuel Pepys' *Diary* is mainly:
A. social B. confessional
C. descriptive D. argumentative

ANSWERS

1	2	3	4	5	6	7	8	9	10
B	C	A	C	D	C	A	C	B	D
11	**12**	**13**	**14**	**15**	**16**	**17**	**18**	**19**	**20**
C	A	C	B	A	D	A	A	B	C
21	**22**	**23**	**24**	**25**					
C	D	A	A	B					

THE EIGHTEENTH CENTURY

THE AUGUSTAN AGE (1700-1740)

In general, the eighteenth century was the age of understanding and enlightenment. The emphasis was on the advancement of the human mind. Sensibility was the guiding principle. This age borrowed the humour and poetic technique of the previous century.

This age is generally called *The Augustan Age* or *The Age of Queen Anne* because the queen patronized the men of letters. The period is also known as the Classical Age. It was an age of tolerance and harmony and was guided by reason. Dryden still wrote and was a contemporary of French authors Corneille, Racine and Moliere. Many English works were translated by the French. Poetry was still for aristocrats and the courts, but prose spread among the common public. People demanded instructions and information and practical hints for living. This led writers to use a simple style to be comprehensible to all.

Poetry

Matthew Prior (1664-1721) began by writing a parody of The Hind and the Panther in which he expounded his opinions on politics. **Sir Samuel Garth (1661-1791)** and **Joseph Addison (1672-1719)** used the heroic couplet of Dryden. Addison described Marlborough's victory at Blenheim in his poem *The Campaign* (1704). But the poetical luminary of the period was **Alexander Pope (1688-1744)**. He polished Dryden's couplet and used it as a weapon of satire, like in the famous *An Essay on Man* (1732-1734). His *An Essay on Criticism* (1711) and *The Rape of the Lock* (1712, 1714) are other great works. The latter is in mock-heroic style and describes the anger of a lady whose lock of hair had been cut off. Pope also translated the Iliad. He wrote *The Dunciad* (1728) to castigate bad poets. His *Imitations of Horace* (1733-1737) is highly admired even today.

Jonathan Swift, usually known as a prose writer, also showed a gift or versification like in his poem *On the Death of Dr. Swift*. **John Gay (1685-1732)** was popular for his fables like *The Hare with Many Friends* and his songs in *The Beggar's Opera.* **Edward Young's (1683-1765)** *The Commaint, or Night Thoughts on Life, Death, and Immortality* (1742), is a poet's delight in meditation underlining the vanity of all earthly glory.

Prose

This period saw an increasing demand for the circulation of facts and ideas among the public. **Daniel Defoe (1659-1731)** was a trail-blazer as a Journalist and his popular works are *The True-Born Englishman* (1701) and *The Shortest Way with the Dissenters* (1702). Defoe wrote the first English novel *Robinson Crusoe* (1719), which is a children's classic or collection of adventure stories. He cultivated the art of reporting and presented his stories as historical narratives which are precise and practical.

Steele, Addison, Swift, Arbuthnot were the other great prose-writers of the time. They introduced a style adorned by figures of speech. The periodicals of Steele and Addison contain essays which deal with practical moral questions and reflect the morals of the time.

Richard Steele (1672-1729) led a dissipated life and was full of remorse for it. He extols the Bible as a guide in life in his work *The Christian Hero*. He launched the journal *The Tatler* in 1709. **Joseph Addison** propagated rational and moderate ideas. He collaborated with Steele on *The Tatler*. Steele then founded *The Spectator* in 1711 and Addison again collaborated. Here they were merely the spectators of the society and its foibles. It epitomizes the whole nation. The character of Sir Roger de Coverley is a masterpiece, a comic personality with eccentricities. Other characters, Sir Andrew Freeport. Will Honeycomb, Captain Sentry capture the imagination of the readers.

Jonathan Swift (1667-1745) enjoyed ridicule rather than correction. He lays bare all the vices of man as something that are beyond correction. He ridiculed the modern authors in his The *Battle of the Books* (1704) and attacked the Papists and Presbyterians in *The Tale of a Tub* (1704). His most popular work is a children's classic, *Gulliver's Travels* (1726), which is also a satire on politics, religions, science and nature of man.

John Arbuthnot (1667-1735) was another humanist and man of wit and is known for his *The History of John Bull* (1712), an amusing allegory on the politics of the time.

During this period a number of deists like Locke, Collins and Tindal propounded a philosophy advocating reasoning rather than superstitious beliefs as advocated by orthodox Christians. Earl of Shaftesbury (1671-1713), Lord Bolingbroke (1678-1751) and Mandeville were other rationalists of the time who wrote many prose works.

THE AGE OF TRANSITION (1740-1800)

Like all other periods of transition, this age was also disturbed and confused. Two movements can be clearly observed in the writings of the time: (*i*) the allegiance to the old order of classicism, and (*ii*) the search after the new order of Romanticism. The period was marked by new learning, new philosophy, growth of historical research and new realism.

This period is also known as the *Age of Johnson* because **Samuel Johnson (1709-1784)**, the greatest English man of letters, flourished during this period. Samuel Johnson was a versatile man of letters translator, journalist, commentator, critic, novelist, biographer and poet. He created two satirical poems, *London* (1738) and *The Vanity of Human Wishes* (1749). He had a supple style and describes his personal reflections in his essays *The Rambler* (1750-1752) and *The Idler* (1758-1760). His *Dictionary of English Language* (1747-1755) shows remarkable precision in definition and a feeling for the correct use of words. Besides the novel *Rasselas, Prince of Abyssinia* (1759) his best works are biographical and literary studies and his edition of *Shakespeare* (1765). His *Lives of the Poets* (1777-1781) is a biographical work. His admirer James Boswell's famous biography of Johnson has made him immortal. He is described here in candid details. His prejudices, excellences and demerits are all laid bare.

Poetry

Poetry showed the influence of Dryden and Pope. It was mainly didactic and satirical and the couplet still was the major form.

Oliver Goldsmith's (1728-1774) *Deserted Village* (1770) is a masterpiece of the period. **James Thomson's (1700-1748)** *The Seasons* (1730) is a praise of the beauties of Nature in all her diversity. Other noteworthy poems of the period are **William Collins' (1721-1759)** *Ode to Evening*, a delightful lyric, and **Thomas Gray's (1716-1771)** *Elegy Written in a Country Churchyard* (1751).

A general belief in human liberty was seen as the French Revolution proceeded. **William Cowper** (1731-1800) who wrote *The Ballad of John Gilpin,* **George Crabbe (1754-1832)**, the Scotsman **Robert Burns (1759-1796)** and the mystic **William Blake (1757-1827)** echoed the sentiments of the period. Burns was a farmer and wrote in original racy dialect thus causing a break from convention. Blake was a visionary and his poems are collected in *Songs of Innocence* (1789) and *Songs of Experience* (1794). In *The Tyger,* he uses the Lamb as a symbol of innocence and of Jesus, and the Tiger as the symbol of evil in the world, of the evil seen in the French Revolution where thousands were sent to the guillotine.

Novel

The period saw the development of the novel. A series of masterpieces came out. In the novel, the author could describe events in detail. Defoe's novels so far were based on strange subjects. Now they concentrated on commonplace events of family life and society. Adventure of earlier novels gave place to character portrayal. The novels were very long and filled with minute details. **Samuel Richardson (1689-1761)** wrote *Pamela, or Virtue Rewarded* (1740) and *Clarissa Harlowe* (1747-1748). **Henry Fielding (1707-1754)** is famous for *Joseph Andrews* (1742) and *Tom Jones* (1749), **Tobias Smollet (1721-1771)** wrote *The Adventures of Roderick*

Random (1748) and *The Expedition of Humphry Clinker* (1771), **Laurence Sterne (1713-1768)** wrote *Tristram Shandy* (1760), and **Oliver Goldsmith** *The Vicar of Wakefield* (1766).

Letter

There were famous letter writers also, like **Lord Chesterfield (1694-1773). Horace Walpole (1719-1797), Thomas Gray and Richardson**. Frequently, a series of letters was bound into book-form. Collections of this kind were the letters of **Lady Mary Wortley Montagu (1689-1762)**, written to Pope from Constantinople, and of Thomas Gray, from the Lake District. Chesterfield's letters to his son contain comments on political and social matters. Richardson's *Pamela* is entirely in letter-form.

Drama

The century was the age of the great novels. Drama lost originality and talent. People saw Shakespeare's plays enacted, but what attracted them was the genius of the actors. However, there were a few good plays written. For instance, Johnson's *Irene* (1749), Fielding's *The Miser*, Goldsmith's anti-sentimental comedy *She Stoops to Conquer* (1773), and Sheridan's *The School for Scandal* (1777) and *The Rivals* (1775).

Historical Work

Towards the last part of the century the history of England was rocked by many revolutionary changes the impact of which were felt in English literature. Till the mid-18th century Victorian England reigned supreme. She was mistress of the seas and her imperial rule covered many colonies. In 1776, America declared her independence and the British Parliament was divided on the issue. Many Britishers favoured the American claims. In 1789, the French Revolution broke out and here too the Britishers were divided into two camps. Inspired by the writings of Rousseau, many believed the Revolution was being fought for the right causes. The Parliament resounded with the speeches of the famous. Some even accused Warren Hastings for his extortion policies in India and some others were against slave-trade.

Treatises on philosophy by **David Hume (1711-1776)** and histories by **William Robertson (1721-1793)** and political economy (*Wealth of Nations*) by **Adam Smith (1723-1790)** came out.

Edmund Burke (1729-1797) read law and began writing to propound his views on human feelings and emotions. His language is as oratorical in Parliament at the trial of Warren Hastings as in his famous writing *A Philosophical Inquiry into the Origin of our Ideas of the Sublime and the Beautiful* (1756).

Other orators who expressed themselves in writing were Tom Paine, Godwin and Jeremy Bentham. **William Godwin (1756-1836)** advocated the elimination of government in *Enquiry Concerning Political Justice* (1793). He proscribed law, marriage, gratitude, everything that limited liberty. His monumental work is *The Decline and Fall of the Roman Empire* (1776-1788) in which he describes the growth of Christianity and his belief in reason rather than the divine. At the same time **William Paley (1743-1805)** wrote *A View of the Evidences of Christianity* (1794) to prove the existence of miracles by logic.

MAJOR AUTHORS AND THEIR WORKS

Alexander Pope (1688-1744)

Pastorals
An Essay on Criticism
Windsor Forest
The Rape of the Lock
Dunciad
Translation of Iliad and Odyssey
To Lord Bathrust
On the Use of the Riches
An Essay on Man
Epistle to Dr. Arbuthnot
Of the Knowledge and Characters of Men
Of the Characters of Women
The Messiah
Satires and Epistles of Horace Imitated

Matthew Prior (1664-1721)
Solomon on the Vanity of the World
Alma : or the Progress of the Mind
The Town and Country Mouse

John Gay (1685-1732)
Fables
The Shepherd's Week
The Rural Sports
Trivia
The Beggar's Opera
The Streets of London

Edward Young (1683-1765)
Night Thoughts

Dr. Samuel Johnson (1709-1784)
The Vanity of Human Wishes
London
The Lives of the Poets
Preface to Shakespeare
Dictionary of the English Language
A Journey to the Western Islands of Scotland
The Rambler
Rasselas
Prince of Abyssinia
The Life of Savage
The Adventurer
The Idler

Daniel Defoe (1661-1731)
Robinson Crusoe
Mall Flanders
Colonel Jack
The Memoirs of a Cavalier
Captain Singleton
Journal of the Plague Year
Roxana

Jonathan Swift (1667-1745)
The Battle of the Books
A Tale of a Tub
Gulliver's Travels
Journal to Stella
The Drapier's Letters
Cadenus and Vanessa

Joseph Addison (1672-1719)
The Spectator
The Campaign
Public Credit
The Vision of Mirza
Cato
Rosamond
The Drummer

Richard Steele (1672-1729)
The Tatler
The Guardian
The Funeral
The Lying Lover
The Tender Husband
The Conscious Lover

Thomas Gray (1716-1771)
Elegy Written in a Country Churchyard
On a Distant Prospect of Eton College
On the Death of a Favourite Cat
The Bard
The Progress of Poesy
The Fatal Sisters
The Descent of Odin

MULTIPLE CHOICE QUESTIONS

1. *The Hind and the Panther* is a parody about:
A. religion
B. society
C. politics
D. human beings in general

2. Which poem is in mock-heroic style?
A. *The Rape of the Lock*
B. *The Christian Hero*
C. *On the Death of Dr. Swift*
D. *The Hare with Many Friends*

3. Who was the first journalist of the age?
A. Dryden B. Daniel Defoe
C. Swift D. Arbuthnot

4. Who wrote the first English dictionary?
A. Goldsmith B. Boswell
C. Webster D. Samuel Johnson

5. Lord Chesterfield is famous as a:
A. Novelist B. Letter-writer
C. Playwright D. Poet

6. The novel written in epistolary or letter form is:
A. *Joseph Andrews* B. *Pamela*
C. *Vicar of Wakefield* D. *Tom Jones*

7. Johnson's biographer was:
A. Boswell B. Irene
C. Swift D. Edmund Burke

8. A play which describes heroes as virtues personified and is full of pompous speeches is:
A. Heroic play
B. Sentimental Comedy
C. Anti-Sentimental Comedy
D. Tragi-Comedy

9. Edmund Burke was:
A. poet and scholar B. playwright
C. orator and writer D. lexicographer

10. *The Decline and Pall of the Roman Empire* is written by:
A. Paley B. Smith
C. Johnson D. Godwin

11. The main reason why papers came out in Queen Anne's time was:
A. People were hungry for information about current events
B. People wanted to contact businessmen
C. People wanted to improve their writing style
D. People liked sensational fiction stories

12. The characters Sir Andrew Freeport, Captain Sentry and Sir Roger are featured in:
A. *The Tatler*
B. *The London Gazette*
C. *The Spectator*
D. *The Review*

13. The countries that influenced British literature and art in the 18th century were:
A. Germany and Holland
B. Sweden and Norway
C. Austria and France
D. France and Italy

14. The religious revival of the 18th century started by John and Charles Weslay was known as:
A. Methodism B. Deism
C. Presbyterianism D. Evangelism

15. *The Hind and the Panther Transvers'd to the Story of the Country and City Mouse* is a poem by:
A. Dryden B. Matthew Prior
C. Pope D. John Gay

16. John Gay is famous for a musical drama named:
A. *The Beggar's Opera* B. *Polly*
C. *The Secretary* D. *Fables*

17. *The Ballad of John Gilpin* is written by:
A. Thomas Gray B. William Cowper
C. William Blake D. Robert Burns

18. The son of a British Prime Minister is famous for his letters and *The Castle of Otranto*, a gruesome play. His (the son's) name was:
A. Robert Walpole B. Horace Walpole
C. William Pitt D. Churchill

19. *Wealth of Nations* is written by:
A. Joshua Reynolds B. Adam Smith
C. Godwin D. David Hume

20. Sheridan was a:
A. poet B. dramatist
C. novelist D. musician

21. *The Rivals* is a play by:
A. Sheridan B. Goldsmith
C. Johnson D. David Garrick

22. *Origin of our Ideas of the Sublime and the Beautiful* is an essay by:
A. Edmund Burke B. Godwin
C. Thomas Paine D. Hume

23. The greatest Scottish poet of the 18th century is:
A. Robert Burns B. Waltor Scott
C. William Cowper D. John Gay

24. The lines, *"O My luve's like a red, red rose,/That's newly sprung in June;...."* are attributed to:
   A. William Blake
   B. Fergusson
   C. Robert Burns
   D. Macpherson

25. Who was known as the "Man of Feeling" after his sentimental novel *The Man of Feeling*?
   A. Francis Burney
   B. Ann Rediliffe
   C. Matthew Lewis
   D. Henry Mackenzie

ANSWERS

1	2	3	4	5	6	7	8	9	10
C	A	B	D	B	B	A	B	C	D
11	**12**	**13**	**14**	**15**	**16**	**17**	**18**	**19**	**20**
A	C	D	A	B	A	B	B	B	B
21	**22**	**23**	**24**	**25**					
A	A	A	C	D					

THE NINETEENTH CENTURY

THE ROMANTIC AGE (1798-1830)

The eighteenth century literature of England was inspired by reason, but the nineteenth century was the age of imagination. The Preface to the *Lyrical Ballads* by William Wordsworth and Samuel Taylor Coleridge in 1798, heralds the period of English Romanticism. The authors of this work were disgusted with the excesses of the French Revolution, they condemned the Rationalist Movement. England turned away from the literature of France and transferred her sympathies to Germany. The philosophical doctrine of Romanticism was inspired by Germany. Romanticism was essentially poetic. Although poles apart in their political beliefs, Wordsworth and Shelley both considered the poet as the guide, prophet and seer of mankind.

Poetry

For the great Romantics — Wordsworth, Shelley, Keats, Byron — the study of the wondrous world of feelings, senses, instincts, of Man' relation to Nature, were of prime importance. Romanticism is shot with *metaphysics*. As M. Lanson puts it, *tout traverse de frissons metaphysique* Alexander Pope had used poetry to depict the thoughts of the philosophers in his *Essay on Man*. The Romantics, dedicated to Romantic imagination — *the esemplastic imagination* as Coleridge called it — were convinced that what was revealed to their poetic intuitions, was right, the Truth. Mysterious forces divine in origin moved the earth, not cold rationalist cause and effect. Pope's couplet was dull and too precise governed by convention. The Romantics sought a lyrical form using unusual images and association of words. They found models for these in the Renaissance and the old popular poetry.

William Wordsworth (1770-1850) is aptly called the "High Priest of Nature". He saw Nature as the *'Stern Daughter of the voice of God'*, man's conscience whose balmy presence never disappointed. He was born in 1770 in the picturesque Lake District of England. Here he spent happy years of his childhood in communion with God and Nature. After study at Cambridge, he went to France in 1791 and was enthused by the cause of the Revolution. But when the Reign of Terror came and thousands died at the guillotine, his fine sensibilities, his search for human equality and peace received a rude shock. He engaged himself in the philosophy of William Godwin for sometime. Finding no solution to the problem of human pain, he finally turned to the study of Nature. In the poems of the Lyrical Ballads he describes the mundane happenings of country life, the activities of humble people. He used their common dialect with its flawed grammar as his style. He decries the coming of the industrial era which mechanized English life. With no ornament, his poetry draws its power from the intensity of his feelings and imagination, In The Prelude (1805), a long poem, Wordsworth set out to look back and retrospect on his life. He follows the growth, the turnings of his poetic genius since childhood, ruminates on his errors and recalls the corrective lessons of Nature. In his great moral poem, The Excursion (1814), he uses a philosophy to refute the pessimism that the Revolution had brought.

Samuel Taylor Coleridge (1772-1834) was Wordsworth's "Spirits Brother". He was guided by the same philosophy of the imagination. While Wordsworth's imagination gave him a special vision of the common things of rustic life, Coleridge stirred up the supernatural. To appreciate his poetry peopled with strange, translunary beings like *The Ancient Mariner,* one needs *'that willing suspension of disbelief that constitutes poetic faith'*. In *The Rime of the Ancient Mariner*, Coleridge describes the strange adventures of a sailor in a ship. Having killed an albatross, the mariner suffers from hallucinations. The poem, with strange rhythm and cadences, creates a wondrous world. Coleridge was a master of lyrical style. His other famous poems are *Christabel* (1816), and *Kubla Khan* (1816). *Kubla Khan* was written as a result of an opium dream and described the wonderful, strange palace of the Chinese king, Kubla Khan. Coleridge certainly fulfils the meaning of *'Renaissance'* as *'a renascence of wonder'*.

Robert Southey (1774-1843) wrote poetry based on outlandish settings and myths like *Thalaba, the Destroyer* (1801), *The Curse of Kehama* (1810), and *Roderick, the Last of the Goths* (1814). His descriptions are rich and graphic and he uses a great variety of verse forms. He wrote a number of poems in ballad form.

Walter Scott (1771-1832) also had an interest in ballad poetry. He translated the *Lenore* from German (1796). His *The Minstrelsy of the Scottish Border* (1802) shows a great romantic interest in the Middle Ages and the days of chivalry.

The second generation of great Romantic poets include Shelley, Keats and Byron.

Percy Bysshe Shelley (1792-1822) gave up his title and wealth to write poetry. His aim was to awaken mankind to the millenium, the coming future, which would remove human anguish and sorrow. His famous ode, *Ode to the West Wind* is an impassioned exhortation — *Make me thy lyre eu'n as the forest is ...... If Winter comes, can Spring be far behind?* He came under the influence of William Godwin, the philosopher. He proclaimed himself an atheist at the age of 21. His works include *Queen Mab* (1813), *Prometheus Unbound* (1818-1819), which shows human revolt against false gods, *To a Skylark, Adonais* (1821), which is an elegy to Keats, and The Cenci (1819). Shelley's style is a mixture of abstractions and visual images.

John Keats (1795-1821) was the most sensuous of the great Romantic poets. As we read his poems, richly laden with imagery and associations, all the senses are stirred up the visual, olfactory, auditory and tactile. It is said he tasted pepper in wine to describe certain lines. His famous odes are *To a Nightingale, To Autumn* and *On a Grecian Urn.*

Lord George Gordon Byron (1788-1824) was a wealthy nobleman who shunned the popular beliefs of his times. He was notorious as a dilletante. At the age of 19, he wrote Hours of Idleness (1807). With the publication of *Childe Harold's Pilgrimage* (1812) he became famous. Childe Harold was Byron himself, the figure of the disillusioned man, the hero fed up of pleasures and debauches. He lives an outlawed life and is rebellious in spirit. He took on more incarnations in his poems, *The Giaour* (1813), *The Corsair* (1814), *The Siege of Corinth* (1815). In these he displayed his own passions and eccentricities. In 1816, divorced from his wife, he retired to Switzerland and then to Italy. He wrote a number of plays — *Manfred* (1817), *Cain* (1821) and *The Deformed Transformed* (1824). The crowning work was his lyrical, satirical *Don Juan*

(1819-1823). He went to Greece to fight for its independence, but died of illness. His satire is political, against England and also against English hypocrisy and cant. His licentious descriptions caused scandals. Don Juan, his magnum opus, is written in ottava rima or eight-line stanzas and is full of wit and mockery.

Thomas Moore (1779-1852), Thomas Campbell (1777-1844), Samuel Rogers (1763-1855), James Hogg (1770-1835), Walter Savage Landor (1775-1864) and **Leigh Hunt (1784-1859)** were other poets of the time.

Novel

Novels of terror and mystery prospered from 1800 to 1830. **Matthew Gregory Lewis** (1775-1818) wrote *Tales of Terror* (1800) and *Tales of Wonder* (1801). **Charles Lamb's (1775-1834)** *Tales from Shakespeare* (1807) is very popular even today. *Mrs Shelley,* the poet's wife, wrote the classic *Frankenstein* in which a scientist creates a monster that turns on its creator and destroys his most beloved ones. It is a novel of prophetic fear. **Miss Mary Mitford** wrote on country life and **Maria Edgeworth (1767-1849)** brought out educational novels like Belinda (1801) and *Tales of Fashionable Life* — novels for children.

Jane Austen (1775-1817) produced half a dozen novels which are drawing-room comedies of life. They study the passion and distress of young ladies and the life of country-folk. The novels — *Pride and Prejudice* (1813), *Sense and Sensibility* (1811), *Emma* (1816), *Persuasion* (1818), *Mansfield Park* (1814), *Northanger Abbey* (1818) — are realistic and witty, full of bracing dialogue.

Walter Scott was Scotland's greatest novelist recreating the past of his country's myths and ballads with rich humour. *Waverly* (1814), *Guy Mannering* (1815), *The Heart of Midlothian* (1818) contain history and direct observation. In *Ivanhoe* (1820), he describes the history of England in the days of the legendary Richard, the Lion Heart. *Kenilworth* (1821), *Quentin Dunward* (1823) were his other famous historical novels. He imbued the Romantic era with a love for the Middle Ages.

Prose/Criticism

The Romantic Age saw a number of reviewers and critics like **Jeremy Bentham (1748-1832)**, who expounded utilitarian doctrines, **Sydney Smith (1771-1845)**, and **William Cobbett (1762-1835)**. Coleridge, the poet, interpreted the doctrines of Kant and Schelling which show the distinction between pure reason and practical reason.

Lamb, Hazlitt, De Quincey and Leigh Hunt were Romantic critics of literature. **Charles Lamb's** essays on Shakespeare's tragedies state that we cannot do justice to them by staging them since the passions which are to be felt in their intensity are torn to tatters by the gimmickry of the actors. **William Hazlitt's (1778-1830)** criticism of some of Shakespeare's characters like Falstaff — *he laughs three inches below the flesh* — is a masterpiece. Coleridge's famous work of criticism, *Biographia Literaria* (1817), marvellously analyses Wordsworth's poetry. The Romantics believed that Shakespeare's art was organic like a work of Nature and *"esemplastic"* — able to blend different elements by imagination. **Thomas De Quincey's (1785-1859)** style is penetrating and incisive when criticizing the poets in *The Confessions of an English Opium Eater* (1821).

MAJOR AUTHORS AND THEIR WORKS

William Wordsworth (1770-1850)

The Lyrical Ballads
The Prelude
The Excursion
Tintern Abbey
Ode on Intimations of Immortality
Michael
The Solitary Reaper
Loadamia
Ode to Duty
To Milton
The Leech-Gatherer
Upon Westminster Abbey
The Rainbow

We Are Seven
The World Is Too Much with Us
To the Cuckoo
The Daffodils
Lucy Gray
Simon Lee
Early Spring
Strange Fits of Passion Have I Known

Walter Scott (1771-1832)

The Bride of Lammermoor
Ivanhoe
Quentin Durward
The Heart of midlothian
Old Mortality
The Antiquity
Guy Mannering
Waverly
Rob Roy
Kenilworth
Red Gauntlet
The Black Dwarf
The Monastery
The Abbot
The Pirate
The Fortunes of Night
The Betrothed
The Talisman
Woodstock
Lives of the Novelists
Life of Napoleon
Tales of Grandfather
The Lay of the Last Minstrel
The Minstrelsy of the Scottish Border
Marmion
The Lady of the Lake
Rockeby

Robert Southey (1774-1843)

Joan of Arc
Wat Tyler
After Blenheim
The Holly Tree
The Scholar
A Vision of Judgement
Madoc
Life of Nelson
Thalaba the Destroyer
Roderick
The Curse of Kehama

S.T. Coleridge (1772-1834)

Biographia Literaria
Table Talk
Aids to Reflection
Christabel
Kubla Khan
The Rime of the Ancient Mariner
France : An Ode
Destiny of Nations
Frost at Midnight
Dejection : An Ode
Youth and Age
Religious Musings

Lord Byron (1788-1824)

Childe Harold's Pilgrimage
Don Juan
The Bride of Abydos
Manfred
The Giaour
Hours of Idleness
The Vision of Judgement
The Prisoner of Chillon
Lara
Marino Faliero
English Bards and Scotch Reviewers
The Siege of Corinth
The Corsair
Cain

P.B. Shelley (1792-1822)

On the Necessity of Atheism
The Revolt of Islam
Prometheus Unbound
The Mask of Anarchy
Hellas

The Cenci
The Witch of Atlas
The Indian Serenade
Ozymandias of Egypt
Epipsychidion
Alaster
Queen Mab
Adonais
Ode to the West Wind
The Cloud
Ode to a Skylark
O World! O Life! O Time!
Defence of Poetry (a Prose Work)
To Night
The Sensitive Plant
A Lament

John Keats (1795-1821)

Endymion
Lamia
Hyperion
The Eve of St. Agnes
Isabella
The Eve of St. Mark
La Belle Dame Sans Merci
Ode to a Nightingale
Ode to Autumn
Ode On a Grecian Urn
Ode to Psyche
On Melancholy
On First Looking into Chapman's Homer
Bright Star

Jane Austen (1775-1871)

Sense and Sensibility
Pride and Prejudice
Mansfield Park
Emma
Persuasion
Northanger Abbey

Charles Lamb (1775-1834)

Essays of Elia
The Last Essays of Elia
John Woodvil
Tales from Shakespeare
Specimens of English Dramatic Poets
The English Comic Writers
The Old Familiar Faces

William Hazlitt (1778-1830)

Characters of Shakespeare's Plays
The English Poets
The English Comic Writers
The Dramatic Literature of the Age of Elizabeth
The Round Table : A Collection of Essays
Table Talk on Men and Manners
The Spirit of the Age

Thomas De Quincey (1785-1859)

Confessions of an English Opium Eater
Joan of Arc
English Mail Coach
Dream Fugue
Murder Considered as One of the Fine Arts
Suspiria de Profundis

Samuel Rogers (1763-1855)

Pleasures of Memory
Italy

James Hogg (1770-1835)

Kilmeny
The Queen's Wake

Thomas Campbell

Pleasures of Hope
Theodoric
Gertrude of Wyoming
Lachiel
Lord Ullin's Daughter
The Last Man
Ye Mariners of England
Hohenlinden
The Battle of Baltic

Thomas Moore (1779-1852)

Lalla Rookh
Irish Melodies

Leigh Hunt (1784-1859)

Story of Rimini
Autobiography

Walter Savage Landor (1775-1864)
Gebir
Hellenics
Imaginary Conversations
The Citations of William Shakespeare
Pericles and Aspasia

THE VICTORIAN ERA (1830-1880)

During this era, the conflict between religion and science, mysticism and rationalism, became intense. There were those who, influenced by Darwin's theory of evolution as expounded in his *On the Origin of Species,* lost their faith in the biblical explanation of man's descent from Adam and Eve. They wanted to shun dogma and accept the scientific spirit. Others lamented the loss of faith and the rising consumer values. Mathew Arnold in his poem *Dover Beach* writes:

"The Sea of Faith was once too at the full.....
But now I only hear its long withdrawing melancholy roar......"

Prose

Carlyle and Ruskin echoed the prophecies of the Romantic era in their prose works. **Thomas Carlyle (1795-1881)**, the Scotsman, abandoned orthodoxy and came under the influence of the German writers Schiller, Novalis, Richter and Goethe. His work *Sartor Resartus* (1833-1834) is a sort of allegory based on a German professor who has written a treatise on clothes. He penetrates through the clothes to the essence of the man's being. Carlyle was also a historian. His historical works are *The French Revolution* (1837) and *The History of Frederich II of Prussia, called frederik the Great* (1858-1865). These are satirical and prophetic, expounding how man and society are organized. He was against materialism and praised the Magi and prophets of the past. He advocates strength and power.

John Ruskin (1819-1900) was indignant about the ugliness of existence brought in by industrialism and the machine. *Unto This Last* (1860), which influenced Gandhiji's economic theories, describes his disgust for soulless labour. He was a student of arts. *Modern Painters* (1843, 1860) is about landscape painters like Turner. He also wrote *The Seven Lamps of Architecture* (1849) and *The Stones of Venice* (1851-1853), praising Gothic art.

Matthew Arnold (1822-1888), the poet, wanted his countrymen to inculcate classical qualities to become harmonious in morals and in creative works. The English must break away from their insular moorings by imbibing the teachings of Greece and the French. He is *the detector-general of the intellectual failings of his own nation*. Poetry, according to him, is important in character formation, and culture is *"the minister of the sweetness and light essential to the perfect character"*. His works include *On translating Homer, The Study of Celtic Literature and Essays in Criticism* (1865, 1889). He wrote St. Paul and Protestantism advocating that dogma should be removed from Christianity and it should adjust itself to the findings of science.

A number of philosophers, historians and scholars wrote in this period. Charles Darwin's theory of evolution dramatically affected human thought. **John Stuart Mill (1806-1873)** expounded the processes of logic and political economy. **Herbert Spencer (1820-1903)** and **Thomas Henry Huxley (1825-1895)** were scientists. **Thomas Babington Macaulay (1800-1859)** was a poet, essayist and historian who advocated English education in India. The Oxford Movement gave rise to religious writers like **John Keble (1792-1866)** and **John Henry Newman (1801-1890)**. Newman's famous work is *Apologia pro Vita Sua* (1864) in which he explains why he had converted to the Roman Church.

Novel

The transition from Walter Scott's novels to Charles Dicken's first novel in 1836 is a great one. When Queen Victoria ascended the throne, **Frederick Marryat (1792-1848)** produced sea-stories; **Edward Bulwer Lytton (1803-1873)** wrote about Byronic heroes, attractive criminals and historical novels like *The Last Days of Pompeii* (1834); **Benjamin Disraeli**

(1804-1881), the Prime Minister of England, wrote *Coningsby: or The New Generation* (1844) and *Sybil: or The Two Nations* (1845) to show that the aristocrats of the society had a duty towards the unfortunate ones. In Disraeli's novels, one finds the politics of Queen Victoria's reign.

Perhaps the greatest Victorian novelist is **Charles Dickens (1812-1870)**, whose identification with the underdog in society was unmatched by any writer. One reason for this is his own troubled childhood led in penury under the shadow of a father who was in debtor's prison. The part of his life comes through vividly in his novel *David Copperfield* (1849-1850) which is also an indictment of the cruel, unimaginative schools of his times. He was a master craftsman in character delineation. A host of characters and their dialogues have become household in the English-speaking world. Thus the incorrigible optimist Micawber, Geakle, Pickwick, Fagin and others are types of characters that may be seen all around us anywhere. Dickens had a forgiving sense of humour. He never let bitterness creep into his recreations of painful events of the past. Among his famous novels are: *Pickwick Papers* (1836; in the picaresque style), *Barnaby Rudge* (1841) and *A Tale of Two Cities* (1859; based on the French Revolution), *Oliver Twist* (1837) and *Hard Times* (1854); novels exposing social conditions. He has a picturesque style and concrete imagination.

William Makepeace Thackeray (1811-1863) made a penetrating analysis of upper middle class and aristocratic society. He was a master of irony. In *The Book of Snobs* (1849), he ridicules the tendency to fawn on nobility and to imitate their manners. *Vanity Fair* (1847-1848), *History of Pendennis* (1848-1850), *The Newcomes* (1853-1855), *The History of Henry Esmond* (1852) and *The Virginians* (1857-1859) are pictures of contemporary life in which he depicts human eccentricities and follies. He was adept at reproducing jargon and idiolects.

The Romantic spirit was still alive in the works of the Bronte sisters. **Charlotte Bronte (1816-1855)** wrote *Jane Eyre* (1847), the story of a governess in a terrifying house. Her sister **Emily Bronte (1818-1848)** wrote *The Wuthering Heights* (1847), set in a wild landscape. Powerful passions and characters have made this one of the greatest novels of all times.

George Eliot (1819-1880), a pen-name for Mary Ann Evans, wrote Adam Bede (1859), the story of a girl who was forced to murder her own baby. *The Mill on the Floss* (1860) and *Romola* (1863) are other novels by her. In *Middlemarch, a Study of Provincial Life* (1871-1872), the novelist builds up, from the lives of a great number of deeply studied characters, the complex picture of the life of a small town.

Poetry

The poetry of this period still shows the influence of the Romantic Era. **Alfred, Lord Tennyson (1809-1892)** was an eclectic, selecting the best of his forerunners. He was first interested in style and metre, but later on ideas started interesting him. A great many poems by him are flawlessly beautiful. If *The Lotus Eaters* is softly languorous, *Ulysses* has a striking severity. Tennyson also experienced the intellectual crisis of his times and shared its anxieties. For instance, *The Princess* (1847) is occupied with the question of feminism. *In Memoriam* (1850) is one of his most beautiful poems. It is an elegy on the premature death of his friend Arthur Hallam. It concerns itself with the belief in immortality, the conflict between the hopes of Christianity and the rationalism of science. It is composed of octosyllabic quatrains. He shows a type of Byronic revolt in Locksley Hall (1886) and Maud (1855). In *Idylls of the King* (1859, 1869, 1889) he took Arthurian legends as his theme.

Robert Browning (1812-1889) was famous for using the technique of dramatic monologue in his poems. Through the protagonists of his poems he gives vent to his feelings, passions and aspirations. Thus in *Paracelsus* (1835), he describes the highly ambitious hero who wanted to transform man's life. We find here Browning's views on truth and philosophy. His other poems include *Sordello* (1840), *Pippa Passes* (1841), *My Last Duchess, Porphyria's Lover* and his masterpiece, *The Ring and the Book* (1868-1869). In his works we find an excess of thought and a rare vocabulary. He uses blank verse dexterously. His brusque speech, broken syntax and uneven rhythm are in contrast to Tennyson's. As Pound and Eliot have said, Browning brought verse nearer to modern colloquial speech. Browning's characters are remote in time and culture. Some of these are Rabbi Ben Ezra, Fra Lippo Lippi and Andrea del Sarto. In *The Ring and the Book* he takes as his subject an Italian crime and explores the minds of all his characters. He strikes a note of hope in his poems. The lines *"God's in his heaven/ And all's well with the world"* lay bare his beliefs. But in general, Browning is considered a difficult poet.

Matthew Arnold (1822-1888) was a reflective poet with a melancholic bent. A deep brooding pensiveness informs his poetry. Dover Beach shows his concern with the loss of faith in a world of science. His epic poem *Sohrab and Rustum, Tristram and Iseult, The Scholar Gypsy* are other famous works.

Dante Gabriel Rossetti, William Morris and Algernon Charles Swinburne together are known as the Pre-Raphaelite poets. They affected Raphael, the Renaissance painter, in their desire to paint sonorous wordpictures which may not have much content to conveyor any philosophy to reveal. It was in accordance with the aestheticism of Ruskin. In fact Rossetti and Morris were painters as well as poets. They worshipped beauty like John Keats did. Robert Buchanan attacked these poets as belonging to *the fleshly school of poetry.*

Dante Gabriel Rossetti (1828-1882) translated the Italian poet Dante's *Vita Nuova*. His *The Blessed Damozel* is an exquisite poem and his best sonnets are contained in *The House of Life* in which he extols his young and beautiful wife. They are full of rich sounds and images and mystic symbols. Rossetti was inspired by the ballads of the Middle Ages. Like the primitive Italian painters, he uses rich colours and depicts warm sensuous feelings.

William Morris (1834-1896) was enchanted by Gothic art of the Middle Ages. His poems drew inspiration from those of Froissart, Chaucer and Malory. He borrowed stories from Scandinavia and Iceland. His poems are like frescoes and are very lyrical in quality. The famous ones are *The Earthly Paradise* (1868-1870) and *The Life and Death of Jason* (1867). These works show rhythm and use of archaism. He strove to bring civilization back to art from the utilitarian industrialization.

Algernon Charles Swinburne (1837-1909) was a prodigy. He was a musician, and a sonority of rhymes filled his poetry. He took romantic themes like revolt against society, hatred of monarchy and struggle against traditional morality. His *Atalanta in Calydon* (1865) is his masterpiece and is known for its choral passages.

To these poets of the Victorian Age must be added the name of **Edward Fitzgerald (1809-1883)** whose **The Rubaiyat of Omar Khayyam (1859)** is a classic.

MAJOR AUTHORS AND THEIR WORKS

Alfred Lord Tennyson (1809-1892)

The Princess
In Memoriam
Maud
Enoch Arden
Idylls of the King
Queen Mary
Harold
Backet
Akbar's Tomb
Crossing the Bar
Locksley Hall
Locksley Hall Sixty Years After
Dora
Poems by Two Brothers
The Falcon
The Cup
Poems Chiefly Lyrical
Ulysses
Poems Chiefly Lyrical
Ulysses
The Lotos-Eaters
The Death of Oenone and Other Poems

Robert Browning (1812-1889)

Pauline
Paracelsus
Strafford
Sordello
Bells and Pomegranates
Christmas Eve and Easter Day
Men and Women
Dramatis Personae
The King and the Book
Asolando
Pippa Passes
Fra Lippo Lippi
Andrea del Sarto
King Victor and King Charles
Dramatic Lyrics
Dramatic Romances and Lyrics

Matthew Arnold (1822-1888)

Sohrab and Rustum
Tristram and Iseult
Balder Dead
Empedocles on Etna
Stanzas from the Grande Chartreuse
The Strayed Reveller and Other Poems
Dover Beach
Thyrsis
Scholar Gypsy
On Translating Homer
New Poems
On the Study of Celtic Literature
Essays in Criticism
Culture and Anarchy
Literature and Dogma
Mixed Essays
Friendship's Garland
God and the Bible

D.G. Rossetti (1828-1882)

The Blessed Damozel
World's Worth
Ave
The White Ship
Sister Helen
Eden Bower
The House of Life
Ballads and Sonnets

Christina Georgina Rossetti (1830-1894)

The Goblin Market
The Prince's Market
A Pageant and Other Poems

William Morris (1834-1896)

The Defence of Guenevere
The Life and Death of Jason
The Earthly Paradise
A Dream of John Bull
News from Nowhere
A Tale of the House of the Wolfings
The Roots of the Mountains
The Story of the Glittering Plain
The Sundering Flood
Hope and Fears for Art
Signs of Change

A.C. Swinburne (1837-1909)

Atalanta in Calydon
Erechtheus
Tristram of Lyonesse
Chasteland
Bathwell
Mary Stuart
William Blake : A Critique
A Study of Shakespeare
A Study of Ben Jonson
Songs Before Sunrise

Edward Fitzgerald (1809-1883)

Euphranor : A Dialogue on Youth
Translation of Rubaiat

Thomas Carlyle (1795-1881)

Sartor Resartus
The French Revolution
Heroes and Hero-Worship
Past and Present
The Letters and Speeches of Oliver Cromwell

Latter-day Pamphlets
Life of John Sterling
History of Frederick the Great
Chartism

John Ruskin (1819-1900)

The Modern Painters
Salsette and Elephanta
The Seven Lamps of Architecture
The Stones of Venice
The Two Paths
Unto This Last
Munera Pulveris
Time and Tide by Wear and Tyne
Fors Clavigera
Sesame and Lilies
The Crown of Wild Olive

T.B. Macaulay (1800-1859)

History of England from the Accession of James II
Lays of Ancient Rome

Charles Dickens (1812-1870)

Pickwick Papers
Nicholas Nickleby
Martin Chuzzlewit
Dombey and Son
David Copperfield
Bleak House
A Tale of Two Cities
Great Expectations
Our Mutual Friend
Edwin Drood
Oliver Twist
Little Dorrit
Baraby Rudge
The Uncommercial Traveller
A Christmas Carol
Hard Times
Old Curiosity Shop

William Makepeace Thackeray (1811-1863)

Vanity Fair
Barry Lyndon
Pendennis
Henry Esmond
The New Comes
The Virginians
Adventures of Philip
The Book of Snobs
The History of Pendennis
Lovel the Widower
The Round about Papers
The English Humorists of the Eighteenth Century
The Four Georges
Rebecca and Rowena
The Rose and The Ring
Ivanhoe—the Legend of the Rhine

George Meredith (1828-1909)

The Ordeal of Richard Feveral
Evan Harrington
Emilia in England
Rhoda Fleming
Vittoria
The Adventures of Harry Richmond
Diana of the Crossways
One of Our Conquerous
The Amazing Marriage
The Egoist
Beauchamp's Career
The Tragic Comedians

Charlotte Bronte (1816-1855)

Jane Eyre
Shirley
The Professor
Villette

Emily Bronte (1818-1848)

Wuthering Heights

George Eliot (1810-1880)
(Mary Ann Evans)

Adam Bede
The Mill on the Floss
Silas Marner
Scenes of Clerical Life
Life of Jesus

Romola
Fleix Holt the Radical
Daniel Deronda
Middlemarch

Benjamin Disraeli (1804-1881)

Vivian Gray
Sybil : Or the Two Nations
The Voyage of Captain Popavilla
Henrietta Temple
Coningsby : or the New Generation
Tancred : or the New Crusade
The Wondrous Tale of Alroy and the Rise of Iskander
Contarini Fleming : A Psychological Autobiography

R.L. Stevenson (1850-1894)

Travels with a Donkey in the Cevennes
An Inland Voyage
Virginibus Pueresque
New Arabian Nights
Treasure Island
The Strange Case of Dr. Jackyll and Mr. Hyde
Kidnapped
The Black Arrow
The Master of Ballantrae
Catriona
Underwords
A Child's Garden of Verses

Thomas Hardy (1840-1828)

Under the Greenwood Tree
Desperate Remedies
A Pair of Blue Eyes
Two on a Tower
Far From the Madding Crowd
The Return of the Native
The Mayor of Casterbridge
Tess of the D'Urbervilles
Jude the Obscure
The Hand of Ethelberta
The Trumpet Major
The Woodlanders
The Well-beloved
A Laodicean
A Group of Noble Dames
Life's Little Ironies
Wessex Poems
The Dynasts
A Changed Man
Winter Words
The Waiting Supper and Other Tales

MULTIPLE CHOICE QUESTIONS

1. *"Bliss was it in that dawn to be alive, But to be young was very heaven!"* These lines have been attributed to:
   A. Wordsworth   B. Shelley
   C. Keats   D. Byron
2. *The Essays of Elia* is written by
   A. De Quincey   B. Charles Lambs
   C. Hazlitt   D. Cobbett
3. The publication of Wordsworth's Lyrical Ballads coincides with the
   A. French Revolution
   B. War for American Independence
   C. Industrial Revolution
   D. Invention of the steam engine
4. The poem Coleridge wrote as a result of an opium-induced dream was:
   A. *The Solitary Reaper*
   B. *Christabel*
   C. *Rime of the Ancient Mariner*
   D. *Kubla Khan*
5. Byron's poem, *The Vision of Judgment,* is an attack on the works of:
   A. Coleridge   B. Keats
   C. Shelley   D. Southey
6. *Childe Harold* is a poem by:
   A. Coleridge   C. Southey
   B. Byron   D. Shelley

7. *Prometheus Unbound* is written by:
A. Browning B. Tennyson
C. Shelley D. Spenser

8. *Adonais* is an elegy on:
A. Keats B. Arthur Hallam
C. Byron D. Shakespeare

9. John Keats is famous for his:
A. odes B. plays
C. blank verse D. masques

10. *Tales from Shakespeare* was written by:
A. Coleridge
B. Lamb and his sister Mary
C. Wordsworth
D. Byron

11. *Confessions of an English Opium Eater* is written by:
A. De Quincey B. Coleridge
C. Byron D. Leigh Hunt

12. William Godwin was a:
A. Psychologist B. Statesman
C. Scotsman D. Philosopher

13. *Don Juan* by Byron is written in:
A. blank verse B. rhyming couplets
C. ottava rima D. quatrains

14. The educational novel written by Maria Edgeworth is:
A. *Waverly* B. *Belinda*
C. *Ivanhoe* D. *Northanger Abbey*

15. Coleridge's *Biographia Literaria* critically analyzes the works of:
A. Byron B. Wordsworth
C. Keats D. Shelley

16. *The Stones of Venice* is a book about:
A. History of Venice
B. Landscapes
C. Romantic Literature
D. Gothic Art

17. Hopkins and Patmore were:
A. religious poets B. nature poets
C. war poets D. critics

18. Swinburne, Rossetti and Morris together were known as the:
A. Decadent poets
B. Pre-Raphaelite poets
C. War poets
D. Absurd poets

19. Christina Rossetti's work containing poems for children is:
A. *The Earthly Paradise*
B. *Scholar Gypsy*
C. *Goblin Market*
D. *The House of Life*

20. Swinburne's masterpiece known for its choral passages is:
A. *Atalanta in Calydon*
B. *Cain*
C. *Sohrab and Rustam*
D. *Queen Mab*

ANSWERS

1	2	3	4	5	6	7	8	9	10
A	B	C	D	D	B	C	A	A	B
11	**12**	**13**	**14**	**15**	**16**	**17**	**18**	**19**	**20**
A	D	C	B	B	D	A	B	C	A

THE MODERN AGE (1880-ONWARDS)

As the 20th century dawned, new values replaced the old ones and shaped the literature of Great Britain. England fast lost its imperial image as her colonies revolted and fought for independence. Industrialization progressed by leaps and bounds and the two World Wars brought economic depression. All this affected the content of literature. Writers sought new vehicles of expression. The findings of **Sigmund Freud** in the realms of psychology took novelists to the subconscious mind. A great number of writers who became famous men of letters in English came from Ireland **(G.B. Shaw, W.B. Yeats, James Joyce and Samuel Beckett)** and from America **(T.S. Eliot and Ezra Pound)**. Socialism became a practising creed and feminism raised her head. Dogmatic Christianity was more or less ignored. Although great strides were made in scientific inventions, science could not provide suitable answers to the deep questioning of the human mind resulting in ethical philosophy. The age saw the end of feudalism. Victorian reticence and prudery gave way to decadence in literature. English writers came under the influence of the French Parnassians and Symbolists. Scandinavia and Russia represented by **Ibsen** and **Tolstoy** also influenced the British men of letters. Many a poet wished to fight free from the fixed rules of versification and wrote in free verse. Many imitated the American poet **Walt Whitman**. English literature became more expansive in its concerns. The life and culture of foreign lands were depicted. Although **Kipling** was an imperialist, his works go beyond England. Being born in India, his works give a graphic view of the country. The great Celtic Revival under Yeats brought a new strain to English literature. Finally, the theatre, lying dormant for a century, now woke up with renewed vigour.

Criticism

The Age began with scholarly works in literary history. **Leslie Stephen (1832-1904)** wrote biographical and critical essays. He produced *The English Utilitarians and the Dictionary of National Biography*. He was an agnostic and rationalist. **A.C. Bradley (1851-1935), H.J.C. Grierson (1866-1960)** and **Edward Dowden (1843-1913)** were other famous critics. Bradley is famous for his critical work on Shakespeare's tragedies.

Walter Horatio Pater (1839-1894) propounded the literary doctrine *Art for Art's Sake* which was a quest for the most refined pleasure. The exquisite in art came from a reflection of the past. He eulogized the accomplishments of the Renaissance. His prose style was rich, musical and classical. His works include *Studies in the History of the Renaissance* (1873) and *Marius the Epicurean* (1885).

John Addington Symonds (1840-1893) was another admirer of the Renaissance. **Oscar Wilde (1856-1900)**, more known as a novelist and dramatist, gave a wider dimension to the theory of Art for Art's Sake by spicing it with wit and paradox. **George Saintsbury (1845-1933)** and **Sir Walter Raleigh (1861-1922)** were other famous critics.

Poetry

Most of the poetry written in this period are the works of those more renowned as novelists: Robert Louis Stevenson, Rudyard Kipling and Thomas Hardy. William Butler Yeats, who pioneered the Celtic Revival, Thomas Steams Eliot, whose *Wasteland* is a watershed leading to modern poetry, Gerard Manley Hopkins, the Catholic poet, are the famous poets of this period.

Rudyard Kipling (1865-1936) wrote on imperialist themes in *Barrack Room Ballads* (1892), *The Seven Seas* (1896) and *Five Nations* (1903). These poems were aimed by their rugged music to rouse people to protest. He combined folk-music with music-hall chorus. It had the sound of drum beats and bugle-calls and even the refinements of chamber music. The poetry of imperialism, heroism of national policy, contained slang and even biblical allusions. In fact, his popularity was that of Walt Whitman, the national poet of America. Many of his subjects were from India, like the poem *Gunga Din*.

W.E. Henley (1849-1903) also wrote poetry which praised Britain's colonial power. *The Song of the Sword, For England's Sake* and *London Voluntaries* are some of his better-known poems.

There were also a group of poets called the Decadents. They were aesthetes and their doctrine was *'Art for Art's Sake'*. **Oscar Wilde** was the leading poet of the group. *The Ballad of Reading Gaol* (1898) is his famous work inspired by his crime and imprisonment.

A group of poets had a pessimistic view of life. **John Davidson (1857-1909), Ernest Dawson (1867-1900)** and **A.E. Housman (1859-1936)** are some of these poets. But the leading pessimist of the age was **Thomas Hardy (1840-1928)**, better known as a novelist. He published *Wessex Poems* (1898) after the novel *Jude the Obscure* failed to receive public acclaim. His poetry was musical and highly individual. He had a disillusioned view of life. From 1903 to 1908, he produced the vast poetical work *The Dynasts*, written under the background of Napoleon's struggle against Europe combining real history with symbolic flashes. His poem, *To an Unborn Pauper Child,* reveals his utter dejection with life: *'Breathe : hid heart',* it begins.

Francis Thompson (1859-1907) and **Gerard Manley Hopkins (1844-1889)** were religious poets of the beginning of the twentieth century. Thompson's poem, *The Hound of Heaven* is a masterpiece. It describes God as a Heavenly Hound chasing man to capture his soul and man fleeing Him in the pleasures of life. The Jesuit, Hopkins invented a new type of verse called *'sprung rhythm'*. It was filled with strange word coinages and is difficult for the ordinary reader to understand. His poetry reflects the conflict within him between his attraction to Roman Catholicism and his joy for the beautiful creation. He wrote a number of religious poems of which *The Wreck of the "Deutschland"* is one of the best. It describes the death of five Franciscan nuns on board the ship, *Deutschland.*

Irish, English and Continental influences met in **W.B. Yeats (1865-1939)**. He was born in Ireland but came to live in London. He was influenced by the strange mystical visions of William Blake, by pre-Raphaelite refinement and even the mysticism and occultism of the Orient, especially of India. His poetry is an attempt to revive Celtic mysticism and Irish mythology. Apparently it was Yeats who introduced Rabindra Nath Tagore to the West. He also came under the influence of Verlaine, a French symbolist poet. His best poetry is in *The Wild Swans at Coole* (1919), *The Tower* (1928) and *The Winding Stair* (1933). Some of his well-known poems are: *Easter* (1916), *The Second Coming, Byzantium, A Prayer for my Daughter, Leda and Swan, Sailing to Byzantium, Meru, Lapis Lazudili, Among School Children,* etc. His progress as a poet can be assessed by comparing the beautiful but simple *Lake Isle of Innisfree* with the beautiful and profound *Byzantium.*

The towering poet of the 20th century is **Thomas Steams Eliot (1888-1965)**. Eliot came on to the scene when the West was passing through tremendous upheavals — belief in religion, especially of the Church was fading, democracy was the new experiment in politics, and many modernist trends were noticeable in literature. Eliot proclaimed himself "a royalist in politics, an Anglo-Catholic in religion and a classicist in literature". Tradition, according to him, was not the dead past but the past living in the present. In his essay *Tradition and the Individual Talent*, he states that "the talent of an artist shows itself not where he differs from the ancients but where, in his work, they assert their immortality". Eliot's poetry shows metaphysical, symbolist and imagist strains, but his individual talent shines forth unmistakeably. An eclectic philosophy, borrowed from his own Christianity and Buddhism and the Upanishads informs his poetry. His poetry, especially *The Wasteland* (1922) is a poem that describes the zeitgeist (spirit of the times) and the *angoisse metaphysique* (metaphysical anguish) of life in post-World War Europe. It begins with the sentence *"April is a cruel month"* and this sets the strain for the whole poem. A brooding sense of futility and human inanity pervades modern life. Eliot achieves this effect by a combination of literary allusions to the past which stirs associations, and by what is called as the *objective correlative*. This last technique means that images are described which call up an emotion or a feeling.

His other poems are *The Lave Song of J. Alfred Prufrock* and *Four Quartets* (1944). These lines from the *Four Quartets* may sum up the disillusionment of the times: *"Footfalls echo in the memory/Down the passage one could not take / To the door one could not open"*. Eliot was a poet of spiritual regeneration.

As the century proceeds, a host of poets make their mark **Stephen Spender (1909-1995), W.H. Auden (1907-1973), C. Day Lewis (1904-1972), Louis MacNeice (1907-1963)** — all of them wrote with a Social awareness, exposing the horror of the bourgeois culture and capitalist exploitation and the terror of totalitarianism.

We cannot end this section of the early modern twentieth century without a reference to **Rupert Brooke (1887-1915), Wilfred Owen (1893-1918)** and **Siegfried Sassoon (1886-1967)** popularly known as the "War poets". They had served the Armed Forces in the First World War, and after 1918, disillusioned by the horrors they had witnessed took their pens to write against the war. The poem *The Soldier* is one of the finest lyrics in the English language. It describes the poet's sense of impending death in battle and his love for his country: *"If I should die/Think only this of me/That there is a part of England/Buried in some foreign land"*. Another poem is Sassoon's *Everyone Sang,* which describes the exultation felt by the soldiers returning home after the General Armistice was signed. They are described as *freed birds.*

Novel

Just like poetry, the novel of this century reflects the great passions and strivings of the age. The discoveries of **Sigmund Freud (1856-1939)** revealed the relationship of man's behaviour to his subconscious mind. The subconscious contains impressions of past experiences which influence a person's attitudes and behaviour. These discoveries led not only to new methods of psychiatric treatment but also to new dramatic techniques in the art of the novel. The stream-of-consciousness method used by James Joyce and Virginia Woolf spring from these discoveries. The modern novel is more and more concerned with an analysis of human behaviour. The focus shifts from a description of the external atmosphere to the thoughts of the characters.

Thomas Hardy's works are tinged with a gloomy pessimism reminiscent of Schopenhauer, and an analogy may be found in his works to Flaubert and Zola from France. Hardy's country Dorsetshire and the surroundings become the 'Wessex' of his novels. His work is full of realistic descriptions of the countryside. The places, full of pre-historic and Roman remains, heaths, have a character, and influence the people living there. The pre-historic past presses on the life of today. He is adept at delineating rustic characters. Man is a puppet of fate and an uncontrollable destiny drives him along life. A bitter helplessness pervades his novels *Far from the Madding Crowd* (1874), *The Return of the Native* (1878), *The Mayor of Casterbridge* (1886), and *Jude the Obscure* (1895). His success reached a climax with *Tess of the d'Urbervilles* (1891). His *Tess of the D'UrberviUes* and *Jude the Obscure,* because of their frank handling of sex and religion, aroused the hostility of the reading public. These two books, however, present Hardy's most moving indictments of the human situation.

The works of George Robert Gissing (1857-1903) produce a sense of absolute dejection. He worked as an ill-paid hack in the poor districts of London and described these places vividly in his books. Although impressed by Charles Dickens, his writings show none of Dickens' humour. One bitter, wretched world, a miserable London, exists in his works. Thus *Demos, a Story of English Socialism* (1886) describes the futility of socialist agitation, *The Nether World* (1889), the wretchedness of the London slums, *New Grub Street* (1891), the hopeless lot of a penniless writer, and *The Odd Women* (1893), the plight of unmarried women. His style is as bare and unaffected as his ideas.

Robert Louis Stevenson (1850-1894) stands in contrast to Hardy and Gissing in his recreation of the life of action and adventure. Although he suffered from an incurable malady, he did not lose faith in himself. He brought out *An Inland Voyage* (1878), *Travels with a Donkey in the Cevennes* (1879), *The Silverado Squatters, Treasure Island* (1833), *Kidnapped* and *The Master of Ballantrae* (1889) among others. The last three are very popular among children the world over. He also wrote children's adventure classics like *The Treasure Island* (1883), *Dr Jekyll and Mr. Hyde* (1886) and *Kidnapped* (1886). In *Dr. Jekyll and Mr Hyde* he touches upon the dual nature of man his good and evil aspects. His style is vivid and full of interesting details.

Another great novelist was the Pole, **Joseph Conrad (1857-1924)**, who perfected his knowledge of English and wrote in a vivid style with a strong foreign accent. His experience of sailing life and work in the English merchant service gave him the ideas to write masterpieces like *The Nigger of the*

Narcissus (1897), and *Lord Jim: A Tale* (1900). Like the Slavs he was preoccupied with the problem of human misery. *Lord Jim* and *The Heart of Darkness* (1902) show his anger at what the white man had done to exploit Africa and other nations. A trait of his narrative technique is the gradual picture of his character formed from fragmentary descriptions of witnesses. He has a rich, sensuous prose style full of striking imagery.

Rudyard Kipling wrote stories about Indian life: *Plain Tales from the Hills* (1888) and *Soldiers Three* (1888). *Plain Tales from the Hills* depicts an Englishman's encounter with the strange East. Kipling was born in Bombay and spent his early life in India. He knew the land and its customs, its people and languages. His best book is *Kim* (1901), the story of a half-Irish boy, who speaks the language of the rustics of India and accompanies a Buddhist Lama on his search for "Nirvana" or Salvation. Kipling is adept at describing the sights and smells of India and its colourful people with their racy dialects. He also wrote two animal epics entitled, *The Jungle Book* (1894) and a series of short stories for children like *Captains Courageous* (1897), *Just So Stories* (1902) and *Puck of Pook's Hill* (1906). Kipling was influenced by Carlyle's doctrine of energy. As a spokesman of the Imperialist theme he believed that it was ideal for a person to sacrifice himself for his tribe. He believed that especially the white man was ordained to rule and lead nations. His works praise Britain's hegemony over her colonies.

Shortly after Kipling, came H. G. Wells and John Galsworthy who were Socialists and criticized the English society. **H.G. Wells** (1866-1946) began by writing stories with a semi-scientific flavour like *The Time Machine* (1895), *The Island of Dr Moreau* (1896), *The Invisible Man* (1897) and *The War of the Worlds* (1898). The stories are ingenuously plotted and thrill and disturb the readers. Later on Wells' interest shifted to social problems. He became a member of the Fabian Society. He wrote *Mankind in the Making* (1903) describing how society would look like when reformed by socialism. He also satirized the society in *Love and Mr Lewisham* (1900), *Kipps* (1905). *Tono-Bungay* (1909) and *Marriage* (1912). He does not glorify Britain's past and he scorns the existing institutions of his country. He wrote a number of remarkable books after the outbreak of World War I in 1914. These show his restless self-examining spirit. Some of these are *Mr Britling Sees it through* (1916) and *The Undying Fire* (1919).

In the works of **John Galsworthy (1867-1933)** we find an artistic conscience. Like Wells, he also attacked the concept of property and commercialism in his novels. He too exposed and criticized national prejudices, especially those existing among his own class, the landed gentry. He was widely read in Continental Literature and was especially influenced by France and Russia. Turgenev with his noble realism was his ideal. He is a detached and impartial observer of his country's decadent values. He advocates a fearless search for truth. *In The Island Pharisees* (1904) he exposes the stagnation of thought among English privileged classes. A similar theme is touched in other novels like *The Country House* (1907), *The Patrician* (1911) and *The Dark Flower* (1913) where country squires, aristocracy and artists are critically studied. *The Forsyte Saga* (1922) is his masterpiece. It is a natural history of the rich upper-middle class family. He describes their attitude to events like the Great War, the growth of socialism, unemployment and the coal strike.

Enoch Arnold Bennett (1867-1931) wrote a number of different types of novels presenting a detailed picture of an industrial district in the provinces. He is a realist like the French nationalists. His masterpiece is *The Old Wives' Tale* (1908).

G.K. Chesterton (1874-1936) was a champion of tradition and he refuted and opposed the attacks of his contemporaries against English society in *Orthodoxy* (1908), *The Napoleon of Notting Hill* (1904). He believed in tradition sanctified by ages of experience and even in the religious bond between men. His style is effective with the use of imagery and comparison and he spices it with plenty of humour.

James Joyce (1882-1941) pioneered a new type of novel with the *stream-of-consciousness* technique.

Characters in *Ulysses* (1922) unreel themselves by a sort of interior monologue. Speech is mimicked and styles are parodied. *Ulysses* is modelled on the *Odyssey* of Homer and set in the slums of Dublin. The thousand pages of this novel cover just one day in the life of Leopold Bloom and Stephen Dedalus. Joyce coined words from several languages and was a master craftsman with wit and conceits. His other famous work is the autobiographical *A Portrait of the Artist as a Young Man* (1916) which describes his adolescence and sensuous tendencies.

Virginia Woolf (1882-1941) continued the stream-of-consciousness technique. Her works *To the Lighthouse* (1927) and *Mrs Dallaway* (1925) reveal the hidden inner life of her characters.

E.M. Forster (1879-1970) was the novelist of cultural relations. In **A Passage to India** (1924) he studies the conflict between the west and the east and takes a favourable stand for the latter. *Where Angels Fear to Tread* (1905) studies how the cultural divide between an Italian girl and her English husband leads to the ruination of their marriage and life.

D.H. Lawrence (1885-1930) was a prolific writer. His outspoken views on sexual relations raised much hue and cry. He considered sex the religion of the blood. His novels were dubbed pornographic. He believed in the free expression of human personality, in being guided by unrestrained primitive instincts. In *Sons and Lovers* (1913) he studies the relationship of son and mother and the social disparity of a father, a coalminer and a mother, a teacher. The novel is autobiographical. Other works by him are *The Rainbow* (1915), *Women in Love* (1921), and *The Plumed Serpent* (1926). *The Rainbow,* suppressed as obscene, treats the conflict between man and woman. *Lady Chatterley's Lover* (1928) was canned for being obscene.

George Orwell (1903-1950) wrote novels which were an indictment of totalitarian government: *Animal Farm* (1945) and *Nineteen Eighty-Four* (1949). **Aldous Huxley's** *Brave New World* (1932) is a prophetic book about the future of civilization in the context of scientific advancement.

Drama

After Shakespeare, **George Bernard Shaw (1856-1950)** is the great playwright whose works enlivened the British stage. Shaw, like Ibsen, believed in drama as a vehicle for ideas. He had a rich Irish sense of humour and his plays are satires on various social and philosophical themes. His general technique was to discuss the problem of his play first in its preface. Often this preface is longer than the play itself. *Widowers' Houses* (1892) was his first play. In this he discusses the problem of Housing. In *Mrs Warren's Profession* (1894) he lays bare the profession of a prostitute. In *Arms and the Man* (1894) the theme is the chocolate-cream soldier. Shaw was an iconoclast breaking well-established idols or myths. Thus this play disillusions us of the romantic image of a soldier. He is not one who is willing to die for his country, but one who loves his life. When the enemy is weak, he attacks, but withdraws and takes to his heels if the enemy is strong. George Bernard Shaw had a keen interest in the English language and formulated a standard pronunciation for it. He studies the theme of how language can influence one's rise in the social ladder. Professor Higgins succeeds in teaching a flower-girl to rid herself of a cockney accent and to speak well enough to pass for royalty! In *Man and Superman* we see Shaw as a master conversationalist. Ideas are discussed without much action taking place in the play. *The Apple Cart* (1929) shows the weaknesses of democracy. Although an Irish man, Shaw did not write on Irish themes as such.

Oscar Wilde reminds one of the Restoration playwrights Sheridan and Congreve in his comedy of manners. His style is full of paradox and verbal wit. Some of his famous plays are *Lady Windermere's Fan* (1892), *A Woman of No Importance* (1893) and *The Importance of Being Ernest* (1895).

John Galsworthy's plays *Strife* (1909), *Justice* (1910) and *Loyalties* (1922) were based on the theme of class exploitation.

W.B. Yeats contributed to the Irish drama. His Celtic theme comes through in *The Countess Cathleen* (1892) and *The Land of Heart's Desire*

(1894). **Sean O'Casey** (1884-1964) and **J. M. Synge** (1871-1909) were other noted Irish playwrights. The latter's plays, *The Playboy of the Western World* (1907) and *Riders to the Sea* (1904) are famous.

T.S. Eliot's contribution to the modern theatre were religious and moral plays. He uses the Greek "chorus" style in *Murder in the Cathedral* (1935) to heighten the dramatic effect of the murder of Thomas Becket by the Archbishop of Canterbury's men. *The Family Reunion* (1939) is a play about sin and expiation. Eliot pruned verse to sound like prose. This is done dexterously in *The Cocktail Party* (1949) and *The Confidential Clerk* (1953) where characters speak verse which sounds like prose.

A group of playwrights came to be known as the "Angry Young Men". **John Osborne (1929-1994)** was the most prominent of them. His play *Look Back in Anger* (1956) catches the mood of the frustrated youth in post-War England. In his plays, he exposes the wretchedness of the working class.

Harold Pinter (1930-2008) mixes comedy and horror in his plays like *The Birthday Party* (1958).

Another group of dramatists drew their inspiration from France. *The Absurd Theatre*, as it was called, began in France with Albert Camus, Jean Genet and Ionesco as its pioneers. In England, **Samuel Beckett (1906-1989)** was the Irish dramatist of this school. His plays *Endgame* (1955), *Krapp's Last Tape* (1958) and *Waiting For Godot* (1906) show the meaninglessness of human action and the unrelieved gloom of existence.

MAJOR AUTHORS AND THEIR WORKS

George Bernard Shaw (1856-1950)

Widowers' Houses
Candida
You Never Can Tell
Man and Superman
Back to Methuselah
Saint Joan
Heartbreak House
The Philanderer
Mrs. Warren's Profession
Caesar and Cleopatra
John Bull's Other Island
Major Barbara
The Doctor's Dilemma
Getting Married
The Apple Cart
Pygmalion
The Dark Lady of the Sonnets
Plays Pleasant and Unpleasant
The Millionaire
The Intelligent Woman's Guide to Socialism
Everybody's Political What is What
Cashel Byron's Profession
Love Among the Artists
Androcles and the Lion
The Devil's Disciple
The Man of Destiny

W.B. Yeats (1865-1939)

The Land of Heart's Desire
The Countess Cathleen
The Shadowy Waters
The Hour-glass
The Resurrection
The King's Threshold
On Baile's Strand
The Cat and the Moon
Ideas of Good and Evil
Discoveries
The Wind among the Reeds
The Wanderings of Oisin
The Tower
The Winding Stair and Other Poems
Lake Isle of Innisfree
Byzantium

John Galsworthy (1867-1933)

The Silver Box
Strife
The Skin Game
The Man of Property
Justice

Loyalties
Escape
The Inn of Tranquility
The Forsyte Saga
The Country House
Fraternity
The Patrician
The Dark Flower
Saint's Progress
Maid in Waiting
Flower Wilderness

Rudyard Kipling (1865-1936)

Kim
The Jungle Book
Barrack-room Ballads
Departmental Ditties
The Seven Seas
The Five Nations
Tales from the Hills
Soldiers Three
Life's Handicap
The Phantom Rickshaw
Many Inventions
The Day's Work
Just-so Stories for Little Children
Rewards and Fairies
Debits and Credits

H.G. Wells (1866-1946)

The Time Machine
Love and Mr. Levisham
Kipps
The History of Mr. Polly
Mr. Britling Sees It Through
Christina Albertas Father
The Wonderful Visit
The Island of Dr. Moreau
The Invisible Man
The War of the Worlds
The First Men in the Moon
The Food of the Gods
Marriage
Experiment in Autobiography
The Contemporary Novel

Joseph Conrad (1857-1924)

The Nigger of the 'Narcissus'
Typhoon
Lord Jim
Victory
Almayer's Folly
An Outcast of the Islands
Youth
Heart of Darkness
The Secret Agent
The Shadow of Line
Suspense-A Napoleonic Novel

Arnold Bennett (1867-1931)

The Old Wives' Tale
Clayhanger
Riceyman Steps
Buried Alive
Hilda Lessways
These Twain
Sacred and Profane Love
The Pretty Lady
The Love Match
The Author's Craft

Walter de la Mare (1873-1956)

Peacock Pie
Memoirs of a Midget
Songs of Childhood
Bells and Grass
The Traveller
Early the Morning
Love

T.S. Eliot (1888-1965)

The Waste Land
Prufrock and Other Observations
Gerontion
The Hollow Men
Ash Wednesday
Four Quartets
Sweeney Agonistes

Murder in the Cathedral
The Rock
The Family Reunion
The Cocktail Party
The Confidential Clerk
The Sacred Wood
After Strange Gods
The Elder Statesman
The Idea of a Christian Society
What is a Classic?
For Lancelot Andrews
The Use of Poetry and the Use of Criticism
Elizabethan Essays
Points of View

Virginia Woolf (1882-1941)

The Voyage Out
Jacob's Room
Mrs. Dalloway
To The Light House
The Waves
Flush
Orlando : A Biography
The Common Reader
Roger Fry
The Death of the Moth
Mr. Bennett and Mrs. Brown
A Room of One's Own
Between the Acts (Unfinished)

E.M. Forster (1879-1970)

Abinger Harvest
Two Cheers for Democracy
A Passage to India
Howard's End
The Hill of Devi
The Celestial Omnibus
Collected Short Stories
Where Angels Fear to Tread
The Longest Journey
The Story of the Siren
A Room with a View
The Eternal Moment

James Joyce (1882-1941)

Ulysses
Portrait of the Artist as a Young Man
Finnegans Wake
Dubliners

D.H. Lawrence (1885-1930)

Sons and Lovers
Woman in Love
Lady Chatterly's Lover
The Rainbow
The White Peacock
Kangaroo
The Plumed Serpent

Aldous Huxley (1894-1963)

Point Counter Point
The Burning Wheel
Those Barren Leaves
Brave New World
After Many a Summer
Eyeless in Gaza
Antic Hay
Time Must Have a Stop
Crome Yellow
The Defeat of Youth
The Perennial Philosophy
The Devils of Loudun

George Orwell (1903-1950)

The Animal Farm
The Road to Wigan Pier
Nineteen Eighty-Four
Burmese Days
Keep the Aspidistra Flying

Oscar Wilde (1854-1900)

The Sphinx
The Ballad of Reeding Gaol
The Canterville Ghost
De Profundis
The Duchess of Padua
The Importance of Being Earnest
An Ideal Husband

Lady Windermere's Fan
Salome
The Picture of Dorian Gray
The Happy Prince and the Other Tales

Harold Pinter (1930-2008)
The Birthday Party
The Dumb Waiter
The Care Taker
A Night Out
The Home Coming
Old Times
Silence

MULTIPLE CHOICE QUESTIONS

1. The Celtic Revival was begun by:
A. George Bernard Shaw
B. W.B. Yeats
C. J.M. Synge
D. James Joyce

2. *The Wasteland* is written by:
A. T.S. Eliot B. John Galsworthy
C. Thomas Hardy D. Virginia Woolf

3. Hardy is famous for his poem:
A. *The Hound of Heaven*
B. *The Dynasts*
C. *Four Quartets*
D. *Wild Swans of Coole*

4. The Irish dramatist, who wrote absurd plays, was
A. W.B. Yeats B. Samuel Beckett
C. Sean O'Casey D. J.M. Synge

5. *Everyone Sang* is a poem about:
A. socialism B. music
C. war D. death

6. *The Old Wives'* Tale is written by:
A. Robert Gissing B. Galsworthy
C. H.G. Wells D. Arnold Bennet

7. Robert Louis Stevenson wrote stories about:
A. adventure B. human nature
C. war D. nature and man

8. *The Invisible Man* is written by:
A. D.H. Lawrence B. H.G. Wells
C. Kipling D. Dickens

9. *Nigger of the Narcissus* is written by:
A. Hardy B. Eliot
C. Lawrence D. Conrad

10. Sex was considered the religion of the blood by:
A. D.H. Lawrence B. Ibsen
C. G.B. Shaw D. Oscar Wilde

11. The British novelist and poet who described India best was:
A. Virginia Woolf B. Graham Greene
C. Rudyard Kipling D. Aldous Huxley

12. Rupert Brooke, Wilfred Owen and Siegfried Sassoon are together known as:
A. Flower Poets B. War Poets
C. Poets of Revolt D. Patriotic Poets

13. Walt Whitman was the national poet of:
A. England B. Poland
C. America D. France

14. *The Wreck of the Deutschland* is a:
A. war poem B. historical poem
C. romantic poem D. religious poem

15. *Sprung rhythm* was invented by:
A. Gerard Manley Hopkins
B. T.S. Eliot
C. Auden
D. Yeats

16. *The Family Reunion* — a play, is written by:
A. W.B. Yeats B. T.S. Eliot
C. Cecil Day Lewis D. Louis MacNiece

17. Gissing's *The Odd Women* is a work on:
A. plight of unmarried women
B. poverty of slum-dwellers
C. war and love
D. the life force

18. *Ulysses* is written by:
A. Virginia Woolf B. George Orwell
C. Arnold Bennett D. James Joyce

19. *The Patrician* is written by:
A. Kipling B. H.G. Wells
C. Henry James D. Galsworthy

20. *Look Back in Anger* is written by:
A. A. J. Cronin B. Aldous Huxley
C. D. H. Lawrence D. John Osborne

ANSWERS

1	2	3	4	5	6	7	8	9	10
B	A	B	B	B	D	A	B	D	A
11	**12**	**13**	**14**	**15**	**16**	**17**	**18**	**19**	**20**
C	B	C	D	A	B	A	D	D	D

INDIAN WRITING IN ENGLISH

ANAND, MULKRAJ (1905-2004)

He was greatly influenced by Premchand on the one hand and Tagore on the other.
Some of his famous novels are :

1. The Village (1939)
2. Across the Black Waters (1940)
3. The Sword and the Sickle (1942)
4. Untouchable (1933) (his first novel)
5. Seven Summers (1951)
6. Private Life of an Indian Prince (1953)
7. The Big Heart (1945)
8. Coolie (1936) (It was recast in seventies)
9. Two Leaves and a Bud (1937)
10. The Old Woman and the Cow (1960)
11. The Road (1961)
12. Death of a Hero (1963)
13. Confession of a Lover (1976)
14. Morning Face (1968)

AUROBINDO, GHOSE (1872-1950)

- He was known as the "firebrand" of India.
- He was a poet, a saint, a philosopher, statesman, yogi and a prophet.
- He is one of the pre-Independence Titanic trio of Indian poets—Tagore, Aurobindo and Sarojini Naidu.
- He is chiefly known for his
  - (*i*) Savitri (1953) a poetic epic on a grand scale.
  - (*ii*) The Life Divine (1939-40)
  - (*iii*) Essays on Gita
- He is a great exponent and proponent of ancient Indian thought.
- According to R. K. Singh, "Aurobindo is sympathetic to the modernist trends in writing and study of poetry and, in fact, himself adopts some of the methods followed by the modern poets."
- To quote Mr. Singh again, "In Aurobindo's literary order, poetry is a means of spiritual expression that helps to open the consciousness..."

CHATTERJEE, BANKIM CHANDRA (1838-94)

- He is generally called 'The Father of Bengali fiction.'
- Today he is most known for his patriotic bent of mind.
- In all he wrote 14 novels.
  - (*i*) Some of them are historical.
  - (*ii*) Others are social.
  - (*iii*) Still others are philosophical with stress on renunciation and non-attachment.
- Some of his novels are :
  - (*i*) *The Poison Tree* (*1884*): It is a story of Hindu life in Bengal of the period
  - (*ii*) Kapalkundala (1885)

(*iii*) Durgeshnandini (1890)
(*iv*) Krishnakanta's Will (1895)
(*v*) The Two Rings (1897)
(*vi*) Rajmohan's Wife (1904) (published posthumously)
(*vii*) Anand Math (1884)

CHAUDHURI, NIRAD, C. (1897-1999)

- He came into limelight with the publication of his "The Autobiography of an Unknown Indian." (1951).
- His other important works are:
  (*i*) A Passage to India (1959)
  (*ii*) Continent of Circe (1966)
  (He received the Duff Cooper Memorial Prize).
  (*iii*) The Intellectual in India (1967)
  (*iv*) To Live or Not to Live (1970)
- He is known for his most correct and chaste prose for which he has earned much acclaim from the scholars and critics, including Khushwant Singh.

DESAI, ANITA (Born-1937)

- She is a renowned novelist and short story writer.
- Some of her famous novels are :
  (*i*) Cry, the Peacock (1963)
  (*ii*) Voices in the City (1965)
  (*iii*) Bye-Bye, Blackbird (1971)
  (*iv*) Fire on the Mountain (1977)
  (*v*) Clear Light of Day (1980)
- Her collection of short stories is captioned "Games at Twilight" (1978)

GANDHI, M.K. (1869-1948)

1. His famous work in English is "My Experiments with Truth."
2. The work is an important autobiographical writing which is held in high esteem for its truthfulness, frankness, simplicity and directness of expression in non-ornamental effective English.

MARKANDAYA, KAMALA (1924-2004)

1. She is one of the modern novelists and is known for her:
   (*i*) Nectar in a Sieve (her first novel) (It is a novel on miserable rural life).
   (*ii*) Some Inner Fury (1955)
   (It is a novel of violence and destruction)
   (*iii*) A Silence of Desire (1960)
   (It is a novel urging the readers to speak out frankly to unburden their hearts).
   (*iv*) Possession (1963)
   (The problem of possession is discussed in this novel).
   (*v*) A Handful of Rice (1966)
   (It depicts the life of the poor classes in Madras).
   (*vi*) The Coffer Danus (1969)
   (*vii*) The Nowhere Man (1972)
   (*viii*) Two Virgins (1973)
   (*ix*) The Golden Honeycomb (1977)
   (*x*) Pleasure City (1982).

KHUSHWANT SINGH (Born-1915)

- He is known for his novels :
  (*i*) Train to Pakistan (his masterpiece)
  (*ii*) I Shall Not Hear the Nightingale (1959). (It describes the social life of a Sikh family during the pre-Independence period).
- "The Mark of Vishnu" is another of his well-known works.
- Some of his known stories
  (*a*) Karma
  (*b*) When Sikh Meets Sikh
  (*c*) The Rape, etc.
- He is also known for his:
  (*i*) A History of the Sikhs
  (*ii*) Translation of Japji Sahib, etc.
- His regular columns appear weekly in some dailies, *e.g.* :
  (*i*) 'With Malice Towards One And All'—The Hindustan Times.
  (*ii*) 'This Above All'—The Tribune.

- Mulk Raj Anand is stated to have said that Khushwant Singh's "Train to Pakistan" is likely to last, while about his other creative literary work, one may have some doubts.
- Among his latest work is "Truth, Love and Little Malice."

MULLER, MAX (1823-1900)

- He was a famous Indologist, German orientalist and linguist, who unearthed a lot of ancient Indian history and Sanskrit scriptures, the Rig Veda, in particular, of which he published six colossal volumes, for which he had got an assignment from the East India Company in 1847.
- Actually he was a student of Sanskrit, who started comparative study of languages and "Avesta" (in 1845) which is the renowned sacred book of the Zoroastrians.
- He gave seven lectures on Indian and ancient Indian philosophy at Cambridge University, which have now been published by Rupa & Co. under the caption: "India : What Can it Teach Us?"
- He distnguishes the highest wisdom of Greece and India by using the terms "to know ourselves" and "to know our self", respectively.
- Muller makes very appreciative comments on the Rig Veda and the Vedic Religion.

NAIDU, SAROJINI (1879-1946)

- She is a well-known Indian English poet who started writing poetry at a very early age and she was inspired by Edmund Gosse to choose Indian themes and scenery rather than imitating the English classics.
- She is now known as 'The Nightingale of India.'
- She took a keen interest in India's struggle for freedom.

Some of her works are :

1. The Golden Threshold (1905)
2. The Bird of Time (1912)
3. The Broken Wing (1917)
4. The Sceptred Flute (1946)
5. The Feather of the Dawn (1961)
   (It appeared posthumously)

Some of her famous poems are :

1. The Queen's Rival
2. Palanquin Bearers
3. To My Fairy Fancies
4. The Pardah Nashin
5. Awake
6. Village Song
7. The Soul's Prayer
8. Fishermen of Coromondel
9. It You Call Me
10. Caprice
11. Summer Woods
12. Songs of Radha
13. The Bird Sanctuary, etc.

NANDY, PRITISH (Born-1947)

- He was the editor of the 'Illustrated Weekly of India' and has now Telecast a T.V. serial over the Doordarshan: "Hungama Unlimited."
- (*i*) He is a prolific poet, though he is still not considered one of the best.
  (*ii*) Most of his poetry has been dismissed by critics as mere experimental gimmickry. Such was Saleem Peeradina.
  (*iii*) Even Nissim Ezekiel dubbed him to be a poetaster.
- Some of his works are :
  (*i*) Gods and Olives (1967)
  (*ii*) On Either Side of Arrogance (1968)
  (*iii*) From the Outer Bank of the Brahmputra (1969)
  (*iv*) Riding the Midnight River (1975)
  (*v*) In secret Anarchy (1979), etc.
- He has written a number of anthologies and translated a number of poets including Agyeya, Amrita Pritam, Kaifi Azmi etc.
- He has also written some short stories and a verse play.

NARAYAN, R.K. (1906-2001)

- Of the three great novelists, Narayan, Anand and Rao, it is Narayan who has won the maximum accolade both in India and abroad.
- One of his great achievements is his creation of the famous town of Malgudi like Hardy's Wessex.
- Narayan is the true master of humour, irony, realism, romance and artistry.
- Most of his novels and stories depict the life of people of South India.
- It is sometimes held that Narayan lacks true pathos, genuine depth of feeling, realistic description of poverty and misery, the elements which go in for making a novelist a great one.
- However, he has earned much popularity as a novelist, and within the range of his own art, he cannot be taken except with due regard and attention.

Some of his famous novels are :

1. Swami and Friends (1935)
2. Bachelor of Arts
3. The English Teacher
4. The Financial Expert
5. Mr. Sampath (1949)
6. The Guide (1958)
7. The Man-eater of Malgudi
8. The Dark Room (1939)
9. Waiting for the Mahatma
10. The Vendor of Sweets
11. The Painter of Signs (1976)

(He won the Sahitya Akademi Award for 'Guide' in 1961)

R.K. NARAYAN (as a short story writer)

- Some of his stories have appeared in the following collections:
  (*i*) Malgudi Days
  (*ii*) Dodu and Other Stories
  (*iii*) Cyclone and Other Stories
  (*iv*) Gods, Demons and Others

Narayan has written a few hundred stories, most of them quite interesting and highly readable:

Some of his famous short stories are :

1. The Golden
2. A Career
3. The Snake Song
4. Man Hunt
5. A Willing Slave
6. An Astrologer's Day
7. The Doctor's word
8. God of Troubles, etc.

NEHRU, JAWAHARLAL (1889-1964)

- He needs no introduction as a freedom fighter, statesman and first Prime Minister of India.
- Some of his literary works are :
  (*i*) An Autobiography (1936)
  (*ii*) Glimpses of World History (1939)
  (*iii*) Discovery of India (1946)
- Children enjoy reading his "Letters from Father to His Daughter."
- He is known for his simple, chaste, poetic English which is a model of natural style.

PRITAM, AMRITA (1919-2005)

- She is the most famous Punjabi Author.
- She won the Jnanpith Award for her "Kagaj Te Kenvas" in 1981.
- Her best known autobiographical work which appeared in the seventies is "Rasidi Ticket."
- (*i*) Her "Shadows of words : An Auto-biography" (a transcreation of the Hindi original by Jyoti Sabharwal) has been published by Macmillan in 2002.
  (*ii*) The book presents "an inner journey down the memory lane" presented by the author, who considers old age the best part of her life, like the last sips of tea, which are usually the sweetest."

RADHAKRISHAN, SARVAPALLI (1888-1975)

- He is known as an outstanding educationist and a philosopher who presented the Hindu/Indian viewpoint to the world.
- His works include
  - (*i*) An Idealist View of Life (Lectures)
  - (*ii*) Indian Philosophy (1923, 1927)
  - (*iii*) The Hindu View of Life (1932)
  - (*iv*) An Idealist View of Life (1932)
  - (*v*) Eastern Religious and Western Thought (1939)
- He wrote in a very simple, intelligible prose-style.

RAO, RAJA (1908-2006)

- His famous works are:
  - (*i*) The Serpent and the Rope (1960)
  - (*ii*) Kanthapura (1938)
  - (*iii*) The Cat and Shakespeare (1965-66)
- (*i*) He was awarded the Sahitya Akademi Award for his 'The Serpent and the Rope' in 1964.

  (*ii*) He was also decorated with Padma Bhushan in 1969.

Raja Rao as a short story writer

- He is also a well-known short story writer.
- His first collection of short stories was "Jauni" which was published in France in 1930.
- The collection: "The Cow of the Barricades" was published in 1947

  Some of his famous short stories are :
  1. Akkayya
  2. The Little Gram-shop
  3. Kanaka Pal
  4. Narsiga

ROY, ARUNDHATI (Born-1961)

She made her debut with her novel: "The God of Small Things" which won her the Booker Prize in 1997, besides a handful amount running into crores as royalty for less than four hundred pages which comprise the said novel.

DE, SHOBHA (Born-1948)

- She is a renowned contemporary Indian English novelist and T.V. serial script writer.
- Some of her novels are prescribed in universities in England and Australias.
- Her T.V. serial "Swabhiman" which ran into numerous episodes was telecast over the Doordarshan.
- (*i*) She has become even more popular with her serial "Kittie Party" telecast over the Zee T.V.

  (*ii*) According to the Tribune, it "is a clever insight into the mind of today's urban Indian women poised at the crossroads of modernity and tradition."

TAGORE, RABINDRANATH (1861-1941)

Tagore was a versatile genius. He was a :

(*i*) poet
(*ii*) novelist
(*iii*) short story writer
(*iv*) dramatist
(*v*) musician
(*vi*) actor (in dramas)
(*vii*) painter
(*viii*) statesman and a host of other things.

Some of his famous novels are :

1. The House and the World (1919)
2. The Wreck (1921)
3. Gora (1923)

VIVEKANANDA, SWAMI (1863-1902)

He is a well-known Indian seer, prophet, recluse preacher, lecturer and poet, who:

(*i*) made the ancient Indian philosophy known to the whole world at the Parliament of Religious in Chicago, USA.

(*ii*) Brought about a wave of resurgence among the Indian masses through his stirring spiritually inspired speeches which were also full of:

(*a*) patriotic fervour
(*b*) love for universal brotherhood.
(*c*) spirit of social uplight, etc.

SOME LITERARY MASTERPIECES

CANTERBURY TALES

by Chaucer

'Canterbury Tales' is a collection of stories in verse by Chaucer. These tales are told by twenty-nine pilgrims who are going on a visit to the shrine of St. Thomas-a-Becket at Canterbury.

Each tale is a complete unit in itself without being intended to be linked with other tales. But, in the narration which is fictional in essence, we have head-links which are actually connecting passages. The headlinks are descriptions of the pilgrims as well as the events that take place in the course of the journey besides valuable digressions.

In those days, the people were very fond of pilgrimages for the sake of religious devotion and fun and they generally travelled in groups to face the dangers of the journey. The tales are written and descriptions of pilgrims given as if Chaucer himself had met such characters and had some experiences like those given.

The pilgrims meet at the Tabard Inn in Southwark on the eve of their departure and there they plan the journey. Chaucer himself is one of the pilgrims and the host of the Inn, Harry Bailly, not only gives a hearty welcome to the pilgrims but also accompanies them to the shrine.

Since the journey is quite tedious, each pilgrim is required to tell two tales on the journey towards the shrine and two during the return journey. But, Chaucer could complete only twenty four tales during his life time and in this sense, the Canterbury Tales is only a fragment.

An important aspect of the tales which brings Chaucer near to a dramatist and a novelist is that the tales differ in character as widely as do those by whom they are told.

The Knight tells, a chivalrous tale, the Clerk a devotional tale while the Miller's and the Reeve's tales are coarse and farcical in complete harmony with their own characters.

UTOPIA

by Thomas More

The period when Renaissance was in full bloom, Utopia was written by Sir Thomas More who lived from 1478-1535. He was imbued with the spirit of humanism.

The Greek word "Utopia" means "nowhere". Hence, it is in this light that Sir More tried to present an imaginary ideal republic of his dreams, which was of course, impossible to be achieved on this earth.

Utopia was originally written in Latin and was published in 1516. Later, it was translated into Italian and French. It was much later, after death of More, that its English translation appeared.

The Important characters in the book are :

1. The writer himself.
2. Peter Giles—writers's friend
3. Raphael Hythloday—a Portuguese traveller.

The book comprises two parts. In part one the protagonist (Hythloday) describes his voyaging with the explorer, Amerigo Vespucci.

In part two Hythloday describes the country of Utopia.

COMMENTS :

Utopia Glorifies

1. A democratic society.
2. A socialistic society with public control over wealth.
3. Religious tolerance
4. Economic equality
5. Peace and prosperity (upto a limit)
6. Love of this world.
7. Love of nature and natural way of living.
8. Love of beauty.
9. Love of the common man.
10. Love of human dignity.

Utopia Condemns

1. Aristocracy
2. Elitism
3. Asceticism and stoicism
4. Other worldliness

5. Fanaticism and bigotry.
6. False Chivalry
7. A Luxurious way of life
8. Scholasticism
9. Narrow-mindedness
10. War, Jingoism and Chauvinism.

GORBODUC

by Thomas Norton & Thomas Sackville

The other name of Gorboduc is Ferrex and Porrex. It is known for being the first regular English tragedy. It was written by Thomas Norton and Thomas Sackville and was first staged in 1562, that is, two years before the birth of Shakespeare. The work became a model for the Renaissance dramatists. It is, in essence, a Senecan tragedy of revenge.

The important characters in this tragedy are :

1. Gorboduc, The king of England
2. Ferrex—Gorboduc's elder son
3. Porrex—Gorboduc's younger son
4. Videna—The Queen
5. The murderers of the king and the queen
6. The nobles
7. The common people, etc.

The story in a nutshell: After the king divides his kingdom between his two sons, the latter begin to quarrel as a result of which Porrex kills Ferrex. The latter is so much loved by the queen that she kills Porrex. The people rise in revolt and kill the king and the queen. The nobles thereafter kill the murderers of the royal couple. This leads to a bloody civil war. There is chaos and anarchy as the question of success remains unsolved.

Senecan Features

1. Division into five acts.
2. Revenge as the chief motive.
3. A chain of murders—one murder leading to the other.
4. A ghost as one of the characters.
5. Lack of humour and any comic relief.
6. All-pervading seriousness and blood and thunder.
7. Avoidance of bloodshed on the stage, as it is reported by the characters through dialogues and monologues.
8. A plethora of rhetorical speeches by the characters.
9. Appearance of the chorus at the end of each act.

The use of blank verse in a drama was for the first time made in Gorboduc.

ASTROPHEL AND STELLA

by Philip Sidney

Astrophel and Stella is a sonnet series written by Sir Philip Sidney, Sidney is known more as a critic for his 'Apologie for Poetry' than as a poet, though his poetic claim is not altogether rejectable. His chief position as a poet rests on Astrophel and Stella.

Significance

1. The work is significant in the sense that it is perhaps the first work in English literature written in the white heat of passion, arising out of a personal and intimate experience.
2. In spite of artificiality of certain sonnets and general Petrarchan extravagance in the series, the work, having arisen out of real experience and genuine feelings, does not altogether look unreal.
3. It sounds real in several respects as in the apostrophe to the moon, in minute, vivid details and descriptions, etc.
4. Though the excessive use of conceits, hyperboles and embellishments mars the series in certain respects, yet its overall significance for the English literature cannot be underestimated.
5. Sidney was, no doubt, influenced by Petrarch. Yet he tries to assert himself every now and then by following a rhyme scheme other than the Petrarchan.
6. His most frequently used rhyme scheme is abba, abba, cdcd, ee. In other words, his sonnets end with a couplet in the Shakespearean style.

DOCTOR FAUSTUS

by Christopher Marlowe

The play opens with the chorus which announces the theme of the play i.e., the story of a scholarly doctor who has his end because of excessive lust for knowledge in the fields of magic and necromancy.

At the start Faustus looks at several fields of study such as Logic, Medicine, Law, Divinity, etc. But he finally settles at Magic. Then appear the Good Angel and the Evil Angel. The former warns Faustus against studying Magic book. He asks him to study the holy books. But the latter encourages him to study the Magic book.

The End of Faustus: His end is as tragic as it can be. He has not indulged or little indulged in sensual pleasures. What makes his sin more serious in theological circles in his association with Satan and the Satanic forces-demons, ghosts, devils etc. So, he gets no forgiveness and relief of any kind despite all his wailings and is taken away to hell by the Devils.

THE WINTER'S TALE

by Robert Green

Robert Greene's prose novel 'Pandosto' or 'The Triumph of Time' was published in 1588 and reprinted in 1607. This became the source for Shakespeare's *The Winter's Tale* which seems to have been composed in 1610 or 1611.

The title signifies an old wives' tale told to the curious children before they go to bed. Hence, such a tale can contain fairy-tale, exaggerative or legendary elements which may be far from reality because of some romantic, imaginary, unreal, absurd persons, incidents and situations.

Characters

Polixenes—the King of Bohemia, Leontes—the King of Sicilia, Hermione—Leontes's wife, Mamillus—Son of Leontes, Camillo—a Gicilian Lord, Cleomenes & Dion—courtiers, Paulina—Antigonus's wife, Emilia—the queen's lady, Florizel—the son of the king of Bohemia, Florizel—known as Doricles, Paulina.

BARTHOLOMEW FAIR

by Johnson

It is one of the most famous of Jonson's comedies which pleases all but hurts none. It is an authentic picture of the London of Queen Elizabeth's times. It was first staged in 1624, in manuscript form. It was published later in 1631.

There is a broad spectrum of humanity in the work at all levels, chiefly low level. Thus we have in the play gallants, gulls, cutpurses and bawds, lovers, squires, servants and justices of peace, etc.

Important Characters

1. **Bartholomew Cokes:** He is a foolish young squire.
2. **Waspe:** He is servant to Cokes who accompanies him to the fair.
3. **Grace Wellborn:** She is the fiancee of Waspe.
4. **Edgeworth:** He is a cutpurse.
5. **Nightingale:** A ballad singer and companion and accomplice of Edgeworth.
6. **Adam Overdo:** A justice of peace.
7. **Zeal-of-the Land Busy:** He is a Puritan who becomes an object of mockery.
8. **Dame Purecraft:** She is a rich widow.
9. **Winwife:** He is a London gallant who is Busy's rival in wooing Purecraft.
10. **Quarlous:** He is a gamester but he is guised as a madman. He is Busy's friend, with whom he finds himself in a quarrel. He at last wins the hand of Purecraft.

Plot: There is virtually no plot in the play but only a presentation of a plethora of incidents and episodes which are mostly left undeveloped. Jonson's chief aim is to hold a mirror to the London life of his times.

The main incidents are

1. Cokes being relieved of purse, sword, cloak and marriage licence at the hands of Edgeworth.
2. Overdo being taken for a pickpocket and put in the stocks.
3. Waspe and Busy being put in the stocks for fighting and creating nuisance.
4. Overdo's escape from the stocks.
5. Quarlous's disclosing to Overdo the real face of Edgeworth.
6. Overdo's invitation to all to dinner.
7. Quarlous's winning of the hand of Purecraft.

Thus, the play proves Jonson to be a gentle satirist who has an ocean of sympathy with his characters of all kinds.

PARADISE LOST

by John Milton

Needless to say that the said Epic is the greatest heroic poem in English literature and one of the greatest of its kind in world literature.

A true epic on classical lines though with several diversional elements, as it is, it has twelve books.

A bookwise "Argument of Paradise Lost" is given by W.J. Long, which may be summarised as under :

Book I

It contains *inter alia*,

(*i*) a statement of the subject, the Fall of Man, and

(*ii*) a noble invocation for light and divine guidance.

Thereafter, in it, we have—

(*i*) description of Satan and the rebel agents. Satan's physical size, his gigantic shield, etc. are on supernatural lines, as can be visualised for a devil of his kind, as in a true epic in particular.
Satan's great power of oratory is also there before us.

(*ii*) the ouster of the rebel angels from heaven by the Almighty.

(*iii*) the diabolical plot of the rebel angels to wreak their vengeance on God by beguiling Adam and Eve, God's children and first parents of mankind, from their state of innocence by bringing about their fall by eating the forbidden fruit in the Eden.

(*iv*) a description of the sulphurous hell-fire and the eternal agonies undergone by the damned spirits there.

(*v*) the raising of Satan's palace, Pandemonium.

Book II

It contains, *inter alia*,

(*i*) a description of the council of devils in the Pandemonium.

(*ii*) Satan's desire to take up the task of beguiling Adam and Eve upon himself.

(*iii*) his journey to the gates of hell, guarded by Sin and Death.

Book III

It contains *inter alia*—

(*i*) God's behest to Raphael to warn Adam and Eve of the imminent danger of disobedience to them.

(*ii*) Son of God's offer to take upon himself the sin of the impending disobedience of man.

(*iii*) Satan's meeting with Uriel, the Angel of the sun, for the purpose of learning the way to earth, the abode of God's new creation.

(*iv*) Satan's journey to the earth in the guise of an angel of light.

Book IV

It contains, *inter alia*—

(*i*) The scenes of Paradise and of Adam and Eve being in the state of innocence.

(*ii*) Eden being guarded by an angel.

(*iii*) The arrest of Satan when he is trying to tempt Eve in a dream.

(*iv*) the setting free of Satan in an unconvincing way.

Book V

It contains, *inter alia*—

(*i*) the description by Eve of her dream to Adam.

(*ii*) Adam and Eve's routine life.

(*iii*) Raphael's visit to Eden.

(*iv*) Raphael's description of the revolt of the fallen angels.

Book VI

It contains, *inter alia*—

a continuation of Raphael's description of the revolt of the fallen angels.

Book VII

It contains a description of the story of creation by Raphael.

Book VIII

It contains Adam's description to Raphael of himself and his meeting with Eve.

Book IX

It contains an account of Satan's temptation of Eve.

Book X

It contains, *inter alia*—

(*i*) God's judgement on Adam and Eve.
(*ii*) Sin and Death's construction of a highway through chaos to the earth.
(*iii*) Satan's return to Pandemonium.
(*iv*) Adam and Eve's repentance.
(*v*) the turning of fallen angels into serpents.

Book XI

(*i*) Acceptance of Adam's repentance by God.
(*ii*) Michael's departure to bring into effect Adam and Eve's banishment from Eden.
(*iii*) Michael's prophecy regarding the destiny of man.

Book XII

It contains *inter alia*—

(*i*) Continuation of Michael's prophecy.
(*ii*) Learning by Adam and Eve of future redemption of mankind.
(*iii*) Adam and Eve's departure out of Eden.

Given below are some extracts from Book I:

The lines given below state the theme: The Fall of Man and present an Invocation to the Muse and the Holy spirit (*i.e.* the spirit of God):

THE WAY OF THE WORLD

by Congreve

As the play opens, we find two men Mirabell and Fainall talking to each other in a Chocolate House.

We learn that Fainall is married to Lady Wishfort's daughter, Arabella who is referred to as Mrs Fainall in the play. We also learn, that Mirabell loves Lady Wishfort's niece, Millament. Lady Wishfort is not only Millament's aunt but also her guardian.

It is learnt that Mirabell often went to Wishfort's house ostensibly to court her but actually to meet Millament. This pretence of Mirabell is at last exposed by Mrs. Marwood.

An enigmatic situation is now created for Millament. Since Lady Wishfort has learnt about Mirabell's sham, she forbids any meeting between him and Millament, Further, in order to inherit the lady's wealth, she has to marry according to her wish. This means that if she marries Mirabell against her wishes, she is likely to be deprived of the fortune of the lady who is fifty-five.

Mirabell has his own plot. He arranges marriage between his servant, Waitwell and Lady Wishfort's maid servant, Foible. The purpose of this marriage is that Waitwell is presented by Mirabell as his (imaginary) uncle, named Sir Rowland.

As Foible has been taken into confidence, she would impress upon Lady Wishfort that Sir Rowland, a wealthy man, has in his heart a deep love and wants to marry her. Through this plan Mirabell wanted to cause embarrassment to Lady Wishfort by revealing the identify of Sir Rowland later and thus compelling her to allow Millament to marry him.

A hindrance is created in the execution of the plot when Mrs. Marwood, Fainall's mistress comes to know about the plan, and she makes her lover aware of it. Besides, not only Millament but also Mrs. Fainall know about this plot.

Mrs. Fainall had once been Mirabell's mistress and in her heart of hearts, she still loves him. Hence, she also does not want that Mirabell should marry Millament, as her heart is burning with the fire of jealousy.

Mr. Fainall is a mean fellow, and he finds it an easy opportunity to blackmail Lady Wishfort. For this, he threatens to divorce Mrs. Fainall. It is further another proof of his avaricious nature that in a deed which is in his possession, he has already arranged the settlement of major part of Mrs. Fainall's estate in his own favour.

It is at the most critical moment when Sir Rowland and Lady Wishfort are busy in constructive prospects and Mirabell and Millament have agreed to marry each other, that Fainall makes his appearance.

Thus Mirabell's apple-cart is disturbed. However, Foible reveals the secret of Fainall's love affair with Mrs. Marwood. However, Fainall, rising on the crest of the situation sets forth certain conditions to remain silent. The conditions concern the fortunes of Mrs. Fainall and Millament and the marriage of Lady Wishfort.

Just then Waitwell presents a deed which is executed by Mrs. Fainall before her marriage with Fainall. In it, she has conferred her then estate on

Mirabell. Thus the deed with Fainall becomes infructuous.

The net result of this *deus ex machina* is that Mirabell and Millament now have no obstacle in tying the nuptial knot to each other.

SENSE AND SENSIBILITY AND PRIDE AND PREJUDICE

by Jane Austen

In essence, the novel *Sense and Sensibility* is a satire on sentimentalism. Elinor represents sense, while sensibility is represented by her sister Marianne. The story, like all stories of Jane Austen, is very simple, but interesting.

Mrs. Henry Dashwood with her three daughters Elinor, Marianne and Margaret, is left in a very straitened situation on the death of her husband. They have to retire to Devonshire where they begin to live in a very humble cottage.

Edward Ferrars is the brother of Mr. John Dashwood. John is the step son of Mr. Henry Dashwood. He had been entrusted by the latter to take care of his wife and daughter after his death. But he does not discharge his responsibilities in this respect.

Edward and Elinor fall in love with each other. Marianne falls in love with a poor, unscrupulous young man, John Willoughby.

Willoughby suddenly leaves for London. Marianne and Elinor go after him. But Willoughby says that he is going to be married to a rich heiress. Elinor also learns that even her lover, Edward, has been untrue to her, as he is already engaged to Lucy Steel who is the niece of Edward.

Edward's mother is not happy with his engagement to Lucy, and settles her property on his younger brother, Robert, who is a fool of the first water. Then Robert and Lucy are married, while Edward stands rejected. Then Edward marries Elinor. Marianna who has been wooed by Colonel Brandon, marries him.

Immature style of Jane Austen is evident in this novel, but her future greatness and maturity is also visible here in seed form. The novel was completed in 1797, though it was published in 1813.

The story of Pride and Prejudice which is regarded as her best work and was published in 1813 is well-known to all scholars and need not be given here. It is in this novel that all the plot and stylistic perfection of Jane Austen comes into play. It is here that the dialogues are most lively, characters life like and her humour at its best.

Whereas in Sense and Sensibility, her characters such as Mrs. Jennings, her stupid daughter, her uncouth son-in-law and Mr. Palmer are some of the humorous characters they are no match for Mr. Collins, Mrs. Bennet, Catherina de Borough and others of Pride and Prejudice.

DAVID COPPERFIELD (1849-50)

***by Charles Dickens** (**1812-70**)*

David Copperfield is perhaps the most popular novel of Dickens. It is an autobiographical novel in which Dickens's power of characterization, depicting humorous and pathetic situations and characters is perhaps the best brought out. The novel is told in the first person.

THE MAYOR OF CASTERBRIDGE

by Thomas Hardy

It was published serially in 1886. It is the story of a man who brings doom upon himself.

THE MILL ON THE FLOSS (1860)

***by George Eliot** (**1819-80**)*

The Mill on the Floss is the most popular novel of George Eliot. It is also perhaps her most auto-biographical novel. The story represents the typical Victorian problem of morality and a moral order which spares nobody.

The Mill mentioned in the title of the novel is the imaginary mill 'Dorlcote Mill' owned by Mr. Tulliver. The mill is situated on the river Floss.

The two main characters in the novel are:

(*i*) Tom Tulliver, and

(*ii*) Maggie Tulliver.

THE WASTELAND

by T.S. Eliot

When the Wasteland was published in book form in 1922, it was soon realized to be the beginning of the emergence of the Modernist Poetry.

Earlier the Georgians and the Imagists had appeared and disappeared but their effect, particularly that of the latter, had been retained in the inner recesses of the minds of the writers, poets included, even though superficially the movement of Imagism had all but spent itself.

It was because Ezra Pound who had occupied a pivotal position in the movement which had such protagonists as Hilda Doolittle and Aldington, also was instrumental in giving the final shape, as were now have, to Eliot's poem.

The Wasteland depicts the collapsing civilization of Europe and, connotatively, the fall of values in the modern world. The poem is highly realistic in this sense, but it promises vaguely some possibility of redemption through some everlasting philosophies such as that of the Buddha and the Upanishadas.

It cannot be disputed that the overwhelming picture of pessimism, death and desolation in the poem is to a great extent the result of the annihilation and mayhem which was witnessed in the First World War that ended in 1917. Then there emerged a particularly distressing mood in the twenties and this mood of depression of the entire period all over the world is very deftly brought about in the poem.

The poem's merit does not lie just in depicting a particular mood, but in its employment of complex symbolism and references to mythology, history, culture, religion and literature from varied sources in modern and medieval world and even the remote ancient times.

SAINT JOAN

by G.B. Shaw

It is one of the most famous plays of G.B. Shaw. It is this play which won him the Nobel Prize. The play was first produced in 1923.

Historical Background to Saint Joan: Saint Joan is a historical play which is based on the life and career of a real character, Joan of Arc. She was a common country girl, who was born in 1412. As a girl, she heard divine voices and had divine visions. But she was sent to the stake on the charges of heresy in 1431.

Social, political and religious conditions of the period are closely related to the story of Joan of Arc.

It was in 1415 that the English forces under the leadership of their young king, Henry V defeated Charles VI, the French King at Agincourt—a decisive battle which aroused waves of nationalism in England.

As a result of this humiliating defeat, the French king had to accept certain most unpleasant terms such as :

1. He had to sign a treaty with the English King in 1420.
2. According to it, he had to :
   - (*i*) disown his own son, the Dauphin, declaring him as illegitimate.
   - (*ii*) marry his infant daughter to the English king.
   - (*iii*) allow the English to keep with them large area of France which they had conquered.

It is to be noted that at that time, France was not one united country. It consisted of a number of estates which were under the control of different feudal lords or barons.

TO THE LIGHT HOUSE

by Virginia Woolf

Virginia Woolf's most famous novel, Mrs. Dalloway was published in 1925. Two years later, another masterpiece of hers was published in 1927.

It is the only novel of Mrs. Woolf which has a Three Part Structure :

- (*i*) Part I: The Window
- (*ii*) Part II: Time Passes
- (*iii*) Part III: The Lighthouse.

The main characters in the novel are:

1. **Mrs. Ramsay:** She is a middle-aged charming woman, a mother of eight children. She is the central figure in the novel.
2. **Mr. Ramsay:** He a scholar and philosopher of great repute and has won several academic honours.
3. **Charles Tansley:** He is an intelligent young student of Mr. Ramsay.

4. **Minta Doyle:** He is a young man who loves Paul Rayley.
5. **Paul Rayley:** She loves Doyle.
6. **Augustus Carmichael:** He is an old man and poet.
7. **Lily Briscoe:** She is a painter.
8. **William Bankes:** He is an old friend of Mr. Ramsay's.
9. **James Ramsay:** He is six year old child of Ramsays.
10. **Cam :** Janes's sister.

The scene is laid in the island of Skye in the Hebrides.

The story is autobiographical in nature in the sense that:

(*i*) Mr. and Mrs. Ramsay resemble Mrs. Woolf's parents.

(*ii*) Lily Briscoe greatly resembles Mrs. Woolf herself.

The novel whether more artistic than Mrs. Dalloway or not, has earned as much if not more popularity than Mrs. Woolf's other masterpiece.

The novel is written on the stream-of-consciousness technique:

(*i*) In the *Window,* not only the personality of Mrs. Ramsay is revealed, but also we have the personality of Mr. Ramsay before us which is laid bare through the eyes of Lily Briscoe, Charles Tansley, William Bankes, etc.

(*ii*) In *Time Passes*, we learn more about Mrs. Ramsay and others through the memory of the Charwoman, Mrs. Mc Nab.

(*iii*) In *Lighthouse* we have another focus on Mrs. Ramsay through the memory of Lily Briscoe.

The novel is poetic, as usually all of Mrs. Woolf's novels are

ADVENTURES OF HUCKLEBERRY FINN

by Mark Twain

The novel opens with a warning to the reader:

"Persons attempting to find a moral in it will be banished; persons attempting to find a plot in it will be shot."

Although Mark Twain wrote this novel as a companion to Tom Sawyer, yet it is much more than that. However, a link with the earlier novel is established in the first chapter.

Huck is adopted by the widow Douglas to "civilize" him. The money which is found at the end of Tom Sawyer is put by Judge Thatcher on interest and it fetches a dollar to each boy 'all the year round.'

Huck is not much interested in Douglas' prescriptions of a strict disciplined moral life. Twain attains a technical tour de force by shifting narrative to the first person. This enables Twain to establish *point of view*. Huck is the model of *radical innocence* and *instinctive knowledge*.

SONS AND LOVERS

by D. H. Lawrence

The family of Morels lived in the mining village of Betswood. Mrs. Morel who has had a puritan nourishment, still upholds the values of refinement and nobility. She gets enamoured of Morel's rich ruddy face and merry laughter as well as wavy black hair. Mr. Morel is also captivated by her. The two get married.

The two have an antithetical nature and temperament. Whereas Mrs. Morel is a puritan lady, Mr. Morel is fond of a sensuous, luxurious life. He tries to domineer over his wife. But she rebels against this and the result is that even the children dislike Mr. Morel.

The estrangement between the couple becomes intense when one day, out of jealousy, Mr. Morel clips off the curls of the young William, whom his mother loves so such.

Mrs. Morel does not give up her efforts to reform her husband. But he rather goes more and more astray in his fondness for drinking, etc.

The couple had two more children. Morel tries to entertain the children, but often, the more Mrs. Morel instigates them against him, the more he teases them.

Mrs. Morel is frightened of her estranged relationship with her husband and focuses all her attention on her sons. She wants to possess her first child William whose love affair with Lily she condemns. But the boy dies of pneumonia.

Then Paul Morel, the third child, and the hero of the novel, falls ill. He is suffering from bronchitis. She nurses him tenderly and virtually treats him as her lover. This is how the famous Oedipus complex gets manifested in the novel.

Paul has relationship with three women, that is, his mother, Miriam and Clara. Among these, Miriam is his beloved.

The relationship between Paul and Miriam develops as Paul goes to the Willey Farm with his mother. He offers to teach her French and algebra and thus a friendship develops between the two. But, as Lawrence himself points out, their friendship is "chaste" and purely spiritual.

This relationship between Paul and Miriam cannot become an everlasting one since Mrs. Morel is afraid that Miriam is going to suck Paul's soul and she herself can ill-afford to lose her son. Paul too realises that as long as his mother is alive, his relationship with any woman cannot be permanent.

Paul is interested not only in a spiritual relationship with Miriam. He wants to have with her a physical contact also, but this she denies to him.

Since Paul cannot get physical satisfaction from Miriam, he enters into physical union with a married woman, Clara, who lives separately from her husband. But, the problem is that the woman is unable to satisfy Paul spiritually. The result is that Paul is thrashed by Clara's husband to his complete discomfiture.

Since Paul feels that his failure with both the women, Miriam and Clara, has been because of his mother's possessive nature towards his soul, he begins to hate her. But, when she falls ill with cancer, he tries to arrange the best medical treatment for her.

Being no longer able to witness the agonising misery of his mother, he ends the story of her life by administering morphia to her.

Now, it was impossible for Paul to establish relationship with any woman. He had to be lonely, and there was no escape for him from this state of affairs.

HAMLET

by Shakespeare

Introduction: The king of Denmark has recently died. On his death, his son, Hamlet, the Prince of Denmark, who is a student at the University of Wittenberg, is summoned to the Danish Court.

Hamlet feels miserable that his father's throne has been seized by his uncle, Claudius and his mother has married him.

Ophelia: Another shock comes to Hamlet when his beloved, Ophelia, rejects his suit on the advice of his father, Polonius.

The Ghost: Hamlet learns from his friend, Horatio, and two officers that they have sighted his father's ghost. As Hamlet himself encounters the ghost, the latter tells him the reality that his father had been poisoned by his uncle. The ghost also burdens Hamlet with the responsibility of avenging his death.

The spies: Claudius appoints two spies, Rosencrantz and Guildenstern to keep a watch on Hamlet. The latter arranges the staging of a play "The Murder of Gonzago" to which the king is also invited. The king's abnormal behaviour while watching the play (in which the murder of a king in a manner similar to that in which Hamlet's father is killed is staged) convinces Hamlet of Claudius's guilt.

Having been convinced of Claudius's and his mother's collusion in the murder of his father, Hamlet scolds his mother in a closed room. But as he hears an echo from behind the curtain, he thrusts his rapier at the person hidden. This is how Polonius who was eavesdropping gets killed.

Cause of Hamlet's Madness: Claudius tries his best to know the real cause of Hamlet's "madness," "ecstasy" or distraction, but having failed in his effort, he decides to send him out to England.

In the Ship: In the ship with the two spies, Rosencrantz and Guildenstern, Hamlet opens the sealed letter which contains the orders for his execution on his reaching England. He cleverly replaces these orders for the execution of the spies who lose their life in the venture.

Ophelia's Madness and Death: On learning about the death of her father, Ophelia goes mad, while her brother Laertes burns with the desire for revenge which is sharpened by Claudius.

The Duel: As Ophelia's dead body is being lowered in the grave, Hamlet grapples with Laertes. The two have a bloody duel in which both of them are badly wounded.

Claudius's end: When the two fighters are dying the villainy of Claudius is divulged by Laertes and Gertrude, the Queen. Hamlet kills Claudius with his poisoned rapier and soon Fortinbras arrives to be the next ruler of Denmark.

A Dialogue between the ghost and Hamlet

There are several extremely interesting scenes in Hamlet. Hamlet's dialogue with the ghost of his father is one of them.

MACBETH

by Shakespeare

Macbeth was the Lord of Glamis. He was related to Duncan, the king of Scotland. As the play begins, he returns with another general, Banquo, after crushing the rebellion of the Lord of Cawdor.

The Three Witches: When the two generals were returning, they met three witches, one of whom addressed Macbeth as the Lord of Cawdor. Macbeth felt greatly excited as he heard the witches' prophecies that he would soon be king and Banquo's descendants would also be kings. Thereafter, they disappeared.

Macbeth's Promotion: Soon thereafter, Macbeth was informed by two nobles that he had been made Lord of Cawdor by the king. This further thrilled Macbeth as he realized that the prophecy of the witches had come out true. He was so curious and enthusiastic that he wanted that the second prophecy of the witches that he would become the king should also turn true as early as possible.

Duncan's visit to Macbeth's Castle: The king Duncan wanted to visit Macbeth's castle to honour him. Meanwhile, Macbeth informed his wife through a letter regarding the witches' prophecies.

Lady Macbeth's Ambition: Lady Macbeth was even more ambitious than Macbeth and wanted to see him king. As Macbeth reached home, at the earliest, she incited her husband to murder Duncan to make the prophecy come out true. Macbeth was hesitant in accepting this advice.

Duncan was warmly welcomed by the Macbeth couple. He loved the peaceful atmosphere of the castle and went to sleep peacefully and without an iota of suspicion in his mind.

Lady Macbeth continued inciting her husband and even called him a coward when he expressed hesitation and his feeling of non-propriety in killing a guest who was also one of their kins.

The couple drugged the guards and they went into a sound sleep. Then Lady Macbeth herself went to kill Duncan, but now the king's face seemed to her as that of her father. So, she could not execute her plan.

The Bloody Dagger: Thereafter, Macbeth went into the king's room, but as he saw the vision of a bloody dagger, he changed his mind. Yet again, he took courage and struck a dagger into Duncan's heart and killed him.

The Voice: As Macbeth told his wife about the deed, he heard a voice: "Macbeth shall sleep no more." As Macbeth was now terribly overtaken by fear and madness, Lady Macbeth, showing greater courage, put the blood-covered dagger by the side of the guards and stained their clothes with blood to put the blame on them.

The Porter: Soon, the gate knocked. As the porter opened the gate, two of Duncan's nobles entered and went into the king's room where they found him dead.

Duncan's sons: As the news of the king's murder was conveyed to Macbeth, he killed the two guards. Meanwhile, as the news reached Scotland, the king's sons began to run for safety. The elder one, Malcom fled to England. Macbeth was then proclaimed king of Scotland.

Banquo: Macbeth was satisfied that the witches' second prophecy had also turned out to be true, but he feared Banquo. It was because the witches had also prophesied that Banquo's descendants would be kings. Hence, to perpetuate his kingdom Macbeth made up his mind to kill not only Banquo but also his son, Fleance.

The Banquet: Macbeth hit upon a plan. He invited all the nobles to a banquet. As Banquo and his son were on their way to Macbeth's castle, two assassins hired by Macbeth waylaid Banquo and his son. In the attempt, Banquo was killed but his son escaped.

Banquo's Ghost: Macbeth saw Banquo's ghost seated in a chair at the banquet. He even heard the ghost's whispers. Those present there were surprised to note Macbeth's strange behaviour.

For a brief period, the ghost disappeared, but soon it appeared again. Macbeth began to tremble and cry wildly. His such behaviour made him a suspect in the eyes of the guests.

The Witches Again: Macbeth went to consult the witches again. As he saw them, they called three ghosts. Macbeth was told the following three prophecies in turn :

(*i*) Macbeth should beware of Macduff.

(*ii*) No man born of woman could harm Macbeth.

(*iii*) Macbeth could never be defeated until Birnam Wood came to Dunsinane hill.

Lady Macbeth's mental state: Lady Macbeth was in an extremely depressed mood. As such she committed suicide. Macduff had run away to England. It was reported to Macbeth that the Birnam wood was marching towards Dunsinane hill. Macbeth felt puzzled. Soon, it was known that the green branches of the wood were being carried by Malcom's soldiers who were marching towards Macbeth.

Macbeth and Macduff: A fight started between Macbeth and Macduff face to face besides their soldiers fighting with their opposites. As Macduff told Macbeth that he was taken from his mother's womb, Macbeth felt so much discouraged that he got killed without a fight. The witches' prophecies had come full circle on Macbeth, as all his ambition was finally dashed to the ground with true poetic justice meeting out to him, which is perhaps not present in any other of Shakespeare's plays.

Macbeth is a great poet and *inter alia,* Macbeth is a wonderful piece of lyrical and dramatic poetry.

ARMS AND THE MAN

by G. B. Shaw

The young, romantic Raina is standing in her balcony to enjoy the beauty of the night in that month of November in 1885. She has all the romantic ideas of heroism of her lover Major Sergius Saranoff who is out taking part in the war between the Bulgarians and the Serbs.

Suddenly, there comes an intruder. He is a Swiss officer, Captain Bluntschli. He threatens Raina with his pistol and orders her to keep quiet.

Soon, a Russian army officer enters Raina's room to search for the fugitive. Raina hides Bluntschli behind the curtain. She tells the officer that nobody has entered her room.

As the officer goes away, Raina offers some chocolate cream to the fugitive. He tells her that he always carries chocolates to the war in place of cartridges. Then he goes to sleep.

It is the 6th of March, 1886. As Major Petkoff, Raina's father returns from the war, he is welcomed by Raina and her mother, Catherine. Major Sergius also comes. He has resigned from the army as he has not been given promotion.

The two family servants, Nicola, the man-servant and Louka, the maid-servent are already engaged. But when Sergius and Louka are alone, Sergius embraces Louka. She tells him that Raina loves a Swiss officer and would marry him.

Bluntschli comes to return the coat lent to him by Raina and Catherine. Major Petkoff instructs Bluntschli to prepare papers for sending three regiments. The papers are then delivered to the messengers.

Raina has already learnt from Bluntschli about non-heroic part of Sergius in the army. Sergius thinks that she is no longer loyal to him.

At last Raina is married to Bluntschli to which both Petkoff and his wife agree. Louka gets married to Serguis.

In this way, the myth of both the heroism of a soldier and the romance of love is exploded by Shaw in his own inimitable, interesting and simple way.

THE PORTRAIT OF A LADY

by Henry James

It is perhaps Henry James' most important novel which was written in 1881. James believed in images rather than in a story. Yet, if the novel is to be studied as a story, it can be said to be the psychological study of Isabel Archer a young American girl who leaves America with her aunt Mrs. Touchett and goes to Europe in a sort of what may be called her spiritual odyssey.

☛ 1. While portraying Isabel, Henry James had the model of his cousin Mary Temple called "Minny" in his mind. The young girl died in 1870 when she was only 24.
2. The European tour is arranged as once dreamed by Minny, though she got no opportunity to fulfil her dream.
3. Minny had died of T.B.; here we find Ralph dying of the same disease.
4. Gardencourt is a 16th Century English mansion– the kind of architecture Henry cherished.
5. Henry was particularly fond of painting and architecture.
6. Isabel's European odyssey comprises a visit to several countries, *e.g.* England, Italy, France, Greece, Turkey and Egypt.
7. It is to be noted that Henry James had a high regard for the European culture with its vast history, but he had no fondness for his native, American culture which had no history except that worth the name.
8. Isabel is shown as having fondness for Browning and George Eliot, as Minny also had. Besides she is also interested in the German philosophy.

THE GUIDE

by R.K. Narayan

Written in 1958, The Guide which won R.K. Narayan the Sahitya Akademi Award is one of his best novels and a masterpiece giving ample proof of his *tour de force* in the matter of artistic technique.

There are two distinct aspects of the story of The Guide. One half of it is supposed to be told by Raju, the hero, to one of his followers (as he turns from a tourist guide to a saint). The entire life story of Raju is however put in a flashback and told as such by the author. This technical achievement is a rare triumph in the modern artistic style.

Again, to understand more clearly, the story of Raju as saint forms the objective aspect and that of Raju as a tourist guide the autobiographical aspect. This artistic pattern is woven in the entire novel and this is what makes it artistically unique.

Simply speaking, it is the story of Raju's life and death. Raju has to indulge in several vocations and avocations, such as:

(*i*) as a food vendor at the railway station.
(*ii*) as a tourist guide.
(*iii*) as a sentimental adulterer.
(*iv*) as a manager to a dancing girl, Rosy.
(*v*) as a prisoner.
(*vi*) as a reluctantly holy martyred saint.

The setting is, as usual with Narayan, Malgudi town. It is at the newly set up railway station that Raj becomes a vendor. As a tourist guide also, he is quite successful.

One day Rosy, the dancer, and Marco, her husband, an archaeologist, engaged Raju as their guide. There were often quarrels between the husband and the wife.

Raju fell in love with Rosy and spent most of his time with her. He wanted to make her a famous dancer. Rosy's husband at last left her and she now lived with Raju. She was his 'snake-girl'.

Raju who was too ambitious, crossed the limit of propriety. He got addicted to habits such as gambling, drinking, etc. But when he forged the signature of Rosy on an important document, he was caught by Rosy's husband. He had to spend two years in jail. Then Rosy parted ways with him.

After completing his jail term, Raju went to a village, Mangal. There the people mistook him for a saint. Raju, depending on the art of simulation and dissimulation, found it a golden opportunity to be something, and if still dilly-dallying, he willy-nilly took it upon himself to be a holy man.

It was Raju's misfortune that his test was too near and too hard and it was beyond his imagination and comprehension. As usual, the villages were a superstitious lot, and as the famine hit the village, they expected of Raju to do some miracle to appease the rain God.

Raju had no grounding in such machinations of the so-called holy men and he had to go on a fast into death to cause the rain god to show his mercy. Once started, it was now impossible to give up the fast, as the whole area had been converted into a hubbub of pilgrims, tourists, visitors and mediamen who were reporting every now and then on Raju's determination and condition.

The days passed by and yet there was no sign of a cloud. It was the twelfth day of his fast. Raju was too weak to walk or even talk. Somehow he managed to reach the bank of the river, the venue of his prayer for rain. He collapsed uttering the words, "Velan, it's raining in the hills. I can feel it coming up under my feet, up my legs."

GORA

by R.N. Tagore

Written in 1923, it is perhaps the most famous novel of Tagore. It is a patriotic novel which expresses the voice of Resurgent India which is arousing to shake up the shackles of slavery. The novel expresses true secularism and a fusion of the oriental and the occidental. Even Gourmohan, the hero, the son of an English lady is brought up in a Hindu household and stands for that universal blend of ideologies and cultures which is so characteristic of Tagore.

MULTIPLE CHOICE QUESTIONS

1. Who wrote *Don Juan*?
A. Shakespeare B. Tennyson
C. Byron D. T.S. Eliot

2. Who wrote *The Life of Johnson*?
A. Boswell
B. Macaulay
C. Churchill
D. Sir Walter Raleigh

3. *Priest's Nun's Tale* was written by
A. Spenser B. Charles Lamb
C. Tennyson D. Chaucer

4. Who is said to have first used the term "Metaphysics"?
A. Matthew Arnold B. Sidney
C. Donne D. Dr. Johnson

5. The writer of *Volpone* is
A. Johnson B. Milton
C. Jonson D. Shelley

6. Which is the correct chronological sequence?
A. Spenser—Chaucer—Milton—Donne
B. Spenser—Wordsworth—Tennyson—T.S. Eliot
C. Milton—Shakespeare—Philip Larkin—Keats
D. Auden—Eliot—Shelley—Keats

7. *Pilgrim's Progress* was written by
A. Milton B. Shelley
C. Swinburne D. John Bunyan

8. The writer of the line : *"Stone walls do not a prison make"* is
A. Lovelace B. Milton
C. W.B. Yeats D. T.S. Eliot

9. *"Monkey's Paw"* is a
A. Poem B. Drama
C. Short story D. Novel

10. Lyrical Ballads appeared in
A. 1690 B. 1798
C. 1802 D. 1800

11. The writer of *'A Pair of Blue Eyes'* is
A. Thackeray B. Dickens
C. George Eliot D. Thomas Hardy

12. *Hard Times* was written by
A. Thackeray B. Dickens
C. Trollope D. Marquese

13. Which of the following poets was most impressed by the German philosophy?
A. Chaucer B. Wordsworth
C. Coleridge D. Southey

14. The two cities referred to in *"A Tale of Two Cities"* are
A. London and Paris B. London and Rome
C. Rome and Paris D. Moscow and Rome

15. *The Peasant's Bread* is a story by
A. Maupassant B. Tagore
C. R.K. Narayan D. Tolstoy

16. *The Financial Express* was written by
A. Raja Rao B. R.K. Narayan
C. Tagore D. Mulk Raj Anand

17. *"Negative Capability"* is a term associated with
A. Tagore B. Shelley
C. Keats D. Coleridge

18. The most impressive treatment of "imagination" has been given by
A. Coleridge B. Shelley
C. Eliot D. Yeats

19. *Lady Chatterley's Lover* was banned because it was considered
A. obscene B. revolutionary
C. obscurantist D. None of these

20. *For Whom The Bell Tolls* was written by
A. Marquese B. Hemingway
C. Hawthorne D. None of these

21. The writer of : *"A Pair of Mustachios"* is
A. Anand B. Tagore
C. Raja Rao D. Anita Desai

22. The writer of *Scarlet Letter* is
A. Henry James B. James Joyce
C. Hawthorne D. None of these

23. Rousseau is associated with
A. French Revolution
B. American War of Independence
C. Russian (Bolshevik) Revolution
D. None of these

24. Who wrote *'Train to Pakistan'*?
A. Narayan
B. Manohar Malgaon
C. Khushwant Singh
D. Anand

25. Who is the writer of *Azadi*?
A. R.K. Narayan B. Khushwant Singh
C. Tagore D. Chaman Nahal

26. *"The God of Small Things"* is written by
A. R.K. Narayan B. Hemingway
C. Graham Greene D. Arundhati Roy

27. Who wrote the poem *"Listeners"*?
A. Tennyson B. Thomas Hood
C. Goldsmith D. Walter de la Mare

28. In writing *"Canterbury Tales"* Chaucer was influenced by
A. Decameron
B. The Divine Comedy
C. The Holy Bible
D. None of these

29. *'Animal Farm'* was written by
A. James Joyce B. Virginia Woolf
C. George Orwell D. Hemingway

30. Shobha De is a
A. poet B. dramatist
C. novelist D. an actress

31. Dunciad was written by
A. Dryden B. Pope
C. Tennyson D. Shelley

32. Bernard Shaw got the Nobel Prize for
A. Pygmalion
B. Man and Superman
C. Saint Joan
D. None of these

33. The Victorian Period is marked by
A. Great political upheavals
B. Great social security
C. Great wars
D. Economic deprivation

34. Swift is known mainly as
A. an essayist B. a poet
C. a satirist D. a short story writer

35. Who is the writer of the novel *"The Village"*?
A. Khushwant Singh B. Anita Desai
C. Mulk Raj Anand D. R.K. Narayan

36. The most famous writer of the heroic couplet is
A. Dryden B. Chaucer
C. Spenser D. Pope

37. *Macflecknoe* is a poem written by
A. Dryden B. Pope
C. Tennyson D. Yeats

38. Who wrote *'Everyman in His Humour'*?
A. Shakespeare B. Jonson
C. Milton D. Keats

39. *'Indian Jugglers'* is an essay by
A. De Quincey B. Gardiner
C. Hazlitt D. Lamb

40. Who wrote *'The Gropes of Wrath'*?
A. Pearl Buck B. Hemingway
C. Virginia Woolf D. John Steinbeck

41. Who rendered into English the ancient Greek tragedy *"Atlanta in Calydon"*?
A. Swinburne
B. Shelley
C. Tennyson
D. Arthur Hugh Clough

42. *The Deserted Village* was written by
A. Cowper B. Goldsmith
C. Keats D. Johnson

43. *'Savitri'* is an epic written by
A. Tagore
B. Prem Chand
C. Aurobindo
D. Bankim Chandra Chatterjee

44. The anthem *"Vande Mataram"* occurs in
A. Godan B. Anand Math
C. Gora D. Train to Pakistan

45. *'All Fool's Day'* is an essay written by
A. Charles Lamb B. Hazlitt
C. A.G. Gardiner D. R.C. Stevenson

46. The drama *Tamburlaine* is written by
A. Shakespeare B. Marlowe
C. Lyly D. Green

47. The book *"Appreciations"* was written by
A. Morris B. Arnold
C. Walter Pater D. Christina Rossetti

48. *"The Admirable Crichton"* was written by
A. Steinbeck B. T.S. Eliot
C. Trollope D. James Barrie

49. *"The Death of a Salesman"* was written by
A. James Barrie B. Eugene O'Neill
C. Arthur Miller D. None of these

50. The Restoration period is said to have started from
A. 1660 B. 1676
C. 1625 D. 1645

51. Who wrote *"The Lady's Not for Burning"*?
A. Barrie B. Christopher Fry
C. Robert Bridges D. T.S. Eliot

52. Who wrote the poem *"Brahma"*?
A. T.S Eliot B. Emerson
C. Whitman D. Frost

53. The writer of *Walden* is
A. Tennyson B. Whitman
C. Thoreau D. Frost

54. In *'Sons and Lovers'* Lawrence has depicted the life of
A. factory workers B. miners
C. farmers D. animals

55. Who wrote *Kim*?
A. Kipling B. Tagore
C. Lawrence D. Narayan

56. *'The Hairy Ape'* is a famous play by
A. Barrie B. Eugene O'Neill
C. Christopher Fry D. T.S. Eliot

57. Who is the writer of *Frankenstein*?
A. George Eliot B. Jane Austen
C. Mary Shelley D. Emile Bronte

58. Who wrote the *'Cries of Children'*?
A. Robert Browning B. Elizabeth Barrett
C. Thomas Hood D. Cowper

59. Which poet is known as poet's poet?
A. Shakespeare B. Milton
C. Spenser D. Shelley

60. Who wrote the maximum number of sonnets?
A. Shakespeare B. Milton
C. Sidney D. Wordsworth

61. *Adonais* is the eulogy written on the death of
A. Coleridge B. Byron
C. Keats D. Wordsworth

62. Who wrote *Mother*?
A. Tolstoy B. Maxim Gorky
C. Chekhov D. Hardy

63. Who is associated with *Malgudi*?
A. Narayan
B. Anand
C. Manohar Malgonkar
D. Anita Desai

64. The author of *Beowulf* is
A. Bede B. Cynewulf
C. Chaucer D. Unknown

65. The Anglo-Saxon period is often said to be from 450 to ......
A. 900 B. 1000
C. 1050 D. 1100

66. *"To a Mountain Daisy"* is a poem by
A. Wordsworth B. Shelley
C. Keats D. Burns

67. Who wrote: *"The Devil's Disciple"*?
A. Galsworthy B. Barrie
C. Shaw D. Fry

68. Who wrote *"The Decline and Fall of the Roman Empire"*?
A. Walter Raleigh B. Trollope
C. Smollett D. Edward Gibbon

69. Richard Hooker was a prose writer of the
A. Victorian period
B. Romantic period
C. Elizabethan period
D. Chaucerian age

70. Alexander Dumas was
A. an English writer B. an American writer
C. a French writer D. a German writer

71. Which one was not one of the Lake poets?
A. Shelley B. Wordsworth
C. Southey D. Coleridge

72. *The Theory of Catharsis* is associated with
A. Plato B. Dryden
C. Aristotle D. Sidney

73. Who wrote *'In Defence of Poetry'*?
A. T.S. Eliot B. Yeats
C. Keats D. Shelley

74. *'The Playboy of the Western World'* is a play by
A. Barrie B. Synge
C. Fry D. Eliot

75. *'Silent Woman'* is a play by
A. Marlowe B. Shakespeare
C. Ben Jonson D. Lyly

76. The Scene of *Beowulf* is laid in
A. England B. France
C. Spain D. None of these

77. *"Kidnapped"* was written by
A. Dickens B. Thackeray
C. Hardy D. R.L. Stevenson

78. *'The Prisoner of Zenda'* was written by
A. Sterne B. Trollope
C. Anthony Hope D. George Eliot

79. What was the full name of Cervantes?
A. Jim Cervantes
B. John Cervantes
C. Miguel de Cervantes
D. Sir Roger Cervantes

80. Besides being a poet, Chaucer was
A. a trader B. a manufacturer
C. a teacher D. a diplomat

81. The name of William Golding's first novel is
A. The Inheritors B. Lord of the Flies
C. Pincher Martin D. The Pyramid

82. The author of *Erewhon* is
A. Hardy B. Marquese
C. Samuel Butler D. Cervantes

83. Which of the following is a *Comedy of Manners*?
A. The Way of the World
B. The Duchess of Malfi
C. The Lady's Not for Burning
D. The Hairy Ape

84. Which one among the following is not a pessimist?
A. Gissing B. Browning
C. Hardy D. Thomson

85. Charles Reade's drama *"Drink"* was adapted from a work of
A. Goethe B. Zola
C. Mallarwe D. Tennyson

86. Which one among the following was not a utilitarian?
A. Rousseau B. James Mill
C. Ricardo D. Bentham

87. *'The Praise of Folly'* was written by
A. Walter Raleigh B. Thomas Moore
C. Charles Lamb D. Ruskin

88. Who wrote: *"In Praise of Idleness"*?
A. Bertrand Russell B. Thomas More
C. Charles Lamb D. Hazlitt

89. The real name of Saki is
A. H.H. Munro B. Samuel Butler
C. George Orwell D. The Duke

90. Who started: *"The Tatler"*?
A. Addison B. Swift
C. Steele D. Stevenson

91. The poem *'The Song of the Shirt'* was written by
A. Mrs. Browning B. Pope
C. Shelley D. Thomas Hood

92. *Sir Roger* was originally the creation of
A. Addison B. Dryden
C. Steele D. Milton

93. Who wrote: *"Areopagitica"*?
A. Charles Lamb B. Hazlitt
C. De Quincey D. Milton

94. *'The Selfish Giant'* is a story written by
A. Tagore B. Oscar Wilde
C. Maupassant D. Tolstoy

95. Who wrote : *"Four Quartets"*?
A. T.S. Eliot B. W.B. Yeats
C. W.H. Auden D. Philip Larkins

96. Who wrote : *"Look Back in Anger"*?
A. Steinbeck B. Christopher Fry
C. John Osborne D. Barrie

97. Who wrote : *"The Devils of Loundun"*?
A. Bertrand Russell B. Aldous Huxley
C. J.B. Priestley D. Hazlitt

98. Who wrote : *"Principles of Human Knowledge"*?
A. Milton B. John Bunyan
C. Nash D. George Berkeley

99. Who wrote : *"Liber Amoris"*?
A. Lamb B. Hazlitt
C. Byron D. Wordsworth

100. *"A Railway Clerk"* is a poem by
A. Keki N. Daruwallah
B. Nissim Ezekiel
C. Shiv K. Kumar
D. Jayanta Mahapatra

101. Who won The Booker of Bookers?
A. Arundhati Roy B. Khushwant Singh
C. Mulk Raj Anand D. Salman Rushdie

102. Who wrote: *"The Battle of Books"*?
A. Bacon B. Hazlitt
C. Swift D. None of these

103. Who wrote: *"Nectar in a Sieve"*?
A. Mulk Raj Anand
B. Manohar Malgonkar
C. Kamala Markandaya
D. Pearl S. Buck

104. *'The Good Earth'* was written by
A. Raja Rao
B. R.K. Narayan
C. Pearl S. Buck
D. Kamala Markandaya

105. The writer of *'The Dove Found No Rest'* is
A. Pearl S Buck B. Hemingway
C. Raja Rao D. Dennis Stoll

106. Who wrote: *"So Many Hungers"*?
A. Bhabani Bhattacharya
B. Kamala Markandaya
C. Manohar Malgonkar
D. Chaman Nahal

107. Who is the writer of *"The Middleman and Other Stories"*?
A. Mulk Raj Anand B. Bharati Mukherjee
C. Tagore D. Prem Chand

108. Cicero was a Roman
A. philologist B. physician
C. orator D. None of these

109. Who is the writer of *"Gita Rahasya"*?
A. Tulsi Das B. Vivekananda
C. Shivananda D. B.G. Tilak

110. *'The Rubaiyat of Omar Khayyam'* was translated into English by
A. Robert Browning B. Tennyson
C. Fitz Gerald D. Hopkins

111. Mayakovsky was the famous poet of
A. France B. Italy
C. Austria D. Russia

112. Marquese originally wrote his *"One Hundred Years of Solitude"* in
A. French B. German
C. Spanish D. Italian

113. Identify Emile Bronte's novel in the following
A. Persuasion
B. Wuthering Heights
C. Jane Eyre
D. Middlemarch

114. Which one is believed to be the first English tragedy?
A. Gorboduc
B. The Spanish Tragedy
C. Dr. Faustus
D. The Jew of Malta

115. Which of the following works is not by Milton?
A. Paradise Lost B. Il Penseroso
C. Lycidas D. Maud

116. *'Music At Night'* is a book of essays by
A. A.G. Gardiner B. Bertrand Russell
C. Aldous Huxley D. Chesterton

117. The character of Sherlock Holmes was created by
A. Arthur Conan DoyleB. Hazlitt
C. I.A. Richards D. Agatha Christie

118. Who wrote the Preface to the *Gitanjali*?
A. W.B. Yeats B. T.S. Eliot
C. Auden D. Philip Larkin

119. What can be said to be the tragic flaw in *Hamlet*?
A. Revenge B. Indecisiveness
C. Hastiness D. Suspicion

120. Who wrote *'The Spanish Tragedy'*?
A. Shakespeare B. Thomas Kyd
C. Marlowe D. Lyly

121. Name the author of *"1984"*
A. George Orwell B. Graham Greene
C. Naipaul D. James Joyce

122. Who is the creator of *Wessex*?
A. Dickens B. Smollett
C. Meredith D. Hardy

123. Whose novel *"The Foundation Pit?"* was discovered only a few years ago?
A. Andrey Platanov B. Cherneshevysky
C. Jane Austen D. George Eliot

124. The novel *"We"* was written by
A. Andrey Platanov B. Tolstoy
C. Maxim Gorky D. Zamayatin

125. Name the writer of *"What Is To Be Done"*
A. Zamayatin B. Gorky
C. Cherneshevysky D. Chekhov

126. Name the writer of the novel *"Les Miserables"*
A. Virginia Woolf B. Mrs. Radcliffe
C. Victor Hugo D. James Joyce

127. Which of the following novels is not by Salman Rushdie?
A. Midnight's Children
B. Grimus
C. The Moor's Last Sigh
D. The Lighthouse

128. A sonnet comprises
A. 16 lines B. 14 lines
C. 12 lines D. 20 lines

129. Who is renowned for his outstanding work *"Holy Sonnets"*?
A. Donne B. Herrick
C. Milton D. Pope

130. Which of the following is not written by Hugo Charteris?
A. Pictures in the Wall
B. A Piece of String
C. The Old Boys
D. The Boarding House

131. Which of the following works is by H.G. Wells?
A. All in a Garden Fair
B. The Invisible Man
C. A Child of the Jago
D. Point Counter Point

132. Who wrote : *"The Ideal of a Christian Church"*?
A. John Keble
B. Newman
C. Nash
D. William George Ward

133. Which of the following odes is not by Keats?
A. Ode on Intimations of Immortality
B. Ode to a Nightingale
C. Ode on a Grecian Urn
D. Ode to Autumn

134. Which of the following works is not that of David Hume?
A. Treatise of Human Nature
B. The Rise and Fall of the Roman Empire
C. Political Discourses
D. History of Great Britain

135. Who is the writer of *'The School for Scandal'*?
A. Ben Jonson B. R.B. Sheridan
C. Congreve D. Webster

136. Who is the writer of the poem *"The Canonization"*?
A. Milton B. Dryden
C. Donne D. Chaucer

137. Name the writer of the poem *"Wind Hour"*?
A. Hopkins B. Eliot
C. Dryden D. Yeats

138. Who is the writer of the poem *"Adam's Course"*?
A. Eliot B. Tagore
C. Yeats D. Shelley

139. Who wrote the poem: *"Lay Your Sleeping Head"*?
A. Auden B. Yeats
C. Stephen Spender D. Ted Hughes

140. The play *"The Birthday Party"* is written by
A. G.B. Shaw B. Galsworthy
C. Harold Pinter D. Osborne

141. Who is believed to be the writer of *"On the Sublime"*?
A. Aristotle B. Longinus
C. Plato D. M. Arnold

142. Name the author of *"An Essay on Dramatic Poesie"*
A. Dryden B. Sidney
C. Shelley D. Arnold

143. Who is the writer of *"Culture and Society"*?
A. Cleanth Brooks
B. Eliot
C. Bertrand Russell
D. Raymond Williams

144. The writer of the *'Mirror and the Lamp'* is
A. Hume B. Lionel Trilling
C. M.H. Abrams D. Sean Lucy

145. The writer of *"Provide Provide"* is
A. Whitman B. Frost
C. Yeats D. Auden

146. Who wrote *"Desire Under the Elms"*?
A. Arthur Miller B. Osborne
C. Eugene O'Neill D. Shaw

147. Who is the writer of *"A Severed Head"*?
A. Iris Murdoch B. Paul Scott
C. Goldwing D. Huxley

148. *'Das Kapital'* is written by
A. Engel B. Freud
C. Marx D. Lawrence

149. *"Waiting for Godot"* is written by
A. Samuel Beckett B. Ibsen
C. Brecht D. Chekhov

150. Who is the writer of *"A House for Mr. Biswas"*?
A. Salman Rushdie
B. V.S. Naipaul
C. Vikram Seth
D. R.K. Narayan

151. Name which is not the work of Marlowe
A. Richard I B. Tambarlaine
C. The Jew of Malta D. Dr. Faustus

152. Name the writer of the poem *"The Weary Blues"*
A. Longfellow B. Whitman
C. Frost D. Langston Hughes

153. Which of the following poems is not written by Robert Lowell?
A. In the Cage B. Dolphin
C. Good Morning D. The Old Flame

154. Which of the following poems is written by Wallace Stevens?
A. Red Sun Blues B. Sunday Morning
C. From Survivor D. "Going"

155. Which of the following poems is not written by Philip Larkin?
A. Art Grass B. Sad Steps
C. Traveller D. Church going

156. *Oedipus Rex* was written by
A. Sophocles B. Homer
C. Seneca D. Aeschylus

157. Flaubert's famous work is
A. Odysseus B. Madame Bovary
C. The Trial D. The Outsider

158. Northrop Fry is basically a
A. Dramatist B. Novelist
C. Poet D. Critic

159. The writer of *"The Beauty in a State"* is
A. Raja Rao
B. Tagore
C. Shelley
D. Ananda Coomaraswami

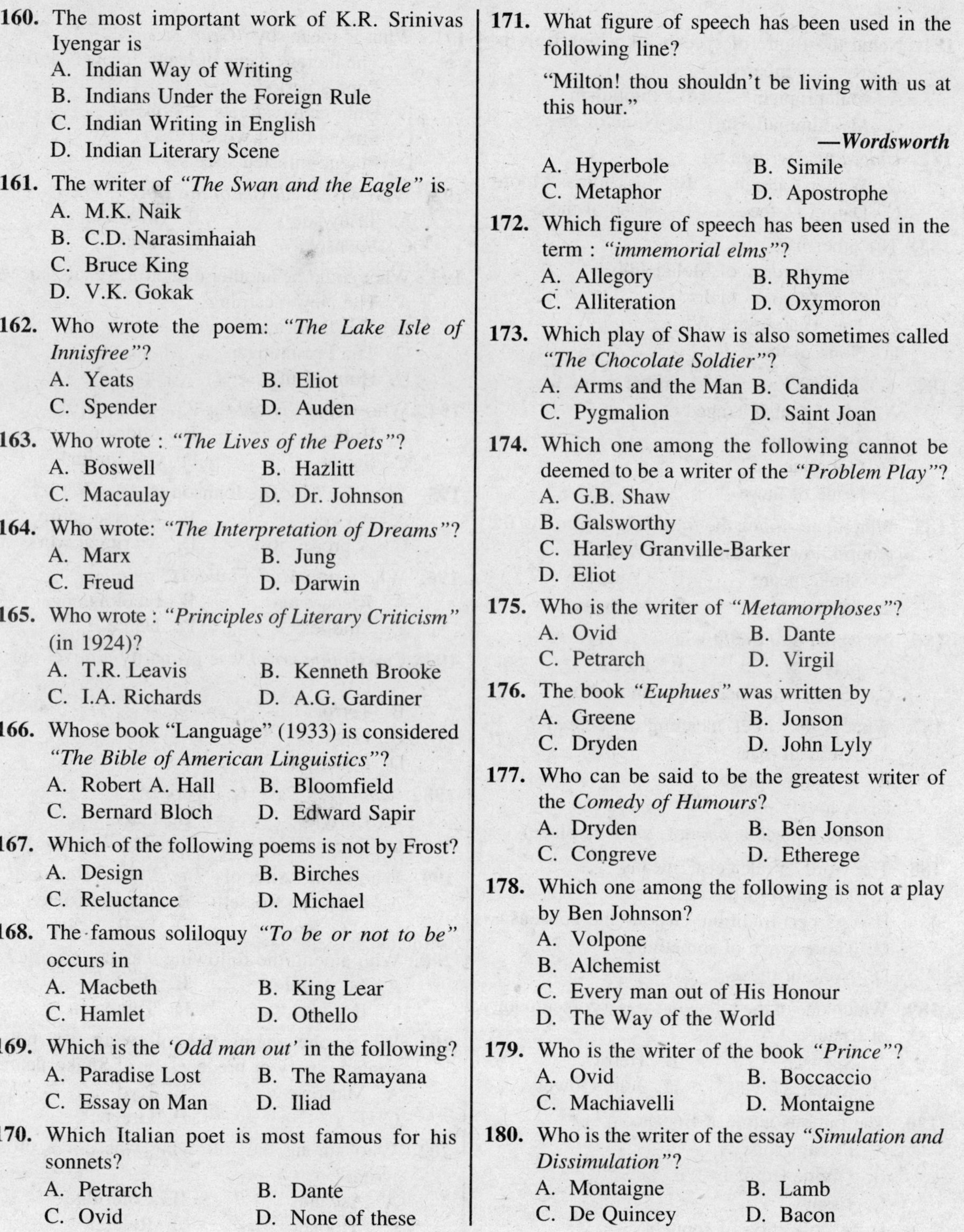

160. The most important work of K.R. Srinivas Iyengar is
A. Indian Way of Writing
B. Indians Under the Foreign Rule
C. Indian Writing in English
D. Indian Literary Scene

161. The writer of *"The Swan and the Eagle"* is
A. M.K. Naik
B. C.D. Narasimhaiah
C. Bruce King
D. V.K. Gokak

162. Who wrote the poem: *"The Lake Isle of Innisfree"*?
A. Yeats B. Eliot
C. Spender D. Auden

163. Who wrote : *"The Lives of the Poets"*?
A. Boswell B. Hazlitt
C. Macaulay D. Dr. Johnson

164. Who wrote: *"The Interpretation of Dreams"*?
A. Marx B. Jung
C. Freud D. Darwin

165. Who wrote : *"Principles of Literary Criticism"* (in 1924)?
A. T.R. Leavis B. Kenneth Brooke
C. I.A. Richards D. A.G. Gardiner

166. Whose book "Language" (1933) is considered *"The Bible of American Linguistics"*?
A. Robert A. Hall B. Bloomfield
C. Bernard Bloch D. Edward Sapir

167. Which of the following poems is not by Frost?
A. Design B. Birches
C. Reluctance D. Michael

168. The famous soliloquy *"To be or not to be"* occurs in
A. Macbeth B. King Lear
C. Hamlet D. Othello

169. Which is the *'Odd man out'* in the following?
A. Paradise Lost B. The Ramayana
C. Essay on Man D. Iliad

170. Which Italian poet is most famous for his sonnets?
A. Petrarch B. Dante
C. Ovid D. None of these

171. What figure of speech has been used in the following line?
"Milton! thou shouldn't be living with us at this hour."
—Wordsworth
A. Hyperbole B. Simile
C. Metaphor D. Apostrophe

172. Which figure of speech has been used in the term : *"immemorial elms"*?
A. Allegory B. Rhyme
C. Alliteration D. Oxymoron

173. Which play of Shaw is also sometimes called *"The Chocolate Soldier"*?
A. Arms and the Man B. Candida
C. Pygmalion D. Saint Joan

174. Which one among the following cannot be deemed to be a writer of the *"Problem Play"*?
A. G.B. Shaw
B. Galsworthy
C. Harley Granville-Barker
D. Eliot

175. Who is the writer of *"Metamorphoses"*?
A. Ovid B. Dante
C. Petrarch D. Virgil

176. The book *"Euphues"* was written by
A. Greene B. Jonson
C. Dryden D. John Lyly

177. Who can be said to be the greatest writer of the *Comedy of Humours*?
A. Dryden B. Ben Jonson
C. Congreve D. Etherege

178. Which one among the following is not a play by Ben Johnson?
A. Volpone
B. Alchemist
C. Every man out of His Honour
D. The Way of the World

179. Who is the writer of the book *"Prince"*?
A. Ovid B. Boccaccio
C. Machiavelli D. Montaigne

180. Who is the writer of the essay *"Simulation and Dissimulation"*?
A. Montaigne B. Lamb
C. De Quincey D. Bacon

181. Name the figure of speech for which Lyly is chiefly remembered
A. Malapropism B. Euphuism
C. Melodramaticism D. None of these

182. *Utopia* was written by
A. Walter Raleigh B. Sir Thomas Moore
C. Daniel Defoe D. None of these

183. The other name for *Euphues* is
A. The Anatomy of Melancholy
B. The Anatomy of Joy
C. The Anatomy of Wit
D. None of these

184. *Ferrex and Porrex* is the other name for
A. The Spanish Tragedy
B. Dr. Faustus
C. Goboduc
D. None of these

185. Which one among the following belongs to the group known as University Wits?
A. Shakespeare B. Congreve
C. Dryden D. Marlowe

186. *Astrophel and Stella* is a
A. play B. novel
C. sonnet sequence D. short story

187. What is the Greek meaning of *'Utopia'*?
A. An ideal place
B. A healthy place
C. A lovely place
D. Not a place (=*ou*=not; *topos*=a place)

188. The word "Volksgeist" means
A. The spirit of the age
B. (As per) tradition, custom and consensus
C. The essence of something
D. None of these

189. Which one of the following was a contemporary of Chaucer?
A. Spenser B. Herrick
C. Robert Graves D. John Gower

190. The famous work of Boccaccio is
A. Decameron
B. Divine Comedy
C. Essays
D. A collection of sonnets

191. What is meant by *"Grub Street"*?
A. The literary scene of hacks' crowds during Pope's period.
B. Unhygienic streets of London
C. Streets full of worms
D. Plague-infested streets

192. Who wrote: *"Idylls of the King"*?
A. Tennyson B. Browning
C. Spenser D. Keats

193. What could be another name for Renaissance?
A. The New Learning
B. The Reformation
C. The Prostantism
D. Humanism

194. Who wrote: *'Hudibras'*?
A. Butler B. Addison
C. Steele D. Goldsmith

195. *"London"* by Dr. Johnson is
A. An epic B. A verse satire
C. A prose satire D. A critical work

196. Who wrote *Moll Flanders*?
A. Richardson B. Fielding
C. Smollett D. Defoe

197. *The Gothic novel* was primarily a novel of
A. Pity
B. Terror
C. Love
D. Description of nature

198. *'Unto This Last'* is a work by
A. Carlyle B. Pater
C. Oscar Wilde D. John Ruskin

199. Who is the writer of *"The Blessed Damozel"*?
A. Christina Rossetti B. Emile Bronte
C. D.G. Rossetti D. W.B. Yeats

200. Who among the following was not a critic?
A. M. Arnold B. Ruskin
C. Dryden D. Tennyson

201. Which one among the following was not a contemporary or predecessor of Shakespeare?
A. Marlowe B. Kyd
C. Fry D. Greene

202. Who among the following was not a prose writer?
A. Ascham B. Coleridge
C. Hooker D. Raleigh

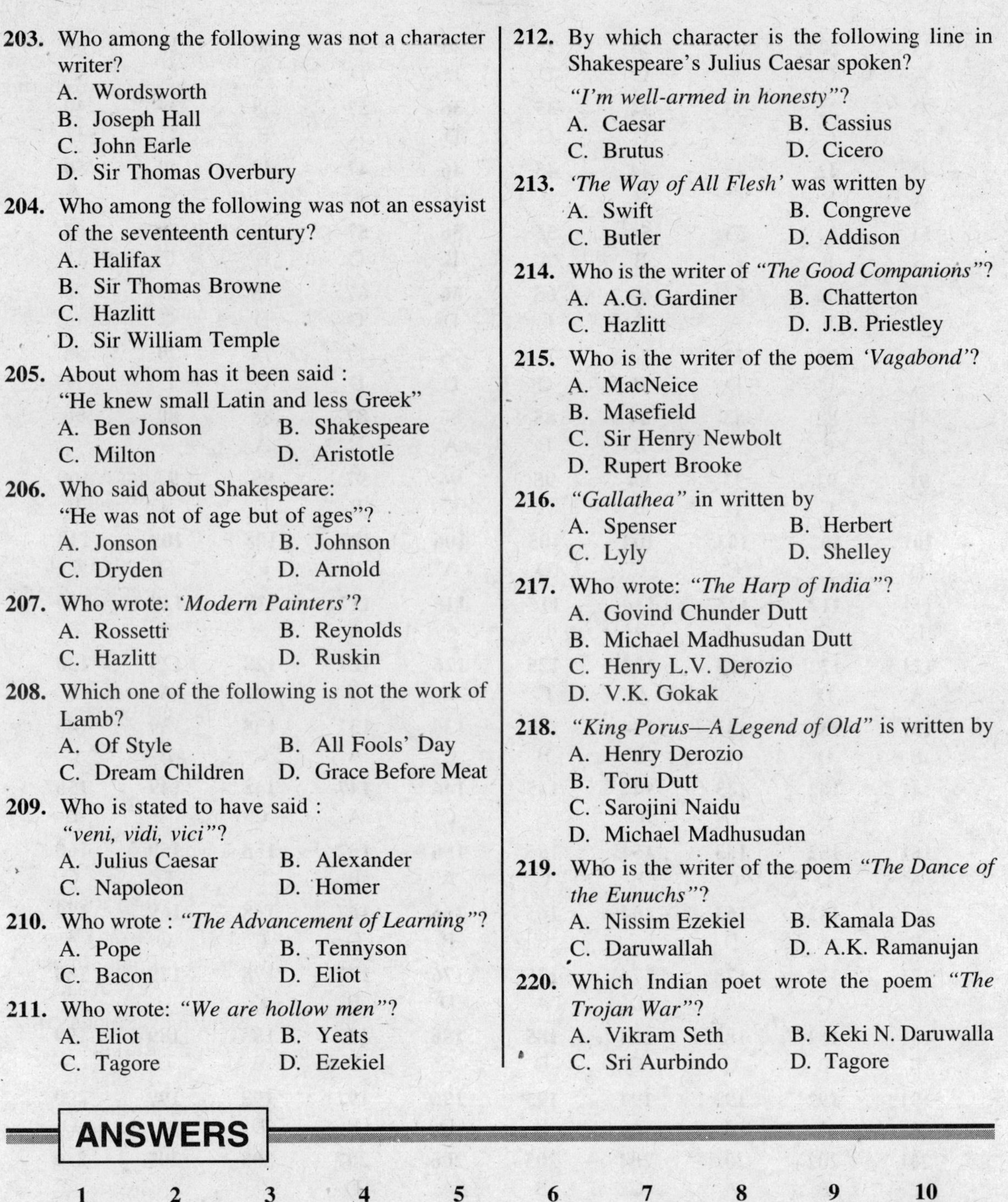

203. Who among the following was not a character writer?
A. Wordsworth
B. Joseph Hall
C. John Earle
D. Sir Thomas Overbury

204. Who among the following was not an essayist of the seventeenth century?
A. Halifax
B. Sir Thomas Browne
C. Hazlitt
D. Sir William Temple

205. About whom has it been said :
"He knew small Latin and less Greek"
A. Ben Jonson B. Shakespeare
C. Milton D. Aristotle

206. Who said about Shakespeare:
"He was not of age but of ages"?
A. Jonson B. Johnson
C. Dryden D. Arnold

207. Who wrote: '*Modern Painters*'?
A. Rossetti B. Reynolds
C. Hazlitt D. Ruskin

208. Which one of the following is not the work of Lamb?
A. Of Style B. All Fools' Day
C. Dream Children D. Grace Before Meat

209. Who is stated to have said :
"veni, vidi, vici"?
A. Julius Caesar B. Alexander
C. Napoleon D. Homer

210. Who wrote : *"The Advancement of Learning"*?
A. Pope B. Tennyson
C. Bacon D. Eliot

211. Who wrote: *"We are hollow men"*?
A. Eliot B. Yeats
C. Tagore D. Ezekiel

212. By which character is the following line in Shakespeare's Julius Caesar spoken?
"I'm well-armed in honesty"?
A. Caesar B. Cassius
C. Brutus D. Cicero

213. *'The Way of All Flesh'* was written by
A. Swift B. Congreve
C. Butler D. Addison

214. Who is the writer of *"The Good Companions"*?
A. A.G. Gardiner B. Chatterton
C. Hazlitt D. J.B. Priestley

215. Who is the writer of the poem *'Vagabond'*?
A. MacNeice
B. Masefield
C. Sir Henry Newbolt
D. Rupert Brooke

216. *"Gallathea"* in written by
A. Spenser B. Herbert
C. Lyly D. Shelley

217. Who wrote: *"The Harp of India"*?
A. Govind Chunder Dutt
B. Michael Madhusudan Dutt
C. Henry L.V. Derozio
D. V.K. Gokak

218. *"King Porus—A Legend of Old"* is written by
A. Henry Derozio
B. Toru Dutt
C. Sarojini Naidu
D. Michael Madhusudan

219. Who is the writer of the poem *"The Dance of the Eunuchs"*?
A. Nissim Ezekiel B. Kamala Das
C. Daruwallah D. A.K. Ramanujan

220. Which Indian poet wrote the poem *"The Trojan War"*?
A. Vikram Seth B. Keki N. Daruwalla
C. Sri Aurbindo D. Tagore

ANSWERS

1	2	3	4	5	6	7	8	9	10
C	A	D	D	C	B	D	A	C	B
11	**12**	**13**	**14**	**15**	**16**	**17**	**18**	**19**	**20**
D	B	C	A	D	B	C	A	A	B

21	22	23	24	25	26	27	28	29	30
A	C	A	C	D	D	D	A	C	C
31	32	33	34	35	36	37	38	39	40
B	C	A	C	C	D	A	B	C	D
41	42	43	44	45	46	47	48	49	50
A	B	C	B	A	B	C	D	C	A
51	52	53	54	55	56	57	58	59	60
B	B	C	B	A	B	C	B	C	D
61	62	63	64	65	66	67	68	69	70
C	B	A	D	C	D	C	D	C	C
71	72	73	74	75	76	77	78	79	80
A	C	D	B	C	D	D	C	C	D
81	82	83	84	85	86	87	88	89	90
B	C	A	B	B	A	B	A	A	C
91	92	93	94	95	96	97	98	99	100
D	C	D	B	A	C	B	D	B	B
101	102	103	104	105	106	107	108	109	110
D	C	C	C	D	A	B	C	D	C
111	112	113	114	115	116	117	118	119	120
D	C	B	A	D	C	A	A	B	B
121	122	123	124	125	126	127	128	129	130
A	D	A	D	C	C	D	B	A	B
131	132	133	134	135	136	137	138	139	140
B	D	A	B	B	C	A	C	A	C
141	142	143	144	145	146	147	148	149	150
B	A	D	C	B	C	A	C	A	B
151	152	153	154	155	156	157	158	159	160
A	D	C	B	C	A	B	D	D	C
161	162	163	164	165	166	167	168	169	170
B	A	D	C	C	B	D	C	C	A
171	172	173	174	175	176	177	178	179	180
D	C	A	D	A	D	B	D	C	D
181	182	183	184	185	186	187	188	189	190
B	B	C	C	D	C	D	B	D	A
191	192	193	194	195	196	197	198	199	200
A	A	A	A	B	D	B	D	C	D
201	202	203	204	205	206	207	208	209	210
C	B	A	C	B	A	D	A	A	C
211	212	213	214	215	216	217	218	219	220
A	C	C	D	B	C	C	D	B	C

●●●

2 Comprehension of Poems

1. TO HIS COY MISTRESS

Had we but world enough, and time,
This coyness, lady, were no crime.
We would sit down and think which way
To walk, and pass our long love's day;
Thou by the Indian Ganges' side
Shouldst rubies find; I by the tide
Of Humber would complain. I would
Love you ten years before the Flood;
And you should, if you please, refuse
Till the conversion of the Jews.
My vegetable love should grow
Vaster than empires, and more slow.
An hundred years should go to praise
Thine eyes, and on they forehead gaze;
Two hundred to adore each breast,
But thirty thousand to the rest;
An age at least to every part,
And the last age should show your heart.
For, lady, you deserve this state,
Nor would I love at lower rate.

But at my back I always hear
Time's winged chariot hurrying near;
And yonder all before us lie
Deserts of vast eternity.
Thy beauty shall no more be found,
Nor, in thy marble vault, shall sound
My echoing song; then worms shall try
That long preserv'd virginity,
And your quaint honour turn to dust,
And into ashes all my lust.
The grave's a fine and private place,
But none I think do there embrace.

Now therefore, while the youthful hue
Sits on thy skin like morning dew,
And while thy willing soul transpires
At every pore with instant fires,
Now let us sport us while we may;
And now, like am'rous birds of prey,
Rather at once our time devour,
Than languish in his slow-chapp'd power.
Let us roll all our strength, and all
Our sweetness, up into one ball;
And tear our pleasures with rough strife
Thorough the iron gates of life.
Thus, though we cannot make our sun
Stand still, yet we will make him run.

—*Andrew Marvell*

QUESTIONS

1. The poem is most similar in style and content to:

A. a lyric B. a panegyric
C. an ode D. a sonnet

2. The first stanza consists of all of the following except:

A. a steady meter B. metaphor
C. end rhymes D. anaphora

3. The word "coyness" in line 2 most likely means:

A. sedentary lifestyle B. hurried state
C. procrastination D. modesty

4. The second stanza differs from the first in that:

I. the imagery changes from libidinous to morbid
II. the tone changes from arrogant to desperate
III. the sound changes from alluring to chilling

A. I and II only
B. I and III only
C. II only
D. II and III only

5. The speaker's strategy in the passage as a whole consists of:
A. an introduction to a problem, deductive reasoning, criticism, and solution
B. soothing sounds, cogent examples, and personal anecdotes
C. seduction, accurate data, and historical examples
D. a major premise, minor premise, and conclusion

6. Which of the following lines contains internal rhyme?
A. line 2 B. line 16
C. line 6 D. line 4

7. The references to the "Indian Ganges" (5), the "Humber" (7), the "Flood" (8), and the "Jews" (10) serve to:
A. flatter and impress
B. confound and shock
C. startle and mystify
D. persuade and elude

8. In line 40, "his" refers to:
A. the speaker B. the addressee
C. "birds of prey" D. time

9. The phrase "vegetable love" (11) is:
A. an example of synesthesia
B. an oxymoron
C. intended to emphasize the speaker's immediate desire
D. a metaphor for the speaker's long-lasting love

10. Which of the following devices enhances the speaker's point in the last two lines of the passage?
A. assonance B. alliteration
C. figures of speech D. pun

11. "Time's winged chariot hurrying near" (22) can best be paraphrased as:
A. we must catch up with time
B. time is our rescuer
C. time flies
D. time is all-powerful like God

12. The words at the ends of lines 23 and 24 and at the ends of lines 27 and 28 are examples of:
A. slant rhyme
B. masculine rhyme
C. iambic pentameter
D. internal rhyme

13. The simile in line 34 serves to:
A. impress the addressee
B. underscore the addressee's ephemeral youth
C. distract the addressee
D. point out the addressee's natural beauty

2. THE AUTHOR TO HER BOOK

Thou ill-form'd off spring of my feeble brain,
Who after birth did'st by my side remain,
Till snatcht from thence by friends, less wise than true,
Who thee abroad exposed to public view,
Made thee in rags, halting to th' press to trudge,
Where errors were not lessened (all may judge).
At thy return my blushing was not small,
My rambling brat (in print) should mother call.
I cast thee by as one unfit for light,
The visage was so irksome in my sight,
Yet being mine own, at length affection would
Thy blemishes amend, if so I could.
I washed thy face, but more defects I saw,
And rubbing off a spot, still made a flaw.
I stretcht thy joints to make thee even feet,
Yet still thou run'st more hobbling than is meet.
In better dress to trim thee was my mind,
But nought save home-spun cloth, i' th' house I find.
In this array, 'mongst vulgars may'st thou roam.
In critics' hands, beware thou dost not come,
And take thy way where yet thou are not known.
If for thy father askt, say, thou hadst none;
And for thy mother, she alas is poor,
Which caused her thus to send thee out of door.

—*Anne Bradstreet*

QUESTIONS

1. The main topic of the poem is:
   A. an artist's relationship with her work
   B. an artist's dislike for her work
   C. the need for editing before publication
   D. unreasonable critics

2. The word "Thou" in line 1 indicates:
   A. the poem is a letter
   B. the poem is an invocation
   C. the speaker is employing apostrophe
   D. the speaker uses arcane vocabulary to make a point

3. The tone of the poem is:
   A. mournful
   B. nurturing
   C. self-deprecating
   D. vengeful

4. The poem is developed mainly through:
   A. rhyme
   B. iambic pentameter
   C. simile
   D. conceit

5. Who is the subject of the verb "Made" (5)?
   A. the press B. friends
   C. the speaker D. the book

6. The words "trudge" (5) and "judge" (6) are examples of:
   A. internal rhyme B. feminine rhyme
   C. slant rhyme D. masculine rhyme

7. The poem's rhythm is composed of:
   I. iambic pentameter
   II. terza rima
   III. heroic couplets
   A. I only
   B. I and II only
   C. II and III only
   D. I and III only

8. The poem contains all of the following devices except:
   A. enjambment
   B. imagery
   C. personification
   D. explicit metaphor

9. The relationship between the speaker and her addressee is most similar to the relationship between:
   A. a teacher and a student
   B. a nurturing father and a child
   C. a boss and an employee
   D. a fastidious artist and her painting

10. The speaker implies her book is all of the following except:
    A. inchoate
    B. disseminated prematurely
    C. fallible
    D. polemical

3. SUCCESS IS COUNTED SWEETEST...

Success is counted sweetest
By those who ne'er succeed.
To comprehend a nectar
Requires sorest need.
Not one of all the purple host
Who took the flag to-day
Can tell the definition,
So clear, of victory,
As he, defeated, dying,
On whose forbidden ear
The distant strains of triumph
Break, agonized and clear!

—*Emily Dickinson*

QUESTIONS

1. The overall tone of the poem is:
   A. pedantic
   B. didactic
   C. moralistic
   D. adagelike

2. The poem can be summarized by which of the following sentences?
   A. Only those who have achieved success understand its sweetness.
   B. Success comes only to those who risk and persevere.
   C. Success is best won through hard work.
   D. Only those who have not achieved success understand its sweetness.

3. The rhythm and beat of the poem as a whole can best be described as consisting of:
   A. three to four feet of iambs
   B. iambic pentameter
   C. iambic trimeter
   D. three to four feet of trochees

4. The structure of the poem consists of:
   A. a hypothesis, reasoning, and a solution
   B. a proposition and evidence
   C. one axiomatic sentence and two sentences with images demonstrating the axiom
   D. a theory and examples

5. The poem's language can be described as consisting of all of the following except:
   A. aphorisms B. homilies
   C. epigrams D. chiasmus

6. The alliteration in the first stanza serves to:
   A. soothe the reader
   B. highlight the envious tone
   C. complement the assonance in the first stanza
   D. emphasize the appeal of success by creating an appealing sound

7. The word "comprehend" in line 3 most likely means:
   A. to eat
   B. to figure out
   C. to determine
   D. to truly know

8. Line 5 is an example of what type of measured beat?
   A. iambic tetrameter
   B. iambic trimeter
   C. trochaic tetrameter
   D. iambic pentameter

9. The words "day" (6) and "victory" (8) provide an example of:
   A. feminine rhyme B. slant rhyme
   C. double entendre D. oxymoron

10. The poem's rhyme scheme is:
   A. *abcb defe ghih*
   B. *abab abab abab*
   C. *abcb abcb abcb*
   D. *abcd efgh ijkl*

4. GOD'S GRANDEUR

The world is charged with the grandeur of God.
It will flame out, like shining from shook foil;
It gathers to a greatness, like the ooze of oil
Crushed. Why do men then now not reck his rod?
Generations have trod, have trod, have trod;
And all is seared with trade; bleared, smeared with toil;
And wears man's smudge and shares man's smell: the soil
Is bare now, nor can foot feel, being shod.
And for all this, nature is never spent;
There lives the dearest freshness deep down things;
And though the last lights off the black West went
Oh, morning, at the brown brink eastward, springs—
Because the Holy Ghost over the bent
World broods with warm breast and with ah! bright wings.

—*Gerard Manley Hopkins*

QUESTIONS

1. The structure and form of the poem indicates that it is:
   A. a pastoral
   B. an elegy
   C. a Petrarchan sonnet
   D. an ode

2. The theme of the poem is best expressed by which one of its phrases?
   A. "It gathers to a greatness, like the ooze of oil" (3)
   B. "all is seared with trade; bleared, smeared with toil" (6)
   C. "Why do men then now not reck his rod" (4)
   D. "nature is never spent" (9)

3. The rhyme scheme of the poem is:
   A. *abbaabba cdccdc*
   B. *abcdefabcdefgg*
   C. *abab cdcd efef gg*
   D. *abbaabba cdcdcd*

4. Lines 1–3 contain an abundance of:
A. alliteration
B. asyndeton
C. anaphora
D. metaphor

5. The change in tone from lines 1–3 to lines 4–8 is:
A. a change from reverential to ambivalent
B. a change from perplexed to dismayed
C. a change from awe-inspired to dirgelike
D. a change from optimism to skepticism

6. The sound devices in line 4 serve to emphasize:
A. the superiority of men to God
B. the unity between men and God
C. the fearless independence of men
D. man's obliviousness to God's grandeur

7. In context, the repetition in line 5 highlights:
A. man's preference for the natural world
B. the inexorable nature of man's mistakes
C. the monotonous demands of an earthly life
D. man's temporary preference for industry and materiality over God

8. Line 6 contains all of the following devices except:
A. internal rhyme B. consonance
C. assonance D. enjambment

9. The change in sound from the first three lines to line 4 is:
A. a change from a mellifluous sound to a harsh sound
B. a change from a tranquil sound to a placid sound
C. a change from a confusing sound to a clear sound
D. a change from an inconsistent sound to a steady sound

10. The last six lines differ from the first eight in that:
A. the sound changes but the tone stays the same
B. God is portrayed as less powerful
C. the focus is more on man than on God
D. they reassure rather than question

11. The alliteration in the final six lines reinforces:
I. God's eminence
II. the speaker's confidence
III. God's harmony with the world
A. I only B. I and II only
C. III only D. I, II, and III

12. The poem ends with:
A. bemusement B. unrestrained awe
C. didacticism D. qualified hope

5. DEFEAT

Defeat, my Defeat, my solitude and my aloofness;
You are dearer to me than a thousand triumphs,
And sweeter to my heart than all world-glory.

Defeat, my Defeat, my self-knowledge and my defiance,
Through you I know that I am yet young and swift of foot
And not to be trapped by withering laurels.
And in you I have found aloneness
And the joy of being shunned and scorned.

Defeat, my Defeat, my shining sword and shield,
In your eyes I have read
That to be enthroned is to be enslaved,
and to be understood is to be leveled down,
And to be grasped is but to reach one's fullness
and like a ripe fruit to fall and be consumed.

Defeat, my Defeat, my bold companion,
You shall hear my songs and my cries and my silences,
And none but you shall speak to me of the beating of wings,
And urging of seas,
And of mountains that burn in the night,
And you alone shall climb my steep and rocky soul.

Defeat, my Defeat, my deathless courage,
You and I shall laugh together with the storm,
And together we shall dig graves for all that die in us,
And we shall stand in the sun with a will,
And we shall be dangerous.

—*Kahlil Gibran*

QUESTIONS

1. The mood that is established by the end of the poem is one of:
   A. confidence B. cynicism
   C. desire D. destruction
2. The poem as a whole is written as a(n):
   A. allegory B. anecdote
   C. letter D. apostrophe
3. The speaker sees "Defeat" primarily as his:
   A. friend B. mentor
   C. adversary D. obstacle
4. The speaker characterizes "Defeat" as all of the following except:
   A. second best to success
   B. distinct
   C. useful
   D. brave
5. The repetitive use of the word "And" at the start of many lines in the poem is:
   A. grammatically incorrect
   B. an example of hyperbole
   C. a device known as asyndeton
   D. a device known as anaphora
6. The metaphor of the "sword and shield" (9) is meant to:
   A. emphasize "Defeat's" emboldening powers
   B. characterize the speaker as invincible
   C. contradict the previous stanza's imagery
   D. change the poem's tone from sarcastic to laudatory
7. In the second stanza, the speaker reveals that:
   A. "Defeat" is a characteristic of the young
   B. "Defeat" is an actual person
   C. he sees value in "Defeat" because it makes him incorrigible
   D. he sees value in "Defeat" because it makes him self-aware
8. The speaker's address to "Defeat" as his "deathless courage" (21) shows:
   A. the poem's ironic tone
   B. the speaker's appreciation of death
   C. that courage and death are opposites
   D. that with "Defeat" comes temerity
9. The third stanza reveals that the speaker thinks success is:
   A. hypocritical
   B. unimaginable
   C. overrated
   D. easily obtained
10. The poem's refrain:
    A. is found in lines 1, 4, 9, 15, and 21 and characterizes "Defeat" as alone
    B. is found in all lines beginning with "And" and highlights the theme
    C. is found in all lines beginning with "And" and emphasizes the speaker's point
    D. is found in lines 1, 4, 9, 15, and 21 and enhances the poem's odelike quality

6. MY COUNTRY AWAKE

Where the mind is without fear and the head is held high;
Where knowledge is free;
Where the world has not been broken up into fragments by narrow
domestic walls;
Where words come out from the depth of truth;
Where tireless striving stretches its arms towards perfection;
Where the clear stream of reason has not lost its way into the
dreary desert sand of dead habit;
Where the mind is led forward by thee into ever-widening thought
and action—
Into that heaven of freedom, my Father, let my country awake.

—Rabindranath Tagore

QUESTIONS

1. The tone of the poem can best be described as:
   A. earnest B. plaintive
   C. pious D. optimistic
2. In the poem, the speaker addresses:
   A. his country B. himself
   C. a political leader D. God

3. The poem as a whole is made up of what type of sentence?
   A. cumulative
   B. compound-complex
   C. periodic
   D. compound

4. The poem as a whole is a:
   I. supplication
   II. prayer
   III. speech
   A. I only B. I and II only
   C. II only D. II and III only

5. The use of the word "Where" at the start of several clauses in the poem is a device known as:
   A. analogy B. apostrophe
   C. parallelism D. anaphora

6. Lines 1, 3, 6, and 8 all contain which sound device?
   A. enjambment B. alliteration
   C. consonance D. assonance

7. The speaker implies his country is all of the following except:
   A. fearful B. limited
   C. fettered D. irreparable

8. The "dreary desert sand of dead habit" (7–8):
   A. is an implied metaphor stressing the hopelessness of chronic behavior
   B. is an explicit metaphor emphasizing desperation
   C. is a conceit that contains alliteration
   D. contains a soothing sound to complement the speaker's dream of a desert country

9. The words "head . . . held" (1) and "desert . . . dead" (8) contain:
   A. consonance and imagery
   B. internal rhyme and assonance
   C. oxymora and alliteration
   D. alliteration and assonance

10. In the grammatical structure of lines 9–10, "the mind" is:
   A. the dependent clause
   B. the predicate
   C. the subject
   D. the object

7. TO THE VIRGINS, TO MAKE MUCH OF TIME

Gather ye rose-buds while ye may:
Old Time is still a-flying;
And this same flower that smiles to-day,
To-morrow will be dying.

The glorious lamp of heaven, the Sun,
The higher he's a-getting,
The sooner will his race be run,
And nearer he's to setting.

That age is best, which is the first,
When youth and blood are warmer;
But being spent, the worse, and worst
Times, still succeed the former.

—Then be not coy, but use your time,
And while ye may, go marry;
For having lost but once your prime,
You may for ever tarry.

—Robert Herrick

QUESTIONS

1. The poem is a(n):
   A. ode B. ballad
   C. sonnet D. lyric

2. In the poem, the speaker's tone can best be described as:
   A. encouraging B. vehement
   C. desperate D. pushy

3. The word "ye" in line 1 refers to:
   A. virgins
   B. the speaker's friend
   C. all women
   D. the reader

4. The device used in line 2 is:
   A. anachronism B. personification
   C. allusion D. sensory imagery

5. The word "tarry" in line 16 most likely means:
   A. marry B. regret
   C. beautiful D. delay

6. Alliteration is evident in which of the following lines?
   A. line 2 B. line 3
   C. line 4 D. line 5

7. The rose-buds are:
   A. dying
   B. an indication that the addressees are carefree
   C. a symbol of young girls' leisure time
   D. a metaphor for the ephemeral nature of youth and beauty

8. In the second stanza, the sun is characterized as:
   I. electric
   II. male
   III. a runner
   A. I only
   B. I and II only
   C. I and III only
   D. I, II, and III

9. In line 9, the words "best" and "first" create:
   A. masculine rhyme
   B. internal rhyme
   C. feminine rhyme
   D. consonance

10. Where does enjambment occur in the poem?
   A. line 4
   B. line 11
   C. line 13
   D. line 14

11. In line 12, "the former" refers to:
   A. the worse times
   B. the worst times
   C. the first age
   D. the time of matrimony

12. A major theme of the poem can best be summarized as:
   A. everything is temporary, especially youth and beauty
   B. time is a formidable foe
   C. young women should indulge in sexual intercourse as soon as possible
   D. "carpe diem"

13. The poem's rhyme scheme is:
   A. *ababcdcdefefghgh*
   B. *aabbccddeeff gghh*
   C. *abab cdcd efef ghgh*
   D. *abab abab abab abab*

8. MORNING AT THE WINDOW

They are rattling breakfast plates in basement kitchens,
And along the trampled edges of the street
I am aware of the damp souls of housemaids
Sprouting despondently at area gates.
The brown waves of fog toss up to me
Twisted faces from the bottom of the street,
And tear from a passer-by with muddy skirts
An aimless smile that hovers in the air
And vanishes along the level of the roofs.

—T. S. Eliot

QUESTIONS

1. The tone of the poem is developed through:
   I. diction
   II. imagery
   III. metaphor
   A. I only
   B. I and II only
   C. II and III only
   D. I, II, and III

2. Regarding the scene he is describing, the speaker is:
   A. removed and observant
   B. obsessed and upset
   C. optimistic
   D. fatalistic

3. The people described in the poem are characterized mostly as:
   A. ghostlike
   B. penurious
   C. starving
   D. pathetic

4. The poem's assonance:
   A. is found in the words "muddy skirts" (7) and emphasizes the ugliness of the scene being described
   B. is found in the words "faces from" (6) and creates a soothing sound to ease the speaker's discomfort
   C. is found in the words "fog toss" (5) and creates a feeling of upward movement to complement the movement of the waves
   D. is found in the words "brown waves" (5) and emphasizes the disparity between ugliness and beauty

5. The speaker is differentiated from the people he describes by:
   I. his wealth
   II. his location
   III. his actions

A. I only B. I and II only
C. II only D. II and III only

6. In line 5, the "waves" are:
   A. so big they reach the speaker's window
   B. a metaphor for the fog that carries the images of faces down below up to the speaker at his window
   C. part of the poem's bigger conceit that compares the scene below to an ocean
   D. part of a hypothetical situation thought up by the speaker

7. The words "fog . . . faces from" (5–6) are an example of:
   A. consonance B. repetition
   C. anaphora D. alliteration

8. The subject to which the word "tear" (7) refers is:
   A. a passer-by B. the speaker
   C. the brown waves D. an aimless smile

9. NOBODY COMES

Tree-leaves labour up and down,
And through them the fainting light
Succumbs to the crawl of night.
Outside in the road the telegraph wire
To the town from the darkening land
Intones to travelers like a spectral lyre
Swept by a spectral hand.

A car comes up, with lamps full-glare,
That flash upon a tree:
It has nothing to do with me,
And whangs along in a world of its own,
Leaving a blacker air;
And mute by the gate I stand again alone,
And nobody pulls up there.

—Thomas Hardy

QUESTIONS

1. The first line of both stanzas:
   I. ends in a word that is never rhymed
   II. sets a scene
   III. contains a steady meter
   A. I only B. I and II only
   C. II and III only D. II only

2. The alliteration in line 11:
   A. contrasts with the consonance in line 13
   B. does not match the content of line 11
   C. emphasizes the speaker's unity with the "world" (11)
   D. coincides with the alliteration in the previous line

3. We can interpret that the "air" becomes "blacker" (12) because of all of the following except:
   A. the speaker's isolation has become more palpable
   B. it mimics the speaker's emotional state
   C. the lights of the car have gone
   D. it is later at night now

4. The overall tone of the poem is:
   A. self-pitying
   B. eerie
   C. nostalgic
   D. irreverent

5. The first stanza contains all of the following devices except:
   A. consonance B. personification
   C. masculine rhyme D. simile

6. What is "Swept by a spectral hand" (7)?
   A. the darkening land B. travelers
   C. an instrument D. the speaker

7. In context, the word "spectral" (6, 7) most likely means:
   A. mythical B. invisible
   C. shining D. ghostly

8. The purpose of the simile in line 6 is:
   A. to offer optimism in a dark situation
   B. to emphasize the telegraph's power by humanizing it
   C. to add a soothing tone to an otherwise ominous mood
   D. to highlight the irony of the telegraph wire

9. The rhyme scheme of the poem is:
   A. *abab cdcd efef gg*
   B. *aabbccddeeff ggh*
   C. *ababcdc ababcdc*
   D. *abbcdcd eff gege*

10. The poem's theme can be interpreted as:
A. the natural environment is lonely
B. the natural world is omnipotent
C. isolation is a common state
D. the benefits of modern technology are dubious

10. O CAPTAIN! MY CAPTAIN!

O Captain! my Captain! our fearful trip is done!
The ship has weathered every wrack, the prize we sought is won.
The port is near, the bells I hear, the people all exulting,
While follow eyes the steady keel, the vessel grim and daring.

But, O heart! heart! heart!
Leave you not the little spot
Where on the deck my Captain lies,
Fallen cold and dead:

O Captain! my Captain! rise up and hear the bells!
Rise up! for you the flag is flung, for you the bugle trills:
For you bouquets and ribboned wreaths; for you the shores a-crowding:
For you they call, the swaying mass, their eager faces turning.

O Captain! dear father!
This arm I push beneath you.
It is some dream that on the deck
You've fallen cold and dead!

My Captain does not answer, his lips are pale and still:
My father does not feel my arm, he has no pulse nor will.
But the ship, the ship is anchored safe, its voyage closed and done:
From fearful trip the victor ship comes in with object won!
Exult, O shores! and ring, O bells!
But I, with silent tread,
Walk the spot my Captain lies,
Fallen cold and dead.

—***Walt Whitman***

QUESTIONS

1. The poem's style and content are most similar to those of:
A. a ballad B. a sestina
C. a sonnet D. an elegy

2. The poem is developed mainly through:
A. a refrain
B. an explicit metaphor
C. a metaphor
D. an extended, implied metaphor

3. The references to the captain change:
A. from exclamations in the first and second segments to calm statements in the third segment
B. to direct addresses in the third segment
C. to internal thoughts in the third segment
D. to dialogue in the second segment

4. The captain in the poem is most likely:
A. a metaphor for a nation's leader
B. an excellent seafarer who has suddenly died
C. a metaphor for the speaker's father
D. a symbol of the mighty naval industry

5. The repetition of the phrase "O Captain! my Captain" is called:
A. a refrain
B. an echo
C. anaphora
D. epistrophe

6. The three segments of the poem are divided according to:
A. the speaker's shock, anger, and disbelief
B. the speaker's discovery, denial, and acceptance
C. death, funeral, and denial
D. theory, research, and conclusion

7. Lines 5–8 can best be summarized as:
A. I should never forget the moment of my captain's death.
B. I love my captain.
C. My heart is breaking upon seeing my captain die.
D. I will never leave this spot where my captain has died.

8. The poem ends with the speaker in a state of:
   A. optimism B. disappointment
   C. celebration D. mourning

9. The form of the poem's third segment differs from the form of the first two segments in that the former:
   A. contains exact end rhymes
   B. contains a steady rhyme scheme
   C. lacks exclamations
   D. does not address the captain

10. In lines 19–20, the ship is like the captain in all of the following ways except:
   A. they have both ended their heroic journeys
   B. they have achieved their goals
   C. they are both metaphors
   D. they have both arrived home safely

11. The "bells," "flag," "bugle," "wreaths," and crowds in the second segment:
   A. are meant to be ironic
   B. are part of the speaker's hallucination
   C. describe both a victory celebration and a funeral
   D. are metonymies for the captain

12. The rhyme of "bells" and "lies" differs from the rhyme of "tread" and "dead" (21–24) in that the former:
   A. is a slant rhyme
   B. is a masculine rhyme
   C. is not a rhyme
   D. is an internal rhyme

11. THAT THE NIGHT COME

She lived in storm and strife.
Her soul had such desire
For what proud death may bring
That it could not endure
The common good of life,
But lived as 'twere a king
That packed his marriage day
With banneret and pennon,
Trumpet and kettledrum,
And the outrageous cannon,
To bundle Time away
That the night come.

—*William Butler Yeats*

QUESTIONS

1. The poem characterizes night as:
   I. remote
   II. a panacea
   III. interminable
   A. I only B. II only
   C. I and III only D. II and III only

2. When measured, the beat and meter of lines 1–5 is called:
   A. trochaic pentameter
   B. iambic trimeter
   C. trochaic tetrameter
   D. iambic tetrameter

3. Lines 1–4 contain which of the following devices?
   A. slant and exact rhyme
   B. assonance and consonance
   C. alliteration and personification
   D. polysyndeton and asyndeton

4. In context, the words "banneret and pennon" most likely mean:
   A. men and women
   B. food and beverage
   C. wedding decorations
   D. types of fanfare

5. The word "it" in line 4 refers to:
   A. "death" B. "Her"
   C. "soul" D. "desire"

6. The simile in line 6 reveals:
   A. the king's superiority to the woman
   B. the king's love for his wife
   C. the woman's anticipation of her wedding night
   D. the woman's excitement about death

7. The use of multiple conjunctions in lines 8–10 is a device called:
   A. asyndeton B. polysyndeton
   C. caesura D. epistrophe

8. The variation in beat is most evident in which line?
   A. line 12 B. line 10
   C. line 7 D. line 8

9. The main difference emphasized in the poem between "Her" and the "king" is:
A. their gender
B. their way of living
C. the object of their desire
D. their attitude

10. The change in sound beginning in line 9 parallels:
A. the woman and the king's impatience
B. the woman's dread
C. the king's excitement
D. the intense energy of a wedding celebration

11. The phrase "To bundle Time away" (11) means:
A. to pass time   B. to protect time
C. to waste time   D. to save time

12. The words "night come" (12) contain what type of beat?
A. anapestic   B. dactylic
C. iambic   D. spondaic

12. CONTEMPORANIA

The corner of a great rain
Steamy with the country
Has fallen upon my garden.

I go back and forth now
And the little leaves follow me
Talking of the great rain,
Of branches broken,
And the farmer's curses!

But I go back and forth
In this corner of a garden
And the green shoots follow me
Praising the great rain.

We are not curst together,
The leaves and I,
Framing devices, flower devices
And other ways of peopling
The barren country.

Truly it was a very great rain
That makes the little leaves follow me.

—William Carlos Williams

1. A theme of the poem is:
A. the harshness of nature
B. the speaker's realization that he is united with powerful nature
C. the greatness of the rain
D. the life cycle

2. The poem's themes and style are most in line with:
A. neoclassicism   B. postmodernism
C. realism   D. imagism

3. The form and structure of the poem can best be described as:
A. a sonnet   B. a villanelle
C. a sestina   D. free verse

4. The title suits the poem in that:
A. the poetic techniques are novel and groundbreaking
B. the speaker describes modernism
C. the poem includes details from contemporary life
D. the poem is an artifact recording a moment in time

5. The rain reminds the speaker of:
I. his fertility
II. the life cycle
III. the similarities he shares with plants
A. I only   B. I and II only
C. II and III only   D. I, II, and III

6. The speaker's attitude toward the rain is similar to:
A. a stargazer's attitude toward the universe
B. an artist's attitude toward his muse
C. an acolyte's attitude toward his idol
D. a husband's attitude toward his wife

7. The poem contains all of the following devices except:
A. repetition   B. consonance
C. personification   D. assonance

8. The exclamation point in line 8 reveals:
A. the speaker's dismay
B. the leaves' points of view
C. the farmer's hatred
D. the greatness of the rain

9. The last two lines of the poem:
A. contain iambic pentameter
B. make up the envoy
C. communicate a theme
D. make up a couplet

10. When the speaker says, "The leaves and I,/ Framing devices, flower devices" (15), he means:
A. the leaves frame and he flowers
B. they are not curst
C. plants frame the land and flower the land
D. both leaves and people liven up the barren land by decorating it and by procreating

13. THE WORLD IS TOO MUCH WITH US

The world is too much with us; late and soon,
Getting and spending, we lay waste our powers:
Little we see in nature that is ours;
We have given our hearts away, a sordid boon!
This Sea that bares her bosom to the moon;
The Winds that will be howling at all hours

And are up-gathered now like sleeping flowers;
For this, for every thing, we are out of tune;
It moves us not—Great God! I'd rather be
A Pagan suckled in a creed outworn;
So might I, standing on this pleasant lea,
Have glimpses that would make me less forlorn;
Have sight of Proteus coming from the sea;
Or hear old Triton blow his wreathed horn.

—William Wordsworth

1. The poem's structure, style, and content are most like those of:
A. a lampoon
B. a lyric
C. a Spenserian sonnet
D. a Petrarchan sonnet

2. The theme of the poem as a whole can best be stated as:
A. nature is better than technology
B. the natural world has more to offer than people
C. the natural world is a panacea for our troubles
D. we should be reproached for having immersed ourselves in industry and lost touch with the natural world

3. The first two lines contain an abundance of:
A. couplets
B. internal rhyme
C. hyperbole
D. alliteration

4. Personification is evident in which of the following lines?
A. line 14
B. line 5
C. line 6
D. line 8

5. The rhyme scheme of the poem is:
A. *aba aba aba aba*
B. *abbaabba cdcdcd*
C. *abab cdcd efef gg*
D. *abaabaabacdcdcd*

6. In context of the poem as a whole, we can infer that the word "world" means:
A. Society
B. England
C. the man-made world
D. nature

7. The phrase "sordid boon" (4) is:
A. a call for an end to industry
B. a sarcastic expletive that mocks our "hearts"
C. a paradox that deplores human nature
D. an oxymoron that points out the irony of society's advancement

8. The change in tone beginning in line 9 is best explained as:
A. a change from being wistful to willful
B. a change from regretful to remorseful
C. a change from scolding to lamenting
D. a change from being forlorn to bitter

9. The metaphor in line 10 compares:
A. a religion to a mother's breast
B. Paganism to an outdated belief system
C. beliefs to mothers
D. religion to breast milk

10. The allusions in lines 13–14 illustrate:
A. the speaker's sanguinity
B. the speaker's predicament
C. the speaker's fantasy
D. the speaker's knowledge

ANSWERS

1. TO HIS COY MISTRESS

1	2	3	4	5	6	7	8	9	10	11	12	13
A	D	D	B	D	C	A	D	D	B	C	A	B

2. THE AUTHOR TO HER BOOK

1	2	3	4	5	6	7	8	9	10
A	C	C	D	B	D	D	D	D	D

3. SUCCESS IS COUNTED SWEETEST...

1	2	3	4	5	6	7	8	9	10
D	D	A	C	D	D	D	A	B	A

4. GOD'S GRANDEUR

1	2	3	4	5	6	7	8	9	10	11	12
C	D	D	A	C	D	B	D	A	D	D	B

5. DEFEAT

1	2	3	4	5	6	7	8	9	10
A	D	B	A	D	A	D	D	C	D

6. MY COUNTRY AWAKE

1	2	3	4	5	6	7	8	9	10
A	D	C	B	D	B	D	A	D	D

7. TO THE VIRGINS, TO MAKE MUCH OF TIME

1	2	3	4	5	6	7	8	9	10	11	12	13
D	A	A	B	D	B	D	D	D	B	A	D	C

8. MORNING AT THE WINDOW

1	2	3	4	5	6	7	8
D	A	A	C	D	B	D	C

9. NOBODY COMES

1	2	3	4	5	6	7	8	9	10
C	A	D	A	A	C	D	D	D	D

10. O CAPTAIN! MY CAPTAIN!

1	2	3	4	5	6	7	8	9	10	11	12
D	D	A	A	A	B	A	D	B	D	C	A

11. THAT THE NIGHT COME

1	2	3	4	5	6	7	8	9	10	11	12
A	B	C	D	C	D	B	A	C	A	A	D

12. CONTEMPORANIA

1	2	3	4	5	6	7	8	9	10
B	D	D	D	D	A	B	D	C	D

13. THE WORLD IS TOO MUCH WITH US

1	2	3	4	5	6	7	8	9	10
D	D	D	B	B	C	D	D	A	C

●●●

Glossary of Literary Terms

ABRIDGED EDITION: Condensed or shortened version of a work.

ABSENCE: It is a modern term which is used to explain a work of art on the basis of aspects which are absent rather than those which are manifestly present in the work.

ACRONYM:

1. A word formed from the initial letters of other words, *e.g.*
   NOIDA for New Okhla Industrial Development Authority.
2. The word may be considered synonymous to 'acrostic'.

ACROSTIC: It is a form of literary exercise in which the first letters of each line in a poem form a word as we read downwards. *e.g.*

"Wait, O little child, wait!
In the wind lies thy message,
Not in the hubbub of the worldly;
Else you may repent, says the sage."
(The word formed is "WINE")

ACT: Major division in a dramatic work.

ADAGEL: Maxim or proverb.

ADDENDUM: Addition or appendix to a book.

AESTHETIC REALISM:

1. According to Hudson, "Esther Waters" by George Moore was a landmark in this movement toward aesthetic realism.
2. This movement was the vehicle of the new realists of which Moore and Gissing were representatives.
3. According to Hudson, "they mistook mere ugliness for frankness and "seeing life steadily and seeing it whole."

ALEXANDRINE:

1. It is a line of six iambic feet instead of five.
2. It is not known for certain how this line originated.
3. It appears that it was evolved by Spenser by adding the Alexandrine to the eight-line stave (a b a b b c b c) of Chaucer that he used in *the Monkeys Tale.*

ALIENATION EFFECT: It was a term devised by the famous German playwright, Bartolt Brecht, who wanted to bring home the need, for realization of a kind of 'alienation' of the audience and the actors from the stage during the performance of a play, as the play being a play and not a part of real life.

ALLEGORY: When the abstract or spiritual ideas are presented through living images, the result is the allegory.

Examples of Allegorical Works

(*i*) The Pilgrim Progress
(*ii*) The Scarlet Letter
(*iii*) The Faerie Queene
(*iv*) Morality Plays, such as "Everyman".
(*v*) Seven Deadly Sins in Dr. Faustus, etc.

ALLITERATION: It signifies the repetition of initial consonant sounds, *e.g.* The furrow followed free.

ALLUSION: Allusion is a reference to a well-known person, place, event, literary work, or work of art. Writers often make allusions to stories from the Bible, the Mahabharata, Greek or Roman mythology, plays by Shakespeare, famous quotes by historical figures such as Mahatma Gandhi, political and historical events, and to other materials with which they can expect their readers to be familiar. By using allusions, writers can bring to mind complex ideas simply and easily. Gandhi used an allusion to the writings of the Bible when he said, "An eye for an eye turns the whole world blind."

ALMANAC: Book or table comprising a calendar of days, weeks and months indicating special occasions or events.

ANAGNORISIS: It means Discovery or Reversal in a Tragedy.

ANAGRAM: Letters or word or phrase which, when re-arranged, form a new word.

ANAPAEST: It comprises two unaccented syllables followed by an accented one:

(*i*) Redeploy
(*ii*) Introduce
(*iii*) Camouflage

ANDROCENTRISM: The term implies the predominance of man in all social and intellectual activities.

ANECDOTE: Brief account or story about an individual.

ANGRY YOUNG MEN: It was a movement which came into existence in the second half of the twentieth century, mainly as a result of Osborn's play: "Look Back In Anger."

ANNOTATION: Textual comment on a book.

ANTAGONIST: Antagonist is a character or force in conflict with a main character, or protagonist. In the Harry Potter series, for example, Voldemort is the antagonist. Not all stories contain antagonists; however, in many stories the conflict between the antagonist and the protagonist is the basis for the plot.

ANTHOLOGY: Collection of poetry or prose from diverse sources.

ANTITHESIS:

1. It signifies the setting of one thing against another, often of opposite sense *e.g.*
   'A *friend never* betrays, an *enemy always* does.'
2. 'Antithesis' can be expressed in literature also by presenting two aspects (of life) side by side, *e.g.* the real and the marvellous.

APHORISM: Short statement of a truth or dogma couched in memorable terms.

APHORISTIC ESSAY: Aphoristic Essays are impersonal essays. They are pithy and short essays packful of the author's knowledge, wisdom and philosophy of life. They are rugged and abrupt and difficult to understand on account of their depth of thought.

APOSTROPHE: It implies an exclamatory address to a person. (usually a dead one), some inanimate object or an abstract idea, *e.g.*

"Milton! thou shouldn't be living with us at this hour..."

ARCHAISM: It is a word or phrase which is no longer in use, *e.g.* loon, quoth, yclept, eftsoon(s), etc.

ARCHETYPAL APPROACH TO CRITICISM:

1. This Approach is also called Mythological, Ritualistic or Totemic Approach.
2. It endeavours to study literature on the basis of myth.

AREOPAGITICA: This is the name of Milton's famous prose pamphlet, pleading for freedom, freedom of the press, in particular.

ARGOT: Slang or coarse vernacular language.

ASIDE:

1. It is a kind of device similar to "soliloquy" (being probably comparatively brief) when a character speaks to himself.

2. The best example of an "aside" may be Shylock's words : "How like a fawning publican he looks" in Act, I sc. 3 of The Merchant of Venice.

ASSONANCE: Unlike the alliteration (which signifies the repetition of consonant sounds), it signifies the repetition of vowel sounds, *e.g.*
I *hear* him *bear* the mark of a *seer* on his head.

AUTOBIOGRAPHY: A form of nonfiction in which a person tells his or her own life story. Notable examples of autobiographies include Gandhi's My Experiments with Truthand Nehru's.Towards Freedom. A memoir is a first-person account of personally or historically significant events in which the writer was a participant or an eyewitness and is a particular kind of autobiography.

AUTO SUGGESTIVE TEXT: The texts of certain very ancient books are not found in their authentic forms. Different editors or publishers modify them in their own way. Efforts should be made to discover their real or authentic form.

AVANT-GARDE: Without going into historical aspects of the word, one can say that it implies those (persons) who support or create the newest ideas, fashions (generally literary or artistic), techniques, styles, etc. in an art, piece of literature, etc.

BALLAD: The word 'Ballad' literally means 'a dance-song'. They generally sang of the brave deeds and heroic exploits of historical or legendary heroes and knights.

BATHOS:

1. It is a term to denote anticlimax.
2. It is generally used when there is sudden descent or fall from the sublime to the trite or ridiculous, *e.g.*
   Delay not thine departure hence,
   For thou mightst have a hot pudding, Awaiting thee.

BELLES LETTERS: Essays on literary studies and the aesthetics of literature.

BIBLIOGRAPHY: List of works on a particular subject or author.

BIOGRAPHY: An account of a person's life.

BLANK VERSE: Poetry with unrhymed line endings (usually written in iambic pentameters).

BLURB: These are the words of praise or description of a book in a nutshell, inserted usually by the publisher on the cover page or jacket of the book, to attract the reader's eye.

BOUND VERSE: Verse based on metrical pattern.

BURLESQUE: Burlesque is defined as 'an incongruous imitation'. It imitates the matter or manner of a serious literary work, or literary genre, but makes the imitations funny and amusing by a ridiculous disparity.

BOWDLERIZE: To 'cleanse' a work by omitting or cutting out indecent passages, phrases or words.

CACOPHONY: When the excessive use of high sounding words is made such that the meaning is lost or diminished in value in the sound, the result is cacophony instead of euphony.

CADENCE: Rhythm and phrasing of language.

CAESURA:

1. In classical prosody, 'Caesura' means "break between words within a metrical foot." (Concise Oxford).
2. In English prosody, it means "pause about middle of line." (ibid.).
3. A Caesura "which does not immediately follow the ictus" is known as 'Feminine Caesura" (Chambers 20th century).

☛ In modern connotation, Caesura implies natural pause in a line of verse and not an unnatural or forced one.

CAMPUS NOVEL: The Campus Novels deal with the life and problems of students in colleges and universities. They highlight the problems of education and careers of students during this formative period.

CANON: Collection of works established as genuine.

CANTO: Division of an epic or narrative poem.

CAPTION: Short description accompanying an illustration.

CARICATURE: The chief characteristics of characters are sometimes so exaggerated by the author that the characters look like some humorous or even funny creatures. The result is the creation of caricatures. This is what Dickens (more than any other author) has done.

CATASTROPHE: The final end of the tragedy is called catastrophe. At this point the hero or the heroine or both meet their tragic death. The tragic end comes through Hamartia and Perpheteia. It signifies the complete (often sudden) devastation of the fortunes of a character (often the hero and/or the heroine) in a play or piece of fiction.

CATALOGUE: List of books or works.

CATHARSIS: This is the term used for the ousting of the emotions of pity and fear in the tragedy.

CAVALIER POETS: The Cavalier Poets were associated with the Court of Charles I. They wrote witty and polished lyrics of live and gallantry. The group included Richard Lovelace, John Suckling, Thomas Carew and Robert Herrick.

CHARACTER: Character is a person or an animal that takes part in the action of a literary work. The following are some terms used to describe various types of characters:

- main character is the one on whom the work focuses
- major characters include the main character and any other characters who play significant roles
- minor character is one who does not play a significant role
- round character is one who is complex and multifaceted, like a real person
- flat character is one who is one-dimensional
- dynamic character is one who changes in the course of a work
- static character is one who does not change in the course of a work
- protagonist is the leading character or main character in a drama, movie, novel or other fictional work
- antagonist is a character or a force which actively opposes or is hostile to the main character or protagonist

CHARACTERIZATION: Characterization the act of creating and developing a character. There are two primary methods of characterization: direct and indirect. In direct characterization, a writer simply states a character's traits, as when F. Scott Fitzgerald writes in his story "Winter Dreams," "He wanted not association with glittering things and glittering people—he wanted the glittering things themselves." In indirect characterization, character is revealed by one of the following means:

1. the words, thoughts or actions of the character
2. descriptions of the character's appearance or background
3. what other characters say about the character
4. the ways in which other characters react to the character.

CHORUS: The term Chorus is taken from Greek drama. In English drama it is applied to a character who speaks the Prologue and Epilogue and also communicates to the audience the exposition, setting and offstage events in the play.

CHRONICLE OR HISTORICAL PLAY: A Chronicle or Historical play deals with the life of a king or with some important historical event. However, the dramatist weaves an imaginative or highly emotional garb around it to make it appealing to the spectators sitting in the theatre.

CIPHER: Writing that employs substitution or transposition of letters.

CLASSIC:

1. A classic (in reality, any book) is "the expression of man" as an individual.
2. It is also the expression of his mindset and the stance taken by him.

CLICHE: Any word, phrase or expression that has lost its real effect for having been too frequently used by authors or laymen is called a cliche which may otherwise be quite lovable, *e.g.*

(*i*) The news is too good to be true.
(*ii*) The sorrow was too deep for tears.
(*iii*) Thanking you in anticipation, etc.

CLIMAX:

1. It is the main point of interest in a play or novel which is reached usually in the third act (or sometimes 4th or a 5th act of a play) or towards the end.
2. The resolution often takes place after the Climax or the forces for it start working or increase their intensity after it.

COLLOQUIAL:

1. In speech, the use of certain words and phrases which are not acceptable in standard speech.
2. Such colloquial expressions should be avoided in all formal speech or writing.

COLONIALISM: The term differs from 'colonization' as the term may imply political or economic control of policies in a political unit without real annexation of land.

COLONISATION: Literarily, the most significant modernist theories in the matter of

(*i*) colonisation
(*ii*) post-colonisation
(*iii*) decolonisation, and
(*iv*) neo-colonisation have been provided and practised by—
(*a*) Ngugiwa Thiong'o
(*b*) Soyinka
(*c*) Achebe Chinua, etc.

COMEDY: Comedy, in general, is a play of love, romance and marriage, joy and delight, wit and humour, light satire and irony exposing the follies and foibles of man good-humouredly. It deals with the light and trivial occurrences of life which are treated in such a manner that the ludicrous and comic element predominates.

COMEDY OF HUMOURS: Ben Jonson was the principal exponent of the Comedy of Humours. The Comedy of Humours was actually satirical comedy based on the classical concept of humours.

COMEDY OF MANNERS: The Comedy of Manners exhibited the artificial manners and low moral values of the high class society of the Restoration Age. They largely displayed the intrigues, witty remarks, sparkling dialogues and verbal fencings between gentleman and sophisticated ladies.

COMIC RELIEF: It is the name given to the brief light or comic dramatic action within the performance of a regular serious play to bring about a relief to the spectators to regain their real selves, for a short while to relax their strained nerves and prepare for further action, often more serious and culminating into breath-taking, gasping climax before denouement.

CONCEIT:

1. A conceit is a far-fetched or highly complex and even obscure or unintelligible comparison between two, often dissimilar, persons or objects.
2. It was commonly used by the Elizabethans particularly the Metaphysical poets, especially Donne.

CONCORDANCE: Alphabetical index of words in a work, or works by a single author.

CONFIDANT/CONFIDANTE:

1. In a play when a character takes upon himself/herself the task of some secret or information characteristic about a character to another, the character indulging in such an activity is known as a "confidant" (mas.) or "confidante" (fem.)

2. Such information or secret is generally in the matter of love.
3. A good example of a 'confidante' is Nerissa in the Merchant of Venice.

CONFLICT: Conflict a struggle between opposing forces. Sometimes this struggle is internal, or within a character; at other times this struggle is external, or between a character and an outside force. Conflict is one of the primary elements of narrative literature because most plots develop from conflicts

CONNOTATION:

1. It signifies the suggested or implied meaning of word as against the transparent or literary meaning.
2. Connotative devices are brought into play by the artists, poets in particular to enhance pleasure and acceptability conveyed by words and other expressions.
3. Poets like Keats and T.S. Eliot frequently resort to the device of suggestiveness which is akin to connotation.

CONSONANCE: Consonance the repetition of similar final consonant sounds at the ends of words or accented syllables. Emily Dickinson uses consonance in the following lines:

But if he ask where you are hid
Until tomorrow–happy letter!
Gesture, coquette, and shake your head!

CONSUMMATION:

1. When a work achieves complete satisfaction on all counts—literary as well as artistic, it is consummation that results.
2. An artist who has the knack, calibre or skill to make this achievement, is a consummate artist.

COPYRIGHT: Protective law to prevent pirating or plagiarism of an author's work.

COUPLET: Two successive rhyming lines in poetry.

COURT COMEDY: It is opposed to the Domestic Comedy in the sense that instead of domestic scenes it contains other elements which attract a different kind of audience, *e.g.*

(*i*) endless play of words
(*ii*) elaborate dialogues
(*iii*) repartees, jests, retorts, etc.

CYCLE: Group of works united by an overall theme.

DACTYL: Dactyl means one accented syllable followed by two unaccented ones, *e.g.*

(*i*) Lazily
(*ii*) Separate
(*iii*) Unspoken.

DEISM: A "deist" is a theist who believes in the existence of God but rejects the idea of a revealed religion.

DENOTATION: Denotation the objective meaning of a word, independent of other associations that the word brings to mind.

DENOUEMENT: The conclusion of a comedy is called denouement. Here all the obstacles and tangles that came in the path of true love are resolved and the lovers get happily married.

DESCRIPTION: Description a portrayal, in words, of something that can be perceived by the senses. Writers create descriptions by using images. Description is one of the major forms of discourse and appears quite often in literary works of all genres.

DESCRIPTIVE CRITICISM OR PRACTICAL CRITICISM: Descriptive Criticism is a study or evaluation of individual works or authors. The critic evaluates their aims, methods and effects, and brings out their aesthetic beauty, emotional effect and literary significance by whatever criteria he deems fit.

DETONATION: When a word refers to its literal meaning independent of the meaning which the author may intend to convey, it is the device of "Detonation" which is at play.

DIABOLUS EX MACHINA:

1. The term literally means "devil out of the machine".

2. When all of a sudden a person or an event spoils the whole good game, causing unmitigated misery, it is the work of "Diabolus Ex Machina".
3. Thus, the term signifies sudden, unexpected turn of events for a plightful situation.

DIALECT: Manner of speaking pertaining to a particular class or geographical region.

DIALECTIC:

1. It was used originally to refer to the nature of a logical argument.
2. Later, it began to be linked to Kant, Hegel and Marx in varying forms.
3. The three generally accepted aspects of 'dialectic' are:
   (*i*) *Thesis:* It is akin to the (original) idea.
   (*ii*) *Antithesis:* It implies the inherent opposition in the thesis, which may operate after some time.
   (*iii*) *Synthesis:* It implies the resolution of the conflict to evolve a higher (or final) truth.

DIALOGUE:

1. Dialogue is something very important in any poetic or prose play or a piece of prose fictions.
2. (*i*) The nature of the dialogue, including its language depends upon the kind of the play—a tragedy, comedy, romance, etc. or the kind of the scene prevailing there at the time and place of the dialogue.
   (*ii*) Much also depends upon the taste of the spectators or audience which again is related to the spirit of the age.

A DIALOGICAL NOVEL: It is a kind of novel in which a number of voices, interactive in the scheme, operate in work, resulting in a kind of dialogue (or series of dialogues) as against the Monologic Presentation.

DIARY: Sequential private record of personal and other events kept by an individual.

DICTION:

1. It refers to the selection, arrangement and order of words.
2. The term which has become more popular in literary world is "Poetic Diction" to which a lot of space has been devoted by Wordsworth in his "Preface to Lyrical Ballads."

DICTIONARY: Book containing the words of a language, and their definitions, alphabetically; two-language dictionaries contain the corresponding words of both languages and their meanings, also alphabetically; any book that gives words and phrases about a particular subject, arranged alphabetically.

DIDACTIC: A work is didactic in nature when it undertakes to teach a moral, *e.g.* much of Wordsworth's poetry.

DIDACTIC LITERATURE: Didactic Literature is that form of literature that directly seeks to teach some moral or religious lesson. Allegorical works like Spenser's *Faerie Queene* or Bunyan's *Pilgrim's Progress* are didactic literature. Most of the eighteenth-century literature is didactic.

DIGEST: Publication where works are abridged.

DIGRESSION:

1. When a writer, instead of carrying on the main plot or incident, starts indulging in a side story, dialogue or descriptive narration, it is digression that results.
2. Digression gives extraneous pleasure which is not inherent in or indispensable to the main story.
3. Digression can sometimes enhance the value of a work but more often it mars its spirit.

DOCUMENTARY: Form of fiction or drama based on documentary evidence provided by newspapers, recent historical reports or other contemporary or recent factual evidence.

DOGGEREL: Rough, ill-constructed verse.

DOMESTIC COMEDY:

1. One of the earliest examples of the Domestic Comedies is "Gammer Gurton's Needle" (Cir. 1562)

2. It presents realistic life of the peasant class of its times.
3. It is full of fun and coarse humour.

DOUBLE ENTENDRE: Ambiguity in a word or expression, one of whose meanings is usually bawdy or frivolous.

DOMESTIC NOVEL: The domestic novels present the day-to-day domestic life of the middle-class families and their friends and relations. The festivals and festivities, functions and celebrations, birthdays and marriage are graphically described in them.

DRAMA: Drama is a long literary composition in prose or verse, developed through dialogues and action to be presented on the stage. While every other form of literature is complete in itself; drama remains incomplete without a stage.

DRAMATIC IRONY: It is a device occurring in a drama when a character on the stage is unaware of a fact which the audience know and understand.

DRAMATIC MONOLOGUE: 'Monologue' literally means 'Dialogue with the self'. In the Dramatic Monologue there is only one character who expresses out his own innermost feelings and thoughts through a long poetic speech. It offers a psychological analysis of the solo-speaker.

DRAMATIS PERSONAE: Characters in a play.

DUOLOGUE: Conversation between two characters in a play, story or poem.

EDITION: Total number of copies of a book printed from unchanged set of type.

ELECTICISM: The term implies the gleaning of facts or ideas from different sources instead of depending on just one source (or a few sources).

ELEGY: Serious meditative poem; often lamenting death.

EMPATHY: In a play or novel, when the reader or spectator begins to feel like the hero/heroine or some particular character as if he/she were that character, it is "empathy" which is at play.

EMPIRICISM: Empiricism implies the importance of experiment and experience in the matter of gaining knowledge.

ENCYCLOPAEDIA: Comprehensive work encompassing and describing many aspects of knowledge; specialist work covering comprehensively a subject or discipline.

EPIC: The Epic is the greatest and most sublime form of poetry. The Epic is a long poem, divided into several books, celebrating the life, heroic deeds and achievements of a national hero, whether historical or legendary.

EPIC STYLE: -

1. It is a style which is dignified and exalted (as grand style is), as:
   (i) *Paradise Lost* by Milton
   (ii) *Aeneid* by Virgil
   (iii) *Iliad* by Homer
   (iv) *Hyperion* by Keats, etc.
2. Sometimes, it is, also referred to as 'heroic' style.'

EPIGRAM: A brief, pointed statement, in prose or in verse, often characterized by use of some rhetorical device or figure of speech.

EPILOGUE: It is the last item in a work of art (as in a drama) which often declares or comments upon the conclusion of the work.

EPIPHANY: Epiphany a sudden revelation or flash of insight.

EPISTLE: Direct address to another person, a 'letter' in the form of verse.

EPISTOLARY NOVEL: The Epistolary Novel is a novel of which the plot develops through the medium of letters. The characters exchange their thoughts and views through letters. There is very little dialogue face to face.

EPITAPH: Valediction to dead person or persons; inscription on a tomb or grave.

EPITHET: It comprises a word or group of words to describe the chief characteristics of a person, *e.g.*

(*i*) Alexander the Great

(*ii*) The Holy Bible.

EPONYMOUS: Person whose name becomes the title of the work.

ERASTIANISM:

1. It implies the doctrine that the state should have supremacy over the church in ecclesiastical matters.
2. Erastianism was one of the doctrines which was vehemently opposed by the followers of the Oxford Movement
3. The doctrine is probably wrongly ascribed to Erastus.

ESSAY: Short composition, usually in prose, discussing a topic or variety of topics.

EUPHEMISM: When an unpleasant expression has to be made in a comparatively pleasant or less harsh way, the mellowed or toned down words which are used express euphemism, *e.g.*

(*i*) Instead of saying about a person "He acted foolishly, we can say, "He should have acted more wisely."

(*ii*) Instead of saying about a person that he has died, we sometimes say, "God Almighty has called him" or "He has left for his heavenly abode."

EUPHONY:

1. It signifies the pleasant combination of words which create desirable rhythms and tonal effects without interfering with the intended meaning.
2. An excessive use of such devices can lead to tautology or bombasticism and sound superficial or facile.
3. The generally accepted antonym of euphony is "Cacophony".

EUPHUISM: An ornate, floral style of writing popularized by Lyly.

EXPOSITION: It signifies a way of writing where explanations are not withheld or suppressed but manifestly made clear to the reader for immediate response based on clarity.

FABLE: A short narrative in prose or verse, often with animals, that points a moral.

FICTION: General term for an imaginative work, usually in prose.

FIGURATIVE LANGUAGE: writing or speech not meant to be taken literally. Writers use figurative language to explain ideas in vivid and imaginative ways.

For example, Emily Dickinson begins one poem with this description:

It sifts from leaden sieves,
It powders all the wood.

By describing the snow as if it were flour, Dickinson renders a precise and compelling picture of it.

FIGURE OF SPEECH (OR OF RHETORIC): It signifies the unusual use of words to heighten their effect.

FIRST PERSON: Style of novel, etc., in which narrator is a character.

FLASHBACK:

1. When a writer while presenting a situation suddenly refers to a past situation or event, it is the device of "flashback" that he exploits.
2. Browning, T.S, Eliot and Stream of consciousness novelists, in particular, take advantage of this device.

FOIL: Foil is a character who provides a contrast to another character. In the Arthur Conan Doyle detective stories, Dr. Watson provides a foil to Sherlock Holmes.

FOLK TALE: Story handed down by word of mouth from generation to generation.

FOOT: In poetry, rhythmic unit of two or three syllables.

FORESHADOWING:

1. It is a device in which the author himself prepares the spectators (or readers) for the catastrophe or some important event which may be on the cards.
2. Such a device checks the readers, etc. from suffering from the malady of disbelief.
3. Shakespeare is probably one of the greatest masters of this device, and it is sometimes believed that one of the main reasons of Shakespeare's grand success was his convincing mastery over the technique of foreshadowing.

FOREWORD: Short introduction to a work.

FREE VERSE (VERS LIBRE): Poetry free from mechanical restrictions such as metre and rhyme, cadenced according to meaningful stress.

FUSTIAN: It means the use of pompous, ornate, Euphuist or bombastic language.

GAZETTEER: Geographical dictionary or index.

GENRE: Genre a division or type, of literature. Literature is commonly divided into three major genres: poetry, prose and drama. Each major genre can in turn be divided into smaller genres. Poetry can be divided into lyric, concrete, dramatic, narrative, and epic poetry. Prose can be divided into fiction (novels and short stories) and nonfiction (biography, autobiography, letters, essays, and reports.) Drama can be divided into serious drama, tragedy, comic drama, melodrama, and farce.

GHOST WRITER: Person who undertakes literary work for another who takes the credit.

GLOSSARY: Alphabetical list of unfamiliar or uncommon words, usually appended to work in which they appear.

GOTHIC: Gothic the use of primitive, medieval, wild, or mysterious elements in literature. Gothic novels feature places like mysterious and gloomy castles, where horrifying, supernatural events take place.

GROTESQUE: Grotesque the use of bizarre, absurd, or fantastic elements in literature. The grotesque is generally characterized by distortions or striking incongruities.

HAIKU: A Haiku is a Japanese poem of seventeen syllables, in three lines of five, seven and five traditionally evoking images of the natural world.

HAMARTIA: Hamartia is the 'tragic flaw' in the character of the tragic hero who is basically a good and great man. This 'tragic flaw' becomes the cause of his fall, doom and death.

HAPLOLOGY: Omission in utterance of a sound resembling neighbouring sounds.

HAPLOGRAPHY: The inadvertent writing once of what should have been written twice.

HEROIC COUPLET: A couplet written in iambic pentametre is known as a 'heroic couplet'.

HEROIC DRAMA: Heroic drama was mainly written in the Restoration Age principally by Dryden. It tried to emulate the dimensions of Epic or Heroic poetry. Its hero was a great warrior whose fate affected the fate of an empire, such as Dryden's *All For Love*.

HEROIC VERSE: A poem written in heroic couplets is known as 'heroic verse,' *e.g.* Pope's poems such as:

(*i*) Essay Man
(*ii*) Essay in Criticism
(*iii*) The Rape of the Lock, etc.

HISTORICAL NOVEL: The Historical Novel draws its theme from some important historical event. But around this historical event the novelist weaves some imaginative and artistic environment to make it an interesting and arresting theme for a novel.

HOMILY:

1. It is a term pertaining to a work which instead of laying stress on artistic or aesthetic standards, undertakes to urge the readers on to a high moral life.
2. It is just like a sermon in a church.
3. Such are the most of the poems of Longfellow.

HOMOGRAPH: It implies a word which has the same spelling and pronunciation as another, but is different in meaning and origin from the other, *e.g.* :

(*i*) bear (*n*) an animal
(*ii*) bear (*v*) (to) tolerate
(*iii*) bear (*v*) (to) carry

HOMONYM:

1. It is "a word having the same sound and perhaps the same spelling as another, but a different meaning and origin"
2. Hence, *Homonymous* means: " having the same name : having different *significations* and origin but the same sound." (ibid.)

HYPERBOLE: It is a figure of speech which expresses an exaggerated statement to heighten the effect of a rhetorical statement, *e.g.*

(*i*) O child, may you never die!
(*ii*) Child is Father of the Man

IAMBIC PENTAMETER: Iambic Pentameter a line of poetry with five iambic feet, each containing one unstressed syllable followed by one stressed syllable. Iambic pentameter may be rhymed or unrhymed. Unrhymed iambic pentameter is called blank verse, which Shakespeare often used in his plays.

IDIOM: Form of expression of phrase peculiar to its language and possessing a meaning other than its literal one.

IDOLATRY: It means the worship of an image which is believed to be the abode of a superhuman being.

IDYLL: The origin of Idyll may be traced back to the Greek poet Theocritus, Idylls are small lyrical poems generally describing the scenes and pleasures of rural countryside. They depict country life as realistically and pictorically as possible.

IMAGE: Image is a word or phrase that appeals to one or more of the five senses—sight, hearing, touch, taste, smell.

IMAGERY: Imagery is the descriptive or figurative language used in literature to create word pictures for the reader. These pictures or images are created by details of sight, sound, taste, touch, smell, or movement. The following stanza, from Kuangchi C. Chang's "Garden of My Childhood," shows how a poet can use imagery to appeal to several sense:

I ran past the old maple by the terraced hall
And the singing crickets under the latticed wall.
And I kept on running down the walk
Paved with pebbles of memory big and small
Without turning to look until I as out of the gate
Through which there be no return at all.

IMAGISM: School of poetry (early 1900s) concerned with precise language, direct treatment, and freedom of form.

IMPERIALISM: It means the state policy for a country (as of England and certain other European countries, in particular during certain periods of history) to expand its area by annexing foreign lands and subduing the natives.

IMPERSONALITY: It means that the author himself should not be palpably visible in a piece of literature, in other words, the work should be done on highly objective lines.

IMPRESSIONISTIC CRITICISM: Impressionistic Criticism is that branch of criticism in which the critic evaluates a work by the impressions it makes upon his own mind. He expresses the attitudes and feelingful responses the work evokes in him as an individual.

INDIANISM: When an expression is commonly used in India but is not used by the English, it is called an "Indianism," *e.g.*

(*i*) 'demise' instead of 'death'
(*ii*) 'bearer' instead of 'waiter'
(*iii*) 'left for his heavenly abode' instead of 'died,' etc.

INTERIOR MONOLOGUE:

1. It is a device, as used by James Joyce in *Ulysses*, to express the thoughts, feelings and emotions of a character on usually more than one levels of consciousness.

2. It is a sort of inner debate which may or may not be conflict in essence.

INTERLUDES: The interludes were generally short entertainments inserted within a longer play or amidst some other festivities or festivals. Their primary function was to entertain the audience by humour or even by farce.

INTRODUCTION: Essay stating author's intention to reader.

INVERSION: It is the figure of speech (much used by Milton but ridiculed by many modern critics) in which words are presented in their unnatural order, *e.g.*

O God's glory I sing,
And to His Mercy I pray.

IRONY: It is a device used to convey a meaning which is the opposite of the apparent meaning, *e.g.* What a brave son of India Jai Chand was!

JINGLE: Verse or verses with strong rhyme and rhythm.

JOURNAL: Paper, periodical or magazine.

JUDICIAL CRITICISM:

1. It is the kind of criticism which is a sort of judgement on a writer or his work of art.
2. Such kind of best example is Pope's *"Essay on Criticism"*.

LEGEND: Story about a particular person containing myth and historical fact; explanation of symbols on a map or chart.

LETTER: Letter is a written message or communication addressed to a reader or readers and generally sent by mail. Letters may be private or public, depending on their intended audience. Letters to the editor are a common form of public letter.

LEXICON: Dictionary, especially for Classical and Middle Eastern languages.

LIMERICK:

1. It is a kind of humorous verse written in five jingling lines.
2. The form seems to have derived "from a refrain formerly used, referring to 'Limerick' in Ireland."

LINGUISTICS: The scientific study of language.

LITOTES:

1. It is akin to "understatement" which is sometimes used by writers to emphasise the desired meaning, *e.g.* India is not lagging in Information Technology.
2. However, more often it is an "understatement used ironically, especially using a negative to express the category as :

   'I shan't be sorry when it's over' meaning 'I shall be very glad', or 'It was no easy matter' for 'It was very difficult.'

LOCAL COLOR: Local Color a literary work of characters and details unique to a particular geographic area. Local color can be created by the use of dialect and by descriptions of customs, clothing, manners, attitudes, scenery, and landscape.

LYRIC: A Lyric is a short musical composition meant to be sung to the accompaniment of a lyre by a single singer. Now the term is used for any short non-narrative poem expressing a single thought or feeling of the poet.

LYRIC POEM: Lyric Poem a melodic poem that expresses the observations and feelings of a single speaker. Unlike a narrative poem, a lyric poem focus on producing a single, unified effect. Types of lyric poems include the elegy, the ode, and the sonnet.

MANUSCRIPT: Book or work written by hand.

MAXIM: Short statement or even sentence containing a general truth about human conduct and human nature.

MELODRAMA:

1. It was a crude form of drama which appealed to the groundings who were not much interested in the artistic minuteness such as the plot, characterization, etc.

2. They wanted only entertainment through striking scenes and absorbing movement of incidents and situations.

METAPHOR: A figure of speech in which one thing is spoken of as though it were something else. The identification suggests a comparison between the two things that are identified as in "death as a long sleep" or "the sleeping dead." A mixed metaphor occurs when two metaphors are jumbled together. For example, thorns and rain are illogically mixed in "the thorns of life rained down on him." A dead metaphor is one that has been overused and has become a common expression, such as "the arm of the chair" or "nightfall." Metaphors are used to make writing more vivid and meaningful.

METAPHYSICAL: The term 'metaphysical' was first used by Dryden in his assessment of the poetry of John Donne. The metaphysical poets were men of learning, and to show their learning was their whole endeavour.

METAPHYSICAL SCHOOL OF POETRY: The term 'Metaphysical' was first used by Dryden and further extended by Dr Johnson. It refers to a group of seventeenth-century poets who employed far-fetched imagery, abstruse arguments, scholastic philosophical terms, and subtle logic.

METRE: The rhythmical pattern if a poem. The pattern is determined by the number and types of stresses or beats in each line. To describe the meter of a poem, scan the lines. Scanning involves marking the stressed and unstressed syllables as follows, with the stressed syllables in bold and the unstressed syllables in italics:

"*Me* **thinks** *the* **la***dy* **doth** *pro***test** *too* **much**"
(Shakespeare's *Macbeth*)

The weak and strong stresses are then divided by vertical lines (/) into groups called feet. The following types of feet are common in poetry written in English:

1. Iamb: a foot with one unstressed syllable followed by one stressed syllable, as in the word: a**round**.
2. Troche: a foot with one stressed syllable followed by one unstressed syllable, as in the word: **bro**ken
3. Anapest: a foot with two unstressed syllables followed by one stressed syllable, as in the phrase: in a**flash**
4. Dactyl: a foot with one stressed syllable followed by two unstressed syllables, as in the word: **ar**gument

Lines of poetry are often described as iambic, trochaic, anapestic or dactylic. Lines are also described in terms of the number of feet that occur in them, as follows:

1. *Monometre :* It means a line (or verse) with a single iamb (foot)
2. *Dimetre:* It means a line with two iambs.
3. *Trimetre:* It means a line with three iambs.
4. *Tetrametre:* It means a line with four iambs.
5. *Penta metre:* It means a line with five iambs.
6. *Hexta metre:* It means a line with six iambs.
7. *Hepta metre:* It means a line with seven iambs.

METONYMY:

1. It implies the use of the name of some person or thing for another person or thing, *e.g.*
   (*i*) Have you studied 'Milton'?
   (Milton here means Milton's works).
   (*ii*) In the 'light' of these remarks:
   ('light' here means in view of....)
   (*iii*) Sceptre and Crown (i.e. monarchy)
   Must tumble down.

MIRACLE PLAY: A Miracle play is basically a religious play. They deal with the lives of saints and the miracles performed by them. The life and martyrdom of a saint formed the central theme of a Miracle play.

MOCK HEROIC: When an apparent epic is presented in a light vein, it is known as a "mock heroic" poem piece of fiction, etc., *e.g. The Rape of the Lock.*

MODERNISM: Towards the close of the 20th century, a movement against such modes as realism and naturalism started in all forms of literature and art such as poetry, drama, novel, music, painting, architecture, sculpture, etc. which continued unabated during the first world war period and partly upto the middle of the century.

MODULATION:

1. Of necessity, poetry is musical.
2. As in music, to avoid poetry from falling into "monotony," there is the system of "modulation" which here means, changing the key or tone, to introduce the element of variety to give or enhance pleasure.

MONOLOGUE: Single person addressing an audience alone, in drama, verse or prose. *Interior monologue*: unspoken but thought speech in verse or prose.

MOOD: Mood is the feeling created in the reader by a literary work or passage. Elements that can influence the mood of a work include its settling, tone, and events.

MORALITY PLAY: Morality Plays are allegorical plays. They present on the stage, personified Virtues and Vices. Everyman is presented as the Hero. Satan personified as Vice, God or Christ as Virtue, and Death as the Reward of Sin.

MOTIVATION: Motivation is a reason that explains a character's thoughts, feelings, actions, or speech. Characters are motivated by their values and by their wants, desires, dreams, wishes, and needs. Sometimes the reasons for a character's actions are stated directly, but other times the motives are implied or stated indirectly.

MYSTERY PLAY: The Mystery Plays basically deal with the themes taken from the Bible. They present in chronological order major events from the creation and fall of man through Nativity, Crucifixion, Resurrection of Christ to The Last Judgement.

MYTH: A fictional tale that explains the actions of gods or heroes or the causes of natural phenomena. Myths that explain the origins of earthly life, as does the Book of Genesis in the Bible and the Rig Veda, are known as origin myths. Other myths express the central values of the people who created them.

NARRATIVE: A story told in fiction, nonfiction, poetry or drama. Narratives are often classified by their content or purpose. An exploration narrative is a firsthand account of an explorer's travels in a new land. A historical narrative is a narrative account of significant historical events. Narrative poems also tell a story in verse form. Three traditional types of narrative verse are ballads, songlike poems that tell stories; epics, long poems about the deeds of gods or heroes, and metrical romances, poems that tell tales of love and chivalry.

NATURALISM: Naturalism was a literary movement among novelists at the end of the nineteenth century and during the early decades of the twentieth century. The Naturalists tended to view people as hapless victims of immutable natural laws. Authors include Jack London and Stephen Crane. Naturalism is a form of realism.

NARRATOLOGY: It means the study of different forms and structures of a narrative work in the matter of its various syntactical, literary and grammatical frameworks.

NEOCLASSICISM: Movement of late 17th and 18th century reviving classical values in English literature, emphasizing discipline, reason and clarity.

NEOLOGISM: Newly-coined word.

NEW WAVE (LA NOUVELLE VAGUE): Movement in literature and cinema originating in France in late 1950s that attempted to eschew fixed values, revealing a character by the way he experienced objects and events, which were often meticulously described.

NOM DE PLUME: Term used to indicate a fictitious name used by a writer to represent his work.

NON-FICTION: Nonfiction prose writing that presents and explains ideas or that tells about real people, places, objects or events. Essays, biographies, autobiographies, journals, and reports are all examples of non-fiction.

NOVEL: A long work of fiction. A novel often has a complicated plot, many major and minor characters, significant theme, and several varied settings. Novels can be classified in many ways, based on the historical periods in which they are written, on the subjects and themes that they treat, on the techniques that are used in them, and on the literary movements that inspired them.

NOVELETTE: Long short-story of some 15,000 words.

NOVELLA: Prose fiction longer than a short story, shorter than a novel (about 30,000 words), concentrating upon a single event. A novella is not as long as a novel but is longer than a short story. Ernest Hemingway's *The Old Man and the Sea* is a novella.

OBSCURITY: When a writer's language is not (or not easily) intelligible to the reader, the work concerned is termed as obscure.

ODE: An Ode is a long lyrical poem, serious in subject, elevated in style and elaborate in its stanzaic structure. It is in the form of an address to the object or the person about whom it is written.

OMNISCIENT AUTHOR: It is a device used by some outstanding modern novelists to move freely from the objective narrative to the internal or subjective psyche of a character or characters and then comment freely and apparently unattached on the significance, possibility or outcome of any or some events.

ONOMATOPOEIA: The use of words that imitate sounds. Examples of such words are buzz, hiss, murmur, and rustle. Isabella Gardner uses onomatopoeia in "Summer Remembered":

Sounds sum and summon the remembering of summers
The humming of the sun
The mumbling in the honey-suckle vine
The whirring in the clovered grass
The pizzicato plinkle of ice in an auburn uncle's amber glass

ORAL TRADITION: the passing of songs, stories and poems from generation to generation by word of mouth.

ORATORY: public speaking that is formal, persuasive, and emotionally appealing.

OXYMORON: It is a figure of speech in which two apparently contradictory words or terms are used to convey, a paradoxical sense, e.g.

(*i*) 'busy-idle days' (Lamb in *Dream children*)

(*ii*) Life in Death (Coleridge in *'Rime.....'*).

PANTOMIME:

1. A Pantomime is a dramatic representation pertaining to some myth, legend or traditional tale (or it may have some fairy element in it).
2. Pantomimes became popular in England particularly in the first quarter of the 18th century.

PARABLE: A story which conveys a moral lesson is known as a parable, as for instance, the biblical parables.

PARADOX: It is a figure of speech in which a truth is brought home through the use of self-contradictory statement, *e.g.*

(*i*) Cowards die many a time before their death.

(*ii*) Discretion is the better part of valour.

(*iii*) After death, we awake into an eternal life.

PARALLELISM:

1. It is a rhetorical device where balancing sentences, phrases or words are used to enhance effect, e.g.
   What is important is not what you say, but what is important is what you mean.
2. Excessive use of this device leads to monotony and superficiality.

PARODY: Comic imitation of serious words, style, sense, subject of a writer to make them appear ridiculous.

PASTORAL: Literature depicting idealized rural life.

PASTORAL ELEGY: It is an elegy cast into the conventional pastoral form. It is presumed that the poet is a shepherd mourning the death of a fellow shepherd. The whole image of goats, sheep, pastures and pastoral gods and goddesses is drawn into it.

PATHETIC FALLACY: When nature is shown as sympathising with human lot, the device used is called "pathetic fallacy," *e.g.*

(*i*) Byron's description of the battle of Waterloo in Childe Harold's Pilgrimage.

(*ii*) The behaviour of slow-moving nature in Tennyson's "Lotos-eaters".

PEDANTRY: The term refers to the excessive display of knowledge such as:

(*i*) Foreign words and phrases

(*ii*) Allusions

(*iii*) Archaic words

(*iv*) High sounding and sesquipedalian words

(*v*) Cataloguing, etc.

when these are not strictly needed within the context of the work.

PERIODIC SENTENCE: A sentence in which the Principal clause occurs at the end when it is preceded by one or more subordinate clauses, such that the sense is clear only when the whole sentence is read, is known as a 'periodic sentence'.

PERIODICAL: Magazine or journal published regularly.

PERIPETEIA: Peripeteia means sudden change in the fortune or position of the hero from good to bad, or high to low. This reversal of fortue happens due to Hamartia in the character of the hero.

PERIPHRASIS:

1. It means a round about way of saying a thing, *e.g.* An idle singer of an empty day, etc.
2. The term is close to circumlocution and euphemism in sense and effect.

PERSONAL ESSAY: According to Hudson, true essay is essentially personal. Montaigne says, "I am myself the subject of my book". In the Personal essay the author gives his own experiences, impressions of reactions about the subjects taken up for writing his essays.

PERSONIFICATION: A figure of speech in which a non-human subject is given human characteristics. In "April Rain Song," Langston Hughes personifies the rain:

Let the rain kiss you
Let the rain sing you a lullaby.

Effective personification of things or ideas makes them seem vital and alive, as if they were human.

PERSUASION: Writing or speech that attempts to convince a reader to think or act in a particular way. Persuasion is used in political arguments as well as in advertising, editorials and sermons.

PESSIMISTS: Although in English literature, we have a number of pessimist poets or a good number of poets expressing at times pessimistic ideas or writing sometimes in a pessimistic mood, yet two of the poets are known in particular, as "Pessimists." They are:

(*i*) Thomas Hardy

(*ii*) A.E. Housman

PHILOLOGY: Study of literature, language and linguistics.

PICARESQUE: Chronicle of adventures of a rogue; originated in 16-century Spain.

PINDARIC ODE: The Pindaric Odes are written on the model of the odes written by Pindar, the great Greak poet. They are choric in character and designed to be sung by a troupe of dancers in churches or public halls.

PLAGIARISM: Wrongful appropriation and publication of another's work as one's own.

PLATITUDE: It means a truth or generalization which is too well-known mainly because of its overuse, *e.g.*

Truth is evergreen.

PLEONASM:

1. It means the use of words more than those which are absolutely necessary, *e.g.*
   (*i*) He sat *down* on the ground.
   (*ii*) He looked up *high* towards the sky.
   (*iii*) He has got *sole* monopoly over such kind of business.
2. In essence, it is akin to Tautology or circumlocution.

PLOT: The plan or sequence of events in a literary work. In most novels, dramas, short stories, and narrative poems, the plot involves both characters and a central conflict. The plot usually begins with an exposition that introduces the setting, the characters, and the basic situation. This is followed by the inciting incident, which introduces the central conflict. The conflict then increases during the development until it reaches a high point of interest or suspense, the climax. The climax is followed by the end, or resolution, of the central conflict. Any events that occur after the resolution make up the denouement. The events that lead up to the climax comprise the rising action. The events that follow the climax comprise the falling action.

POEM: Literary work which may be in rhyme, blank verse or a combination of the two.

POETIC DICTION:

1. Diction stands chiefly for choice of words.
2. In poetry, poetic diction is unavoidable as mere metre is not enough to make a poem a literary piece of work.
3. In other words, mere versification or combination of words in rhyme or any other verse form does not make poetry.
4. The poets resort to several devices in this regard, some of which are :
   (*i*) Use of similes, metaphors, symbols, inversions, and other figures of speech as such as hyperbole, irony, antithesis, personification, etc.
   (*ii*) Omission of some parts of speech or grammatical rules.
   (*iii*) Use of archaic or uncommon words.
   (*iv*) Change in order of words, etc.
   (*v*) Use of picturesque phrases and expressions
   (*vi*) Use of other ornamental devices such as epithets
   (*vii*) Use of highly musical lies, fanciful flights etc.

POETIC JUSTICE: The term 'Poetic Justice' was coined by Thomas Rhymer. It means exact reward or punishment given to a character according to his good or bad deeds. This exactness of justice is possible only in the world of poetry.

POETIC LICENCE: By 'Poetic Licence' it is meant a certain amount of liberty enjoyed by the poets in the use of grammar, word-order or coinage of words in order to produce greater poetic effects.

POETRY: One of the three major types of literature, in which form and content are closely connected, like the two faces of a single coin. Poems are often divided into lines and stanzas and often employ regular rhythmical patterns, or meters. Most poems make use of highly concise, musical, and emotionally charged language. Many also make use of imagery, figurative language, and special devices such as rhyme.

POINT OF VIEW: The perspective or vantage point from which a story is told. Three commonly used points of view are first person, omniscient third person, and limited third person.

In *first person point of view*, the narrator is a character in the story and refers to himself or herself with the first-person pronoun "I."

The two kinds of *third-person point of view, limited* and *omniscient*, are called "third person" because the narrator uses third-person pronouns such as "he" and "she" to refer to the characters. There is no "I" telling the story.

In stories told from the *omniscient third person point of view*, the narrator knows and tells about what each character feels and thinks.

In stories told from the *limited third-person point of view*, the narrator relates the inner thoughts and feelings of only one character; and everything is viewed from this character's perspective. The *Harry Potter* series by J.K. Rowlings is told from the limited third-person point of view.

PORNOGRAPHY: Work in which there is a deliberate emphasis on the sexual behaviour of characters, in order to arouse sexual excitement.

POTBOILER: Work written essentially to gain the author a livelihood.

PRECIS: Concise statement; short summary of a work.

PREFACE: Introduction to a work.

PRE-RAPHAELITE SCHOOL OF POETS: A group of painter-poets led by D.G. Rossetti founded the Pre-Raphaelite School of poetry. Other poets of this school were Christina Rosetti, Swinburne, and William Morris. They wrote highly sensuous, pictorial and symbolical poems which could be painted with equal effect.

PROLOGUE: It is often the original statement by the writer (as in a drama) which highlights the chief aim of the work which is going to be unfolded or staged.

PROPAGANDA: Work devoted to the dissemination of an idea or belief, usually biased.

PROPHETIC NOVEL: The Prophetic Novels try to forecast what the future would be like. They do not claim to be absolutely correct. They only give a tentative picture of the future on the basis of the tendencies prevailing in the present.

PROSE: The ordinary form of written language. Most writing that is not poetry, drama or song is considered prose. It occurs in fiction and nonfiction.

(MODERN) PROSE STYLE:

1. The English prose style started by Bacon, flourished in the hands of Addison and Steele and numerous essayists and prose stylists that followed.
2. As a fine example of the latest modern prose style, Naipaul who won the Nobel Prize for Literature in 2001 deserves to be mentioned.

PROSODY: Study of the handling of language in poetry.

PROSOPOPAEIA: This figure of speech is used when:

(*i*) The past (called the Historic Present) is written in the present tense:

Sohrab and Rustam clash with their full might.

(*ii*) The (anticipated) future is written in the present tense:

Here, we go to our new house tomorrow with all our belongings carried in a lorry and then tucked in elegant mahogany almirahs.

PSEUDONYM: Name other than the true one used by an author to represent his work.

PSYCHOLOGICAL NOVEL: The Psychological Novels are also known as the "Stream of Consciousness Novels'. These novels probe into the working of human psychology at the conscious, subconscious and unconscious levels.

PSYCHOLOGICAL PROCESS: It is the process applied to the study of a piece of literature to penetrate another's mind and to study the activities, utterances, etc. of various characters, as, for instance, to arrive at the exact nature of Hamlet's madness whether there was "method" in it or not.

PUN:

1. When a word gives several meanings (often for fun) as in a play, it is the "pun" that is used.
2. Shakespeare is a great master of this device.
3. **Example :**
   (*i*) This is the *book*.
   (*ii*) It means
   (*a*) any book
   (*b*) a holy book, often the Bible.

REALISM: Literature that attempts to depict life objectively and faithfully.

REFORMATION: Reformation was a religious Movement led by Martin Luther in the fifteenth century. It protested against the practices of the Roman Catholic Church. It advocated complete faith in the Bible and in one's own soul for salvation.

REFRAIN: Phrase, line or lines repeated at intervals or at the end of a stanza in poetry.

REGIONAL NOVEL: The Regional Novel is a novel which describes the social and family life, customs and manners, language and dress, occupations and professions of the people of a particular region. The entire novel is woven around these factors of the region.

RENAISSANCE: The term Renaissance literally means re-birth on revival. In Art and Literature it meant the rebirth or revival of Greek art, literature, culture and pattern of life which had been partly or largely destroyed by the repeated invasions of the Turks.

REVIEW: Notice or critical article on musical, artistic or literary work.

REVUE: Theatrical entertainment made up of sketches, dances, songs, recitals and improvised pieces, usually humorous, satirical or topical.

RHETORIC: Art of using language, in speaking or writing, to persuade. The persuasive style (rather than the content) of a work.

RHYTHM:

1. It signifies the measured regular beat or movement of sounded words in language.
2. Rhythm is a must in poetry as well as prose, as it introduces or enhances the element of pleasure, interest and curiosity.

RHYME: Echoing sound or audible similarity in two or more words, especially at endings. Device used to construct much poetry.

RIDDLE: Puzzle, question or enigma; conundrum.

ROMAN A CLEF: Novel based upon actual people under disguised names.

ROMANCE: Tale of chivalry, originally written in verse (Medieval times); term applied now to any wonderful or mysterious tale far removed from reality.

ROMANCE LANGUAGES: Languages which have emerged straightaway from Latin and/or Greek, are called Romance Languages.

ROMANTICISM: Romanticism has been variously defined by various critics and scholars. According to Walter Peter, "Romanticism is the addition of curiosity to the desire of beauty.

ROMANTIC COMEDY: The Romantic Comedy is basically a love comedy. There is usually a story of triangular love with two heroes and one heroine, or two heroines and one hero, but finally the play ends in happy marriage.

SAGA: Lengthy prose work, sometimes in several parts, describing the history and events surrounding medieval kings, warrriors and, recently, fictitious families.

SATIRE: Dryden defines the Satire as "a literary composition whose principal aim is to ridicule folly or vice. The true end of Satire is the amendment of vices by correction." A healthy satire good-humouredly exposes one's folly or vice.

SCIENCE FICTION: Literature based on scientific fact or fantasy, on earth or on other worlds in space, often set in periods in the distant future.

SEMANTICS: Branch of linguistics dealing with meaning, and the change of meaning, in words.

SEMIOLOGY: General study or science of signs with which humans communicate with each other (including words and their use in every context).

SERMON: Verbal instruction of some length, usually religious.

SHORT STORY: Work of fiction usually revolving around single event.

SIC: Included in brackets after a printed word or quoted passage to indicate that it is quoted accurately, however actually incorrect.

SIMILE:

1. When we draw comparison between two persons by using (usually 'like', as-so or as) it is the 'simile' that we make use of, *e.g.*
   (*i*) As red as a rose
   (*ii*) As happy as a lark
   (*iii*) She looked like a violet, half-hidden behind the rock.
2. *An Exaggerated Simile:* It is a simile in which the sense is clearly exaggerated, *e.g.*
   (*i*) He ran as fast as lightning
   (*ii*) He has in himself the force as much as there is in ten horses.

SLANG: Colourful and vernacular language of the street, marketplace, barrackroom, workplace, sportsplace and playground.

SOLILOQUY: Kind of monologue in which a stage character expresses his thoughts and feelings.

SONG: Poem or verse set to music.

SONNET: 14-line poem of set rhyme-scheme; Elizabethan (Shakespearean) *ababcdcdefefgg*, Italian *abbaabba cdcdcd* (or *cdecde*).

STANZA: A group of lines in a poem that are considered to be a unit. Many poems are divided into stanzas that are separated by spaces. Stanzas often function just like paragraphs in prose. Each stanza states and develops a single main idea.

STREAM OF CONSCIOUSNESS: A narrative technique that presents thoughts as if they were coming directly from a character's mind. Instead of being arranged in chronological order, the events of the story are presented from the character's point of view, mixed in with the character's feelings and memories just as they might spontaneously occur in the mind of a real person. Stream-of-consciousness writing reveals a character's complex psychology and presents it in realistic detail.

STROPHE AND ANTI STROPHE:

1. Strophe is "the song sung by the chorus (in a Greek play) as it moved towards one side, answered by an exact counterpart."
2. Anti-Strophe is the term for the Strophe, "as it returned : part of any ode thus answered..."

STYLE: A writer's typical way of writing. Style includes word choice, tone, degree of formality, figurative language, rhythm, grammatical structure, sentence length, organization-in short, every feature of a writer's use of language. Ernest Hemingway in The Old Man and the Sea and Aravind Ardiga in The White Tiger, for example, use a simple or informal prose style that contrasts with V. S. Naipaul's more formal style of writing.

STOCK MATERIAL: Material necessary for a writer to write.

STOCK CHARACTERS: Characters that are commonly found in most of pieces of dramas or fiction.

STOCK SITUATIONS: Situations which are frequently presented by authors in their works.

SUSPENSE: A feeling of growing uncertainty about the outcome of events in a literary work. Writers create suspense by raising questions in the minds of the readers. Suspense builds until the climax of the plot, at which point the suspense reaches its peak.

SYMBOL: Anything that stands for or represents something else. A conventional symbol is one that is widely known and accepted, such as a voyage symbolizing life or a skull symbolizing death. A personal symbol is one developed for a particular work by a particular author. Examples include Melville's white whale in *Moby Dick.*

SYNTHESIS, POETRY OF: The term "Poetry of Synthesis" is referred to by I.A. Richards, and it has been thus explained by Cleanth Brooks—

"... a poetry which does not leave out what is apparently hostile to its dominant tone, and which, because it is able to fuse the irrelevant and disordant, has come to terms with itself and invulnerable to irony."

STRUCTURE: The structure meant is a structure of meaning, evaluations and interpretations; and the principle of unity which informs it seems to one of balancing and harmonizing connotations, attitudes and meanings.

SUBLIMITY: It is a term which is used to describe inexplicable beauty which is beyond any rules to describe or measure.

SYMBOLISM: French poetic movement of late 19th century that developed as revolt against realism, concentrating on evoking emotions by use of indirect suggestion (symbol and metaphor); flourished in Russia at turn of century as literary movement, and later in British novel.

SYNECDOCHE:

1. This figure of speech is used when the understanding of one thing by means of another is employed.
2. This can be done in several ways, some of which are mentioned below :
   (*i*) When a part stands for a whole or genus, e.g.
   We have fifty *hands* in our factory.
   (hands = workers)
   (*ii*) When a whole or genus stands for a part, e.g. He belongs to a different *world* from yors (world = category, social set-up, economic status, etc.)
   (*iii*) When an individual represents a class, *e.g.* He is the *Nestor* of our village.
   (Nestor = the oldest man)

SYNTAX: It means:

(*i*) The way a sentence is constructed
(*ii*) Arrangement of words in writing (or in speech) according to the rules of grammar
(*iii*) Rules pertaining to this system or arrangement.

SYNONYM: A word similar in meaning to another.

SYNOPSIS: Outline of the main points of a work; a summary.

TALE: Spoken or written narrative.

TAUTOLOGY: Overuse of synonyms or repetition of ideas in sentence.

THEME: A central message or insight into life revealed by a literary work. An essay's theme is often directly stated in its thesis statement. In most works of fiction, the theme is only indirectly stated: a story, poem, or play most often has an implied theme. In some forms of didactic literature, which is intended to be morally instructive, such as a fable or a parable, the theme can be stated outright at the end as the "moral of the story." In some modern literature, the theme can be very subtle and abstract.

THESIS: Long essay or treatise on a subject, usually expository; work presented to examiners for academic qualification.

THIRD PERSON: Style of novel, etc., in which narrator is outside action.

TONE: The writer's attitude towards his or her subject, characters, or audience. A writer's tone may be formal or informal, friendly or distant, personal or pompous.

TRACT: Short printed treatise on religious or political subject.

TRAGEDY: The Tragedy is the tragic story of a good and great man who, on account of a slight flaw in his character, passes through a harrowing emotional and spiritual crisis, and finally meets his doom and death.

TRAGEDY OF BLOOD (AND THUNDER):

1. It was basically a melodramatic presentation of horrible, gory scenes.
2. The first famous tragedy of this kind is Kyd's "Spanish Tragedy".

TRAGIC-COMEDY: A Tragic-Comedy is an artistic combination of both tragedy and comedy. It develops as a tragedy to the point of climax, and then takes a happy turn and finally ends into a happy denouement.

TRAGIC FLAW: In Shakespeare's tragedies, in particular, we often find a particular flaw in the character of the hero which ultimately leads to the fall of his destiny, along with the fall of his state or estate.

TRANSFERRED EPITHET: When an epithet is transferred from a person to a thing, it is known as a 'transferred epithet', *e.g.*

(*i*) It is a *foolish* idea

(*ii*) Let *happy* days come.

TRANSLATION: Rendering of a work into another language.

TREATISE: Formal work examining a subject and the principles underlying it.

TROCHAIC LINE METRE:

1. A line in verse is known as a *"trochaic" line* when the first, third and other odd syllables in it are accented (as in the 'Iambic metre') irrespective of the length of the line.
2. A poem comprising such lines is known as having been written in the "Trochaic" metre.

UNDERSTATEMENT: It is practically the opposite of hyperbole and is sometimes used by the writers to emphasise indirectly the desired meaning.

VADE MECUM: Manual or handbook carried for frequent reference.

VERISIMILITUDE: It is the likeness of truth presented in a work of art that makes it similar to the characteristics or situation in real life and that enables the readers to accept it ungrudgingly as truth (and may be, sometimes, more than real happening in life).

VERNACULAR: Domestic or native language.

VERSIFICATION: Study of how traditional verse is constructed.

WIT: Dryden defines (in "Annus Mirabilis") wit as "delightful imagining of persons, actions, passions or things."

YARN: Story or tale, sometimes improbable and far-fetched.

●●●

DESCRIPTIVE ENGLISH
(FOR ESSAY TYPE QUESTIONS)

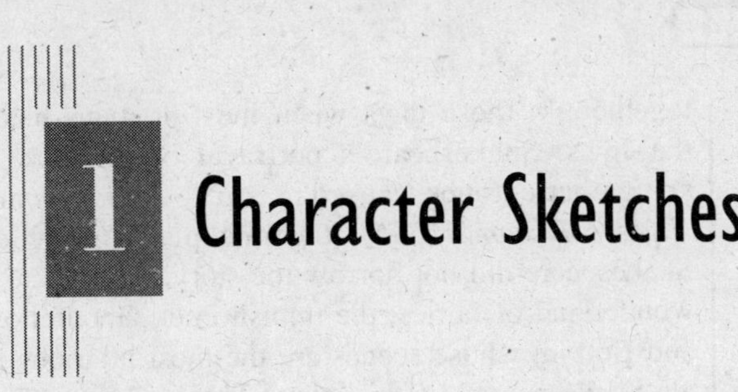

1 Character Sketches

WILLIAM SHAKESPEARE (1564-1616)

Life

William Shakespeare was born on 23rd April 1564 at Stratford-on-Avon. His father was a grain-dealer. His business deteriorated when William was yet a child and so William could not study more than a few years in the local grammar school and left it at the age of about 13 to help out in his family's business. He married at the age of 18 to Anne Hathaway, who was eight years his senior. They had three children, but the marriage was not happy. According to tradition, William was caught poaching deer and rabbits in Thomas Lucy's park at Charlecote. He was lynched and ran away from home, gradually reaching London. There he got a job as a holder of visitors' horses at a theatre. He later on got a job as an actor and is supposed to have done the roles of the type of Ghost in *Hamlet* and Adam in *As You Like it.* Shakespeare very soon got the hang of the theatre and began revising plays or writing plays based on English translations of Greek and Latin stories. These plays were very successful with audiences and provoked the jealousy of rivals like Greene who denounces Shakespeare in a pamphlet entitled *A Groatsworth of Wit* (1592). Greene describes him as "an upstart crow beautified with our feathers, that with his Tyger's heart wrapped in a player's hide ....".

From then on there was no stopping of Shakespeare's upward rise in career. He was attached to and wrote his plays for the Earl of Leicester's Players. In 1595, his name appears on the Payroll of the Lord Chamberlain's and finally of the King's Servants. These companies performed at The Rose, The Curtain and The Theatre. The company finally bought the Globe and Shakespeare, growing prosperous, became a partner of the Globe Theatre and later of the Blackfriars.

Shakespeare wrote and published for twenty years from 1591 to 1611. During this period he wrote 37 plays and more than 154 sonnets. The first 126 of the sonnets are addressed to a man Mr. W.H., the Earl of Southampton, who introduced him to the important courtiers, and the remainder to a "dark lady". He grew prosperous day by day, acquired estate, got his father to apply for a coat of arms and became a gentleman by inheritance. He bought New Place, the largest house at Stratford and retired there after 1611. After a drinking bout in 1616, he fell sick and died.

Works

Shakespeare wrote the famous love poems, *Venus and Adonis* (1593) and *The Rape of Lucrece* (1594) dedicated to the Earl of Southampton. These poems in themselves entitle him to a place among the immortals. But he was destined to become famous and known to posterity as England's greatest dramatist. He began, as was the custom of the times, by collaborating with Marlowe and Kyd in revising and touching up old plays like *Titus Andronicus, Henry VI* and *Richard III.* The exact sequence of dates in which his plays came out is not known, but only sixteen were published in quarto form during his life-time. There were copyright laws at the time and unscrupulous writer 'pirates' took down bits of the plays as they were enacted and published them in different editions. In 1623, seven years after his death, two of Shakespeare's friends and fellow-actors, Heminge and Condell, published all his plays as the first folio in memory of their worthy friend. This folio contains all the plays except *Pericles.* There are references to Shakespeare's plays in *Palladis Tamia, Wit's Treasury* (1593) by Francis Meres. The date of composition is guessed by topical and contemporary allusions in the plays and the tone and metre used.

In the earlier plays there is in general a youthful exuberance, a lot of verbal wit, strange conceits and light-heartedness. The blank verse used is end-stopped (the sense ends with each line) and rhyming couplets are used. As the plays grow in maturity and Shakespeare's art advances he uses run-on lines in which the sense of one line carries on to the next. This allows the verse to express a greater range of emotions. Still later on, feminine endings are used, that is, a number of unstressed syllables are added at the ends of lines. In the last plays, rhyme completely disappears.

Shakespeare's plays were written in three periods. Although their date of writing is based on conjecture, the periods give a clue to the gradual development of his art.

Early Period (1590-1596)

Henry VI (three plays), *Richard III, Richard II, Love's Labour Lost, A Midsummer Night's Dream, Romeo and Juliet.*

Middle Period (1596-1608)

Herry IV (two plays), *The Merchant of Venice, As You Like It, Julius Caesar, Hamlet, Othello, Macbeth, Twelfth Night, King Lear, Antony and Cleopatra,* etc.

Late Period (1608-1613)

Cymbeline, The Tempest, Pericles, The Winter's Tale, etc.

The above are some of the 37 plays he wrote. An analysis of the plays reveals some common characteristics of the different categories like comedies and tragedies. The comedies are boisterous and farcical. They show Shakespeare's immature period. *The Merchant of Venice* (1596) is one of his most popular comedies with several episodes woven together. In those days when the Christians hated the Jews, Shakespeare's portrayal of Shylock in sympathetic tones caused a stir. *A Midsummer Night's Dream* (1595), the one play for which Shakespeare did not borrow the story, takes us to a wonderland of fairies, the impish Puck Goodfellow and Bottom whose scenes are the most hilarious in all Shakespeare. In this play, Theseus says *"The lunatic, the lover, and the poet/Are of imagination all compact."* This line refers to Shakespeare's own weird fancies as he creates them in his plays. *The Merry Wives of Windsor* (1600) was written on the behest of Queen Elizabeth. The character Falstaff is one of Shakespeare's best creations. According to the critic Hazlitt, Falstaff is all laughter and merriment, "laughing 3 inches below the skin". *Much Ado about Nothing* (1598) contains bracing wit-combats between Benedick and Beatrice. *As You Like It* (1600) provides glimpses of an emotionally rich life in the forest of Arden. *Twelfth Night* (1601) is a hilarious comedy. Through Malvolio, Shakespeare satirizes Puritanism.

Histories like *Richard III* (1593) and *Richard II* (1596) show the influence of Marlowe on Shakespeare. He wrote the three parts of *Henry VI* (1591-92) in collaboration with Marlowe. Most of these histories show the patriotic victory of kings.

The tragedies show Shakespeare's maturity in character delineation. *Titus Andronicus* (1594) is a horror play. *Romeo and Juliet* (1594) is a romantic tragedy which has become immortal. The four great tragedies of Shakespeare are psychological plays which show how a man of high rank falls from grace, becomes a plaything of destiny and ends up wretchedly all because of a "fatal flaw" in his character. In Greek tragedy, man was a complete puppet whose destiny was in the hands of the gods. Shakespeare often alludes to this: *"As flies to wanton boys are we to the gods/They kill us for their sport"*. But he gives his tragic characters "will-power". The tragic flaw in their characters, however, becomes the cause of their undoing. Thus with *Julius Caesar* (1599), it is his inordinate ambition; with *King Lear* (1605) it is dotedness and bad temper; with *Hamlet* (1601), it is over-refinement of thought leading to indecision; and with *Othello* (1604), it is simplicity causing suspicion. *Timon of Athens* (1607) is the tragedy of a misanthrope. *Coriolanus* (1606) depicts how pride leads to downfall. The last plays — *Pericles* (1608), *Cymbeline* (1609), *The Winter's Tale* (1610) and *The Tempest* (1611) have happy endings. With *The tempest* Shakespeare bid farewell to the theatre just as Prospero in the play puts away his wand and magic books.

To estimate the complete contribution of Shakespeare to English literature and the literature of the world is a difficult task. Thousands of books have been written on Shakespeare by scholars from all over the world and his plays have been translated into all the major languages. They are enacted everywhere and the Russians even claim he was a Slav! Even after 400 years his fame is on the rise. In *Julius Caesar,* Brutus says, *"How many times will this scene of ours be acted over/In states unborn and accents yet unknown"*. This indeed was a prophetic statement about his own plays.

Dryden stated that Shakespeare had 'a universal mind' and Ben Jonson said, "Shakespeare was not of an age but for all times." Indeed Shakespeare's characters — a gallery of 800 — are types of characters that have inhabited this planet throughout the human history. Shakespeare could enter into his characters and present them so vividly that they are more real than life itself. Master of the whole keyboard of emotions and expressions, the subtlest feelings are expressed in his plays. No wonder we quote him the most after the Bible.

Another aspect of his genius is that he excelled many of his contemporaries in whatever they invented. Thus he took Marlowe's 'mighty line' or the blank verse and made it a supple instrument for expressing many intense feelings. Ben Jonson described the 'humours' or human moods in his plays; Shakespeare bettered him in the description of greed, vice, folly and virtue.

Many have expressed doubt about his claim to the authorship of 37 plays in just 20 years. Yet there is no cause for doubt here. After all, he borrowed the stories from Latin and Greek translations and enlivened them with his genius. One of the sources of his Roman histories like *Julius Caesar,* for example, was Plutarch's *Lives of the Noble Romans* translated by North.

Shakespeare undoubtedly had many demerits, but these are overwhelmed and eclipsed by his outstanding gifts. Shakespeare, not being educated more than a few years in grammar school, was thrown upon his own resources. He observed Nature and human behaviour very keenly and had rare intuition and imagination. So he was trained in the school of life. His faults of grammar so prevalent in his plays are glossed off as poetic licence. In fact, he created his own grammar, using nouns as adjectives and inventing syntax. These have become expressions so apt, it is impossible to change or correct them without reducing the impact.

What was Shakespeare's philosophy? Was he a Christian? Shakespeare's ideas as expressed through his noble characters show universal virtue free from dogma and any religious denomination. They are virtues in the human spirit. He was capable of seeing good in all people.

"There is a soul of goodness
In things evil
Distil it if we may".

His advocacy of the cause of Shylock, the Jew, in the days when rank hatred existed for them among the Christians, shows the truth of the above lines. It reinforces the view that Shylock was a man *"more sinned against than sinning"*. Portia's speech on mercy and forgiveness in *The Merchant of Venice* is one of the most beautiful passages of his plays: *"The quality of mercy is not strained/It droppeth like the gentle rain from above/This mightiest in the mightiests"*.

The great range and variety of human behaviour treated by Shakespeare gives his plays an everlasting interest. We may ascribe to the Bard what he himself makes Enobarbus say of Cleopatra:

"Age cannot wither her
Nor custom state her infinite variety".

BEN JONSON (1573-1637)

Ben Jonson was only second to Shakespeare as a playwright. He had a chequered career. He was educated at Westminster School, but did not go up to university. Both Oxford and Cambridge Universities, however, honoured him. Jonson did stints as bricklayer, soldier and then actor. Being of a hot temperament, he picked up quarrels with fellow-actors and even killed one in a brawl for which crime he was branded in the left hand. He was both an admirer and a rival of Shakespeare. He offended King James and the Scots by his comedy *Eastward Hoe!* (written with George Chapman and John Marston), was imprisoned and almost lost his ears and nose. He lived for sometime with William Drummond, the Scottish poet, at Hawthornden. Drummond has left us an account of Ben Jonson's fiery nature. Like Samuel Johnson later on, Jonson later on, Jonson behaved like a literary dictator in the last period of his life gathering fawning admirers who were called the tribe of Ben. He died a poor man. On his tomb in Westminster Abbey, it is inscribed "O rare Ben Jonson!".

Ben Jonson was a neo-classical and revived the theories of drama that existed among the classical Greeks and Romans. Thus unlike Shakespeare, he maintained the classical rules of the unities of time, place and action in his plays. In this way, he wished to reform the Elizabethan theatre. Although he worshipped Shakespeare "this side of idolatory", he derided his lack of classical taste. At the Mermaid Tavern, he had witty combats with Shakespeare. Jonson did a lot of research into historical facts and documented his famous plays *Sejanus* and *Catiline* which turned out to be dull and pedantic. He was more successful in comedies and attacked romantic conventions used by his contemporaries. The comedies are realistic portrayals of the fads and follies of contemporary London. The best of his comedies are *Everyman in His Humour* (1598), *Epicoene or The Silent Woman* (1609), *The Alchemist* (1610) and *Volpone* (1605), the story of criminals.

Ben Jonson's comedies were "comedies of humour". In medieval medical parlance, a honour was one of the four fluids — choler, bite, phlegm and blood which determined a person's disposition by its preponderance. Thus choler or rather too much of it made one bad-tempered. Ben Jonson thus used it to mean a typical trait or idiosyncracy of a person. He exaggerated this and blew it out of all proportions to create comedy. Characters are given tell-tale names like Morose in *Epicoene.* Thus his characters were personifications of various qualities and resembled moralities. This was a method Charles Dickens was to employ later on, but on a larger canvas. Morose in Ben Jonson's play is eccentric about noise. He cannot tolerate the least noise. He oils his locks and doors and lives in a narrow street where no traffic is possible. His house is carpeted to absorb sound. Servants communicate in signs and one loses the job if the boots squeak. Morose agrees to his nephew marrying if he can get a perfectly silent woman. This he finds. But after marriage the wife becomes a loud mouth. The nephew celebrates the marriage with a noisy band. Horrified, Morose looks for a divorce. Here too he meets with disaster since he accosts two lawyers wrangling noisily. The nephew agrees to get rid of his wife if Morose leaves him an inheritance. He gets Morose to make a bond for this. Then he pulls of his wife's wig to reveal a boy!

Jonson's other plays are tedious and satirical — *Everyman out of His Humour* (1599), *Cynthis's Revels* (1600) and *The Poetaster* (1601). Jonson also wrote pastoral drama. His *Eastward Hoe!* gives a realistic picture of London life that surpasses all of Shakespeare's descriptions of the city. His plays contain some very beautiful lyrics like *"Drink to me only with thine eyes"*.

Ben Jonson was original and showed great technical skill in plot construction. His language is witty and vigorous, but his characters are not immortal because satire dominated his plays. Jonson's style was coarse and he was more concerned about his own age.

JOHN DONNE (1573-1631)

John Donne led a dissipated and tempestuous life before he took religious orders and rose to become Dean of St. Paul's. He wrote both secular and religious poems depicting his great ambivalent nature — passionate eroticism and deep meditation. Donne despised convention which followed Spenser's style of ornate language and smooth lyricism. To rebel against this he adopted a crabbed style and used a deliberately colloquial language. Ben Jonson, who otherwise admired him, said that for not keeping metre properly Donne deserved hanging. Donne's subjects were not allegory, pastoral or platonic love, but as mentioned earlier, a wild and passionate love. He was given the name of metaphysical because he and his followers like Henry Vaughan, George Herbert and Crashaw affected the metaphysical philosophers. They were all learned men and exhibited their learning by subtlety of thought or philosophical rumination as expressed in their poetry. The idea of his poem *The Extasie* could be described or expressed in straight and simple language, but Donne invests it with strange arguments and it requires tortured imagination to understand his reasoning. Thoughts and feelings are blended in a strange manner. Preposterous conceits are used. Conceits are images in which two contrastive ideas are yoked together or the sense jumps abruptly from the sublime to the ridiculous. Thus his mandrake song — *"Go and catch a falling star/ Get with child a mandrake root/ Tell me where all past years are/ Or who cleft the Devil's foot"* — describes how after travelling far and wide a man reports that there is no woman existing who is fair and true. Donne was unkind to the opposite sex. In one of his poems, he describes how after his death he would visit his disdainful mistress and as a ghost watch her making love to her new lover.

In some of his divine poems like *Death, be not proud,* he displays great forcefulness of reasoning. Because of the obscurity of his thoughts, Donne lost his admirers in the 18th and 19th centuries, but T.S. Eliot and the moderns revived interest in him, by having recourse to imagery and metre like his to express a tortured conscience.

JOHN MILTON (1608-1674)

Life

John Milton was born on December 9, 1608 in London. His father was a lawyer-cum-banker. Although a Puritan, he loved art and literature and was known as a musician. Milton was trained in music and inherited a love for music. He was charming and aloof. After his education at St. Paul's School he joined Christs' College, Cambridge. But he was rusticated from college for protesting against the curriculum.

Even while he was at Cambridge, he wrote Latin and Italian poems. The best one was *Ode on the Morning of Christ's Nativity* written at the age of twenty-one. In this poem he celebrates the end of paganism and "the death of Pan". The style is rich with Elizabethan devices.

He refused ordination as minister or taking holy orders under the Church of England because this would have fettered his liberated conscience. He settled at Horton near London and devoted himself to writing poems. *L' Allegro* and *Il Penseroso* and two masques *Arcades* and *Comus* and the famous elegy, *Lycidas,* are the works of this period.

In 1638 he left for a tour of the Continent. He won many friends in Italy because of his interest in and mastery of Latin and Italian. But before he could go to Greece, he heard of the conflict between the King and the Parliament and hurried back to England to support the latter. He also taught for a time at a school and wrote a tract on education.

Between 1640 and 1660 he wrote prose pamphlets and some sonnets. When the Commonwealth was established, he was appointed Latin Secretary to the department of foreign affairs. He married Mary Powell in 1643. The marriage was an unhappy one. The daughter of a Cavalier Royalist, she could not tolerate Milton's puritanical ways and left him after marriage. He was much aggrieved and wrote tract pleading for a change in divorce laws. Mary returned to him after two years and he had three daughters by her.

Milton turned fully blind in 1653. Andrew Marvell and others assisted him in his work of writing. He accepted his blindness as the will of God in his beautiful sonnet *On His Blindness: "They also serve who only stand and wait".*

He married Catherine Woodcock after his first wife died. But Catherine also expired within fifteen months. When monarchy was restored, Milton lost his post and was arrested. He was soon released. He lost some of his property. Now Milton set himself to writing the work that was to make him immortal. In 1667, he completed the *Paradise Lost.* During this period he married for the third time. He finished *Paradise Regained* and *Samson Agonistes* in 1671. He died on November 8, 1674.

Milton was a tolerant Puritan. That is why he got along well with a Royalist father-in-law and a Catholic brother. In later life he became an Arian and did not accept Christ as the divine son. He kept away from wine and women in order to concentrate on higher goals. An unshakeable idealist, he could not understand man completely. His desire to reform mankind was too ambitious and failed. His poetry is remembered today for its magnificent grandeur rather than for any message.

Works

There are four clear-cut periods in Milton's career as a poet: (1) At Cambridge till 1632, (2) At Horton from 1632 to 1638, (3) The period of journalism from 1640 to 1660, (4) The final period of his masterpieces.

The period of his youth produced the famous *Ode on the Morning of Christ's Nativity* (1629). The poem is marred by exaggeration and metaphysical conceits in describing his devotion to the infant Jesus. He also wrote a number of Latin and Italian poems which have been translated into English.

In 1632, he wrote the exquisite *"L' Allegro"* and *Il Penseroso.* The titles only are in Italian. The poems and their spirit are quite English. The first one describes the poet's thoughts in a gay mood and *Il Penseroso* describes the gloomy side of his thinking. The poems are written in octosyllabic couplets and have a haunting music. *L'Allegro* means *'the cheerful man'* and describes his revels, his delight in a castle or a theatre and *Il Penseroso,* his pensive thoughts. Dr. Johnson is said to have admired these poems very much. The poems depict not so much natural scenes as moods of the mind. Milton seeks pure pleasure. In *L'Allegro*, it is Mirth, fresh, rosy and vigorous, dancing on tiptoe. In *Il Penseroso,* divine Melancholy is presented as a pensive nun *"devout and pure .... with even step and musing gait".*

Milton's inner conflict, the moral problem before him, is the theme in the masques *Arcades* and *Comus.* Although these are Renaissance in form, the spirit is grave, austere and Miltonic. *Comus* (1634) is a paean to chastity. It is obviously didactic and lacks any dramatic power to thrill. A young, immaculate heroine is confronted by the magician, Comus, who is drunk and sensual. He tries to have her beautiful virginity, but she is successful in warding him off. The poem is full of discourses and learned reminiscences of the classics and lyrical grace. The morality is high and only the select few could appreciate it.

In *Lycidas* (1637) Milton laments the death of a friend by drowning. The elegy asks the question that if a young man full of promise is carried away in the prime of youth then what avails in this life? Pleasure, therefore, calls him to *"sport with Amaryllis in the shade, Or with the tangles of Neaera's hair".* But another voice, that of fame, calls him away to a life of virtue.

Milton wrote in prose for twenty years. He also composed some exquisite sonnets including the one *On His Blindness* where he regrets he might be incapable of performing God's wish on earth because of his impairment, but consoles himself that even through poetry he can fulfill his life:

"And that one talent which is death to hide
Lodged with me useless
But Patience to prevent that murmur soon replies
They also serve who only stand and wait".

The Restoration of 1660 deprived him of his post for sometime. Poverty, blindness and leisure brought forth his best works: *Paradise Lost* (1667), *Paradise Regained* and *Samson Agonistes* (1671). Here we read in magniloquent lines through great biblical allegories of his personal unhappiness and a nation's agony. He is Beelzebub Satan and Samson in rebellion. Thrown out of Heaven by God, Satan exhorts:

"What though the field be lost
All is not lost
The unconquerable will to survive".

He wrote in blank verse only and used choruses in *Samson Agonistes. Paradise Lost* is his magnum opus, a Puritan's meditation of the Bible or his interpretation of it. The story of Adam and Eve becomes the drama of conscience, the exposure to temptation. The Bible has the ingredients of his own life. *Paradise Regained* is a reply to *Paradise Lost.* This poem is an allegory based on the story of Christ's fast for forty days where he resists the three temptations of Satan and destroys the latter's reign on earth. Christ is seen not as divine incarnation, but as a superman. In fact, Milton himself is Christ, like in that he resists the great temptation for worldly fame by mastering Greek culture and becoming a poet. Literature, philosophy and art are all vain compared to the true wisdom of the Bible.

In *Samson Agonistes,* we again see Milton. He is Samson betrayed by Delilah. He is alone and isolated, blind and helpless, the last of the Republicans among the triumphant Royalists. He lashes out against woman, as the inferior of the human race, deceitful and untrustworthy. The poem is like a Hellenic drama, but lacks movement. There is unending dialectics and reasoning.

JOHN DRYDEN (1631-1700)

Dryden was the greatest man of letters in the Restoration Period. In fact, he dominated the literary scene in poetry, prose and drama and the dates of his life 1640 to 1702 are known as the *Age of Dryden* and covers the reigns of Charles II, James II and William III. After 1660, a decisive change came over English thought and style. It became practical and utilitarian and shunned the speculative and the imaginative. One reason for this was the influence of French models like Moliere in literature. English writers copied French plots. Secondly, the writers were dissatisfied with the past. The Renaissance with its emphasis on wonder and imagination had ruled long. The grandeur of Milton was too much for the common masses, Shakespeare's great works were followed by degenerate writers, and the Puritans had made literature very moralistic and morose. Now there was a general desire for change. It is in this light that Dryden's works must be considered.

Life

Dryden was born in 1631 in a respectable family and was educated at Westminster School and Trinity College. His earlier poems: *"Heroic stanzas on the Death of Oliver Cromwell"* (1659), and *Astraea Redux* (1660) were based on contemporary events, the latter on the happy Restoration of Charles II. He was married to an Earl's daughter and wrote plays for fifteen years to make a decent living. During the Great Plague he withdrew to the country where he composed the famous *Essay of Dramatick Poesie.* He became the poet laureate after Davenant. When the revolution came he was deprived of the post of poet laureate because he wrote *The Hind and the Panther* (1687) in defence of the Roman Catholic Church. He spent the remaining twelve years of his life in writing plays and translating Virgil and the *Fables.* He died in May 1700 and was buried in Westminster Abbey.

Dryden had no fixed religious or political loyalties and changed sides to suit his needs. He was patronized by the king and more than once got involved in brawls.

Poetry

Some of his poems are:

1. *Heroic Stanzas on the Death of Cromwell* — written in quatrains (1659).
2. *Astraea Redux* to celebrate the return of Charles II — written in heroic couplets (1660).
3. *Annus Mirabilis* (Wonderful Year) describing the Great Fire of London and the Dutch War (1667).
4. *To the Memory of Mrs. Anne Killigrew.*
5. *Song for St. Cecilia's Day* (1687).
6. *Alexander's Feast* (1697).

The first three were based on contemporary events. The last three are known still for their lyrical beauty. *Alexander's Feast* is the best poem in which the power of music is brought out through the sound and rhythm of the words and lines.

Absalom and Achitophel (1681) is one of the best political satires in English. It was written in the background of the bogus Popish Plot. The anti-

Catholics used the opportunity to stir up a hysteria against Catholics and James who was to succeed Charles to the throne. The anti-Catholics also tried to get the Exclusion Bills passed in Parliament to prevent James from succession, but the King dissolved the Parliament. The Earl of Shaftesbury tried to put the Duke of Monmouth on the throne, but was arrested. But when he was acquitted, the Whigs struck a medal to acknowledge him as a hero. Dryden based it on the story from the Bible. Charles II is portrayed as David, Duke of Monmouth is Absalom and Shaftesbury, his evil counsellor, is Achitophel. The poem derides Shaftesbury who flees to Holland and dies in exile. The satire is immortal for its wonderful pen-pictures of the Earl of Shaftesbury and the Duke of Buckingham (Zimri).

Dryden wrote other satires like *The Medal* (1682) again on Shaftesbury. Shadwell, a former friend of Dryden, wrote a counter to this entitled, *The Medal of John Bayes.* To this last Dryden replied with another, *Mac Flecknoe* (1682) — satirizing Shadwell.

In Dryden's age, politics and religion were mixed up and Dryden wrote verse arguing for or against the Church. He wrote *Religio Laice* (religion of the layman) which is a defence of the Church of England against the Roman Catholic Church. When he became a convert to the Catholic faith, he wrote *The Hind and the Panther.* The Roman Church is a milk-white Hind and the Anglican is represented as a fierce Panther. The argumentation is remarkable.

Dryden wrote free translations / paraphrases of Virgil and the *Fables* or *Tales* of Chaucer and Boccaccio.

In most of his poetry, Dryden shows his mastery of the heroic couplet often interspersed with triplets.

Drama

When Dryden began writing plays, the Restoration stage underwent significant changes. The theatre companies called the King's Players and the Duke of York's Players, got patents to stage plays, and theatre began to be patronized exclusively by the aristocracy. The Royalists used the stage to ridicule the Puritans and their excessive pre-occupation with morality. Stage machinery like scenery came to be used and actresses took parts instead of boys for female roles. Shakespeare's plays like *Romeo and Juliet* were rewritten with happy endings. Dryden joined the Restoration drama scene by vulgarizing *The Tempest* by adding coarse touches to it. French drama, especially Moliere's comedies and Corneille's tragedies, began to influence Restoration drama. Restoration tragedy was called 'heroic' since the hero and the heroine were grand and declaimed speeches in decasyllabic couplets full of rant and bombast. Love and honour were of an extravagant type and heroic feats were accomplished. Owing to his mastery of the heroic couplet, Dryden excelled others in this. His *The Conquest of Granada* (1669-1670) has a preface defending heroic drama. He defended the use of rhyme in the *Essay of Dramatick Poesie*. He also wrote blank verse tragedies like *All for Love* (1678) in the Elizabethan tradition. This play is his own version of Shakespeare's *Antony and Cleopatra* and is probably his best. Comedy is more characteristic of Restoration literature. Here too Dryden led the age. Although his first comedy *The Wild Gallant* (1663) was a failure. he, wrote the successful *Marriage a la Mode.*

Prose

Dryden was also the greatest prose writer of his age. He wrote essays, prefaces to his plays, dedications, prologues to his works of poetry, propounding his views on literature. Dryden's prose style was plain, elegant, forceful and modern. His *Preface to the Fables* written in a conversational style consists of the wonderful appreciation of Chaucer's personality and genius. *The Essay of Dramatick Poesie* (1668) is a dialogue between four friends representing and comparing the merits of classical, French, Elizabethan and the new English drama. His defence of rhyme in drama and his praise of Shakespeare stand out as excellent prose pieces. Dr. Johnson aptly called Dryden the Father of English Criticism.

DANIEL DEFOE (1659-1731)

Daniel Defoe belonged to the Age of Queen Anne which is also known as the *Age of Prose.* The political satire was the speciality of the works of fiction or novels. Journalism began with periodical essays in *The Tatler* and *The Spectator*. Prose style became simple, plain and was moulded to express clearly narration, description, exposition argument and speculation.

Daniel Defoe, who is world-renowned for his novel *Robinson Crusoe,* began his career as a journalist and went on to novels. He belonged to the Dissenting Schools where a modern and practical education was given. Having failed to start a number of trades, he took to writing pamphlets where his flair for controversy found expression. His first verse satire was *The True-Born Englishman* (1701), in which he defended King William III who was being ridiculed by his English subjects for being Dutch. In his second work *The Shortest Way with the Dissenters* (1702), he argues that the best way of tackling dissenters is to liquidate them. He was convicted of sedition and was imprisoned. In the prison he wrote *A Hymn to the Pillory*. He became a hero in the public eye and was released on the instance of Lord Oxford. He started a non-political paper *The Review* (1704) discussing current politics. A ghost story *True Relation of the Apparition of one Mrs Veal* came out in 1706 in this paper and was much acclaimed.

He joined Lord Oxford as a secret agent and negotiated the Union in Scotland. He was arrested for writing some anti-Jacobite pamphlets but then released on bail. He became a Tory journalist and spied on the Tories for the Whigs. It was late in life when he was sixty that he published *Robinson Crusoe* (1719) and other works like *Moll Flanders* (1722), *Captain Singleton* (1720), *Colonel Jack* (1722), etc. He wrote prolifically on travel, trade and other subjects. His heroes are low characters like pirates and prostitutes. *A Journal of the Plague Year* (1722) is notable for its authentic account of the plague of 1664-65. Gifted with a versatile and powerful imagination, Defoe's stories are narrated by a fictitious hero. He uses a lot of vivid details. A puritan by upbringing, he moralizes and writes for a free conscience. His *Review* trail-blazed the essays of Steele and his novels were the cue for the great works of Richardson and Fielding.

JONATHAN SWIFT (1667-1745)

Life

Jonathan Swift was born posthumously in Ireland. His uncle brought him up sending him to Trinity College, Dublin. Being hot-tempered and vitriolic by nature, he said that his uncle had given him the education of a dog. He worked as secretary to Sir William Temple but could not tolerate subordination. He was ordained a minister in Ireland, but finding the life dull, returned to work for Temple for the rest of his life. In 1697, he defended Temple and his favour for the Ancients in *The Battle of the Books,* published in 1704.

After Temple's death he returned to find work in Ireland. From 1699 to 1710 he socialized with the Whigs like Steele; Addison and Congreve in London. He took to writing pamphlets to support the Church and the Whigs. One of these was *Argument against Abolishing Christianity.* He also contributed essays to the *Tatler* denouncing the vulgar style of the journals of the time.

When he found that his support of the Church and the Whigs did not pay him, he switched his favours to the Tories. He became the editor of the Tory paper *The Examiner.* He wrote pamphlets like *The Conduct of the Allies* (1711) to support the cause of peace with France and ending of the War of Spanish Succession. His *Journal to Stella* is a work of great merit.

The Tories made him Dean of St Patrick's Cathedral, Dublin, for his services. But he was disappointed because he wanted to be a Bishop. When Queen Anne died and the Tories fell, he became entirely heart-broken and lived the last thirty years in exile in Ireland, a country he detested. But the wretchedness of the poor moved him to write for their cause in various pamphlets like *Drapier's Letters* (1724), *A Short View of the Present State of Ireland* and the famous *A Modest Proposal. Gulliver's Travels* came out in 1726. He suffered from a disease of the brain and became insane in the end. His will, strangely, bestowed part of his income to set up a lunatic asylum.

Character and Works

Swift was a bundle of contradictions. Although he loved and was admired by two women, and political bigwigs sought his company, he was a great misanthrope or hater of mankind, as the mad ravings in his novels reveal. Since he suffered from congenital deformity and abnormality in the brain, his callousness and snobbery are understandable. He could snub lords and ladies in his writings.

A Tale of the Tub (1704) is an argument among the three faiths prevalent — Roman Catholicism, Anglicanism and Puritanism. Basing his satire on reason, he attacked religion, science and philosophy. *Journal to Stella* is based on his relationship with Esther Johnson whom he loved. He also loved Vanessa and the triangle of love was an interesting phenomenon of his personality. The journal consists of letters which show Swift's rarely soft, human nature and gives details of his daily life from 1710-1713.

A Modest Proposal was written to call public attention to the plight of poor children in Ireland. Swift recommended that the best solution was that the rich should devour infants and poor children upto the age of eighteen months. A rather repulsive proposal!

The most famous work of Swift which has become the children's classic is his satire *Gulliver's Travels* (1726). The hero finds himself ship-wrecked at Lilliput, a land of diminutive humans. He mocks at their wars, civil strifes and pomp. There are disputes between the high heels and the low heels and between the Big-endians and the Little-endians on the fatuous question of whether eggs should be broken on their big or their little heads! The satire was aimed at the religious and political controversies of his time. When Gulliver reaches Brobdingnag, he encounters a race of giants. To them, he represents *"a race of pernicious, odious vermin"* or humans. At Laputa, Swift aims his satire at the philosophers, historians and scientists of the time. At the Academy of Projectors, a scientist is engaged for the past eight years in extracting sunshine from cucumbers! Later on he pours vitriol on Houyhnhnms, horses who can reason and the Yahoos full of animal corruption.

Swift was gifted by a very mordant style of satire and wrote out of sheer malice and bitterness. While we admire his genius, we are repelled by his hatred of mankind.

RICHARD STEELE (1672-1729)

Richard Steele was a colourful man who had a chequered career. Born in Ireland, he was educated in the Charterhouse school at London and then went off to Oxford where Addison was a classmate. He left Oxford without a degree and joined the army. He soon became a captain for having written a poem to support the Whigs when Queen Mary died. Although partly puritanical, he was a licentious like a Restoration Cavalier and was falling into debts for his extravagance. He wrote *Christian Hero* (1701) to show the importance of religion in ennobling man. He married twice. He was gentleman waiter to Prince George of Denmark, Queen Anne's husband. He edited the *"London Gazette"* and then brought out a number of papers in succession, like *The Tatler* (1709), *The Spectator* (1711), *The Guardian* (1713), *The Englishman* (1713), etc. He was appointed member of Parliament in 1713, but when he favoured Hanoverian succession in his pamphlet *The Crisis,* he was expelled. He apologized for this in another autobiographical tract. With the accession of George I, he returned to parliament and was knighted. He became the manager of Drury Fane Theatre. He kept writing essays for journals till he left London in 1724 because of financial problems. He also wrote a number of comedies whose interest today is merely historical.

JOSEPH ADDISÓN (1672-1719)

Joseph Addison's father was a clergyman. He went to school at Charterhouse and to college at Oxford. At both places Richard Steele was his fellow student. He became a classical scholar and a fellow of Magdalen College. He won an annual pension of 300 pounds by writing poems to flatter William III and the ministers. He could use his finances to travel across the Continent for four years during which he learnt a lot about public life. With the death of the King his pension was stopped. He then turned to the Whigs for favours and praised their policies in *The*

Whig Examiner. He celebrated the British victory at Blenheim in *The Campaign* (1704) and was promoted to parliament. When the Tories came to power, he engaged in writing for the newspapers begun by Richard Steele — *The Tatler, The Spectator* and *The Guardian.* When the Whigs returned, he defended their policies again in *The Freeholder.* In 1716, he married the Countess of Warwick and towards the end of his life became a Secretary of State.

ALEXANDER POPE (1688-1744)

Alexander Pope was born in London and as a child lived at Binfield in Windsor Forest. His father was a linen-draper. As a poor Catholic he was denied a good education and was taught by a family priest and at a Catholic school. He suffered from congenital deformity and was always physically weak which is generally regarded as the reason for his peevish, spiteful and revengeful nature. His works, like Swift's, are often motivated by malice and he uses poetry to lampoon and lambaste other writers like Addison, Grub Street hacks, Theobald and Colley Cibber. When he was jilted by Lady Montagu, a bluestocking, he made her the subject of a vulgar satire. His habits showed him to be miserly. He wrote on the reverse blanks of letters and on scraps of paper. Swift called him the "paper-saving Pope". He encouraged younger writers, and the saving grace in his character was his affection for his mother whom he tended very lovingly in her old age. He already had paternal property and his translation of Homer proved a bonanza, bringing him 10,000 pounds. He bought a house at Twickenham and made a beautiful garden. There he lived a comfortable life.

Pope's first collection of poems *Pastorals* was written in 1709 when he was only sixteen. In 1711, he published *An Essay on Criticism,* which brought him into the poetic limelight. In this work, he uses a verse very near to prose in form. The work sums up the art of poetry as propounded by Horace under the influence of Boileau, the French poet-critic. We see here Pope's mastery of terse epigrammatic style that has made him the most quoted writer after Shakespeare. His style is a counterpart of the pithy maxims of Francis Bacon in prose. Pope took Dryden's heroic couplet and made it smoother but rigid. Pope subordinates the content or matter to the form. Some of his more famous lines often quoted are:

"A little learning is a dangerous thing".
"To err is human, to forgive divine".

In his satire, *The Rape of the Lock,* published in 1714, he satirizes the fashions of high society in mock-heroic style. In probable imitation of Boileau's *Lutrin,* he creates an epic where spirits like gnomes and fairies take part. The context is the trivial matter of one Lord Petre who clips off a lock of hair from Arabella Fermor's head. This leads to a quarrel between their families. Pope brings in all the paraphernalia of fashionable society — tea parties, billet-doux and lap-dogs. According to Doctor Johnson, the poem is the most ingenious of Pope's works.

Eloisa to Abelard treats of the love between a theologian teacher of Paris and Eloisa who has dedicated her life to God. Their love is carried out through the passionate lines of correspondence.

Pope translated the *Iliad* in ten years and followed it up with a translation of the *Odyssey* for which Fenton and Broome helped him. Since Pope's verse, or rather the couplets he wrote, are mechanical in structure, it is difficult to distinguish contributions made by others to the translation. Many scholars criticized the translations as unauthentic in the sense that he could not bring in the grandeur of the classics into his works. But for the general public it was a great boon. For the first time they had the classic stories in language comprehensible to them.

In 1725, Alexander Pope published an edition of Shakespeare which was berated by the Shakespeare scholar Theobald for its many factual errors. Pope wrote *The Dunciad* (the *'Iliad'* of Dunces) to avenge himself on Theobald. He also attacked hack writers of Grub Street and the mediocre actor-dramatist Colley Cibber who had been made poet laureate. The poem is a merciless attack on dullness.

It is said that Pope took Dryden as his model and the *Dunciad* was inspired by *MacFlecknoe*. But instead of imitating the gracious Dryden, Pope was bent on personal revenge and malice.

An Essay on Man (1733-34) is again verse in aphorisms. Its aim was to *"vindicate the ways of God to man"*. It elaborates the general philosophy common to most religions that man cannot understand God's inscrutable ways and therefore finds faults with the universal order. Our vision cannot 'see' the mysterious perfection of Creation. The famous lines, often quoted, are:

"All Nature is but Art, unknown to thee;
All Chance, Direction which thou canst not see:
And spite of Pride, in erring Reason's spite
One truth is clear, Whatever is, is Right".

Epistle to Dr. Arbuthnot (1735) has an autobiographical element in it. The satire is famous for the portrayal of Addison, or Atticus in the poem.

Pope's stature as a poet has undergone shifts since his times. In his own age, he was looked upon as a genius of the heroic couplet, the best wit of the times. But when Wordsworth and Coleridge published their *Lyrical Ballads* in 1798, they derided his stiff, epigrammatic style and his malicious wit. His image fell very low in the 19th century for writing poetry that was almost prose. In modern times, poetry that seeks deviated ways to express thoughts is extolled and so Pope is back in the list of the greats.

Pope himself laid down the main principle of his poetry.

"True wit is nature to advantage dressed,
What oft was thought but ne'er so well express'd".

'Nature' in Pope's times human nature and behaviour in general. Pope mechanized Dryden's couplet by sticking to the iambic beat with well-marked caesuras or pauses. He forced all his ideas into the straight-jacketted body of his verse. His poetry is full of moral principles and has given us a great number of pithy, epigrammatic statements to be quoted in our essays and speeches.

SAMUEL JOHNSON (1709-1784)

Doctor Samuel Johnson was the literary dictator of the third part of the 18th century. Although his contribution to poetry and drama is admirable, he is chiefly known for his prose works — biographies, criticism, letters, prefaces, essays and the dictionary. He has become known to the world more through the biography of him written by his devoted disciple and secretary, Boswell. Boswell's masterly protrayal of Johnson is one of the best biographies in English literature. It paints Johnson bigger than life and makes his personality overshadow his great contributions to literature. The biography, in fact, made both the master and the disciple immortal. It has given us numerous anecdotes from the life of Samuel Johnson and numerous quotations of the great man of letters.

Samuel Johnson, the son of a bookseller, was born at Lichfield. From early childhood he knew poverty and had to struggle for subsistence when he drifted to London in 1737. Johnson found London full of corruption and wretchedness of the poor. In his famous poem *London* (1738), he describes the crimes, intrigues, squalor, slums and poverty of the metropolis. He finds a vast concourse of humanity engaged in the worship of Mammon, the god of gold. He is tired of the inane human quest for glory and fame. He describes the lives of the great and famous in his poem, *The Vanity of Human Wishes* (1749).

After *The Tatler* and *The Spectator* the art of essay-writing died down. Johnson revived it and brought out *The Rambler* (1750-52) and *The Idler*. The first one was not well received since it was of a serious, moralizing type. The latter was in the lighter vein and was much acclaimed. Johnson also wrote a tragedy, the *Irene* (1749), on the neo-classic model. He wrote *Rasselas* (1759) to pay for the charges of his mother's funeral. Later on he became famous and was acknowledged as a great master of literature. The government gave him a pension of 300 pounds annually which allowed him to live comfortably for the rest of his life with a circle of admirers at the coffee-house and club. Johnson defined "Pension" in his famous dictionary as an allowance given to a person for *"treason to his country"*. This, of course, does not show his ingratitude but strange humour. Johnson first proposed his idea of composing his famous dictionary to Lord Chesterfield in a letter. The Lord did not respond and Johnson felt snubbed. Later on when after eight years of monumental hard labour, Johnson's dictionary, the first ever in the English language, came out. Chesterfield wanted to cash on it for fame by writing a preface. Johnson then wrote a famous except taking Chesterfield to task. The dictionary is unique in that the definitions are often subjective and contain Johnson's personal opinions. For instance, Oats is described as a grain used to feed horses in England, but supports the people in Scotland!

A group of booksellers deputed Johnson to write on the *Lives of the Poets*. The work was finished in 1781, and is his contribution to literary criticism. A staunch neo-classicist, he judges poets by the rules of the classics. Although he points to Shakespeare's disregard of the unities, he allows concessions in his case saying there is always an appeal from criticism to nature. Pope is Johnson's great poet for observing a strict mechanical metre. Johnson is callous to the imaginative flights of the poets. The shortcoming of the *Lives* is the selection of poets. Many minor poets are discussed and important contemporaries are left out.

Today, the image of Doctor Johnson, the eccentric, far overshadows his contributions to literature. Boswell described him as a bundle of contradictions. He could be humorous in public always, yet he suffered from melancholic depression throughout his life. He married a widow, twenty years older than himself. Johnson was always cynical of people. When Boswell first introduced himself as coming from Scotland, Johnson replied, *"That is something most of your countrymen cannot help"*. Yet despite all rebuffs and snubs, Boswell admired him and having failed to join the bar, followed the Doctor. Johnson was born with scrofula which made his face swollen and ugly like a mask. He would stammer and spit while talking and had uncouth table manners. Yet he was the most admired man of his times and had a circle of literary greats around him. He frequented the coffee houses and clubs and was the most suave conversationalist of his times. Boswell records many details of his talks. Boswell accompanied the master to the Scottish Isles and both wrote separate accounts on this. Johnson's was called *Journal of a Tour to the Hebrides.*

Johnson's literary style, which was pedantic, ponderous and full of Latinisms, goes by the name of Johnsonese. Today we admire him as the greatest man of letters of his age.

THOMAS GRAY (1716-1771)

Thomas Gray has his own unique place in English literature. He is famous today and remembered chiefly for his long poem *Elegy Written in a Country Churchyard* (1751). General Wolfe is said to have commented, "I would rather be remembered as the man who wrote the Elegy than the conqueror of Quebec!" Palgrave would have left it out of his Golden Treasury because of its length had Tennyson not insisted. Doctor Johnson who was usually hard on Gray, praised its universal nature — it echoed the finer sentiments of all mankind.

Gray was educated at Eton and Cambridge and because he had independent means of money, he lived a quiet scholarly life in the university. He was extremely well-read in the Greek classics and traces all poetry to its Hellenic source in his *Progress of Poesy*. He also studied European literature and produced *The Descent of Odin* from Icelandic myths. The undergraduates of his college played a practical joke on him startling him on a false fire alarm. This made him shift from Peterhouse to Pembroke. His mother lived estranged from his ill-tempered father and this might have contributed to the melancholic strain in most of his poetry. The Elegy is a meditation on the futility of all human endeavour. Notice these off-quoted lines:

Full many a gem of purest ray serene
The dark unfathom'd caves of ocean bear.
Full many a flower is born to blush unseen,
And waste its sweetness on the desert air.
The boast of heraldry, the pomp of pow'r
And all that beauty, all that wealth e'er gave,
Awaits alike th' inevitable hour.
The paths of glory lead but to the grave".

Another poem *The Bard* is one of the best Pindaric odes in the English language. It is based on the Welsh legend of King Edward's cruel conquest of Wales. It describes how Edward had all the Welsh bards killed and one bard survived and gathered with the ghosts of slain bards to curse Edward and foretell his doom in the Wars of the Roses: *"Ruin seize thee, ruthless king!"*. The Tudors would reign supreme and the great poets of the Elizabethan age would achieve eminence. The surviving bard hurls himself from a mountain into a river below.

Gray was also capable of humour as may be seen in his *Ode on the Death of a Favourite Cat*. A Lord's cat is drowned in a water jar while trying to catch goldfish in it. Gray makes the comments: "A fev'rite has no friend" and "What female heart can gold despise? What cat's averse to fish?" Gray wrote other odes like *On Spring, On a Distant Prospect of Eton College,* and *On Adversity.*

Gray has written less but whatever he has produced is sterling poetry, a mixture of classical restraint and romantic imagination and varied, regular music.

OLIVER GOLDSMITH (1728-1774)

Goldsmith is remembered today for his famous poems *The Deserted Village* (1770) and *The Traveller* (1764). Also well-known are his poems, *Elegy on the Death of a Mad Dog,* the fine lines beginning "When lovely woman stoops to folly", and *Retaliation.*

Oliver Goldsmith was the son of an Irish clergyman. After school, he attended Trinity College, Dublin. He was temporarily sent out of college for some misdemeanour, but rejoined to obtain a degree in 1749. He was rejected from the priesthood and for a time worked as a tutor to support his family. He studied medicine at Edinburgh and then at Leyden, Holland. He went on a walking-tour of some countries in Europe and wrote down his experiences in his poem *The Traveller* in which he describes the different gifts of scenery and culture bestowed by Nature on different countries.

On return to England, he had stints at different jobs — chemists assistant, proof-reader, school master and even a roving player. He worked as a hack-writer for sometime. In 1759, he published *an Enquiry into the Present State of Polite Learning in Europe*. He edited a periodical called *Bee*. He wrote prolifically for magazines like Smollett's *British Magazine*. He brought out a series of *Chinese Letters in the Public Ledger*. His works included histories, biographies and books of popular science.

An interesting event led to the publication of his novel, *The Vicar of Wakefield,* in 1766. He was pestered by his landlady for not paying his rent. She put pressure on him to accept marriage with her. Flustered, he sent a message to Doctor Johnson who arrived soon after and discovered the manuscript of *The Vicar* and sold it off for 60 pounds.

Goldsmith's enemies like Garrick and Boswell exaggerated his vices. It is true Goldsmith was unpleasant in appearance, extravagant and led a luxurious lifestyle and got into debt for it. Despite all this, we cannot deny his contribution to literature. The characters of his essays, poems and plays stand out unforgettably.

Goldsmith was inspired by the Restoration comedy and wrote *The Good-natured Man* (1768) and *She Stoops to Conquer* (1773) which are anti-sentimental comedies. As Goldsmith writes in the preface of the latter play, the true spirit of comedy had died since the sentimental comedy of his times had no laughter in it. It was merely a maudlin display or tear-jerker making the reader and audience indulge in sobs.

To regain health it was necessary to restore gaiety and laughter. For this he pleads with Doctor Johnson to administer the cure. *The Good-natural Man* was produced at Covent Garden in 1768. Doctor Johnson recommended the play. The play portrays a character called Croaker who is Benjonsonian in his *'humour'*. It is the story of Mr Honeywood, a warm-hearted simpleton who gives money in charity without finding out the genuine neediness of the recipients. In the end his uncle opens his eyes to his folly.

She Stoops to Conquer is a much more successful play. It was produced at Covent Garden in 1773. It has numerous sub-plots but all pivot around *The mistakes of a night,* the other title of the play. The characters of the son-pampering Mrs

Hardcastle, Tony Lumpkin, the mischievous scoundrel son of Mrs Hardcastle and of the ambivalent Marlow are unforgettable. Some scenes are uproariously funny — the servants being trained to entertain guests, Tony Lumpkin takes his guests round and round the house in the dark to land them in a horse-pond.

WILLIAM BLAKE (1757-1827)

William Blake was a revolutionary eighteenth century poet. He admired Milton but did not use his blank verse. In fact, he wrote his poetry in a type of rhythmical prose. He was far beyond his time. Of the Romantic vein of which he was a forerunner, he exercised his imagination to the extreme. So much so that he reaches levels of obscurity impossible to fathom.

Blake was the son of a London hosier and himself took to painting nad engraving. His earlier poetry was written as commentary to his book of paintings.

Most of his earlier poetry is simple and imbued with a lyrical sweetness. They are contained in two anthologies — *Songs of Innocence* (1789) and *Songs of Experience* (1794). His latter poetry is very mystical and difficult to understand. Blake had mystic visions of God and angels in childhood and they are described in his poetry. He created a symbolism of his own. The horrors of the French Revolution shocked him and this is symbolized in his poem *The Tyger:*

"Tyger, Tyger, burning bright!
In the forests of the night.
What immortal hand or eye
Could frame thy fearful symmetry?"

Christ as Eternal goodness was symbolized by the Lamb. *The Songs of Innocence,* therefore, represent experiences under divine grace and *The Songs of Experience,* the power of evil in the world.

Blake's contemporaries thought of him as insane and one living in a strange, unreal world. But Wordsworth described Blake thus: "The madness of Blake interests us more than the sanity of others".

WILLIAM WORDSWORTH (1770-1850)

Life

William Wordsworth was born on April 7, 1770 at Cockermouth in the Cumberland highlands. His father was a lawyer and land agent. He lost both the parents by the age of fourteen. His school days at Hawkeshead was full of joy, spent in games and reading. He joined St John's College, Cambridge when he was seventeen and went on a walking tour of France during one of his vacations. Taking his degree in 1791 he went to France to stay. The cause of the French Revolution — liberty and equality — attracted him much. He spent 1797-98 mostly with Coleridge and published *Lyrical Ballads* in collaboration with him. After this he visited Germany with his sister Dorothy. Finally he returned to Grasmere in the Lake district of England. Here he published the second volume of the *Lyrical Ballads* and married his cousin Mary Hutchinson.

Wordsworth's life was spent in quiet contemplation and meditation in the beautiful Lake district. Here nature inspired him to write his poetry. He also visited Wales, Scotland and Ireland. He was left a legacy of money by a kind man and got a job as sinecure — distributor of stamps. A man of simple living and high thinking, he could lead a comfortable life and devote himself to poetry. In 1842, the Government provided him a pension of £ 300 a year.

Earlier Wordsworth's poetry received no recognition. In fact, there was adverse criticism of it. But during the last two decades of his life, recognition came to him. He received an honorary degree from the Universities of Durham and Oxford. In 1843 he was appointed poet-laureate. He died in 1850.

Wordsworth was of hardy north-country stock. In austerity he reminds us of Milton. Wordsworth's egotism came in the way of appreciation of the poetry of others.

Works

Wordsworth's works like *The Prelude* and *The Excursion* make him worthy of the recognition he received as poet-laureate. First and foremost, Wordsworth was the High Priest of Nature. While Cowper, Burns, Blake, Byron, Shelley and Keats all loved Nature 'it was only the external forms'. The Wordsworth Nature was where the Spirit of the Supreme Being dwelt. Nature revealed God's peace and mystery. He had a mystic understanding of Nature. Nature showed the bonds that united all forms of life together — birds, animals and humans. To love all was the message of Nature, Nature was a great teacher. In his own words:

"One impulse from a vernal wood
May teach you more of man,
Of moral evil and of good,
Than all the sages can".

To be able to learn such lessons, Wordsworth advocated a receptive heart. If one bared oneself to the influence of Nature one received wisdom, health, beauty, grace and peace of mind. In one of his *Lucy* poems he says:

"And beauty born of murmuring sound
Shall pass into her face".

When England went to war with France, his mind was in conflict between patriotic loyalty and his love and admiration for the Revolution. War shattered all hopes. He returned to Nature to restore his faith in divine providence and found Nature a great healer.

Nature was a teacher of morals. *"Stern Daughter of the voice of God,"* he called her. His attitude to Nature developed in stages. First, he saw the visionary gleams of childhood in the *Ode on the Intimations of Childhood.*

"There was a time when valley, rock and hill
Seem'd apparelled in celestial light".

Later he developed a passion for Nature which gave him *"aching joys."* Finally, Nature in all its manifestations gave him a lesson in living: *"the meanest flower that blows"* gave him *"thoughts that do often lie too deep for tears".*

Once when Wordsworth was returning home from Cambridge, he passed through a very beautiful landscape of mountains and the sea and that moment of enchantment with Nature was a flash of illumination. He realized that his mission of life was to teach mankind. He wished to bring mankind back to Nature for healing and morals. He set out to write the long poem *The Recluse,* consisting of two parts *The Prelude* (1850) and *The Excursion* (1814). He could not finish the work. Wordsworth claimed that his work as a poet was to teach and this is what he does. The poem is marred by too much moralizing.

Wordsworth felt that the real characters for his poetry must be common, noble men, not Lords and Ladies. He, therefore, wrote a number of poems like *The Idiot Boy, Harry Gill* and *Peter Bell* (1819) in which metre is ignored and common everyday speech is used. The effect is prosaic poetry — dull and ineffective. The real great poetry of Wordsworth is that which springs from his genius, not his poetic beliefs. Wordsworth's great poetry shows spiritual depths of calm reflection. As he writes in *Laodamia,* his classical poem, *"For the Gods approve / The depth and not the tumult of the soul".*

Wordsworth wrote a great variety of poems — odes, lyrics and almost 400 sonnets of which *Upon Westminster Bridge, On Milton* and *The World is too much with Us* are famous.

According to Wordsworth, poetry was "emotion recollected in transquillity". *The Solitary Reaper, To a Highland Girl, The Daffodils, Tintern Abbey* and the *Immortality Ode* were written after sometime had elapsed from the event described. These events were moments of perception and when the time had passed the emotions stirred by those moments surfaced clearly. These emotions are then put into words.

JANE AUSTEN (1775-1817)

Jane Austen was the daughter of a Hampshire rector. She and her sisters were educated at home. Jane's life was spent at country parishes and at the health resort at Bath. Her life was hardly disturbed by any major upheaval and was for the most part uneventful. Even the Napoleonic Wars of the time never touched her thinking. Her brothers were in the navy, and naval exercises took place in her village. Naval officers like Wickham and Wentworth appear in her novels as only eligible bachelors for the girls. Jane Austen was intensely familiar with the social life of Hampshire and she makes this the limited canvas of her novels. A country mansion drawing room and a few young girls and boys were enough stuff for her to mould her novels. Witty dialogues, understatements and humour are used to delineate characters — an art in which she had no equal in her age. Her novels are *comedies of manners* and she excels in them and is probably unique in this genre. Her characters belong to the middle class which she knew very well and portrayed in six wonderful novels. *Pride and Prejudice, Sense and Sensibility, Mansfield Park* and *Emma* were published between 1811 and 1815. *Northanger Abbey* and *Persuasion* were published posthumously in 1818. These dates do not correspond to the dates of writing. For instance *Northanger* was published last but was the first to be written, in 1797.

In the beginning, Jane Austen could not get a publisher easily, but she emerged into limelight when the novel *Emma* was praised in the *Quarterly Review* by an anonymous writer who later on turned out to be Walter Scott, the great Scottish novelist. He wrote, "That young lady has a talent for describing the involvements and feelings and characters of ordinary life which is to me the most wonderful I ever met with .... the exquisite touch which renders, ordinary commonplace things and characters interesting, from the truth of the description and the sentiment, is denied to me".

Jane Austen did not practise any new or invented art of novel writing, yet her plots are most ingeniously constructed, the sub-plots dovetailing wonderfully. She did not seek to moralize, either. All she set out to do and succeeded in, was to entertain her readers by a faithful representation of life around her. She was not romantic in view and her descriptions are most matter-of-fact. She ridiculed the Radcliffian novel of terror and mystery in *Northanger Abbey.* She ridicules Marianne's sentimental nature in *Sense and Sensibility.* Her novels are one around of domestic work, balls, gossips, teas, love-affairs, visits and money matters — the common paraphernalia of any human life. Touched by her sparkling wit, these trivial affairs burst into life.

She was adept at charting the sentiments of love in a female heart. It is not so much the hero and heroine who impart life to her novels as the secondary characters — the Collins and the Bennetts. She does not indulge in hairsplitting psychology like Henry James or Virginia Woolf. A few broad strokes are enough to assess a character. Characters have both their good and bad sides. Even villains like Wickham Willoughby, Crawfords, Frank Churchill display gaiety and charm.

Irony is a major device in character portrayal. In *Sense and Sensibility* the selfishness of John Dashwood is revealed through ironic dialogue in which John begins by intending to give 3000 pounds to his step-mother and step-sisters. He whittles this down gradually to zero and finally reasons out that they had better give him something! She is excellent in exposing hypocrisy and the foibles of society. Mrs Musgrove in *Persuasion* is ridiculed as exhibiting hysterical grief (crocodile tears) on her deceased son.

Financial wholeness is the bedrock of a happy life. A realist by nature, Austen believed that we cannot change the world, but must adjust ourselves to it. She derided people who claimed superiority on the basis of birth, but she acknowledged class distinctions as no snobbery.

ALFRED TENNYSON (1809-1892)

Lord Alfred Tennyson was the third son of a Lincolnshire clergyman and went to Louth Grammar School and Trinity College, Cambridge. His earlier poetry received scant praise from critics. They include *Poems by two Brothers* (1827), *Timbuctoo* (1829) which received the Chancellor's prize, *Poems, Chiefly Lyrical* (1830) and the Volume *Lady Shàlott and Other Poems* (1833). In 1842, he published two slim anthologies, revising some older poems. These won recognition. In 1850, he was made Poet Laureate. In the same year, he published his famous elegy *In Memoriam,* on the death of a friend Arthur Hallam. He became a peer in 1884. He died at the age of 83 in 1892.

When Tennyson brought out his two volumes of poetry in 1842, people claimed him as a successor to Keats because of his romantic spirit. But he did not ignore the classical correctness of form in which there are no redundant ornaments of style. There is a great sense for pictures and sounds but this is not overdone. He shunned adherence to any strict poetic diction or too much imagination and imbued his poetry with philosophy. He also, like Wordsworth, wrote to instruct his readers. He wanted to enlighten and edify his readers. He came to be regarded a prophet who voiced the thoughts of the Victorians.

As a youth, Tennyson believed in the grandeur of his country, in the institution of Parliament and democracy. He also believed that science would help to take the world to glorious heights. But as time went on he was filled with doubts. In religion, the Darwinian theory of man's evolution from natural selection of species threatened the biblical story of Adam and Eve and weaned men away from their traditional faith. Socialism was leading to too much materialism. Tennyson warned his country-men not to take up any extreme stand. Scientific progress must not drive out religious feelings of charity and love.

The Princess (1847) deals with women's rights, the need to give them a higher education. Tennyson's thoughts on religion come through in *In Memoriam* (1850) and *The Idylls of the King* (1859, 1869, 1889). In *Maud* (1855) he exposes the folly of materialsm.

One of Tennyson's demerits was that his narration in the longer poems like *In Memoriam* is rambling and vague. *Maud* is excellent for its diverse metre but is on the whole unbalanced and melodramatic. *The Princess* is very popular with its romance, humour, pathos, songs and philosophy.

Tennyson's excellence lies mainly in his lyrical gifts especially in his shorter poems. He displays domestic pathos and rustic humour in *Enoch Arden* (1864) and a number of poems. In these he describes the life of ordinary men and women he knew in Lincolnshire and the Isle of Wight. He is quite authentic in his description of farmers, cobblers and people of the common classes.

Tennyson was aware of evil in his age. He described Earth as "teeming with liars, and madmen and knaves, and wearied of Autocrats, Anarchs and slaves". Yet he was optimistic of a bright future for humanity. He was a seer and spoke from the depths of the heart. No wonder his poems strike us and we quote so much from his poems now-a-days. Here are some of the more popular lines:

"There lives more faith in honest doubt
Believe me, than in half the creeds"
(In Memoriam)

" 'tis better to have loved and lost
Than never to have loved at all".
(In Memoriam)

"For men may come and men may go,
But I go on forever". (The Brook)

"The old order changeth, yielding place to new,
And God fulfils himself in many ways
Lest one good custom should corrupt the world".
(Morte d' Arthur)

Tennyson suited his verse to different themes, moods, feelings and atmosphere. Rhyme and blank verse were used to match form and matter. Many poems are replete with graphic descriptions of nature. For example, in *Mariana* he describes Mariana's farm-house which is decaying and desolate:

"With blackest moss the flower-pots
Were thickly crusted, one and all;
The rusted nails fell from the knots
That held the pear to the gable-wall".

There is a nostalgia and pathos in the lines of his poems *Break, Break, Break* and *Tears, idle tears*; there is a yearning *For the days that are no more*.

Tennyson was hailed as a prophet of his age.

ROBERT BROWNING (1812-1889)

Robert Browning was educated at home and in private schools. His father was a clerk in the Bank of England. His mother was of mixed stock and a dissenter. In 1846, he married the poetess Elizabeth Barret. He lived in Italy until her death in 1861. After this he returned to London. He died in 1889 and was buried in Westminster Abbey.

His major works include:

Pauline (1833) in which he shows his admiration for an anonymous poet who may be guessed to be Shelley.

Paracelsus (1835) is the story of a Swiss physician who searched for perfect knowledge and the secrets of the universe. But having no power to love, he did not achieve his goal.

Sordello (1840) is a poem based on the life of a 12th century poet. This poem is very difficult to understand.

Browning also wrote two plays, *Strafford* (1837) and *A Blot on the 'Scutcheon* (1843). Among other well-known poems are *Pippa Passes* (1841), *The Pied Piper of Hamelin, The Lost Leader, My Last Duchess* and *Andrea del Sarto. The Ring and the Book* (1868-1869) is one of the longest poems in the English language and was his masterpiece.

Robert Browning was a complete contrast to Tennyson. While Tennyson interested himself in the political affairs of the Victorian times, the glory of England and democratic traditions, the Parliament of Man, Browning's poetry shows no reference to the political or religious questions of his times. *Home Thoughts from Abroad,* however, does show some patriotic feelings. While Tennyson's mind was filled with the doubts about God and faith, Browning strongly believed in God. Browning was a philosopher and did not care much for beauty and melody like Keats and Tennyson did in their poetry. He is more like John Donne, filled with intellectual curiosity for the strange and unconventional. He did not ignore the beauties of Nature as is evident from his poems *Pippa Passes* and *Saul*.

According to Browning, God and Immortality are unquestioned truths of existence. God is evident in the love that is visible in Man and Nature. He believed that as man evolved from age to age, his ideals in life became higher. Man must struggle ceaselessly to overcome his failures and imperfections: *"Ah, but a man's reach should exceed his grasp/ Or what's a Heaven for"?* Failures are stepping stones to success. His philosophy is a positive one. He was an optimist, *"God's in His heaven and all's right with the world"*.

Browning's love for his wife, Elizabeth Barrett, inspired many of his love poems, like *By the fireside* and *O Lyric Love.*

Browning's poetry is famous for the technique known as the *dramatic monologue*. Characters are made to speak out their minds and unfold their hidden thoughts. This was a device to etch out characters like the Bishop Bloryam and in this he excelled.

One of the demerits of Browning's poetry is obscurity. The common reader cannot understand his poetry. He chose events and characters from the past like Fra Lippo Lippi and Andrea del Sarto. Not many were interested among them. His style is compressed leaving out pronouns and grammatical connectives which makes the meaning vague. But he is popular today for his simpler poems like *The Pied Piper* and *A Grammarian's Funeral.*

CHARLES DICKENS (1812-1870)

Life

Charles Dickens was the son of a navy office clerk, John Dickens. The young Charles moved with his father from Postmouth to Chatham and then to London. His father underwent many financial problems and had to spend time in debtor's prison in Marshalsea. Charles survived by working in a blacking factory and roaming the streets of London as a vagrant. These bitter experiences left a deep, traumatic effect on his life and were recreated in his novels in the characters of David Copperfield, Little Nell, Oliver, Paul Dombey and Pip.

Charles Dickens did not get a smooth education, breaking off from schools according to whether his father could pay or not. The schools he went to were also centres of persecution. When he was only fifteen he became a lawyer's clerk and at 19, a reporter of Parliamentary speeches. At 21, he became a reporter on *The Morning Chronicle* to which he contributed various imaginary sketches of social life which were later published as *Sketches by Boz* (1836). Dickens wrote his masterpiece *Pickwick Papers* in monthly installments in 1836-37. In 1937, Queen Victoria came to the throne. The world of characters he created caught the imagination of the people like anything and he became a resounding success. He also became rich at 25.

In 1848, his wife Catherine left him since she believed he was having an affair with Ellen Ternan, an actress. The scandal sent tremor through the literary world.

Dickens visited America twice, in 1842 and 1867, and also the Continent, and read out his works in a dramatic style. At the age of 59, he died of cerebral bleeding and was buried at Westminster Abbey.

Works

The Pickwick Papers was his masterpiece. It firmly enthroned Dickens in the hearts of the readers throughout Europe, America and later in the whole English-speaking world. Almost 300 characters were created in this series. Each character is a universal type that may be found in any age and land. In this, Dickens is compared to Shakespeare. Dickens created almost 2000 character-types. His unique gift for minute description is unparalleled. Dickens' characters are household words today. We have come to describe people as Pickwickian or Dickensian when they display oddity or eccentricity. Thus the loyal Sam Weller, a servant, is a type of the witty, resourceful and loyal; Jingle as a rascal using a clipped telegraphese; the wily Uriah Heep; the incorrigible optimist Micawber and hundreds of others are types of the universal panorama of human beings.

Dickens' novels are loosely constructed. His later novels like *Bleak House* (1852), *David Copperfield* (1849), *Great Expectations* (1860) which show a maturer craftsman at work, are appealing because of their humour and pathos. Dickens used his novels to muster public opinion against many social injustices. Thus *Nicholas Nickleby* (1838) is a satire on the horrible condition of Yorkshire schools like Dotheboys Hall with its cruel schoolmaster Squares. Later on these schools were forced to close down. Dickens called his weekly *Household Words (1849)*, a gentle mouthpiece of reform. Most of his satire was garbed in humour, so it did not hurt. In *Household Words* and *All the Year Round* (1859), Dickens campaigned for free trade, abolition of Corn Laws, improvement of sanitation, etc. He exposed the appalling conditions of labour in the Midlands and the North in *The Curiosity Shop* (1840) and *Hard Times* (1854). This led to reform in factory laws. Thanks to Dickens' description of debtor's imprisonment in *Little Dorrit* (1855) the laws were altered, Fleet Prison and Marshalsea (where his father was imprisoned) were demolished. Dickens ridiculed obstructive bureaucratic interference through his description of the Barnacles and the Civil Service. His suggestive name for bureaucratic red tape was the Circumlocution Office. Although Dickens had no faith in the functioning of Parliament, he was in favour of democracy if practised in spirit. Bernard Shaw remarked that *Little Dorrit* was a more revolutionary book than Marx's *Das Capital*!

Dickens came to be known as the family novelist of the Victorians. His main aim was to convey moral precepts to his countrymen through a personal relationship in his serialized publications. In *Martin Chuzzlewit* (1843), he condemns selfishness and greed; in *Dombey and Son* (1846), pride is reviled; *Our Mutual Friend* (1864) shows the corrupting influence of wealth; the most sublime is his teaching of unselfish love and generosity in *A Christmas Carol* (1843). Dickens lived in an age of sexual prudery. It was very corrupt to mention 'sex'. Marriage was the only sacred bond. He shows how Emily who is seduced by Steerforth in *David Copperfield* is disgraced by society.

Some of the demerits of Dickens' writings have been described as: (*a*) he is often verbose, using more words than necessary; (*b*) his plots are not properly constructed; (*c*) he does not describe sublime thoughts, and (*d*) his novels are too grounded in the Victorian age to have any meaning now. Many critics have refuted these charges. If there are faults of diction in Dickens it is owing to his irregular education. But, like Shakespeare, his very faults are qualities of his genius. His powerful, graphic descriptions, the dialogues he puts into his characters — all remain unsurpassed despite oddities of syntax. He was educated in the cruel school of life and he was a keen observer. His descriptions and characterization give his novels an enduring value. It is ridiculous to say that Dickens does not deal in sublime thoughts. Love and charity are the essence of Christ's doctrines and like Christ's own simple language in the gospels, Dickens uses a layman's diction to express these.

Dickens is certainly the greatest novelist of English literature.

MATTHEW ARNOLD (1822-1888)

Matthew's father was the headmaster of Rugby College and he was educated at Rugby and Balliol College, Oxford. In 1851 he was appointed Inspector of Schools and he married the daughter of a judge. He was Professor of Poetry at Oxford for ten years. His famous poems are *The Strayed Reveller and other poems* (1849), *Empedocles on Etna* (1852), *Sohrab and Rustum* (an epic based on the Shah-Nama of Persia), *Switzerland, Dover Beach* and *The Scholar Gypsy.*

Matthew Arnold was a versatile writer trying his hand in poetry and criticism. In his age he was seen as a prophet and apostle of culture. His literary criticism is contained in the preface of his *Poems* (1853 volume) and in *Essays in Criticism* (1865, 1889). He was also a prose writer of renown.

Arnold's poetry reflects most the Victorian loss of faith in the face of materialism and the progress of science. His famous poem, *Dover Beach,* best brings this out.

"The sea of Faith
Was once, too, at the full and round earth's shore
Lay like the fold of a bright girdle furl'd.
But now I only hear
Its long withdrawing melancholy, roar ......"

Arnold admired the classical rule of clarity of expression which must be subordinated to the thought. He condemned poets including Shakespeare who used ornamental patches with no solid thought content. Arnold did not use much rhyme. *Sohrab and Rustum* is in blank verse. From Wordsworth and Goethe he learnt to use poetry to convey morals. In *Resignation,* he recommends that we reflect on life calmly and impersonally.

Arnold used poetry to express experiences about "actions, human actions, possessing an inherent interest in themselves". He also used poetry to convey personal feelings of a deep nature. *The Forsaken Merman, Scholar Gypsy, Thyrsis* and even *Sohrab and Rustum* are romantic poems in which his own feelings are uppermost. Thirteen of his poems including two *Obermann* poems and *Grande Chartreuse* are elegiac and contain his philosophy.

Arnold was influenced by the Greek classical form in poetry, but lacked their joy. Peace which is the aim of life, according to him, is difficult to achieve in the sick hurry of Victorian living. There is, therefore, a nostalgic desire to live in the past like his scholar gypsy who joins a roving band. His Obermann retires to a Swiss mountain to meditate and Empedocles cannot bear society or solitude and throw himself into the Crater at Etna. For Arnold, the best path was one of quiet work and self-dependence. *Love Nature* and *Know Thyself,* he prescribes. Like Wordsworth he believed that Nature had a healing touch. Arnold defined poetry as "a criticism of life" and, though intellectual in spirit, it is not cold and unspontaneous.

THOMAS HARDY (1840-1928)

Thomas Hardy was born near Dorchester (the country which was to be part and parcel and permanent landscape of his novels). By profession he was an architect and his sense of symmetry and design may be responsible for the perfect organization of the plots of his novels. His first great novel *Far from the Madding Crowd* (1874) brought him fame and money and he was able to devote himself more completely to his literary pursuits. He married twice, the second time in 1914 at the age of 74. In 1910, he was awarded the Order of Merit.

Hardy wrote many novels of which five are world-famous. *Far from the Madding Crowd* is about Bathsheba Everdene, a farmer who is loved by a shepherd called Gabriel Oak who serves her for many years with devotion. But Bathsheba falls in love with a selfish sergeant Troy and she realizes the greater, more permanent love of Gabriel Oak. She marries him.

Hardy's second great novel is *The Return of the Native* (1878). His great work of tragedy is *The Mayor of Casterbridge* (1886) which contains his vision of life. Man has very little free will and the great power of the universe control him as seen in the fate of Henchard who in a drunken state sells his wife and undergoes unlimited sorrows. A blind Universal Will controls destiny. Shakespeare believed that a tragic flaw was responsible for the downfall of his great characters. Hardy went much further and truly echoes Shakespeare's words, *"As flies to wanton boys are we to the gods. They kill us for their sport"*. Hardy's other great tragic novel *Tess of the D'Urbervilles* (1891) ends with the lines *"The President of the Immortals had finished his sport with Tess"*. Hardy's novel, *Jude the Obscure* (1895) deals with the social question of marriage.

Hardy was a pressimist. He knew the rustic life of his Dorsetshire very well and used this as the landscape of his novels. In fact, landmarks like Egdon Heath assume the nature of a character in the novel. Hardy described the seasons and aspects of Nature very realistically and the past plays an important role. Historical relics like Stonehenge, Roman roads and references to Napoleonic Wars are all there.

Hardy usually wrote in plain and direct style and his portrayal of rural life is unromantic. But sometimes he clutters his language with technical words. His rustics have a sense of humour which is too sophisticated to believe. His women characters are passionate and impulsive and love is a major theme in his fiction. His plots do not seem convincing. Many events are obviously contrived and seem quite illogical. There are too many coincidences.

Hardy was also a poet. He used his poetry to express his philosophy of fatalism. In fact, he took to writing poetry because his last novel, *Jude the Obscure,* was not well received by critics and readers. His *Wessex Poems,* a volume of poems, came out in 1898. He wrote the long novel or epic *The Dynasts* (1903, 1906, 1908) with the Napoleonic Wars as the background. Other notable poems by him are: *The Darkling Thrush* and *To an Unborn Paper Child.*

Hardy is certainly one of the greatest literary figures of English literature.

GEORGE BERNARD SHAW (1856-1950)

George Bernard Shaw was an Irish protestant playwright based in the United Kingdom. He was uniquely the winner of the Nobel Prize in Literature and an Academy Award for writing adapted screenplay.

George Bernard Shaw was born on 1856 in Dublin, in a lower middle-class family of Scottish-Protestant ancestry. His father was a failed corn-merchant, with a drinking problem and a squint, and his mother was a professional singer, the disciple of Vandeleur Lee, a voice teacher claiming to have a unique and original approach to singing.

When Shaw was just short of his sixteenth birthday, his mother left her husband and son, and moved with Vandeleur Lee to London, where the two set up a household, along with Shaw's elder sister, Lucy. There, Shaw's mother worked as a clerk for an estate office.

In 1876, Shaw left Dublin and his father, and moved to London. He went with his mother's *menage*. There he lived with his mother and sister while pursuing a career in journalism and writing. The first medium he tried as a creative writer was prose, completing five novels before any of them were published. He read voraciously, in public libraries and in the British Museum reading room.

In 1891, at the invitation of J.T. Grein, a merchant, theatre critic, and director of a progressive private new-play society, The Independent Theatre, Shaw wrote his first play, *Widower's Houses*. For the next twelve years, he wrote close to a dozen plays, though he generally failed to persuade the managers of the London Theatres to produce them. A few were produced abroad; one (*Arms and the Man*) was produced under the auspices of an experimental management; one (*Mrs Warren's Profession*) was censored by the Lord Chamberlain's Examiner of Plays and several were presented in single performances by private societies.

In 1898, after a serious illness, Shaw resigned as theatre critic, and moved out of his mother's house where he was still living to marry Charlotte Payne-Townsend, an Irish woman of independent means. Their marriage lasted until Charlotte's death in 1943.

In 1904, Harley Granville Barker, an actor, director and playwright, twenty years younger than Shaw who had appeared in a private theatre society's production of Shaw's *Candida*, took over the management of the Court Theatre on Sloane Square in Chelsea and set it up as an experimental theatre specializing in new and progressive drama. Over the next three seasons, Barker produced ten plays by Shaw, and he began writing new plays with Barker's management specifically in mind.

Over the next ten years, all but one of Shaw's plays, (*Pygmalion* in 1914) was produced either by Barker or by Barker's friends and colleagues in the other experimental theatre managements around England. With royalties from his plays, Shaw, who had become financially independent on marrying, now became quite wealthy. Throughout the decade, he remained active in the Fabian Society, in city government, and on committees dedicated to ending dramatic censorship, and to establishing a subsidised National Theatre.

The outbreak of war in 1914 changed Shaw's life. For Shaw, the war represented the bankruptcy of the capitalist system, the last desperate gasps of the nineteenth-century empires, and a tragic waste of young lives, all under the guise of patriotism. He expressed his opinions in a series of newspaper articles under the title, *Common Sense About the War*.

After the war, Shaw found his dramatic voice again and rebuilt his reputation, first with a series of five plays about "creative evolution," *Back to Methuselah*, and then, in 1923, with *Saint Joan*. In 1925, he was awarded the Nobel Prize for Literature. He donated the cash award towards an English edition of the Swedish playwright, August Strindberg, who had never been recognised with a Nobel prize by the Swedish Academy. Shaw's plays were regularly produced and revived in London. He lived the rest of his life as an international celebrity, travelling the world, continually involved in local and international politics. And he continued to write thousands of letters and over a dozen more plays.

In 1950, Shaw fell off a ladder while trimming a tree on his property at Ayot St. Lawrence in Hertfordshire, outside London, and died a few days later of complications from the injury, at the age of 94. He had been at work on yet another play (*Why She Would Not*). In his will, he left a large part of his estate to a project to revamp the English alphabet. After that, the project failed, the estate was divided among the other beneficiaries in his will: the National Gallery of Ireland, the British Museum, and the Royal Academy of Dramatic Art.

●●●

2 Short Answer Type Questions

Q. 1. What does the word Renaissance mean? In what way did ancient Rome and Greece inspire the Renaissance in England?

Ans. *Renaissance* means *Rebirth* or a flowering again of culture. It inculcated a sense of wonder in all things.

The great writers of the English Renaissance borrowed the ideas and the style of the works in Latin and Greek in English translation. Thus Shakespeare borrowed and adapted numerous stories from Plutarch's *Lives of the Noble Romans* translated into English from the original Latin by Thomas North. Italian writers like Boccaccio and Straparola provided the impetus for many English novels.

Q. 2. What is *"euphuism"*?

Ans. Euphuism was a style of writing invented by John Lyly. The word comes from the title of his famous romance, *Euphues, the Anatomy of Wit* (1579). The style is characterized by the use of figures of speech like alliteration and antithesis and of fantastic metaphors and similes based on mythology, flora and fauna. Inanimate objects are endowed with human feelings and sensations — a figure of speech called *pathetic fallacy.*

Q. 3. Why was England called *a nest of singing birds* during the Renaissance?

Ans. Thomas Campion, Ben Jonson, Thomas Dekker, Shakespeare and others wrote beautiful songs in their plays. Many sonnets were also written. Those by Shakespeare addressed to a dark lover are exquisite and well-known. Thomas Campion published a book of songs in an anthology entitled *Two Books of Ayres* which contains the brilliant lines:

"There is a garden in her face
Where roses and white lilies grow
A heavenly paradise in that place
Where all pleasant fruits do grow".

Q. 4. What is a metaphysical conceit?

Ans. Made popular by John Donne, a metaphysical conceit is yoking together of two antithetical ideas for striking effect. One example is the poem *The Flea*. The insect bites the poet and then bites his mistress. The poet does not wish to kill it because:

"This flea is you and I, and this
Our marriage bed, and marriage temple is".

Q. 5. How did the revised edition of the Bible influence English style?

Ans. Commissioned by King James I, the revisers put the Bible into a beautiful prose nearer the language of the common man, yet full of poetry. The archaic expressions are not there and the syntax has a strange rhythm that elevates and edifies human feelings. The writers of the period were greatly influenced by the biblical style and tried to adopt it in their writings.

Q. 6. Comment briefly on Francis Bacon's achievements.

Ans. Bacon (1561-1626) was vastly read from different fields. His writings are philosophical and practical as contained in his work *Novum*

Organum. His ideas also influenced the formulation of the *Royal Society for Improving Natural Knowledge* in 1645. His most popular work is his *Essays*. The essays contained in it are on diverse topics and are especially distilled wisdom on human nature and on life. The style is terse. Epigrams abound which are often quoted by writers and orators.

Q. 7. What did the stage look like in the Elizabethan Age?

Ans. One of the earliest stages was the Globe in which Shakespeare's plays were enacted. It was an open air theatre. A platform jutted out as a stage. All around it sat the groundlings or ordinary folk who munched apples and threw brick-bats at actors if bored up. There were rising galleries all around where the elite gentry sat. Boys acted the roles of females. A poster was brought on stage to indicate change of scenes. The unities of time, place and action were disregarded.

Q. 8. What did Ben Jonson mean when he said "Poets are born and not made"?

Ans. In original Latin the statement is *Poeta nascitur non fit*. Jonson meant that Shakespeare was born with talent for drama. He studied in a grammar school for a few years but remained uneducated generally. He keenly observed life. He read English translations of Latin and Greek stories and adapted them for his plays. He invested the stories with a life and passion which show his genius. Each of his 800 or so characters live up to reality and his themes are universally applicable to all countries and periods of human history.

Q. 9. What were the general characteristics of the Restoration drama?

Ans. They depicted the licence and ridicule of the Puritan's moral code. The theatre was a place of vice. Scenery played an important role and now actresses replaced boys for female roles. Shakespeare's tragedies were rewritten to have happy endings. Under French influence, superhuman feats were described and heroes were presented as ideals.

Q. 10. Comment on Shakespeare's sonnets briefly.

Ans. Shakespeare wrote about 140 sonnets. Most of them are addressed to a certain dark lady who had betrayed him. There are some addressed to his friend, an Earl. The Shakespearean sonnet has three quartrains clinched by a couplet. The first quartrain depicts the problem, the next two develop it and the couplet presents a sort of solution. Some of his famous sonnets are *"Shall I compare thee to a summer's day"* and *"When to the sessions of sweet silent thought"*.

Q. 11. Why is the 18th century called the *Age of Understanding and Enlightenment*?

Ans. During this age there was a great emphasis on the advancement of the mind. People wanted to read books in simple and practical hints for living. Journalism as a genre began to cope with the demand for the circulation of facts and ideas. A number of deists like Locke, Collins and Tindal advocated reasoning.

Q. 12. Write a brief note on the growth of journalism in the 18th century.

Ans. During this age people wanted to know more and more about diverse subjects. Richard Steele and Addison brought out papers called the *Spectator* and *The Tatler*. As observers of society they wrote of its foibles in the character of Sir Roger de Coverley. Daniel Defoe brought out journalistic writings like *The Shortest Way with the Dissenters*.

Q. 13. What type of satire was written in the 18th century?

Ans. Jonathan Swift (1667-1745) was the foremost satirist of the age. He was adept at ridiculing the vices of men. These were supposed to be incorrigible. In *The Battle of the Books* he attacked modern people. In *The Tale of the*

Tub he attacked the Pepists and the Presbyterians. He attacks man's religion, politics and science in *Gulliver's Travels* and calls man a pernicious creature. John Arbuthnot wrote an allegory on politics in *The History of John Bull*.

Q. 14. Comment on Dr. Johnson's versatility.

Ans. Dr. Johnson was a versatile man of letters. As a lexicographer, he wrote the first English Dictionary which is remarkable for personal insights. As a novelist, he wrote *Rasselas* and as a playwright, *Irene*. He was also a poet. *London* and *The Vanity of Human Wishes* are his famous poems. He was also a translator critic, biographer and journalist.

Q. 15. How did the novel develop?

Ans. The 18th century is known as the age of the novel proper. Character portrayal, family and social life became the important subjects, and minute details filled the book. *Pamela*, and *Clarissa Harlowe* were written by Richardson. Henry Fielding wrote *Joseph Andrews,* and *Tom Jones,* Tobias Smollet wrote *Roderick Random* and *Humphry Clinker*.

Q. 16. What changes took place in the West which influenced the writings of Englishmen in the last part of the 18th century?

Ans. England saw the revolt of her colonies. Many in the British Parliament favoured the claims of America to secede from the crown. In 1776, America declared her independence. Rousseau's writings inspired many Englishmen. He wrote, *"Man is born free, but everywhere he is chains"*. Many therefore believed that the French Revolution was being fought for the right causes.

Q. 17. Why is Blake called a mystic poet?

Ans. William Blake was a visionary. He described his strange visions in poems like *The Tiger* which was written against the background of the French Revolution. *The Tiger* represented the forces of evil and the Lamb, goodness and meekness.

Q. 18. What is the special characteristic of the major Romantic poets?

Ans. Wordsworth is known as the High Priest of Nature. He worshipped Nature as the healer of the bruised soul, the voice of God and bestower of peace. Shelley was the poet of the millenium or the bright future of mankind. The burden of his song was *"If Winter comes, can Spring be far behind?"* Byron was a tempestuous rebel against social mores. Ostracized as a Casanova or womanizer, he spent his years in Italy and Greece. His poems castigate the hypocrisy and cant of English society. Keats was the poet of sensuous delights. Coleridge created a dream world in his poems, a few of which were inspired by opium-induced dreams.

Q. 19. Write a note on Keat's Odes.

Ans. The *Ode to the Nightingale* shows Keats' desire to withdraw from the world of reality by the power of imagination (*'wings of poesy'*). Keats' brother died of consumption and he felt life to be meaningless. A nightingale singing outside his house inspired the ode. *The Ode on a Grécian Urn* shows the Hellenic traits of his poetry. The Urn becomes the subject of Keat's philosophizing on the aspect of timelessness of art. *"Beauty is Truth and Truth Beauty"*, he concludes. *Ode to Autumn* is laden with the descriptions of rich smells and colours of autumn season. *Ode to Psyche* is another of his odes.

Q. 20. What is the characteristic of Pre-Raphaelite poetry?

Ans. Swinburne, D.G. Rossetti and William Morris wrote poems which are colourful paintings or musicals in words. Colour and sound predominate in Pre-Raphaelite poetry.

Q. 21. Write a short note on Wordsworth's *The Prelude*.

Ans. *The Prelude* is the autobiographical poem of Wordsworth. It records the development of Wordsworth as a poet. Although the poem had already been written by 1805, it was not published until 1850, after the poet's death. The entire poem runs to fourteen books. It describes the formative influence of nature with exaltation and awe. Writen in blank verse, some of its famous passages are on skating and boating.

Q. 22. Write a few lines on Jane Austen's novels.

Ans. Austen's first novel was *Pride and Prejudice* (1813), which is considered her masterpiece because of its smooth and unobstrusive style. Her other novels are *Sense and Sensibility* (1811), *Northanger Abbey* (1818), *Mansfield Park* (1814), *Emma* (1816), and *Persuasion* (1818). Her novels, such as the *Emma*, are the pictures of everyday existence. Her characters are not types, but individuals. Her method of portrayal is based upon acute observation and incisive irony.

Q. 23. What changes took place at the beginning of the twentieth century that were reflected in literature?

Ans. England began to lose her colonies and shrunk in size. Science progressed and many inventions were made. The World War caused economic depression. Sigmund Freud made discoveries in the human subconscious.

Q. 24. What foreign influences were noticed in the English literature of the early 20th century?

Ans. Writers in England borrowed ideas and techniques from the French Parnassians and Symbolists, from Ibsen in Norway and Leo Tolstoy in Russia. They imitated the free verse of Walt Whitman of America. They described the culture of distant lands which now had become accessible through navigation and air travel and colonization.

Q. 25. What does "Art for Art's Sake" mean?

Ans. This theory was propounded by Walter Pater. It was based on a contemplation of the achievements of the past, especially of the Renaissance. The theory in literature advocated refined pleasure. Symonds, Oscar Wilde and Saintsbury were other followers of this school.

Q. 26. What is the "Celtic Revival"?

Ans. It was the study and rejuvenated interest in Irish tradition and mythology. W.B. Yeats was its pioneer.

Q. 27. Why is Rudyard Kipling known as an imperialist?

Ans. Kipling glorified the achievements of the Anglo-Saxon race, especially in ruling her colonies. According to him, the white man was ordained to rule the seas and lands.

Q. 28. What was Hardy's view of life?

Ans. Hardy was a pessimist. He believed life was unrelieved gloom. Man was a helpless victim of his destiny, the plaything of uncontrollable forces.

Q. 29. How does Eliot's poetry describe Post-World War Europe?

Ans. Europe after the war brought out the anguish of people who had lost their dear ones. Human life ceased to have much meaning since death and destruction stalked it everywhere.

Q. 30. What is the meaning of "Objective Correlative"?

Ans. It was Eliot's poetic technique. He used a number of images or word pictures in his poetry. These images stimulate certain associations lying buried in the universal human subconscious. The associations create feelings and sensations of futility, doom, frustration as the poet wanted to depict.

Q. 31. What did the War poets describe in their poetry?

Ans. They had been soldiers who fought in World War I. They had seen the senseless killing and horror of war-machines. War destroys love and all human virtues. Freedom to live is man's greatest right which war eliminates. Wars must end forever on our planet. Such is the burden of their songs.

Q. 32. In what way did Freud's discoveries affect English literature?

Ans. Freud discovered the three layers of human consciousness. The subconscious is man's retained impressions of all his experiences — good and bitter. These continue to control his attitudes and behaviour in the present. Modern novelists like James Joyce and Virginia Woolf described characters unreeling an interior monologue where the voices of the past speak so as to say. These past thoughts buried in the deep mind surface without order of logic of time. This technique is known as the steam-of-consciousness. Virginia Woolf defined it thus: "Life is not a series of jiglamps but a luminous halo that has been from time immemorial".

Q. 33. What social problems were discussed by Shaw, Wells and Galsworthy?

Ans. Wells was a member of the Fabian Society and criticized existing institutions in Britain. Galsworthy exposed the landed gentry's snobbery and decadence and class exploitation. Shaw was an iconoclast, destroying age-old myths about the soldier's life, the life of a prostitute and the weakness of democracy.

Q. 34. How does Milton's poetry reveal his Puritanism?

Ans. Most of Milton's poetry is austere in spirit. His only gay poem is *L'Allegro* which reveals lively, happy moods. *Il Penseroso* is a direct counterpart to *L'Allegro*. It describes Nature in a pensive mood, a pure, devout nun. *Paradise Lost* shown Satan's fall from heaven and grace and *Samson Agonistes*, the helpless blind Samson betrayed by his fiancee, Deliah. *Comus* is a masque which extols feminine virtue to the extreme.

Q. 35. What is autobiographical in *Paradise Lost*?

Ans. *Paradise Lost* is ostensibly the story of Satan's or Beelzebub's fall from Heaven. He is thrown out for being rebellious. The story recalls Milton's loss of his post when monarchy returns, his humiliation at the hands of the Royalists. The temptation of Christ during his forty days' fast recalls Milton's conflict between divine virtue and the desire for literary fame.

Q. 36. What was Wordsworth's poetic philosophy?

Ans. Wordsworth believed that a poet's first task was to teach. His poems, especially *The Recluse*, are full of moralizing. He believed in Nature as the voice of God. Every manifestation of Nature — hills, rivers and meadows — breathed the universal spirit. In this he was a pantheist. He called Nature *"Stern Daughter of the voice of God"*. Nature was a healer of tired minds. It taught simple living and high thinking, love of one's fellows, faith in divine Providence, control of one's hopes and desires, and obedience to the divine law.

Q. 37. How much formal education did William Shakespeare receive? Why is it said that he was educated in the school of life?

Ans. Shakespeare went to study at the grammar school at Stratford-on-Avon. He had to leave it at the age of 13 to help his father in the grain business. So, actually, he had little or negligible formal education. As Ben Jonson said about him, *Poeta nascitur non fit* meaning "Poets are born not made". Shakespeare had an inborn intuition to a high degree for his plays and his characterization show him to be the master of the keyboard of human feelings. The eight hundred or so gallery of characters he created show how observant he must have been of human nature or how much imagination he had to enter into other people's minds. He knew "little Latin and less Greek", yet read works in English translation voraciously. He used plots of existing stories which he endowed with a life of his own.

Q. 38. Throw light on Shakespeare's sonnets.

Ans. Shakespeare wrote more than 154 sonnets, many of which are found in his plays and many are on their own. The Petrarchan sonnets from Italy were addressed to Laura and were sonnets of love. The early English just translated or borrowed the ideas of these sonnets and wrote to praise a Celia as a paragon of beauty. Shakespeare also wrote sonnets of love in praise of an unknown dark lady and the Earl of Southampton, his friend. He is full of wrath for the lady who jilted him. Many of Shakespeare's sonnets are merely quibbles and full of conceits, but some are famous for their imagination, good diction and fine lyrical quality. Among the famous ones are:

"Shall I compare thee to a summer's day?"
"When to the sessions of sweet silent thought".

The sonnets contain 14 lines. There are three quatrains which develop a problem and these are followed by a couplet which clinches it all with a solution.

Q. 39. Point out some of the demerits of Shakespeare's plays. How did contemporary writers react to them?

Ans. Shakespeare violates many rules of conventional grammar. For instance, parts of speech are mixed up in their function — nouns are used as adjectives and adverbs, there is discord between nouns and verbs, etc. Yet, the errors so admirably portray the feeling or description that to correct them would be to spoil the whole effect and rhythm. So such deviations are passed off as "poetic licence". In fact, in modern poetry like that of Hopkins, deviance is a device for communicating unusual thoughts and feelings.

Shakespeare violated the classical unities of time, place and action. A scene could jump suddenly from Athens to a forest elsewhere. Ben Jonson pointed out this error, yet made concessions for Shakespeare, "There is always an appeal to Nature". Such a concession from the scorching pen of Ben Jonson is indeed a recognition of Shakespeare's genius and spontaneity which would not brook rules.

Q. 40. What was Shakespeare's religion and philosophy?

Ans. There is no evidence whether Shakespeare was a faithful churchgoer or not. But his plays give ample proof that he had a generous, catholic view of human life. There was a place for Christian mercy and charity and a heart for the Jew Shylock in *Merchant of Venice,* and the pagan Moor (*Othello*). He was open-minded encompassing the knowledge of different climes: *"There are more things in Heaven and Earth than have been dreamt of in your philosophy, Horatio" (Hamlet).*

It would be more apt to say Shakespeare had "a universal mind" than a merely Christian heart.

Q. 41. Why is it said that Ben Jonson was the literary dictator of his time?

Ans. There was something hot and fiery in Ben Jonson's temperament. He got into brawls with fellow-actors and even killed one for which he was branded in the left hand. He was a rival of the great Shakespeare and berated him for not keeping to the classical rules of drama, for not keeping the unities of time, place and action. Yet he admired him, "this side of idolatory". He offended King James of Scotland by his comedy, *Eastward Hoe!* He thus got imprisoned and almost had his ears and nose chopped off.

He exercised an influence on the Elizabethan theatre. His plays, *Sejanus* and *Catiline* are well-documented in historical facts. He attacked romantic conventions and the follies of London life.

Q. 42. What is the meaning of "humour" in Ben Jonson's plays?

Ans. Ben Jonson took the medieval meaning of humour used in medicine. There are four humours or liquids — bile, phlegm, choler and blood — in the human body. These not only regulate a person's metaboslism but also determine his predominant character-trait. Thus anger, greed, gluttony, etc. are human vice which Ben Jonson attacked in his plays

Every Man in His Humour and *Volpone*. In *The Silent Woman*, Morose is an eccentric who has a phobia about noise. He oils his door hinges regularly and carpets his floors. Servants who cannot maintain silence are dismissed. His nephew blackmails him for his inheritance by marrying a loud-mouthed woman.

Q. 43. In what way is Tennyson regarded as the prophet of his age, the Victorian Age?

Ans. Tennyson's poetry voice the major concerns of the English people of his age. Belief in parliamentary democracy and fundamental human rights, the tension between the traditional faith of the Bible and the scientific rationality generated by Darwin' discovery (*In Memoriam* and *Idylls*), the question of women's rights (*The Princess*), were all touched upon in his poetry. These, in fact, were the major concerns of the Victorians.

Q. 44. In what way is Browning an optimist?

Ans. Browning believed that man is evolving to higher states of consciousness. A man must achieve or strive towards perfection by conscious effort and by overcoming his shortcomings. *"God's in his Heaven/And all's well with the world"* was his chief message through *Pippa Passes*.

Q. 45. What were the main themes of Arnold's poetry?

Ans. Matthew Arnold was concerned with the Victorian loss of faith in God. He describes it beautifully and nostalgically in *Dover Beach*.

"The Sea of Faith was once too at the full....
But now I only hear its long withdrawing melancholy roar
Retreating to the breath of the night wind...."

Arnold believed in quiet hardwork and withdrawal from the sick hurry of Victorian living. His heroes do this. Thus Obermann retires to a Swiss mountain and Empedocles throws himself into a crater. Nature has a healing touch.

Q. 46. Briefly describe Hardy's vision of human life. How does it differ from Shakespeare's?

Ans. Hardy is the most pessimistic writer of English. Life was one long penance for man. Uncontrollable powers directed man's will and buffetted him on the waves of existence. Man is a puppet led to a tragic doom. Hardy's heroes and heroines never know peace for long. Death stalks them. To be born is a curse, he explains in his poem, *To an Unborn Pauper Child.* While Shakespeare believed that man had a will to direct his fate (*"The fault is not in our stars that we are underlings"*) yet he could be led astray by some tragic flaw in his character. For Hardy man had no hope whatsoever.

Q. 47. What do we mean when we call someone Dickensian?

Ans. Dickens' characters are now symbols of oddities and idiosyncracies of character. Dickens created a galaxy of 2000 characters in his works. Micawber stands for an incorrigible optimist. Likewise Uriah Heep for a scheming rogue. A person is Dickensian if he has traits which may be the subject of humorous consideration.

Q. 48. Discuss Dickens as a social reformer.

Ans. Dickens dealt with the inefficiency of public schools in *Nicholas Nickleby* and of prisons in *Little Dorrit.* These were based on personal childhood experience. He also exposed the poor plight of labour in the novels *Old Curiosity Shop* and *Hard Times.* These books caused government reforms in these areas.

Q. 49. In what sense is *Macbeth* a tragedy?

Ans. Tragedy explores man's relationship with the universe. It shows man contending with forces such as Death and Fate which are far more powerful than him. The Greeks believed man to be a helpless puppet in the hands of the gods, a plaything of chance stumbling from one situation to another till he succumbs to death. He had no free will. This was more or less the view of Thomas Hardy. Shakespeare's idea of tragedy was based on the Greek ideology. A man in high status — Macbeth as a general, Caesar as a general, Hamlet as a Prince and King Lear as a king — suffers from a tragic flaw (*hamartia*) which is usually pride or *"Hubris"* that leads to his downfall. In Shakespeare, these tragic heroes have a free will, but they succumb to their major weakness. They have a choice and power to take a decision but pride or their tragic flaw leads them astray.

Tragedy concerns itself with man's very existence with, the meaning and purpose of his life. Tragedy deals with a serious action having serious implications. The tragic character is always defeated by powerful internal forces, (like Macbeth by his vaulting ambition) and external forces (his wife's persuasions, the promptings of the witches). He has to die in the end. But though death overcomes him, his courage leaves its mark in the world.

Q. 50. Can we call Macbeth a tragic hero?

Ans. Macbeth, the protagonist of the play, has committed many heinous crimes. He kills the king, Duncan, who he acknowledges is "full of the milk of human kindness". He follows it up by hiring assassins to finish off contenders to the throne. Thus Lord Banquo is done away with. He has Macduff's wife and children killed. He takes to wanton killing till his subjects rise against him. Can we call such a person a "hero"? It is certainly difficult to acknowledge this, yet Shakespeare has presented him as one. Macbeth has great self-awareness and has a deeper vision of life than others in the play. He can imagine the path to further greater achievement. He is sensitive and has uncommon vitality and intelligence. He is agonized by his thoughts and deeds. These values then make him a hero though he is alone and isolated in the world.

Q. 51. Write a brief note on the supernatural in *Macbeth*.

Ans. *Macbeth* has a number of incidents and events that add a sense of mystery and otherworldliness to the play. Shakespeare introduced these so-called supernatural elements to please his audience in his days since they believed in such things. Thus, the three witches are first seen on the blasted heath accosting Macbeth and Banquo and forewarning them of events to come. Their statements are couched in ambiguous language and they mislead Macbeth into thinking that he will be the king and nothing can kill him. The witches prepare a hideous concoction of animal and human parts and chant strange incantations. They can vanish into thin air as they are made of ethereal substances. They can materialize themselves at will, foretell the future and pull heads and babies out of cauldrons. Their prophecy makes it clear that Macbeth's kingship and defeat are both fated.

Lady Macbeth's invocation to the powers of evil arise from her desire to gain power but once her conscience surfaces, she goes insane. Other seemingly supernatural events can be explained in logical terms. Thus Birnam forest does not move but it is the enemy who are camouflaged in green branches. That Macduff is not born of woman is explained by the fact that his mother underwent a Caesarean operation. The supernatural unleashes Macbeth's *'hubris'* — his pride or tragic flaw. By ironical statements the witches mislead him.

Q. 52. Write a brief sketch of Lady Macbeth.

Ans. Lady Macbeth is often called the fourth witch of the play. Some of her actions make us conclude that she is similar to the three witches who materialize on the blasted heath. She invokes evil powers by her incantations and is supposed to mislead Macbeth to a bloody ambition by her provocations. Many critics, however, do not agree with this epithet of fourth witch. It is not Lady Macbeth but Macbeth himself who, goaded by an internal craze for power, allows himself to be influenced by her. In fact, after Duncan's death she tries to dissuade him from murdering Banquo, Fleance and Macduff. Her invocation of evil is just her desire to achieve her goal. She suppresses her conscience but it resurfaces to plague her. She grows insane and walks and talks in her sleep and has a light burning by her side always. Not all the sweet scents of Arabia can wash this blood from her hands, she thinks. The doctors attending on her declare that she needs more the divine help for treatment than medicine. She does not approve any of Macbeth's actions after Duncan's death. She states that he is stepping the limits of ambition, his murders are heinous and he might go mad.

Lady Macbeth's great saving grace is her support of Macbeth to the throne. She wants to strengthen his will-power. Her speech shows her more manly than Macbeth, who wavers before the assassination. Lady Macbeth almost verges on revulsive cruelty when she declares she can smash the head of a child whom she has breast-fed. During Elizabethan times, women played a subsidiary role to men as it was a patriarchal society. Therefore, Lady Macbeth is presented as one who cannot act on her own. She can only initiate the action. But she rebels against social norms and shows man-like courage and fortitude.

Q. 53. Write a note on the minor characters of *Macbeth*.

Ans. Duncan provides the role of the king who is to be killed; but he is much subordinate to Macbeth and Lady Macbeth. He helps to raise issues. People in the Elizabethan age were much concerned about the question of the divine right of a king. Scholars spent time and effort to decide whether a bad person should be allowed to rule just because the king was considered 'divine'. Shakespeare presents both sides of the argument. On the one hand, the murder of a king is the highest form of sin because he is divine irrespective of whether he is good or bad. The other picture is that the most able person should be the king since it is survival of the fittest which counts.

Shakespeare compares Duncan to King Edward who is saintly and able to perform miraculous cures. Duncan, on the other hand, deceives Macbeth. He showers tributes of titles on him but knows that ultimately he will make his own son the king.

Banquo is presented as a foil to Macbeth. His reactions to the prophecy of the witches differs from those of Macbeth. He is a complex personality and hides his intentions and feelings. He is murdered quite early in the play.

Macduff is loyal and devoted to King Duncan and works to restore the throne to Malcohn — Duncan's son, the rightful heir, according to him. Where Macbeth is full of sin and crime, Macduff is a normal person who bears the suffering caused by Macbeth who kills his whole family.

Ross and Angus, the porter, the Doctor who attends on Lady Macbeth and Macbeth's valet are choric characters. They comment and offer perspectives. When Macbeth reacts to their news that he has been made Thane of Cawdor, Ross and Angus comment on it. They also comment on Macbeth's state of mind when he sees the ghost of Banquo. The porter's speech provides comic relief. He represents the porter at the gates of Hell. He leads to the discovery of Duncan's death. The Doctor and maid provide us information on the pitiable state of Lady Macbeth's mind — her derangement and her estrangement from her husband. Finally, the old man comes like an angel to warn Macbeth of his last chance to save himself from complete ruin, but fails.

Q. 54. What is the function of imagery in *Macbeth*?

Ans. An image is a comparison between two things, ideas or persons or animals. It helps to describe some state, character or personality better. Macbeth usually compares his mind, a person or a state to an animal. His ambition vaults like a horse; his disturbed and guilty mind is "full of scorpions"; he finds himself tied "bear-like to the stake"; Banquo is "scotched" snake. These images point to a wild state of mind, a rebel against the laws of humanity, the potential criminal. Duncan uses images related to nature. The air 'smells wooingly' at Inverness Castle and the temple martlet "builds its nest as if it were a peaceful place".

The other imagery in *Macbeth* is generally related to food and feasts, clothes, and natural disasters like earthquakes and fires. Unlike his contemporaries, Shakespeare has not taken any imagery from medicine, science, law, exploration, etc.

Q. 55. How does Shakespeare use dramatic irony in *Macbeth*?

Ans. In the play, we know all along that Duncan is going to be murdered because of Macbeth's plan. But Duncan is quite unaware of it. When he reaches the Castle at Inverness, he praises the beautiful surroundings and clean, healthy, fresh air. He seems quite at peace with himself. But the reader knows that the hour of his assassination is at hand. This prior knowledge makes the play interesting. It adds a certain sense of awe and excitement. This is called dramatic irony.

Q. 56. What are the sources of the story of *Macbeth*?

Ans. Shakespeare usually borrowed the story of his plays from Greek and Roman classics in English translation. He also used books of Italian, Scottish and other sources. He gave the story a new vitality by infusing it with more human element and philosophy. The ideas for Macbeth came from a number of sources. Thus, Holinshed's *Chronicle of Kings* and important figures of England, Ireland and Scotland supplied the historical facts. Three books on witchcraft and demonology by Reginald Scott and a book on witchcraft by King James I himself were other sources. *Macbeth* is not a good source for accurate information on Scotland though Macbeth was a Scottish King. But the play offers much information about Shakespeare's England when Elizabeth and James ruled. The interest in witchcraft, the question of the divine rights of kings engaged the minds of thinkers in that age.

Q. 57. What information does the *Macbeth* about the beliefs of Shakespeare's age?

Ans. The Elizabethans believed in the Great Chain of Being. God was manifest in all His creation. From God power manifested itself in the king, then men, then women, the animals and vegetable kingdoms. The king was God's representative on earth. No one was to question his actions and deeds. It was sacrilege. This was actually a theory propounded by the royal court to maintain the supremacy of the king.

On the other hand, people questioned Elizabeth's being the Queen. It was believed (and so the priests propagated it) that woman was inferior to man and must be kept in her place. Elizabeth being a woman, it was unnatural for her to rule over men. So the divine right became controversial.

Everything in Nature was Order — a manifestation of God. Any chaos and disorder was a sign of evil. Women who tried to assert themselves were burnt as witches at the stake.

Q. 58. Show the importance of Act 1 of *Macbeth*.

Ans. The whole first Act of the play is an exposition of the major characters and themes of the play. The readers or spectators are introduced to the fundamentals of the plot. The main images and symbols that describe the major concerns are also introduced. The protagonist, Macbeth, his wife, King Duncan, Lord Banquo — all come on the stage. Their status and the chief traits in their characters are delineated. The Act shows us the main issue at hand. Macbeth has suppressed single-handedly a rebellion against the King. Duncan rewards him with titles, yet nominates his own son, Malcolm, heir to the throne. Macbeth feels this is wrong. The prophecy of the witches and his wife's provocations egg him on to plot the assassination of the King.

Q. 59. What is the importance of the first scene of *Macbeth*?

Ans. When the play opens we are taken to a vast blasted heath or open space with a bleak and bare look. Nothing grows there. There is a lot of thunder in the sky, and in the flashes of lightning, we see three horrible hag-ridden witches. In ancient Greek tragedies, Sybil a mythological creature, appeared. She would ask the protagonist a "riddle". If the protagonist answered this correctly, it would lead to their prosperity, otherwise they would fall a victim to destruction and ruin. In *Macbeth,* the three witches are like Sybil in that they ask strange riddles. Macbeth cannot understand the full meaning of these but is encouraged by the prophecies they make of his becoming the king to plot the assassination of Duncan. The witches' speech goes like this:

"When shall we meet again?
In thunder, lightning or in rain?"
"When the hurly-burly's done
When the battle's lost and won".

The 'hurly-burly' may refer to the storm raging outside. It may refer to Macbeth's internal state of mind in which a conflict is about to begin. The 'battle's lost and won' probably means that Macbeth has won a battle but might lose the next since he will kill Duncan and lose his soul or conscience.

The gruesome atmosphere and setting of the play is further established when the witches depart saying:

"Fair is foul and foul is fair,
Hover through the fog and filthy air".

Probably this denotes that the moral atmosphere was polluted in Scotland and corruption held sway. 'Fair' and 'foul' were the good and the bad of the time. Good could become bad and vice versa.

The first scene prepares the reader to understand the whole play by introducing all the main themes or issues. In Greek mythology, fate was represented by three sisters who were blind in that they were indifferent to the fate of the people whose lives they controlled. The witches here were intent on misleading and harming people. They, therefore, set the mood of destruction that will follow Macbeth to his grave.

Q. 60. Write a note on the 'soliloquy' on Time and Action made by Macbeth.

Ans. 'Soliloquy' means speaking alone. An actor speaks out to reveal his innermost thoughts — the ones he would never have uttered to anyone. In speaking so he or she contemplates on a philosophical issue that is important for the action of the play.

In his soliloquy on Time and Action made in Act I Scene VII, Macbeth explores the nature of Time and its relationship to human action, of crime and its relationship to punishment. According to one belief, Time only has meaning if we believe in the existence of God. Time began and will end with God. Every action is a part of the general scheme of God. According to another theory, God does not exist. Time is a natural phenomenon. Macbeth is concerned about the issue because he is afraid of divine punishment falling on him for his action of deciding to kill Duncan. So by denying God and the idea of laws, he wishes to suppress his conscience.

Q. 61. What is the importance of the vision of the dagger Macbeth has before attempting the murder?

Ans. In his second soliloquy Macbeth is shown reacting to the vision of the dagger that appears before him. He asks himself if this is a real dagger or an illusion of his fevered brain. The plan to murder Duncan has set off a conflict in his mind. His conscience is troubled. And the dagger is a projection of his troubled state. It seems the dagger symbolizes the fact that by murdering Duncan he will be murdering his own conscience. The dagger also eggs him on to commit the deed. In his soliloquy he tells himself that he must not allow his plans to stop with thinking. He must also act, otherwise his thoughts are mere day-dreaming and lack substance like the dagger. Thus the dagger is used to justify his future actions. Macbeth has thus taken up a stand against morality and has adopted evil as his guide.

Q. 62. Compare and contrast Macbeth's state of mind with Lady Macbeth's before the murder is committed.

Ans. Macbeth and Lady Macbeth talk under their breath in a tense and nervous manner. Their speech is abrupt and jerky, the sentences break at wrong places and the speakers go breathless. Lady Macbeth says that Duncan looked like her father in sleep, otherwise she herself would have murdered him. This shows that her conscience is lurking behind her evil desires. She even fears they will be discovered and punished. She wants, however, to succeed in their plans to enjoy a few moments of glory. The desire for power and glory by defying the laws of nature is an idea that was studied by Marlowe in his play, *Dr. Faustus*. Lady Macbeth's attitude is matter-of-fact and practical. They will wash off the blood from their hands and thereby put aside the thoughts of the event of murder. Macbeth's conscience, on the other hand, is troubled. He knows he will never sleep peacefully anymore. He has lost his soul. While Lady Macbeth tries to cover up their deed with rhetoric and commonsense, Macbeth is weighed with sin and repentance.

Q. 63. Write a note on the life and works of George Bernard Shaw.

Ans. George Bernard Shaw was one of the greatest of Irish men of letters who wrote plays in English. He was born on July 26, 1856 in Dublin. He worked as a clerk and cashier in a land agent's office till he was fifteen. His father could not earn a proper livelihood to keep his family happy, so Bernard Shaw left Dublin with his mother and sisters and settled down in London when he was sixteen.

Since his mother was more devoted to music than her children, George Bernard Shaw had to develop independently and he grew strong in mind and spirit. He developed an ability to analyze human life — its customs and prejudices — and to pass judgement on them. He had learnt to appreciate music from his mother and had developed a fine ear so that when he began writing his plays, the dialogues had the rhythm of spoken language and came very naturally to the actors and held the audience spellbound. He also became a music critic for *The Star* (1888). Later he reviewed plays for *The Saturday Review* (1895-98). These were very highly acclaimed.

Shaw socialized with great men of London and was able to imbibe their ideas and ideals. He came under the influence of the American economist, Henry George, and was impressed by his social doctrines. He also became a member of the Fabian Society whose aim was to change society by a gradual process of non-violent revolution. Shaw's ideas led Mrs Annie Besant to join the Fabian Society.

Shaw began writing plays to discuss social, political and religious problems of his times. Thus his characters were his mouthpieces for change. He explained many of his ideas in his prefaces to the plays. These prefaces sometimes were longer than the plays themselves. Shaw believed in the philosophy of Life Force. Woman was impelled to chase man in a bid to continue the species. His first popular play was *John Bull's Other*

Island (1904) — a comedy about Irish politics. Shaw's comedy is full of lively, bristling, witty dialogues. His plays came out under two collections — *The Unpleasant Plays* and *Pleasant Plays*.

He ruled the literary roost for more than half a century before his death in 1950. Some of his more important plays are:

1. *The Philanderer* (1893): love and marriage is a game between the sexes.
2. *Mrs Warren's Profession* (1894): about prostitution.
3. *Arms and the Man* (1894): an anti-romantic play about love and war.
4. *Caesar and Cleopatra* (1899): famous for the portrayal of Caesar.
5. *Man and Superman* (1905): an exposition of Shaw's theory of Life Force.
6. *Back to Methuselah* (1921): shows his gospel of creative evaluation and belief in the Life Force. Life is not the survival of the physically fittest as Darwin believed, but of the person with superior intelligence.
7. *St Joan* (1923): about a protestant martyr who believed she heard the voice of God and was condemned.
8. *The Apple Cart* (1929): which shows him as a Modernist.

Q. 64. Comment on the title of the play *Arms and the Man*.

Ans. Dryden translated the *Aeneid* of Virgil from Latin. The opening lines read:

"Arms and the Man I sing, who forced by fate,
And haughty Juno's unrelenting hate."

George Bernard Shaw has taken the title of his play from the opening line, but he has presented the opposite of *Aeneid's* view about war and heroism. According to *Aeneid*, war is a glorious thing and man can achieve heroic deeds through it. Thus 'man' and his 'arms' or weapons are praised. In his play, *Arms and the Man,* Bernard Shaw gives an ironic meaning to the words. Shaw does not see any glory in war or in soldiers. His soldier, Bluntschli is "a chocolate-cream soldier". He fights in the war for the Serbs though he is from Switzerland. He fights to earn a living. He fights because he has to. But his main aim is to live as long as possible and to avoid getting killed. He carries chocolates in his pockets. There are, according to him, two types of soldiers: the young ones who carry pistols and cartridges; the old ones who carry food in their pockets. Bluntschli makes fun at the way in which the Bulgarians under Sergius attacked the Serbs. It was foolhardy, suicidal for a cavalry to charge a battery of machine guns. They could have all been wiped off if the guns went off.

Thus the title of the play indicates Shaw's concern with soldiers, warfare and weapons.

Q. 65. In what way is *Arms and the Man* an anti-romantic comedy?

Ans. Bernard Shaw's beliefs were influenced by realism and reasoning, not by emotions and sentiments. Although a realist, he is not a cynic. He treats his subject matter with light humour and wit. The subtitle of the play is: An *Anti-Romantic Comedy in Three Acts.* "Romance" means "a form of fiction, distinguished from the novel or tale because it does not bind itself to verisimilitude or reality, but gives scope to imagination and idealization.

The first scene itself is romantic. We see Raina standing at the window, gazing at the snowy Balkan mountains. She is thinking deeply of her beloved Sergius who is fighting for the Bulgarians. Her ideas of love and romance are based on the poetry of Lord Byron and the novels of Alexander Pushkin. She has also seen the opera at Bucharest and knows of romantic tales. Sergius has become the hero of the Slivnitza battle. In a romantic gesture, Raina picks up his picture and gazes at it proudly. Her "feelings are beyond expression". She does not kiss it, but only picks it up like a holy act. She must be loyal to Sergius' love, always she promises.

Suddenly Bluntschli, running away from the enemy, climbs up the pipe leading to Raina's room and clambers in. His sudden appearance dispels Raina's romantic mood.

In the conversation that follows between Raina and Bluntschli, Raina is shocked to learn of Bluntschli's anti-romantic views about war. He is fighting in the war to earn his bread and butter. He finds nothing glorious about war. When Raina finds he is carrying chocolates, she scorns at him and gives him a few chocolate-creams. Bluntschli is quite unashamed of his conduct. He is hiding in Raina's bedroom to escape the enemy. He falls asleep with fatigue. Raina, who thought soldiers were very tough and could go without food and sleep, is disillusioned. This is Bernard Shaw's humorous way of presenting his anti-romantic views Slowly Raina realizes that her pride in his aristocratic upbringing and her lofty ideals are in illusion.

In Act Two, Shaw takes up the idea of higher love. Sergius and Raina are proud to be higher lovers. Raina adores Sergius as a hero. Sergius says that she is his inspiration. He fought the war like a knight imagining his lady love watching the tournament. But Sergius is shown falling in love with maid Louka and Raina flirts with Bluntschli. Sergius admits that it is very tiring to keep up the higher love. Physical love is a necessity too. Shaw is trying to prove what a sham higher love is. Thus in this sense, too, the play is an anti-romantic comedy.

Q. 66. Write a note on Bluntschli on the basis of your reading the play *Arms and the Man*.

Ans. Bernard Shaw gives us a pen-picture of Bluntschli as soon as he enters Raina's room. He is about 35 years of age and of a middle stature. His appearance is not distinguished. There is nothing specially attractive about him. But he is well-built with a strong neck and shoulders. He has an obstinate appearance, short crisp bronze curls hang on his head. Although shabbily dressed and exhausted, he is alert.

Although Swiss, Bluntschli joined the Serbian army to earn a livelihood. He is matter-of-fact and practical in his outlook about war. A war is won by strategy and cunning. There is nothing heroic about it. It is the duty of the soldier to attack when he is in a strong position and to retreat and save his life when in a weak position. When he enters Raina's room, he uses her cloak to prevent her from coming out and shouting. "It's good enough for a man with only you to stand between him and death", he says about the cloak. When he sees Raina sit on his pistol, he shrieks and when she throws out the empty box of chocolates, he shies away frightened. But actually this is not owing to cowardice. He is nervous and tired because he has been under fire for three days. He is shrewd and understands how to exploit a situation. He uses Raina's cloak to prevent her from going out to disclose him. But he is not indecent since he returns the cloak to her when leaving. When working for Petkoff and Sergius, he shows intelligent military sense and hard work. War has erased his softer feelings. He does not show sorrow on hearing of his father's death. He gives in to romance and love with Raina when the chance arises, but leaves her immediately when duty calls.

Q. 67. Write a brief sketch of Raina Petkoff on the basis of your reading the play *Arms and the Man*.

Ans. Raina is a young and beautiful girl who is full of romantic ideas about love and war gathered from the books of Byron and Pushkin. According to her a soldier is a hero always and war is full of glory. She thinks she loves Sergius who has just succeeded in leading a Bulgarian cavalry charge against the Serbians. A soldier does not suffer from physical pain or hunger. Her love for Sergius is the higher love. She adores him. When she takes up his picture she holds it aloft with pride like a priestess but does not kiss it. When Sergius returns to her after the war, she floods him with praises:

Raina: "You have been out in the world, on the field of battle, able to prove yourself there worthy of any woman in the world."

Raina: "And you have never been absent from my thoughts even for a moment."

Her dialogue is obviously artificial and affected, suffused with romantic ideas. She is merely posing, imitating the romantic ideals of books she has read. However, it is difficult to maintain this higher love for very long. She starts flirting with Bluntschli.

At first, Bluntschli's behaviour and ideas prove a rude shock to her romantic ideas. He tells her that a soldier really cares for his own life and even carries chocolates in his pockets. He uses her cloak to stop her from shouting. But gradually she begins to like him for he shows himself a gentleman by returning her cloak. Raina displays courage when Bluntschli intrudes into her room. She is also capable of sympathy and pities the 'chocolate-cream soldier' when he is depressed. She begins to see the logic in his ideas about war and admires his realism.

Bernard Shaw believed that the Life Force in nature forced woman to chase man to find a mate to breed a higher type of human. Here Raina falls in love with Bluntschli and wants to marry him. When she sees Sergius and Louka together she does not suspect them, but once she knows that they are flirting, she breaks off from Sergius and takes Bluntschli as husband.

Q. 68. Describe the character of Sergius Saranoff on the basis of your reading the play *Arms and the Man*.

Ans. Sergius is a tall, handsome, well-built soldier. He too is romantic and has the imagination of 'a mountaineer chieftain'. He is civilized. Again, like Raina, his fiancee, he has picked up romance from Byron and Pushkin. He imagines himself a knight during the cavalry charge he led against the Serbs, and imagines Raina standing at her window watching and inspiring him with her beauty. Raina is a model of perfection to him. He showers her with praises: "Dearest! all my deeds have been yours." "My lady and my saint!" But his romantic idea of higher love receives a blow when he sees Raina flirting with Bluntschli.

Sergius is conceited. He refuses to admit that he blundered on the field of battle by charging at the battery of guns which might have blown his cavalry to bits. "This hand is more used to the sword than to the pen", he says to hide his fault. He falls into the trap of Louka, the maid. He says things like "I never apologize", I am never sorry", "Nothing binds me", all showing his stubborn pride.

He has a few good qualities. When he is charmed by Louka, he refuses to hear anything ill against Raina. "Take care, Louka, I may be worthless enough to betray the higher love; but do not you insult it."

●●●

3 Long Answer Type Questions

Q. 1. Do you think the women's novels in nineteenth-century England have common characteristics which would enable us to constitute women's fiction as a category? Discuss with examples.

Ans. The academic discipline of Women's Writing as a discrete area of literary studies is based on the notion that the experience of women, historically, has been shaped by their gender, and so women writers by definition are a group worthy of separate study: "Their texts emerge from and intervene in conditions usually very different from those which produced most writing by men." It is not a question of the subject matter or political stance of a particular author, but of her gender, *i.e.*, her position as a woman within the literary world. Women's writing, as a discrete area of literary studies and practice, is recognized explicitly by the numbers of dedicated journals, organizations, awards, and conferences which focus mainly or exclusively on texts produced by women.

As far as nineteenth-century women writers are concerned, they were women first, artists second to their contemporaries. A woman novelist, unless she disguised herself with a male pseudonym, had to expect critics to focus on her femininity and rank her with the other women writers of her day, no matter how diverse their subjects or styles. The knowledge that their individual achievement would be subsumed under a relatively unfavorable group stereotype acted as a constant irritant to feminine novelists. George Eliot protested against being compared to Dinah Mulock; Charlotte Brontë tried to delay the publication of Villette so that it would not be reviewed along with Mrs. Gaskell's Ruth. Brontë particularly wanted to prevent the male literary establishment from making women writers into competitors and rivals for the same small space: "It is the nature of writers to be invidious," she wrote to Mrs. Gaskell, but "we shall set them at defiance; they shall not make us foes."

Through the 1850s and 1860s there was a great increase in theoretical and specific criticism of women novelists. Hardly a journal failed to publish an essay on women's literature; hardly a critic failed to express himself upon its innate and potential qualities. This situation, similar to the expanded market for literature by and about women in the late 1960s, suggests that the Victorians were responding to what seemed like a revolutionary, and in many ways a very threatening, phenomenon. As the number of important novels by women increased through the 1850s and 1860s, male journalists were forced to acknowledge that women were excelling in the creation of fiction, not just in England, but also in Europe and America. As it became apparent that Jane Austen and Maria Edgeworth were not aberrations, but the forerunners of female participation in the development of the novel, jokes about dancing dogs no longer seemed an adequate response.

Therefore, women's fiction in nineteenth-century England should not be as a category. The women novelists in this period had dealt with almost every aspect of society. For example, Jane Austen depicts a society which, for all its seeming privileges (pleasant houses, endless hours of leisure), closely monitors behaviour. Her heroines in particular discover in the course of the novel that individual happiness cannot exist separately from our responsibilities to others. Emma Woodhouse's cruel taunting of Miss Bates during the picnic at Box Hill and Mr Knightley's swift reproof are a case in point: "How could you be so insolent in your wit to a woman of her character, age, and situation?—Emma, I had not thought it possible." Emma is mortified: 'The truth of his representation there was no denying. She felt it at her heart.' Austen never suggests that our choices in life include freedom to act independently of wider obligations. If we are fortunate (as Emma is), we have a duty of kindness and protection to those who are not; society, in the form of public opinion or the judgement of other individuals, like Mr Knightley, provides a check on conduct. "[Miss Bates's] situation", argues Mr Knightley to Emma, "should secure your compassion".

Charlotte Brontë was not overtly radical in her social views. On reading an article in the Westminster Review (1851), which argued for women's rights to vote and to work despite the spirit of rebelliousness which flows through Jane Eyre, she writes to the novelist Elizabeth Gaskell that while she approves of many of the writer's arguments she feels they are lacking in 'heart' and tender feelings. While Brontë does not approve of women voting, she does believe they should be allowed to work. In the novel, Jane makes a passionate plea for women to be allowed to use their talents, and not to be confined to the home 'making puddings and knitting stocking, ...playing on the piano and embroidering bags. When Jane Eyre (1847) was published by Charlotte Brontë under the masculine pseudonym Currer Bell, it was received with great acclaim by some critics, and harsh criticism by others. The conservative Lady Eastlake suggested that if the book was by a woman 'she had long forfeited the society of her own sex'. In addition to this lack of femininity, she also diagnosed a spirit of rebellion which she likened to the working class uprisings of the Chartists, with their demands for votes for the working people, and also the political revolutions which were then sweeping across Europe. She challenged 19th-century conceptions of appropriate female behaviour through the creation of a heroine Her sister Emile Bronte depicted a socio-economic England in her famous novel *Wuthering Heights* unlike Charlotte Bronte. The novel opens in 1801, a date Q.D. Leavis believes Brontë chose in order "to fix its happenings at a time when the old rough farming culture, based on a naturally patriarchal family life, was to be challenged, tamed and routed by social and cultural changes; these changes produced Victorian class consciousness and 'unnatural' ideal of gentility." In 1801 the Industrial Revolution was under way in England; when Emily Brontë was writing in 1847, it was a dominant force in English economy and society, and the traditional relationship of social classes was being disrupted by mushroom-new fortunes and an upwardly-aspiring middle class. A new standard for defining a gentleman, money, was challenging the traditional criteria of breeding and family and the more recent criterion of character. This social-economic reality provides the context for socio-economic readings of the novel.

More examples can be given. But, from these examples we can come to a conclusion that, women's fiction in the nineteenth-century cannot be branded as a category, because they had dealt with many topics and problems of the then England and their way of representation was also different.

Q. 2. How does feminist and/or queer theory help to understand gender equations in literary texts? Discuss any one text of your choice identifying specific theories and theorists you may be drawing your inferences from.

Ans. Queer theory is a field of critical theory that emerged in the early 1990s out of the fields of queer studies and women's studies. Queer theory includes both queer readings of texts and the theorisation of 'queerness' itself. Heavily influenced by the work of Lauren Berlant, Leo Bersani, Judith Butler, Lee Edelman, Jack Halberstam, and Eve Kosofsky Sedgwick, queer theory builds both upon feminist challenges to the idea that gender is part of the essential self and upon gay/lesbian studies' close examination of the socially constructed nature of sexual acts and identities.

Queer theory "focuses on mismatches between sex, gender and desire". Queerness has been associated most prominently with bisexual, lesbian and gay subjects, but its analytic framework also includes such topics as cross-dressing, intersex bodies and identities, gender ambiguity and gender-corrective surgery. Queer theory's attempted debunking of stable (and correlated) sexes, genders, and sexualities develops out of the specifically lesbian and gay reworking of the post-structuralist figuring of identity as a constellation of multiple and unstable positions. Queer theory examines the discourses of homosexuality developed in the last century in order to place the "queer" into historical context, deconstructing contemporary arguments both for and against this latest terminology.

Let us discuss about the book "Gender Trouble", by Judith Butler. Arguing that traditional feminism is wrong to look to a natural, 'essential' notion of the female, or indeed of sex or gender, Butler starts by questioning the category 'woman' and continues in this vein with examinations of 'the masculine' and 'the feminine'. Best known however, but also most often misinterpreted, is Butler's concept of gender as a reiterated social performance rather than the expression of a prior reality. She criticizes one of the central assumptions of feminist theory: that there exists an identity and a subject that requires representation in politics and language. For Butler, "women" and "woman" are categories complicated by factors such as class, ethnicity, and sexuality. Moreover, the universality presumed by these terms parallels the assumed universality of the patriarchy, and erases the particularity of oppression in distinct times and places. Butler thus eschews identity politics in favor of a new, coalitional feminism that critiques the basis of identity and gender. She challenges assumptions about the distinction often made between sex and gender, according to which sex is biological while gender is culturally constructed. Butler argues that this false distinction introduces a split into the supposedly unified subject of feminism. Sexed bodies cannot signify without gender, and the apparent existence of sex prior to discourse and cultural imposition is only an effect of the functioning of gender. Sex and gender are both constructed.

Q. 3. Explain Bakhtin's concept of dialogism. How useful is it for understanding the novel as a literary form? Answer with the help of suitable examples.

Ans. The English terms dialogic and dialogism often refer to the concept used by the Russian philosopher Mikhail Bakhtin in his work of literary theory, The Dialogic Imagination. Bakhtin contrasts the dialogic and the "monologic" work of literature. Bakhtin was a thinker interested in the social relations inherent in any form of speech or writing. He contrasts the unitary, single-voiced speech of the monologue, where only one person is speaking, with the idea of dialogue, where two or more voices engage with each other from different points of view. Monologue, or monologia, is associated with the idea of a centralized power system, a single voice speaking the only truth that can exist, without challenge or interplay. Dialogic speech, on the other hand, always involves a multiplicity of speakers and a variety of perspectives; truth becomes something negotiated and debated, rather than something pronounced from on high. Monologic speech seems to come from God or nowhere; it is dissociated from the speaker who originates it, and from the social relations in which that speaker is embedded. Dialogic speech acknowledges sets of social relations between and among speakers, and is thus more descriptive of historical and cultural realities.

Bakhtin uses the concept of dialogism in discussing the distinction between novels and poetry as literary forms. In poetry, Bakhtin argues, words are used monologically, as if they have no connection to social or historical relations; a word has meaning only in reference to language itself. In prose fiction, by contrast, words are used dialogically, as having both etymological meaning and social meaning. The form of the novel, as exemplified in Dostoevsky, encourages dialogic speech, as different characters speak in recognizably different voices, and engage with each other in debating worldviews, rather than affi rming a single worldview. Another aspect of Bakhtin's dialogics appears in his discussions of the "double-voiced" word, a term he uses to describe irony or parody, or words used in quotation marks. A double-voiced word contains two meanings: a literal or monologic meaning, that is, a dictionary definition, and an implied or dialogic meaning, which appears in the social relationship between the two participants in a dialogue. An example is the word "smart." A monologic utterance would come from an authority, like a professor, who would describe a student by saying "she is very smart," which the listener would take at face value. Said between two students who dislike this person, however, "she is very smart" takes on another tone, one of irony or disbelief—an added "yeah, right" that designates a worldview shared by the two speakers, but not by the person referred to. This double-voiced word is similar to the concept of the double-voiced discourse articulated by W. E. B. du Bois in discussing the experience of African Americans who learn to speak two languages: that of the dominant white culture and that of their black subculture. Bakhtin suggests four aspects of the general characteristics of the novel: "the novel should not be 'poetic,' as the word 'poetic' is used in other genres of imaginative literature;" the hero should not be heroic like in an epic; the hero should not be portrayed as unchanging or already completed but instead should be shown as in a state of becoming; "the novel should become for the contemporary world what the epic was for the ancient world".

In his essay, *Epic and Novel: Towards a Methodology for the Study of the Novel* Bakhtin attempts to outline a theory of the novel and its unique properties by comparing it to other literary forms, in particular the epic. Bakhtin sees the novel as capable of achieving much of what other forms cannot, including an ability to engage with contemporary reality, and an ability to re-conceptualize the individual in a complex way that interrogates his subjectivity and offers the possibility of redefining his own image. He also stresses the novel's flexibility: he argues it is a genre with the unique ability to constantly adapt and change, partly because there is no generic canon of the novel as there is for epic or lyric poetry.

While Bakhtin does make reference to proto-novels in antiquity, he dates the rise of the modern novel with the Renaissance and suggests that it developed then precisely because of a new temporal perspective: man had become conscious of the present not only as a continuation of the past, but also as a 'heroic and new beginning'. This allowed the novel, a genre that was concerned with the possibilities of the present, to flourish. The novel, therefore, is 'the only genre born of this new world and in total affinity with it' *i.e.*, the most apt form for literary expression in the modern world.

Q. 4. Examine how deconstructive modes of reading cultural, literary and philosophical texts have transformed the way we read these texts.

Ans. Deconstruction is a poststructuralist theory, based largely but not exclusively on the writings of the Paris-based Jacques Derrida. It is in the first instance a philosophical theory and a theory directed towards the (re)reading of philosophical writings. Its impact on literature is based in part on the fact that deconstruction sees all writing as a complex historical, cultural process rooted in the relations of texts to each other and in the institutions and conventions of writing, in part on the sophistication and intensity of its sense that human knowledge is not as controllable or as cogent as Western thought would have it and that language operates in subtle and often contradictory ways, so that certainty will always elude us.

Deconstructive reading, which is a re-reading in the sense of interpreting afresh in the presence of all pre-existent interpretations, adopts a three-pronged approach to deal with dualities. It first exposes how the oppositions are configured hierarchically. Secondly, it upends the hierarchy provisionally to make the text reverse what it appeared to mean primarily. Finally, it reaffirms the binary opposites within a non-hierarchical correlation of difference. Exhibiting that these conceptual distinctions are non-stable, reversible, and reciprocally dependent, deconstruction celebrates limitless singular interpretations of meaning without proposing any objective reality or truth. Further, deconstruction reads a text to observe where it tends to posit its own centre (a privileged idea/concept) to hold the whole structure of the text together and how it constructs its own system of language to yield meaning, and then looks to see how it contradicts itself and what will happen to the structure if the centre is taken away. Thus, deconstruction is a strategy of reading that looks for places where the structure gets shaken up and where more "play" (Derrida, "Structure" 89) of signifiers occurs. Deconstruction does not unbuild the structure of a text. Rather, it tries its level best to manifest that the text has already unbuilt itself. To unravel the inconsistencies and prevarications inherent in key concept(s)/theme(s)/idea(s), which make a text possible, deconstructionism has to go beyond binarism too. While examining the logicality and rhetoricity of a text, a deconstructionist has to read between the lines to 'trace' the aporias, shifts in argument/tenor, and other orthodoxly overlooked details like footnotes/endnotes, casual metaphors, etymologies, use of slashes/brackets/commas, changes in word-order, repetition of words, solecisms, etc. A deconstructive reading (writing), which is based completely on the subjective opinion of the reader (writer), is a counter-writing which keeps postponing its final version.

Deconstruction also nurtures imagination, ingenuity, creativeness and criticality by employing newer ways of explicating texts/language. It emphasizes that any text, including that which is aware of its self-deconstructive nature as well as that which has been deconstructed (at least once), can be subjected to a deconstructive reading as each such reading remains preliminary and unfinished. In agreement with the spirit of deconstruction, the division between what is within the text and what is beyond the text also can be deconstructed. It will offer the deconstructor the liberty to contextualize the uncertainties of the text with its outside factors such as cultural and linguistic circumstances which propelled its writing, or the personal life of its author, etc. Also, by deconstructing such customary limitations of the method, it will help deconstruction extend its boundaries with each fresh reading.

It is imperative to realize that to deconstruct a text does not imply to tear it apart or leave it meaningless. Rather, the aim is to survey and expand the horizon of its possible logical and rhetorical meanings to understand it more and better and thus provide democratic dimensions to its interpretation.

Finally, deconstructive modes of reading have transformed the way we read the texts because, deconstructive reading paves the way for the disclosure of inherent instability, ambiguities and multiplicities of meaning, and dichotomies within texts. As says Vincent Leitch: "[Deconstruction] aims to decipher the stable truths of a work, employing conventional 'passive' tactics of reading; and it seeks to question and subvert such truths in an active production of enigmatic undecidables." Further, "deconstruction as a mode of interpretation is concerned, it has often been condemned for its incapacity to provide any concluding thesis as regards the drift of a particular work, and accused of having "little philosophical sensitivity," lacking "precision and accuracy" and being "an apocalyptic manner of a conspiracy against all literary values" (Gasch). It has also been criticized for being a self-indulgent intellectual subculture which ignores rational appreciation from the outside. Nevertheless, deconstructionism owing to its interstitial hovering between philosophy and literature has immensely influenced interdisciplines like linguistics, psychology, cultural studies, sociology, and anthropology throughout, maintaining its critical rigor in present times as well.

Q. 5. In what way was dress related to identity in Early Modern England? How are the violations of dress code represented in Elizabethan and Jacobean drama? Discuss with reference to two plays.

Ans. Dress occupies a complex and important position in relation to human experience. Not just utilitarian, dress gives form to a society's ideas about the sacred and secular, about exclusion and inclusion, about age, beauty, sexuality and status. In dressing the Elite, garments held multiple meanings in early modern England. Dress was used to promote health and physical well-being, and to manage and structure, life transitions. It helped individuals create social identities and also to disguise them. Indeed, so culturally powerful was the manipulation of appearances that authorities sought its control. Laws regulated access to the dress styles of the elite, and through less formal strategies, techniques of disguise were kept as the perquisites of the powerful. Dress was not just a form of cultural expression but in turn contributed to societal formation. Clothes shaped the configurations of the body, affected spaces and interactions between people and altered the perceptions of the wearers and viewers. People put on and manipulated their garments, but in turn dress also exercised a reverse influence. Clothes made not just the man and the woman, but also the categories of gender itself. Topics covered include cross-dressing, sumptuary laws, mourning apparel and individual styles.

The Elizabethan Era was a period in English history dominated by the Class structure. People who lived in the Elizabethan era were not allowed to wear whatever they liked. It did not matter how wealthy they were—the fabric, and even the styles of their clothes were dictated by their rank, status or position and these strict rules were enforced by English Law. These laws about clothing in the Elizabethan era were called Sumptuary Laws.

During the late 1500s, Queen Elizabeth-I passed a series of strict laws relating to dress codes. The laws ensured that people across the social spectrum dressed according to their rank and class. At this time, England was importing great quantities of luxury fabrics, and the Queen expressed concern that her subjects were spending too much money on 'unnecessary foreign wares' and 'vain devices'. The laws allowed her to curb extravagant spending, and to define and set the distinctions between the different strata of society. Those found dressed in inappropriate clothing could be fined. This document specifies the fabrics and types of clothing that each social rank was permitted to wear, such as specific types of embroidered silks, 'tinseled' satins, furs or 'purpures'—a type of purple or crimson robe.

In Elizabethan and Jacobean time, clothes reflected a person's status in society—there were laws controlling what you could wear. As plays had kings, queens and wealthy people in them, the actors' costumes reflected their characters social status. Costumes were mainly the modern dress of the time. So for less important roles, actors might wear their own clothes. However, for a play set in ancient Greece or Rome, the company might try for an 'ancient' look for the important characters by giving the main characters to gas over their normal clothes. The company reused costumes if they could—changing a cloak, or putting on some expensive lace. Sometimes they had to have a new costume made. In Shakespeare's time all actors were male. Men and boys played all the female parts. As with the men, women's costumes were usually ordinary clothes that reflected the social status of the character the actor was playing. They also wore wigs which, by their colour and styles, showed the age and status of their character. Costumes themselves were expensive, so usually players wore contemporary clothing regardless of the time period of the play. The most expensive pieces were given to higher class characters because costuming was used to identify social status on stage. The fabrics within a playhouse would indicate the wealth of the company itself. The fabrics used the most were: velvet, satin, silk, cloth-of-gold, lace, and ermine. For less significant characters; actors would use their own clothes. Actors also left clothes in their will for following actors to use. Masters would also leave clothes for servants in their will, but servants weren't allowed to wear fancy clothing, instead, they sold the clothes back to theatre companies. In the Elizabethan era, there was a law stating that certain classes could only wear clothing fitting of their status in society. There was a discrimination of status within the classes. Higher classes flaunted their wealth and power through the appearance of clothing, however, actors were the only exception. If actors belonged to a licensed acting company, they were allowed to dress above their standing in society for specific roles in a production.

Q. 6. "Even in the West color is a whole lot more than hue. It is the combustible mix of attraction and repulsion towards colour that owes more than a little to the Western experience of colonization as colored otherness." Respond critically with examples from literary texts.

Ans. This has been taken from the book "What Color is the Sacred" written by Michael Taussig. He wrote these words in order to discuss the face of world history. He cited the example of the German playwright Goethe. In his book on colour, Goethe wrote, "Men in a state of nature, uncivilized nations and children, have a great fondness for colours in their utmost brightness." What Goethe and through him Michael Taussig wanted to tell us that, people have a fondness for brightness. They do not like any fade colour which in no way appealing from the point of view of brightness. We can cite examples from the Western experience as stated in Taussig's aforesaid book. According to Taussig fondness of and attraction towards deep colour could be applied to southern Europeans, especially the women with their bright-colored bodices and ribbons. Again the author turned to Goethe and wrote that Goethe recalled a German mercenary returned from America who had painted his face with vivid colors in the manner of the Indians, the effect of which was not disagreeable: On the other hand, in northern Europe at the time in which Goethe wrote in the early nineteenth century, people of refinement had a disinclination to colors, women wearing white, the men, black. And not only in dress. When it came to what he called "pathological colours"; Goethe wrote that people of refinement avoid vivid colors in the objects around them and seem inclined to banish vivid colors from their presence altogether. It is as if there are two presences glowering at each other, shifting uncomfortably from one foot to the other. It is as much a body thing, a presence thing, as conscious intellection. One "presence" is people of refinement. The other is vivid colour. Colour attracts not only kids, primitives and Southern women, but attracts war also. If brightly colored uniforms have given way to today's camouflage, we will to wonder whether camouflage is not, in its own right, a play in vivid colour as well as a fashion statement for the warring class. The generals look good in camouflage, too, even though they never get close to anything more dangerous than Fox news. But the medals come colored. French soldiers hung on the longest. Beginning his "storm of steel" in 1915 near the village of Orainville in Champagne, the German soldier Ernst Junger saw them dead and red in the sugar-beet fields lit by moonlight. They wore bright red pants well into the First World War, when it was suggested that their appalling losses might be reduced if they decolored, a fate that was, according to Goethe, Europe's lot for many a year, "women wearing white, the men, black": Yet Goethe's primitives are engraved in the European image of what warriors should be.

To equate calor with color as did Isidore of Seville detaches us from a purely visual approach to vision and makes color the cutting edge of such a shift. Color vision becomes less a retinal and more a total bodily activity to the fairytale extent that in looking at something, we may even pass into the image. Three of my favorite authors relish this power of color: Walter Benjamin, William Burroughs, and Marcel Proust. They see color as something alive, like an animal, and all three expend considerable verbal talent in getting this across: Benjamin concentrating on the child's view of color and colored illustrations in early children's books; Burroughs on drugs, sex, and games with language; Proust on the fullness of involuntary memory transporting one's body to the event by chance recalled. All of which is to say color comes across here as more a presence than a sign, more a force than a code, and more as color, which is why, so I believe, John Ruskin declared in his book Modern Painters that "colour is the most sacred element of all visible things"? This or something like it can be experienced acutely in many non-Western societies, as when an anthropologist casually spoke of indigenous Australians as "color mad" (a compliment), and Ticio Escobar writes of the Chamacoco Indians of Paraguay in the 1980s as obsessed with colors, dyeing, as he puts it, the deepest conceptions of their culture. Here colors illuminate the backdrop of myths and set the body alight during ceremonies. Colors "force the object to release hidden meanings, meanings that are neither complete nor lasting, to be sure, but that can gesture, ever so obliquely, to truths that remain otherwise concealed."

Goethe did not go far enough. Not nearly as far as the German soldier who painted his face in the manner of the North American Indians, For while who it may appear that people of refinement, unlike "man in a state of nature" are averse to vivid color the situation both in Goethe's time and in our own seems averse to me even stranger; that this distaste for vivid color is actually an unstable mix of attraction and repulsion, which the face-painted soldier got right. When Walter Benjamin, Marcel Proust, and William Burroughs bring out the fact that even in the West color is a whole lot more than hue, that color is not secondary to form, that it is not an overlay draped like a skin over a shape—they are not saying that "man in a state of nature" has gotten this right and we in the West are nonsensuous creatures who are frightened of passions and the body. To the contrary, it is the combustible mix of attraction and repulsion towards color that brings out its sacred qualities which, as Goethe's face-painted mercenary suggests, owe more than a little to the Western experience of colonization as colored otherness.

Q. 7. Write an essay on the significance of time and memory, choosing two modernist texts (novels, poems or plays).

Ans. ***Significance of Time and Memory***

Time is a theme in literature; all poems, plays and prose writings are set in a time. A work of literature can be thought of as involving four different and potentially quite separate time frames: author time (when the work was originally written or published); narrator time (when the narrator in a work of fiction supposedly narrates the story); plot time (when the action depicted actually takes place); and reader or audience time (when a reader reads the work or sees it performed). These may all be relatively close together, but they may not be—consider Walter Scott's novel *Rob Roy*, for example: although we may read it in the early 21st Century, it was written and published in 1817, it deals with plot events around a century earlier (1715), and it is narrated by an old man looking back some 50 years or so at his youth—four different time frames over a three hundred year period. Let us cite the example of Virginia Woolf's *Mrs Dalloway* as an example of significance of time. Her original title, *The Hours*, indicates the importance of time as one of the novel's themes. By looking at Woolf's writing style, critiquing her use of clocks, and analyzing Clarissa's thoughts, the reader finds a philosophical message about time, powerfully expressed.

The lyrical, flowing pattern of Woolf's writing easily slides in and out of different characters' thoughts. Her ability to show the random yet patterned working of our minds gives us a realistic sense of mental time. Woolf's sentences quickly cross the boundaries of the past, present, and future. She saw the writer's task as "being able to go beyond the 'formal railway line of sentences' and to show how people feel or think or dream all over the place". She wanted to express a point of view, not a plot. Her stream-of-consciousness writing allows us insight into a variety of characters. For example, within the first moments that we meet Clarissa, we rapidly travel between her present, her past, and her thoughts about the future. In the process, we understand pieces of her life which create the woman we come to know in a single day. We see the lifetime culmination of beautiful moments and painful moments embodied in Woolf's characters.

Woolf's style impresses upon the reader the time which exists in our minds. Mental time does not progress steadily forward, like the clock time we follow. This point is illustrated by Clarissa's arrival at the flower shop in the morning; her senses are effortlessly taken to evening time as she thinks,

And it was the moment between six and seven when every flower-roses, carnations, irises, lilac-glows; white, violet, red, deep orange; every flower seems to burn by itself, softly, purely in the misty beds; and how she loved the grey-white moths spinning in and out, over the cherry pie, over the evening primroses!

This passage flows easily from her seeing the flowers in the present to being drawn back to memories and sensations from her past. If Woolf wrote in any other way, her layered message about time would not be as successfully or beautifully expressed. Critic Bernard Blackstone wrote that "*Mrs. Dalloway* is an experiment with time. It is a mingling of present experience and memory". Essentially, Woolf's style adds emphasis to her idea of time as a constant flow-time that is the present but also the past; linear but sporadic; eternal but vanishing.

Big Ben and St. Margaret's represent different rates of time: one marching straight ahead without looking back, the other gently making its presence known. Woolf's use of Big Ben serves two purposes. First, its concise tolling indicates the time that we lose each day. It shows the constant forward movement of the hours. Second, the fame of Big Ben suggests that the mark we leave on the world be something grand, something renowned. The bell of Big Ben agitates Clarissa: "The sound of Big Ben flooded Clarissa's drawing-room where she sat, ever so annoyed, at her writing table; worried; annoyed". The clock tells her she is running out of time and reminds her of her middle-age. Its toll reminds her that she has done nothing civilization would consider impressive. She feels "a suspense before Big Ben strikes. There! Out it boomed. First a warning, musical; then the hour, irrevocable. The leaden circles dissolved in the air". Woolf's description of the bell as a "warning" and the hour as "irrevocable" (used more than once) clearly states a negative idea of Big Ben time. The strike of the clock cautions that another hour has passed-time that we will never have to live again.

While Big Ben reminds Clarissa of her mortality, St. Margaret's serves another purpose. With St. Margaret's, Woolf presents a time that appeals to the human spirit. It chimes in a little late, gliding "into the recesses of the heart and buries itself, to be, with a tremor of delight, at rest". Although not a famous bell tower, St. Margaret's attracts the attention of those who hear it. Therefore, it contradicts the message of Big Ben-to leave behind something famous to be remembered by when we die. Instead, St. Margaret's suggests that we not be overly consumed with losing time and that we be aware of it in our own way. In comparison with Big Ben, St. Margaret's suggests that time meanders and passes subtly. The tower's bell represents an approach to life that accepts the moment. It makes the listener aware of time to appreciate it, not to fear it.

In short, Woolf suggests that time exists in different forms. It exists in the external world, but also—and perhaps more importantly—in our internal world. Her description of the loud and rushing civilization suggests that we push ahead in the name of progress, without fully appreciating the moment. Through the character of Clarissa, Woolf challenges the usual definition of success. Perhaps we need not leave some magnificent gift behind in the form of a building or a concrete art piece. Instead, maybe it is how we live our lives and our appreciation for the present that are truly more powerful and eternal. The small gifts we offer others, like bringing people together through a party, can touch people differently than a monument.

Secondly, time and memory is found in TS Eliot's *The Waste Land* also. Eliot, as an inter-war interpreter or experimenter, deals with time in the poem "The Waste Land" as the most significant and instructive thing of the universe and of the human being. Eliot overtly contrasts the glories of the past with the sordidness of the present. He experiments with both the idea of human time and the stream of consciousness.

The time structure of the poem, however, may well be the most significant key to its understanding. The intricate and complex movement within time is achieved by the constant use of citation, allusions, reference and adaptation. The opening line of the poem places the poem in time; 'April is the cruelest month'; here, April is the now of the poem.

In the epigraph, the speaker says "with my own eyes", indicating that he is physically present at the event. But he says that he saw 'Sibyl'; this describes an event of the past. Time shifts in a number of directions; The reader's present to Eliot's present (reader's past) Eliot's present to Petronius's present (Eliot's past) Petronius's present to the Sibyl's present (Petronius's past).

Every human being knows that a given period of cloak-time may appear longer or shorter depending upon the circumstances. A period spent pleasurably is likely to seem to fly, while a period spent painfully is likely to seem endless. In the physical world, any given event occupies a measurable quantity of clock-time, but in the world of mind, time is not measurable; rather, it is relative to events. Experiments with the reproduction of thought patterns necessitate experiments with duration in the human rather than in the cloak sense.

As far as memory is concerned in *The Waste Land*, the opening lines strangely tell us that spring is an awful time of year. "April is the cruellest month, breeding Lilacs out of the dead land, mixing Memory and desire, stirring Dull roots with spring rain." We might not like how wet the ground is, but isn't spring the traditional time of love and rebirth? Not so much for Eliot, because for him, all the spring rain does is stir "dull roots." These dull roots are connected to human memory and desire, which seem to be so dead in this opening scene that nothing will bring them to life. In this passage, Eliot connects memory to a feeling of longing that can never be fulfilled, just as the desire to return to the past can never be fulfilled. This would suggest that memory can only connect us to a past that is gone forever, so it only has the power to make us feel numb.

We have to stare at these lines for a long time before they start making any sense at all, but after a while, you start to realize that they are spoken by the woman named Marie who has gotten old, and is no longer the sled lovin' child she was in her younger days. In these lines, we're told about present-day Marie, who only finds adventure by reading books in the night. Her tendency to travel south in the winter is important, too, since it contrasts with the exciting winters she once spent in the snow-covered mountains. Eliot might open the poem with this passage about Marie to show us that society as a whole is too removed from its innocent and playful days. Now, people might want to be too safe, and simply read books about the world instead of experiencing it.

Q. 8. Explain the differences in artistic form between literary narratives and visual texts such as painting, sculpture and film.

Ans. Although it is commonplace to speak of the spatial arts, painting and sculpture, as narrative arts—a way of speaking which suggests the intimate relations between image and text—pictorial artists obviously do not narrate stories in the same way that writers do. In a certain sense, they do not narrate at all. To speak of an artist as a teller of stories is a figure of speech, since painters and sculptors do not "tell," they "show." As some critics have observed, pictorial artists imply a narrative by referring to what has been said in words, but surely such allusions are not the same thing as a narrative in words.

We can trace the comparison of painting and literature back to classical antiquity, to Homer who implicitly compares his own account of the shield of Achilles to the images rendered on that great work by Hephaistos. The idea of such similitude has been sustained over a period of nearly three millennia by the notion of painting as "mute poetry" or "visible speech," and it is still very much alive. We must always remember, however, that the comparison of literature and painting is imperfect, since it is based on an analogy and is not an identity.

The modern idea of the pictorial artist as storyteller nonetheless has important roots in Leon Battista Alberti's treatise, On Painting of 1435, in which the author, himself an artist and writer both, writes famously about painting as a historia. The word historia, which means a "story," suggests something written. When Alberti says that a historia is a composition, he implicitly compares art to literature, since the word "composition" was traditionally used to describe literature. He further implicitly compares painting and literature when he says that in painting a historia the painter should seek the advice of poets and orators. Nevertheless, speaking of a historia as the representation of various bodies and things—human beings, animals, and other subjects or objects—he refers primarily to an image composed in space. He is not expressly concerned here with the passage of time, which is the province of literature. Of course to examine the spatial composition of a pictorial image takes time, but we are not talking here about the time it takes to read a story, but about the time that passes within the story itself.

In Renaissance art, pictorial composition, the arrangement of figures in space, often conflicts sharply with an image's implicit associations with the temporal character of a literary narrative. This is so because the episodes of the story that a painter or sculptor presents are not always placed in an obviously identifiable sequence within the space defined by the painter. The figures of a single episode or series of episodes in a "continuous narrative" so-called are dispersed through space, above all, as a way of making the spatial composition harmonious and not necessarily or primarily as a means of making the allusion to a narrative obvious.

Two hundred years after Alberti wrote about painting as a historia, Gotthold Ephraim Lessing underscored the fundamental difference between art, which is spatial, and literature, which is temporal, by emphasizing the intrinsic limits of both art forms. In his classic work, *Laocoön*, Lessing objected to a spatial art that aspires to suggest the passage of time. I do not wish to take up here Lessing's argument against spatial art that aspires to be temporal. I want, instead, to suggest that any spatial art that calls to mind a story unfolding in time must take license in some degree with the temporal narrative to which it refers, since the pictorial artist's principal concern is with the disposition of figures across the picture plane or within its spatial illusion. It is important to keep in mind those cases where the chronological narrative is at odds with the pictorial composition, because these instances remind us of fundamental differences between literature and art that we can too easily forget or ignore.

In order to underscore the basic distinction between a pictorial image and a text, let us turn our attention to the canonical Renaissance historia of Jacob and Esau, which Ghiberti made for the *Gates of Paradise* at the very moment when Alberti wrote about painting as historia. This scene is widely appreciated as a tour de force of Renaissance perspective, which is an ideal vehicle for rendering the subject, since it provides a space, indeed a stage upon which the artist can arrange his figures or actors. The space in which the artist distributes his figures is the place where he suggests the relations of his image to a story. The Jacob and Esau panel is especially fascinating because its historia or "story" is not always fully obvious in the way of many so-called "continuous narratives," where one can easily recognize the suggestion of a narrative through time. Whereas Ghiberti's pictorial composition of figures and architecture is beautifully and harmoniously conceived, the implicit temporal sequence of the story to which he alludes is radically interrupted or disrupted by pictorial considerations both planar and spatial. In the literature inspired by Ghiberti's image there is indeed a tension between the appreciation of the panel's harmonious composition and the full understanding of the narrative to which the scene alludes.

Q. 9. Discuss the representation of social reality in an Indian novel of your choice from the nineteenth century or the first half of the twentieth century, focusing on gender, class or caste relations in the novel.

Ans. Literature has thousands of threads which can weave the beautiful piece of art. Each thread has its own importance in the creative work. In the same way, there are different narrative techniques for the narration of literature. Among the narrative techniques, Realism, in literature, is an approach that attempts to describe life without idealization or romantic subjectivity.

Realism is a style of writing that gives the impression of recording or 'reflecting' faithfully an actual way of life. The term refers, sometimes confusingly, both to a literary method based on detailed accuracy of 79 description and to a more general attitude that rejects idealization, escapism, and other extravagant qualities of romance in favor of recognizing soberly the actual problems of life. Modern criticism frequently insists that realism is not a direct or simple reproduction of reality (a 'slice of life') but a system of conventions producing a lifelike illusion of some 'real' world outside the text, by processes of selection, exclusion, description, and manners of addressing the reader. In its methods and attitudes, realism may be found as an element in many kinds of writing prior to the century ago.

Realism in literature is the theory or practice of fidelity to nature or to real life and to accurate representation without idealization of everyday life. The Indian novels dealing with social realism were ushered in by famous novelists like Munshi Prem Chand in Hindi and Sarat Chandra Chattopadhyay in Bengali during the 1920s. The direct involvement in values and experience in the Indian context now became apparent. The problems of social life of the common people soon became amalgamated with burning public issues of the day, particularly by the Indian Freedom Struggle, which provided rich and ready material for the writers. The purely social reform novels were inflamed by politics, since any desire to improve the lot of the people was bound to be linked with political independence. If the nineteenth century Indian novels are taken for study, it is seen that the Indian social situation, so very different from the western, was often moulded and manipulated to meet the requirements of the new western literary mode. The realistic novel could come into existence because the tension between the individual and the society had attained a certain intensity. If this tension had not existed or had not been exploited, narrative fiction may have continued to retain qualities associated with the epic or romance. If the social transformation of the nineteenth century had not set in motion certain dialectical forces among the English educated class, the novel in its realistic form might not have taken root in India. So it can be said that social and fictional realism had a close affinity in the nineteenth century in India and continued to do so. *Anandamath*

(Bengali-1882), *Indulekha* (Malyalam-1888), *Lakshyant Kon Gheto* (Marathi-1890), *Umrao Jaan Ada* (Urdu-1899) are examples of such novels. Around the 1930s, the Indian English novel acquired a distinctive shape and character when it started voicing the aspirations of the people against colonial oppression and awakening them to the need of putting their society on the path of freedom, hope and aspiration. This can be said about Mulk Raj Anand whose novels embody a strong sense of consciousness about the evils of social injustice, particularly exploitation, caste divisions, caste wars etc. In short, the Indian social novels subject the social system to a thorough scrutiny. Even today, these novels continue to be relevant for their, engaging cultural and social debates. A discussion about the social and political aspects of the Indian English novel is incomplete without talking about the Indian Freedom Movement. The Freedom Movement made a sporadic start from around the later part of the nineteenth century after the First War of Indian Independence (1857) and gained great impetus during the 1920s and 1930s until the achievement of independence in 1947. The freedom struggle provided rich and ready material for the writers, particularly the Indian poets and novelists in the regional languages, and Indian English writers were no exception to the rule. The Indian Freedom Movement contributed greatly to the mass social emancipation of the Indian people.

The creative writers of Indian English have made use of the country's freedom struggle and the Partition as the background of their novels. In many of these novels, Gandhi figures prominently as also his ideology and philosophy. As for example, M.R. Anand, Raja Rao and R.K.Narayan, who published their first works during the 1930s were strongly influenced by Gandhi. In the immediate post-independence era when there was a great outpouring of fiction, the notable works to be influenced by Gandhi—the man and his principles were Bhabani Bhattacharyya's *So Many Hungers* (1947), K.A. Abbas's *Inquitab* (1955), K. Markandaya's *Some Inner Fury* (1957) R.K. Narayan's *Waiting for the Mahatma* (1958), etc.

Society and life in India is an interesting conglomeration of tradition and change. As a critic says, "Tradition in India is wrapped up in the crannies of nature, in the rituals and religion, in the collective; simple living of the villagers, in the emotional integration of large families." However, with the pace and march of modern life, change has become an inevitable part of Indian life. The orbit of fiction will become narrow, even stifling, if it is concerned with only a single, isolated phenomenon. In Bhabani Bhattacharyya's *Music for Mohini*, Jayadev, the quiet scholar and Mohini, the young city-bred wife, worked as forces of progress which were resisted initially by the mother who is finally reconciled with the changing times.

Indian society has always been a congregated one; the atomisation of the west is still foreign. Thus even individual dramas tend to have a broad social content, and one life reflects another. One sees this in the tension between minority groups and those who still seek to uphold monolithic class barriers. This can also be seen in the conflicts between the new urbanized class and their village kinsmen, between the masses and those in public office, between students and teachers, and most strikingly between the young and the middle aged (and often bewildered parents). These conflicts are re-enacted in a million forms in modern India.

Q. 10. What is Cultural Studies? How has it affected our conceptions of literary value?

Ans. Cultural studies is an innovative interdisciplinary field of research and teaching that investigates the ways in which "culture" creates and transforms individual experiences, everyday life, social relations and power. Research and teaching in the field explores the relations between culture understood as human expressive and symbolic activities, and cultures understood as distinctive ways of life. Combining the strengths of the social sciences and the humanities, cultural studies draws on methods and theories from literary studies, sociology, communications studies, history, cultural anthropology, and economics. By working across the boundaries among these fields, cultural studies addresses new questions and problems of today's world. Rather than seeking answers that will hold for all time, cultural studies develops flexible tools that adapt to this rapidly changing world.

Arising from the social turmoil of the 1960s, Cultural Studies is an academic discipline which combines political economy, communication, sociology, social theory, literary theory, media theory, film studies, cultural anthropology, philosophy, art history/ criticism etc. to study cultural phenomena in various societies. Cultural Studies researches often focus on how a particular phenomenon relates matters of ideology, nationality, ethnicity, social class and gender.

Since culture is now considered as the source of art and literature, cultural criticism has gained ground, and therefore, Raymond Williams' term "cultural materialism", Stephen Greenblatt's "cultural poetics" and Bakhtin's term "cultural prosaic", have become significant in the field of Cultural Studies and cultural criticism.

The works of Stuart Hall and Richard Hoggart with the Birmingham Centre, later expanded through the writings of David Morley, Tony Bennett and others. Cultural Studies is interested in the process by which power relations organize cultural artefacts (food habits, music, cinema, sport events etc.). It looks at popular culture and everyday life, which had hitherto been dismissed as "inferior" and unworthy of academic study. Cultural Studies' approaches: (1) transcend the confines of a particular discipline such as literary criticism or history (2) are politically engaged (3) reject the distinction between "high" and "low" art or "elite" and "popular" culture (4) analyse not only the cultural works but also the means of production.

In Cultural Studies, representation is a key concept and denotes a language in which all objects and relationships get defined, a language related to issues of class, power and ideology, and situated within the context of "discourse". The cultural practice of giving dolls to girls can be read within the patriarchal discourse of femininity that girls are weaker and delicate and need to be given soft things, and that grooming, care etc. are feminine duties which dolls will help them learn. This discourse of femininity is itself related to the discourse of masculinity and the larger context of power relations in culture. Identity, for Culture Studies, is constituted through experience, which involves representation—the consumption of signs, the making of meaning from signs and the knowledge of meaning.

Cultural Studies views everyday life as fragmented, multiple, where meanings are hybridized and contested; *i.e.*, identities that were more or less homogeneous in terms of ethnicities and patterns of consumption, are now completely hybrid, especially in the metropolis. With the globalization of urban spaces, local cultures are linked to global economies, markets and needs, and hence any study of contemporary culture has to examine the role of a non-local market/ money which requires a postcolonial awareness of the exploitative relationship between the First World and the Third World even today.

Q. 11. Choose at least two prominent Indian texts that you consider a part of 'World Literature'. Explain the reasons for your choices as well as what you mean by 'World Literature'.

Ans. World literature is sometimes used to refer to the sum total of the world's national literatures, but usually it refers to the circulation of works into the wider world beyond their country of origin. Often used in the past primarily for masterpieces of Western European literature, world literature today is increasingly seen in global context. Readers today have access to an unprecedented range of works from around the world in excellent translations, and since the mid-1990s a lively debate has grown up concerning both the aesthetic and the political values and limitations of an emphasis on global processes over national traditions.

The two prominent texts considered a part of world literature are (*i*) *The Glass Palace* by Amitav Ghosh and (*ii*) *God of Small Things* by Arundhati Roy.

Q. 12. How does the concept of race feature in sixteenth and seventeenth century England? Discuss the role of race in a play of your choice belonging to the period.

Ans. The first clear evidence of racism occurred at the end of the 16th century, with the start of the slave trade from Africa to Britain and America CLR James in Modern Politics wrote "the conception of dividing people by race begins with its slave trade. Thus this (the slave trade) was so shocking, so opposed to all the conceptions of society which religious and philosophers had, the only justification by which humanity could face it was to divide people into races and decide that Africans were an inferior race". What he means is that when the slave trade began, people started dividing others into groups and deciding that the Africans were an inferior race and that they were below all other groups of people. Racism was made as an attempt to justify the inhuman treatment of black people in that time. By the end of the 17th century, racism became common among the people as the justification for the most degrading form of slavery. As the slave trade declined, so did the mistreatment of the black people. In the 1840's, Racism took on another form, and was for the justification of the empire taking over. Concepts such as the "white man's burden" became well known in England and Britain. As time went on, racism became the ideological justification for capitalism's expansion into conquering countries, taking their wealth and exploiting their natives. Misdemeanors Capital Offenses Wandering in a drunken state—wear a barrel publicly like a shirt Gossiping, speaking too freely would put a cage like contraption on the offenders head. A metal strip called the "brank" rested on the tongue and was covered with spikes. Any movement caused severe injuries to the tongue. A public whipping for anyone who stole less then 12 pence Murder, Manslaughter, Rape, Arson or Witchcraft were a mandatory death sentence—Commoners were hung and noblemen beheaded High Treason was dealt with by a hanging, then they were taken down before dead, dragged face first through the streets by horses tail and then cut into four pieces and displayed publicly. The penalty for cheating, especially when an African American was involved was severe. In your face! Racism in 16th century was during the slave trade. Moors were considered barbarians, and were treated as such. Moors were accused for crimes and blamed for society's problems. In the 17th Century slave trades were coming to an end. Many black people were demanding their rights for equality. Queen Elizabeth granted the Moors "full diplomatic recognition" out of gratitude for their help in conquering Spain, in 6101 she deported them, citing concerns about their irregular behaviour and a fear that allowing then to stay in England would lead to overpopulation. The book "To Kill A Mockingbird" is a great example of the 17th century. Black people were blamed for crimes they did not commit if they were up against a white person. Free women married to

African American bond labor between 1664 and 1692 were bound to serve their husband.

However, playwrights like William Shakespeare paid respect to the black people and did not support racism. Shakespeare's presentation of the noble, dignified Othello as the hero of a tragedy must have been startling to Elizabethan audiences. "Othello is a man of action whose achievement was immediately obvious to an Elizabethan audience, in spite of his exotic colour and background, because of his position as the commanding general for the greatest commercial power of the preceding century" studied Gerald Eades Bentley. Several characters in the play, especially Iago, are racially prejudiced. Iago's racism is the source of his hatred of Othello.

Q. 13. Discuss the characteristics of Epistolary Novel using textual examples.

Ans. An epistolary novel is a novel written as a series of documents. The usual form is letters, although diary entries, newspaper clippings and other documents are sometimes used. Recently, electronic "documents" such as recordings and radio, blogs, and e-mails have also come into use. The word epistolary is derived from Latin from the Greek word *epistole*, meaning a letter. The epistolary form can add greater realism to a story, because it mimics the workings of real life. It is thus able to demonstrate differing points of view without recourse to the device of an omniscient narrator. The founder of the epistolary novel in English is said by many to be James Howell (1594-1666) with "Familiar Letters" (1645-50), who writes of prison, foreign adventure, and the love of women.

The first novel to expose the complex play that the genre allows was Aphra Behn's *Love-Letters Between a Nobleman and His Sister*, which appeared in three volumes in 1684, 1685, and 1687. The first truly epistolary novel, the Spanish "Prison of Love" (Cárcel de amor) (c.1485) by Diego de San Pedro, belongs to a tradition of novels in which a large number of inserted letters already dominated the narrative. Other well-known examples of early epistolary novels are closely related to the tradition of letter-books and miscellanies of letters. The epistolary novel as a genre became popular in the 18th century in the works of such authors as Samuel Richardson, with his immensely successful novels *Pamela* (1740) and *Clarissa* (1749).

Q. 14. Discuss the characteristics of Ode using textual examples.

Ans. An ode is a type of lyrical stanza. It is an elaborately structured poem praising or glorifying an event or individual, describing nature intellectually as well as emotionally. A classic ode is structured in three major parts: the strophe, the antistrophe, and the epode. Different forms such as the homostrophic ode and the irregular ode also exist.

There are three typical forms of odes: the Pindaric, Horatian, and irregular. Pindaric odes follow the form and style of Pindar. Horatian odes follow conventions of Horace; the odes of Horace deliberately imitated the Greek lyricists such as Alcaeus and Anacreon. Irregular odes use rhyme, but not the three-part form of the Pindaric ode, nor the two- or four-line stanza of the Horatian ode. The ode is a lyric poem. It conveys exalted and inspired emotions. It is a lyric in an elaborate form, expressed in a language that is imaginative, dignified and sincere. Like the lyric, it is of Greek origin. An English ode is a lyrical stanza in praise of, or dedicated to someone or something that captures the poet's interest or serves as an inspiration for the ode. The lyrics can be on various themes. The earliest odes in the English language, using the word in its strict form, were the *Epithalamium and Prothalamium* of Edmund Spenser. Perhaps the greatest odes of the 19th century, however, were Keats's Five Great Odes of 1819, which included "Ode to a Nightingale", "Ode on Melancholy", "Ode on a Grecian Urn", "Ode to Psyche", and "To Autumn". After Keats, there have been comparatively few major odes in English. One major exception is the fourth verse of the poem *For the Fallen* by Laurence Binyon, which is often known as *The Ode to the Fallen*, or simply as *The Ode*.

Q. 15. Discuss the characteristics of Sentimental Comedy using textual examples.

Ans. Sentimental comedy is an 18th-century dramatic genre which sprang up as a reaction to the immoral tone of English Restoration plays. In Sentimental comedies middle-class protagonists triumphantly overcome a series of moral trials. These plays aimed to produce tears rather than laughter and reflected contemporary philosophical conceptions of humans as inherently good but capable of being led astray by bad example. By appealing to his noble sentiments, a man could be reformed and set back on the path of virtue. While the plays contained characters whose natures seemed overly virtuous and whose problems were too easily resolved, they were accepted by audiences as truthful representations of the human predicament.

The characters in sentimental comedy are either strictly good or bad. Heroes have no faults or bad habits, villains are thoroughly evil or morally degraded. The authors' purpose was to show the audience the innate goodness of people and that through morality people who have been led astray can find the path of righteousness. The playwrights of this genre aimed to bring the audience to tears, not laughter, as the name sentimental comedy might suggest. They believed that noisy laughter inhibited the silent sympathy and thought of the audience. The best known work of this genre is Sir Richard Steele's *The Conscious Lovers* (1722), in which the penniless heroine Indiana faces various tests until the discovery that she is an heiress, leads to the necessary happy ending. The first sentimental comedy, *Love's Last Shift* was written by Colley Cibber, an actor-manager, writer, and poet laureate, in order to give himself a role. The play did establish him as both an actor and a playwright, and though some of his 25 plays were praised, his political adaptations of well-known works met with much criticism.

Q. 16. Evaluate the contribution of Dalit studies to literary studies.

Ans. Dalit is a Sanskrit word which means "oppressed" and "downtrodden." It was appropriated in the 1970s by "untouchable" writers and activists to describe their community, both in the present and in historical contexts. Starting with the Dalit Panther movement, led by writers in the 1970s, the term "Dalit" acquired a radical new meaning of self-identification that signified a new oppositional consciousness. Today it is a widely used term in the Indian public sphere, especially in academic and literary fields.

Dalits constitute nearly 17 per cent of India's population—210 million people as per the 2011 census. They are considered untouchable by orthodox Hindus and Hindu theology because of their association in rural areas with impure occupations such as leather work, sanitary work, removing dead animals, and midwifery.

Dalit studies is a new field of research in India which looks at the problem of marginalised groups, namely Dalits, tribals, religious minorities, women from excluded groups, denotified tribes, physically challenged and similar groups in economic, social and political spheres. Dalit studies scholars also undertake research on the nature and forms of discrimination and social exclusion faced by marginalised groups.

The major objective of Dalit studies is to offer new perspectives for the study of India. First, to foreground dignity and humiliation as key ethical categories that have shaped political struggles and ideological agendas in India. Second, Dalit studies historicizes the persistence of caste inequality and discrimination that have acquired new forms in a modern and democratic India. Given these objectives, a key aim of Dalit studies is to recover histories of struggles for human dignity and caste discrimination by highlighting Dalit intellectual and political activism.

For a long time, Dalit Studies would have only meant discussing the 'problems' of the Dalit communities and 'helping' them-more in the spirit of a remedial program than social science, whereas the real challenges of Dalit Studies are generating new material, finding new ways of teaching and consistently fighting the lack of recognition of these alternate ways. Now that it has become a standard practice to name anything raising voice against the Brahminical knowledge and academic practice as 'anti-national', Dalit Studies is also becoming a platform to fight the criminalization of its exponents as well as rest of the activists who work within the anti-caste movements. Of course, this is not something that can be accomplished without the presence of the Dalit scholars themselves. Otherwise, the field would end up replicating the upper caste notion of 'uplifting the downtrodden' an example of which might be found in the Gandhian practice of coining the Bangis (a caste group that primarily worked as scavengers) as 'Harijans', eternally identifying Dalits as scavengers, devaluating other prominent Dalit castes and devaluating the complex theory of discrimination in general, thus creating an oversimplified "caricature" of the whole issue. Since the nation never recognized social movements based on caste discrimination such as 'Self-Respect movement', entering temples, claiming space, untouchability, etc. as part of the national agenda, it inevitably comes down to the 'anti-nationals' to redefine certain social norms—both academically and in everyday life.

One of the first Dalit writers was Madara Chennaiah, an 11th-century cobbler-saint who lived during the reign of Western Chalukyas and who is also regarded by some scholars as the "father of Vachana poetry". Another poet who finds mention is Dohara Kakkaiah, a Dalit by birth, whose six confessional poems survive. In 1958, the term "Dalit literature" was used at the first conference of Maharashtra Dalit Sahitya Sangha (Maharashtra Dalit Literature Society) in Mumbai Baburao Bagul (1930-2008) wrote in Marathi. His first collection of stories, *Jevha Mi Jat Chorali* (English *When I had Concealed My Caste*), published in 1963, depicted a cruel society and thus brought in new momentum to Dalit literature in Marathi; today it is seen by many critics as an epic portraying lives of the Dalits, and was later made into a film by actor-director Vinay Apte. Gradually with other writers like, Namdeo Dhasal (who founded Dalit Panther), these Dalit writings paved way for the strengthening of Dalit movement.

In 1993, Ambedkari Sahitya Parishad, Wardha organized the first Akhil Bharatiya Ambedkari Sahitya Sammelan (All India Ambedkarite Literature Convention) in Wardha, Maharashtra to re-conceptualize and transform Dalit Sahitya (Dalit literature) into Ambedkari Sahitya, after the name of the Dalit modern-age hero, scholar and inspiration Dr. B.R. Ambedkar, who had successfully campaigned against caste-discrimination and was a strong advocate of Dalit rights. Ambedkari Sahitya Parishad then successfully organized the Third Akhil Bharatiya Ambedkari Sahitya Sammelan in 1996 and became a voice of advocacy for awareness and transformation. Since then ten similar Sahitya Sammelans, or literary gatherings, were held in various places.

Dalit literature started being mainstream in India with the appearance of the English translations of Marathi Dalit writing. *An Anthology of Dalit Literature*, edited by Mulk Raj Anand and Eleanor Zelliot, and *Poisoned Bread : Translations from Modern Marathi Dalit Literature*, originally published in three volumes and later collected in a single volume, edited by Arjun Dangle, both published in 1992, were perhaps the first books that popularised the genre throughout India.

According to Satyanarayana and Tharu, "although it is possible to identify a few Dalit writers from earlier times, the real originality and force of Dalit writing, which today comprises a substantial and growing body of work, can be traced to the decades following the late 1960s. Those are the years when the Dalit Panthers revisit and embrace the ideas of Babasaheb Ambedkar, and elaborate his disagreements with the essentially Gandhian mode of Indian nationalism, to begin a new social movement. In the following decades, Dalit writing becomes an all-India phenomenon. This writing reformulates the caste question and reassesses the significance of colonialism and of missionary activity. It resists the reduction of caste to class or to non-Brahminism and vividly describes and analyzes the contemporary workings of caste power."

Asserting the importance of Dalit literature Arundhati Roy has observed: "I do believe that in India we practice a form of apartheid that goes unnoticed by the rest of the world. And it is as important for Dalits to tell their stories as it has been for colonized peoples to write their own histories. When Dalit literature has blossomed and is in full stride, then contemporary (upper caste) Indian literature's amazing ability to ignore the true brutality and ugliness of the society in which we live, will be seen for what it is: bad literature.

Q. 17. Critically examine any two contemporary texts using the interpretive framework of the theory of *Rasa*.

Ans. A *rasa* literally means "juice, essence or taste". It connotes a concept in Indian arts about the aesthetic flavor of any visual, literary or musical work, that evokes an emotion or feeling in the reader or audience, but that cannot be described.

The *rasa* theory is mentioned in Chapter 6 of the ancient Sanskrit text *Natya Shastra* attributed to Bharata Muni, but its most complete exposition in drama, songs and other performance arts is found in the works of the Kashmiri Shaivite philosopher Abhinavagupta (c. 1000 CE). According to the *Rasa* theory of the *Natya Shastra*, entertainment is a desired effect of performance arts but not the primary goal, and that the primary goal is to transport the individual in the audience into another parallel reality, full of wonder and bliss, where he experiences the essence of his own consciousness, and reflects on spiritual and moral questions.

Although the concept of *rasa* is fundamental to many forms of Indian arts including dance, music, theatre, painting, sculpture, and literature, the interpretation and implementation of a particular *rasa* differs between different styles and schools. The Indian theory of *rasa* is also found in the Hindu arts and *Ramayana* musical productions in Bali and Java (Indonesia), but with regional creative evolution.

●●●

4 Writing Critical Review

Purpose of a Critical Review

The critical review is a writing task that asks you to summarise and evaluate a text. The critical review can be of a book, a chapter, a poem or a journal article. Writing the critical review usually requires you to read the selected text in detail and to also read other related texts so that you can present a fair and reasonable evaluation of the selected text.

What is meant by Critical?

At university, to be critical does not mean to criticise in a negative manner. Rather it requires you to question the information and opinions in a text and present your evaluation or judgement of the text. To do this well, you should attempt to understand the topic from different perspectives (i.e. read related texts) and in relation to the theories, approaches and frameworks in your course.

What is meant by Evaluation or Judgement?

Here you decide the strengths and weaknesses of a text. This is usually based on specific criteria. Evaluating requires an understanding of not just the content of the text, but also an understanding of a text's purpose, the intended audience and why it is structured the way it is.

The determination of the book review is to communicate to the readers mind the ideas and sensations book reviewer experienced while researching the content, in this way explaining the reader what exact meaning the author presumed to transmit, or what did the reviewer experienced while during the reading. The book reviewer, then, stands as reporter, who informs the third party of the events, as an analyst, who makes judgments basing them on own experience, and as the observer from the side, who pretends to act as the reader him/herself should do by expressing own opinion, desires and expectations.

Making book review implies some special skills, as well as obliges with some precise responsibilities. Professional reviewer has not just to read and scrutinize the text, but to realize concealed, implied meaning the author obviously had dropped hints about. Skilled book reviewers' explanations make the reader feel this "that is just what I thought" sensation. The reviewer must also state the main points of the reviewed book. While some aspects are less meaningful, others have to be marked out as prerogative issues. The task is even more complicated as the writer could unintentionally imply the idea the reviewer of the book can notice.

What is meant by Analysis?

Analysing requires separating the content and concepts of a text into their main components and then understanding how these interrelate, connect and possibly influence each other.

The book review is assigned to develop analytical skills. First, the reviewer has to depict the content, regardless of the type of novel, an historical or critical book. In the subsequent narration the goal of the book reviewer is to discuss the content of the book and provide analysis of what he/she had read, and deduce if the author managed to reveal the core, whether he/she kept to the thesis or properly achieved the purpose of the book. The last thing the reviewer has to do is to speculate on the topic himself/herself. The book reviewer should also undertake through their own research to discuss the theme, assess the authors ability to express and explore this theme, and provide an opinion of the novel.

Summarising and Paraphrasing for the Critical Review

Summarising and paraphrasing are essential skills for academic writing and in particular, the critical review. To summarise means to reduce a text to its main points and its most important ideas. The length of your summary for a critical review should only be about one quarter to one third of the whole critical review.

The best way to summarise is to:

1. Scan the text. Look for information that can be deduced from the introduction, conclusion and the title and headings. What do these tell you about the main points of the article?
2. Locate the topic sentences and highlight the main points as you read.
3. Reread the text and make separate notes of the main points. Examples and evidence do not need to be included at this stage. Usually they are used selectively in your critique.

Paraphrasing means putting it into your own words. Paraphrasing offers an alternative to using direct quotations in your summary (and the critique) and can be an efficient way to integrate your summary notes. The best way to paraphrase is to:

1. Review your summary notes
2. Rewrite them in your own words and in complete sentences
3. Use reporting verbs and phrases (*e.g.,* The author describes…, Smith argues that …).
4. If you include unique or specialist phrases from the text, use quotation marks.

Structure of a Critical Review

Critical reviews, both short (one page) and long (four pages), usually have a similar structure. Check your assignment instructions for formatting and structural specifications. Headings are usually optional for longer reviews and can be helpful for the reader.

Introduction

The length of an introduction is usually one paragraph for a journal article review and two or three paragraphs for a longer book review. Include a few opening sentences that announce the author(s) and the title, and briefly explain the topic of the text. Present the aim of the text and summarise the main finding or key argument. Conclude the introduction with a brief statement of your evaluation of the text. This can be a positive or negative evaluation or, as is usually the case, a mixed response.

Summary

Present a summary of the key points along with a limited number of examples. You can also briefly explain the author's purpose/intentions throughout the text and you may briefly describe how the text is organised. The summary should only make up about a third of the critical review.

Critique

The critique should be a balanced discussion and evaluation of the strengths, weakness and notable features of the text. Remember to base your discussion on specific criteria. Good reviews also include other sources to support your evaluation (remember to reference).

You can choose how to sequence your critique. Here are some examples to get you started:

- Most important to least important conclusions you make about the text.
- If your critique is more positive than negative, then present the negative points first and the positive last.
- If your critique is more negative than positive, then present the positive points first and the negative last.
- If there are both strengths and weakness for each criterion you use, you need to decide overall what your judgement is. For example, you may want to comment on a key idea in the text and have both positive and negative comments. You could begin by stating what is

good about the idea and then concede and explain how it is limited in some way. While this example shows a mixed evaluation, overall you are probably being more negative than positive.

- In long reviews, you can address each criteria you choose in a paragraph, including both negative and positive points. For very short critical reviews (one page or less) where your comments will be briefer, include a paragraph of positive aspects and another of negative.
- You can also include recommendations for how the text can be improved in terms of ideas, research approach; theories or frameworks used can also be included in the critique section.

Conclusion

This is usually a very short paragraph.

- Restate your overall opinion of the text.
- Briefly present recommendations.
- If necessary some further qualification or explanation of your judgement can be included. This can help your critique sound fair and reasonable.

References

If you have used other sources in your review you should also include a list of references at the end of the review.

Critical Review of a Poem or Text

Critical Analysis of a Poem

With poetry, the author is always very deliberate with his word choice and format to convey meaning. Poems are meant to be read aloud, which is why they have a very lyrical quality or at least have an interesting rhythm that punctuates the elements of the poem. A critical analysis of the poem allows the reader to have a better understanding of the symbols and language used in the piece. This often offers a more intimate appreciation of the work.

Important Steps

1. Find a specific theme in the work that gives the poem larger meaning. Consider the entire piece, including the title. Perhaps the poem is a symbol about growing old or a loss of innocence or maybe the overarching theme is the importance of the environment. If so, the context for the theme is hidden in the words and presentation.
2. Create a critical analysis checklist that you can follow when reviewing the piece. This allows you to dissect the poem into individual pieces that helps you understand the poem as a whole. For example, make a checklist that lists title, setting, point of view, rhyme scheme, meter, genre, conflict or context. Use these elements as a guide for your analysis.
3. Review the plot of the poem. Answer the questions: What is happening? To whom is it happening? Once you have an understanding of what is being described in the poem, you can start to apply its meaning in your analysis.
4. Analyse the rhyme scheme of the poem, if any. Not all poetry has to rhyme. However, poems are often written for the intention of being read, so there should be a rhythm when read aloud. When performing your analysis, be sure to read the poem aloud alone or with a friend to hear the way it sounds, not just to see the words on the page.
5. Consider the format of the poem. It could be free form, without any identifiable pattern, or it can fit into a specific writing scheme. This is often a deliberate act on the part of the author. In your analysis, you should describe what this format could mean and how it helps or hinders communication of the message.
6. Review the figurative language of the poem. Poetry is known for using literary devices, such as simile, metaphor, personification, irony and metonymy in the work. This not only

constitutes the body of the poem, it demonstrates the author's control over language. Evaluation of this language is a crucial part of your analysis.

7. Form a thesis statement based on your understanding of the poem's meaning. When writing any sort of academic work, your paper should have a clear thesis. For example, "The pitfalls of arrogance and power as described in the poem 'Ozymandius.'"
8. Find parts of the poem that support your thesis statement. Throughout the body of your analysis, you should provide clear clues as to where you got your thesis. Use actual lines from the text, as well as a thorough analysis of word choice.

Analysis of Sylvia Plath's Poem—Mirror

I am silver and exact. I have no preconceptions.
Whatever I see I swallow immediately
Just as it is, unmisted by love or dislike.
I am not cruel, only truthful,
The eye of a little god, four-cornered.
Most of the time I meditate on the opposite wall.
It is pink, with speckles. I have looked at it so long
I think it is part of my heart. But it flickers.
Faces and darkness separate us over and over.

Now I am a lake. A woman bends over me,
Searching my reaches for what she really is.
Then she turns to those liars, the candles or the moon.
I see her back, and reflect it faithfully.
She rewards me with tears and an agitation of hands.
I am important to her. She comes and goes.
Each morning it is her face that replaces the darkness.
In me she has drowned a young girl, and in me an old woman
Rises toward her day after day, like a terrible fish.

Sylvia Plath's poem 'Mirror' is an objectively serious poem which reveals the similarities between poems and the obsessive interest in the truth of reflections and the unhealthy dissatisfaction resulting from dwelling too long on an "exact" image of the present. Plath uses interesting perspective, significant structure, and deep metaphors to also illustrate the similarity between the truthful qualities of poets and mirrors.

The use of first person "I" in the poem 'Mirror' by Sylvia Plath gives an intimate perspective and reveals the mirror's unbiased thoughts. This personified mirror speaking in first person reflects an objective outlook on life from the perspective of a detached observer. Like the mirror's reflection, a poet must also show a clear truth in poetry. The mirror and reflection are metaphors representing the absolute truth of present realities which poets explore and release into the world. The mirror is "unmisted" by prejudice human "preconceptions" and reveals "only" the "truthful" aspects of the world directly in front of it. The mirror's attitudes on life are like a poet's in that they may show a true observation which common people do not wish or are unable to see. Poetry can cut through and unlock social barriers. Though an appearance of a person or situation may be viewed as negative, through a different lens of vision it may then be found to have positive effects. Unlike poetry, mirrors only reflect the present and are unable to predict the future appearance of the area being reflected.

In the second stanza the speaker changes its physical form into a "lake" from a "mirror". The poem is divided by a focus on the mirror itself and the woman who interacts with her reflection in the lake. The division of the poem can also be interpreted as the past and present or present and future of the earth. Just as mirrors reflect images and faces, lakes are giant reflecting pools which claim to show reality, not "cruel" criticism. Reflections are used as a way to measure progress over time. This progress can often become an obsession. The lake is a reference to Narcissus, a youth who fell in love with his image in a lake. The pessimistic woman who visits the lake "each morning" in dedication, like Narcissus, finds herself less young and desirable than the previous days. Though the outcome of aging is inevitable, the woman refuses to accept the laws of nature and continues to be heartbroken by her reflection. The lake is interestingly rewarded with "tears and an agitation of hands", actions which do not hold pleasant appreciation for "truthful" reflections. The woman is so concerned with her appearance compared to her younger days that she is unable to enjoy the present. The woman represents most women's desire to appear young, attractive, and successful all their days. If one lives in the past one will find that each day is a "terrible fish" which holds no hope or happiness. The "terrible fish" is representative of disappointment, unhappiness, and regret stemming from opportunities not seized and an inability to enjoy life as it comes. Instead of embracing and cherishing the time at hand, the woman has "drowned" her youth by disrespecting the truth of the present reflection. This relationship between woman and lake can be translated and applied to many challenges in life. The second stanza is a tragedy because the woman is not "seizing the day" and living out her potential, but is wasting her valuable time. Appearance to the world holds such a great "importance" that it generates an obsession with the worshiped godlike and reflective object.

Mirror by Sylvia Plath has a serious and objective tone to provide an honest interpretation of the people and images which are watched by the square "eye of a little god". The short precise declarative statements create a feeling of detached loneliness. The mirror has grown fond of the familiar and constant "pink" wall "with speckles" and has a slight resentment toward the faces and "dark" nights which force the wall to retreat. Poets will often inform the public about "dark" events in history or everyday life through poetry. Plath creates a dark fateful image by using relatively simple diction. The prominent consonant sounds of the precise word choice create a descriptive scene without a superfluous amount of words. Plath uses figurative language to describe the "mirror" and the woman's reflection in the "lake" to create a similarity of hopeless truth for the future of each object.

Plath's Mirror is a reflection on the way absolute realities of society and the greedy nature of many human's desire for immortality and success can be viewed through objective poems and immediate feedback. The "darkness" of judgment surrounds the young woman and hides the "wall" that has become the "heart" of the "four-cornered" mirror. Poems and Poets can also reflect an accurate or "truthful" picture of present realities. Plath's careful and succinct word choice creates a sparse environment in which the classic situation takes place. The "mirror" knows only truth and is immune from the subliminal judgment which plagues every person's perception of the world. This poem has a distinct correlation between a poet's poem and a mirror's truthful reflection.

Mirror—Summary

In this poem, the mirror is the speaker. It is an autobiographical poem. The mirror talks about itself, its surroundings and the woman who uses it. In this way, it gives its observations in an objective way without any personal bias. The mirror say that its appearance is silver and exact. It does not have any pre-conceptions or anything else about its existence. It is just what it is "Unmisted by love or dislike". It is neither cruel nor biased nor prejudiced, only truthful.

It can be called the eye of a little god, four-cornered, that is, it is framed in a four cornered frame and it remains fixed on the wall and sees the opposite wall and only when someone comes between it and the wall or at night or in darkness, the reflection of the opposite wall goes away.

The mirror is like a lake, it drowns the face of the woman, who tries to see her reflection in it. She searches for her, beauty which she had in her youth. She grows sad to see herself old now. She then turns to "candles" or the "moon" which the mirror calls "liars" because these create a misted kind of surrounding around the woman's face due to which she does not see the wrinkles or signs of old age. But the woman's real identity is revealed by the mirror. Seeing her changed face, the woman sheds some tears and moves her hands angrily.

The mirror is very important to the woman. Every morning she sees herself and she is filled with fear at her reflection of having grown old. She feels like a fish out of water, but the mirror can't do anything as it reflects only the truth—that is what one really is. So, in this way, the mirror claims to be a very objective opinion-giver or reflector of images.

Summary and Analysis of Wordsworth's Poem—The Solitary Reaper

Behold her, single in the field,
Yon solitary Highland Lass!
Reaping and singing by herself;
Stop here, or gently pass!
Alone she cuts and binds the grain,
And sings a melancholy strain;
O listen! for the Vale profound
Is overflowing with the sound.
No Nightingale did ever chaunt
More welcome notes to weary bands
Of travellers in some shady haunt,
Among Arabian sands:
A voice so thrilling ne'er was heard
In spring-time from the Cuckoo-bird,
Breaking the silence of the seas
Among the farthest Hebrides.
Will no one tell me what she sings?--
Perhaps the plaintive numbers flow
For old, unhappy, far-off things,
And battles long ago:
Or is it some more humble lay,
Familiar matter of today?
Some natural sorrow, loss, or pain,
That has been, and may be again?
Whate'er the theme, the Maiden sang
As if her song could have no ending;
I saw her singing at her work,
And o'er the sickle bending;
I listened, motionless and still;
And, as I mounted up the hill
The music in my heart I bore,
Long after it was heard no more.

In the first stanza the speaker comes across a beautiful girl working alone in the fields of Scotland (the Highland). She is "Reaping and singing by herself." He tells the reader not to interrupt her, and then mentions that the valley is full of song.

The second stanza is a list of things that cannot equal the beauty of the girl's singing.

In the third stanza the reader learns that the speaker cannot understand the words being sung. He can only guess at what she might be singing about.

In the fourth and final stanza the speaker tells the reader that even though he did not know what she was singing about, the music stayed in his heart as he continued up the hill.

Analysis

"The Solitary Reaper" was written on November 5, 1805 and published in 1807. The poem is broken into four eight-line stanzas (32 lines total). Most of the poem is in iambic tetrameter. The rhyme scheme for the stanzas is either abcbddee or ababccdd. (In the first and last stanzas the first and third lines don't rhyme, while in the other two stanzas they do.)

This poem is unique in Wordsworth's oeuvre because while most of his work is based closely on his own experiences, "The Solitary Reaper" is based on the experience of someone else: Thomas Wilkinson, as described in his Tours to the British Mountains. The passage that inspired Wordsworth is the following: "Passed a female who was reaping alone: she sung in Erse [the Gaelic language of Scotland] as she bended over her sickle; the sweetest human voice I ever heard: her strains were tenderly melancholy, and felt delicious, long after they were heard no more" (as quoted in The Norton Anthology English Literature).

Part of what makes this poem so intriguing is the fact that the speaker does not understand the words being sung by the beautiful young lady. In the third stanza, he is forced to imagine what she might be singing about. He supposes that she may be singing about history and things that happened long ago, or some sadness that has happened in her own time and will happen again.

As the speaker moves on, he carries the music of the young lady with him in his heart. This is a prevalent theme in much of Wordsworth's poetry. For instance, the same idea is used in "I wandered lonely as a cloud" when the speaker takes the memory of the field of daffodils with him to cheer him up on bad days.

Analysis of John Donne's Poem—Death be not Proud

Death be not proud, though some have called thee
Mighty and dreadfull, for, thou art not soe,
For, those, whom thou think'st, thou dost overthrow,
Die not, poore death, nor yet canst thou kill mee.
From rest and sleepe, which but thy pictures bee,
Much pleasure, then from thee, much more must flow,
And soonest our best men with thee doe goe,
Rest of their bones, and soules deliverie.
Thou art slave to Fate, Chance, kings, and desperate men,
And dost with poyson, warre, and sicknesse dwell,
And poppie, or charmes can make us sleepe as well,
And better then thy stroake; why swell'st thou then?
One short sleepe past, wee wake eternally,
And death shall be no more; death, thou shalt die.

The sonnet "Death Be Not Proud", written by John Donne in England around the year 1618, is one sonnet of nineteen that are part of a collection entitled The Holy Sonnets. Through the use of literary terms and techniques, "Death, Be Not Proud", exemplifies the popular Christian philosophy of the period, that heaven is eternal. John Donne starts the poem "Death Be Not Proud" in utilizing the figurative language of personification, "Death, be not proud, though some have called thee mighty and dreadful, for thou art not so". In using this technique thc author is able to apply human qualities which make Death tangible and a being in which the narrator can entertain an argument and eventually win his case based upon Christian philosophy. Additionally, in the personification of treating Death, the embodiment of non-living as a living being, the author has also utilized the literary term irony. It can be seen that through the use of personification and irony John Donne has set the stage for Death to become just as undone as any man. The continued unraveling of Death is illustrated in lines 5 and 6 through the use of metaphor, "... From rest and sleep, which but thy pictures be, much pleasure; then from thee much more must flow". The narrator is claiming that rest and sleep are nothing but pictures of death, an image of what death is, and that they provide much pleasure so when death actually does happen the pleasure will be much greater. This line of conversation brings death who imagines himself to be mighty and feared in line 1 and 2 down to a being who now brings much pleasure instead of fear. Then in lines 9 and 10, "Thou art slave to fate, chance, kings, and desperate men, and dost with poison, war, and sickness dwell," through the use of imagery John Donne hands Death a crushing blow to his fearsome image.

Death is presented as a slave to Fate, Chance. Kings, and Desperate men. It is shown that death's home, his dwelling is with poison, war and sickness, and that he must await the outcome and decisions of his masters, the true powers that be fate, chance, kings and desperate men. Finally, in the last two lines of 13 and 14 through the author's further use of irony, Death is told, he "...shall be no more; Death, thou shalt die.". Much of the irony here is that it is only due to Christian philosophy, the belief that there is no death, that the argument is won for the narrator. With the death of ones physical body, man awakens to an eternal spiritual life, and death is over, man wins. It can be seen throughout the poem "Death, Be Not Proud" that the use of literary terms and techniques helped highlight and explore the views of Christian philosophy which during the time of John Donne was eternal life, the only option to believe.

Critical Response of Sylvia Plath's Poem—Words

Axes
After whose stroke the wood rings,
And the echoes!
Echoes traveling
Off from the center like horses.

The sap
Wells like tears, like the
Water striving
To re-establish its mirror
Over the rock

That drops and turns,
A white skull,
Eaten by weedy greens.
Years later I
Encounter them on the road...

Words dry and riderless,
The indefatigable hoof-taps.
While
From the bottom of the pool, fixed stars
Govern a life.

"Words" is a short poem of four stanzas, five lines each. It is written in an open form with irregular meter and only occasional rhyme. Since the poem is written entirely in metaphor, the title serves as an important clue to meaning. The poem exists as a separate entity, to be met by any traveler on the road of life.

The landscape of "Words" is mental, rather than physical, so its effects on the reader can be disorienting. There is no hand on the axe that strikes, no riders on the horses, no eyes behind the welling tears. One does not encounter the narrator until near the end of the third stanza. At this point, one sees that the poem is written in the first person, and it becomes clearer that preceding stanzas are the thoughts of the poet as she meditates on her subject, words. "Words" is structured as a series of stanza-paragraphs each exploring a different aspect of the subject. Distinct but interlocking images unify the ideas and reveal a progression of perceptions about the nature of the poetic utterance. The dominant image pattern of movement radiating from a centre is established immediately. The almost physical sense of vibration coupled with the repetition of the word "echoes" links the axes image to that of horses galloping. Plath often uses horse imagery to denote creative energy.

In the second stanza, the mood changes, becoming quieter. Welling sap ties this stanza to the preceding as imagery, and likening sap to tears places the imagery in a human context. Poets, particularly those of the confessional school to which Plath belongs, often use their work as catharsis, as a way in healing. In the middle of the second stanza, the imagery changes to water into which a stone has been dropped. One expects a continuation of healing ideas, due to the similarity of the images. The implication here shifts subtly from healing to concealing, Certainly there is a sense of attempted healing in the sap that tries to seal the wounded flesh of the tree and tears that can release psychic pain.

In the third stanza, the poetic landscape changes almost imperceptibly from the real to the surreal. As the stone sinks beneath the surface of water, it drops and turns changing to a skull. The ringing power of the "axe" has given way to the inertness of the "rock", which in its tumbling, changes into a macabre remnant of creative energy, a breached skull. The idea of lifelessness is reinforced by the next lines. The reader is jerked back to the surface world, but the boundaries of reality are still blurred. In a reversal of the usual metaphoric technique in the first stanza where horses represented words, words are now spoken as if they were horses. The power and purpose behind the purpose is gone; however, they are dry and are riderless. The words seem to have taken on a power of their own, outside the control of their creator. Finally, as if to escape those "indefatigable hoof-taps", the poem, like the skull, sinks to the bottom of the pool, away from the energy, the pain, and the nightmarish confusion, to a place of certainty.

Metaphor is the overriding device of "Words". Because, there is no narrative framework, even a superficial reading requires some interpretation of its metaphor. Plath uses metaphor as more than a device for seeing experience in a new light. In this poem, she uses progressive linking of subtly changing imagery to mirror a changing mental state. Plath does not make the reader's task easy, but she does supply the clues.

Plath is an enigmatic poet. She veers from life to death, from tenderness to violence. She is not in control of her fate, as she sees it, but she is in control of her life and thus suicide is her sole power. The stream represents her life and the rocks represent her suffering and emotional issues - they churn up the stream. Lying in the bottom of the pool everything is calm because she finally has control over her life (through death).

This is one of the last poems she wrote before her death and reflects the inner turmoil of one desperately seeking help. Her critics, father and husband reject her. She acknowledges the power of their words in the first line \'Axes\'. Words are her weapon and her defence. It is no wonder this poem is named after them.

Critical Examination of "The Rape of the Lock"

The Rape of the Lock, originally published as *The Rape of the Lock : An Heroic-Comical Poem* in 1712, is a mock-epic based upon an actual disagreement between two aristocratic English families during the eighteenth century. Lord Petre (the Baron in the poem) surprises the beautiful Arabella Fermor (Belinda) by clipping off a lock of hair. At the suggestion of his friend and with Arabella Fermor's approval, Alexander Pope used imagination, hyperbole, wit, and gentle satire to inflate this, trivial social slip-up into an earthshaking catastrophe of cosmic consequence. The poem is generally described as one of Pope's most brilliant satires. The poem makes serious demands upon the reader, not only because of its length, but also because it requires a background knowledge of epic literature and some understanding of the trapping of upper-crust England.

The poem reflects the picture of the contemporary society. *The Rape of the Lock* mirrors eighteenth century elegant society and life in London with all its fashions, follies, frivolities and vices. The poem is a witty social document which mirrors false ideology. Morality intrigue debauchery, corruption, social scandals mostly sexual pleasure and fashion of the ladies, the tawdriness of the morality of the beau-demon is revealed through the poem.

The poem constantly shifts between mocking silly social conventions of the aristocracy, (such as elaborate courtship rituals) and satirizing serious literary conventions of traditional epic literature (such as its lofty style, exhaustive descriptions of warriors readying for battle, and heavy doses of mythology). With many allusions to Homer's Iliad and Odyssey, Virgil's *Aeneid*, and John Milton's *Paradise Lost*, the speaker compares the loss of Belinda's hair to the great battles of classic epic literature. The speaker describes Belinda applying makeup as if she was a warrior going to battle. While playing a game of cards, the Baron sneaks up behind Belinda and perform the "tragic" snipping of the lock of hair. An army of gnomes and sprites attempts to protect Belinda to no avail. Belinda demands the restoration of her lock and another "battle" ensues. Finally, the lock ascends skyward as a new star to beautify the heavens.

The poem ridicules the silly social manners of the aristocracy and deflates the elevated sense of importance in the affairs of wealthy ladies and gentlemen. Yet, the poem also displays some fondness for the grace and beauty of that world. Pope enjoys all the ivory and tortoise shell, cosmetics and diamonds, expensive furniture, silver coffee service, fancy china, and light conversation—this was the world in which he moved attempting to find patronage for his poetry.

The Rape of the Lock is the perfect example of mock-heroic poem. The characteristics of a mock heroic poem—the discrepancy the triviality of the subject matter, the Invocation to the muse, epic similes, the sonorous and grand speeches, use of epic machinery, journey to the underworld, a voyage on board are present here.

Critical Examination of "Middlemarch: A Study of Provincial Life"

Modestly subtitled "A Study of Provincial Life," George Eliot's *Middlemarch* has long been recognized as a work of great psychological and moral penetration. The novel is set in the fictitious Midlands town of Middlemarch during 1829-32, and it comprises several distinct (though intersecting) stories and a large cast of characters.

The theme of the novel itself, however, revolves around the slenderest of threads: the mating of "unimportant" people. This theme, which engages the talents of such other great writers as Jane Austen, Thomas Hardy, Henry James, and D. H. Lawrence, allows Eliot the scope to examine the whole range of human nature. She is concerned with the mating of lovers because people in love are most vulnerable and most easily the victims of romantic illusions. Each of the three sets of lovers in *Middlemarch*—Dorothea Brooke, Edward Casaubon, and Will Ladislaw; Rosamond Vincy and Tertius Lydgate; and Mary Garth and Fred Vincy—mistake illusion for reality. Significant themes include the status of women, the nature of marriage, idealism, self-interest, religion, hypocrisy, political reform, and education.

Eliot's novel is set in the fictional town of Middlemarch, North Loamshire, which is probably based on Coventry, in the county of Warwickshire, where she had lived prior to moving to London. Like Coventry, Middlemarch is described as being a silk-ribbon manufacturing town.

The subtitle of the novel—*A Study of Provincial Life*—has been viewed as significant, with one critic viewing the unity of *Middlemarch* as being achieved through "the fusion of the two senses of 'provincial' ", that is on the one hand the geographical, meaning "all parts of the country except the capital"; and on the other hand, a person who is "unsophisticated" or "narrow-minded". Through its sub-title Middlemarch represents the lives of ordinary people, not the grand adventures of princes and kings. Middlemarch represents the spirit of nineteenth-century England through the unknown, historically unremarkable common people. The small community of Middlemarch is thrown into relief against the background of larger social transformations, rather than the other way around.

Although it has some comical elements and comically named characters. *Middlemarch* is a work of realism. Through the voices and opinions of different characters we become aware of various issues of the day: the Great Reform Bill, the beginnings of the railways, the death of King George IV, and the succession of his brother, the Duke of Clarence. We learn something of the state of contemporary medical science. We also encounter the deeply reactionary mindset within a settled community facing the prospect of what too many is unwelcome change.

England is the process of rapid industrialization. Social mobility is growing rapidly. With the rise of the merchant middle class, one's birth no longer necessarily determines one's social class for life. Chance occurrences can make or break a person's success. Moreover, there is no single coherent religious order. Evangelical Protestants, Catholics, and Anglicans live side by side. As a result, religious conflicts abound in the novel, particularly those centering on the rise of Evangelical Protestantism, a primarily middle-class religion that created heated doctrinal controversy.

Eliot continually uses the metaphor of a web to describe the town's social relations. She intricately weaves together the disparate life experiences of a large cast of characters. Many characters subscribe to a world-view; others want to find a world-view to organize their lives. The absence of a single, triumphant world-view to organize all life is the basic design of *Middlemarch*. No one occupies the center of the novel as the most important or influential person. *Middlemarch* social relations are indeed like a web, but the web has no center. Each individual occupies a point in the web, affecting and affected by the other points. Eliot's admirable effort to represent this web in great detail makes her novel epic in length and scope. Unlike in an epic, however, no single point in the web and no single world-view reign triumphant.

As a matter of fact, even "Middlemarch", an imaginary provincial town, has a symbolical not a topical significance. It is provincial, because it is bereft of the glamour of heroic adventure and passionate dedication to high ideals; and this not because the characters are no longer capable of dedication, but because the time for uncommon fits is forever gone. Those who still crave for them look quixotically ridiculous and helpless. Provincial, because intellectual enterprise no longer leads to momentous scientific systems and discoveries but only to provisional results and diminutive steps in collectively undertaken projects.

Critical Examination of "Gulliver's Travels"

Jonathan Swift had at least two aims in *Gulliver's Travels* besides merely telling a good adventure story. Behind the disguise of his narrative, he was satirizing the pettiness of human nature in general and attacking the Whigs in particular. Emphasizing the six-inch height of the Lilliputians, he graphically diminished the stature of politicians and indeed the stature of all human nature. And in using the fire in the Queen's chambers, the rope dancers, the bill of particulars drawn against Gulliver, and the inventory of Gulliver's pockets, he presented a series of allusions that were identifiable to his contemporaries as critical of Whig politics.

Why, one might ask, did Swift have such a consuming contempt for the Whigs? This hatred began when Swift entered politics as the representative of the Irish church. Representing the Irish bishops, Swift tried to get Queen Anne and the Whigs to grant some financial aid to the Irish church. They refused, and Swift turned against them even though he had considered them his friends and had helped them while he worked for Sir William Temple. Swift turned to the Tories for political allegiance and devoted his propaganda talents to their services. Using certain political events of 1714-18, he described in *Gulliver's Travels* many things that would remind his readers that Lilliputian folly was also English folly—and, particularly, Whig folly. The method, for example, which Gulliver must use to swear his allegiance to the Lilliputian emperor parallels the absurd difficulty that the Whigs created concerning the credentials of the Tory ambassadors who signed the Treaty of Utrecht.

Within the broad scheme of *Gulliver's Travels*, Gulliver seems to be an average man in eighteenth-century England. He is concerned with family and with his job, yet he is confronted by the pigmies that politics and political theorizing make of people. Gulliver is utterly incapable of the stupidity of the Lilliputian politicians, and, therefore, he and the Lilliputians are ever-present contrasts for us. We are always aware of the difference between the imperfect (but normal) moral life of Gulliver, and the petty and stupid political life of emperors, prime ministers, and informers.

In the second book of the *Travels*, Swift reverses the size relationship that he used in Book-I. In Lilliput, Gulliver was a giant; in Brobdingnag, Gulliver is a midget. Swift uses this difference to express a difference in morality. Gulliver was an ordinary man compared to the amoral political midgets in Lilliput. Now, Gulliver remains an ordinary man, but the Brobdingnagians are moral men. They are not perfect, but they are consistently moral. Only children and the deformed are intentionally evil.

Set against a moral background, Gulliver's "ordinariness" exposes many of its faults. Gulliver is revealed to be a very proud man and one who accepts the madness and malice of European politics, parties, and society as natural. What's more, he even lies to conceal what is despicable about them. The Brobdingnagian king, however, is not fooled by Gulliver. The English, he says, are "odious vermin."

The Houyhnhnms are super-reasonable. They have all the virtues that the stoics and Deists advocated. They speak clearly, they act justly, and they have simple laws. They do not quarrel or argue since each knows what is true and right. They do not suffer from the uncertainties of reasoning that afflict Man. But they are so reasonable that they have no emotions. They are untroubled by greed, politics, or lust. They act from undifferentiated benevolence. They would never prefer the welfare of one of their own children to the welfare of another Houyhnhnm simply on the basis of kinship.

Very simply, the Houyhnhnms are horses; they are not humans. And this physical difference parallels the abstract difference. They are fully rational, innocent, and undepraved. Man is capable of reason, but never wholly or continuously, and he is—but never wholly or continuously—passionate, proud, and depraved.

In contrast to the Houyhnhnms, Swift presents their precise opposite: the Yahoos, creatures who exhibit the essence of sensual human sinfulness. The Yahoos are not merely animals; they are animals who are naturally vicious. Swift describes them in deliberately filthy and disgusting terms, often using metaphors drawn from dung. The Yahoos plainly represent Mankind depraved.

Swift uses the technique of making abstractions concrete to show us that super-reasonable horses are impossible and useless models for humans. They have never fallen and therefore have never been redeemed. They are incapable of the Christian virtues that unite passion and reason: Neither they nor the Yahoos are touched by grace or charity. In contrast, the Christian virtues of Pedro de Mendez and the Brobdingnagians (the "least corrupted" of mankind) are possible to humans. These virtues are the result of grace and redemption. Swift does not press this theological point, however. He is, after all, writing a satire, not a religious tract.

Critical Examination of "Othello"

Othello (The Tragedy of Othello, the Moor of Venice) is a tragedy by William Shakespeare, believed to have been written in 1603. The story revolves around its two central characters: Othello, a Moorish general in the Venetian army and his unfaithful ensign, Iago. Given its varied and enduring themes of racism, love, jealousy, betrayal, revenge and repentance, *Othello* is still often performed in professional and community theatre alike, and has been the source for numerous operatic, film, and literary adaptations.

Othello was crafted at the dawn of the 17th century, shaped by complex social and geopolitical issues that new historicist critics, who seek to place literary works within a historical framework, have recently sought to unravel. Yet from its first staging to the present, *Othello* has also been among the few Shakespearean plays to be repeatedly staged to enthusiastic audiences, not only in England, but across the globe. This continuing appeal suggests that the tragedy transcends the time and location in which it was written, provoking new interpretations from generation to generation, place to place. In order to fully appreciate Othello, we need to see it in its multifaceted historical context—then—and consider the myriad ways it speaks to audiences now.

Shakespeare draws upon the Christian-Turkish binary but also undercuts it by making the play's most villainous character a Venetian and its hero an outsider. Fearful of vesting military power in one of its own citizens, Venice's republican government contracted with foreign mercenaries who could easily be dismissed once the crisis was over (as Othello is in Act 5). Although Othello has been chosen by the Venetian government to lead its army, 'the Moor' (a term that originally referred to practitioners of Islam) remains an alien in Venice. Like the liminal island of Cyprus, he is caught in the middle, neither European nor Turk yet embodying both, and in his suicide he highlights his service as a Christian hero by killing the 'turbaned Turk' within, who 'beat a Venetian and traduced the state'.

Othello's geopolitical impact is not limited, however, to conflicts between Venice and the Ottoman Empire. Othello's blackness and his background as a foreign mercenary prefigures the hybridity postcolonial theorists have identified in colonial subjects. Brabantio and Desdemona are fascinated by his strange stories of cannibals and anthropophagi; Othello's first gift to her is a handkerchief given to him by an Egyptian charmer, 'dyed in mummy [a black liquid distilled from corpses] and steeped in the ancient lore of charmers, sibyls and magic'. The Moor's stories allow Desdemona to experience the exotic/erotic delight found by many early modern readers in travel narratives that described the 'antres vast' of unexplored territories in Africa, the East and the New World.

Critical Examination of "Sons and Lovers"

Sons and Lovers is a 1913 novel by the English writer D. H. Lawrence, originally published by B.W. Huebsch Publishers. They placed it ninth on their list of the 100 best novels of the 20th century. While the novel initially received a lukewarm critical reception, along with allegations of obscenity, it is today regarded as a masterpiece by many critics and is often regarded as Lawrence's finest achievement.

Sons and Lovers is a text that cries out for a psychoanalytic interpretation. One of Freud's most famous theories is the Oedipus complex, which deals with a child's emerging sexuality. Freud used the story of Sophocles' Oedipus Rex to help illustrate his theory. In the story, Oedipus unwittingly kills his father and marries his mother. According to Freud, all male children form an erotic attachment to their mother and are jealous of the relationship the father has with the mother. The male child fears he will be castrated by the father so he represses the sexual desire for the mother and waits for his own sexual experience. However, if the boy does not fulfill these steps, then he will carry the oedipal complex with him into adulthood (Dobie 52-53). As a result, having this complex makes it very difficult to form adult relationships with others. In other words, if the child never grows out of this type of behavior, he will be dysfunctional in adulthood.

Sons and Lovers is a study of human relationships. Gertrude Morel, because of her turbulent and odd relationship with her husband, ends up developing deep emotional relations with her two eldest sons'. The second eldest in particular, Paul, is the receiver of most of this deep emotion. Because of these feelings and the deeper-than-usual emotional bond between the two, Paul has difficulty being comfortable in his own relationships. Paul's relationship with Miriam is plagued by his mother's disapproval, jealousy, and Miriam's own spirituality.

In *Sons and Lovers* the themes we find are—bondage, contradictions and oppositions, nature and flowers, apart from Oedipus complex discussed earlier. Lawrence discusses bondage, or servitude, in two major ways: social and romantic. Socially, Mrs. Morel feels bound by her status as a woman and by industrialism. She complains of feeling "buried alive," a logical lament for someone married to a miner, and even the children feel they are in a "tight place of anxiety." Though she joins a women's group, she must remain a housewife for life, and thus is jealous of Miriam, who is able to utilize her intellect in more opportunities. Romantic bondage is given far more emphasis in the novel. Paul (and William, to a somewhat lesser extent) feels bound to his mother, and cannot imagine ever abandoning her or even marrying anyone else. He is preoccupied with the notion of lovers "belonging" to each other, and his true desire, revealed at the end, is for a woman to claim him forcefully as her own. He feels the sacrificial Miriam fails in this regard and that Clara always belonged to Baxter Dawes.

Lawrence demonstrates how contradictions emerge so easily in human nature, especially with love and hate. Paul vacillates between hatred and love for all the women in his life, including his mother at times. Often he loves and hates at the same time, especially with Miriam. Mrs. Morel, too, has some reserve of love for her husband even when she hates him, although this love dissipates over time.

Lawrence also uses the opposition of the body and mind to expose the contradictory nature of desire; frequently, characters pair up with someone who is quite unlike them. Mrs. Morel initially likes the hearty, vigorous Morel because he is so far removed from her dainty, refined, intellectual nature. Paul's attraction to Miriam, his spiritual soul mate, is less intense than his desire for the sensual, physical Clara.

The decay of the body also influences the spiritual relationships. When Mrs. Morel dies, Morel grows more sensitive, though he still refuses to look at her body. Dawes's illness, too, removes his threat to Paul, who befriends his ailing rival.

Sons and Lovers has a great deal of description of the natural environment. Often, the weather and environment reflect the characters' emotions through the literary technique of pathetic fallacy. The description is frequently eroticized, both to indicate sexual energy and to slip pass the censors in Lawrence's repressive time.

Lawrence's characters also experience moments of transcendence while alone in nature, much as the Romantics did. More frequently, characters bond deeply while in nature. Lawrence uses flowers throughout the novel to symbolize these deep connections. However, flowers are sometimes agents of division, as when Paul is repulsed by Miriam's fawning behavior towards the daffodil.

Critical Examination of "A Portrait of the Artist as a Young Man"

A Portrait of the Artist as a Young Man by James Joyce is possibly the greatest example in the English language of the bildungsroman, a novel tracing the physical, mental, and spiritual growth and education of a young person. It details events which closely correspond with those of Joyce's first twenty years. According to Joyce's celebrated biographer, Richard Ellman, Joyce hoped that his *Portrait* would be an autobiographical novel, "turning his life into fiction." While scholars disagree on the extent to which Joyce's life affected his fictional narrative in the novel, most of them concur that Stephen Dedalus is both the protagonist of the novel, as well as the persona (Latin, meaning "mask") behind which Joyce paints his fictional "portrait" of the "artist" and of the "young man." We must keep in mind, however, that many of the people and the situations of the novel have been presented in the form of satire. We must also be aware that the author selected this technique to emphasize how the life of an artist differs from that of others who share his world.

This novel depicts Joyce's innovative use of stream of consciousness, a style in which the author directly transcribes the thoughts and sensations that go through a character's mind, rather than simply describing those sensations from the external standpoint of an observer. Joyce's use of stream of consciousness makes *A Portrait of the Artist as a Young Man* a story of the development of Stephen's mind. In the first chapter, the very young Stephen is only capable of describing his world in simple words and phrases. The sensations that he experiences are all jumbled together with a child's lack of attention to cause and effect. Later, when Stephen is a teenager obsessed with religion, he is able to think in a clearer, more adult manner.

We must keep in mind, however, that many of the people and the situations of the novel have been presented in the form of satire. We must also be aware that the author selected this technique to emphasize how the life of an artist differs from that of others who share his world.

In *A Portrait*, the reader learns through the particular experiences of Stephen Dedalus how an artist perceives his surroundings, as well as his views on faith, family, and country, and how these perceptions often conflict with those prescribed for him by society. As a result, the artist feels distanced from the world. Unfortunately, this feeling of distance and detachment is misconstrued by others to be the prideful attitude of an egoist. Thus the artist, already feeling isolated, is increasingly aware of a certain growing, painful social alienation.

Stephen's thoughts, associations, feelings, and language (both cerebral and verbal) serve as the primary vehicles by which the reader shares with Stephen the pain and pleasures of adolescence, as well as the exhilarating experiences of intellectual, sexual, and spiritual discoveries.

In "Portrait," Joyce ventures inside that part of our identity for which no language yet exists, probing into the space between what belongs to the individual alone and what is ours together, exploring the shifts of mind, the currents of our moods and feelings as they flow blindly this way and that, and mapping the unarticulated, more or less salient presence of the soul, that part of our inner being that rises when we are enthused and falls when we are afraid or despairing. "Portrait" is about this, a young man's soul, and what makes Joyce's novel so magical, what makes it essentially literary, is that his conquest of what belongs to the individual alone—what is special, and to Joyce's mind unique about Stephen Dedalus—is also a conquest of what belongs, and is unique, to each of us.

A Portrait of the Artist as a Young Man explores what it means to become an artist. Stephen's decision at the end of the novel—to leave his family and friends behind and go into exile in order to become an artist-suggests that Joyce sees the artist as a necessarily isolated figure. In his decision, Stephen turns his back on his community, refusing to accept the constraints of political involvement, religious devotion, and family commitment that the community places on its members.

●●●

5 Writing Brief Notes

AMERICAN TRANSCENDENTALISM

American transcendentalism is essentially a kind of practice by which the world of facts and the categories of common sense are temporarily exchanged for the world of ideas and the categories of imagination. The point of this exchange is to make life better by lifting us above the conflicts and struggles that weigh on our souls.

Transcendentalism emerged from "English and German Romanticism, the Biblical criticism of Johann Gottfried Herder and Friedrich Schleiermacher, the skepticism of David Hume", and the transcendental philosophy of Immanuel Kant and German Idealism. Miller and Versluis regard Emanuel Swedenborg as a pervasive influence on transcendentalism. It was also influenced by Hindu texts on philosophy of the mind and spirituality, especially the Upanishads.

A core belief of transcendentalism is in the inherent goodness of people and nature. Adherents believe that society and its institutions have corrupted the purity of the individual, and they have faith that people are at their best when truly "self-reliant" and independent.

Transcendentalism emphasizes subjective intuition over objective empiricism. Adherents believe that individuals are capable of generating completely original insights with little attention and deference to past masters.

The transcendentalists were suspended between imagination and common sense. If they had been consistent empiricists or materialists, their theories might have been securely founded on facts. Had they been fully fledged idealists or rationalists, their theories might have been firmly fixed on logical relations. In reality, they were neither consistent nor fully fledged theorists. Emerson complained of a see-saw in his voice. Yet what is most valuable in the legacy of transcendentalism is not theoretical and is not in need of theoretical backing. It is the practices by which the transcendentalists managed, at least occasionally, to re-make the world in the image of what they loved.

BLACK ARTS MOVEMENT

The Black Arts Movement, Black Aesthetics Movement or BAM is the artistic outgrowth of the Black Power movement that was prominent in the 1960s and early 1970s. Time magazine describes the Black Arts Movement as the "single most controversial movement in the history of African-American literature—possibly in American literature as a whole." The Black Arts Repertory Theatre is a key institution of the Black Arts Movement. The movement has been seen as one of the most important times in African-American literature. It inspired black people to establish their own publishing houses, magazines, journals and art institutions. It led to the creation of African-American Studies programs within universities. The movement was triggered by the assassination of Malcolm X. Among the well-known writers who were involved with the movement are Nikki Giovanni, Sonia

Sanchez, Maya Angelou, Hoyt W. Fuller, and Rosa Guy. Although not strictly part of the Movement, other notable African-American writers such as novelists Toni Morrison and Ishmael Reed share some of its artistic and thematic concerns. BAM influenced the world of literature with the portrayal of different ethnic voices. Before the movement, the literary canon lacked diversity, and the ability to express ideas from the point of view of racial and ethnic minorities, which was not valued by the mainstream at the time.

SURREALISM

Surrealism is a cultural movement that began in the early 1920s in France, and is best known for its visual artworks and writings. Artists painted unnerving, illogical scenes with photographic precision, created strange creatures from everyday objects, and developed painting techniques that allowed the unconscious to express itself. Its aim was to "resolve the previously contradictory conditions of dream and reality into an absolute reality, a super-reality".

Surrealist works feature the element of surprise, unexpected juxtapositions and non sequitur; however, many Surrealist artists and writers regard their work as an expression of the philosophical movement first and foremost, with the works being an artifact. Leader André Breton was explicit in his assertion that Surrealism was, above all, a revolutionary movement.

Surrealism developed out of the Dada activities during World War I and the most important center of the movement was Paris. From the 1920s onward, the movement spread around the globe, eventually affecting the visual arts, literature, film, and music of many countries and languages, as well as political thought and practice, philosophy, and social theory.

DALIT PANTHER MOVEMENT AND ITS LITERATURE

Dalit Panthers is a social organisation that seeks to combat caste discrimination. It was founded by Namdeo Dhasal and J. V. Pawaron 29 May 1972 in the Indian state of Maharashtra. The movement saw its heyday in the 1970s and through the 1980s, and was later joined many Dalit-Buddhist activists. The Dalit Panthers were inspired by the Black Panther Party, a socialist movement that sought to combat racial discrimination against African-Americans, during Civil Rights Movement in the United States, which occurred in the mid-20th century. The initiative to form the Dalit Panther Movement was taken up by Namdeo Dhasal, J. V. Pawar, and Arun Kamble in Bombay. They conceived the movement as a radical departure from earlier Dalit movements, due to its initial emphasis on militancy and revolutionary attitudes, akin to attitudes espoused by their Black American counterparts. The Dalit Panthers emerged to fill the vacuum created in Dalit politics resulting from B.R. Ambedkar's Republican Party of India splitting into factions. The Dalit Panthers led to a renaissance in Marathi literature and arts. They advocated for and practised radical politics, fusing the ideologies of Ambedkar, Jyotirao Phule and Karl Marx. Crucially, the Dalit Panthers helped invigorate the use of the term Dalit to refer to lower-caste communities. This manifesto, issued in 1973, combines the Ambedkarite spirit with a broader Marxist framework and heralds the rise of autonomous Dalit perspective in post-Independence India.

Dalit literature has its origins in the exploitation of Dalits and symbolises a quest for equality and a rational attitude towards the problems of society. The exploitation and persecution of Dalits was sanctified by irrational religious dogma propagated by the Hindu orthodoxy. Thus, challenging this persecution necessitated taking a rational attitude towards society's problems. In this sense one can say that the teachings of Bhagwan Buddha can be counted among the first pieces of Dalit literature. In modern times, the writings of Mahatma Phule and Savitribai were instrumental in again bringing major shift in the domain of Dalit literature. Mahatma Phule critically analysed the history of India and with irrefutable evidence established that Shudras and Ati Shudras are original inhabitants of this land and thus rightful owners of resources. He glorified *shrama* (labour) which is a basic requirement of economic growth. He devised very effective ways of spreading his literary work through the oral traditions. Powada (ballads) and Kalapathak (stage performance) were immensely popular among the weaker section, particularly Dalits in rural Maharashtra. He revolutionised the life of Shudras and Ati Shudras and his writings formed the roots of modern Dalit literature.

KARUNA RASA

Karuna rasa is a very essential part of the Natyashastra. It refers to the "pathetic sentiment" used in dramatic performance (natya). It is a Sanskrit compound composed of the words of *karuna* (pathetic) and *rasa* ('sentiment'). This sentiment is produced from a combination of determinants, consequents and complementary psychological states. The dominant emotion or the Sthayi Bhava in Karuna rasa is soka or sorrow. The *Vibhavas* or determinants of Karuna rasa are curse, distress, downfall, calamity, and separation from the near and dear ones, loss of wealth, murder, imprisonment, flight, dangerous accidents and misfortunes. Its presentation in the stage is through the following *Anubhavas*, viz. discharge of tears, lamentation, parched throat and mouth, pallor of the face, drooping of the limbs, gasping for breath, loss of memory and other similar things. The Vyabhicari Bhavas of Karuna rasa are dejectedness, in difference, languor, anxiety, yearning excited state, illusion, loss of sense, sadness, ailments, lethargy, sluggishness, epileptic loss of memory, fear, death, paralysis, tremor, pallor in the face, shedding of tears, loss of speech and the kindred feelings. The Natyashastra states that the Karuna Rasa takes its origin through different Bhavas either at the sight of the death (or murder) of the dear one or when unpleasant words have an adverse impact. It is to be presented in the stage through sighs, lamentations, loss of sense, weeping bitterly and other similar gestures.

ART ON THE INTERNET

Internet art (often referred to as net art) is a form of digital artwork distributed via the Internet. This form of art has circumvented the traditional dominance of the gallery and museum system, delivering aesthetic experiences via the Internet. In many cases, the viewer is drawn into some kind of interaction with the work of art. Artists working in this manner are sometimes referred to as net artists.

Internet art can happen outside the technical structure of the Internet, such as when artists use specific social or cultural Internet traditions in a project outside it. Internet art is often—but not always—interactive, participatory, and multimedia-based. Internet art can be used to spread a message, either political or social, using human interactions.

The term Internet art typically does not refer to art that has been simply digitized and uploaded to be viewable over the Internet. This can be done through a web browser, such as images of paintings uploaded for viewing in an online gallery. Rather, this genre relies intrinsically on the Internet to exist, taking advantage of such aspects as an interactive interface and connectivity to multiple social and economic cultures and micro-cultures. It refers to the Internet as a whole, not only to web-based works.

Theorist and curator Jon Ippolito defined "Ten Myths" about Internet art in 2002. He cites the above stipulations, as well as defining it as distinct from commercial web design, and touching on issues of permanence, archivability, and collecting in a fluid medium.

THE GOD OF SMALL THINGS

The God of Small Things (1996) is the debut novel of Indian writer Arundhati Roy. It is a story about the childhood experiences of fraternal twins whose lives are destroyed by the "Love Laws" that lay down "who should be loved, and how. And how much." The book explores how the small things affect people's behavior and their lives. It won the Booker Prize in 1997.

The story is set in Ayemenem, now part of Kottayam district in Kerala, India. The temporal setting shifts back and forth between 1969, when fraternal twins Rahel and Esthappen are seven years old, and 1993, when the twins are reunited at the age of 31. Malayalam words are liberally used in conjunction with English. Facets of Kerala life captured by the novel are Communism, the caste system, and the Keralite Syrian Christian way of life.

BELOVED

Beloved is a 1987 novel by the American writer Toni Morrison. Set after the American Civil War (1861-65), it is inspired by the story of an African-American slave, Margaret Garner, who escaped slavery in Kentucky late January 1856 by fleeing to Ohio, a free state. Morrison had come across the story "A Visit to the Slave Mother who Killed Her Child" in an 1856 newspaper article published in the *American Advocate* and reproduced in The Black Book, a miscellaneous compilation of black history and culture that Morrison edited in 1974. The book is the story of Sethe and her daughter Denver after their escape from slavery. Their home in Cincinnati is haunted by a revenant, whom they believe to be the ghost of Sethe's daughter. Because of the haunting—which often involves objects being thrown around the room—Sethe's youngest daughter Denver is shy, friendless, and housebound, and her sons, Howard and Buglar, have run away from home by the age of 13. Baby Suggs, the mother of Sethe's husband Halle, dies in her bed soon afterwards.

The novel won the Pulitzer Prize for Fiction in 1988 and was a finalist for the 1987 National Book Award. It was adapted during 1998 into a movie of the same name starring Oprah Winfrey. A *New York Times* survey of writers and literary critics ranked it the best work of American fiction from 1981 to 2006.

The book's dedication reads "Sixty Million and more", referring to the Africans and their descendants who died as a result of the Atlantic slave trade.

MY NAME IS RED

My Name Is Red is a 1998 Turkish novel by writer Orhan Pamuk translated into English by Erda Göknar in 2001. Pamuk would later receive the 2006 Nobel Prize in Literature. The novel, concerning miniaturists in the Ottoman Empire of 1591, established Pamuk's international reputation and contributed to his Nobel Prize. The influences of Joyce, Kafka, Mann, Nabokov and Proust and above all Eco can be seen in Pamuk's work.

The main characters in the novel are miniaturists in the Ottoman Empire, one of whom is murdered in the first chapter. From this point, Pamuk—in a postmodern style reminiscent of Jorge Luis Borges—plays with the reader and with literary conventions. The novel incorporates metafiction in such ways as making frequent reference to the reader and to the narrators' awareness that they are characters in a book.

THE CANTERBURY TALES

The Canterbury Tales is a collection of 24 stories that runs to over 17,000 lines written in Middle English by Geoffrey Chaucer between 1387 and 1400. In 1386, Chaucer became Controller of Customs and Justice of Peace and, in 1389, Clerk of the King's work. It was during these years that Chaucer began working on his most famous text, *The Canterbury Tales*. The tales (mostly written in verse, although some are in prose) are presented as part of a story-telling contest by a group of pilgrims as they travel together on a journey from London to Canterbury to visit the shrine of Saint Thomas Becket at Canterbury Cathedral. The prize for this contest is a free meal at the Tabard Inn at Southwark on their return.

The question of whether *The Canterbury Tales* is a finished work has not been answered to date. There are 84 manuscripts and four incunable editions of the work, dating from the late medieval and early Renaissance periods, more than for any other vernacular literary text with the exception of *The Prick of Conscience*. This is taken as evidence of the Tales' popularity during the century after Chaucer's death. Fifty-five of these manuscripts are thought to have been originally complete, while 28 are so fragmentary that it is difficult to ascertain whether they were copied individually or as part of a set. *The Tales* vary in both minor and major ways from manuscript to manuscript; many of the minor variations are due to copyists' errors, while it is suggested that in other cases Chaucer both added to his work and revised it as it was being copied and possibly as it was being distributed. Determining the text of the work is complicated by the question of the narrator's voice which Chaucer made part of his literary structure.

WAITING FOR GODOT

Waiting for Godot is a play by Samuel Beckett, in which two characters, Vladimir and Estragon, wait for the arrival of someone named Godot who never arrives, and while waiting they engage in a variety of discussions and encounter three other characters. Waiting for Godot is Beckett's translation of his own original French play, *En attendant Godot*, and is subtitled (in English only) "a tragicomedy in two acts". The original French text was composed between 9 October 1948 and 29 January 1949. The premiere was on 5 January 1953 in the Théâtre de Babylone, Paris. The English language version was premiered in London in 1955. In a poll conducted by the British Royal National Theatre in 1990 it was voted the "most significant English language play of the 20th century".

The play opens (Act 1) on an outdoor scene of two bedraggled companions: the philosophical Vladimir and the weary Estragon who, at the moment, cannot remove his boots from his aching feet, finally muttering, "Nothing to be done." Vladimir takes up the thought loftily, while Estragon vaguely recalls having been beaten the night before. Finally, his boots come off, while the pair ramble and bicker pointlessly. When Estragon suddenly decides to leave, Vladimir reminds him that they must stay and wait for an unspecified person called Godot—a segment of dialogue that repeats often. Unfortunately, the pair cannot agree on where or when they are expected to meet with this Godot. They only know to wait at a tree, and there is indeed a leafless one nearby.

PROMETHEUS UNBOUND

Prometheus Unbound, lyrical drama in four acts by Percy Bysshe Shelley, published in 1820. The work, considered Shelley's masterpiece, was a reply to Aeschylus's *Prometheus Bound*, in which the Titan Prometheus stole fire from heaven to give to mortals and was punished by Zeus (Jupiter). Shelley's heroic Prometheus strikes against oppression as represented by a power-mad Jupiter. This brilliant but uneven work represented the culmination of the poet's lyrical gifts and political thought.

Prometheus, tortured, is tempted to yield to Jupiter's tyranny but instead forgives him. In this act, Shelley suggests, lies his salvation. Panthea and her sister Asia, symbol of ideal love, decide to free Prometheus by confronting Demogorgon, the volcanic power of the underworld, who vanquishes Jupiter in a violent eruption. Prometheus is reunited with his beloved Asia, and the liberation of human society is foretold. The last act, written months after the first three, describes this joyful transformation but warns that evil must be checked lest tyranny reign once more.

THE NEIGHBOURS OF INDIA

India is the second largest country in the world in the matter of population and the seventh largest one in the matter of area. She is the largest democracy in the world. There are six countries whose boundaries touch the boundary of India. They are Pakistan and Afghanistan in the north-west, Bangladesh and China in the north-east, Burma (Myanmar) in the east and Nepal in the north. India has good religious, social and cultural ties with Nepal. She has entered into treaties of peaceful co-existence with Burma and Bangladesh. Only a small border of hers touches Afghanistan. China and Pakistan have long borders with India. China attacked India in 1962 annexed a large chunk of her territory. But now negotiations are going on in a very cordial atmosphere. However, in view of her massive nuclear and other weaponry, India has to be vigilant. Pakistan is a great headache to India. She attacked India in 1948, 1965, 1971 and in 1999 but even all the time having been defeated, she hasn't given up her belligerent attitude against India. Taliban, a Muslim fundamentalist group is backed by Pakistan, so, India has to be very wary. India has become a nuclear power now and there should be no slackness in defence preparedness.

AN INDIAN GIRL'S MARRIAGE

An Indian marriage is an expensive and noisy affair which presents a series of pompous and glittering scenes and a lot of greediness and superstition. Last week the marriage of my sister was celebrated. She had for days been kept at home and was not allowed to go out. My mother had collected all kinds of precious clothes, jewellery, furniture, etc., to be given to her in-laws in dowry. My father had purchased a brand new motorcycle, a refrigerator, a colour television set and so many other items for her. We could not afford to give a car. As the boy also belongs to a lower middle class family, there was no demand for a car. In fact, no demand was made by the boy or his parents, but we had to follow the customs to maintain our due respect in society. There was a ladies' sangeet (musical concert for ladies) two days before the marriage. Sweets were distributed to all our relatives, friends and neighbours who then gave us 'shagun'. On the appointed day and at the time as determined by the priest, seven rounds around the holy fire were taken by the boy and my sister. The priest also administered them vows of fidelity, protection, purity, etc. We gave many gifts and a sumptuous feast to the noisy marriage-party and my sister was seen off with the boy with tears in our eyes.

THE SECRET OF HAPPINESS

Happiness is not a commodity that can be purchased in the market. It is chiefly a state of mind which the rich as well as the poor can have if they have the will to have the same. We can hear the poor, penniless and hard working housemaids humming tags from popular songs while doing their tedious chores which the rich ladies disdain to touch. A speck of dust in the drawing room raises the blood pressure of a rich lady, but the dung and dirt which lie on the floor of a slum dweller give him the necessary comfort and rest and an ideal place for reclining and even sitting to have his meals. A recent study has shown that the happy moments are almost equal in the lives of the rich and the poor. The rich live in a fool's paradise if they think that they are better off than the poor in the matter of happiness. What is then the secret of happiness? Just positive attitude! We can't say that the Christ was unhappy on the crucifixion or Socrates was unhappy while drinking the cup of hemlock.

HORRORS OF WAR

No doubt, war is a horrible thing. In olden times, wars were not so dangerous. The warriors or armies fought and the common people remained untouched. In those days, weapons were also crude and less dangerous—bows and arrows, spears, daggers and swords. Later came guns and cannon. But in modern times, we have AK-47 and other sophisticated rifles and revolvers, bombs, missiles and so many horrible things. There are chemical and biological weapons. The atomic weapons can destroy the whole world in the twinkling of an eye. Now the warplanes and long range guns and missiles do not differentiate much between military and civilian targets. As a result of it, crops are destroyed and buildings including factories, hospitals, houses, educational institutions and places of worship are demolished. There is a great loss of human life. Innumerable women become widows and children become orphans. Prices rise and unemployment increases. There is a tremendous strain on nerves due to war-shocks. Let man come to senses and banish war.

TO BE A TRUE POLITICIAN

Gandhiji tempered politics with morality for which many people have the misnomer as religion. For example, Gandhiji never went the whole hog for any religion and he didn't accept all Hindu rituals and superstitions. He offered one "Talisman" (or touchstone) for anything we do and that is: will it be in anyway beneficial to the poorest, the lowliest and the lost? And this is pure morality, though socio-economic morality, a kind of welfare economics. Gandhiji didn't just preach: he practised what he preached. It is he who coined the word "Harijan" (*i.e.* man of God) for the untouchables. How many politicians, swearing by Gandhism, follow Gandhiji's principles? One can find any loophole in Gandhian philosophy, but nobody can lay the charge of corruption or selfishness on Gandhiji. How many leaders can now be counted as true Gandhians? Now, every Tom, Dick and Harry who has some money and land and property tries to fish in the troubled waters of politics. If he is a political leader merely by virtue of his wealth, how is he a true politician swearing by Gandhiji who neither had a penny in his pocket nor ownership over an inch of land?

MY WEAKNESSES

It is very difficult to talk about one's own weaknesses. Sometimes, one is not even aware of the same. However, I have a few weaknesses of which I'm aware and have the guts to talk about. My first weakness is that I'm very suspicious by nature. Sometimes, I reject even a well-intentioned proposal suspecting it to be based on some vested interest. Later, I have to repent for having lost the opportunity. My second weakness is that I can't express my attachment to a person properly such that the person concerned thinks that I've no interest in him and he begins to ignore or neglect me. In this way, I've lost a number of good friends. My third weakness is that I'm very impulsive by nature. I feel irritated if I don't find the things happening the way I wish them. This way, I've sometimes to face an unnecessary opposition or embarrassing admonition from somebody. I'm trying my best to overcome my weakness.

MY STRONG POINTS

To talk of one's own strong points may be something from the region of boastfulness. Yet, I'm ready to take the risk since I'm proud of my strong points. My first strong point is that I can't be allured into any temptation. If I'm an official of any rank in an office, I can't be bribed in any way. My second strong point is that I'm very hard working. Others may be more intelligent than I, but I often steal a march over them by dint of hard work and they are astonished. My third strong point is that I always keep my promise to the best of my ability and capacity. Therefore, all consider me a reliable person. My fourth strong point is that I'm very punctual. I have always reached my classes in time. I have never missed a train or bus. I have always maintained my appointments except on two occassions due to some unavoidable reasons and then I expressed my apologies in abundant measure.

ADDRESS TO THE YOUTH

Should an old man address the youth in this manner: "O the erring obstinate youth! You have chosen the path of destruction. Your fall from the precipice is certain and imminent. You have ignored the path of simplicity, sincerity and hard work to which I tried to lead you. You are after glitter and glamour, the snares of which are hard to break." Or do the youth deserve the address as under: "O the flowers of this ancient holy land! The future of this land depends on you. You are the torch-bearer of the future, a beacon light for the coming generations. Try to learn from experience and avoid the mistakes that I committed, and mend your ways so that you may be able to lead successful and prosperous lives. Live all of you like brothers, equitably sharing your resources and income and with a spirit of cooperation, tolerance, goodwill and mutual adjustment, without heating up controversies to a volatile state."

SUPERSTITIONS

How many of us are there who don't believe in superstitions in one way or the other, notwithstanding their claim to the contrary? The first and foremost superstition may be belief in God. Nobody can prove the existence of God. Can anybody do so? Of course, those who say God is not there, also cannot prove their point. One can say with Sir Roger de Coverley, that much can be said on either side. Then what about the belief in past and future births? What the religious Gurus, astrologers and tantriks are most afraid of, is questioning *i.e.*, rationalism. There are certain rationalist societies and clubs which try to explain all the mysterious phenomena to enable the people to get rid of superstitions. An average Indian is scared if either of his eyes or any of his limbs throbs or if a cat or someone with fire in his hand crosses his way. If a man meets a Brahmin early in the morning, he is scared. If a man has an itching sensation in either of his palms, he believes he's going to get money from somewhere. When a particular superstition turns out false, we never think about it and continue believing in such non-existent things.

MORALS AND MANNERS

In the present curricula, the teaching of morals virtually means teaching about God or religions or just mannerism. Morals as taught in the schools, do not just leave the sphere of manners to touch, much less enter, the sphere of real morality. For instance, it is not taught if a choice has to be made between manners and morals, which should be preferred? Manners to morals or morals to manners? It is for the man of prudence to decide whether a child has the right to ask his parents. "Is the car in which I'm taken to school bought with money earned through honest means? Is the big house in which we are living built with money earned through fair means? Are my hefty fees and pocket money paid from honest earnings?" And can he refuse to accept such money if he finds it tainted? It is for the field experts to decide. Then it will be for the educationists to decide whether, the child can be taught to put such questions to his parents? Since parents adopt dishonest means to earn money mainly for their children, if the latter refuse to accept such money, the problem of dishonesty may probably be solved to some extent. But who is to teach such morals to students—parents or teachers? May be, the proposition needs a lot of discussion, as no conclusion is possible in haste.

THE ART OF FLATTERY

There are two peculiarities in modern man which at once make him higher and lower than animals. One is that he has no tail to wag. The other is that his tongue serves the purpose of a tail alongwith its quality of speaking. Shakespeare says about Julius Caesar that he felt the most flattered when he was told that he didn't like flattery. Those who are masters in the art of flattery have the subtle ways to flatter besides simply praising. They offer flowers, banquets, gifts by one pretext or the other such as articles like wristwatches, boxes of sweets, chocolates or biscuits, silk suits, toys, show pieces, etc. But evidently praise is the commonest method, e.g. praising a boss's son or dog, his house, car, dress, neck-tie, shoes, furniture, hairstyle, moustaches, complexion, aesthetic sense, politeness, honesty, way of speaking, his intelligence, resourcefulness, presence of mind, hospitality and so on. Praising a boss's shaving is no different from shaving him off his sense of proportion if he is taken in!

HAPPINESS AND CONTENTMENT

The renowned Augustan poet, Alexander Pope, in his famous poem: 'Ode to Solitude,' says:

"Happy the man whose wish and care
A few paternal acres bound."

The poet means to say that man is happy who is contented with his lot. Such a man does not have very high ambitions which are often unachievable and which make him restless. Even Lord Buddha says that we should control our wants and desires. The basic reason for man's unhappiness and restiveness is his longing for more and more things, particularly the objects of luxury. Lust for money does not let man rest. Once man has achieved his target to get a particular amount of money, his target rises further high and he remains as restless as he was. If we think that happiness is the aim of life, we shall have to lead a life of simplicity and contentment by controlling our wants. It does not mean that we should not endeavour to make progress. We can have a healthy competition. Once Jawahar Lal Nehru said that there could be no progress without healthy ambition. The main point is that we should not be jealous of others' progress and we should not use underhand methods to achieve our aim; otherwise, we can find ourselves in soup. When we have made a desirable amount of progress, we should be contented and charitable.

A MODERN GIRL

Modernity stands for progress. A modern girl, therefore, is an emancipated girl who cannot be subjugated or subdued by the panopticon gaze of patriarchy. She is proud of her sex and is capable of challenging the gendered vision of her class. She is not dependant on her father, brother, husband or son. She ventures out and earns her own livelihood.

Unlike her predecessors, she is vociferous about her rights and asserts them when necessary. She doesn't spend her life resigned to fate. She is educated and smart. She is articulate and doesn't shy away when confronted with the vagaries of fate. She has eliminated the 'gender discrimination' that her predecessors suffered for centuries. She has retained the age old womanly virtues like tolerance, sacrifice, sympathy, compassion, determination and care but she has fought off any attempt of subjection.

THE GIRL CHILD

It is the duty of the parents and the society to take care of their children. Strangely enough, the elephants consider it the duty of the entire herd to take care of their young ones, but the human beings lack this instinct. The result is that among human beings if a child is born of rich parents, he becomes lovely, clean and intelligent and lovable as he enjoys all luxuries and is welcome everywhere, but a poor man's child who lacks all facilities of diet, health, education and training is an abominable creature whom the society looks down upon for his squalor and lack of manners. This is, in particular, the case with the girl child, more if by God's curse she is born an ugly black-skinned one. Who is responsible for this inequality and inequity? When will our society learn to respect children particularly the girl children and give them their rights to education, to health, and due regard as we should know an educated, enlightened girl child can prove to be a great asset to the family and the nation in the matter of national projects like population control, spread of literacy, good morals and manners, etc.?

ECONOMIC JUSTICE IN INDIA

Our constitution guarantees social as well as economic justice to all the citizens of India. Economic justice means providing an economic environment in which there is no poverty; there is no inequality; no concentration of wealth in few hands; and no economic exploitation of the unprivileged class by the privileged class. Economic justice also envisages equal employment opportunities for all; equitable distribution of goods and services; and equal access to economic activities for all. Unfortunately the above mentioned parameters of economic justice are yet to be adequately achieved in India. No doubt, we have taken spectacular strides forward in the area of economic development, especially after the New Economic Policy of 1991 which introduced the concepts of Liberalisation, Privatisation and Globalisation. India has become an international economic power to reckon with. But, the expected 'trickle down effect' that the Nehru-Mahalanobis plan anticipated, failed to take place. The rich became richer and the poor became poorer. The former used the resources that should have benefitted all the citizens but due to defective delivery mechanism and a lackadaisical administrative approach, the plans failed to make much breakthrough and the unscrupulous proletariats continued their unjust enrichment at the cost of the poor who remained at the receiving end. It seems they have been doomed to bottomless perdition and all routes to salvation have been clogged by the haves. Economic justice is still elusive in our country and this fact is corroborated by the incidents of farmers' suicides and self-immolation by the unemployed youth.

EASY LIFE BUT ENDANGERED LIFE

Scientific advancements have considerably contributed to the growth of our civilization. Scientists have improved the quality of our lives immeasurably, for example, computers, telephones, televisions, airplanes, etc. Science is man's only hope against diseases which were incurable in the past. But science has also produced problems—problems that are inherently hazardous and detrimental to the very human existence. For example, pollution. Global warming and the fear of global inundation are the fallouts of pollution. Nuclear weapons have led to a constant apprehension of annihilating warfares. There is also the scare of an obnoxious biological warfare that might lead to painful destruction of our race. On a less hazardous front, we see that people have become lethargic and obese because of the conveniences in excess. A mechanised lifestyle has led to the break down of human communication.

People are becoming distant islands—indifferent towards each other and without tender emotions. Excess dependance on science could bring a cataclysmic end of our earth.

VISION 2020

'India vision 2020' is the plan proposed by former Indian president Dr. APJ Abdul Kalam to make India a developed country by 2020. According to the plan, for transforming the nation into a developed country, five areas in combination have been identified, based on India's core competence, natural resources and talented manpower for integrated action to double the growth rate of GDP and realize the vision of developed India. These are agriculture and food processing with a target of doubling the present production of food; infrastructure with reliable electric power including solar farming for all providing urban amenities in rural areas and interlinking of rivers; education and healthcare; information and communication technology—as this can be used for tele-education, tele-medicine and e-governance; nuclear technology; and space technology in conjunction with defence technology. The vision aims at sustaining at least 10% growth (GDP) rate for ten years, reducing rural urban divide, providing equal access for all to energy and water; corruption-poverty-illiteracy free India; eliminating crime against women and children; and education for all.

BETTER ALONE THAN IN BAD COMPANY

"Man is a social animal," says Aristotle, one of the greatest philosophers of the world. It is also said, "A man who lives alone, must either be a beast or a God." As human beings we are bound to live in company only, man being a gregarious animal. The earliest men lived in tribes and clans. Then grew the family and society. The emergence of nations is only a recent phenomenon. But, unfortunately, sometimes in life, man is surrounded by such people who have a dubious reputation and are hell-bent to lead him on a wrong path. Despite all one's remonstrances, things may not taper off to any progressional or salubrious end with the result that man must either fall in line with others, however, suspicious their credentials, or fend for oneself alone. The sane counsel in such an eventuality is: "Shun, bad company whatever the price" or "Better alone than in bad company."

CHILD IS THE FATHER OF MAN

In his famous Ode to nature, William Wordsworth says that the child in every person teaches him to appreciate nature and the natural wonders. What we think as children will help to determine how we think as adults. The poet hopes to always love nature as he did as a child. A child can teach human qualities to an adult who has been defiled by the artificial human civilization. A child is selfless, innocent, exuberant, indiscriminate and open. He never conceals his emotions. He has nothing to hide. When we grow up we get conditioned by the conventions of the society. Our mind gets polluted by the ideas of casteism, communalism, regionalism, linguistic parochialism, narcissism etc. Children play pranks whereas adults play sanguinary wars. Thus, we need to go back to our roots and relearn all those virtues we lost while growing up. In this respect children can guide men. That is why Wordsworth, states metaphorically that 'child is the father of man'.

●●●

6 Essay Writing

An essay is a written composition containing an expression of one's personal opinions or ideas on a subject. A good essay must hold its readers' attention from the beginning to the end. For this, it must possess certain qualities which make a piece of writing readable and enjoyable.
Every essay depends on two things: (a) its subject matter, and (b) its language.
To write an essay you require 'material'—clear ideas based on experience, reading and observation. These ideas have to be put into words and these words must convey what you wish to say. For this you should know the right words and the most appropriate way to put them together.

CONTEMPORARY INDIAN WRITING IN ENGLISH

The seed of Indian Writing in English was sown during the period of the British rule in India. Now the seed has blossomed into an ever green tree, fragrant flowers and ripe fruits. The fruits are being tasted not only by the native people, but they are also being 'chewed and digested' by the foreigners. It happened only after the constant caring, pruning and feeding. Gardeners' like Tagore, Sri Aurobindo, R.K. Narayan, Raja Rao—to name only a few, looked after the tender plant night and day. In modern time, it is guarded by a number of writers who are getting awards and accolades all over the world.

Indian English Literature (IEL) refers to the body of work by writers in India who write in the English language and whose native or co-native language could be one of the numerous languages of India. Its early history began with the works of Michael Madhusudan Dutt followed by R. K. Narayan, Mulk Raj Anand and Raja Rao who contributed to Indian fiction in the 1930s. The noteworthy contemporary writers in English language are Salman Rushdie, V. S. Naipaul, Ruskin Bond, Vikram Seth, Amitav Ghosh, Anita Desai, Kiran Desai, Shashi Tharur, Suketu Mehta, Bharati Mukherjee, Jhumpa Lahiri, Arvind Adiga, David Davidar, Kovid Gupta, Agha Shahid Ali and Rohinton Mistry. All of them are of Indian descent.

Among the contemporary writers, the most notable is Salman Rushdie, born in India, now living in the USA. Rushdie with his famous work *Midnight's Children* (Booker Prize 1981, Booker of Bookers 1992, and Best of the Bookers 2008) ushered in a new trend of writing. He used a hybrid language—English generously peppered with Indian terms—to convey a theme that could be seen as representing the vast canvas of India. He is usually categorised under the magic realism mode of writing most famously associated with Gabriel García Márquez. Anita Desai, who was shortlisted for the Booker Prize three times, received a Sahitya Akademi Award in 1978 for her novel *Fire on the Mountain* and a British Guardian Prize for *The Village by the Sea*. Her daughter Kiran Desai won the 2006 Man Booker Prize for her second novel, *The Inheritance of Loss*. Ruskin Bond received Sahitya Akademy Award for his collection of short stories *Our Trees Still Grow in Dehra* in 1992. He is also the author of a historical novel *A Flight of Pigeons*, which is based on an episode during the Indian Rebellion of 1857. Vikram Seth, author of *The Golden Gate* (1986) and *A Suitable Boy* (1994) is a writer who uses a purer English and more realistic themes. Being a self-confessed fan of Jane Austen, his attention is on the story, its details and its twists and turns. Vikram Seth is notable both as an accomplished novelist and poet. Vikram Seth's outstanding achievement as a versatile and prolific poet remains largely and unfairly neglected. Another writer who has contributed immensely to the Indian English Literature is Amitav Ghosh who is the author of *The Circle of Reason* (his 1986 debut novel), *The Shadow Lines* (1988), *The Calcutta Chromosome* (1995), *The Glass Palace* (2000), *The Hungry Tide* (2004), and *Sea of Poppies* (2008), the first volume of The Ibis trilogy, set in the 1830s, just before the Opium War, which encapsulates the colonial history of the East. Ghosh's latest work of fiction is *River of Smoke* (2011), the second volume of *The Ibis trilogy*. *The God of Small Things* (1997), Arundhati Roy's debut novel, didn't just win the Booker Prize, but also became the biggest selling book by a non-expatriate Indian author. Roy, known for her strong political stances and commentary, is one of the most followed writers in contemporary India today. Her work also includes several collections of essays including *War Talk* (2003) and *Capitalism : A Ghost Story* (2014).

Rohinton Mistry is an India born Canadian author who is a Neustadt International Prize winner for Literature laureate (2012). His first book *Tales from Firozsha Baag* (1987) published by Penguin Books Canada is a collection of 11 short stories. His novels *Such a Long Journey* (1991) and *A Fine Balance* (1995) earned him great acclaim. Shashi Tharoor, in his *The Great Indian Novel* (1989), follows a story-telling (though in a satirical) mode as in the Mahabharata drawing his ideas by going back and forth in time. His work as UN official living outside India has given him a vantage point that helps construct an objective Indianness. Vikram Chandra is another author who shuffles between India and the United States and has received critical acclaim for his first novel *Red Earth and Pouring Rain* (1995) and collection of short stories *Love and Longing in Bombay* (1997). His namesake Vikram A. Chandra is a renowned journalist and the author of *The Srinagar Conspiracy* (2000). Suketu Mehta is another writer currently based in the United States who authored *Maximum City* (2004), an autobiographical account of his experiences in the city of Mumbai. In 2008, Arvind Adiga received the Man Booker Prize for his debut novel *The White Tiger*.

Bharati Mukherjee (1940), the expatriate of the Indian origin in the U.S.A, is one of the remarkable women writers to have contributed an explicit fiction to the much debated vein of post-modernist literature. Bharati Mukherjee has established herself as a powerful member of the American literary scene with her novels like *The Tiger's Daughter* (1972), *Jasmine* (1989), *Wife* (1975) and anthologies of short stories such as *Middleman and Other Stories* (1988) and *Darkness* (1985). *The Holder of the World* (1993) and *Leave It to Me* (1997) are two other novels by Bharati Mukherji. The writer of a posterior vision and dehumanizing trend of negative capability has made the case of untraditional experience dominating issue over a detached kind of living in future. The methods adopted by Bharathi to portray her sense of the life are not the sensibilities, incorporating the elements of the disassociating and alienated self.

Author of *A Walk Through the Yellow Pages* (1987), *The Half-Inch Himalayas* (1987), *A Nostalgist's Map of America* (1991), *The Country Without a Post Office* (1997), Agha Shahid Ali is among the premiere English language poets born in 20th century India. The Kashmiri poet who moved to the United States later in his life is credited with having introduced the Ghazal form in American poetry. Jhumpa Lahiri's debut short story collection, *Interpreter of Maladies*, was released in 1999. The stories address sensitive dilemmas in the lives of Indians or Indian immigrants, with themes such as marital difficulties, the bereavement over a stillborn child, and the disconnection between first and second generation United States immigrants. In

2003, Lahiri published *The Namesake*, her first novel. The story spans over 30 years in the life of the Ganguli family. The Calcutta-born parents immigrated as young adults to the United States, where their children, Gogol and Sonia, grow up experiencing the constant generational and cultural gap with their parents. Lahiri's second collection of short stories, *Unaccustomed Earth*, was released on April 1, 2008. Upon its publication, *Unaccustomed Earth* achieved the rare distinction of debuting at number 1 on *The New York Times* best seller list. *New York Times Book Review* editor, Dwight Garner, stated, "It's hard to remember the last genuinely serious, well-written work of fiction—particularly a book of stories—that leapt straight to No. 1; it's a powerful demonstration of Lahiri's newfound commercial clout." Lahiri's writing is characterized by her "plain" language and her characters, often Indian immigrants to America who must navigate between the cultural values of their homeland and their adopted home. Lahiri's fiction is autobiographical and frequently draws upon her own experiences as well as those of her parents, friends, acquaintances, and others in the Bengali communities with which she is familiar. Lahiri examines her characters' struggles, anxieties, and biases to chronicle the nuances and details of immigrant psychology and behaviour.

The other contemporary Indian writers in English like Shashi Tharur, David Davidar, Kovid Gupta and others have written books in English which are worth reading. All the Indian writers in English have made India proud of their prolific writing talent and command over English.

SHAKESPEAREAN TRAGEDY

Shakespearean tragedy is the designation given to most tragedies written by playwright William Shakespeare. Many of his history plays share the qualifiers of a Shakespearean tragedy, but because they are based on real figures throughout the History of England, they were classified as "histories" in the First Folio. The Roman tragedies—*Julius Caesar, Antony and Cleopatra* and *Coriolanus*—are also based on historical figures, but because their source stories were foreign and ancient they are almost always classified as tragedies rather than histories. Shakespeare's romances (tragicomic plays) were written late in his career and published originally as either tragedy or comedy. They share some elements of tragedy featuring a high status central character but end happily like Shakespearean comedies. Several hundred years after Shakespeare's death, scholar F.S. Boas also coined a fifth category, the "problem play," for plays that do not fit neatly into a single classification because of their subject matter,. setting, or ending. The classifications of certain Shakespeare plays are still debated among scholars.

There are 9 elements in Shakespeare's tragedies at a glance—Tragic hero; A struggle between good and evil; Hamartia; Tragic Waste; External conflict; Internal conflict; Catharsis; Supernatural elements; Absence of Poetic Justice and Comic relief.

- **Tragic Hero:** A tragic hero is one of the most significant elements of a Shakespearean tragedy. This type of tragedy is essentially a one-man show. It is a story about one, or sometimes two, characters. The hero may be either male or female and he or she must suffer because of some flaw of character, because of inevitable fate, or both. The hero must be the most tragic personality in the play. According to Andrew Cecil Bradley, a noted 20th century Shakespeare scholar, a Shakespearean tragedy "is essentially a tale of suffering and calamity conducting to death." (Usually the hero has to face death in the end.)

  An important feature of the tragic hero is that he or she is a towering personality in his/her state/kingdom/country. This person hails from the elite stratum of society and holds a high position, often one of royalty. Tragic heroes are kings, princes, or military generals, who are very important to their subjects. Take Hamlet, prince of Denmark; he is intellectual, highly educated, sociable, charming, and of a philosophic bent. The hero is such an important person that his/her death gives rise to full-scale turmoil, disturbance, and chaos throughout the land. When Hamlet takes revenge for the death of his father, he is not only killing his uncle but inviting his own death at the hands of Laertes. And as a direct result of his death, the army of Fortinbras enters Denmark to take control.

- **A Struggle Between Good and Evil:** Shakespearean tragedies play out the struggle between good and evil. Most of them deal with the supremacy of evil and suppression of good. According to Edward Dowden, a 19th century noted poet and literary critic, "Tragedy as conceived by Shakespeare is concerned with the ruin or restoration of the soul and of the life of man. In other words, its subject is the struggle of Good and Evil in the world." Evil is presented in Shakespearean tragedies in a way that suggests its existence is an indispensable and ever-enduring thing. For example, in *Hamlet*, the reader is given the impression that something rotten will definitely happen to Denmark (foreshadowing). Though the reader gets an inkling, typically the common people of the play are unaware of the impending evil.

  In *Julius Caesar*, the mob is unaware of the struggle between good and evil within King Caesar. They are also ignorant of the furtive and sneaky motives of Cassius. Goodness never beats evil in the tragedies of Shakespeare. Evil conquers goodness. The reason for this is that the evil element is always disguised, while goodness is open and freely visible to all. The main character (the most pious and honest person in the tragedy) is assigned the task of defeating the supreme evil because of his goodness. As a result, he suffers terribly and ultimately fails due to his fatal flaw. This tragic sentiment is perfectly illustrated by Hamlet in the following lines:

  "O cursed spite,

  That ever I was born to set it right."

- **Hamartia:** Hamartia is the Greek word for "sin" or "error", which derives from the verb *hamatanein*, meaning "to err" or "to miss the mark". In other words, hamartia refers to the hero's tragic flaw. It is another absolutely critical element of a Shakespearean tragedy. Every hero falls due to some flaw in his or her character. Here I will once again reference A.C. Bradley, who asserts, "The calamities and catastrophe follow inevitably from the deeds of men and the main source of these deeds is character." As a result of the fatal flaw, the hero falls from a high position, which usually leads to his/her unavoidable death.

  A good example of hamartia can be seen in *Hamlet* when Hamlet's faltering judgment and failure to act lead him to his untimely death. He suffers from procrastination. He finds a number of opportunities to kill his uncle, but he fails because of his indecisive and procrastinating nature. Every time, he delays taking action. In one case he finds an opportunity to kill Claudius while Claudius is praying. Still, Hamlet forgoes the excellent opportunity to achieve his goal with the excuse that he doesn't want to kill a man while he is praying. He wants to kill Claudius when he is in the act of committing a sin. It is this perfectionism, failure to act, and uncertainty about the correct path that ultimately results in Hamlet's death and lead Denmark into chaos.

- **Tragic Waste:** In Shakespearean tragedies, the hero usually dies along with his opponent. The death of a hero is not an ordinary death; it encompasses the loss of an exceptionally intellectual, honest, intelligent, noble, and virtuous person. In a tragedy, when good is destroyed along with evil, the loss is known as a "tragic waste." Shakespearean tragedy always includes a tragic waste of goodness. *Hamlet* is a perfect example of tragic waste. Even though Hamlet succeeds in uprooting the evil from Denmark, he does so at the cost of his death. In this case, the good (Hamlet) gets destroyed along with evil (Claudius). Neither of them wins. Instead, they fail together.

- **External Conflict:** External conflict plays a vital role in the tragedies of Shakespeare. External conflict causes internal conflict in the mind of the tragic hero. Every tragic hero in a Shakespearean play is confronted with external conflicts that must be addressed. Hamlet, for example, is confronted with external conflict in the shape of his uncle, Claudius. He has to take revenge, but as a result of his uncle's craftiness and effective security, Hamlet isn't able to translate his ideas into action. This external conflict gives rise to internal conflict, which hinders Hamlet from taking any action.
- **Internal Conflict:** Internal conflict is one of the most essential elements in a Shakespearean tragedy. It refers to the confusion in the mind of the hero. Internal conflict is responsible for the hero's fall, along with fate or destiny. The tragic hero always faces a critical dilemma. Often, he cannot make a decision, which results in his ultimate failure. Again, Hamlet is a perfect example. He is usually a doer, but over the course of the play, his indecision and frequent philosophical hangups create a barrier to action. Internal conflict is what causes Hamlet to spare the life of Claudius while he is praying.
- **Catharsis:** Catharsis is a remarkable feature of a Shakespearean tragedy. It refers to the cleansing of the audience's pent-up emotions. In other words, Shakespearean tragedies help the audience to feel and release emotions through the aid of tragedy. When we watch a tragedy, we identify with the characters and take their losses personally. A Shakespearean tragedy gives us an opportunity to feel pity for a certain character and fear for another, almost as if we are playing the roles ourselves. The hero's hardships compel us to empathize with him. The villain's cruel deeds cause us to feel wrath toward him. Tears flow freely when a hero like Hamlet dies. At the same time we feel both sorry for Hamlet and happy that Claudius has received his proper punishment.
- **Supernatural Elements:** Supernatural elements are another key aspect of a Shakespearean tragedy. They play an import role in creating an atmosphere of awe, wonder, and sometimes fear. Supernatural elements are typically used to advance the story and drive the plot. The ghost Hamlet sees plays an important role in stirring up internal conflict. It is the ghost who tells Hamlet his father was killed by his uncle Claudius and assigns him the duty of taking revenge. Similarly, the witches in *Macbeth* play a significant role in the plot. These witches are responsible for motivating Macbeth to resort to murder in order to ascend the throne of Scotland.
- **Absence of Poetic Justice:** Poetic Justice means good is rewarded and evil is punished; it refers to a situation in which everything comes to a fitting and just end. There is no poetic justice in the tragedies of Shakespeare, rather, these plays contain only partial justice. Shakespeare understood that poetic justice rarely occurs outside of fiction. Good deeds often go without reward and immoral people are often free to enjoy life to its fullest. *"Do good and have good"* was considered an outdated ethos in the time of Shakespeare, which is why we don't find any poetic justice in his tragedies. Good is crushed along with evil. Hamlet dies along with Claudius.

Comic Relief: Comic relief is our final key element. Shakespeare didn't follow in the footsteps of his classical predecessors when writing tragedies. Greek and Roman writers didn't use comic relief. But Shakespeare wanted to relieve the tension for the reader and lighten up the mood here and there. A few examples of comic relief scenes include the grave digger scene in *Hamlet*, the drunken port scene in *Macbeth*, the fool is smarter than the king dialogue in *King Lear*, and the Polonius in the wings speech in *Hamlet*. We also have the following scene in *Romeo and Juliet*:

MERCUTIO: *"No, 'tis not so deep as a well, nor so wide as a church-door, but 'tis enough; 'twill serve. Ask for me to-morrow, and you shall find me a grave man. I am pepper'd, I warrant, for this world."*

Shakespearean tragedy usually works on a five-part structure, corresponding to the five acts: Part One, the exposition, outlines the situation, introduces the main characters, and begins the action. Part Two, the development, continues the action and introduces complications. Part Three, the crisis (or climax), brings everything to a head. In this part, a change of direction occurs or understanding is precipitated. Part Four includes further developments leading inevitably to Part Five, in which the final crisis of action or revelation and resolution are explained. *Othello* follows this pattern.

THE USES OF LINGUISTICS

Linguistics is the scientific study of language, and involves an analysis of language form, language meaning, and language in context. The earliest activities in the documentation and description of language have been attributed to the 4th century BCE Indian grammarian Panini, who wrote a formal description of the Sanskrit language in his *Astadhyayi*.

Linguists traditionally analyse human language by observing an interplay between sound and meaning. Phonetics is the study of speech and non-speech sounds, and delves into their acoustic and articulatory properties. The study of language meaning, on the other hand, deals with how languages encode relations between entities, properties, and other aspects of the world to convey, process, and assign meaning, as well as manage and resolve ambiguity. While the study of semantics typically concerns itself with truth conditions, pragmatics deals with how situational context influences the production of meaning.

Grammar is a system of rules which governs the production and use of utterances in a given language. These rules apply to sound as well as meaning, and include componential subsets of rules, such as those pertaining to phonology (the organisation of phonetic sound systems), morphology (the formation and composition of words), and syntax (the formation and composition of phrases and sentences). Modern theories that deal with the principles of grammar are largely based within Noam Chomsky's framework of generative linguistics.

The uses of Linguistics are many. Linguists investigate how people acquire their knowledge about language, how this knowledge interacts with other cognitive processes, how it varies across speakers and geographic regions, and how to model this knowledge computationally. They study how to represent the structure of the various aspects of language (such as sounds or meaning), how to account for different linguistic patterns theoretically, and how the different components of language interact with each other. Linguists develop and test scientific hypotheses. Many linguists appeal to statistical analysis, mathematics, and logical formalism to account for the patterns they observe.

Linguistics is an important subject that gives us insight into one of the most intriguing aspects of human knowledge and behaviour. Learning linguistics means that we will learn about many aspects of human language, including sounds (phonetics, phonology), words (morphology), sentences (syntax), and meaning (semantics). It can involve looking at how languages change over time (historical linguistics); how language varies from situation to situation, group to group, and place to place (sociolinguistics, dialectology); how people use language in context (pragmatics, discourse analysis); how to model aspects of language (computational linguistics); how people acquire or learn language (language acquisition); and how people process language (psycholinguistics, experimental linguistics).

Linguistics programs may be organized around different aspects of the field. For example, in addition to or instead of the above areas, a program might choose to focus on a particular language or group of languages; how language relates to historical, social, and cultural issues (anthropological linguistics); how language is taught in a classroom setting, or how students learn language (applied linguistics); or how linguistics is situated in the cognitive sciences.

A degree in linguistics helps students to acquire valuable intellectual skills, such as analytical reasoning, critical thinking, argumentation, and clarity of expression. This means making insightful observations, formulating clear, testable hypotheses, generating predictions, making arguments and drawing conclusions, and communicating findings to a wider community. Linguistics majors are therefore well equipped for a variety of graduate-level and professional programs and careers. Some may require additional training or skills, but not all do.

As far as professional aspects are concerned, the importance of linguistics is immense. Training in linguistics can equip you to work on speech recognition, text-to-speech synthesis, artificial intelligence, natural language processing, user research, and computer-mediated language learning, among many other areas. People with a background in linguistics and education can develop materials for different populations, train teachers, design assessments, find effective ways to teach language-related topics in specific communities, or use the language of a community effectively in instruction. Many applied linguists are involved in teacher education and educational research. If one is professionally qualified in linguistics one might teach in departments such as Linguistics, Philosophy, Psychology, Speech/ Communication Sciences, Anthropology, English, and departments focused on specific foreign languages. Skilled translators and interpreters are needed everywhere, from government to hospitals to courts of law. For this line of work, a high level of proficiency in the relevant language(s) is necessary, and additional specialized training may be required. Some agencies and institutes seek linguists to work with language consultants in order to document, analyze, and revitalize languages (many of which are endangered). Some organizations engage in language-related fieldwork, conducting language surveys, establishing literacy programs, and translating documents of cultural heritage. People qualified in Linguistics can help the actors need training in pronunciation, intonation, and different elements of grammar in order to sound like real speakers of a language or dialect. They may even need to know how to make mistakes to sound like an authentic non-native speaker. Linguistics people can work with the companies that specialize in advertising. These companies often do extensive linguistic research on the associations that people make with particular sounds and classes of sounds and the kind of wording that would appeal to potential consumers. Therefore, Linguistics can help us in many ways.

MY NATION, MY LANGUAGE

My nation, *i.e.*, India is one of the oldest civilizations in the world, spanning a period of more than 4000 years, and witnessing the fusion of several customs and traditions, which are reflective of the rich culture and heritage of the Country.

The history of the nation gives a glimpse into the magnanimity of its evolution—from a Country reeling under colonialism, to one of the leading economies in the global scenario within a span of fifty years. More than anything, the nationalistic fervour of the people is the contributing force behind the culmination of such a development. This transformation of the nation instills a sense of national pride in the heart of every Indian within the Country and abroad. Historians, writers, politicians and other eminent personalities across the Globe have greatly appreciated India and its contribution to rest of the world. Though these remarks are only a partial reflection of the greatness of India, they certainly make us feel proud of our motherland. The world-famous scientist Albert Einstein once said,

"We owe a lot to the Indians, who taught us how to count, without which no worthwhile scientific discovery could have been made!" The world-famous French scholar Romaine Rolland once said about India, "If there is one place on the face of earth where all the dreams of living men have found a home from the very earliest days when man began the dream of existence, it is India!" And so on.

The facets of my India is first, the Code of Conduct of the Indian National Flag, which has been dubbed as Flag Code of India, 2002 is an attempt to bring together laws, conventions, practices, and instructions for the guidance and benefit of everyone concerned and secondly, the song Jana-gana-mana, composed originally in Bengali by Rabindranath Tagore, was adopted in its Hindi version by the Constituent Assembly as the National Anthem of India on 24 January 1950. We have a National Song also, *i.e.*, *Vandemataram*, written by renowned Bengali novelist Bankimchandra Chattopadhyay. I am proud of my nation because, we are one. Ours is a multi-religious and multi-lingual country, but still mentally we are not detached of our country, and do not bear any provincial identity. We always feel that we are Indian—people of one nation only. We are a very old civilization and a peace-loving nation. Our great monk Swami Vivekananda highlighted India and unfurled her victorious flag in 1893 in the World Religious Congress held in Chicago, the USA. He once said, "Civilizations have arisen in other parts of the world. In ancient and modern times, wonderful ideas have been carried forward from one race to another. But mark you, my friends, it has been always with the blast of war trumpets and the march of embattled cohorts. Each idea had to be soaked in a deluge of blood..... Each word of power had to be followed by the groans of millions, by the wails of orphans, by the tears of widows. This, many other nations have taught; but India for thousands of years peacefully existed. Here activity prevailed when even Greece did not exist... Even earlier, when history has no record, and tradition dares not peer into the gloom of that intense past, even from until now, idea after idea has marched out from her, but every word has been spoken with a blessing behind it and peace before it. We, of all nations of the world, have never been a conquering race, and that blessing is on our head, and therefore we live....!" Therefore I am proud to become a part of that nation.

Secondly, in a multi-lingual country like ours, not all the languages can be "my language", because not all the countrymen can speak all the languages of a multi-lingual country. Despite being an Indian, I also can't speak or follow all the languages prevalent in India. Though I have a high regard for all the languages of India including Hindi, because Hindi has tied up all the Indians, but my language is my mother tongue. I feel easy and comfortable when I speak in my mother tongue, share pleasantries or exchange views with the people of my mother tongue. There are so many languages, not only in my country, but also in the entire world, but I find myself incomplete if I can't get a scope to speak in my mother-tongue. Even a renowned polyglot also, at some moment, wants to relieve himself mentally by speaking in his mother tongue. He then goes in search of people of same language. Every language is rich with its invaluable literature and every language has given birth to people, famous in many spheres of life. My language is also no exception to it. Therefore, the first priority is my language. I like the other languages but I love my language.

IF I WERE A SPARROW

It is sometimes said, "if wishes were horses, beggars would ride them." I fully agree with those who say this, still, I do not think anything wrong if I were to run the horses of my imagination.

Accordingly, I'm in a mood to imagine myself a sparrow. Hence, I want to contemplate how I would look and feel and behave if I were a sparrow.

Naturally, if I were a sparrow, I'd have a small body which would be well equipped with soft wings and feathers like every bird. I do not here want to go into the intricacies of difference in wings and feathers of various kinds of birds. It is because I do not want to divide the world of birds on any pretext like the artificial division among human beings on the basis of colors, race, caste, creed, nationality, etc.

There are several reasons that I want to be a sparrow. First of all, if I were a sparrow, I could fly up in the sky, if not very high and breath the fresh air that I have never enjoyed before. In the sky, I don't have to care too much about others' feelings and thoughts and I can just enjoy the feeling of freedom and carelessness. Secondly, I could travel to different countries and wander in multiple breathtaking landscapes and exotic architectures to feast my eyes. In this way, I could expand my horizons. Thirdly, except from travelling between diverse countries, I could also choose where to live on my own will. Instead of any tree, I could build my nest in the ventilator. What a wonderful thing it is! The last but not the least, I don't have to worry about the future if I were a sparrow and only have to live in the present rather than living in the purpose-driven life. In the above mentioned, there are plenty of advantages to live a bird life. No matter how far-reaching that kind of dream it is, I still believe that if I could be a sparrow, it must be the most amazing thing in my life.

The most remarkable thing that I'd do is that I'd fly in the sky unhindered as the king or queen of skies as the case may be. It won't be impossible for me to feel like Shelley's Skylark to be somewhere near heaven from which height I'd pour my wisdom of ages down on the curious, puzzled humanity. Man is habituated to looking before and after and that is the cause of his misery. I'd teach him how to soar in the infinite skies selflessly.

Perhaps human spaceships which display the feats can be no match for me since my flight is entirely selfless and arises out of sheer happiness and love for freedom and adventure, whereas any and every human activity of whatever dimension is a part of some selfish motive lurking somewhere somehow without fail.

WHY I LIKE INDIAN FILMS

I like Indian films because of many reasons. First, beyond the aesthetic impact of politics, the thematic content of many Indian films naturally reflects Indian history and politics. Countless films deal with rebellions against the British, or remember rebellion against the British fondly. The partition between India and Pakistan is a frequent subject as well, with political tensions between the two countries providing stories for everything from Cold War-style espionage between the two countries to doomed romances between an Indian boy and a Pakistani girl, to—this being India—both at the same time.

Even a cursory, surface-level understanding of events like this can help greatly in understanding the context of Indian films—not because they'd be incomprehensible without it, but because they are made, for the most part, for Indian audiences familiar with all these events, so occasionally details are elided to avoid over-explaining. It's not that one can't "get" Indian films without that, it just helps one get them in a different way.

Moreover, I am fond of colourful characters which I find in Indian films. I am specially fond of Indian actors gutsy enough to go totally extreme with their outfits and their roles. The saris, kurtas, and even "normal" clothes are fun, bright, and always come with scarves. The fashion is very good, it's contagious. I like Indian films because of various other reasons. First, Indian films in general have more romance than Hollywood films, both in the volume and in the level of romance in the movie itself. The Indian culture is also generally more conservative than the West, so the romance tends to be less physical and more emotional, which I appreciate, if only because it's something different. Secondly, stories and plot constructions in Indian movies are unique. These two features always attract me. Thirdly, a very interesting feature of Indian films is that the music is not usually performed by the actors in the film, but by professional singers whose primary job is to sing for Indian movies. Fourthly, like singing, dancing is also a part of Indian movie. Like singing, dancing also entertains us but never seems that it is an extra item, irrelevant to the film. Both singing and dancing complement an Indian film.

The final reason of my fondness for Indian films is, Indian films are pretty different from the films of the West. We won't have to read the sub-title of a film while watching it, as the language is more or less comprehensible to us, at least our mother tongue and the languages which surround us and the stars are also our familiar ones.

RESERVATION POLICY IN INDIA

Two thousand years ago, the great philosopher Aristotle said, "injustice arises equally". This profound statement is what lies at the heart of equality—a fundamental human right. Every human simply by virtue of being a human being is entitled to equal treatment.

The most significant, pervasive and violent discrimination in our country is the centuries old caste system. It was abolished by the Constitution in 1952 and untouchability was declared a crime. There was a category of people called dalits outside this system who were discriminated and treated as untouchables. They were thus given reservation by the government.

Reservation in India is the process of setting aside a certain percentage of seats (vacancies) in government institutions for members of backward and under-represented communities (defined primarily by caste and tribe). It is a form of quota-based affirmative action. Scheduled Castes, Scheduled Tribes and other backward classes are the primary beneficiaries of the reservation policies under the Constitution with the objective of ensuring a 'level' playing field.

The Constitution of India states in Article 15(4) that, "All citizens shall have equal opportunities of receiving education. Nothing herein contained shall prevent the state from providing special facilities for educationally backward sections".

It also states that, "The State shall promote with special care the educational and economic interests of the weaker sections of society and shall protect them from 'social injustice' and all forms of exploitation". The Article further states that nothing in Article 15(4) will prevent the nation from helping SCs and STs for their betterment.

In 1982, the Constitution specified 15% and 7.5% of vacancies in public sector and government-aided educational institutes as a quota reserved for the SC and ST candidates respectively for a period of five years, after which it was to be reviewed. This period was routinely extended by the succeeding governments. The Supreme Court of India ruled that reservations cannot exceed 50% and put a cap on reservations.

However, there are State laws that exceed this 50% limit and these are under litigation in the Supreme Court. For example, caste based reservation stands at 69% and the same is applicable to about 87% of the population in the State of Tamil Nadu.

In 1990, then Prime Minister VP Singh announced that 27% of government positions would be set aside for OBCs in addition to the 22.5% already set aside for SCs and STs. This was followed according to the Mandal Commission which was established in India in 1978 by the Janata Party government under Prime Minister Morarji Desai with a mandate to "identify the socially or educationally backward".

Now, the question arises whether there is a need to review the reservation policy in India or should continue with the tradition? The basic idea of reservation was undoubtedly superb as it was in all good intent, meant to improve till now the status of those sections of the society which had hitherto been left uncared for. However, as we see it today, the policy of reservation has completely changed in the past few years. There has been unlimited extension of the policy for no one knows how long, it appears as though the policy has come to stay forever and its extension is also as though unlimited, with several more sections joining the band wagon of the classes under reservation.

If we look at the reservation policy in India, we are the only country in the world that provides affirmative action based on individual caste identities. It is a well established fact that reservations are tools of upliftment for those disadvantaged groups who have suffered years of discrimination and oppression at the hands of the higher castes.

We the people of India, believe in the concept of 'Vasudhaiva Kutumbakam' where we take each and every person on equal terms and also take the path of fraternity into its ambit. The reservation policy in India gave a change to the backward and downtrodden people to be on equal terms with the other classes of the society. It not only helped them in improving their lives and status in the society but also provided them with an opportunity to represent themselves in various aspects of the decision-making part of society, something which has denied to them for a long time.

Reservation has come up in educational institutions, in jobs, in state assemblies, in Parliament and in every feasible sphere. It will be a wonder if this system is really going to help us to raise our standards in every sphere or will this become just a tool in the hands of a few, to forward their own interests, as has been upto this juncture. The reservation policy has taken only few families of weaker sections and not the masses, in general, in its purposed ambit. If we do not revise this preferential discrimination policy, we are going to see more division, more resentment and more violence. We need a policy which really helps people who are deprived of education and means of better life. Reserving certain percentage of seats in the higher education of institutions and jobs in the high ranks of the government is not going to help solve problems of 85% of total backward castes population.

The government need to review its reservation policy instead of extending its benefits to the other sections also who call themselves backwards. The criterion for reservation should be totally restructured as we need to set certain definitions straight all over again before we decide whom to give reservation or not to give it at all. If equality is the aim, reservation should be given to people with lower income group so that they feel at par with the rest of the society.

Economic background must be considered if reservations are actually to help deserving people. The current reservation policy and its persistence is likely to increase the caste gap which is most likely to solidify distinctions in the society producing unnecessary rancour. It should be kept in mind that lowering the standard of education for anyone is not the solution, it is important to raise the standards of facilities provided to people so that they become self-reliant and come out of the vicious circle of caste and quotas. Reservation should not be looked at as the only tool for empowering the marginalised backward communities of the society.

CYBER CRIME

The past two decades have witnessed an invasion by technology in almost all the spheres of human life. This has led to an increased dependency on technology. Thanks to information technology, the world is making paradigm shifts from the offline to the online domain. Everything from banking, stock exchange, healthcare, education can be controlled and monitored using technology. As there are two sides of a coin, the technology also has two sides to it *i.e.*, its pros and cons. One of the major cons of the technology is cyber crime.

Cyber crime is defined as a crime in which a computer is the object of the crimes such as, hacking, phishing, spamming or is used as a tool to commit an offense (child pornography, hate crimes). Cyber criminals may use computer technology to access personal information, business trade secrets or use the internet for malicious purposes such as online monitoring of another person's activities, unauthorised users who can access their personal and sensitive information.

A person who gains unatuthorised access to the system is known as a hacker. Theft involves the download of copyrighted material by violating the copyrights. In the case of electronic fund transfer crime, a person illegally gains access to another person's bank details and this may lead to financial losses. E-mail bombing involves sending a large number of mails over the network in order to crash the server. A very common cyber crime act is sending the virus as an attachment via mails. This virus can be used to extract the data from the system and jeopardise it in some cases.

National and international financial institutions, banks and security agencies fall victim to the cyber criminals. In many cases, they have to pay a lot of money to the criminals in order to prevent the misuse of their data. The social media is driving the world crazy. But, at the same time, it has become a breeding ground and platform for cyber crime. Thanks to the sharing culture of social media, people tend to share a lot over the social media platforms. This information is used by cyber criminals to extract personal and sensitive information of others which can be misused later on. The imposters create fake social media accounts and post misleading information about the concerned person. This commonly happens with public figures and is done with an intention to malign and harm the image of the person.

In this world dominated by technology, smartphones have become imperative. The smartphones have given way to mobile applications. A large number of private and public sector banks, e-commerce websites, railways and airlines have launched their mobile applications. The ease of operations of smartphone applications prompts the users to install and operate them. With millions of users, these applications are a lucrative source of data.

Many times, the users unknowingly grant certain permissions to the application, which allows it to access their personal information. This gives the application provider with personal information about the individual. So, the user need to be careful while installing mobile applications and be sure of the permissions granted to them.

India is taking giant strides towards digitali-sation with initiatives such as 'Digital India'. This necessitates the people to learn to tackle with the different aspects of cyber crime. Although, people have become tech-savvy, their knowledge about cyber crime is limited. The cyber crime needs to be dealt at two levels—one will be at the individual level and the other will be at the service provider level.

People need to be very careful about their acquaintances and the degree to which they divulge their personal information on social media. It is best to stay away and not accept invites, as well as requests, from unknown people. One should avoid sharing sensitive information such as passwords with anyone.

The passwords need to be strong enough so that the hacker cannot crack them. In order to increase the strength of the password, one can make use of alpha-numeric values and special symbols. In fact, one needs to make sure that there is never a common password for all accounts.

It is best to refrain from clicking on the pop-ups and unknown website links. One needs to make sure that all the transactions that are done online happen through a secured gateway. One must abstain from saving the bank account details on the websites. The mails which make claims about winning a prize money are malicious and must be ignored. A good quality anti-virus must be installed in the system. This anti-virus must be regularly updated.

E-mail service providers as well as many other online platforms have started multi-step verification process in order to secure the user's account. It is always better to spend some extra amount of time and go in for the verification in order to secure one's account.

The service provider can encrypt the data in order to protect it. Encryption is a technique to convert plain text into cipher text. Cipher text is the coded text and it is only the recipient of the data who can decrypt it using a special private key. In this way, except for the recipient, nobody can access the information. A wall can be created between the users and possible intruders. This wall is known as the Firewall. The firewall allows the flow of information only to the computers which are registered and recognised by the host. Digital signatures can be used in case of banking and other such industries. These are created by cryptography and are safe to use.

The biggest concern with regards to cyber crime is that it gets tough to uncover the identity of the criminal. A skilled law enforcing agency is required to deal with this crime. The Information Technology Act, 2000 passed by Indian

Government deals with the domain of cyber crime. But this act has certain loopholes that need to be plugged in order to strengthen the cyber security. Besides, it is important for the government to create awareness among the people about the exponentially rising cyber crime and ways to deal with it.

There will always be new and unexpected challenges to stay ahead of cyber criminals and cyber terrorists but we can win only through partnership and collaboration of both individuals and government. There is much we can do to ensure a safe, secure and trustworthy computing environment. It is crucial not only to our national sense of well-being, but also to our national security and economy.

CHILD LABOUR IN INDIA

Childhood is considered to be the golden period of one's life but this doesn't hold true for some children who struggle to make their both ends meet during their childhood years. At a tender age, which is supposed to be an age of playing and going to school, they are compelled to work in factories, industries, offices or as domestic helps. Child labour means employment of children in any kind of work that hampers their physical and mental development, deprives them of their basic educational and recreational requirements. It is a blot on our society and speaks volumes about the inability of our society to provide a congenial environment for the growth and development of the children.

Earlier, the children used to help their parents in agricultural practices such as sowing, harvesting, reaping and taking care of cattle etc. But industrialisation and urbanisation have in a way encouraged child labour. Children are employed in hazardous work such as bidi rolling, cracker industry, pencil, matchbox and bangle making industries etc. In the bidi industry, children are expected to perform all the chores of rolling, binding and closing the ends of bidis using their nimble fingers. The cracker industry poses threat to the lives of the children due to their direct exposure to the explosive material. The bangle and pencil making industries make the child susceptible to different respiratory problems and lung cancer, in the worst cases. Besides, children are employed as labourers in the garment, leather, jewellery and sericulture industry.

A number of other factors could be attributed to the rise of this menace. In the poor and lower strata families, children are considered to be an extra earning hand. These families have a conviction that every child is an earner so, more the number of children more the earning. The children are expected to shoulder their parents' responsibilities. Parental illiteracy is also one of the contributors to this problem. Education tends to take a backseat in the lives of these children. The uneducated parents consider education as an investment in comparison to the returns which they get in the form of earnings of their children. The child labourers are subjected to unhygienic conditions, late working hours and different atrocities which have a direct effect on their cognitive development. The young and immature minds of the children find it difficult to cope with such situations leading to different emotional and physical problems. Employers also prefer child labourers in comparison to the adults. This is because they can extract more work and still afford to pay the children lesser amount. Bonded child labour is one of the worst forms of child labour. In this, the children are made to work in order to pay off a loan or debt of the family.

It can be considered as a form of slavery where the children assist their parents as they inherit the debt from them. Bonded labourers are most commonly employed in the agriculture sector. Bonded labour has resulted into trafficking of the children from rural to urban areas in order to work as domestic helps or in small production houses.

The government has an important role to play in this fight against child labour. As poverty is one of the major cause of child labour in India, the government needs to assure that it provides basic amenities to all its citizens and there is an equal distribution of wealth. It needs to generate sufficient jobs to assure employability to the poor.

At the same time, NGOs can provide vocational training to people in order to get them good jobs. The government, in collaboration with NGOs, should reach out to the poor people to make them understand the importance of education. The parents as well as the children should be made aware of the government's initiative to provide free education to all the children between the age group of 6-14 years. The parents must be encouraged to send their children to schools instead of work places.

To prohibit the child labour in India Nobel Prize winner Kailash Satyarthi took an initiative. He is the founder of Bachpan Bachao Aandolan (BBA), and organisation dedicated towards the eradication of child labour and rehabilitation of the rescued former child workers. Educated citizens can contribute significantly in doing away with child labour. They can play an important role in spreading the word about the harmful effect of child labour on the oerall development of a child. Affluent and high income group families can pool in funds to support the education of poor children. In fact, the schools and colleges can come up with innovative teaching programmes for the poor children. The principle of 'Each one, teach one' can be followed. Children of the support staff (peons, clerks etc of schools and colleges) can be offered free education.

The Indian Government has enacted many laws to protect child rights, namely the Child and Adolescent Labour (Prohibition and Regulation) Act, 1986, the Factories Act, 1948, the Mines Act, 1952, the Bonded Labour System Abolition Act and the Juvenile Justice (Care and Protection of Children) Act, 2000. Most of these acts prohibit the employment of children below the age of 14 years in factories, hazardous occupations or in bondage. The Right of Children to Free and Compulsory Education Act, 2009 mandates free and compulsory education to all children between the age group of 6 to 14 years. Apart from this, it also reserves 25 per cent seats in every private school for Economically Weaker Sections (EWS) of the society.

The National Policy on Child Labour, 1987 looks into the rehabilitation of children working in hazardous occupations. The Article 39 of the Indian Constitution declares the duty of the state to provide the children the facilities to develop in a healthy and congenial environment and in conditions of freedom and dignity. In May 2015, the government approved a proposal allowing children below 14 years of age to work in family enterprises or entertainment industry with specific conditions.

But there should be a total ban on the employment of small children in any activity other than going to school and getting educated. The government needs to ensure that it has foolproof laws and they are properly executed as well as implemented. Strict measures need to be taken against those who encourage child labour in any form.

Children are the future of a country and it is the childhood which has a profound impact on the future of a child. So, it becomes the collective responsibility of the citizens, society and the government to provide them an environment which helps them to bring out the best of their capabilities, thus participate in the nation building process.

Children are the future citizens of a country. Childhood experiences and foundation will have a great impact on these children's overall development. A nation full of poverty ridden illiterate children cannot make progress. It should be the collective responsibility of the society and the government to provide children with a healthy and conducive environment which will help them to develop their innate capabilities and use their skills effectively.

The need of the hour is to expand the machinery for enforcing the various laws on child labour. If child labour is to be eradicated from India, the government and those responsible for the enforcement need to do their jobs sincerely. Success can be achieved only through social engineering on a major scale combined with broad based economic growth.

PLACE OF WOMEN IN SOCIETY

Today, we find women walking shoulder to shoulder in all fields of life. They are there in the fields of education, medicine, law, engineering, administration, management, etc. Now, we have women teachers, doctors, nurses, air-hostesses, engineers, architects, clerks, officers and even pilots and drivers.

However, all this seems to be on the surface. Women form about one half of the population. Have they got a quota of 50% in all walks of life? The answer is big NO. So, liberation and empowerment of women is still a dream. Only a small fraction of women belonging to higher sections of society have been able to reach the top. Most of them are still languishing behind in this male-dominated society. The condition for women is particularly miserable in poor families and rural areas.

Our constitution gives equal rights to women along with men. Girls are getting education equal to boys at least in the urban areas. Reservation for women has been made in the Panchayati Raj. But such reservation is still not there in the union and state legislatures. In the Parliament and state assemblies, there is a vast gap between the number of men and women legislators.

Still, great cruelties are being inflicted on women. Some of the most heinous crimes in society are taking place against women. Thus, we have female foeticide, bride-burning, dowry system, rapes, molestations, murders of women, eve-teasing, etc.

It is imperative that laws pertaining to women such as anti-dowry laws, sex-determination tests, etc. should be made more stringent and much severer punishments should be given to violaters. Women themselves should also assert at all levels.

Women should be treated equal to men. Girls and women should be given the same type of food, education, clothing, employment opportunities, health opportunities, etc. as boys and men. In other words, women should be empowered further and made self-dependent to give them real freedom and empowerment. Seats for them should be reserved in educational, medical and engineering colleges and particularly in legislatures. It is commendable that Women's Reservation Bill has at last been passed in the Rajya Sabha on 10th March 2010 which gives moral empowerment to women in politics.

PRICE RISE

India is a land of problems. One of the most serious problem is the problem of price rise. Whenever we go to market, we often find that the prices of all the essential articles have risen. Now, the situation has become more serious because of unprecedented rise in the prices of food items.

It is very difficult for a common man to make both ends meet. The income of the common people does not rise so much as the prices of goods. The salaried people and those who live on pensions are hit the most as they have only a fixed income. The condition of those who live on interest income is even worse as the interests have so many times been decreased during the last few years.

One great reason for the rise in prices is the rapid increase in population. Another reason is that most of the people are trying to raise their standards of living. Now people are giving more attention to food, clothing, health, housing, entertainment, education of children, etc. Many people have ACs, cars, desert coolers, geysers, mixers, refrigerators, television sets, telephones, etc. in their homes which previously they did not have. All this increases their expenditure and prices of goods.

Goods are not produced at the same rate as the population and demand rise. Many people waste money on luxuries and functions and marriages. The government does not care to control its expenditure. Taxation system is also defective in our country. Then, there are so many ministers and legislators and government employees who have to be paid from treasury. Not much money is left with the government for development purposes.

India has to import a lot of petroleum products and gas to meet her energy requirements. There is much wastage of petrol on running luxury cars. Black money and corruption also lead to price rise. Some traders hoard essential items and raise prices to earn more profits. Famines, floods and strikes also cause price rise.

To check prices, population should be controlled. Strikes should be avoided. Taxation system should be overhauled. Wastage should be avoided. Black money and corruption should be dealt with strictly. Unnecessary imports should be avoided, particularly the imports of luxury items. More attention should be given to exports. Production should be increased. More attention should be given to energy resources.

Much expenditure has to be done on defence. This cannot be helped. However, it should be avoided wherever the security of the country is not compromised. Good relations with neighbouring countries should be established to minimise expenditure on wars and encounters.

With the coming of the GST system of taxation, people hoped that the prices of goods would by and large go down to a considerable extent. But this has not happened. Let the government and people cooperate with each other to solve all problems, including the problem of price rise.

POPULATION EXPLOSION

The rapidly increasing population may be a matter which can cause scare in the minds of all thinking people. It is a kind of explosion no less horrible than the explosion of an atom bomb.

At the time India got Independence in 1947, she had the population of about 35 crore. Now, she is inhabited by more than 125 crore people. The world over population has greatly increased. It is around 700 crore mark at present. It also means that every 7th person in the world is an Indian. Population is increasing more rapidly in developing countries than in developed countries. It means industrialisation or development is an answer to the rising trend in population.

India is second only to China in the matter of population. But in India, population is increasing much more rapidly than in China. It is estimated by the demographers that within the next two decades India may overtake China in the matter of population and will become number one in the world.

There are several reasons for this rapid increase of population. One of the reasons is the improved healthcare facilities. These facilities have reduced the number of infant mortality and increased the life span. Another reason is illiteracy. Many people, mostly in slum and rural areas do not have much knowledge of means of family planning.

Still, another reason is poverty. Many poor people want more and more children to increase the earning capacity of their family as they put their children to some sort of work at a very early age. Child marriages and early marriages are other reasons.

It is very important that awareness should be brought about among the people to adopt the means of family planning especially, the traditional and religious-minded people of poor families should be brought around to adopt these methods.

FEMALE FOETICIDE

Of all the crimes and immoral acts, perhaps female foeticide is the most heinous. Female foeticide means killing the girl child in the womb. It is no different from killing a girl who is born, as a girl in the womb is as much a living being. She is only at a developing stage.

The main reason for female foeticide is that the girls are not a desirable child in our society. It is mainly because of our faulty social customs. A girl is considered a burden on the parents. It is because as per the common social practice in our country, the girl's parents have to give a very rich dowry on her marriage. In fact, they have to continue giving money and material to the girl's in-laws all her life. Therefore, if the problem of female foeticide is to be solved in right earnest, the problem of dowry system must also be solved on equal footing along with it.

Indians are fond of having a male child to continue the lineage. Those who have one or more girl children go in for female foeticide till they get a male child. In this respect, the use of ultrasonic machines has played a negative role. As a matter of fact, these machines are very useful for scanning purposes to determine the presence of any abnormality in the body. But they are being used unscrupulously for knowing the sex of the infant in the womb. No doubt, there is an Anti-prenatal sex determination law, but the unhealthy practice of knowing the sex of the unborn child is going on secretly. For this, the greedy practitioners charge a hefty amount which the parents of the unborn child gladly pay.

The sex ratio against girls has been declining during the last few decades. It is particularly the condition in some of the northern states, Punjab and Haryana in particular. The situation has become alarming after the arrival of ultrasound scanning machines.

If this trend continues, a stage may come when girls will be a rare breed. Already there are so many crimes against women in society such as rapes, murders, bride-burning, immoral trafficking, etc. We will certainly shudder to think of final stage and that is the world without women. If there are no women, there will be no mankind. So, if we do not take any drastic steps right from now, we may be heading towards a womanless world which means the end of mankind. Hence all the educationists, students, teachers, parents, government, NGO's and the media should strain every nerve to enlighten the people and put an end to this unhealthy practice positively.

RELIGION IS THE OPIUM OF THE MASSES

Religion is the most dominant social force in the society and is next only to technology and materialism. It is surprising to note that but we are bound to hit the next century within a year we have not been able to overcome the harmful effects of religion. The opium of religion is still intoxicating our people and we have received more harm than good due to its existence.

Take the modern urban man as an example. His contribution towards religious causes is very low. He devotes a small time period in temples, mosques or churches; his busy schedule does not allow him to get overindulgent in religious affairs. He is a machine which must churn out money and materialistic assets. Then, how could he possibly devote his entire time to religion? Strange it many seem but we must take note of the fact that ignorance of religion in the urban areas is harmful to the urban masses. The peace of mind and mental satisfaction are no longer the keywords in urban settings. The lust for money, power, cars, mobile phones and factories is increasing and this is giving more tantrums to the urban society. We therefore, feel that "fear of God" and a will to remain on the right path should be inculcated by religion in the urban areas. The "cog in the machine" concept has made the urban people devoid of religious feelings; even if they rely upon religion, it is only an escape for their sins or a platform for their politico-religious machinations.

Now let us have a look at the rural religious landscape. The rural masses are credulous and gullible. They are simple and do not have evil depths in their hearts. They take the statements at their face values and are sans all evil manipulations. So the religious leaders and the politicians use their innocence to their own advantage and exploit them to the core. The sixth anniversary of Babri Masjid demolition fell on December 6, 1998 and there were fears of reprisals from the Muslim militants and fundamentalists. The USA had warned her citizens residing in India that there could be bloodshed on December 6, 1998. The rural areas are the worst hit by the religious turmoils. The master manipulators, politicians, the resource rich people and antisocial elements exploit such tense situations to their advantage. It must be noted that in a total contrast to the urban scenario, the moral values are upheld properly in the rural areas. But still, the rural people are more conforming to religious practices than their urban counterparts. They need not cleanse themselves as they do not have wicked hearts. But they are forced to take a diabolical recourse to religion. What an irony!

This blood and gore would have to be stopped. India is a multi-cultural and multi-ethnic society. We are secular to the core. There are no communal differences or strikes in the rural areas. The political and religious groups create these differences for their vested interests. The ultimate losers are the villagers, the farmers, the rural industries and finally, the national economy. We have to put a check on the communal frenzy at all costs. Our record as a "diverse but united nation" must remain intact.

The communication revolution — through satellite television, Internet, cable TV networks and telephone networks — could deliver the message of communal harmony to the rural masses. Community workshops must be organised in sensitive pockets in order to preach non-violence and brotherhood among the masses. Cinema and theatre could play vital role in this context. If facts are put before the public in the right perspective, then the public would take the criminal elements to task. The police and judiciary should extend all cooperation and support in this regard.

It is very important to educate the masses so that they could distinguish between communalism and religion. An educated individual would have a conscience but an uneducated individual would only have a religion-based motivation for performing any task. Education would inculcate logic, rationale and communal brotherhood among the various communities. After all, we have been living together for the past 5,000 years. A few stray incidents cannot tear our national fabric. We are a strong and united national organism and time has made this glaring fact known to the world.

Religion should dominate our personal and spiritual lives. It should be separated from politics and economic problems. We have entered the new millennium. We have to shed most of the features of the past. Communal violence and hatred is one such evil, which must be done away within the national context. Already, this demon has consumed lakhs of people and property worth billions. Let this demon know that we all are united and would oppose all those forces, which tend to divide us. We shall emerge victorious in the long run as we are on the right path. Our sacrifices would not go in vain. We have already faced enough of communal violence.

SECULARISM

All the politicians in India commit themselves to national unity and security. They pledge their allegiance to a secular India. But all of them play the communal card to their advantage as communalism propagates their interests. They always try to rake up communal issues in some part of the country or another. This helps them in tarnishing the image of other political party and consolidating their own positions in the ensuing elections. If we listen to the gibe of any politician, we would never find him to be telling a lie. They seem to be so natural and patriotic that one may be forced to think that they could have done very well in theatre or cinema.

India is a secular State. The word 'secular' has been inserted in the Constitution (42nd Amendment) Act, 1976. Our secular character has been kept intact by our previous governments and should be kept so in future as well. Our record as a united nation (despite many cultural and religious diversities) is very enviable viz-a-viz our other Asian and African neighbours. How can India cease to exist as a secular entity while it is a glaring fact that our leaders and nation-builders emphasised upon this fact while starting our journey from the dawn of independence in 1947? We had some ideals to cherish, some dreams to realise and some moral values to adopt and nurture. Is our secularism so phoney that it could break under the stress of communal riots merely after 50 years of Independence? No! There is something wrong with our political, social and moral systems and during the task of nation building, we have not been able to take care of some important aspects of our secularism and nationalism. Let us analyse some of the issues at stake :

We did not take adequate care of the interests of the minorities. We tried to reserve seats for SCs, STs and OBCs. We tried to give more privileges to all the tribal masses. But we did not understand that people were proud to be Muslims, Christians and Sikhs. They were in minority but they needed our affection and care. They did not ask for reservations as Muslims, Sikhs or Christians but they deserved our love and empathy.

The planners of our country did well to promote our country as a secular one. But they did not understand that a Hindu, a Muslim or a Christian lives according to his social beliefs, customs and religious rituals. Religion touches his life on a daily basis. We cannot ignore the fact that he needs religion on a day-to-day basis even if he breathes in a secular country. Our 'secular' character cannot overshadow the religious devotion of the masses. For example, a Muslim is an Indian but he is a Muslim as well. He has to attend the mosque for prayers five times a day. He has to fast during the *Ramzan* days and he would certainly celebrate Eid. Our Constitution guarantees the right to accept and follow any religion and the State does not interfere in this right of the individual.

Our leaders failed to understand that the right of all the minorities are equal to the rights of the majority. Therefore, if a citizen of India misuses religion and tries to disrupt the secular fabric of the nation (e.g., terrorism in Punjab), then the State must not tolerate such type of deviation on the part of that citizen and it can use long arm of the law to counter such moves. But if the poor citizen is leading a peaceful life and his religion does not hurt others, then the State does not have any right to impose any ritual, prayer, religious compulsion or tax upon him. For example, it is quite natural that the Hindu Code Bill is not applicable to Muslims as they are governed by Muslim Personal Law.

In this context, we can rightly conclude that the attacks on the minorities, their religious places or places of worship, the incidents of communal carnage and the illegal support of the ruling majority to the anti-social elements (for suppressing the minorities) are deplorable and would not suit the long term secular interests of our nation. We would live in better manner and would grow to new heights if we continue to retain our secular character on national and state levels. We respect and love all the faiths and need blessings of all the forms of Almighty in order to become a stronger and a more prosperous nation.

ENVIRONMENTAL POLLUTION

Important elements constituting the earth are air, soil and water. These together comprise the environment. The earth has a cover of air around it which is called atmosphere. More than two-thirds of the area of the earth comprises oceans and seas which contain water.

All the elements together form climate. All the living beings can live only in a particular type of climate. We are living on the earth because a climate suitable for our living is available on this planet. Our earth took more than 400 crores of years to evolve the present climate.

It is quite clear that if the climate at present available on the earth is disturbed excessively, life on this planet may be in danger. Unfortunately, this is what man is doing at present. His actions are causing the depletion of ozone and oxygen and increasing the production of harmful gases such as carbon dioxide, carbon monoxide, sulphur dioxide, etc. These gases are produced by the smoke released by chimneys of factories, automobiles, burning of wood, etc. Such gases also cause greenhouse effect. They cause increase in temperature all over the earth. This undue increase in temperature is melting the snow on mountain-tops. This can lead to increase in the volume of water in oceans. The result of this can be the merger of many islands and coastal areas in many countries under the water.

Man is at present cutting down forests recklessly. Forests cause rain and maintain a balance of oxygen in the atmosphere.

The excessive use of pesticides and insecticides and the use of spurious fertilizers is polluting the soil. The water channels are being polluted due to the toxic matter released by factories. Non-disposal or improper disposal of medical and domestic waste is also polluting the soil and water.

Another kind of pollution is the noise pollution. We have so much noise in cities and towns. We hear sounds of factory hooters and generators, noises made by hawkers and customers in markets and loudspeakers used at religious places and functions of all types, including religions and political functions and social gatherings such as marriages, etc. Loud noises have an adverse effect on human nerves and they affect the brain and the hearing system of the body. If man wants to continue living on this planet, he will have to mend his ways. Otherwise, there is no certainty that mankind will live for more than a century on it.

DRUG-ADDICTION

When the Hippies came to India, they brought not only strange dresses but also drugs. It is common knowledge that the young people are greatly influenced by anything strange and new.

At present, our country is under the grip of drug-addiction. Most of the drug-addicts live in cities. They include both boys and girls. University, college and school hostels are particularly full of drug-addicts.

Drug-addiction is, however, not restricted to urban areas only. Even in the rural areas there are so many drug-addicts. There are not only men but also women in large numbers who take drugs. This vice has invaded all sections of society. Many rickshaw-pullers, factory workers, government employees and even businessmen can be seen who are given to the habit of drug-taking.

Most often it so happens that a person takes a drug just for the thrill of it. Then he takes it the second or third time to repeat the experience. When he takes it a number of times, he forms the habit. Then a time comes when he wants to get rid of it. But he cannot do so because he feels restlessness if he does not take the drug.

Most of the young people start this habit in the company of their friends in hostels. One reason for this wide-spread practice is that drugs are easily available everywhere. There are so many peddlers who sell drugs. Drugs are of many kinds such as heroin, smack, LSD, opium, ganja, charas, etc. All drugs are habit-forming.

A drug-addict gets his health spoiled. He also wastes his precious money on drugs. Some of these drugs such as heroin are very costly. But those who are addicted to drugs cannot get rid of them easily. If they do not have money to purchase a drug, they steal money from home or from wherever they can. They can even commit some more serious crime to get money for drugs.

Drug-taking makes a person lazy. It can cause even death. Young people should be taught in schools and colleges to avoid this bad habit. If a youth falls a prey to this habit, he should be taken to the drug-deaddiction centre as early as possible. Strict action should be taken against drug-peddlers, chemists, and others who sell drugs.

One reason for this menace is that the young people feel frustrated. They find the education system worthless. They do not get proper love from parents. They are unemployed and have no hope of getting a job. The parents, teachers, NGO's, social workers, government agencies and media should join hands to save the youth of our country from this menace.

PATRIOTISM / NATIONALISM AND NATIONAL INTEGRATION

Some people believe that the concept of nationalism is new to India. They are of the opinion that this concept came in India with the British and the western education.

This, however, is a fallacy. Even in ancient times, people had the concept of India as one country. Their thinking might not have been entirely based on political reality. But the concept of India being one country even politically was not totally absent. Chandragupta Maurya, for instance, under the able guidance of Chanakya, wanted to establish his rule all over India. His capital was Patliputra which is modern Patna in Bihar. Chandragupta marched all over from Patliputra to north India to defeat Alexander's general Seleukas who had attacked India. After him, Ashoka's kingdom covered almost the whole of India and even a part of Afghanistan. Even earlier, India was called "Aryavrat" or "Bharat" which meant the whole of India.

Later, in the middle ages, Adi Shankaracharya established his ashrams in four corners of India. It is clear that people in general had the concept of India as being one country. They travelled to places of pilgrimages which were spread in different parts of the country. It must, however, be admitted that the concept of a nation state as at present was perhaps not there then among the Indians.

In earlier times, the common people pursued their occupation in their villages where most of them lived and they were not much concerned with the kinds of kings and governments ruling at the centre.

India was a vast country inhabited by people of different religions, castes, communities and races, all speaking different languages, wearing different dresses and having different food habits. So, separatist tendencies in people's minds could also not be ruled out. Such tendencies were responsible for the enslavement of the Indian people when one ruler did not help the other ruler who was attacked by some foreign invader. This was mostly witnessed in the middle ages. This enabled even the British rulers to play policy of "divide and rule."

With the emergence of the Indian National Congress towards the close of the 19th century, the love for freedom for the whole country was awakened among the Indian people and it became stronger and stronger as the Independence movement gained momentum. India was fortunate in having selfless, patriotic leaders like Mahatma Gandhi, Bal Gangadhar Tilak, Lala Lajpat Rai, Jawaharlal Nehru, Subhash Chandra Bose and others.

After attainment of Independence, India chose democracy to be the form of government. In this respect too, India has been fortunate for the reason of having such leaders as Jawaharlal Nehru, Lal Bahadur Shastri, Sardar Patel and others.

Later, though fortunately, the democratic set-up in the country has been allowed to continue, the nefarious designs of later narrow-minded leaders slowly landed the country where national integration could be endangered. They encouraged regionalism, linguism, casteism, nepotism and other parochial institutions. The result was a demand from different regions for autonomy, if not secession. Such voices were heard in Kashmir, Punjab, Tamil Nadu, eastern states, etc. By stages new states such as Himachal Pradesh, Haryana, Uttarakhand, Jharkhand, etc. came into being. Again, fortunately, for the Indian people, there has been no secession from the Indian union.

Constitutionally, no state can secede from the union. But what is more important is that the people should have emotional integration. They should consider the nation above any social, religious, communal or racial considerations. There should be a national cohesion among the people. For this, the newspapers, TV, radio and other means of media should play a positive role. Parents, teachers, social workers, students and leaders of all parties should join hands to achieve the end of national integration.

It should be understood clearly that we live if India lives. Who lives if India doesn't? So, national integration is the need of the hour. Let's meet the challenge bravely and unitedly whatever hard work we might have to do.

EXAMINATIONS : RIGHT OR WRONG

Life is all along an examination and all of us have to face one or the other tough task daily, wherever and in whatever position we may be.

Most of the students are virtually in a state of depression near the examinations, though strictly in medical terms, this state may not be technically admitted to be such a state. But, we can say with jubilation "The examination blues!" And jubilation not at the poor fellows who suffer these blues but at the finding out of a term even like Galileo who exclaimed, "Eureka! Eureka! Eureka!" on a new astronomical discovery.

We learn from the counsellors about the students' common complaints like lack of appetite, insomnia, fear of failure, fear of being rebuked by parents, fear of loss of status among the student community in particular and society in general, etc. Sometimes, even suicidal tendencies are noticed by these counsellors. In certain cases, students who have shown remarkable performance in the previous classes are afraid that they may not be able to repeat the performance and be taken to task by their parents. In certain cities, helplines are available round the clock. Even the CBSE has been running such helplines for students.

Some of such helplines for students in blues, to make some queries to get rid of them, are Disha, Snehi, Sarthak, CBSE, etc. It deserves to be noted that not always calls are made by the students themselves, sometimes, even parents make a fervent call about their ward and at times even express their anger over the phone at the defective examination system, which reduces the students to robots and automatons, snatching all the emotions, charm and joy from their life.

Since many of us will be inclined to say that after a lot of experimentation in several ways, the net decision for the present seems to be that examinations in one form or the other are unavoidable. They may be called a necessary evil. In whatever form they may be, they are, after all examinations and there is hardly a student who does not shudder at the sheer mention of the word "Examination."

A great bane of the modern examination system is that we have too many examinations. Even to get admission in the nursery or pre-nursery class, the child has to take a test. Not only the child but also its parents have to appear for an interview. Then throughout the career of the poor child, there are tests and examinations galore such as daily, weekly, monthly, bimonthly, semester-related, annual, etc.

If a student has to seek admission in any other institution for any reason, he has to take a test. Even after getting a certificate, diploma or degree, one has to appear in a test, examination and/or interview or viva voce, group discussion and what not in order to join a vocational, technical or professional course or a job.

We have a pertinent saying: "Excess of everything is bad." This should and does equally apply to the examinations. The examinations always keep the students on tenterhooks. They are often a worried lot. It is hard to find a ray of cheerfulness on the faces of most of the students. Then in this world of hard competition and pressing demands on the students from their parents and teachers, many students fall a prey to such unethical practices as copying. Gone are the days when students like Gandhiji refused to copy the spelling of a word from another student's exercise book even when he was urged by his teacher to do so. Now, not only the students themselves but also many times even their parents and well-wishers try to exhort the student to indulge in the unhealthy practice of copying.

Another great menace, perhaps the greatest of all other menaces, is the menace of leakage of papers of various examinations. There have been reports about the leakage of PMT papers right from the beginning. Similarly, leakage of papers of many other examinations has sporadically taken place in the past. During the recent few years, however, the leakage of papers pertaining to various examinations has taken the shape of an epidemic.

The leakage of All India Pre-Medical Test (AIPMT) was detected in Delhi. It is a different matter that two students were arrested. And, now we hear a well-organised racket has been caught in Chandigarh engaged in facilitating copying in post-graduate medical course admissions tests through high-tech devices such as bluetooth and pen-scanners. They are even said to have placed dummy candidates for this job.

Such a state of affairs can make the students lethargic. They can seriously and sincerely think that if they can get through an examination just by buying a question paper a few hours or a day before the examination, why should they lick the books the whole year? What they now actually need is a few lakhs of rupees for which their parents may be willing even more. Let the nation, society and the world go to hell! So this is what the present examination system makes them and from what. How raw they were and how crude, rude and rough now they are!

Let some methods be devised to uplift the moral standard of not only the students but also the parents, teachers, government functionaries and all others concerned.

India's education and examination systems are now being lauded all over the world for being of quite high quality, though we still find several deficiencies in them. A positive factor in this context is the will for constant rethinking and making changes where necessary. An example can be given in the matter of rethinking about the examinations pertaining to Class X. One of the proposals mooted mainly by the CBSE was concerning making class X examinations optional. The boards, however, did not find favour with this proposal. Instead, the council, allowing flexibility to students, agreed to implement the grading system and also made a case for including internal assessment in schools. It allowed students. The new idea emerged is that the annual examinations should be spread over a couple of months so that a student can take a few papers in one month and the rest in the subsequent months, instead of appearing in the examinations in one go. However, it was agreed that the results should be declared in one go. It was believed that the system would prevent the students from neglecting their school education.

UNITY IS STRENGTH

The advantages of unity have always been manifested themselves on the social, personal and national scales. The family, the society and the country survive only due to the coherence of their components. Unity is a very beneficial and exhilirating spirit of every phenomenon. A united society or a nation would be able to face any challenge or crisis. Let us analyse.

Now-a-days, the concept of nuclear family is catching up very fast. The joint family system is breaking up simply due to the fact that the young boys and girls move towards urban areas in order to earn and to achieve professional satisfaction. The unity of the joint family is sacrificed in terms of prosperity, protection from the world, aid during disease and other disasters. But the nuclear families do not have any such type of security. Hence, they suffer on account of lack of security from the joint family system. An individual cannot fight a war. But some individuals can fight a war together and in all probability, they would be able to win all the wars.

Another example could be given from the Indian history. We lost our crucial wars due to the cracks within our social, religious and political organisations. We have many traitors to curse; Mir Jaffer, Jai Chand, Jai Gopal, Najeebullah etc. are only a few names to mention. The traitors went to the groups of the powerful marauders and let the Indian natives suffer the worst ever defeats. For example, had Jai Chand not invited Muhammed Ghauri from Afghanistan, Prithvi Raj Chauhan would certainly have expanded his empire in the Northern and the Western parts of the country. He could have stopped the onslaught of foreign mercenaries and marauders with the senews of steel. But Jai Chand fought a savage battle with him through Muhammad Ghauri and the righteous king had to give up his life and kingdom in his last war. Our history is full of many such shameful examples.

Let us now turn to the modern times. India has fought five wars so far — in 1948, 1962, 1965, 1971 and in 1999. In all these wars, our brave soldiers, our courageous paramilitary forces, our committed civilians and above all, love for the motherland helped us fight the enemy forces bravely. We lost the 1962 war but we were united as a nation. We won the 1971 and 1999 war due to the courage and united efforts to win over the enemy forces. We were united and would always be united in our endeavour for peace, prosperity and global welfare. Our unity is our strength.

Similar examples of strength in unity could be quoted in the fields of business, warfare, sciences, engineering, sociology, environmental regulations, struggle for Indian independence, the two world wars etc. Human history is full of those stories which proved beyond doubt that when men of courage joined hands for a pious objective, they achieved their coveted aims with flying colours. The ecstacy of success was due to the commitment either to the group norms or to national ideals.

We are now convinced that unity is strength. Then why do we not implement the spirit of unity in our lives? The reason is simple. We are now more materialistic and individualistic than ever before. The lust for money forces us to think in individual terms. The individualistic culture has been developed in the urban areas of India due to Western influences. For example, many people in the West do not marry. They live as couples and leave the partners when they get 'bored' with each other. Similar culture is dominating the urban life in India. Rural areas would also be affected sooner or later. Hence, the individuals fight for money, jobs, family values, prestige, fortune or fame. They do not get any financial, moral or political support from their friends, relatives or parents. Hence, they loose most of the battles in their lives.

We must not ape the West. We must remain united as a family, as a society and as a nation. It is in our best interests to remain united as a nation as the nation would lead us to political, social, economic and moral salvation. Our society believes in unity in diversity. That is why, this multi-lingual, multi-racial and multi-cultural nation has survived for 5,000 years. This resilience itself proves that unity is strength.

MERCY KILLING

Mercy Killing or Euthanasia refers to the practice of ending a life in a manner which relieves pain and suffering. It is a deliberate intervention undertaken with the express intention of ending a life, to relieve intractable suffering.

Euthanasia may be classified according to whether a person gives informed consent into three types: voluntary, non-voluntary and involuntary.

There is a debate within the medical and bioethics literature about whether or not the non-voluntary (and by extension, involuntary) killing of patients can be regarded as euthanasia, irrespective of intent or the patient's circumstances. According to few experts, consent on the part of the patient is not considered necessary. However, others see consent as essential. Medicalized killing of a person without the person's consent, whether non-voluntary (where the person is unable to give consent) or involuntary (against the person's will) is not euthanasia: it is murder. Hence, euthanasia can be voluntary only.

Euthanasia conducted with the consent of the patient is termed voluntary euthanasia. Euthanasia conducted where the consent of the patient is unavailable is termed non-voluntary euthanasia. Examples include child euthanasia, which is illegal worldwide but decriminalised under certain specific circumstances in the Netherlands under the Groningen Protocol. Euthanasia conducted against the will of the patient is termed involuntary euthanasia.

In a country like ours, the religious aspects also have to be considered before taking such decisions. The Bible says, "Thou shalt not kill" And even Islam does not allow anyone to take away life. Is our society mature enough to understand the implications of this? We have cases, where doctors are often beaten up if the patient was not treated properly, what would happen to a doctor if he merely suggested euthanasia to the relatives? Will the relatives be able to understand the suffering of the patient?

Life is a gift, and even a life of pain is a life at least. Some people feel we don't choose when to be born and we should not be given the right to choose when to die. On the contrary, others feel that a life of pain is not a life but an imposition and we should be at least allowed to end it in a dignified peaceful manner. Euthanasia could be legalized, but the laws would have to be very stringent. Every case will have to be carefully monitored taking into consideration the point of views of the patient, the relatives and the doctors. But whether Indian society is mature enough to face this, is yet to be seen, after all it's a matter of life and death.

DRINKING HABITS AMONG YOUTHS

The three "Ws"—"wealth, wine and women" have always been considered the root cause of human fall, for centuries for excess of any of these things leads to physical or psychological or moral decline. Adam was thrown out of Paradise falling prey to Eve's temptations. Wealth brings even ordinary humans on cloud nine and his imaginations get free flight as it revolutionizes human physical entity and the suppressed desires and wishes to throw away the barriers of social, ethical and moral hurdles.

Drinking means alcoholic liquids which, in excess may cause sensuary imbalance among the people. Any drink apart from water which has alcohol as the leading ingredient may derail the mental thinking power which ultimately results in physical aberration like wine, whiskey and scotch.

India has a long association with drink as 'Madira' had been widely prevalent during ancient times. However wine as a regular drink has been widely prevalent in western societies for in European countries weather plays an important role. In metros bigger percentage are addicted to drinks where parties and celebrations would be unthinkable if alcohol is not properly served. Hence, the habit grows more out of fashion and etiquette than the physical requirements, and once it becomes a habit a lot of money is wasted in drinking.

Young men are more tempted to social trends and if professionals with tons of official pressure take refuge under the spell of a glass of scotch or whisky, the broad impact is perceptable. As metropolis are coming up with more and more bars, casinos and pubs where wealth, women and wine associate in an orgy of merry making the social barriers becomes a non-entity. Not only drinking becomes a personal habit but it is a human right as well. The government also supports drinking by lifting restrictions cn alcoholic consumption in recent years as more and more 'wine shops' or 'beer shops' are being opened on the highway. Prices are slashed whereby long queues in front of these shops are constant scences coupled with unprecedented sales. For the aged and creative human, drink can be supportive, but to youths it infects more harm than benefits. Formative years are full of passion and sentiments and alcohol acts as fuel to the fire. If the habits get generated in unemployed youth, it takes the form of addiction and will always result in alarming consequences for if taken to soothe the restlessness born out of failure in love or examinations, it can lead to disastrous ends. A strong urge of drink and no money in the pocket will certainly lead the restless youth to follow the illegal path and anti-social norms. Wine is the mother of all crimes and wealth is the benevolent father of wine who exhausts itself out in order to please his daughter and women is the beloved of wine.

Youths must shun this habit as it not only hampers the studies and professional career but it also takes its toll on the physical, psychological and moral body. Hence, over-socialisation, partying and celebrations should be curtailed as peer pressure compel an individual to swim in alcohol irrespective of his/her health. But yes, at the same time there is no harm in enjoying on odd drink amid in moderate quantity when one feels like. Only it must not be made a regular habiit.

INDIAN SOCIETY NEEDS REFORMS

India is proud to be cradle of the oldest civilisation in the world. It has many firsts to its credit: the Vedas were written here; the Puranas were compiled here; the epics were written in this land. India indeed, had a glorious past. Its social cutsoms, moral values and knowledge levels were respected around the world and India was regarded as the moral and spiritual leader of the mankind during ancient and medieval period.

The concept of joint family system was promoted by Hindu sages. Strict marriage rituals, commitment to the ideals of the family, pride in one's work and profession, love for the nation, commitment towards one super-soul and finally, the willingness to acquire more knowledge about this universe were some of the positive aspects of our ancient culture. During those times, people never locked their homes as there were no thieves. There were only scholars, agricultural workers, courtiers, Kshatriyas and landlords. The country was divided into several kingdoms. The cultural influences and social beliefs were the same throughout India.

But this golden era came to an end. Huns, Pathans, Afghans, Dutch, British and French invaded India and looted her wealth for over 1,000 years. They also brought new cultural beliefs, procedures and a commitment towards materialism. Therefore, the synergistic effect of this combination (of Indian culture with the invading cultures) led to the development of a new Indian society. New religions, social ideologies and political concepts changed our national and social fabrics. Today, we are essentially a Vedic-Western cultural nation and no longer Indians in the strict sense of the word. There were influences of Islam, Christianity and Hinduism on our society and these have led to the creation of a new religious canvass across the nation; the Indian Muslim, the Indian Hindu and the Indian Christian—are the three vital components of this new religious hue.

Indian society needs a serious scrutiny. The chief limitation of modern Indian society is that it has been trying to retain those obsolete values with us which are beneficial only for a smaller section of the society and are not wiling to eliminate the evils of the society as they are still serving the base objectives. The examples of Sati, dowry, early childhood marriage etc could be cited in this regard.

Further, Indian people are aping the West in a shameless manner but have never accepted the norms of the West in terms of efficiency, productivity and hard work in social and business lives. In sum, this generation is more comfortable with the club culture, satellite TV and pornography but would not like to work for sixteen hours a day, as is being or done in the West. Why should India adopt these double standards?

The next vital issue is that of social awareness. Our illiteracy levels are very high. An illiterate mother cannot offer future to her children. The vicious cycle of poverty continues to engulf the rural masses as education has not been able to reach out to the mass levels.

The resistance to change is another vital area in Indian context. Indian mind wants to adopt new technologies and modern social beliefs at a very slow pace but are more than willing to get a cable TV connection so that we could entertain ourselves through indecent entertainment software. Indians do not want to adopt new computer software techniques, production methodologies and living styles as we not want to get out of our Indian shell. But we are always trying to get imported whiskies, electronic gadgets and items of luxury, which would not improve our psyche. This leads to reduction in actual production, efficiency and satisfaction at the economic, societal and industrial levels. We must remember that the society, the industry and the nation are living organisms and each one of these supports the existence and growth of one another.

Even in the new millennium Indian society is not ready to accept the challenges of this era. Nonetheless social reforms would help us in economic growth and overall national progress. The responsibility of these reforms is of the masses; we have to change our psyche in order to become a modern society. The State, the judiciary and the institutions would also have to play key roles in this herculean task. This process would be painfully slow and agonising.

JUDICIAL ACTIVISM IN INDIA

Judicial activism has introduced a new dimension regarding judiciary's involvement in public administration. Judicial activism was made possible in India, thanks to PIL (Public Interest Litigation).

After the Constitution (Twenty fifth Amendment) Act, 1971, by which primacy was accorded to a limited extent to the Directive Principles vis-a-vis the Fundamental Rights making the former enforceable rights, the expectations of the public soared high and the demands on the courts to improve the administration by giving appropriate directions for ensuring compliance with statutory and constitutional prescriptions have increased.

The judicial power under our Constitution is vested in the Supreme Court and the High Courts which are empowered to exercise the power of judicial review both in regard to legislative and executive actions. Judges cannot shirk their responsibilities as adjudicators of legal and constitutional matters.

A common criticism we hear about judicial activism is that in the name of interpreting the provisions of the Constitution and legislative enactments, the judiciary often rewrites them undermining the authority of the legislature and the executive by encroaching upon the spheres reserved for them.

Judicial creativity even when it takes the form of judicial activism should not result in rewriting of the Constitution or any legislative enactments. In the name of doing justice and taking shelter under institutional self-righteousness, the judiciary cannot act in a manner disturbing the delicate balance between the three wings of the State.

Judicial activist fervour should not flood the fields constitutionally earmarked for the legislature and the executive. That would spell disaster. Governmental machinery cannot be run by judges. Any populist views aired by judges would undermine their authority and disturb the institutional balance.

Judicial activism characterised by moderation and self-restraint is bound to restore the faith of the people in the efficacy of the democratic institutions which alone, in turn, will activate the executive and the legislature to function effectively under the vigilant eye of the judiciary as ordained by the Constitution.

CORRUPTION IS AN ACCEPTED NORM

The standard definition of corruption is — the use of public office for private gain. Its roots and seductions lie much deeper in the quality of human relationships that characterize a society.

Corruption and Indian society are inter-woven closely. Each and every office whether it comes under Central or State administration is no exception. Corruption is simply a consequence of the fact that the state has wide discretionary powers.

The motivations that produce and sustain corruption are of course complex. Avarice and ambition doubtless play an important part.

The experience of both state and society in India is profoundly alienating in more ways than one can list and many forms of corruption stem directly from this experience. Indian society is profoundly inegalitarian. Vast disparities of income and power exist almost everywhere, but the depth, to which in India inequality has subjected individuals to a million humiliations, small and large, is almost unprecedented.

Generally, all this corruption goes on under a cloak, although one can almost see it happening before one's eyes, Bureaucracy is also moulded and influenced to take decisions favourable to vested interest due to corruption. In case of large contracts rules are relaxed and then negotiated without transparency. Not a new phenomenon in India or in many other countries.

If the senior bureaucrat or officer disassociates himself/herself from wrong decisions and does so on the files, wrongdoing or corruption would diminish greatly.

But India is considered especially as a case of its own *i.e.* it is only when the higher bureaucracy or officer becomes compliant and suitably "cooks the case", then corrupt practice could occur. But any one with even a mild conscience will hesitate to do so.

It has been rightly pointed that in a society in which honesty and patriotism are laughed at and poked fun of; corruption is going to be all pervading because there is no moral barrier to it at any level. And also an honest officer is always looked down upon as incapable person who is not suiting to the present environment.

●●●

GENERAL AWARENESS

NATIONAL SYMBOLS

STATE EMBLEM

State Emblem of India is an adaptation from the Sarnath Lion Capital of Ashoka. It was adopted by the Government of India on January 26, 1950. In the adapted form, only three lions are visible, the fourth being hidden from the view. The wheel (Dharma Chakra) appears in relief in the centre of the abacus with a bull on the right and a horse on the left.

The bell-shaped lotus has been omitted. The words ''Satyameva Jayate'' meaning ''Truth alone triumphs'' are inscribed below the Emblem in Devanagari script.

NATIONAL FLAG

The National Flag of India is a horizontal tricolour of deep saffron (Kesari), white and dark green in equal proportion. In the centre of the white band there is a wheel in navy blue colour. It has 24 spokes. The ratio of the length and the breadth of the flag is 3 : 2. Its design was adopted by the Constituent Assembly of India on July 22, 1947.

NATIONAL ANTHEM

Rabindranath Tagore's song 'Jana-gana-mana' was adopted by the Constituent Assembly as the National Anthem of India on January 24, 1950.

Jana-gan-mana-adhinayaka jaya he, Bharata-bhagya-vidhata
Punjab-Sindh-Gujarat-Maratha-Dravida-Utkala-Banga
Vindhya-Himachala-Yamuna-Ganga Uchhala-jaladhi-taranga.
Tava subha name jage, Tava subha asisa mange, Gahe tava jaya gatha,
Jana-gana-mangala-dayak, jaya he Bharata bhagya vidhata,
Jaya he, jaya he, jaya he, Jaya jaya jaya, jaya he.

NATIONAL SONG

Bankim Chandra Chatterji's 'Vande Mataram' which was a source of inspiration to the people in their struggle for freedom, has been adopted as National Song. It has an equal status with the National Anthem.

Vande Mataram
Sujalam, suphalam, malayaja-shitalam,
Shasya shyamalam, Mataram
Shubhrajyotsna,pulkita yaminim,
Phulla kusumita drumadalashobhinim,
Subhasinim sumadhura—bhashinim,
Sukhadam, Varadam, Mataram.

NATIONAL CALENDAR

It is based on the Saka era with Chaitra as its first month and a normal year of 365 days. It was adopted from March 22, 1957. Dates of the national calendar have a permanent correspondence with dates of Gregorian calendar as Chaitra I falls on March 22 in a normal year and March 21 in a leap year. In official communications, both Saka and Gregorian calendar dates are written. Months of the national calendar are Chaitra, Vaishakha, Jaishtha, Ashada, Shravan, Bhadra, Ashvina, Kartika, Margashirsha, Pausha, Magha and Phalguna.

NATIONAL ANIMAL

The magnificent tiger — Panthera tigris (Linnaeus) is the national animal of India. Tiger is found in several parts of the country and is known for its grace, strength, agility and enormous power. 'Project Tiger' was launched in 1973 to check their dwindling population in India.

NATIONAL BIRD

The Indian Peacock — Pavo Christatus (Linnaeus) is the national bird of India. It is a colourful, swan-sized bird with a fan-shaped crest of feathers on its head and a long-slander neck. The male species is more colourful with blue breast and a spectacular bronze-green train of around 200 elongated feathers.

National Flower—Lotus

National Tree—Banyan

National Fruit—Mango

National Currency—Rupee '₹'

(One Rupee = 100 Paise)

National Aquatic Animal—Dolphin

BOOKS AND AUTHORS

Name of Book	Author
Ain-e-Akbari	Abul Fazal
Anand Math	Bankim Chandra Chatterjee
An Unknown Indian	Nirad C. Chaudhuri
Arthshastra	Kautilya
Coolie	Mulk Raj Anand
Das Kapital	Karl Marx
Discovery of India	Jawaharlal Nehru
Eternal India	Mrs. Indira Gandhi
Godan	Prem Chand
Gitanjali	Rabindranath Tagore
Gora	Rabindranath Tagore
Geet Govinda	Jayadeva
Harsha Charit	Bana Bhatta
Hindu View of Life	Dr. S. Radhakrishnan
India Wins Freedom	Maulana Abul Kalam Azad
Jobs of Millions	V.V. Giri
Jungle Book	Rudyard Kipling
Kamayani	Jai Shankar Prasad
Kadambari	Bana Bhatta
Life Divine	Sri Aurobindo
Last days of Netaji	G.D. Khosla
Les Miserables	Victor Hugo
Mahabharat	Veda Vyas
Macbeth	William Shakespeare
Mein Kempf	Hitler
Meghduta	Kalidas
Mother (Maa)	Maxim Gorky
Mother India	Katherine Mayo
My Experiments with Truth	Mahatma Gandhi
My Presidential Years	R. Venkataraman
Neeti Shatak	Bhartrihari
Nehru and His Vision	Dr. K.R. Narayanan
Old Man and the Sea	Ernest Hemingway
One World	Wendell Wilkie
Panchtantra	Vishnu Sharma
Paradise Lost	John Milton
Ramayana	Valmiki (in Sanskrit)
Raghuvansham	Kalidas
Rajtarangini	Kalhan
Ram Charit Manas	Tulsi Das
Abhijnan Shakuntalam	Kalidas
Satanic Verses	Salman Rushdie
Saket	Maithili Sharan Gupta
Speed Post	Shobha De
The God of Small Things	Arundhati Roy
Treasure Island	R.L. Stevenson
Twelfth Night	William Shakespeare
Train to Pakistan	Khuswant Singh
Uttara Ram Charitra	Bhava Bhuti
Vanity Fair	W.M. Thackeray
War and Peace	Leo Tolstoy
Wealth of Nations	Adam Smith
Wake up India	Annie Besant

INVENTIONS AND DISCOVERIES

Geographical Discoveries

Discovery	Discoverer
America	Columbus
Brazil	Cabral
North Pole	Robert Peary
Everest (Conquered)	Tabie Junko
Planetary Motion	Kepler
Hawaiian Islands	Captain Cook
South Pole	Amundsen
Solar System	Copernicus

Chemistry and Physics

Discovery	Discoverer
Atom Bomb	Otto Hahn
Atomic Theory	Dalton
Atomic Numbers	Moseley
Cosmic Rays	R.S. Millikan
Dynamite	Alfred Nobel
Electrons Theory	Bohr
Electricity (current)	Volta
Electric Telegraphy (Code)	S. Morse

Discovery	Discoverer
Gravitation	Newton
Gas Light	Murdock
Oxygen	J. Priestly
Photography	L. Daguerre
Printing for the blind	Louis Braille
Radium	Madame Curie
Telegraph	Samuel Morse
Television	J.L. Baird
Telephone	Graham Bell
Wireless	G. Marconi
X-rays	W.K. Roentgen
Mechanical	
Aeroplane	Wright Brothers
Bicycle	Macmillan
Computer	Charles Babbage
Dynamo	Michal Faraday
Diesel Engine	Rudolf Diesel
Engine (Railway)	Stephenson
Fountain Pen	Waterman
Gramophone	Edison
Locomotive Power of Steam	James Watt
Helicopter	Brequet
Life Boat	Henry Greathead

Discovery	Discoverer
Microscope	Z. Jansen
Printing Press	Gutenberg
Revolver	Colt
Sewing Machine	Elias Howe
Thermometer	Fahrenheit
Transistor	W. Shockley
Typewriter	Sholes
Telescope	Hans Lippershey
Tank (Military)	Swinton
Medical	
Antiseptic Surgery	Lord Joseph Lister
Bacteria	Leeuwenhock
Circulation of Blood	William Harvey
Homoeopathy (Discovered)	Hahnemann
Insulin	F. Banting
Penicillin	Alexander Flemming
Malaria Parasite	Dr. Ronald Ross
Stethoscope	Laennec
Vitamins	Funk
Anti-Rabies Treatment	Pasteur
General	
Nylon	Carouthers
Science of Geometry	Euclids

WORLD'S GEOGRAPHICAL SURNAMES

• City of Sky-scrapers—New York • City of Seven Hills—Rome • City of Dreaming Spires—Oxford • City of Golden Gate—San Francisco • City of Magnificent Buildings—Washington D.C. • City of Eternal Springs—Quito (S. America) • China's Sorrow—Hwang Ho • Cockpit of Europe—Belgium • Dark Continent—Africa • Emerald Isle—Ireland • Eternal City—Rome • Empire City—New York • Forbidden City—Lhasa (Tibet) • Garden City—Chicago • Gate of Tears—Strait of Bab-el-Mandeb • Gift of the Nile—Egypt • Granite City—Aberdeen (Scotland) • Hermit Kingdom—Korea • Herring Pond—Atlantic Ocean • Holy Land—Jerusalem • Island Continent—Australia • Islands of Cloves—Zanzibar • Isle of Pearls—Bahrein (Persian Gulf) • Key to the Mediterranean—Gibralter • Land of Lakes—Scotland • Land of Golden Fleece—Australia • Land of Maple Leaf—Canada • Land of Morning Calm—Korea • Land of Midnight Sun—Norway • Land of the Thousand Lakes—Finland • Land of the Thunderbolt—Bhutan • Land of White Elephant—Thailand • Land of Thousand Elephants—Laos • Land of Rising Sun—Japan • Loneliest Island—Tristan De Gunha (Mid-Atlantic) • Manchester of Japan—Osaka • Pillars of Hercules—Strait of Gibraltar • Pearl of the Antilles—Cuba • Playground of Europe—Switzerland • Quaker City—Philadelphia • Queen of the Adriatic—Venice • Roof of the World—The Pamirs, Central Asia • Sugar bowl of the world—Cuba • Venice of the North—Stockholm • Windy City—Chicago • Whiteman's grave—Guinea Coast of Africa • Yellow River—Huang Ho (China) • Sickman of Europe—Turkiye

CAPITALS AND CURRENCIES OF COUNTRIES

Country	Capital	Currency
Afghanistan	Kabul	Afghani
Algeria	Algiers	Dinar
Angola	Luanda	New Kwanza
Argentina	Buenos Aires	Peso
Armenia	Yeravan	Dram
Australia	Canberra	Dollar
Austria	Vienna	Euro
Azerbaijan	Baku	Monat
Bahrain	Manama	Dinar
Bangladesh	Dhaka	Taka
Barbados	Bridgetown	Dollar
Belgium	Brussels	Euro
Bhutan	Thimphu	Ngultrum
Bolivia	La paz	Boliviano
Brazil	Brasilia	Cruzeiro
Bulgaria	Sofia	Lev
Byelorussia	Minsk	Zaichik
Cambodia	Phnom-Penh	Riel
Canada	Ottawa	Dollar
Chile	Santiago	Peso
China	Beijing	Yuan
Colombia	Bogota	Peso
Congo	Brazzaville	Franc
Croatia	Zagreb	Kuna
Cuba	Havana	Peso
Cyprus	Nicosia	Euro
Czech Republic	Prague	Crown
Denmark	Copenhagen	Krone
Egypt	Cairo	Pound
Estonia	Tallinn	Kroon
Ethiopia	Addis Ababa	Birr
Fiji	Suva	Dollar
Finland	Helsinki	Euro
France	Paris	Euro
Georgia	Tbilisi	Lari
Germany	Berlin	Euro
Ghana	Accra	Cedi
Greece	Athens	Euro
Guatemala	Guatemala City	Quetzal
Hong Kong	Victoria	Dollar
Hungary	Budapest	Forints
Iceland	Reykjavik	Krona
India	New Delhi	Rupee

Country	Capital	Currency
Indonesia	Jakarta	Rupiah
Iran	Teheran	Rial
Iraq	Baghdad	Dinar
Ireland	Dublin	Euro
Israel	Jerusalem	Shekel
Italy	Rome	Euro
Jamaica	Kingston	Dollar
Japan	Tokyo	Yen
Jordan	Amman	Dinar
Kazakhstan	Akmola	Tenge
Kenya	Nairobi	Shilling
Korea (S)	Seoul	Won
Korea (N)	Pyongyang	Won
Kyrgyzstan	Bishkek	Som
Kuwait	Kuwait City	Dinar
Laos	Vientiane	Kip
Latvia	Riga	Lat
Lebanon	Beirut	Pound
Libya	Tripoli	Dinar
Lithuania	Vilnius	Litas
Malaysia	Kuala Lumpur	Ringgit
Maldives	Male	Rufiyya
Mauritius	Port Louis	Rupee
Moldavia	Chisinau	Leu
Mexico	Mexico City	Peso
Morocco	Rabat	Dirham
Mozambique	Maputo	Metical
Myanmar (Burma)	Nay Pyi Taw	Kyat
Nepal	Kathmandu	Rupee
Netherlands	Amsterdam	Euro
New Zealand	Wellington	Dollar
Nigeria	Abuja	Naira
Norway	Oslo	Krone
Oman	Muscat	Rial
Pakistan	Islamabad	Rupee
Philippines	Manila	Peso
Poland	Warsaw	Zloty
Portugal	Lisbon	Euro
Qatar	Doha	Riyal
Romania	Bucharest	Leu
Russia	Moscow	Ruble
Saudi Arabia	Riyadh	Rial

Country	Capital	Currency
Slovakia	Bratislava	Euro
Spain	Madrid	Euro
Sri Lanka	Colombo	Rupee
Sudan	Khartoum	Dinar
Sweden	Stockholm	Krona
Switzerland	Berne	Swiss Francs
Syria	Damascus	Pound
South Africa	Capetown (Legislative) Pretoria (Administrative)	Rand
Tajikistan	Dushanbe	Somoni
Taiwan	Taipei	Dollar
Tanzania	Dodoma	Shilling
Thailand	Bangkok	Baht
Turkiye	Ankara	Turkish Lira
Turkmania	Ashikabad	Manat
Uganda	Kampala	Shilling
Ukraine	Kiev	Hyrvna
United Arab Emirates	Abu Dhabi	Dirham
U.K.	London	Pound Sterling
U.S.A.	Washington	Dollar
Uzbekistan	Tashkent	Som
Vietnam	Hanoi	Dong
Yemen	Sana'a	Rial/Dinar
Zimbabwe	Harare	Dollar
Congo (Democratic Republic)	Kinshasa	Franc
Zambia	Lusaka	Kwacha

INDIAN CITIES AND THEIR RIVERS

City	State	River
Agra	U.P.	Yamuna
Ahmedabad	Gujarat	Sabarmati
Alwaye	Kerala	Periyar
Kolkata	West Bengal	Hooghly
Cuttack	Odisha	Mahanadi
Delhi	Delhi	Yamuna
Haridwar	Uttarakhand	Ganga
Kanpur	Uttar Pradesh	Ganga
Ludhiana	Punjab	Sutlej
Lucknow	Uttar Pradesh	Gomati
Nasik	Maharashtra	Godavari
Patna	Bihar	Ganga
Prayagraj	U.P.	Confluence of the Ganga, Yamuna, and invisible Saraswati
Srinagar	J & K	Jhelum
Surat	Gujarat	Tapti
Tiruchirapally	Tamil Nadu	Kaveri
Ujjain	Madhya Pradesh	Shipra
Vijayawada	Andhra Pradesh	Krishna
Varanasi	Uttar Pradesh	Ganga

WONDERS OF THE WORLD

Seven Wonders of the Ancient World: (1) the Pyramids of Egypt, built in approximately 2700 BC; (2) the Hanging Gardens at Babylon; (3) the temple of Artemis at Emphesus; (4) the statue of Zeus at Olympia; (5) the tomb of Mausolus at Halicarnassus, built in nearly 350 BC; (6) the Colossus of Rhodes, built in nearly 280 BC; (7) the Pharos Lighthouse at Alexandria.

Seven Wonders of the Medieval World: (1) the Colosseum of Rome; (2) the Great Wall of China; (3) the Porcelain Tower of Nanking; (4) the Mosque at St. Sophia (Constantinople); (5) Stonehenge; (6) the Catacombs of Rome; (7) the Leaning Tower of Pisa.

Seven New Wonders of the World: (1) Taj Mahal of Agra (India); (2) Pyramid at Chichen Itza (Mexico); (3) Machu Picchu (Peru); (4) Statue of Christ The Redeemer (Brazil); (5) Great Wall of China; (6) Roman Colosseum, Italy; (7) Ruins of Petra, Jordan.

STATES & UNION TERRITORIES OF INDIA (CAPITALS, PRINCIPAL LANGUAGES)

States & Union Territories	*Capitals*	*Principal Languages*
■ Andhra Pradesh	Amravati	*Telgu and Urdu*
■ Arunachal Pradesh	Itanagar	*Monpa, Adi, Nissi etc.*
■ Assam	Dispur	*Assamese and Bengali*
■ Bihar	Patna	*Hindi and Maithili*
■ Chhattishgarh	Raipur	*Hindi*
■ Goa	Panaji	*Konkani*
■ Gujarat	GandhiNagar	*Gujarati*
■ Haryana	Chandigarh	*Hindi*
■ Himachal Pradesh	Shimla	*Hindi and Pahari*
■ Jharkhand	Ranchi	*Hindi*
■ Kerala	Thiruvananthpuram	*Malyalam*
■ Karnataka	Bengluru	*Kannada*
■ Madhya Pradesh	Bhopal	*Hindi*
■ Maharashtra	Mumbai	*Marathi*
■ Meghalaya	Shillong	*Khashi, Jayantia and Garo*
■ Manipur	Imphal	*Manipuri*
■ Mizoram	Aizawl	*Mizo and English*
■ Nagaland	Kohima	*Naga, Assamese and English*
■ Odisha	Bhubaneshwar	*Odiya*
■ Punjab	Chandigarh	*Punjabi*
■ Rajasthan	Jaipur	*Hindi, Rajasthani*
■ Sikkim	Gangtok	*Sikkimese and Gorkhali*
■ Tamil Nadu	Chennai	*Tamil*
■ Tripura	Agartala	*Bengali, Tripuri*
■ Uttar Pradesh	Lucknow	*Hindi*
■ Uttarakhand	Dehradun	*Hindi*
■ West Bengal	Kolkata	*Bengali*
■ Telangana	Hyderabad	*Telgu and Urdu*
■ Jammu & Kashmir	Srinagar/Jammu	*Kashmiri, Dongri, Urdu, Dardi and Pahari*
■ Andaman and Nicobar Islands	Port Blair	*Hindi, Nicobarese, Bengali, Malayalam, Tamil, Telugu*
■ Chandigarh	Chandigarh	*Hindi, Punjabi, English*
■ Dadar and Nagar Haveli and Daman and Diu	Daman	*Gujarati, Hindi*
■ Delhi	Delhi	*Hindi, Punjabi*
■ Lakshadweep	Kavaratti	*Malayalam*
■ Puducherry	Puducherry	*Tamil, Telugu, Malayalam, English and French*
■ Ladakh	Leh	*Ladakhi*

HIGH COURTS IN INDIA

Name	*Territorial Jurisdiction*	*Seat*
Allahabad	Uttar Pradesh	Prayagraj (Bench at Lucknow)
Andhra Pradesh	Andhra Pradesh	Amaravati
Bombay	Maharashtra, Goa Dadar and Nagar Haveli and Daman and Diu	Mumbai (Benches at Nagpur, Panaji, and Aurangabad)
Calcutta	West Bengal and Andaman & Nicobar Islands	Kolkata (Circuit Benches at Port Blair and Jalpaiguri)
Chhattisgarh	Chhattisgarh	Bilaspur
Delhi	New Delhi	NCT of Delhi
Gauhati	Assam, Nagaland, Mizoram and Arunachal Pradesh	Guwahati (Benches at Kohima, Aizawl and Itanagar)
Gujarat	Gujarat	Ahmedabad
Himachal Pradesh	Himachal Pradesh	Shimla
Jammu & Kashmir and Ladakh	Jammu & Kashmir/Ladakh	Srinagar and Jammu
Jharkhand	Jharkhand	Ranchi
Karnataka	Karnataka	Bengaluru (Circuit Benches at Dharwar and Gulbarga)
Kerala	Kerala & Lakshadweep	Ernakulam
Madhya Pradesh	Madhya Pradesh	Jabalpur (Benches at Gwalior and Indore)
Madras	Tamil Nadu & Puducherry	Chennai (Bench at Madurai)
Orissa	Odisha	Cuttack
Patna	Bihar	Patna
Punjab and Haryana	Punjab, Haryana and Chandigarh	Chandigarh
Rajasthan	Rajasthan	Jodhpur (Bench at Jaipur)
Sikkim	Sikkim	Gangtok
Uttarakhand	Uttarakhand	Nainital
Tripura	Tripura	Agartala
Meghalaya	Meghalaya	Shillong
Manipur	Manipur	Imphal
Telangana	Telangana	Hyderabad

FAMOUS HILL STATIONS

Hill Station	State/UT
1. Almora, Mussoorie Nainital	: Uttarakhand
2. Cherrapunji (Shillong), Khasi Hills (Shillong)	: Meghalaya
3. Ooty, Kodaikanal Yereaud	: Tamil Nadu
4. Dalhousie, Kassauli	: Himachal Pradesh
5. Darjeeling	: West Bengal
6. Gulmarg, Srinagar	: Jammu and Kashmir
7. Mahabaleshwar	: Maharashtra
8. Mt. Abu	: Rajasthan
9. Panchmarhi	: Madhya Pradesh

FAMOUS NATIONAL PARKS

1. Corbett National Park : Nainital, Uttarakhand
2. Dudhwa National Park : Lakhimpur Kheri, Uttar Pradesh
3. Kaziranga National Park : Jorhat, Assam
4. Kanha National Park : Jabalpur, Bhedaghat
5. Gir National Park : Rajkot, Junagarh, Gujarat
6. Guindy National Park : Guindy, Chennai, Tamil Nadu
7. Nagairhole National Park : Coorg, Karnataka
8. Bandipur National Park : Mysore, Karnataka

FAMOUS NATIONAL WILDLIFE SANCTUARIES

1. Dachigam Wildlife Sanctuary : Srinagar, Jammu and Kashmir
2. Sariska : Alwar, Rajasthan
3. Hazaribagh Wildlife Sanctuary : Hazaribagh, Jharkhand
4. Tiger Project : Sawai Madhopur, Rajasthan
5. Mudhumali Wildlife Sanctuary : Mudhumalia, Nilgiri, Tamil Nadu
6. Periyar Wildlife Sanctuary : Idukki, Kottayam, Kerala

HOLY PLACES IN INDIA

1. Amarnath	Jammu and Kashmir
2. Ayodhya	Uttar Pradesh
3. Badrinath	Uttarakhand
4. Dwarka	Gujarat
5. Haridwar	Uttarakhand
6. Kancheepuram	Tamil Nadu
7. Kedarnath	Uttarakhand
8. Mathura	Uttar Pradesh
9. Puri	Odisha
10. Rameswaram	Tamil Nadu
11. Tirupati	Andhra Pradesh
12. Ujjain	Madhya Pradesh
13. Varanasi	Uttar Pradesh
14. Bodh Gaya	Bihar

SPORTS

Terms Associated With Sports :

Cricket : Ashes, Bye, Bodyline, Bowling, Break, Cover-point, Creases, Chinaman, Chucker, Drive, Duck, Follow on, Googly, Hit-Wicket, Hat-trick, Leg-before-wicket, Leg break, Leg-bye, Maiden over, No ball, Night-watchman, Runner, Run-out, Stumped, Silly-point, Slip.

Football : Handball, Corner kick, Dribble, Free Kick, Hat-trick, Off-side, Penalty Kick, Try, Throw in, Wembley.

Hockey : Bully, Carry, Corner kick, Corner, Penalty stroke, Off-side, Penalty, Roll in scoop, Sticks, Sudden death, Striking circle, Short Corner, Scoop, Tie-breaker, Under-cutting, Hat-trick.

Tennis : Backhand drive, Deuce, Fault, Half-volley, Net, Let, Volley, Smash, Service.

Billiards : Break, Cannons, Cue, Pot, Jigger, Scratch, In Bauk, In, Off.

Bridge : Dummy, Finesse, Grand-slam, Little Slam, Revoke, Ruff slam, Trump, Tricks, Vulnerable.

Volley Ball : Booster, Love, Service, Volley, Smasher.

Badminton : Smash, Drop, Let.

Chess : Check, Checkmate, Gambit, State-mate.

Golf : Bogy, Caddie, Hole, Links, Stymie, Tee, Put.

Polo : Chukker, Mallet, Bunder.

Baseball : Bunting, Diamond, Pitcher, Put-out, Strike, Home.

Boxing : Knockout, Punch, Upper-cut, Jab, Hook.

FAMOUS TROPHIES

Agha Khan Cup	Hockey
Beighton Cup	Hockey
Corbillion Cup	World Table Tennis (Women)
Davis Cup	Lawn Tennis
Duleep Trophy	Cricket
Durand Cup	Football
Ezra Cup	Polo
I.F.A. Shield	Football
Irani Cup	Cricket (India)
Jayalaxmi Cup	Table Tennis (Women)
Lady Rattan Tata Trophy	Hockey (Women)
Nehru Cup	Hockey (India)
Obaidullah Cup	Hockey
Ranji Trophy	Cricket (India)
Rangaswamy Cup	Hockey (India)
Rovers Cup	Football (India)
Santosh Trophy	Football (India)
Subroto Cup	Football
Thomas Cup	Badminton
Uber Cup	Badminton (Women)
Wellington Trophy	Rowing (India)

BIGGEST, LARGEST, TALLEST OF THE WORLD

Airport, *Largest*—King Fahd International Airport, Dammon (Saudi Arabia)

Animal, *Tallest*—Giraffe (Average height 6.09 m); *Largest and Heaviest*—Blue Whale (190 tonnes)

Longest recorded Animal—Boot lace Worm (55 m); *Fastest*—Cheetah (Approximately 100 km/hr)

Bay, *Largest*—Bay of Bengal

Continent, *biggest*—Asia (31,845,872 km^2); *Smallest*—Australia Mainland (Area 76,17,930 km^2)

Desert, *Largest*—Sahara (N. Africa; maximum length 5,150 km EW; maximum width 3,200 km NS)

Dome, *Largest*—Singapore National Stadium (310 m)

Fish, *Largest fresh water*—Plabeuk (China, Laos and Thailand); *Most abundant*—Bristle mouth; *Most venomous*—Stone Fish (Indo-Pacific Waters)

Fountain, *Tallest*—King Fahd's Fountain (Jeddah, Saudi Arabia)

Gulf, *Largest*—Gulf of Mexico (1,544,000 sq. km)

Island, *Biggest*—Greenland (Kalaatdlit Nunaat-2,175,000 sq km)

Lake, *Largest*—Caspian Sea (Azerbaijan, Russia, Iran border: 37.18 lakh km^2); *Deepest*—Baikal (Siberia); *Largest (fresh water)*—Superior Lake (USA---Canada border: 82,350 km^2)

Mountain, *Highest peak*—Mt. Everest (8848 m; Nepal); *Highest range*—Himalayas, Asia (upto 4200 m); *Greatest mountain range*—Himalaya-Karakoram (96 out of 109 peaks over 7315 m are here)

Museum, *Largest*—American Museum of Natural History, New York

Ocean, *Largest and Deepest*—The Pacific (Area: 166,240,000 km^2; Depth: 10,924 m)

Platform, *Longest (rail)*—Shri Siddharoodha Swamiji Railway Station, Hubballi (Karnataka; India, 1507 m. long)

Railway Station, *Largest*—Grand Central Terminal (New York City; 19 hc)

Rivers, *Longest*—(i) Nile (6650 km) (ii) Amazon (6437 km)

Sea, *Largest*—Philippine Sea (5,695,000 sq. km)

Star, *Brightest*—Sirius A (also called Dog Star)

Temple, *Largest*—Angkor Vat (Cambodia: 402 acres)

Tunnel, *Longest (railway)*—Gotthard Base Rail Tunnel (Switzerland; 57.1 km); *Largest (road)*—Laerdal, Norway (24.51 km)

FIRST IN INDIA

Governor General of Independent India — Lord Mountbatten

Cosmonaut — Sq. Ldr. Rakesh Sharma

Field Marshal — S.H.F.J. Manekshaw

Indian Governor General of Indian Union — C. Rajagopalachari

Indian I.C.S. Officer — Satyendra Nath Tagore

Indian to swim across English Channel — Mihir Sen

Indian Women to swim across English Channel — Miss Arti Saha

Man to climb Mount Everest — Tenzing Norgay

Man to climb Mount Everest without Oxygen — Phu Dorjee

Man to climb Mount Everest twice — Nwang Gombu

Nobel Prize Winner — Rabindra Nath Tagore

President of Indian National Congress — W.C. Banerjee

President of Indian Republic — Dr. Rajendra Prasad

Talkie Film — Alam Ara (1931)

Test Tube Baby (Documented) — Indira

Viceroy of India — Lord Canning

Woman Minister of Indian Union — Rajkumari Amrit Kaur

Woman Governor — Mrs. Sarojini Naidu

Woman President of Indian National Congress — Dr. Annie Besant

Woman Prime Minister — Mrs. Indira Gandhi

Woman Speaker of a State Assembly — Mrs. Shanno Devi

Prime Minister of India — Pt. Jawaharlal Nehru

Muslim President of Indian Union — Dr. Zakir Hussain

Speaker of Lok Sabha — G.V. Mavlankar

Women to Climb Mount Everest — Bachhendri Pal

Woman Judge in Supreme Court — Mrs. Meera Sahib Fatima Biwi

Women Chief Justice of a High Court — Smt. Leela Seth

The First Indian Weightlifter to Win bronze medal in Olympics — Karnam Malleshwari (Sydney, in 2000)

Chief of Defence Staff (CDS) —General Bipin Rawat

World Chess Champion — Vishwanathan Anand

India's First Woman Merchant Navy Officer — Sonali Banerjee

The First Woman Air Vice-Marshal — P. Bandopadhyaya

The First Indian to be appointed as United Nations Civilian Police Advisor — Ms. Kiran Bedi

The First Women to be appointed Deputy Governor of Reserve Bank of India — K.J. Udeshi

The First Indian Lady to win a medal in World Athletic Championship — Anju Bobby George

The First Sikh Prime Minister of India — Dr. Manmohan Singh

IMPORTANT DAYS

15th January	—	Army Day
26th January	—	Republic Day
30th January	—	Leprosy Eradication Day/ Martyr's Day
28th February	—	National Science Day
8th march	—	International Women's Day
15th March	—	World Consumer's Day
21st March	—	World Disabled Day
5th April	—	National Marine Day
7th April	—	World Health Day
18th April	—	World Heritage Day
22nd April	—	International Earth Day
Ist May	—	Worker's Day
3rd May	—	International Sun Day
21st May	—	Anti-Terrorism Day
24th May	—	Commonwealth Day
31st May	—	World No Tobacco Day
5th June	—	World Environment Day
21st June	—	World Yoga Day
26th June	—	International Day against Drug Abuse
11th July	—	World Population Day
15th August	—	Independence Day
24th August	—	Sanskrit Day
5th September	—	Teacher's Day
8th September	—	World Literacy Day
27th September	—	World Tourism Day
1st October	—	World Elder's Day
4th October	—	World Animal Day
8th October	—	Air Force Day
10th October	—	National Solidarity Day
16th October	—	World Food Day
24th October	—	U.N. Day
14th November	—	World Diabetes Day
14th November	—	Children's Day
19th November	—	National Integration Day
26th November	—	Law Day
1st December	—	World AIDS Day
4th December	—	Navy Day
7th December	—	Flag Day
10th December	—	Human Rights Day

PARLIAMENTS OF IMPORTANT COUNTRIES

Afghanistan	—	Shora
Britain	—	Parliament House of Commons, House of Lords
Denmark	—	Folketing
The Netherlands	—	States General
India	—	Sansad
Israel	—	Knesset
Iran	—	Majlis
Ireland	—	Airetann
Iceland	—	Althing
Japan	—	Diet
Norway	—	Storting
Russia	—	Supreme Soviet
Spain	—	Cortes
Sweden	—	Riksdag
U.S.A.	—	Congress Senate
Germany	—	Bundestag

MINERAL RESOURCES OF THE WORLD

Mineral	Largest Producers
Iron Ore	China, Japan, Russia
Tin	China, Indonesia, Peru
Lead	China, Australia, U.S.A.
Zinc	China, Australia, Peru
Manganese	South Africa, Brazil, Australia
Aluminium	China, Russia, Canada
Petroleum	Saudi Arabia, Russia, USA
Silver	Peru, Mexico, China
Coal	China, USA, India

WORLD'S LARGEST PRODUCERS

Articles	Producers	Articles	Producers
Carpets	Iran	Cheese	USA
Cocoa	Cote d'Ivoire	Coffee	Brazil
Copper	Chile	Cotton	China
Diamonds	Russia	Jute	India
Rice	China	Rubber	Thailand
Silk	China	Steel	China
Sugar	Brazil	Tea	China
Tin	China	Wheat	China
Wool	Australia		

TEN LARGEST COUNTRIES BY AREAS

Rank by Area	Country	Area (sq. km.)
1.	Russia	17,075,400
2.	Canada	9,976,139
3.	China	9,561,000
4.	U.S.A.	9,363,123
5.	Brazil	8,511,965
6.	Australia	7,686,848
7.	India	3,287,263
8.	Argentina	2,776,889
9.	Kazakhstan	2,724,900
10.	Algeria	2,381,741

PRESIDENT OF INDIA

He is the constitutional head of the Republic but not the real executive.

Qualifications: (1) Indian citizen; (2) age not less than 35 years; (3) should have qualifications for election to Lok Sabha; (4) should not hold any office of profit; (5) should not be a Member of Parliament or State Legislature.

Election: He is elected by the elected Members of Parliament and State Legislative Assemblies in accordance with the system of proportional representation by means of single transferable vote.

Powers: He makes appointment to all the Constitutional posts. He can address either House of Parliament and send message to them. He can summon and prorogue either House of Parliament and dissolve Lok Sabha. All Bills passed by Parliament must receive his assent to become an Act. He issues Ordinance when Parliament is not in session. No money Bill can be introduced in Lok Sabha without his recommendation. He can grant pardon, reprieve or remit punishment and he can commute death sentences. He can declare national emergency, state emergency and financial emergency.

VICE-PRESIDENT OF INDIA

The Vice-President acts as the ex-officio Chairman of Rajya Sabha and acts as the President when the latter is unable to discharge his functions due to illness, absence or any other reason, or till the election of a new President when a vacancy is caused by the death, resignation or removal of the President.

The Vice-President is elected by an electoral college consisting of the members of both Houses of Parliament in accordance with the system of proportional representation by means of the single transferable vote. He must be a citizen of India, not less than 35 years of age, and should be eligible for election as a member of the Council of States.

PRIME MINISTER OF INDIA

The Prime Minister is the leader of the majority party in the Parliament and the President cannot exercise his discretion in the appointment of the Prime Minister. He stays in office till the majority of the members of Lok Sabha has confidence in him. He occupies an important posi-tion in relation to the council of Ministers. He recommends the names of the persons to be included in the Council of Ministers. He allocates portfolios among them and can ask any minister to tender resignation. He can drop a minister while reshuffling the ministry. He coordinates the administration of various departments. He is the chief link between the President and the Council. He is the leader of the majority party and so, he has a great influence on the Parliament and the party. The Prime Minister enjoys such extensive powers as have been described as the virtual ruler of the country.

THE SOLAR SYSTEM: SOME FACTS

Number of Planets: 8—Mercury, Venus, Earth, Mars, Jupiter, Saturn, Uranus and Neptune.

Largest most

Massive planet .... Jupiter

Brightest planet .... Venus

Brightest star .... Sirius

Fastest orbiting planet .... Mercury

Longest (Synodic) day .... Mercury

Planet with largest moon .... Jupiter

Greatest average density .... Jupiter

Tallest mountain .... Earth

Strongest magnetic fields .... Jupiter

Most circular orbit .... Venus

Shortest (synodic) day .... Jupiter

Hottest planet .... Venus

No moons .... Mercury, Venus

Planet with moon with most eccentric orbit .... Neptune

Lowest average density .... Saturn

Deepest Oceans .... Jupiter

Greatest amount of liquid on the surface .... Earth

THE EARTH: FACTS AND DATA

Composition of the Earth: Aluminium (0.4%), Sulphur (2.7%), Silicon (13%), Oxygen (28%), Calcium (1.2%), Nickel (2.7%), Magnesium (17%), Iron (35%)

Surface area	: 510100500 sq km
Land Surface (29.1%)	: 148950800 sq km
Ocean Surface (70.9%)	: 361149700 sq km
Type of water	: 97% salt, 3% fresh
Total area of water	: 382672000 sq km
Equatorial diameter	: 12753 km
Equatorial Circumference	: 40066 km
Polar Circumference	: 39992 km
Polar diameter	: 12710 km
Equatorial radius	: 6376 km
Polar radius	: 6335 km
Mass (estimated weight)	: 594×10^{19} metric tons
Mean distance from the Sun	: 149407000 km

Earth's orbit speed (around sun)	: 107320 kmph	Time of Rotation (on its axis)	: 23 hrs 56 min 4.09 seconds
Period of Revolution (round the sun)	: 365 days 5 hrs 48 min. 45.51 seconds	Inclination of the axis (to the plane of the ecliptic)	: 23°27'

PRINCIPAL MOUNTAIN PEAKS OF THE WORLD

Mountains	Height in Metres	Range	Date of First Ascent
1. Mount Everest	8,848	Himalayas	May 29, 1953
2. K-2 (Godwin Austen)	8,611	Karakoram	July 31, 1954
3. Kanchenjunga	8,597	Himalayas	May 25, 1955
4. Lhotse	8,511	Himalayas	May 18, 1956
5. Makalu I	8,481	Himalayas	May 15, 1955
6. Dhaulagiri I	8,167	Himalayas	May 13, 1960
7. Mansalu I	8,156	Himalayas	May 9, 1956
8. Chollyo	8,153	Himalayas	Oct. 19, 1954
9. Nanga Parbat	8,124	Himalayas	July 3, 1953
10. Annapurna I	8,091	Himalayas	June 3, 1950
11. Gasherbrum I	8,068	Karakoram	July 5, 1958
12. Broad Peak I	8,047	Karakoram	June 9, 1957
13. Gasherbrum II	8,034	Karakoram	July 7, 1956
14. Shisha Pangma (Gosainthan)	8,014	Himalayas	May 2, 1964
15. Gasherbrum III	7,952	Karakoram	Aug. 11, 1975

POPULAR NICK NAMES OF SOME FAMOUS PERSONALITIES

Andhra Kesari	T. Prakasam
Anna	C.N. Anna Durai
Bang Bandhu	Sheikh Mujibur Rehman
Bapu	Mahatma Gandhi
Bard of Avon	William Shakespeare
Chachaji	Jawaharlal Nehru
Desh Bandhu	C.R. Das
Frontier Gandhi	Khan Abdul Gaffar Khan
Fuhrer	Adolf Hitler
G.B.S.	George Bernard Shaw
Grand Old Man of India	Dadabhai Naoroji
Grand Old Man of Britain	Gladstone
Guru Dev	Rabindra Nath Tagore
Guruji	M.S. Golwalkar
Iron Man of India	Sardar Patel
Lok Nayak	Jayaprakash Narayan
Lady with the Lamp	Florence Nightingale
Lal, Bal, Pal	Lala Lajpat Rai, Bal Gangadhar Tilak, Bipin Chandra Pal
Little Corporal	Napoleon Bonaparte
Lokmanya	Bal Gangadhar Tilak
Mahamana	Pt. Madan Mohan Malaviya
Maid of Orleans	Joan of Arc
Maiden Queen	Queen Elizabeth I
Missile Man	A.P.J. Abdul Kalam
Man of Destiny	Napoleon Bonaparte
Netaji	Subhash Chandra Bose
Nightingale of India	Sarojini Naidu
Panditji	Jawaharlal Nehru
Punjab Kesari	Lala Lajpat Rai
Shastriji	Lal Bahadur Shastri
Uncle Ho	Ho Chi Minh
Wizard of the North	Walter Scott

FAMOUS INTERNATIONAL ORGANISATIONS, HEADQUARTERS

International Organisations	*Headquarters*
United Nations Organisations (U.N.O.)	New York
International Monetary Fund (I.M.F.)	Washington D.C.
World Health Organisation (W.H.O.)	Geneva
Food & Agricultural Organisation (FAO)	Rome
International Labour Organisation (ILO)	Geneva
UNESCO	Paris
International Court of Justice	The Hague
Universal Postal Union (UPU)	Berne
International Civil Aviation Organisation (ICAO)	Montreal
UNIDO	Vienna
International Atomic Energy Agency (IAEA)	Vienna
International Finance Corporation (IFC)	Washington
United Nations Development Programme (UNDP)	New York
UNICEF	New York
International Maritime Organisation (IMO)	London
World Meteorological Organisation (WMO)	Geneva
International Telecommunication Union (ITU)	Geneva
Arab League	Cairo
Commonwealth of Nations	London
World Trade Organisation (WTO)	Geneva
International Development Association (IDA)	Washington D.C.
International Bank for Reconstruction and Development (IBRD)	Washington D.C.
World Intellectual Property Organisation (WIPO)	Geneva
Organisation of Islamic Conference (OIC)	Jeddah (Saudi Arabia)
European Union	Brussels
Red Cross	Geneva
Interpol	Lyons (France)
Asian Development Bank (ADB)	Manila
North Atlantic Treaty Organisation (NATO)	Brussels
Association of South East Asian Nations (ASEAN)	Jakarta

BHARAT RATNA AWARD WINNERS

1. C. Rajagopalachari	1954	**18.** Mother Teresa	1980	**35.** Jaya Prakash Narayan*	1999
2. Dr. S. Radhakrishnan	1954	**19.** Acharya Vinoba Bhave*	1983	**36.** Prof. Amartya Sen	1999
3. Dr. C.V. Raman	1954	**20.** Khan Abdul Ghaffar Khan	1987	**37.** Pt. Ravi Shankar	1999
4. Dr. Bhagwan Das	1955	**21.** M.G. Ramachandran*	1988	**38.** Gopinath Bardoloi	1999
5. Dr. M. Visvesvaraya	1955	**22.** Dr. B.R. Ambedkar*	1990	**39.** Lata Mangeshkar	2001
6. Jawaharlal Nehru	1955	**23.** Dr. Nelson R. Mandela	1990	**40.** Bismillah Khan	2001
7. Govind Ballabh Pant	1957	**24.** Rajiv Gandhi*	1991	**41.** Bhimsen Joshi	2009
8. Dr. D.K. Karve	1958	**25.** Sardar Vallabhbhai Patel*	1991	**42.** C.N.R. Rao	2014
9. Dr. Bidhan Chandra Roy	1961	**26.** Morarji R. Desai	1991	**43.** Sachin Tendulkar	2014
10. Purushottam Das Tandon	1961	**27.** Maulana Abdul Kalam Azad*	1992	**44.** Madan Mohan Malaviya*	2015
11. Dr. Rajendra Prasad	1962	**28.** Jehangir Ratanji Dadabhai Tata	1992	**45.** Atal Bihari Vajpayee	2015
12. Dr. Zakir Hussain	1963	**29.** Satyajit Roy	1992	**46.** Nanaji Deshmukh*	2019
13. Dr. Pandurang Vaman Kane	1963	**30.** Gulzari Lal Nanda	1997	**47.** Bhupen Hazarika*	2019
14. Lal Bahadur Shastri*	1966	**31.** Mrs. Aruna Asaf Ali*	1997	**48.** Pranab Mukherjee	2019
15. Indira Gandhi	1971	**32.** Dr. A.P.J. Abdul Kalam	1997	**49.** Karpoori Thakur*	2024
16. V.V. Giri	1975	**33.** M.S. Subbalakshmi	1998	**50.** Lal Krishna Advani	2024
17. K. Kamraj*	1976	**34.** C. Subramaniam	1998	**51.** Charan Singh*	2024
				52. P.V. Narasimha Rao*	2024
				53. M.S. Swaminathan*	2024

* Posthumous

ART AND CULTURE

☞ Classical Dances

Dance	*State*	*Famous Artists*
Bharat Natyam	Tamil Nadu	Yamini Krishnamurthy, Rukmini Devi Arundale, Swapna Sundari, Sonal Mansingh, Vaijanti Mala, Mrinalini Sarabhai, Chandralekha, Indrani, Ram Gopal, Bal Saraswati
Kathakali	Kerala	Gopinath, K.K. Nayar, Kunju-Kurup, T.K. Chandu
Kuchipudi	Andhra Pradesh/ Telangana	Sapna Sundari, Raja Reddy, Shobha Nayar, Radha Reddy, Vedantam Satyanarayan, Vimpanti Chinna Satyam.
Kathak	North India	Birju Maharaj, Gopi Krishna, Shambhu Maharaj, Sitara Devi, Vishnu Sharma, Durga Lal, Shobhana Narayan
Odissi	Odisha	Kelucharan Mahapatra, Indrani Rehman, Madhavi Mudgal, Pratima Bedi, Samyukta Panigrahi, Sonal Mansingh, Debudas
Manipuri	Manipur	Uday Shankar, Bipin Singh, Suryamukhi, Darohra Jhaveri

☞ Famous Folk Dances

State/UT	*Folk Dance*	*State/UT*	*Folk Dance*
Andhra Pradesh/ Telangana	Dandari, Banjara	Kerala	Mohini Attam, Padayuni
Assam	Bihu, Keli Gopal, Sataria	Madhya Pradesh	Lota Nritya, Jawara
Bihar	Chhau, Magahi, Durga dance	Maharashtra	Tamasha, Dahi Handi, Gof, Deepak Dindi
W. Bengal	Kirtan, Kalatri, Asweabadh, Brita, Kalidance	Manipur	Dhol Cholam
Chhattisgarh	Saila, Karama, Bhagoria	Meghalaya	Nongakarem
Gujarat	Garba, Rasalila, Tippani, Dandia,	Nagaland	Bamboo dance
		Odisha	Chhau, Maya Shabari, Dalachai
Haryana	Damyal, Lahoor	Punjab	Gidda, Bhangra, Panihari
Himachal Pradesh	Dussehra dance, Hikat, Notio	Rajasthan	Thumar, Kathaputali, Tera Tali
Jammu & Kashmir	Dumhal	Tamil Nadu	Terukalathu, Kabalatam, Kargam, Pulivesham
		Tripura	Hazagiri
Jharkhand	Jhau, Ghumakudia, Jadur, Sarhul, Soharai, Karama, Vaima, Loojhari, Jat-Jatin, Vidayat	Uttar Pradesh	Rasalila, Nautanki, Thali, Dhurang, Jhumela, Huraka, Bol.
		Uttarakhand	Kajari, Karan
Karnataka	Yakshagan, Dolu Kunitha	Goa	Dhode Modini

MUSIC

Main Schools of Classical Music

- There are two main schools of classical music, namely, the Hindustani and the Carnatic. The Hindustani school of classical music is in vogue in north-western India, eastern India and northern parts of the South India.

Musical Instruments

- *They are:* Tabla, Mridangam, Pakhawaj, Chandai, Dholak, Veena, Sitar, Sarod, Gootuvadhyam, Sarangi, Flute, Nadaswaram, Shehnai, Shringi and Turahi.

FAMOUS INTERNATIONAL AIR SERVICES

Air Service	*Name of Country*	*Air Service*	*Name of Country*
Air India	India	Lufthansa Airlines	Germany
British Overseas Airways Corporation	Britain	Iraqi Airways	Iraq
Trans World Airlines	America	National Airlines	Iran
Russian Airlines	Russia	Quantas Airlines	Australia
Japan Airlines	Japan	Hong-Kong Airlines	Hong-Kong
Pakistan International Airlines	Pakistan	Egypt Airlines	Egypt
Malaysia Airlines	Malaysia	Slovak Airlines	Slovakia
Royal Nepal Airlines	Nepal	S.I.A.	Singapore
Swiss Airways	Switzerland	Garuda Airways	Indonesia
Air France	France	Bangladesh Viman Sewa	Bangladesh
Kuwait Airways	Kuwait	Air Lanka	Sri Lanka
Pan American World Airways	America	Elitalia Airlines	Italy
K.L.M. Royal Airlines	The Netherlands (Holland)	Air Canada	Canada

FAMOUS RELIGIONS, FOUNDERS, HOLY BOOKS & PLACES OF WORSHIP

Religion	*Founder*	*Holy Books*	*Place of Worship*
Hinduism	Hinduism has no one Founder. (This religion is based upon the religion of original Aryan Settlers)	Ramayan, Vedas, Puranas and Geeta	Temple
Sikh	Guru Nanak Dev	Guru Grantha Sahib	Gurdwara
Christianity	Jesus Christ	Bible	Church
Islam	Prophet Mohammed	Koran (Quran)	Mosque
Parsi	Zoroaster	Zend Avesta	Fire Temple
Jainism	Adinath Rishavdev	Jain Granth	Jain Temple
Buddhism	Gautam Buddha	Tripitaka	Buddha Temple
Jew	Moosa	Torah	Synagogue

INTELLIGENCE AGENCIES OF SOME PROMINENT COUNTRIES

Country	*Intelligence Agency*	*Country*	*Intelligence Agency*
India	Research & Analysis Wing (RAW), Intelligence Bureau (I.B.), Central Bureau of Investigation (C.B.I.)	Russia	K.G.B. (Komitel Gosudarstvennoy Bezopasnosty) (Committee for State Security)
Pakistan	Inter Service Intelligence (I.S.I.)	Canada	Security Intelligence Service
U.S.A.	Central Intelligence Agency, Federal Bureau of Investigation	S. Africa	Bureau of State Security
		Iran	Sabak
Britain	Military Intelligence (M.I.)-5 and 6, Special Branch, Ultra, Joint Intelligence Organisation	Iraq	Al-Mukhabarat
		Australia	Australian Security and Intelligence Organisation
Israel	Mosad	France	S.D.E.C.E.
Egypt	Mukhabarat	Spain	C.E.S.I.D.
Japan	Nicho	Cuba	D.G.I.

SOME PROMINENT RACES OF THE WORLD

Races	Country/Area	Races	Country/Area	Races	Country/Area	Races	Country/Area
Veddas	Sri Lanka	Pygmy	Congo Basin	Eskimo	Canada, Tundra Region	Bushman	Kalahari Desert
Somaid	West Siberia	Bantu	Central and South Africa	Lapps	European Tundra	Red Indian	North America
Masai	East Africa	Tartars	Siberia	Hausa	Nigeria		
Muree	New Zealand	Baddu	Arab's Desert	Kirghiz	Steppes (Russia)		
Yakoot	Russian Tundra	Semang	Malaysia				
Papuans	New Guyana						

FAMOUS STRAITS OF THE WORLD

Strait	Between	Country
Malacca Strait	Andaman Sea and South China Sea	Indonesia
Palk Strait	Mannar and Bay of Bengal	India-Sri Lanka
Magellan Strait	Pacific and South Atlantic Ocean	Chile
Dover Strait	English Channel and North Sea	England-France
Berring Strait	Berring Sea and Chukasi Sea	Alaska-Russia
Sugaroo Strait	Japan Sea and Pacific Ocean	Japan
Sunda Strait	Java and Indian Ocean	Indonesia
Gibralter Strait	Mediterranean Sea and Atlantic Ocean	Spain
Harmuj Strait	Persia and Bay of Oman	Oman-Iran
Hudson Strait	Bay of Hudson and Atlantic Ocean	Canada

FAMOUS NEWSPAPERS OF THE WORLD

Newspaper	Place of Publishing	Language
Daily News	New York (America)	English
Guardian	London (Britain)	English
Pravada	Moscow (Russia)	Russian
Al-Ahram	Cairo (Egypt)	Arabic
Merdeca	Jakarta (Indonesia)	Indonesian
Times	London (Britain)	English
People's Daily	Beijing (China)	Chinese
New Statesman	Britain	English
Daily Mirror	Britain	English

Newspaper	Place of Publishing	Language
Hindu, Hindustan, Times of India, Tribune, Statesman, Indian Express, Economic Times	India	English
Hindustan, Nav Bharat Times, Dainik Bhaskar, Dainik Jagaran, Punjab Kesari	India	Hindi

IMPORTANT BOUNDARY LINES

Boundary Line	Countries
Durand Line	Pakistan and Afghanistan
Hindenberg Line	Germany-Poland
Maginot Line	France and Germany
Mannerhein Line	Russia-Finland
Mc Mahon Line	India-China
Order Niesse Line	Germany-Poland
Radcliff Line	India-Pakistan
Seigfrid Line	Germany-France
24th Parallel	India-Pakistan

Boundary Line	Countries
17th Parallel	The line which defined the boundary between North Vietnam and South Vietnam before the two were united.
38th Parallel	North Korea and South Korea
49th Parallel	U.S.A. and Canada

SIGNALS/SIGNS AND MEANING

Signal/Sign	*Meaning*	*Signal/Sign*	*Meaning*
Red Triangle	Family Planning	White Flag	Treaty or Surrender
Red Cross	Medical Help	Yellow Flag	Vehicles with patients of contagious diseases
Red Light	Danger, 'Stop' for the movement of vehicles	Two Bones across with a Skull	Danger of electricity
Green Light	Go	Half mast flown Flag	National mourning
Olive Branch	Peace	Lotus and culture	Sign of civilization
White Pigeon or Dove	Peace	Wheel (Chakra)	Sign of Progress
Black Strip on Arm	(i) Opposition (ii) Sorrow	A blind folded woman with scale in hand	Sign of Justice
Black Flag	Opposition	Reversed flown	National calamity flag
Red Flag	(i) Danger (ii) Revolution		

NATIONAL EMBLEMS OF IMPORTANT COUNTRIES

Country	*National Emblem*	*Country*	*National Emblem*
America	Golden Rod	New Zealand	Kiwi, Fern Southern Cross
Australia	Kangaroo	Norway	Lion
Ireland	Shamrock	Nepal	Kukri
Italy	White Lily	Pakistan	Crescent
Israel	Candelabrum	Poland	Eagle
Iran	Rose	France	Lily
Canada	White Lily	Belgium	Lion
Great Britain	Rose	Bangladesh	Water Lily
Chile	Candor and Huemul	Mongolia	The Soyombo
Germany	Corn Flower	Russia	Double headed eagle
Japan	Chrysanthemum	Lebanon	Cedar Tree
Zimbabwe	Zimbabwe Bird	Sudan	Secretary Bird
Denmark	Beach	Syria	Eagle
Turkiye	Crescent and Star	India	Lioned Capital
The Netherlands	Lion		

THE CONTINENTS OF THE WORLD

Name	*Population (2021) (In million)*	*Per cent of the world's population*
Asia	4,584	59.1
Africa	1,375	17.4
Europe	747	9.8
North America	373	4.8
South America	651	8.4
Australia	41.66	0.5
Antarctica	NA	NA

COMPUTER

The computer is the system of that electronic device through which various informations are processed on the basis of a definite set of instructions called program and mathematical (numerical) and non-mathematical both types of informations are processed.

The first mechanical computer was composed or fabricated by Blaise Pascal in 1642 and it is called Pascalene. But in 1833, Charles Babbage first time conceived an automatic calculator or computer. Charles Babbage is called the father of modern computer. Herman made an electronic tabulating machine based on punch cards which operates automatically.

In 1937, first mechanical computer mark-I was fabricated by Howard Akeen. The most outstanding contribution in the development of modern computer goes to John Wan Newmaan who brought the 2nd revolution in the area of computer in 1951. He discovered EDVAC (Electronic Discrete Variable Automatic Computer) and utilised the stored program and the binary number system in the computer.

FUNCTIONS OF COMPUTER

1. Collection and composition (input) of datas;
2. Storage of datas.
3. Processing of datas.
4. Retrieval or output of the proccessed informations and datas.

UNITS OF COMPUTER

1. Input unit.
2. Central processing unit–CPU.
3. External Memory unit.
4. Output unit.

The CPU of the computer is called brain of the computer and sometimes CPU is also called Micro Processor of the computer. The data is entered through the input unit in the computer and through the central processing unit with the help of External Memory Unit datas are arranged and processed. Ultimately by the output unit these datas or informations are issued or released.

PARTS OF COMPUTER

- **Monitor :** The monitor of the computer is like a television in which the picture appears in the form of doted points on the screen and these are called pixcels.
- **Hard Disc and Floppy Disc :** The Hard Disc is the permanent disc in the computers while the Floppy Disc is the disc utilised when datas or informations are to be transferred from one computer to another.
- **Mouse :** The mouse of the computer is like the remote control of TV through which computer is directly regulated or controlled without utilising the key-board.
- **Printer :** The printer is a device which prints any documents or processed informations of the computer.

SOME HIGH LEVEL LANGUAGES

1. **FORTRAN :** This language was developed for solving the mathematical formulae very quickly and conveniently.
2. **COBOL :** This language was developed for the commerical purposes. For the processing of this language a group of sentences is selected called paragraph and all paragraphs composed are called a section, while all sections composed are called a division.
3. **BASIC :** In basic a definite part of the prescribed instruction is only inserted in the computer.
4. **ALGOL :** This was basically fabricated and designed for the complex algebraic calculations.
5. **PASCAL :** It is an amplified and modified form of ALGOL.
6. **COMAL :** This computer language is used for the students of secondary level.
7. **LOGO :** This language is used for children and kids for drawing Graphic line diagrams.
8. **PROLOG :** This language is developed in 1973 in France and this language is used for Artificial Intelligence which is capable and equivalent to the logical program.

9. **FORTH :** This language was invented by Charles Mure which is frequently used in all types of the works in the computer.

COMPUTER VIRUS

The computer virus is an electronic code which is used to abolish or erradicate the inclusive informations or programs of the computer. Some important computer viruses are Micheleanjalo, Dork Avangor, kilo, filip, Macmug, Scores, Casecade, Jeruslem, Date crime, Coloumbs crime, Internet virus, Pachcom, Pach EXE, COM-EXE, Marizuana, C-brain, bloody, Chenge Mungu and Desi etc.

COMPUTER NETWORKING

There are two types of networkings which are usually occur—Local Area Networking (LAN) and Wide Area Networking (WAN). By LAN all the computers of the same buildings are connected like the computers of university premises, computers of offices etc.

By WAN all the comptuers of a large area are connected like the computers of all the offices of a city or town etc. In India a very large computer network namely INDONET has been installing through which all the main towns and cities has to be interlinked.

COMPUTER TERMINOLOGY

- **Bit :** The bit is a unit of measurement of the electronic data. One bit is either 0 or 1 but not both. On composing 8 bits, 1 byte is formed.
- **Bug :** The Bug is the error in the computer program or system and its eradication is called Debug.
- **Byte :** Total eight bits compose a byte. Thus 8 bits = 1 byte.
- **CD-ROM :** A CD like of music CD in which data can be stored substantially called CD-ROM. In a CD with comparison to floppy extremely more datas can be stored but one problem in it is that one time recorded data can not be deleted or modified.
- **Chip :** It is a thin slice on which by a special mechanism a circuit is designed which is normally made from Silicon.
- **Memory System :** The place where computer data and program are temporarily kept is called Memory system. Usually memory is implied from RAM.
- **Modem :** The device which converts digital signals into analogue signals and vice-versa is called Modem.
- **RAM :** It is Random Access Memory (a place) where datas to be processed are kept temporarily and it is unstable memory.
- **ROM :** It is Read Only Memory and it is stable or Non-valatile memory which doesn't ended after power off.
- **Scanner :** It is a device through which graphic image is transformed to digital image and the scanners are of usually two types one desktop and another hand operating.

PROGRAMING

Computers perform phenomenal feats of calculation, but they do not do so in a complicated way. They actually carry out very simple operations, such as addition and subtraction. They achieve their fantastic computing power by carrying out these operations at incredible speed.

The programme, or set of instructions for operating the computer, is therefore written as a sequence of very simple steps. (See box below) Several computer languages have been developed for different applications, including BASIC, COBOL, FORTRAN and PASCAL. Writing programmes is very skilled and time-consuming work. But for most typical computer applications ready-written programmes are available, called "packages".

☞ How A Programme Works

Without a programme to tell it what to do and how to do it, a computer is unable to function. If, for example, you wanted to know how many times the word 'the' appears in this paragraph, or in the whole book, it would not be enough merely to put the text into a computer and then ask it how many times the word appears. For the computer to accomplish the calculations it has to be told what to do in simple steps. The instructions might be:

1. Scan the text until a space followed by 'T' or 't' is found.
2. If the next letter is not 'h', go back to step 1.
3. If the letter is 'h', is the next letter 'e'?
4. If not, go back to step 1. If it is, go to step 5.
5. If 'e' is followed by a space, add 1 to the total.
6. Go back to step 1.

A full computer programme for this operation would need to be broken down into even more simple steps but a series of such programmes could enable a computer to analyse any amount of text in great detail.

DEFENCE

The Supreme Command of the Armed Forces is vested in the hands of the President of the Country. The responsibility for national defence, however, rests with the Cabinet. All important questions having a bearing on defence are decided by the Cabinet Committee on Political Affairs, which is presided over by the Prime Minister. The Defence Minister is responsible to Parliament for all matters concerning the Defence Services. All the administrative and operational control of Armed Forces are exercised by the Ministry of Defence. The three services – Army, Navy and Air Force function through their respective service headquarters headed by the chief of Staff.

COMMISSIONED RANKS IN DEFENCE SERVICES

Army	*Navy*	*Air Force*
General	Admiral	Air Chief Marshal
Lieutenant-General	Vice-Admiral	Air Marshal
Major-General	Rear-Admiral	Air Vice-Marshal
Brigadier	Commodor	Air Commodor
Colonel	Captain	Group Captain
Lieutenant-Colonel	Commander	Wing Commander
Major	Lt.Commander	Squadron Leader
Captain	Lieutenant	Flight Lieutenant
Lieutenant	Sub-Lieutenant	Flying Officer

INTERNAL SECURITY ORGANISATIONS OF INDIA

S. No	*Name of Organisation*	*Year of Creation*	*Headquarters*
1.	Assam Rifles (A.R.)	1835	Shillong
2.	Central Reserve Police Force (C.R.P.F.)	1939	New Delhi
3.	National Cadet Corps (N.C.C.)	1948	New Delhi
4.	Territorial Army	1948	In different States
5.	Indo-Tibetan Border Police	1962	New Delhi
6.	Home Guard	1962	In different States
7.	Coast Guard	1978	New Delhi
8.	Border Security Force (B.S.F.)	1965	New Delhi
9.	Central Industrial Security Force (C.I.S.F.)	1969	New Delhi
10.	National Security Guard	1984	New Delhi
11.	Police	—	In different States

COMMANDER-IN-CHIEFS OF INDIA

1. General Sir Rob Lockhart	Aug. 15, 1947 — Dec. 31, 1947
2. General Sir Roy Bucher	Jan. 1, 1948 — Jan. 14, 1949
3. General K. M. Kariappa	Jan. 15, 1949 — Jan. 14, 1953
4. General Maharaj Rajendra Sinhji	Jan. 15, 1953 — March 31, 1955

FIRST INDIAN CHIEFS OF STAFF OF INDIAN FORCES

1. General Maharaj Rajendra Sinhji (Army Staff)	April 1, 1955 — May 14, 1955
2. Vice Admiral R.D. Katari (Naval Staff)	April 22, 1958 — June 4, 1962
3. Air Marshal S. Mukherjee (Air Staff)	April 1, 1954 — Nov. 8, 1960

ARMY INSTITUTES

1. Sainik Schools upto +2 Level	33 places in India
2. Rashtriya Indian Military College (prepare for entrance to N.D.A)	Dehradun
3. National Defence Academy (three services)	Khadakwasla, Pune
4. Indian Military Academy (Army)	Dehradun
5. Officers Training Academy (3 services) Short Courses	Chennai
6. National Defence College	New Delhi
7. The College of Combat	Mhow
8. The College of Military Engineering	Kirkee
9. Military College of Telecommunication Engineering	Mhow
10. The armoured Corps Centre and School	Ahmed Nagar
11. The School Artillery	Deolali
12. The Infantry School	Mhow and Belgaum
13. College of Material Management	Jabalpur

AIR FORCE INSTITUTIONS

Air Force Academy	Hyderabad
Helicopter Training School	Hakimpet
Flying Instructors School	Tambaram, Chennai
The College of Air Warfare	Secunderabad
Air Force Administrative College	Coimbatore
Air Force Technical College	Jalahalli

DEFENCE PRODUCTION UNITS

1. Bharat Dynamites Ltd.	Hyderabad
2. Praga Tools	Hyderabad
3. Mishra Dattu Nigam	Hyderabad
4. Bharat Electronics Ltd.	Bangalore
5. Bharath Earthmovers Ltd.	Bangalore
6. Heavy Vehicles Ltd.	Avadi, Chennai
7. Garden Reach Ship Builders and Engineers Ltd.	Kolkata
8. Mazagaon Dock	Mumbai
9. Goa Shipyard	Marmugao
10. Hindustan Shipyard Ltd.	Vishakhapatnam
11. Hindustan Aeronautics Ltd.	Bangalore, Hyderabad, Nasik, Koraput, Kanpur, Lucknow

☞ Indian Army Commands

Command	HQ Location	Command	HQ Location
Eastern Command	Kolkata	Western Command	Chandigarh
Northern Command	Udhampur	Southern Command	Pune
Central Command	Lucknow	Training Command	Shimla
South-Western Command	Jaipur		

☞ Indian Air Force Commands

Command	HQ Location	Command	HQ Location
Western Air Command	New Delhi	South-Western Air Command	Gandhinagar
Central Air Command	Prayagraj	Eastern Air Command	Shillong
Southern Air Command	Thiruvananthapuram	Training Command	Bengaluru

☞ Indian Navy Commands

Command	HQ Location	Command	HQ Location
Eastern Naval Command	Vishakhapatnam	Western Naval Command	Mumbai
Southern Naval Command	Kochi		

☞ Missile and Other Weapons

Name	Class	Range
✶ Agni I	SRBM	850 km
✶ Agni II	MRBM	2500 km
✶ Agni III	IRBM	3500 km-5500 km
✶ Agni IV *or* Agni II Prime	IRBM	4000 km
✶ Agni V	ICBM	5000 km-6000 km
✶ Agni VI	ICBM	8000 km-10000 km
✶ Agni 3SL	ICBM	5200 km-11600 km
✶ Dhanush	SRBM	350 km
✶ Nirbhay	Subsonic Cruise Missile	1000 km

Name	Class	Range
✶ Brahmos	Supersonic Cruise Missile	290 km
✶ Brahmos 2	Hypersonic Cruise Missile	290 km
✶ Prithvi I	SRBM	150 km
✶ Prithvi III	SRBM	350 km
✶ Sagarika	SLBM	700 km-2200 km
✶ Shaurya	TBM	700 km-2200 km
✶ Astra	Air to Air Missile	80 km-100 km
✶ Barak-I	SRSAM	12 km
✶ Barak-8	SRSAM	90 km

☞ Chief of Defence Staff (CDS)

To bring in reform in higher defence management in the country, the post of Chief of Defence Staff (CDS) was created in the rank of a four-star General with salary and prerequisites equivalent to a Service Chief. The Chief of Defence Staff will also head the Department of Military Affairs (DMA), to be created within the Ministry of Defence and functions as its Secretary. Gen. Bipin Rawat was the first CDS of the country from January 1, 2020 to December 08, 2021. Gen. Anil Chauhan assumed the charge of the second CDS on September 30, 2022.

MULTIPLE CHOICE QUESTIONS

1. Match List-I with List-II and select the correct answer from the codes given below the lists:

List-I

(*a*) Napoleon Bonaparte
(*b*) Jean Jacques Rousseau
(*c*) Croce
(*d*) Madame Roland

List-II

1. 'A history is contemporary history'
2. 'Liberty what crimes are committed in thy name'
3. 'Man is born free but everywhere he is in chains.'
4. 'I am the Child of Revolution'

Codes :

	(*a*)	(*b*)	(*c*)	(*d*)
A.	1	2	3	4
B.	4	3	1	2
C.	3	4	2	1
D.	3	4	1	2

2. Abraham Lincon was elected the President of United States in:
A. 1862 B. 1860
C. 1875 D. 1855

3. Who was known as the 'Prince of Humanists'?
A. Francisco Petrarch B. Dante
C. Boccacio D. Erasmus

4. D-Day is the day when:
A. Germany declared war on Britain
B. US dropped the atom bomb on Hiroshima.
C. Allied Troops landed in Normandy
D. Germany surrendered to the allies

5. Whose teachings inspired the French Revolution?
A. Locke
B. Rousseau
C. Hegel
D. Plato

6. At a time when empires in Europe were crumbling before the might of Napoleon which one of the following Governor-Generals kept the British flag flying high in India?
A. Warren Hastings B. Lord Cornwallis
C. Lord Wellesley D. Lord Hastings

7. Which one of the following statements regarding Fascism in Italy is *not* true?
A. The Fascists came to power as a result of popular uprising
B. In 1926, all political parties except Mussolini's party were banned
C. The Fascists suppressed the Socialist movement
D. The Fascists were hostile to the Communists

8. The fall of Czar Nicholas-II is known as:
A. Bloody Sunday
B. Bolshevik Revolution
C. February Revolution
D. October Revolution

9. Industrial Revolution took place first in:
A. France B. Germany
C. United Kingdom D. Japan

10. The British Prime Minister at the outbreak of World War II was :
A. Churchill B. Baldwin
C. Attlee D. Chemberlain

11. The 'Great Depression' (1929) economic crisis was met by adopting the policy of
A. Stimulus B. Marshall Plan
C. New Deal D. Open Door

12. The slogan "No taxation without representation" was raised during the:
A. American War of Independence
B. Russian Revolution
C. French Revolution
D. Indian Freedom struggle

13. In the nineteenth century the people of Europe started moving from the villages to the cities due to the impact of :
A. Epidemics
B. War
C. Industrialisation
D. Population explosion in villages

14. The important cause of the Civil War in America was:
A. Abolition of slavery
B. Quest for freedom
C. Industrialisation
D. Rebellion by the native Americans

15. Industrial Revolution could not have come about without:
A. Merchant capitalism
B. The Enclosure Movement
C. The services of the proletariat class
D. An agricultural revolution

16. Consider the following statements :
The French Revolution came about mainly due to the :
1. Extreme poverty of the people
2. Impact of the works of great writers
3. Cruelty of the rulers
4. Impact of impulsive reaction
Which of the above statements are correct?
A. 1, 2 and 4 B. 2 and 3
C. 1, 3 and 4 D. 1, 2, 3 and 4

17. Asia's oldest and largest Buddhist monastery is situated in :
A. Tawang (Arunachal Pardesh)
B. Lhasa (Tibet)
C. Trincomallee (Sri Lanka)
D. Ulan Bator (Mongolia)

18. Who was the main architect of the Russian Revolution?
A. Karl Marx B. Lenin
C. Stalin D. Tolstoy

19. V.I. Lenin is associated with :
A. Russian Revolution of 1917
B. Chinese Revolution of 1949
C. German Revolution
D. French Revolution of 1789

20. Which one of the following statements is *not* correct?
A. Voltaire believed in Natural Religion
B. Rousseau wrote *Social Contract*
C. Montesquieu authored *The Spirit of Laws*
D. Necker believed in 'General Will'

21. 6th April, 1930 is well known in the history of India because this date is associated with..........
A. Dandi March by Mahatma Gandhi
B. Quit India Movement
C. Partition of Bengal
D. Partition of India

22. Which ruler enforced the system of 'Price Control' in India?
A. Mohammad Tughlak
B. Razia Begum
C. Alauddin Khilji
D. Sher Shah Suri

23. The concept of 'Din-e-Elahi' was founded by which king?
A. Dara Shikoh B. Akbar
C. Sher Shah Suri D. Shahjahan

24. Who are supposed to be the earliest inhabitants of India? Where did they come from?
A. Aryans from Central Asia
B. Dravidians from Mediterranean
C. Negroids from Africa
D. Bhils and the Santhals from West Asia

25. The one chief characteristic of temple architecture of the Gupta Age was :
A. Absence of dome
B. Huge size
C. Beautiful carvings
D. absence of a covered courtyard for the gathering of worshippers

26. The Rigveda consists of :
A. 1000 hymns B. 2028 hymns
C. 1028 hymns D. 1038 hymns

27. The central point in Ashoka's dharma was :
A. royalty to kings
B. peace and non-violence
C. respect to elders
D. religious tolerance

28. The social evil which was conspicuously absent during ancient India was :
A. *Sati*-System B. *Devadasi*-System
C. Polygamy D. *Purdah*-System

29. Which, among the following, can be accepted as a novelty introduced by Mughal emperors to their buildings?
A. Domes B. Minarets
C. Arches D. Attached gardens

30. The first ruler of India who defeated Muhammud of Ghur was :
A. Mularaja II of Gujarat
B. Prithviraja Chauhan of Delhi
C. Jayachand of Kannauj
D. Parmaldeva of Bundelkhand

31. What important event happened in India in 1911?
A. Bengal was partitioned
B. Non-Cooperation movement was launched
C. India's capital was shifted from Calcutta to Delhi
D. Mahatma Gandhi presided over the Congress session

32. The first phase of the Congress Party (1885-1905) was characterized by its efforts to secure:
A. limited independence
B. complete freedom
C. Indianization of services
D. constitutional reforms

33. The Muslim League demanded a separate homeland for the Indian Muslims openly for the first time at its annual session held in Lahore in the year :
A. 1931 A.D. B. 1936 A.D.
C. 1940 A.D. D. 1941 A.D.

34. Under whose governorship did the East India Company secure the Diwani Rights in Bengal, Bihar and Odisha from Emperor Shah Alam?
A. Lord Cornwallis
B. Lord William Bentinck
C. Lord Clive
D. Lord Wellesley

35. The Simon Commission was generally boycotted by the Indian political parties. What was the reason for this general non-cooperation?
A. the Commission aimed at dividing the people
B. it was an 'all white' Commission
C. it came after the Jallianwala Bagh carnage
D. it was an eye wash

36. Aligarh Muslim University was founded by :
A. Dr. Saifuddin Kitchlu
B. Mohammad Ali Jinnah
C. Sir Syed Ahmed Khan
D. Maulana Mohammad Ali

37. Ibn Batutah was an African traveller visiting India during the time of :
A. Alivardi Khan
B. Ala-ud-din Khalji
C. Iltutmish
D. Mohammad-bin-Tughlaq

38. The battle of Wandiawash was fought in :
A. 1726 B. 1760
C. 1818 D. 1857

39. The abolition of *Sati* by government regulation was at the time of :
A. Warren Hastings B. Lord Wellesley
C. Lord Bentinck D. Lord Ahmerst

40. Pick out the wrong combination :
A. Dilwara Temple : Mt. Abu
B. Pashupati Temple : Kathmandu
C. Padmanabh Temple : Bangalore
D. Minakshi Temple : Madurai

41. Match the following:
(*a*) Chanhudaro (*b*) Kalibangan
(*c*) Lothal (*d*) Surkotada
1. Alleged discovery of the skeleton of horse.
2. Bead making.
3. Traces of a dock and ship on seal.
4. Evidence of ploughing the fields.

The Correct code is :

	(*a*)	(*b*)	(*c*)	(*d*)
A.	2	4	3	1
B.	2	1	3	4
C.	1	2	3	4
D.	2	1	4	3

42. Match the Harappan settlements with the banks of rivers on which they were located :

(*a*)	Harappa	1.	Ravi
(*b*)	Mohenjodaro	2.	Indus
(*c*)	Ropar	3.	Sutlej
(*d*)	Kalibangan	4.	Ghaggar
(*e*)	Lothal	5.	Bhogava

Codes :

	(*a*)	(*b*)	(*c*)	(*d*)	(*e*)
A.	1	2	3	4	5
B.	1	2	3	5	4
C.	2	1	3	5	4
D.	2	1	4	3	5

43. The Goddess 'Kannagi' whose many temples were erected during the 'Sangam Age' was the goddess of :

A. Chastity B. Love
C. Prowess D. Wisdom

44. The Jain goal of life is to attain deliverance from the fetters of mudane existence, the way to which lies through three jewels. Which one of the following was not included among the 'three jewels' of Jainism?

A. Right faith B. Right action
C. Right knowledge D. Right conduct

45. The most striking feature of the Ashokan pillar is polish. Name the Ashokan pillar which is considered to be the most graceful of all Ashokan pillars.

A. Sarnath
B. Rampurva
C. Laurya-Nandangarh
D. Rummindei

46. Which are the correct statements?

1. The land grants, started in Satavahana period, paved the way for feudal developments in India.
2. Silk and spices were the Chief Indian export articles of Indo-Roman trade.
3. The Guptas issued the largest number of gold coins in ancient India.
4. The first memorial of a 'SATI' dated 510 A.D. is found at Eran in Madhya Pradesh.

A. 1 and 2 B. 1, 3, and 4
C. 1 and 4 D. 1, 2, 3 and 4

47. Who among the following patronised the 'Gandhara' (Indo-Greek style) School of Art?

A. Ashoka, the Great
B. Harsha Vardhana
C. Kanishka
D. Chandragupta Vikramaditya

48. The Sultanate of Delhi had five ruling dynasties. The dynasty having longest and shortest period were :

A. Ilbari and Khalji
B. Tughlaq and Khalji
C. Tughlaq and Sayyid
D. Ilbari and Lodis

49. Which one of the following events took place at the last during reign of Muhammad-bin-Tughlaq?

A. Introduction of token currency
B. Increase of land-revenue in Doab
C. Transfer of Capital from Delhi to Devagiri.
D. Conquest of Khurasan and Iraq

50. The most learned medieval Muslim ruler who was well versed in various branches of learning including astronomy, mathematics and medicine was :

A. Jalaluddin Khilji
B. Sikander Lodi
C. Ghiyasuddin Tughlaq
D. Muhammad-bin-Tughlaq

51. The 'Sufis' had 12 silsilas. They propounded the idea of Union with God through:

A. Love B. Rituals
C. Fasts D. Prayers

52. Match the following:

(*a*) Peshwa	1.	Foreign affairs
(*b*) Panditrao	2.	Audit and accounts
(*c*) Amatya	3.	Providing grants to scholars
(*d*) Sumant	4.	General supervision
	5.	Military affairs

Select the correct code :

	(*a*)	(*b*)	(*c*)	(*d*)
A.	2	3	4	5
B.	4	1	2	3
C.	4	3	2	1
D.	3	1	4	2

53. The Regulating Act of 1773 can be regarded as the first measure to :
A. assert the right of British Parliament to legislate for India
B. separate the legislature from the executive
C. separate the judiciary from the executive
D. centralise law-making

54. What was the exact constitutional status of the Indian Republic on 26th January, 1950?
A. A Democratic Republic
B. A Sovereign, Democratic Republic
C. A Sovereign, Secular, Democratic Republic
D. A Sovereign, Socialist, Secular, Democratic Republic

55. When the British obtained the grant of Diwani of Bengal, Bihar and Odisha they acquired the right to :
A. maintain law and order in these territories
B. administer civil justice and collect revenue in these territories
C. collect revenue and establish revenue administration in these territories
D. militarily defend these territories

56. Which of the following were responsible for the growth of nationalism in India during the British rule?
1. Economic exploitation of India.
2. Impact of western education.
3. Role of the Press.
Select the correct answer using the codes given below :
Codes:
A. 1, 2 and 3 B. 1 and 2
C. 2 and 3 D. 1 and 3

57. Which one of the following nationalist leaders has been described as being radical in politics but conservative on social issues?
A. G.K. Gokhale
B. B.G. Tilak
C. Lala Lajpat Rai
D. Madan Mohan Malviya

58. Provincial Autonomy in British India was envisaged by the :
A. Act of 1909 B. Act of 1919
C. Act of 1935 D. Act of 1947

59. Dyarchy means :
A. double government
B. a government in which the centre is very powerful
C. a government based on division of power between centre and provinces
D. None of the above

60. The Indian National Congress observed 'Independence Day' for the first time on 26th January in :
A. 1920 B. 1925
C. 1930 D. 1947

61. ....is situated near the banks of Sabarmati River
A. Bhavnagar B. Aurangabad
C. Ahmedabad D. Rajkot

62. Sericulture is:
A. science of the various kinds of serum
B. artificial rearing of fish
C. art of silkworm breeding
D. study of various cultures of a community

63. The most abundant constituents of earth's crust are:
A. Igneous rocks
B. Sedimentary rocks
C. Metamorphic rocks
D. Granite

64. Indian Standard Time is based on:
A. 80°E longitude B. 82½°E longitude
C. 110°E longitude D. 25°E longitude

65. Tides in the oceans are caused by :
A. Gravitational pull of the moon on the earth's surface including sea water
B. Gravitational pull of the sun on the earth's surface only and not on the sea water
C. Gravitational pull of the moon and the sun on the earth's surface including the sea water
D. None of these

66. Nagarjunasagar Project is situated on the river:
A. Tungabhadra
B. Cauvery
C. Krishna
D. Godavari

67. The difference between the Indian Standard Time and the Greenwich Mean Time is:

A. – 3½ hours B. + 3½ hours
C. – 5½ hours D. + 5½ hours

68. Which of the following dams is not on Narmada river?

A. Indira-Sagar Project
B. Maheshwar Hydel Power Project
C. Jobat Project
D. Koyna Power Project

69. Which of the following statements is **not true** about the availability of water on the earth, the crisis for which is going to increase in the years to come?

A. About 97.5 per cent of the total volume of water available on the earth is salty
B. 80 per cent of the water available to us for use comes in bursts as monsoons
C. About 2.5 per cent of the total water available on the earth is polluted water and cannot be used for human activities
D. Possibility is that some big glaciers will melt in the coming ten-fifteen years and sea level will rise by 3-4 metres all over the earth

70. Which of the following is **not** a cash crop?

A. Jute B. Paddy
C. Cashewnut D. Sugarcane

71. Through which States does Cauvery River flow?

A. Gujarat, M.P., Tamil Nadu
B. Karnataka, Kerala, Tamil Nadu
C. Karnataka, Kerala, Andhra Pradesh
D. M.P., Maharashtra, Tamil Nadu

72. Indian Standard Time is the local time of 82½°E which passes through :

A. Guntur B. Delhi
C. Allahabad D. Kolkata

73. The 17th parallel defines the boundary between:

A. North and South Korea
B. USA and Canada
C. North and South Vietnam
D. China and Russia

74. During the period of south-west monsoon, Tamil Nadu remains dry because:

A. the winds do not reach this area
B. there are no mountains in this area
C. it lies in the rain shadow area
D. the temperature is too high to let the winds cool down

75. Which country does top in producing cocoa?

A. Cote d'Ivoire B. Brazil
C. Croatia D. Nigeria

76. The biggest reserves of thorium are in :

A. India B. China
C. The Soviet Union D. U.S.A.

77. The Girnar Hills are situated in which of the following states?

A. Gujarat B. Karnataka
C. Madhya Pradesh D. Maharashtra

78. During December 22nd the sun is vertically over:

A. Tropic of Cancer
B. Tropic of Capricorn
C. The Equator
D. None of the above

79. Photosphere is described as the :

A. Lower layer of atmosphere
B. Visible surface of the sun from which radiation emanates
C. Wavelength of solar spectrum
D. None of the above

80. Broadly, there are three layers of the earth of the crust, the mantle and the core. The crust forms what percentage of the volume of the earth?

A. 0.5% B. 2.5%
C. 7.5% D. 12.5%

81. The grassland of Argentina is known as :

A. Pampas B. Campos
C. Savanna D. None of the above

82. Different seasons are formed because :

A. Sun is moving around the earth
B. of revolution of the earth around the Sun on its orbit
C. of rotation of the earth around its axis
D. All of the above

83. Eskers and Drumlins are features formed by:
A. underground water
B. running water
C. the action of wind
D. glacial action

84. Match List-I and List-II and select the correct answer using the codes given below the Lists :

List-I (*Rivers*)	List-II (*Towns*)
(*a*) Ghaghara	1. Lucknow
(*b*) Brahmaputra	2. Hoshangabad
(*c*) Narmada	3. Ahmedabad
(*d*) Sabarmati	4. Guwahati
	5. Ayodhya

	(*a*)	(*b*)	(*c*)	(*d*)
A.	4	5	1	2
B.	5	4	2	3
C.	5	4	3	1
D.	3	5	2	1

85. Which of the statements as regards the consequences of the movement of the earth is not correct?
A. Revolution of the earth is the cause of the change of seasons.
B. Rotation of the earth is the cause of days and nights.
C. Rotation of the earth causes variation in the duration of days and nights.
D. Rotation of the earth effects the movement of winds and ocean currents.

86. The world is divided into :
A. 12 time zones
B. 20 time zones
C. 24 time zones
D. 36 time zones

87. The 'Kiel' canal links the :
A. Pacific and Atlantic Oceans
B. Mediterranean Sea and Red Sea
C. Mediterranean Sea and Black Sea
D. North Sea and Baltic Sea

88. Match the following :

List-I	List-II
(*a*) Himadri	1. Outer Himalayas
(*b*) Shivalik	2. Inner Himalayas
(*c*) Himanchal	3. Middle Himalayas
(*d*) Sahyadri	4. Western Ghats

Codes:

	(*a*)	(*b*)	(*c*)	(*d*)
A.	1	2	3	4
B.	4	2	3	1
C.	2	1	3	4
D.	1	2	3	4

89. The term 'Regur' refers to:
A. Laterite soils
B. Black Cotton soils
C. Red Soils
D. Deltaic Alluvial Soils

90. Location of sugar industry in India is shifting from north to south because of:
A. cheap labour
B. expanding regional market
C. cheap and abundant supply of power
D. high yield and high sugar content in sugarcane

91. Consider the following statements :
1. Ozone is found mostly in the Stratosphere.
2. Ozone layer lies 55-75 km above the surface of the earth.
3. Ozone absorbs ultraviolet radiation from the Sun.
4. Ozone layer has no significance for life on the earth.

Which of the above statements are correct?
A. 1 and 3 B. 2 and 4
C. 2 and 3 D. 1 and 4

92. Match List-I with List-II and select the correct answer using the codes given below the Lists :

List-I (*Crops*)	List-II (*Producer*)
(*a*) Banana	1. Brazil
(*b*) Cocoa	2. Cote d'Ivoire
(*c*) Coffee	3. India
(*d*) Tea	4. China

Codes :

	(*a*)	(*b*)	(*c*)	(*d*)
A.	2	3	1	4
B.	3	2	1	4
C.	3	2	4	1
D.	2	3	4	1

93. Darjeeling and Dharamsala would be the right places to visit if one wanted to get a clear view respectively of :
A. Kanchanjunga and Dhauladhar ranges
B. Nandadevi and Dhauladhar ranges
C. Kanchanjunga and Nandadevi ranges
D. Nandadevi and Nanga Parvat

94. Atmosphere exists because:
A. The Gravitational force of the Earth
B. Revolution of the Earth
C. Rotation of the Earth
D. Weight of the gases of atmosphere

95. Victoria lake is located in the continent:
A. Africa
B. Asia
C. North America
D. South America

96. The famous Lagoon Lake of India is :
A. Dal Lake B. Chilka Lake
C. Pulicat Lake D. Mansarover

97. Where are most of the earth's active volcanoes concentrated?
A. Indian Ocean B. Pacific Ocean
C. Aral Sea D. Atlantic Ocean

98. Through which of the following states does the river Chambal flow?
A. U.P., M.P., Rajasthan
B. M.P., Gujarat, U.P.
C. Rajasthan, M.P., Bihar
D. Gujarat, M.P., U.P.

99. Which country is called the sugar bowl of the world?
A. Cuba B. India
C. Argentina D. USA

100. The area covered by forest in India is about:
A. 46% B. 33%
C. 23% D. 21.71%

101. A closed economy is the one which :
A. does not permit emigration or immigration
B. permits emigration but no immigration
C. engages in no foreign trade
D. engages in no foreign and domestic trade or transit

102. In a developed economy the major share of employment originates in the :
A. primary sector B. tertiary sector
C. secondary sector D. any of the above

103. The Economic and Social Commission for Asia and Pacific (ESCAP) is located at :
A. Bangkok B. Kuala Lumpur
C. Manila D. Singapore

104. Commercial vehicles are not produced by which of the following companies in India?
A. TELCO B. Ashok Leyland
C. DCM Daewoo D. Birla Yamaha

105. In India, the Public Sector is most dominant in:
A. transport
B. steel production
C. commercial banking
D. organised term-lending financial institutions

106. The main argument advanced in favour of small scale and cottage industries in India is that:
A. cost of production is low
B. they require small capital investment
C. they advance the goal of equitable distribution of wealth
D. they generate a large volume of employment

107. The most serious economic problems of India are:
A. Poverty and unemployment
B. Stagnation, not poverty
C. Unemployment, not poverty
D. Underdevelopment, not poverty

108. Which of the following is not one of the three central problems of an economy?
A. What to produce
B. How to produce
C. When to produce
D. For whom to produce

109. If saving exceeds investment, the national income will:
A. fall B. rise
C. fluctuate D. remain constant

110. In which of the following industries in India are the maximum number of workers employed?
A. Sugar B. Jute
C. Textiles D. Iron and Steel

111. Terrace Cultivation is practiced mostly:
A. in urban areas
B. on slopes of mountains
C. on tops of hills
D. in undulating tracts

112. Which of the following is a Selective Credit Control method?
A. Bank Rate
B. RBI directives
C. Cash Reserve Ratio
D. Open market operations

113. Which of the following taxes is not shared by the Central Government with the States?
A. Union excise duties
B. Customs duty
C. Income tax
D. Estate duty

114. ICICI is the name of a:
A. Financial Institution
B. Chemical Industry
C. Cotton Industry
D. Chamber of Commerce and Industry

115. Structural Unemployment arises due to
A. Deflationary conditions
B. Heavy industry bias
C. Shortage of raw material
D. Inadequate productive capacity

116. Which Commission replaced the Planning Commission in 2015?
A. NIYAM Aayog
B. NAGRIK Aayog
C. NITI Aayog
D. Jan Aayog

117. The largest public sector bank in India is:
A. Central Bank of India
B. Punjab National Bank
C. State Bank of India
D. Indian Overseas Bank

118. Which of the following statements best explains the term contraband goods?
A. Goods produced only for exports
B. Goods produced in joint sector only
C. Goods for the trading of which licence is not required
D. Goods that are forbidden, from export, import or even possession, by law

119. Price in the market is fixed by:
A. Stock exchange rates
B. The demand and supply ruling in the market at a particular time
C. The Finance Minister
D. None of the above

120. Devaluation of currency helps to promote:
A. National Income
B. Savings
C. Imports at lower cost
D. Exports

121. Balanced economic growth can be achieved only if:
A. All the sectors of economy grow at the same rate
B. Population growth is arrested
C. All the inter dependent sectors grow in harmony
D. Basic and heavy industries are assigned highest priority

122. P.V. Sindhu is associated with which of the following sports?
A. Badminton
B. Weightlifting
C. Swimming
D. Tennis

123. 'MODVAT' stands for:
A. Modified Value Added Tax
B. Deduction of cost of inputs from the value of output
C. Reduction in import duties
D. Imposition of tax on professions

124. Who among the following is the first to receive 'Dada Saheb Phalke' award?
A. Shivaji Ganeson B. Devika Rani
C. Dr. Raj Kumar D. None of the above

125. The term 'devaluation' means:
A. Reducing the value of a currency in terms of another currency
B. Increasing the value of a currency
C. Revising the value of a currency
D. None of the above

126. Per capita net availability of pulses has shown a tendency of:
A. Increase over time
B. Decrease over time
C. Constant over time
D. First increase then decrease

127. National Income is the same as:
A. Net national product at market price
B. Net domestic product at market price
C. Net national product at factor cost
D. Net domestic product at factor cost

128. Which one of the following is not an example of indirect tax?
A. Sales tax
B. Excise duty
C. Customs duty
D. Expenditure tax

129. The major aim of devaluation is to:
A. encourage imports
B. encourage exports
C. encourage both exports and imports
D. discourage both exports and imports

130. Structural unemployment arises due to:
A. deflationary conditions
B. heavy industry bias
C. shortage of raw materials
D. inadequate productive capacity

131. When was the Family Planning Programme officially started in India?
A. 1950
B. 1952
C. 1956
D. 1962

132. When was the Reserve Bank of India nationalised?
A. 1947
B. 1949
C. 1950
D. 1951

133. Which of the following is *not* a feature of the Indian economy?
A. High rate of population growth
B. Disguised unemployment
C. Lowest rate of adult literacy
D. High rate of exports

134. The 'Relative Deprivation' approach for measuring poverty has been adopted by:
A. developing countries
B. developed countries
C. under-developed countries
D. None of the above

135. One of the main factors that led to rapid expansion of Indian exports is:
A. Imposition of import duties
B. Liberalisation of the economy
C. Recession in other countries
D. Diversification of exports

136. Sustainable economic development means an increase in the rate of growth of real:
A. total and per capita product
B. total and per capita product and level of literacy rate
C. total and per capita product and life expectancy at birth
D. total and per capita product, taking into account the cost of degradation of the quality of environment in this process

137. Functional unemployment occurs when:
A. unemployed have no qualification for job
B. people frequently change their job
C. people were thrown out from job due to recession
D. None of these

138. Which among the following does **not** have a 'free trade zone'?
A. Kandla
B. Mumbai
C. Visakhapatnam
D. Thiruvanantpuram

139. Sun Belt of USA is important for which one of the following industries?
A. Cotton textile
B. Petrochemicals
C. Hi-tech electronics
D. Food Processing

140. Commercial banking system in India is
A. unit banking
B. branch banking
C. mixed banking
D. None of the above

141. Who gives recognition to political parties in India?
A. Parliament

B. President
C. Supreme Court
D. Election Commission

142. The Quorum of the Legislative Council is :
A. one-fourth of its total membership
B. one-third of its membership
C. one-tenth of its membership
D. 25

143. The Indian Constitution is:
A. federal
B. unitary
C. a happy mixture of the federal and unitary
D. federal in normal times and unitary in times of emergency

144. Universal adult franchise implies a right to vote to all:
A. adult residents of the State
B. adult male citizens of the State
C. residents of the State
D. adult citizens of the State

145. When a resolution prefering a charge against the President has been passed by a specified majority in the House, it is sent to the other House for investigation. If, as a result of such an investigation, a resolution is passed through a specified majority by the other House, declaring that the charge has been sustained, the President shall leave his office. The specified special majority must not be less than :
A. two-third of the members present and voting
B. one-third of the members present and voting
C. three-fourth of the members present and voting and two-third of the total membership
D. two-third of the total membership

146. Which one of the following judicial powers of the President of India has been *wrongly* listed?
A. he appoints the Chief Justice and other judges of the Supreme Court
B. he can remove the judges of the Supreme Court on grounds of misconduct
C. he can consult the Supreme Court on any question of law or fact which is of public importance
D. he can grant pardon, reprieves and respites to persons punished under Union Law

147. The Vice-president of India can be removed from his office before the expiry of his term if :
A. the Rajya Sabha passes a resolution by a majority of its members and the Lok Sabha agrees with the resolution
B. if the Supreme Court of India recommends his removal
C. the President so desires
D. None of the above

148. The Chief Justice of a High Court in India is appointed by the :
A. Governor of the State
B. Prime Minister of India
C. Chief Justice of the Supreme Court
D. President of India

149. Which of the following statements is constitutionally not true about the passing of the Union Budgets, Railway Budgets and Finance Bill in India?
1. Under the law, Finance Bill should be adopted by both the Houses of the Parliament within 45 days of its introduction.
2. If the Finance Bill is not adopted within specified period, the government loses its authority to levy the taxes proposed in the budgets.
3. In the absence of full budget, a vote-on-account gives the power to the government to spend.
4. Government cannot raise revenues without a proper approval of the Finance Bill

A. Only 2 B. Only 3
C. Only 4 D. Only 1, 2 and 3

150. Normally, on whose advice the President's Rule is imposed in a State?
A. Chief Minister
B. Legislative Assembly
C. Governor
D. Chief Justice of High Court

151. Which Article of the Indian Constitution deals with Amendment procedure?

A. Article 368 B. Article 358
C. Article 367 D. All of these

152. Government is the agency through which the will of :

A. the state is expressed
B. the people is expressed
C. the head of the state is expressed
D. the majority is expressed

153. In a unitary system of government :

A. The centre is all powerful
B. The centre is weaker than the states
C. The centre and states stand at par
D. The states and centre are supreme in their respective spheres

154. In Cabinet System of Government the real executive authority rests with :

A. The Council of Ministers
B. The Prime Minister
C. The Constitution
D. The Parliament

155. The Head of the State under a parliamentary government:

A. is an elected representative
B. is a hereditary person
C. is a nominated person
D. may be any one of the above

156. In the event of a ministerial proposal being defeated on the floor of the legislature, under the parliamentary system :

A. the government waits for a general no-confidence motion
B. the minister concerned is taken to task by the Prime Minister
C. the minister is forced to resign
D. the whole Council of Ministers resign

157. The "due process of law" is an essential characteristic of the judicial system of:

A. UK B. France
C. USA D. India

158. Under the Constitution it is :

A. obligatory for the President to accept the advice of the Council of Ministers but is not obliged to follow it
B. obligatory for the President to accept the advice of the Council of Ministers
C. not obligatory for the President to seek or accept the advice of the Council of Ministers
D. obligatory for the President to seek the advice of the Council of Ministers if his own party is in power

159. Which one of the following statements is correct?

A. the Presiding Officer of Rajya Sabha is elected every year
B. the Presiding Officer of Rajya Sabha is elected for a term of two years at a time
C. the Presiding Officer of Rajya Sabha is elected for a term of six years
D. the Vice-President of India is the ex-officio Presiding Officer of Rajya Sabha

160. The introduction of "no confidence" motion in the Lok Sabha requires the support of at least:

A. 50 members B. 70 members
C. 60 members D. 80 members

161. The High Court comes under :

A. State List B. Union List
C. Concurrent List D. None of the above

162. Which one of the following has been wrongly listed as a Fundamental Duty of the Indian citizens?

A. to develop scientific temper, humanism and spirit of inquiry and reform
B. to work for raising the prestige of the country in the international sphere
C. to protect and improve the natural environment
D. to strive towards excellence in all spheres of individual and collective activity

163. Which one of the following is not a Fundamental Duty as outlined in Article 51A of the Constitution?

A. to abide by the Constitution and respect its ideals
B. to defend the country and render national service when called upon to do so

C. to work for the moral upliftment of the weaker sections of society
D. to preserve the rich heritage

164. The main characteristics of the Directive Principles of State Policy given in the Indian Constitution are :
A. not enforceable by any court
B. fundamental in the governance of the country
C. 'Like instruments, instructions, political manifesto and a code of moral precepts which have to guide governors of the country'
D. no law can be passed, which is opposed to these principles

165. Of the following which are true?
A. In a State, the Legislative Council is dominant with regard to non-financial bills and the Legislative Assembly with regard to financial (money) bills
B. Vidhan Parishad can virtually block legisla-tion even if the same is passed by the Vidhan Sabha
C. In case of a tie between the two Houses, the Governor is duty-bound to call a joint session of the two Houses to have the issue settled on a majority verdict
D. If a Bill is twice approved by the Vidhan Sabha, it becomes law even if rejected by the Vidhan Parishad

166. Which one of the following types of emergency can be declared by the President?
A. Emergency due to threat of war and external aggresion
B. Emergency due to break-down of constitu-tional machinery in a State
C. Financial emergency on account of threat to the financial credit of India
D. all the three emergencies

167. The chairman of which of the following parliamentary committees is invariably from the members of ruling party?
A. Committee on public undertakings
B. Public accounts committee
C. Estimates committee
D. Committee on delegated legislation

168. Which of the following is not a formally prescribed device available to the members of parliament?
A. Question hour
B. Zero hour
C. Half-an-hour discussion
D. Short duration discussion

169. Which of the following is not a tool of executive control over public administration?
A. Power of appointment and removal
B. Line agencies
C. Appeal to public opinion
D. Civil services code

170. If the Speaker of the State Legislative Assembly decides to resign, he should submit his resignation to the:
A. Judges of the High Court
B. Deputy Speaker
C. Chief Minister
D. Finance Minister

171. Who was the first Home Minister of Independent India?
A. Rajendra Prasad
B. Jawahar Lal Nehru
C. B.R. Ambedkar
D. Sardar Vallabh Bhai Patel

172. India is a Federal State because of:
A. dual judiciary
B. dual citizenship prevalent here
C. share of power between the Centre and the States
D. rigid Constitution

173. Residuary Subjects are those subjects which are:
A. contained in the State list
B. contained in the Union list
C. contained in the Concurrent list
D. not covered by any of the three lists

174. Which of the following writs can be issued, by the Supreme Court, to enforce Fundamental Rights?
A. Writ of Habeas Corpus
B. Writ of Mandamus
C. Writ of Quo Warranto
D. All of these

175. When the offices of both the President and the Vice-President of India are vacant, who will discharge their functions?
A. Prime Minister
B. Home Minister
C. Chief Justice of India
D. The Speaker

176. The Supreme Court tenders advice to the President of India on a matter of law or fact:
A. on its own
B. only when such advice is sought
C. only if the matter relates to some basic issue
D. only if the issue poses a threat to the unity and integrity of the country

177. Six months shall **not** intervene between two sessions of the Indian Parliament because :
A. it is the customary practice
B. it is the British convention followed in India
C. it is an obligation under the Constitution of India
D. None of the above

178. The States of the Indian Union can be recognised or their boundaries altered by:
A. the Union Parliament by a simple majority in the ordinary process of legislation
B. two-thirds majority of both the Houses of Parliament
C. two-thirds majority of both the Houses of Parliament and the consent of the legislatures of concerned States
D. an executive order of the Union government with the consent of the concerned State governments

179. The Basic Feature theory of the Constitution of India was propounded by the Supreme Court in the case of :
A. Minerva Mills Vs. Union of India
B. Golaknath Vs. State of Punjab
C. Maneka Gandhi Vs. Union of India
D. Keshavananda Vs. State of Kerala

180. Which one of the following writs is issued by a court in case of illegal detention of a person?
A. Habeas corpus B. Mandamus
C. Certiorari D. Quo-warranto

181. Name the instrument with the help of which a sailor in a submarine can see the objects on the surface of the sea.
A. Telescope B. Periscope
C. Gycroscope D. Stereoscope

182. 'HEMOPHILLIA' is the disease of ....
A. liver B. blood
C. brain D. bones

183. Vitamin A is abundantly found in ....
A. Brinjal B. Tomato
C. Carrot D. Cabbage

184. .... is not soluble in water.
A. Vitamin A B. Vitamin B
C. Vitamin C D. None of these

185. The blood vessels with the smallest diameter are called ....
A. capillaries B. arterioles
C. venules D. lymphatics

186. Out of the following .... has the greatest elasticity.
A. steel B. rubber
C. aluminium D. annealed copper

187. Cooking gas is a mixture of which of the following two gases?
A. Carbon Dioxide and Oxygen
B. Butane and Propane
C. Carbon Monoxide and Carbon Dioxide
D. Methane and Ethylene

188. The substance most commonly used as a food preservative is:
A. sodium carbonate B. tartaric acid
C. acetic acid D. benzoic acid

189. Normally, the substances that fight against diseases in human systems are known as:
A. dioxyribonucleic acids
B. carbohydrates
C. enzymes
D. antibodies

190. The SI unit of temperature is ....
A. Kelvin B. Celsius
C. Fahrenheit D. None of the above

191. One of the common fungal diseases of man is :
A. plague B. ringworm
C. cholera D. typhoid

192. A clear sky is blue because:
A. red light is scattered more than blue
B. ultraviolet light has been absorbed
C. blue light is scattered more than red
D. blue light has been absorbed

193. Jenner introduced the method of making people immune to :
A. small pox B. rabies
C. cholera D. polio

194. The largest cell in the human body is :
A. Nerve cell B. Live cell
C. Muscle cell D. Kidney cell

195. What is the device that steps up or steps down the voltage?
A. Dynamo B. Conductor
C. Inductor D. Transformer

196. The protein deficiency disease is known as :
A. Kwashiorker B. Cirrhosis
C. Eczema D. Clycoses

197. Iron deficiency causes :
A. rickets B. anaemia
C. cirrhosis D. goitre

198. Blood group of an individual is controlled by :
A. Haemoglobin B. Shape of RBC
C. Shape of WBC D. Genes

199. In a normal man the amount of blood pumped out by the heart per minute is about :
A. 1 litre B. 3 litres
C. 4 litres D. 5 litres

200. Red/green colour blindness in man is known as :
A. Protanopia
B. Deutetanopia
C. Both A and B above
D. Marfan's syndrome

201. The blue colour of the water in the sea is due to :
A. Reflection of the blue light by the impurities in sea water
B. Reflection of the blue sky by sea water and scattering of blue light by water molecules
C. Absorption of other colours by water molecules
D. None of the above

202. The image formed on the retina of the eye is:
A. upright and real
B. larger than the object
C. small and inverted
D. enlarged and real

203. Unit of loudness of sound is:
A. bel B. decibel
C. phon D. none of these

204. Oil rises up the wick in a lamp :
A. because oil is volatile
B. due to the capillary action phenomenon
C. due to the surface tension phenomenon
D. because oil is very light

205. The 'stones' formed in human kidney consist mostly of :
A. calcium oxalate
B. sodium acetate
C. magnesium sulphate
D. calcium

206. We hear the sound later, while the light is seen earlier:
A. because light's speed is more than that of sound
B. because lights travel in a straight direction while sound in a zigzag direction
C. because sound's frequency is lower than light
D. All of the above

207. Which part of an eye is transplanted?
A. Cornea B. Retina
C. Iris D. Sciera

208. The Universal donor group of blood is:
A. O B. A
C. B D. AB

209. The green colour of the leaf is due to :
A. Presence of Chloroplast
B. Presence of Chromium
C. Presence of Nicoplast
D. Presence of excess of oxygen

210. Voice of a child is more shrill than that of an elderly person because:
A. the pitch of the child's voice is higher than that of the person
B. the pitch is lower
C. the child is more energetic
D. None of the above

ANSWERS

1	2	3	4	5	6	7	8	9	10
B	C	D	C	B	C	A	C	C	D
11	12	13	14	15	16	17	18	19	20
C	A	C	A	A	D	A	B	A	D
21	22	23	24	25	26	27	28	29	30
A	C	B	C	D	C	B	D	D	B
31	32	33	34	35	36	37	38	39	40
C	D	C	C	B	C	D	B	C	C
41	42	43	44	45	46	47	48	49	50
A	A	A	B	C	D	C	B	B	D
51	52	53	54	55	56	57	58	59	60
A	C	A	B	B	A	B	C	A	C
61	62	63	64	65	66	67	68	69	70
C	C	B	B	C	C	D	D	D	B
71	72	73	74	75	76	77	78	79	80
B	C	C	C	A	A	A	B	B	A
81	82	83	84	85	86	87	88	89	90
A	B	D	B	C	C	D	C	B	D
91	92	93	94	95	96	97	98	99	100
A	B	A	A	A	B	B	A	A	D
101	102	103	104	105	106	107	108	109	110
C	B	A	D	D	D	A	C	D	C
111	112	113	114	115	116	117	118	119	120
B	B	B	A	D	C	C	D	B	D
121	122	123	124	125	126	127	128	129	130
C	A	A	B	A	D	C	D	B	D
131	132	133	134	135	136	137	138	139	140
B	B	D	A	B	D	B	D	D	C
141	142	143	144	145	146	147	148	149	150
D	C	D	D	D	B	A	D	C	C
151	152	153	154	155	156	157	158	159	160
A	B	A	A	A	D	C	B	D	A
161	162	163	164	165	166	167	168	169	170
B	B	C	B	D	D	C	B	B	B
171	172	173	174	175	176	177	178	179	180
D	C	D	D	C	B	C	A	D	A
181	182	183	184	185	186	187	188	189	190
B	B	C	A	A	A	B	D	D	A
191	192	193	194	195	196	197	198	199	200
B	C	A	A	D	A	B	D	D	A
201	202	203	204	205	206	207	208	209	210
B	B	B	B	A	A	A	A	A	A